FOUNDATIONS
OF SOCIAL RESEARCH

FOUNDATIONS OF SOCIAL RESEARCH

NAN LIN

Department of Sociology
State University of New York at Albany

McGRAW-HILL BOOK COMPANY

New York   St. Louis   San Francisco   Auckland
Düsseldorf   Johannesburg   Kuala Lumpur   London
Mexico   Montreal   New Delhi   Panama   Paris
São Paulo   Singapore   Sydney   Tokyo   Toronto

FOUNDATIONS
OF SOCIAL RESEARCH

1 2 3 4 5 6 7 8 9 0 KPKP 7 9 8 7 6

This book was set in Times Roman by Maryland Composition Incorporated.
The editors were Lyle Linder and Susan Gamer;
the cover was designed by Nicholas Krenitsky;
the production supervisor was Sam Ratkewitch.
The drawings were done by Danmark & Michaels, Inc.
Kingsport Press, Inc., was printer and binder.

Library of Congress Cataloging in Publication Data

Lin, Nan.
    Foundations of social research.

    Includes index.
    1. Sociological research. I. Title.
HM48.L54   301'.01'8   75-25603
ISBN 0-07-037867-3

Contents

PART ONE: CONCEPTUALIZATION AND VERIFICATION

PART TWO: USE OF STATISTICS IN SOCIAL RESEARCH

PART THREE: RESEARCH INITIATION, SAMPLING, AND MEASUREMENT

PART FOUR: DATA COLLECTION

PART FIVE: DATA ANALYSIS

PART SIX: PRESENTATION AND USE OF SOCIAL RESEARCH

Preface

This is an introductory text on social research, useful for a student or a practitioner who has had limited background training, or no training, in methodology. It differs from other existing texts in that equal treatment has been given to three topics which are usually either treated separately or given different amounts of attention: theory construction, the use of statistics, and the procedures of social research (generally known as "research methods").

Usually, a textbook dealing with "methods" treats the "methodological" aspects of social research superficially, if at all. There are perhaps two reasons why "methodology," addressed to the logic of research and therefore to the process of theory construction, is left out. First, it is considered too "sophisticated" for students at this level to comprehend; second, it is considered as being independent of "how-to" discussions about research procedures—the methods themselves. It is my belief, however, that in view of recent advances in conceptualizing the process of social research, these two reasons are no longer valid. I have used many portions of this text in lower-level undergraduate social research courses that I have taught in the past five years; and the students have convinced me that they are as capable, as new graduate students without training in methodology of absorbing and integrating both "methodology" and "methods." Also, students enjoy discussions of theory and empirical work just as much, as a course taught in the "popular" format—"let's work out a questionnaire and do a survey." The latter approach usually leaves out large chunks of materials, which must eventually be covered by other courses and instructors. In this volume, theory construction receives extensive discussion and is involved in the discussion of all other phases of social research.

Statistics is also omitted from most existing textbooks on social research. Many texts provide a few graphs and equations without distinguishing the two functions of statistics in social research—description and inference. Few books introduce statistics until the section on data analysis appears. I do not argue that all social research must be statistical in nature. But the essential phases of social research, such as measurement (scaling, reliability, and validity) and sampling, must be explained by means of the basic statistical notions of descriptions and inference. Further, the logical linkage of statistical estimations and hypothesis testing with theory construction constitutes a most crucial endeavor of social research. In this text, the use of statistics is discussed in two sections. Descriptive statistics and the notion of statistical inference are introduced before sampling and measurement. After data collection has been taken up, another section provides more extensive treatment of statistical tests and multivariate techniques in inferential data analysis.

Two other innovative chapters deal with structural (sociometric) analysis and policy research. My theoretical concern with the unnecessary distinction between "macro-level" and "micro-level" analysis has led me to introduce structural analysis—its first appearance, as far as I know, in an introductory text. The discussion is necessarily kept at a low level of mathematical sophistication and within a relatively narrow range of topics. I hope that this topic will in the future be more integrated in research books.

The last chapter of the book is devoted entirely to the issues and problems of policy research. Currently, more and more research investment is being channelled to "socially relevant" topics and projects. The chapter deals with the pitfalls as well as the potential benefits of social research in solving social problems.

Throughout the text, I have pointed out problems relating to each aspect of social research. Whenever possible, constructive criticisms are offered so that the student is not only made aware of problems but also alerted to ways and means of dealing with them or avoiding them.

Although this text is broad in scope, it nevertheless reflects my own experience, expertise, and preferences in certain areas of social research. Thus, for example, the survey and the experiment receive more attention than other methods of data collection. Linear models of statistical techniques receive the major portion of discussions on inferential statistics. I do feel, however, that these topics also reflect current trends in the use and development of techniques in social research.

Ideally, this text should be used as a two-semester course; but it has been organized so that several alternative teaching plans, with different emphases, are possible, as is shown on the next page.

Plan A—one semester, with emphasis on a basic understanding of the process of social research. This plan uses nine chapters (Chapters 1, 8, 9, 10, 11, 12, 13, 18 and 19). It assumes that the student is interested in simply acquiring a general understanding of how research is conducted. The materials selected focus on initiation of research, sampling, measurement, data collection, presentation, and use. The experiment is not introduced, as this is too complicated a topic for a brief introduction. Plan A is probably best suited to a community college curriculum.

Plan B—one semester, with emphasis on practical use of social research. This plan uses twelve chapters (Chapters 1, 5, 6, 8, 9, 10, 11, 12, 13, part of Chapter 14, and part of Chapters 17, 18, and 19). It assumes that the student is interested in doing research for pragmatic reasons but not in the pursuit of a career in the social sciences. The selected materials focus on the procedures of social research and descriptive statistics, with a minimal understanding of inferential statistics, structural analysis, and experimentation. This plan is suitable for a four-year college curriculum.

Plan C—two semesters. The first semester covers Chapters 1 through 10, on theory construction, introduction to statistics, initiation of research, sampling, and measurement. The second semester covers Chapters 11 through 19, on data collection, data analysis, and presentation and use of research. This plan is suitable for a university curriculum for the combined methods and statistics requirements.

Plan D—one semester covering all the chapters. This plan assumes that the students have a certain amount of familiarity with social research and are planning to advance to the next level of learning but must brush up on the basics. Thus, it is best suited for a first course on research methods in a graduate curriculum.

The actual examples of social research in the text are sufficient to equip a student to undertake independent research. The student is urged to use this text in conjunction with *Conducting Social Research* (Nan Lin, Ronald S. Burt, and John Vaughn, McGraw-Hill, 1976), which provides the necessary exercises and was prepared with this text in mind.

I wish to thank many colleagues for their critical readings and comments on various drafts of the volume. Substantial revisions resulted from their suggestions. However, I am entirely responsible for any faults, shortcomings, and biases which remain. Ronald Burt and John Vaughn interacted with me throughout the period of the writing, and their insights and arguments benefited the text enormously.

Nan Lin

FOUNDATIONS
OF SOCIAL RESEARCH

Chapter 1

Introduction

This is a book about the *hows* and *whys* of social research. The term *social* refers to the relations between and among persons, groups (be they families, neighborhoods, or bridge clubs), institutions (schools, communities, organizations, prisons, etc.), and larger environments (countries, cultures, or continents). The study of any of these relationships, with an empirical rather than a philosophical orientation, is called *social research*.

This book is intended to do three things:

    1 Help the reader understand how social researchers construct generalities (theories) about social activities
    2 Help the reader learn the procedures used in conducting social research
    3 Show the reader the problems social researchers must face in constructing theories and in conducting social research

In this chapter, we shall discuss some of the specific studies which fall within the range of social research, the aims of social research, and its major phases. Finally, we shall provide an overview of what the chapters of the book will cover.

SCOPE OF SOCIAL RESEARCH

Social research covers a wide range of phenomena. Any relationship involving two or more persons may constitute a legitimate topic for social research. In

1

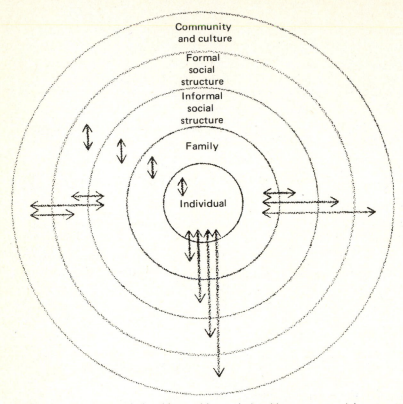

Figure 1.1   The intrarelationships and interrelationships among social components.

other words, social research examines not only the relationships among individuals, but also those between individuals and their families, informal social structures, formal social structures, and communities and cultures. Likewise, not only different relationships within the family component are examined, but also the relationships between the family and the informal social structures, formal social structures, and communities and cultures. Thus, social research covers interunit as well as intraunit relationships across the various social components. Figure 1.1 represents the social components and their intra- and interrelationships, all of which are legitimate arenas for the enterprise of social research.

Let us look at some examples which will illustrate the studies of relationships within and across various social components.

There has been concern about the kinds of children who tend to watch violent television programs. It has been found that children who are frequent viewers of television programs depicting crime and violence tend to have fewer friends, poorer relationships with their parents, and more aggressive personalities than those who are not frequent viewers of such programs.[1] In other words, watching

[1] Donald F. Roberts, "Communication and Children: A Developmental Approach," in W. Schramm et al. (eds.), *Handbook of Communication*, Rand McNally, Chicago, 1973, pp. 174–215.

violent television programs seems to be related to the breakdown of some social and psychological support of individual children. This kind of investigation cuts across four social components, namely, the individual, the family, the informal social structure, and the formal social structure (the mass media). It explores the effects of the individual, the familial, and the informal social structural characteristics on the interaction between the individual and the formal social structure (children watching certain programs on television).

Another area of research concern in sociology has been the examination of the relative effects of father's educational achievement, father's occupational status, and son's educational achievement on the son's eventual occupational status. In the United States, for example, it was found that one's own educational achievement is much more important than one's father's education or occupational status in attaining higher occupational status.[2] In Costa Rica, on the other hand, father's occupational status is more important than son's educational achievement in the son's attainment of higher occupational status.[3]

We might assume that father's occupational status affects son's occupational status because it has a *prescribing* value. Fathers in better occupational positions can utilize their social influence in obtaining better jobs for their sons. Son's educational achievement, then, affects his occupational attainment because of its *ascribing* value; educational achievement prepares a person for a better job. The focus of these investigations is to ascertain the relative importance of a person's prescribed status versus his ascribed status in his attaining a better job. On this basis, we may interpret the findings from the United States and Costa Rica to mean that, as a society progresses industrially, the relative importance of one's prescribed status decreases and that of one's ascribed status increases as regards an individual's attainment of higher social status (social status being indicated by the occupational structure). This kind of analysis involves the social components of the individual, the family, and the formal social structure. It studies the relative importance of the parent-child relationship (father's educational achievement and occupational status) and the individual–formal structure relationship (educational achievement) to another individual–formal structure relationship (occupational status).

Still another example is the question of whether socioeconomic background or school environment affects educational performance more. One such study suggests that socioeconomic background is much more important than school environment (such as equipment, financial expenditure, teacher quality, etc.) in contributing to educational performance.[4] However, school environment (especially the ethnic composition of the student body) affects socially and economically disadvantaged students much more than it does advantaged students. For example, black children perform much better in schools where whites

---

[2] Peter M. Blau and Otis Dudley Duncan, *The American Occupational Structure*, Wiley, New York, 1967, p. 170.

[3] Nan Lin and Daniel Yauger, "The Process of Occupational Status Achievement: A Preliminary Cross-National Comparison," *American Journal of Sociology*, November 1975.

[4] James S. Coleman et al., *Equality of Educational Opportunity*, U.S. Government Printing Office, Washington, D.C., 1966, pp. 21–23.

constitute the majority than in schools where blacks are in the majority. This difference holds even when the black students' socioeconomic characteristics in different classroom situations are taken into account. This kind of study focuses on the effect of the family versus that of the formal social structure (the school environment) on the functioning and achievement of individuals in the formal social structure.

Deviant behavior is another area where a great deal of research attention has converged. Deviance may be defined as the behavioral patterns considered improper by the majority of members of a community or culture. Thus, homosexual behavior is deviant in most cultures and communities, as is committing suicide. It has been suggested that deviance is a result of a person's frequent interaction with individuals who already possess a deviant trait.[5] This does not tell us how these other individuals acquired the deviant trait, nor does it tell us why or how the person interacts with them. But it does tell us that, if a person interacts frequently with those possessing a deviant trait, it then becomes likely that he will also acquire the deviant trait. This suggestion is generally known in deviance as the *hypothesis of differential association.* It taps the social components of the individual and the informal social structure.

Another area of research which has fascinated sociologists is what makes population growth rates differ from one society to another. It was found in the early stages of world industrialization that the process of industrialization led to the reduction of population growth.[6] Typical examples were the European countries where, once industrialization had been in progress for a while, the population growth rates dropped appreciably. The explanation is that, while the death rate dropped because of medical advances, this happened slowly because the self-generated economic and scientific progress was gradual. Mortality gains were met by a declining birthrate, since a smaller family size was advantageous under the conditions of industrialization and urbanization. As a result of the declining deathrate and birthrate, population growth rate was stabilized.

On the other hand, this process apparently does not occur in the developing countries today. Many countries are developing industrially by borrowing technologies from other countries. The death rate has dropped substantially, because of imported health care techniques. However, the reduced mortality rate is not matched by lower birthrates, because the family structure and the culturally rooted belief in the importance of sons have remained substantially intact. As long as education does not penetrate to the masses of people and transform the cultural values, the birthrate will drop only slightly and not enough to match the decreasing death rate. Thus the overall population growth rate will remain high. This kind of investigation into population patterns explores the social components of family, formal structure (process of industrialization), and community and culture (the birthrate, the death rate, and cultural values).

These examples demonstrate the complexity and breadth of social research.

[5] Edwin H. Sutherland and Donald R. Cressey, *Criminology,* 8th ed., Lippincott, Philadelphia, 1970.

[6] Kingsley Davis, "The Demographic Transition," in A. Etzioni and E. Etzioni (eds.), *Social Change,* Basic Books, New York, 1964, pp. 187–194.

AIMS OF SOCIAL RESEARCH

Why do we conduct social research? We may offer two main reasons. Social research is conducted, first of all, to detect regularities in the various social relations. It is also conducted to provide clues to possible solutions to social problems. The first reason is a conceptual or theoretical one, and the second a pragmatic or applied one.

Because of the breadth and depth of human activities involved in the enterprise of social research, it is conceivable that, if we were to conduct a separate study for every social activity we are interested in, everybody in the world would have to become a social researcher and we would have to spend an incredible amount of time and money to conduct all our studies. This is totally infeasible. The alternative is to conduct research in such a manner that we can say something from a single study about a whole set of social activities rather than about a single social activity, and from a small number of individuals studied about a large number of people. This process involves generalization of results from a specific study and a sample of respondents to a set of social concepts or terms and a population. By the rules of social research, which are statistical, logical, or both, the researcher hopefully will isolate certain regularities which apply to a large number of social activities and people.

Social research is also useful as a means of uncovering necessary clues for the evaluation or solution of social problems. It may project what will happen in the future, describe what is happening now, or record what has happened in the past. This evidence can then be helpful when decisions about or solutions to problems must be formulated. But we must bear in mind that such evidence should never be misconstrued as the decision or solution itself.

PHASES OF SOCIAL RESEARCH

Social research follows a sequence of phases, although the phases may not all appear in a given research project and the sequence of their appearance may vary. These phases are (1) formulation of a theoretical or pragmatic issue, (2) formulation of a research problem, (3) sampling of respondents, (4) measurement of information items, (5) data collection, (6) data analysis, (7) interpretation and reporting, and (8) integration of findings in theory or pragmatic use. We will now briefly describe these phases, as shown in Figure 1.2.

Formulation of a Research Issue

There are two types of interest which may lead a researcher eventually to conduct a social research project. He may be interested in either a theoretical or a pragmatic issue.

The ultimate goal of science is to explain events with theories. A *theory* may be defined as a set of interrelated propositions, some of which can be tested empirically. We shall discuss theory and theory construction in detail in the next three chapters. It is sufficient here to say that theories are summary statements about many observed social activities. If the theories are valid, a limited number

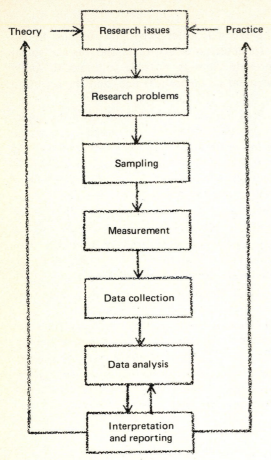

Theory   Research issues   Practice

Research problems

Sampling

Measurement

Data collection

Data analysis

Interpretation
and reporting

Figure 1.2   Phases of social research.

of theoretical propositions should be able to explain many observed social activities. Thus, theory construction becomes the overriding concern of much social research.

The work of Emile Durkheim[7] provides an example. Durkheim was a French sociologist who sought an explanation for egoistic suicide (suicide not for a common cause such as the good of a group, nation, or community). He tested various causal ideas before coming up with his own explanation, namely, that egoistic suicide may result from a person's isolation from cohesive social groups. In other words, isolation from cohesive groups tends to lead individuals toward psychological stress which in turn is expressed in various forms of self-destruction, such as suicide. If this theory is a good one, we would expect the suicide rate among regular churchgoers to be lower than that among nonattenders, the rate

[7] Emile Durkheim, *Suicide: A Study in Sociology,* Free Press, Glencoe, Ill., 1951.

among individuals from broken homes to be higher than that among those whose families are intact, and suicides among urban dwellers to outpace those among country folk.

The effect of participation in social groups on psychological stress and depression should also lead us to predict that suicide is less likely during the days leading up to a social occasion which is important to the individual. For example, we would predict that the suicide rate would decrease as Christmas approaches, at least for those who celebrate that holiday. Similarly, we would predict that one is less likely to commit suicide when his birthday is near, if he usually celebrates it with friends and relatives. In fact, there is evidence that, for the aged, even the death rate tends to be lower before important social occasions such as birthdays, New Year's Day, presidential elections, and the Jewish Day of Atonement than after these occasions.[8]

These examples show how theoretical considerations can originate from and lead to social research. Research can also arise from practical needs or interests. Each social group, institution, community, society, or culture has what it considers its own most urgent problems. In one community, the critical problem may be a housing shortage; in another, racial tension; in yet another, the organization of health services. Because of the uniqueness of each community, research which focuses on the particular problem of one community may not be applicable to others. While such research may not offer theoretical guidance or interest, it is just as legitimate as research leading to or deriving from theoretical issues.

Formulation of a Research Problem

Once a research issue has arisen from theory, practice, or both, the next step is for the researcher to refine the issue into a researchable problem. He cannot merely state his area of interest (such as deviant behavior, urban development, group interaction, race relations, or family structure) and proceed to conduct research. These ideas provide only the general framework within which specific research problems must be formulated. For example, if the researcher is interested in deviance, he should ask himself what kind or kinds of questions can be asked about deviance and what kinds of answers his research should be able to verify.

A research question must inquire about the relationship between two or more activities or behaviors. For example, Does involvement in a deviant environment increase the chances of a person's engaging in deviant behavior? Does being called deviant increase the frequency of deviant behavior? The researcher hopes to be able to answer such questions, not with an absolute "yes" or "no" but with probabilistic statements about the extent to which a relationship exists or does not exist.

After a series of questions has been raised within the framework set out by theoretical or practical considerations, a series of propositions (statements) can

---

[8] David Phillips, "Death Takes a Holiday," in J. Tanur (ed.), *Statistics: A Guide to the Unknown,* Holden-Day, San Francisco, 1972, pp. 52–65; David P. Phillips and Kenneth A. Feldman, "A Dip in Deaths before Ceremonial Occasions: Some New Relationships between Social Integration and Mortality," *American Sociological Review,* vol. 38, no. 6, pp. 678–696, December 1973.

be formulated. These propositions restate the questions in such a form that they specify the relations among the activities and behaviors so that the relations can be examined by using observations of ongoing social activities. Statements which can be directly examined with observations of ongoing social activities are called *hypotheses*.

Formulating a specific research problem within a general area reduces the scope of a potential research project to a manageable size. While concern for world peace can be the motivation for a research project, it is infeasible to study the subject of world peace in its entirety. For a beginner in social research, the first research project should be extremely limited in range. This is not to suggest that it should be insignificant. But it must allow for the fact that the beginning social researcher has minimal financial and personnel support. Rather than gathering information from world leaders on their opinions about world peace, the researcher may have to settle for United Nations records of the past voting practices of various countries on world peace issues. Instead of interviewing every homosexual in town, he or she may decide to observe the behavior of homosexuals at certain gay bars. Narrowing down the research problem to a manageable size also helps to bring central issues into focus. The researcher must shape and reshape the research problem until a research project within the various limitations emerges.

Selection of the Appropriate Type of Study

After formulating a research problem, the researcher must select the type of study most appropriate for its investigation. The selection of a particular type of study is related to the nature of the research problem, the availability of data sources, and the level of knowledge about the research problem.

There are research problems which call for a specific kind of study. For example, if we are interested in a general research area such as urban problems, but have no definite ideas about what questions or propositions are appropriate, we may conduct an *exploratory* study. This allows us to collect preliminary information on a whole range of activities related to urban problems, so we can gain insight into potentially important questions. These questions can then be formulated into explicit research problems for our future efforts.

If, on the other hand, the main purpose of our research project is to obtain an elementary comprehension of certain activities and behaviors, then the study to be undertaken is *descriptive* in nature. For example, to find out how legislators make decisions about how to vote, a good study might describe the activities of legislators which lead up to their voting behaviors.

In some situations, rather than simply describing social activities, we may want to study relationships among two or more social activities. We may not have a proposition or hypothesis about the form a certain relationship will take, but only a general feeling about the relationship. Consequently, we will want to conduct a study which will allow us to generate hypotheses for testing in the future. A *hypothesis-generating* study allows examination of various factors which could play important roles in possible hypotheses. After the data are analyzed, hypotheses can be formulated and the researcher is ready to design another series of studies to test them.

A *hypothesis-testing* study is called for when our understanding of the research problem is rather advanced, that is, when previous research has indicated the kind of behavior pattern or relationship that is to be expected. In this case, the research problem is restated as a hypothesis, and the study entails examination of the hypothesis using appropriate empirical observations.

Because the goal of this type of study is to test a hypothesis, maximal control and precision must be incorporated so that the results may not be attributed to factors other than the relationship stated in the hypothesis. For example, to test the hypothesis that integrated housing leads to more favorable racial attitudes than segregated housing, the researcher must control for other factors such as the racial attitudes of residents before moving into an integrated or segregated housing development. Thus the possibility that it might be previous racial attitudes rather than housing arrangements which lead to more favorable racial attitudes among respondents living in integrated housing is taken into account. The researcher isolates the influence of the factor he is investigating from the influence of other factors.

Sampling of Respondents

Ideally, the researcher wishes to examine every single case which meets certain criteria of his interest. He may want to study all United States citizens, all women of childbearing age in New York City, or all residents of certain housing developments. However, the cost and effort involved inevitably would be prohibitive. Rarely can a researcher study every case in the target population. Usually a subset of cases is selected for inclusion in a study. This subset of cases from the population of all cases which meet the defined criteria (e.g., United States citizens, women of childbearing age in New York City, residents of certain housing developments) is called a *sample* of the population.

Since the researcher is able to study only the sample, does this mean that his results can be applied only to the sampled cases? Fortunately it does not have to. With the help of statistics, if the selection of the sample is based on some probabilistic strategy, the researcher can still generalize the results of his research to the population as a whole. This generalization of course involves errors, since it is practically impossible to select a sample which represents completely all the behaviors and relationships in the population. However, if the selection of the sample, called *sampling,* follows certain statistical rules, the extent of probable error will be known to the researcher. The results can be interpreted with regard to the population with more or less confidence, depending on the extent of the error that is likely to have occurred. The process of generalizing results from a sample to a population is called *inference*.

Measurement

When the research questions and propositions have been formulated, the research problem reduced to manageable size, the appropriate type of study selected, and respondents sampled, the researcher must devise ways of examining the propositions. Certain observations of ongoing social activities may be taken as evidence of support or lack of support for the propositions. Devices (items and response categories) which detect these social activities and measure their frequency or magnitude are called *instruments,* and the process of constructing instruments is called *instrumentation.* One of the most crucial tasks in instrumentation is the assignment of numbers to the response categories—measurement. *Measurement* is the link between a theoretically formulated research problem and the data to be gathered from observations.

To examine the research statement that housing arrangements with regard to the proximity of different races affect racial attitudes, the researcher must devise instruments which will provide indications of both (1) different kinds of housing arrangements and (2) differential racial attitudes. For example, he may wish to tap two kinds of housing arrangements—segregated and integrated housing developments. To detect racial attitudes, he may ask residents of each housing development a series of questions on topics such as how often they interact with persons of other ethnic backgrounds, how strongly they are for or against having their children play with children of other ethnic backgrounds, etc. These questions form an instrument, and the responses by the residents will provide indications of their racial attitudes.

Data Collection

When the researcher has selected the type of study, constructed the instrument, and sampled the respondents, his next task is to generate data from the respondents. The data-collection phase actually consists of two subphases: the pretest and the main study. Before the actual gathering of data from the respondents, it is important for the researcher to know that his instrument works and that the design is appropriate for his respondents. One way to ensure that these requirements are met is to conduct a small-scale study or pretest prior to the main study, using the same instruments and design. The pretest data are collected from individuals other than the sampled respondents, but with similar characteristics. The pretest is usually administered to between five and fifty individuals. It provides an opportunity for last-minute evaluation and possible revision of the instrument, as well as the data-collection method for the main study. If the study involves interviewers, the pretest also provides them with field experience and allows assessment of their competence.

There are many methods of data collection, ranging from observing respondents and going over existing documents, through asking respondents questions using either a written form such as a questionnaire or an interviewer (face to face or over the telephone), to performing manipulations on the respondents before data are gathered from them. These methods are called *observation* (in which the researcher may be either a participant or a nonparticipant in the ongoing social activities of the respondents), *documentary-historical methods* (using census data, police records, diaries, mass media, etc.), *surveying* (including the questionnaire survey, the telephone survey, and the interview), and *experimentation* (in either a laboratory or a natural setting).

Data Analysis

Once the data are gathered, the researcher faces another demanding task, namely, to organize the "raw" data in a form in which they can be analyzed and to find the most suitable techniques for this analysis. Data analysis is often equated with statistical analysis by social researchers. This is quite unfortunate, because the process of data analysis is much more complicated than performing statistical operations on the data. The data received from respondents or observers usually need considerable organization before any meaningful analysis can be carried out on them. They need to be properly coded, transferred to a form that machines, usually computers, can understand (such as punched cards or tapes), and transformed (for example, by forming an index of socioeconomic or occupational status) before the statistical analysis can take place. The task of coding, transferring, and transforming, in many cases, takes more time and effort on the part of the researcher than does statistical analysis of the data.

Statistical analysis itself, of course, still constitutes an important aspect of social research. It provides an important link between the data gathered by a researcher and his hypotheses. In other words, it is the link between data and the theoretical assertions made by the researcher in his statement of the research problem. There are numerous statistical methods available for use by the social researcher. The selection of the appropriate statistical methods for a particular set of data is dictated by (1) the nature of the measurement of the data, and (2) the purpose of the research effort. Different statistical and analytical techniques make different assumptions about the measurement of the data and how the responses are distributed. Therefore, given the specific kind of measurement and pattern of responses, a researcher can ascertain which statistical method is appropriate for a study. Furthermore, he or she must consider the purpose of the study. Is it to describe some characteristics or activities in a population? Is it to formulate a hypothesis? Or is it to test a hypothesis? Each research design requires a certain type of statistics. Inappropriate use of statistics may lead to incorrect interpretations of the data.

Interpretation and Reporting

After the data are analyzed, the researcher must interpret the results. His interpretation follows certain logical rules. These rules are explicit if certain statistics are used in the data analysis. Otherwise they are less explicit and require some conceptual and theoretical thinking. The researcher should always be conservative in interpreting data. The interpretation should never go beyond the ground covered by the data analysis. The conservative approach ensures that what appears in the report and in the literature is solidly supported by data. When the researcher wishes to extend an interpretation into conjecture, it must be clearly stated that this is being done. A researcher must guard against overenthusiasm.

In the social sciences, few insignificant results are accepted and published in the important professional journals. Thus, it might be tempting for the social researcher to liven up his results or stretch his findings. These are poor practices and should be guarded against at all costs. In evaluating others' research reports, it is important to determine whether such misdemeanors have been perpetrated. A piece of research should be evaluated according to its objectivity of interpretation and reporting at least as much as by the significance of its results.

Integration of Findings in Theory or Policy

The research task does not end with a research report. In fact, in most cases the research report signals the beginning of more exciting research activities. A particular research project should lead to more theoretical questions and the formulation of new research problems. This is how scientific knowledge grows and how a researcher grows. Each research project is a new experience for the researcher, and in social research no study is perfect. Therefore, each should offer insight into how better to conduct similar studies, as well as suggesting new research problems.

Application of research findings to ongoing social activities is another area of extension of the research effort. More and more, social scientists are asked the relevance of their work to "real" social problems. While not every social scientist is obligated to conduct research for the sake of applying the results to ongoing activities, social research is increasingly being directed toward such an objective. The federal agencies which offer research funds, such as the National Science Foundation, the National Institutes of Health, the National Institute of Education, and the National Cancer Institute have all stressed the need for "applied" research.

OVERVIEW OF THE BOOK

This book contains six parts: (1) conceptualization and verification; (2) use of statistics in social research; (3) research initiation, sampling, and measurement; (4) data collection; (5) data analysis; and (6) presentation and use of social research. Part One introduces the concepts and elements of theory and theory construction. Part Two introduces the elementary concepts and use of statistics and statistical inference in social research, preparing the reader for the use of symbols in the planning, execution, and analysis of data. Part Three begins the actual phases of social research. Data collection in its variety of methods is discussed in the next part, Four. Part Five discusses data analysis as a way of inferring from the sample data to a population and a theoretical structure, as well as structural (sociometric) analytic methods. Part Six informs the reader how to interpret and report research as well as how to use social research, focusing on the implications of social research for policy.

Part One

Conceptualization and Verification

Chapter 2

Theory and Social Research

A social researcher can seldom conduct his work without any concern for theory, whether theory plays an explicit part in his work or not. In many cases, the social researcher has some specific theoretical ideas in mind when he begins his research project. At other times he emerges from working with his data and says something like, "It looks as though people with more education get better, steadier jobs and higher pay." Whether he thinks about it before or after conducting his research project, the social researcher is attempting to construct a theory. He is trying to generalize what he finds in a specific research project to a certain relationship between factors which may be true not only for his respondents, but for people in larger or other social systems.

However, if theory construction were merely a part of the thinking, conscious or unconscious, of a researcher, there could have been an infinite number of theories. Since it is human nature to speculate about and generalize our experiences, one person's "theory" would be as good as anyone else's. It would not make sense to collect all such "theories." We therefore restrict the term *theory* to a certain type of statement which serves a specific purpose in scientific research.

Theory, in its scientific sense, serves one important purpose: *It explains the relationships among observed activities.*

This chapter will deal with the purpose, structure, and empirical testing of theory.

PURPOSE OF THEORY

First of all, a theory should be able to predict the behavior of one phenomenon from that of another. For example, one may have a theory about the relationship between education and income. If one knows how much education someone has, the theory ought to allow us to predict his approximate income. Predictions can be made for relationships between activities (1) over time, (2) in different physical locations, or (3) for a defined group of social units (a population). The prediction from education to income is essentially an over-time prediction, since we assume that people usually complete their education before taking full-time steady jobs. The prediction that instability of the American government (such as that stemming from the Watergate incident) would lead to a decline in the value of the dollar is a prediction over physical distance. The Watergate affair was strictly an American internal problem, yet from that activity we could predict what would happen in the monetary markets of London, Paris, or Tokyo. But most commonly, a prediction is made about a set of activities observed for a given set of individuals or social units. For example, Durkheim's prediction that isolation from cohesive social groups leads to the tendency to commit suicide was made over a set of observations (Protestants versus Catholics). Thus, the statement should hold over time and physical distance. This type of prediction deals with the *concomitant occurrence* of activities.

However, a theory should do more than simply predict. The purpose of theory is to explain the relationships among social activities. All theoretical statements must be not only predictive, but also explanatory. *Explanation* may be defined as the capability of a statement about a certain relationship to describe a number of observable social activities. A theory should contain simple statements which have explanatory power for a large number of social activities. For example, Durkheim's theory about the relationship between social isolation and psychological stress was used to explain the observed different suicide rates among religious groups which require differential degrees of member participation.

It is possible that several theories provide explanations of similar social phenomena. How, then, can one consider a theory as being superior to others? The superiority of a theory over other competing theories is determined by three criteria: (1) the parsimony of its structure, (2) the accuracy of its explanation, and (3) its pervasiveness over different social phenomena. These three criteria determine the explanatory power of a theory.

A theory consists of a number of related statements or propositions, as shall be discussed shortly. The fewer such statements necessary, the more powerful a theory is considered in comparison with a competing theory. The second criterion, accuracy of explanation, gives more power to a theory when it explains certain phenomena more accurately than other theories. Thus, a theory which explains a set of social phenomena more accurately than another is considered to be more powerful than the other theory. Finally, the more types or varieties of social phenomena a theory can explain, the more powerful the theory is considered. Thus, a theory explaining how some people obtain better jobs than others is considered to be more powerful than another theory, if it can also explain why some people have more friends than others while the second theory cannot.

While these three criteria should be consistent in determining the explanatory power of theories, they are not necessarily always consistent. A theory may be more parsimonious than another, but less accurate or pervasive in its explanation. When two or more theories do not show a consistent ranking pattern on the three criteria outlined above, then all the theories should be retained until a theory more powerful than all of them, showing a consistent superiority over the others when analyzed with the three criteria, emerges. Then, the single most powerful theory should supersede all the preceding theories.

The greater the explanatory power of a theory, the more useful it is. The ultimate goal of science is to compile a limited set of theories which will be able to explain many of the phenomena we observe, be they physical or social.

STRUCTURE OF THEORY

What is a theory? A *theory* is defined here as a set of interrelated propositions, some of which can be empirically tested. Thus, a theory has three important characteristics: (1) it consists of a set of propositions; (2) these propositions are interrelated; and (3) some of them are empirically testable. Before these three characteristics are discussed in detail, it is important to point out that a theory is always preceded by a set of assumptions.

Assumptions

A theory differs from a law in the sense that a law can be universally applied, whereas a theory may be valid only in certain situations. The situations in which a theory applies are described by the assumptions spelled out in the theory. These assumptions thus provide a boundary within which a theory applies. In social sciences, it is not unusual for a theory to exist without the assumptions explicitly spelled out. The consequence is that, in the testing and application of the theory, confusion arises as to whether the theory does not work because it is not "good" enough, or because it should not be applied to the particular situation since it violates the assumptions required for the theory. Thus, it is important that a researcher proposing a theory spells out these assumptions.

Assumptions of a theory are a set of statements describing valid circumstances in which the theory is applicable. These statements are not for testing, since it is admitted that they are true in certain situations and not true in others. However, these statements describe the valid situations in which the theory should apply. In other words, if a given situation violates one or more of the assumptions of a theory, then it is not legitimate to apply the theory. Violation of the assumptions of a theory does not necessarily challenge the validity of the theory. Rather, the knowledge of the assumptions promotes the proper testing and application of the theory. An illustration may help.

One of the best known theoretical orientations in sociology is structural functionalism.[1] It suggests that a social system can be considered as a set of interlinking relations of roles and statuses defined by shared norms and values for the purpose of providing necessary functions for the benefit of the system. We shall not deal with the definitions and substantive issues of the orientation. But, as Dahrendorf points out,[2] this view should be discussed under the following assumptions:

    1   That every society is a relatively stable and persistent constellation of elements
    2   That every society is a relatively well-integrated constellation of elements
    3   That every element in society contributes to its stability
    4   That society is held together by a consensus of its members

When any of these assumptions is violated, then the theoretical orientation loses its validity. In other words, structural functionalism should be applied and considered only when the assumptions hold up in the situations under discussion.

Assumptions of a theory thus are not for testing. They are "taken for granted" by the theorist as specifications of the circumstances where the theory should be applied.

Unless the assumptions about a theory are spelled out, a theory can be wrongly tested and applied. In the construction of any theory, therefore, it is important for the researcher to identify and delineate the underlying assumptions, the statements describing the situations in which the theory should be considered.

Propositions

A *proposition* is a statement about the relationship between two or more concepts. It connects concepts in relational form. Typical propositions are: "The greater the *A*, the greater the *B*"; "An increase in *A* is related to a decrease in *B*"; "*A* is positively (or negatively) related to *B*"; "A positive change in *A* results in a positive change in *B*"; and "A positive change in *A* leads to a negative change in *B*." In these statements, *A* and *B* stand for concepts. Their relationships are specified in the various propositions by phrases such as "the greater . . . the greater," "an increase . . . is related to a decrease," "positively (or negatively) related."

---

[1] Some claim that structural functionalism is a theory. However, it lacks certain characteristics of a theory to be discussed later in the chapter. For a critical view of the work of the most important contemporary spokesman of this orientation, Talcott Parsons, see George C. Homans, "Contemporary Theory in Sociology," in Robert E. L. Faris (ed.), *Handbook of Modern Sociology,* Rand McNally, Chicago, 1964, pp. 951–977. These theoretical orientations are also called theoretical sketches, as they merely outline potential theories.
[2] Ralf Dahrendorf, *Class and Class Conflict in Industrial Society,* Stanford University Press, Stanford, Calif., 1959.

Formation of a Concept   A *concept* is a term which has been assigned some specific semantic meaning. In general, concepts originate in four ways. The first is *through our own imagination*. We may realize through observation that no name has yet been given to a certain set of activities. Or, although a name is available, for our purposes we may wish to group several sets of activities or divide a set into several subsets. In these situations we may legitimately create concepts which refer to the set, aggregated set, or subsets of activities. The only restriction is that the concepts created do not use already accepted labels in an unconventional manner.

For example, social researchers at one time found that certain social activities could be used to assign individuals to rank-ordered groups (such as differential job prestige or income). The concept of "socioeconomic status" was created for such activities. An individual researcher, finding that the only socioeconomic status phenomenon of interest was job differentiation, might use the concept "occupational status" in his research.

Another way of defining concepts is *by experience*. Experience includes personal observations of social activities. As sociologists observed certain human groups achieving preset goals or producing products, they also noted that the rank ordering of individuals in these groups was well-specified. There always seemed to be a small set of individuals who took orders from no one but gave orders to everyone else in the group. These groups came to be known, in sociological terms as well as sometimes in the vernacular, as *organizations*. It may not be possible for everyone actually to observe an organization. But once its characteristics have been spelled out, the concept should allow the identification of most organizations as understood by everyone using the word. It should also guide the exclusion of those human groups to which most people would not apply the word.

A third method of defining concepts is *by convention*. Many terms have conventional meanings for a group, community, or culture. These provide convenient sources of concepts for social theories. Terms like *minority, adolescence, mass media,* etc., have found their way into theoretical statements.

Concepts may also be constructed *from other concepts*. For example, while exploring the concept of socioeconomic status, sociologists became interested in the individual who ranked relatively high on one socioeconomic status index (e.g., education) but low on another (e.g., occupation). This discrepancy became the focus of some theoretical statements and led to a new concept, "status inconsistency."[3] Then, in studying interactions between individuals, sociologists observed that in some interactions the participants had similar socioeconomic status, whereas in others their status was dissimilar. For example, person A might be a bank manager with a college degree, earning $27,000 a year. Person B might be a janitor in the public library who dropped out of school after the fifth grade and earns $6,000 a year. Their interaction is an example of status inconsistency *across*

[3] Gerhard Lenski, "Status Crystallization: A Non-Vertical Dimension of Social Status," *American Sociological Review,* vol. 19, pp. 405–413, August 1954; *Power and Privilege,* McGraw-Hill, New York, 1966; "Status Inconsistency and the Vote: A Four Nation Test," *American Sociological Review,* vol. 32, pp. 298–301, April 1967.

individuals. To avoid confusion with the conventional use of the concept "status inconsistency," a polarized set of concepts was coined. "Homophily" suggests the extent to which interaction participants have similar socioeconomic status, and "heterophily" the extent to which they have dissimilar socioeconomic status.[4]

While concepts can be formulated in a number of ways, it is important for theorists and researchers to adhere to two principles in their construction: (1) convention, and (2) avoidance of unnecessary new concepts. Concepts are expressed in words and should comply with the conventional use of the words. They should not be created simply for their novelty. Sometimes conventional words or concepts need minor modification for specific use in a research project. The researcher need not then coin new concepts. It is sufficient for him clearly to state his own definitions of the conventional ones to indicate how he had modified their usage.

Even when the social researcher does not intentionally modify conventional concepts, misunderstanding of the meaning can occur. It is therefore always advisable for him to provide his own definitions of whatever concepts he uses.

Types of Relations among Concepts   We defined a proposition above as a statement about the relationship between two or more concepts. Having discussed concepts, we shall now consider relationships. A *relationship* is any aspect or quality that can link or connect two or more activities or concepts. There are two main types of relationships (also called *relations*) which can specify the connection between two or more concepts. These are (1) covariational and (2) causal.

Covariational relations   A *covariational* relation indicates the corresponding changes in certain directions of two or more concepts. Typical propositions stating covariational relations are: "The higher the *A*, the higher the *B*"; "The higher the *C*, the lower the *D*"; and "The lower the *E*, the lower the *F*." The first proposition states a positive covariational relation, and the second a negative covariational relation. The third proposition, a reversal of the first, is also a positive relation.

Propositions about covariational relations concern only the cooccurrence or concomitance of two or more activities. They provide no information about which activity is cause and which is effect. For example, the covariational proposition, "Prestige varies directly with power," suggests that a person who has a lot of prestige, however defined, is likely also to have a lot of power over others. The proposition does not tell us whether he gains prestige because he is powerful or becomes powerful as a result of his prestige.

Causal relations   A *causal* relation is involved when a proposition specifically states that a change in one concept in a certain direction causes (leads to, results in, produces, induces) a change in another concept in a certain direction.

[4] Paul F. Lazarsfeld and Robert K. Merton, "Friendship as a Social Process: A Substantive and Methodological Analysis," in Monroe Berger et al. (eds.), *Freedom and Control in Modern Society,* Van Nostrand, New York, 1954, pp. 18–66; Everett M. Rogers and Delip K. Bhowmik, "Homophily-Heterophily: Relational Concepts for Communication Research," *Public Opinion Quarterly,* vol. 34, pp. 523–538, Winter 1970–1971.

To be causal, the relation in the proposition, "An increase in *A* leads to an increase in *B*," must simultaneously fulfill three conditions: (1) *A* and *B* vary concomitantly, (2) *A* and *B* covary without spuriousness, and (3) the increase in *A* temporally precedes the increase in *B*.

The first condition stipulates that *A* and *B* are covariational to begin with. The second states that the relation between *A* and *B* must not be *spurious* or inauthentic. That is, the covariation between *A* and *B* is not due to other factors (perhaps *C, D,* and *E*). For example, we may state as a causal relation, "Social integration leads to innovative behavior." We are saying here not only that social integration (the degree to which a person interacts with others in a social group or community) and innovative behavior (the likelihood of a person's behaving differently from the majority of people in the group or community) covary. We also imply that if other factors which might also covary with innovative behavior (such as socioeconomic status, age, and sex) are taken into account, social integration and innovative behavior will still covary.

Likewise, to prove that cigarette smoking causes lung cancer, not only must a covariation between smoking and lung cancer be established (the more a person smokes, the more likely it is that he will have lung cancer), but it must also be demonstrated that there is no other factor or combination of factors which induces both smoking and lung cancer. Two illustrations of possible spurious covariation between smoking and lung cancer are shown in Figure 2.1. In one

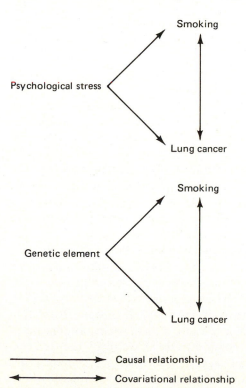

Figure **2.1** Possible spurious covariations between smoking and lung cancer.

situation, both smoking and lung cancer are found to be caused in fact by psychological stress. Thus, although smoking and lung cancer covary strongly, that covariation is due mostly to the covariation between psychological stress and smoking, and between psychological stress and lung cancer. In another situation, the covariation between smoking and lung cancer is similarly attributed to another factor, a genetic element which promotes both smoking and lung cancer in certain individuals.

Demonstrating the nonspuriousness of a covariation between two concepts is no easy matter. Ideally, the theorist should be responsible for the identification of all other factors which may induce changes in the major concepts being considered. He should demonstrate that, even after all these other factors have been taken into account, the major concepts still covary. But, in reality, these demands can seldom be met. For one thing, because most social theories are still in the infant stage, identification of all the factors which could possibly reveal the spuriousness of a covariation is almost always impossible. Also, even if a theorist is hardy enough to try, the pursuit of further factors may eventually turn into an endless exercise. The question of where it all begins will keep pushing the theorist to dig deeper. The problem of where to stop in the endless reduction of factors to their constituent parts, and then those parts to theirs, will probably never be resolved unless it is someday demonstrated that all social activities can actually be explained at some point by physiological variations. This, we suspect, will never occur.

That the problem of spuriousness is unsolvable does not relieve the theorist from concern for it. He must still attempt to identify any other factors he thinks should be taken into account while the causal relation between the primary concepts in his propositions is being examined. An important aspect of his theorizing can help in this task. This is a list of the assumptions under which his propositions hold. These assumptions will provide hints as to the factors that may come into play if they (the assumptions) are not fulfilled. His statement of the assumptions should include a rendering of how these factors would then affect the relations of the concepts advanced in his theory.

The third condition governing causal relationships is the temporal sequence of the concepts. The purportedly causing concept must precede the other concept in time. In order for isolation from social groups to lead to suicide, it must happen before the suicide occurs. Attention to this temporal sequence can sometimes also aid in ascertaining nonspuriousness in a causal relation.

In summation, in order for a relation between two concepts to be designated causal, we must demonstrate that the two concepts covary, that this covariation is not due to any other concepts, and that the causal concept (either its occurrence or its change, depending on the nature of the concept and our measurement of it) precedes in time the occurrence of or change in the effectual concept. Nonfulfillment of any one of these conditions labels a relation, if there is any, as noncausal.

Causal relations, however, can exist either directly or indirectly between concepts. Furthermore, a causal relation can suggest either that one concept is the sole or major cause of another concept, or that it is one of several causes. In

Figure 2.2, we present a number of variations of a causal relation between *A* and *B*, where *A* is the causal or *antecedent* concept and *B* is the effectual or *consequent* concept. In Figure 2.2*a*, *A* appears as the sole and direct cause of *B*. Figure 2.2*b* shows *A* as the sole but indirect cause of *B*. The influence of *A* on *B* is mediated through another concept, *C*. In Figure 2.2*c*, *A* is the sole cause of *B*, but the influence of *A* on *B* involves both direct and indirect paths. *A* influences *B* both directly and indirectly through another concept, *C*. In Figure 2.2*d* through *f*, *A* is not the sole cause of *B*. These multiple-cause relations again show that the influence from *A* and other causes such as *C* may be direct, indirect, or both direct and indirect even when *A* and *C* covary (represented by the line with double arrows).

Confusion of covariational and causal relations   Ideally, theoretical propositions should state explicitly whether the relations postulated are causal or not. They should also indicate whether (1) single or multiple causes and (2) direct influences, indirect influences, or both are expected. Unfortunately, very few propositions in the social sciences have done so. Covariational and causal relations are often confused. Sometimes a proposition is stated in the form, "The greater the *A*, the greater the *B*," and the researcher then proceeds to discuss his theory or findings as if the relation is a causal one. Or a proposition is stated as, "An increase in *A* results in an increase in *B*," while in fact the researcher treats

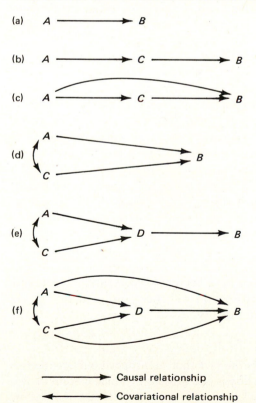

Causal relationship
Covariational relationship

Figure 2.2   Variations in the causal relations between *A* and *B*.

the concepts only as covariational. Hopefully, of course, social scientists will do better in the future, as we realize the possible confusion and distortion which may result.

In the meantime, in evaluating propositions presented in the literature, we must take precautions by following these rules:

1   Unless the authors specifically demonstrate that the relations postulated are causal, we must assume them to be covariational. We should never take for granted that relations are causal simply because terms such as *causes, results in,* or *induces* are used.

2   Unless it is specifically stated whether the causal relations postulated have single or multiple causes, we must assume that they have multiple causes. If the authors do not mention other potential causes, we must assume that these exist and have simply been neglected.

3   If it is not specifically indicated whether the causal relations postulated are direct or indirect, we must assume that they are direct.

These stringent rules, if followed, would sort out some confusion which exists in the current literature. They are conservative in nature. The rules instruct us, when in doubt, to consider propositions as covariational rather than causal, and incomplete rather than complete. They require the researcher to state explicitly the intended nature of his postulated relations, so that the potential contribution of the propositions to the theory can be properly evaluated.

The Null Relation   There is yet a third type of relationship between concepts—the null relation. The null relation states that, given information about one concept, it is difficult to predict how the other concept varies. An example is the assertion, "There is no relationship between sex and racial prejudice." This suggests that, given information about whether a person is of the male or the female sex, it is difficult to predict how racially prejudiced he or she will be (as compared with a person of the other sex). In other words, the null relation indicates that no prediction can be made from one concept to another. Because the null relation does not allow prediction, it is not a legitimate relation for a proposition. However, it plays an important part in the research process, since statistical procedures usually allow testing of the null relation (the null hypothesis). If the null hypothesis is rejected, the researcher gives more credence to the relation among the concepts as stated in the theoretical proposition. This topic will be covered in depth in Chapters 4 and 7.

In the discussion so far, propositions have been defined in terms of concepts and relations among concepts. The next section will focus on the nature of the interrelationships among propositions in a theory.

Interrelationships among Propositions

The second characteristic of a theory is the fact that its propositions are interrelated. This occurs by deduction. *Deduction* is the process in which certain known propositions or premises make other unknown propositions or conclusions follow logically, empirically, or both. The known propositions or premises may be called *postulates,* and the unknown propositions or conclusions may be called *deductions.* The simplest example of deduction is:

Postulates:
1   If *A*, then *B*.
2   If *B*, then *C*.

Deduction:
3   If *A*, then *C*.

Thus, given the first two propositions, the third follows logically.

Three types of deduction are practiced in the social sciences. The first is the *logical* deductive system, in the form just presented. The second is the *empirical* deductive system, where the propositions link theoretical terms (concepts) with empirical, observable terms (variables). The third type is a *combination* of the logical and empirical deductive systems, where deduction of both the logical and the empirical types occurs.

Logical Deduction

There are two variations of the logical deductive system. In one form, the deduction is made for the relations among definitions. A typical definitional logical deductive system is as follows:

Postulates:
1   All men are mortal.
2   Socrates is a man.

Deduction:
3   Thus, Socrates is mortal.

Each statement contains a definition, and the deduction connects the definitions. Note also that in the definitional logical deductive system, the statements are made on an either-or basis. Men are either mortal or not, there is either a Socrates or none, and Socrates is either a man or not a man.

The other form of the logical deductive system is the *propositional.* A typical propositional logical deductive system looks as follows:

Postulates:
1   The greater the prestige a person has in a group, the more likely it is that he possesses knowledge about the activities of the group.
2   The greater the knowledge a person has about the activities of a group, the more likely it is that he will be relied on to represent the group in negotiations with other groups.

Deduction:
3   The greater the prestige a person has in a group, the more likely it is that he will be relied on to represent the group in negotiations with other groups.

One important feature of the propositional deductive system is that the relations between concepts are stated as probabilistic rather than definitive. That is, given the occurrence of a particular value of a concept, the statement merely describes the likelihood of occurrence of a value of another concept. For example, given the fact that a person has a lot of prestige, the first postulate suggests only that he is more likely to possess knowledge about the activities of the group. It does not suggest, as would a definitional statement, that all persons with high prestige have great knowledge about their group.

Problems of Logical Deductions   The most serious problem of the logical deductive approach has to do with the fact that the deduced proposition does not have to hold "logically," if no further assumptions about the relations are specified. To illustrate this problem, let us use the following general example:

Postulates:
  1   The greater the X, the greater the Y.
  2   The greater the Y, the greater the Z.

The postulated propositions can be represented in diagrams as in Figure 2.3. A circle is used to represent each concept. The overlapping portions of the circles indicate the extent of relationships between the concepts. Proposition 1, which postulates a relationship between X and Y, is illustrated by the Venn diagram in the upper left-hand corner of Figure 2.3. Similarly, proposition 2 is shown in the upper right-hand corner.

However, given these two postulates, four different logical deductions are possible:

Deductions:
  3a   The greater the X, the greater the Z.
  3b   The greater the X, the slightly but not significantly greater the Z.
  3c   The greater the X, the much greater the Z. Or:
  3d   As X becomes greater, the change in Z is unknown.

These four possible deductive outcomes are also shown in Figure 2.3. Deduction 3a shows a substantial overlap of X, Y, and Z. Deduction 3b shows a much lesser degree of overlap between X and Z, while the overlaps between X and Y and between Y and Z are still substantial. Deduction 3c is the reverse of deduction 3b, in that while the relations between X and Y and between Y and Z are still about the same as in deduction 3a, the overlap between X and Z is now much greater. In other words, from knowledge of the relations between X and Y and between Y and Z, we gain only a little knowledge about the relation between X and Z. Finally, deduction 3d shows the situation in which, while X and Y as well as Y and Z overlap, there is no overlap between X and Z. In this case, even with the information given in propositions 1 and 2 about the relations between X and Y and between Y and Z, knowledge of X does not help us predict anything about Z.

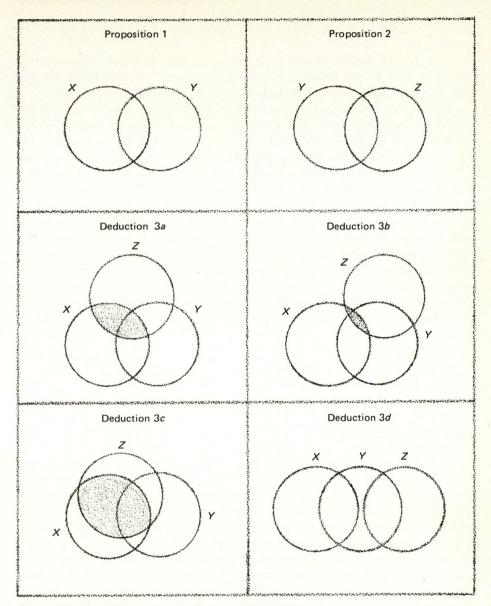

Figure 2.3   Deductions from logically related propositions.

While the logical deductive system holds to varying degrees in deductions 3a, 3b, and 3c, it collapses completely in deduction 3d. There is presently no completely satisfactory solution to this problem. However, several general rules have been suggested to minimize the difficulty.

Rule 1   To make sure that the situation illustrated by deduced proposition 3d does not occur, the overlaps between X and Y and between Y and Z should exceed the totality of Y.[5] In other words, this rule assures that X and Z will at least overlap.

Rule 2   The theorist should state explicitly, if he can, how much overlap between X and Y and between Y and Z is expected. If past literature and knowledge provide him with no clues as to what to expect, he should so state.

Rule 3   No logically postulated propositions should be accepted as true unless they are supported by research evidence or can be tested with observations.

Rule 4   If the theorist is uncertain that rule 1 holds, he should fulfill the following three conditions: (1) the postulated propositions are stated in causal (asymmetric) form; (2) the common concept in the two postulated propositions is prior to one but not both of the other two concepts in the temporal sequence; and (3) it can be assumed that there are no overlaps among the concepts except as stated in the postulated propositions. In other words, X and Z are related only insofar as each is related to Y as stated in the postulated propositions (and in a causal relation, mediated through Y).[6]

Under either rule 1 or rule 4, we are assured that X and Y overlap. However, we do not know the extent of this overlap. Rule 3 strongly suggests that we not venture into an elaborate deductive system of theory without empirical support. Any theory related to social research should be solidly grounded in empirical observation.

Many logically sound deductive systems of theory have no use in social research. Some may even lead to absurd social theories.

For example, consider the three theoretical structures presented in Figure 2.4. All are based on logical deductive systems. The deductions of the first two are identical, although based on different postulates. The deduction of the third is opposite that of the others, although it stems from an admixture of several of their postulates.

If we test only the two different deductions, at best we may be able to discredit one or the other of them.[7] We are fortunate if the deduction supported by empirical evidence is the second ($+A$ varies with $-Z$). In this case we may tentatively accept the third theoretical structure. But if it is the first deduction that is empirically vindicated, there is no way to decide which of the two theoretical structures leading to it deserves more credence. In fact, we could have extended the exercise indefinitely and provided a large number of logically sound sets of postulated propositions all arriving at the same deduction. This would, of course, eventually make it impossible for a social researcher to find empirical evidence to support any particular theoretical structure.

How can this crucial problem be resolved? First, one must realize that there is no ideal solution as long as the logical deductive system prevails in theory

---

[5] Herbert L. Costner and Robert K. Leik, "Deductions from 'Axiomatic Theory,'" *American Sociological Review,* Vol. 29, pp. 819–835, December 1964. The correlational formula suggested is: $r_{XY}{}^2 + r_{YZ}{}^2 > 1$, when variables are measured in deviations. Explanation of the r^2's can be found in Chapter 16.

[6] Costner and Leik, ibid.

[7] There is, of course, a third possible but theoretically trivial outcome: The evidence could fail to support either deduction.

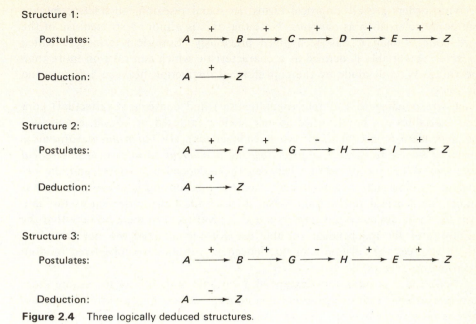

Figure 2.4 Three logically deduced structures.

construction. And at this time, there does not seem to be a better alternative available. However, one can demand that all theories have a strong foundation in empirical evidence. This requirement may be applied not only to deduced propositions, but also to postulated propositions.[8] The manner in which empirical testing helps us resolve the difficulties presented by the logical deductive system will be discussed later in the chapter, when we consider the third characteristic of a theory: the empirical testability of some of its propositions.

The logical deductive system is one of three types of deduction used in the social sciences. The second is the empirical deductive system.

Empirical Deduction

In the empirical deductive system, propositions link theoretical or abstract terms with empirical terms. An *abstract* term is one which does not correspond directly to any observable social activity. For example, "industrialization" cannot be observed directly. Similarly, *social status, group cohesion, decision making, power,* and *prestige* are all abstract terms. On the other hand, an *empirical* term is one which corresponds directly to some observable social activity. Number of cars produced, number of nominations as "best friend" in a high school, frequency of gatherings of a group, relative frequency of an administrator's giving rather than

[8] According to some theorists, postulated propositions may be used if the first and last concepts in the logical set can be measured using observable social activities. Thus, two concepts with observable indicants are connected logically by others lacking such. The concepts without observable indicants are assumed to represent intervening processes. However, if bound by this rule, social research can never falsify a theory, since none of the postulated intervening processes can be refuted.

receiving orders are all empirical terms. In social research, abstract terms are commonly referred to as *concepts*. Note that this is a more restricted use of the word *concept* than it has been given previously. Empirical terms are called *variables*. A variable is defined as a characteristic which can take on more than one value. We will abide by the conventional distinction between concepts and variables.

Corresponding to the antecedent (causal) and consequent (effectual) concepts, variables can be identified as independent (antecedent, causal, exogenous) and dependent (consequent, effectual, endogenous). *An independent variable is perceived by the researcher as preceding the dependent variable in a theoretical structure.* While the distinction between the independent variable and the dependent variable may not be crucial when the relationship is covariational, it is critical for a causal relationship. Also, it has important consequences for data analysis, to be discussed in Chapters 6 and 16. Suffice it to mention here that the variations of the independent variable are considered fixed (do not have "errors"), whereas the variations of the dependent variable are considered random (may involve "errors").

Note that the important feature of a variable is its ability to assume more than one value. "Industrialization" is a concept rather than a variable, because there is no observable social activity we can measure in order to attach different values to industrialization. (We may, however, talk about the degree of industrialization on an abstract level.) On the other hand, number of cars produced by a specific country within a given period is a variable, because it can take on values ranging from none to very large but specific numbers.

An empirical deductive system connects the concepts in a theory with variables. A typical empirical deductive system looks like this:

Postulates:
   1 Across different societies, industrialization varies inversely with interpersonal interaction.
   2 Industrialization varies directly with the number of cars produced per year.
   3 Interpersonal interaction varies directly with the frequency of face-to-face visits.

Deduction:
   4 Across different societies, the number of cars produced per year varies inversely with the frequency of face-to-face visits.

In this theoretical structure, proposition 1 postulates a relationship between two concepts, industrialization and interpersonal interaction, neither of which can be observed directly. This proposition involves no empirical terms. Propositions 2 and 3 each postulate a relation between one of the concepts and a variable. From these three postulated propositions, we deduce proposition 4 which links the two variables.

The empirical deduction involved in this example appears in Figure 2.5.

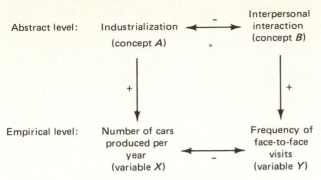

Figure 2.5   An illustration of empirical deduction.

Following convention, logical relations are represented horizontally and empirical relations vertically. Further, in the empirical deductions, the lowest level is used to represent the variables—the observable activities, and the higher level or levels indicate higher levels of abstraction. The deduction linking a concept and a variable is also known as the *epistemic proposition* or *correlation.*

The importance of the empirical deductive system is that it allows the "translation" of theoretical statements containing concepts to statements containing only variables, so that empirical tests of a theory can be made. This function is crucial, since empirical testability is the third characteristic of a theory. A discussion on empirical testability shall follow an examination of the empirical deductive system in detail with sociological examples.

Problems of Empirical Deductions   The empirical deductive system has weaknesses similar to those of the logical deductive system in that the epistemic correspondences between concepts and variables are only postulated. The variables are treated as specific indicators of the concepts, but they may be good or poor indicators. There is much variation in the extent to which they are actually part of the concepts they are supposed to represent.

Let us consider some of these variations in the epistemic correspondence between a variable and a concept. Four of them are presented in Figure 2.6: (*a*) the variable represents only a small portion of the concept, (*b*) the variable represents a large portion of the concept, (*c*) the variable represents a portion of the concept and of another concept or concept(s), and (*d*) the variable represents no portion of the concept.

These variations in correspondence affect the viability of an empirical deductive system. A number of possible effects are illustrated in Figure 2.7. We will discuss them with regard to the example empirical deductive system presented earlier. In Figure 2.7*a*, the concepts overlap, indicating that to some extent proposition 1 is true. However, the variables do not compose large enough portions of their respective concepts to overlap also. As a result, the deduced proposition containing the variables is not true. In Figure 2.7*b*, the concepts and the variables both overlap. Thus, all propositions in the theoretical structure are

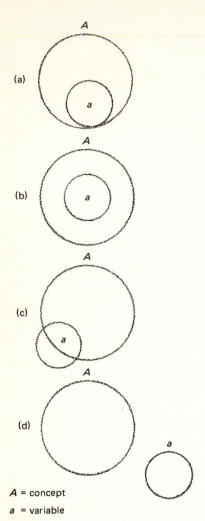

A = concept
a = variable

Figure 2.6 Variations in the correspondence of a concept and a variable.

true to some extent. In Figure 2.7*e* the concepts are not related, but the variables
are. The postulated proposition relating the concepts is therefore not true, but
those connecting the concepts and the variables are, and so is the deduction. In
Figure 2.7*g* the concepts do not overlap; the variables do, but they do not
compose any portion of the concepts. In this case the deduction is true, but none
of the postulates are.

In summary, for an empirical deductive system of theory to be true to a
certain extent, the following conditions must all be met: (1) the concepts are related; (2) the concepts and variables are related as postulated; and (3) the
variables are related as deduced. The absence of one or more of these conditions
will pose different kinds of problems for social researchers.

If condition 1 is not fulfilled but condition 3 is, the social researcher may be
misled into interpreting a relationship between the concepts whether condition 2

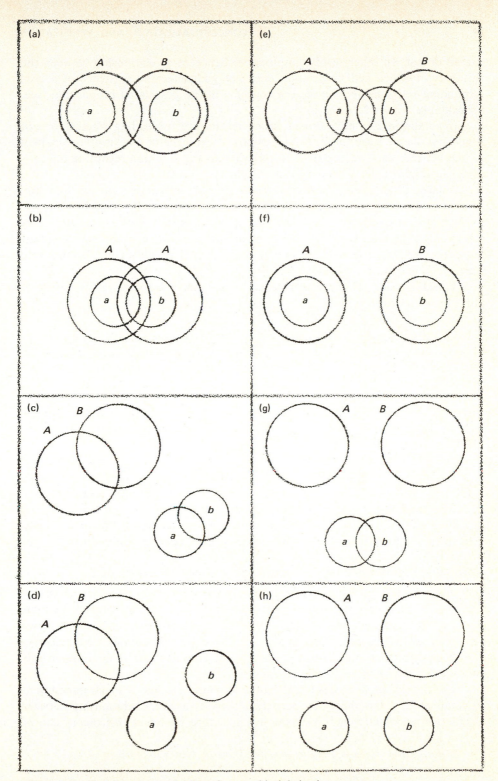

Figure 2.7 Variations in the viability of an empirical deductive system.

is true or not. In other words, empirical evidence of a relationship between the variables in a deduced proposition does not guarantee the existence of a corresponding relationship between the concepts in the postulated proposition (see, for example, Figure 2.7e and g).

If condition 2 is not fulfilled, study results are misleading whether or not conditions 1 and 3 are fulfilled. Any empirical evidence of a relation or the lack of one between the two variables is irrelevant to the situation regarding the concepts (see Figure 2.7c, d, g, and h).

Finally, if condition 3 is not fulfilled, again the researcher cannot draw any conclusion about the relationship between the concepts (see Figure 2.7a, d, f, and h). However, if condition 2, the relationship between the concepts and their corresponding variables, is fulfilled while condition 3 is not, he must conclude that there are at least minimal portions of the concepts which *do not* overlap (see Figure 2.7a and f).

Thus, in using the empirical deductive system, the social researcher must abide by two precautions:

1   When empirical evidence reveals a relationship between variables, it can be assumed that the postulated relationship between concepts explains the observed relationship only to the extent that the variables actually represent the concepts and that the latter are in fact related.

2   When empirical evidence fails to show a relationship between the variables, nothing can be concluded about the relationship or the lack of one between the concepts unless it is known that the variables accurately represent them.

While empirical evidence can be gathered about relationships between variables, how can conclusions about relationships between concepts and epistemic correspondence between concepts and variables be drawn with any degree of confidence? This is where the third characteristic of a theory, the empirical testability of at least some of its propositions, becomes important.

Integrating Logical and Empirical Deduction: Sociological Examples

Before we discuss the third characteristic of a theory, we shall summarize the integration of logical and empirical deduction in a theoretical structure with some sociological examples. *The structure of a theory should involve minimally two concepts and two variables.* Maximally it can be extremely complicated, requiring elaborate theoretical and empirical deductions. However, we shall consider only two well-known sociological theoretical structures.

The first example comes from George Homans' studies of social interactions in small groups. His theory suggests that there is a direct relationship between interaction and sentiment.[9] A theoretical structure based on this theory can be

---

[9] George Caspar Homans, *The Human Group,* Harcourt, New York, 1950.

constructed as follows:

Postulates:
   1 Interaction varies directly with sentiment.
   2 Interaction varies directly with the frequency of telephone calls between two persons.
   3 Sentiment varies directly with the frequency of hugging between two persons.

Deduction:
   4 For a given pair of persons, the frequency of telephone calls varies directly with the frequency of hugging.

The first proposition connects the two concepts and is the only purely abstract statement in the theoretical structure. Propositions 2 and 3 link each concept with a variable and are empirical deductive statements. Proposition 4, the deduction, links the two variables.

This theoretical structure is represented in Figure 2.8. Here, on the abstract level, interaction and sentiment covary. On the empirical level two variables, frequency of telephone calls and frequency of hugging, were used as indicators of the two concepts. These are only two of many possible indicators of interaction and sentiment.

Durkheim[10] proposed a theory about suicide. A theoretical structure stemming from it could read:

Postulates:
   1 Lack of social integration leads to greater psychological stress.
   2 Psychological stress leads to more deviant behavior.
   3 Lack of social integration varies directly with being Protestant rather than Catholic.
   4 Deviant behavior varies directly with the suicide rate.

Deduction:
   5 Therefore, the suicide rate among Protestants should be higher than that among Catholics.

This theoretical structure is slightly more complicated than the last one. First of all, the theory implies causal relations among the three concepts, with lack of social integration leading to psychological stress, and that in turn to deviant behavior. This is in contrast to the previous example, in which the concepts of interaction and sentiment simply covaried. Second, the logical deductive system is also more elaborate. Three concepts are connected in propositions 1 and 2, with psychological stress as the intervening concept. Only two of the three concepts are linked to variables in propositions 3 and 4; psychological stress is omitted.

[10] Emile Durkheim, *Suicide, A Study in Sociology,* Free Press, Glencoe, Ill., 1951.

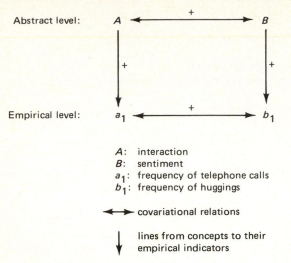

A: interaction
B: sentiment
a_1: frequency of telephone calls
b_1: frequency of huggings

◀───▶ covariational relations

│
▼   lines from concepts to their
     empirical indicators

Figure 2.8   A graphic representation of a theory by Homans.

The rationale for this procedure is that psychological stress would be very difficult to represent using an observable indicator. To avoid risking an inappropriate linkage between this concept and a variable, the concept is omitted from the deduction. This practice of omitting intervening concepts which are difficult to represent with empirical variables is rather common in social research. However, this does not imply that such concepts play an insignificant role in the actual process of social research. This issue will be discussed in more detail in Chapter 10.

The theory on suicide is represented in Figure 2.9. Again, the concepts are presented on the abstract level, and the two variables on the empirical level. The causal relations are shown both among the concepts and between the variables.

These examples have shown concepts at only one level of abstraction. In many theoretical structures, there are different levels of abstraction. Each higher level is more theoretical than the one below it. The indicators of its terms appear in the lower level. Thus, the lowest level of abstraction in a theoretical structure contains empirical variables only.

Empirical Testability of a Theory

As mentioned above, for a theoretical structure to have any credibility, it must have some assurance that the concepts are actually related, that the variables representing various concepts are in fact portions of those concepts, and that the variables are in fact related as stated in the deduction. There is presently no method which can guarantee the first two of these conditions. However, empirical testing helps us to a great extent in approaching their fulfillment. *Empirical testability* is defined as the ability of a theory to be verified using observable social activities.

A deduction in a theoretical structure which contains only variables can

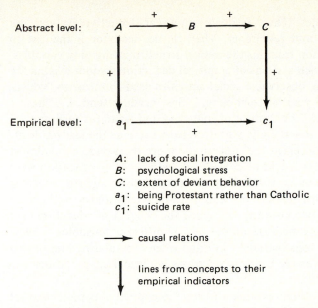

Figure 2.9   A graphic representation of a theory by Durkheim.

readily test the relations among these variables using observable social activities. Thus, it is important for a theory to have such a deduction.

Further, the proposition relating concepts in the theoretical structure can be given more credibility if each concept has a multiple number of epistemically corresponding variables. Confidence in the relation between two concepts is increased as more and more empirical indicators for the two concepts are found to be related. In summary, empirical testability increases credibility of a postulated relationship between two concepts, as it provides tests of a relationship of epistemically corresponding variables (indicators for the variables). *The more such tests involving multiple indicators, the greater the opportunity to assess the credibility of the postulated relationship between the two concepts.*

Unfortunately, many existing sociological theories lack empirical deductions, either explicitly or implicitly stated. At best, such theories should be considered incomplete. This does not mean that every social theorist must map out his deduction or deductions in every detail. However, the process of empirical deduction is especially crucial in the social sciences. Let us elaborate.

Explicit Statement of Variables   In the physical sciences, empirical deduction in most cases is uniform. The empirical variables representing specific concepts are few in number and enjoy a consensus of use among scientists. *Each concept has either a unique variable epistemically corresponding to it, or a set of variables which are interchangeable according to a precise calculus.* For example, the concept of distance is empirically measured in feet, meters, or some other variable. These variables are universally accepted, and their interchangeability follows precise rules. The concepts of mass and heat are similarly represented by universally accepted variables. Thus, intricate empirical deductive systems are available to every theorist and researcher. There is no need for a theorist to specify the empirical deduction from his theoretical structure using only variables.

Such precise and universal systems of empirical deduction seldom exist in the social sciences. For example, observable social activities used to measure "education" could be "number of years of schooling," "last grade attended," "has or has not ever attended school," or "can or cannot read and write his own name." But the number of years of schooling is not always the same as the last grade attended, since it is possible to repeat the same grade more than once. And almost everyone in the United States would be considered "educated" if education were measured by the criteria often appropriate in less industrialized societies, such as "has or has not ever attended school" or "can or cannot read and write his own name." Tests of theoretical propositions containing the concept of education may have disparate results simply because of the use of different variables. Unless social researchers have the same variables in mind when formulating and testing their theories, arguments over the validity of various empirical examinations can continue indefinitely.

Thus, it is wise for the social researcher to state as explicitly as possible what variables should be used for empirical testing of his theories. Each researcher proposing a theory should at least suggest empirical propositions he considers valid tests of his theoretical propositions. If a theoretical structure lacks empirical propositions, it should be considered incomplete. Variables may be deduced from its theoretical propositions and empirically examined by other social researchers. However, they risk inconsistency with the intent of the original work.

Suggestion of Empirical Evidence Besides the explicit statement of variables, empirical testability of theory imposes another constraint on the theorist. He must provide some evidence in addition to logic for his postulated relations among concepts. As shown earlier, mere logical viability is no indication that a theory can be empirically grounded. Logical deductive systems offer infinite variety. However, only those concepts which have corresponding empirical variables should be considered by social researchers. We suggest that a theorist search for empirical evidence even before proceeding to construct theoretical propositions.

At the present stage of instrumentation, it is simply impossible to gather empirical evidence for many potentially useful theories. However, theory construction in sociology and allied disciplines has heretofore showed a lack of success partly attributable to a neglect of empirical verification. Serious social researchers should therefore be aware of the importance of empirical evidence in building theoretical structures.

In short, to promote the empirical testability of a theoretical structure, a theorist should always consider the following:

   1 Empirical evidence must be taken into account prior to the formulation and construction of theoretical propositions and a theoretical structure. Such evidence should be cited as a source of the theoretical structure.

2   In presenting a theoretical structure, the theorist should facilitate its empirical testing by suggesting means of empirical examination, providing deductions containing only empirical variables wherever such can be found for the concepts involved, or both.

Suppose a theorist observes that people making more telephone calls to one another tend to exhibit more hand-holding behavior than others. Furthermore, people who tend to hold hands are likely to share a residence. He constructs the following theoretical structure:

Postulates:
   1   Interaction leads to sentiment.
   2   Sentiment leads to resource sharing.

Deduction:
   3   Interaction leads to resource sharing.

He has formulated a theoretical structure on the basis of earlier empirical observations. The variable "frequency of telephone calls" served as the source of the concept "interaction"; "frequency of hand-holding behavior" suggested the concept "sentiment"; and "likelihood of sharing a residence" became "resource sharing."

Now, in order to make his theoretical structure empirically testable, the theorist can suggest the conditions under which another researcher may be able to observe the relation between frequency of telephone calls and the likelihood of sharing a residence. He should also state that his theoretical structure will be verified most reliably if the relations between interaction and sentiment and between sentiment and resource sharing are examined as well as that between interaction and resource sharing. He thus directs attention to the postulated relations as well as the deduced relation in his theoretical structure. Logical deduction will then be supplemented with empirical evidence.

Multiple Indicators (Variables) for Each Concept   The theorist can also specify other variables which could be used as indicators of the same concepts. Interaction might be measured through the frequency of face-to-face meetings, sentiment by the frequency of hugging, and resource sharing by the frequency of going "Dutch."

A theorist increases the credibility of the relations postulated in a theory by thus providing a list of multiple variables for each concept. That is, he offers a series of empirical deductions from his logical deductive system. This allows multiple empirical tests of the theoretical structure. In general, the theorist can present the following theoretical structure:

Postulates:
   1   An increase in X leads to an increase in Y.
   2a   An increase in X covaries with an increase in x_1.
   3a   An increase in Y covaries with an increase in y_1.

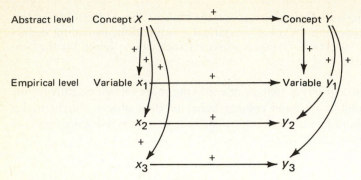

Figure 2.10   Multiple empirical deductive system.

2b   An increase in X covaries with an increase in x_2.
3b   An increase in Y covaries with an increase in y_2.
2c   An increase in X covaries with an increase in x_3.
3c   An increase in Y covaries with an increase in y_3.

Deductions:
4a   An increase in x_1 leads to an increase in y_1.
4b   An increase in x_2 leads to an increase in y_2.
4c   An increase in x_3 leads to an increase in y_3.

In this theoretical structure, X and Y are the concepts, and x_1, x_2, x_3, y_1, y_2, and y_3 are the variables. For each concept, the empirical deductive system contains three variables. As a result, there are three deduced propositions instead of one (see Figure 2.10).

Multiple empirical deductive systems reduce the probability of concepts not being related while variables are (see page 33). The more deduced propositions involving the variables that are empirically supported, the more confidence we have in the relation between the concepts. Conversely, the fewer deduced propositions involving the variables that are empirically supported, the more confidence we have in a lack of relation between the concepts. Since the relation between the concepts cannot be empirically tested directly, multiple deductive systems provide important indirect evidence for the validity of postulated relations.[11]

All these activities on the part of the theorist in the formulation and presentation of his theoretical structure facilitate its empirical testing. When a theoretical structure is presented along with previous empirical evidence, suggestions of means of empirical verification, or both, we may then call it a theory.

[11] The more different the variables in a multiple deductive system are, the better they serve to test the postulate about the concepts. If deduced propositions involving dissimilar variables are empirically supported, the postulated relation between the concepts gains indirect support over a wide range of empirical activities and greater generalizability. See Arthur Stinchcombe, *Constructing Social Theories,* Harcourt, New York, 1968, pp. 15–28.

SUMMARY

In this chapter, the structure of theory as it applies to social research has been introduced. A theory is defined as a set of interrelated propositions, some of which can be empirically tested. Theories are used mainly for explaining social activities which we observe. A proposition is a statement about the relationship between two or more concepts. The concepts may be either abstract or empirical. When a concept is empirical, it is usually called a variable. Concepts can originate from a theorist's own imagination or experience, from convention, or from other concepts.

There are two different kinds of relations among the concepts in propositions. A covariational relation simply suggests that the concepts occur or change in a corresponding manner, whereas a causal relation states that the occurrence of or change in one concept is one cause of the occurrence of or change in the other concept. The causal relation implies not only that the concepts are covariational, but also that such covariation cannot be accounted for by other factors or concepts and that the occurrence of or change in the causal concept precedes the occurrence of or change in the effectual concept.

The propositions in a theory are interrelated by deduction. Logical deduction connects concepts, and empirical deduction links concepts with variables. Logical deduction should be used with extreme caution in social research, since there is no direct empirical test for deduced relations among concepts.

Empirical testability is a requirement for a complete theory. It is promoted by the theorist who utilizes empirical evidence in the construction of his theoretical structure or, if he provides no empirical deductions, at least offers suggestions as to what means of empirical examination would constitute an adequate test of his theory. Multiple empirical deductions allow strong tests of postulated relations between concepts.

Chapter 3

Modeling Theoretical Structures

Having discussed the elements and structure of theories, we now proceed to their construction. This chapter will deal with the use of models in theory construction, and the elaboration of complex theoretical structures.

The discussion of theories has so far been rather abstract. While it is difficult to specify all the ways of using one's imagination in the construction of theories, certain procedures are frequently useful. One of these is the utilization of models.

MODELS: MEANS OF CONSTRUCTING AND EVALUATING POTENTIAL THEORIES

The utilization of models constitutes one effective way of constructing and evaluating potential theories. A model is defined here as a representation of some aspect of a theory. This definition differs from those of most philosophy of science books. Philosophers of science tend to view the model as an analogy to theory[1] or yet-to-be-validated theory.[2] It is viewed here as a tool in theory construction.

---

[1] May Brodbeck, *Readings in the Philosophy of the Social Sciences,* Macmillan, New York, 1968, pp. 579–600.
[2] David Willer, *Scientific Sociology,* Prentice-Hall, Englewood Cliffs, N.J., 1967, p. 15.

A model of a theory differs from the theory itself in at least two aspects. First of all, models do not contain epistemic propositions linking concepts and variables. Instead, they contain only statements linking concepts or variables.[3] At best, they represent the logically deduced propositions in a theory. Further, a model also lacks the complexity of a theoretical structure in that a model may represent a single proposition containing merely a selected number of concepts or variables in the theoretical structure. The lack of epistemological demonstration and a partial structure emphasize that a model is only an "imperfect" theory in the sense that certain aspects of a theory are missing.

Once a model contains all the logically deduced propositions necessary for a theoretical structure, it has accomplished its purpose as a tool for theory construction. For, by adding epistemic propositions, the theoretical structure will be complete. Once a theory has been constructed, models are no longer useful.

With the given definition of a model, it should become possible to enumerate different types of models in terms of the extent to which each resembles the logically deduced propositions contained in a theoretical structure. It is suggested that four types of such models be differentiated. At the most primitive level is the classificatory model. Next comes the typological model, followed by the contingency, associative, and functional models. Each type of model builds on the previous types and more closely approximates a theory. The functional stage is tantamount to logically deduced propositions and exhausts the usefulness of the modeling process. Models facilitate a researcher's progress from the fundamental elements of a theory toward a realized one. Let us examine the various levels of modeling in detail.

Classificatory Model

A classificatory model specifies the values, categories, or classes of a concept. It is also known as the *classification model*. As defined by Hempel,[4] the model must contain a set of two or more criteria which are mutually exclusive and jointly exhaustive such that "every element in the domain of D satisfies exactly one of these criteria." An example is the classification of sex using the two categories "male" and "female." These categories are mutually exclusive, in that a person can belong in one and only one category. They are exhaustive insofar as they allow the classification of any person observed. Classical examples of classificatory models in sociology can be found in Durkheim's identification of several types of suicide[5] and Weber's conceptualization of society as being stratified in three basic dimensions—economic class, status, and power.[6]

[3] R. B. Braithwaite, *Scientific Explanation,* Cambridge University Press, London, 1953, pp. 88–93.

[4] Carl G. Hempel, *Fundamentals of Concept Formation in Empirical Science,* International Encyclopedia of United Science, vol. II, no. 7, University of Chicago Press, Chicago, 1952, p. 51.

[5] Emile Durkheim, *Suicide,* John H. Spaulding (trans.) and Georg Simpson (ed.), Free Press, Glencoe, Ill., 1951.

[6] Max Weber, *The Theory of Social and Economic Organization,* A. M. Henderson and Talcott Parsons (trans.), Oxford University Press, New York, 1947; Kurt B. Mayer, *Class and Society,* Random House, New York, 1955.

A classificatory model may be constructed either from conceptualization or empirical observations. For example, conceptually derived classificatory models appear in much of Parson's classification work on the social system, which he considered "exhaustive of the relevant logical possibilities at a particular level of analysis.[7] An empirically derived classificatory model can be exemplified in Osgood and his associates' derivations of three dimensions of meaning as contained in the polarized adjectives (e.g. good-bad, strong-weak, fast-slow) found in various languages, such as evaluation, potency, and activity.[8]

A classificatory model can be challenged for its categories' mutual exclusivity and joint exhaustiveness. For example, suicides other than egoistic, altruistic, and anomie types might be proposed, and meaning may be conveyed by words or nonverbal gestures other than adjectives.

Not all concepts can be easily broken down into categories.[9] Psychological concepts dealing with attitudes and beliefs fall more naturally along continua than into distinct categories. The same is true of many social concepts (e.g., status, role, opinion, leadership, and even education). In these cases, special care must be taken in constructing categories so that they represent (1) the full range of values, and (2) the proper distribution form. The first requirement ensures that exhaustiveness is approximated. Attention to the proper distribution form should result in observations falling into many of the categories rather than clustering in one or two.

For example, a sociologist who is studying the stratificaton process in different countries might begin by constructing categories like those commonly used in the United States to measure occupational prestige, such as Siegel's index.[10] This model may result in the following distributions for data from the United States:[11]

Occupational prestige	Percentage of respondents
10–19	10
20–29	10
30–39	23
40–49	39
50–59	13
60–69	4
70–79	1
80+	1

However, if this classificatory model were applied in the rural areas of a less

[7] Talcott Parsons, *The Social System,* Free Press, Glencoe, Ill., 1951, p. 66.

[8] Charles E. Osgood, G. J. Suci, and Percy H. Tannenbaum, *The Measurement of Meaning,* University of Illinois Press, Urbana, Ill., 1957.

[9] Carl G. Hempel, op. cit., pp. 34–42.

[10] Paul M. Siegel, "Prestige in the American Occupational Structure," unpublished Ph.D. dissertation, Department of Sociology, University of Chicago, 1971. Also, see Appendix B.

[11] Analysis of National Opinion Research Center 1972 General Social Survey data for all working respondents ($N = 1,347$).

developed nation, such as Haiti, where the occupational system is just beginning to differentiate, the eventual observations might look like this:[12]

Occupational prestige	Percentage of respondents
10–19	86
20–29	3
30–39	7
40–49	3
50–59	1
60–69	0
70–79	0
80+	0

The great majority of observations fall into the first category. Obviously, this distribution is not in the proper form. The data thus challenge the validity of applying the classificatory model to societies such as Haiti, calling for either a different classificatory model or a different concept for measuring social status in such societies.

In summation, classificatory models specify the categories of the concept, which are the building blocks of potential theories. They may arise either from theory or from data. The classificatory model is not theory-like, as it deals with one concept or variable, thus not fulfilling one requirement of a theoretical proposition that two or more concepts or variables be involved.

Typological Model

A typological model specifies the cross-distribution of two or more concepts. Thus, the basic requirement for a typological model is that a dimensional model must be constructed for each concept involved. The two or more concepts are then cross-classified according to the dimensions of each.

The typological model is also known in the literature as the classificatory model,[13] the taxonomical model,[14] and the type-concept.[15] As Stinchcombe pointed out, this model serves two functions: (1) it simplifies conceptualization, and (2) it is a convenient way of writing a function of two or more variables in such a way that interaction effects can be simply stated.

The typological model is popular among sociologists. Many so-called theories are actually typologies. For example, in his analysis of power, Parsons[16]

---

[12] Data taken from a survey of rural Haiti villages for all working males ($N = 199$), in Nan Lin and Daniel Yauger, "The Process of Occupational Status Achievement: A Preliminary Cross-National Comparison," *American Journal of Sociology,* November, 1975.

[13] Ernest Nagel, *The Structure of Science,* Harcourt, New York, 1961; David Bohn, *Causality and Chance in Modern Physics,* Routledge, London, 1957.

[14] Hans L. Zetterberg, *On Theory and Verification in Sociology,* Bedminister Press, Totawa, N.J., 1963.

[15] Arthur L. Stinchcombe, *Constructing Social Theories,* Harcourt, New York, 1968.

[16] Talcott Parsons, "On the Concept of Influence," *Public Opinion Quarterly,* vol. 27, pp. 37–62, 1963.

Table 3.1   Specialized Media of Social Interaction

Sanction	Channel	
	Intentional	Situational
Positive	Persuasion	Inducement
Negative	Activation of commitments	Deterrence

Source: Talcott Parsons, "On the Concept of Influence," *Public Opinion Quarterly,* vol. 27, pp. 37–62, 1963.

suggested that social interactions utilize a generalized medium, the language, and some specialized media. The latter can be categorized according to a typology constructed by cross-classifying the concepts of *sanction* (whether the source of an interaction makes a positive or a negative assertion about the idea being discussed), and *channel* (whether the source attempts to commit the receiver to the intrinsic value of the idea or simply to its acting-out in a situation). The typology of specialized media appears in Table 3.1.

Thus, Parsons defined power as the medium which combines negative sanction and a situational channel for the purpose of deterrence. His analysis consisted in effect of a typological model.

Merton[17] suggested that individual adaptations in a social structure can be defined in terms of acceptance or rejection of (1) cultural goals and (2) institutionalized means. The two-concept typology is shown in Table 3.2.

The four main individual adaptive modes are identified as conformity, ritualism, innovation, and retreatism. Merton also described a fifth mode, rebellion, which occurs when existing cultural goals and means are rejected and new goals and means substituted.

Typological models help the researcher bring into focus patterns or types of activities arising from interaction of the categories of two or more concepts. Since they depend on the soundness of the dimensions of the concepts involved, it is important to ascertain that these concepts fulfill the criteria of mutual exclusivity and exhaustiveness. The danger inherent in the typological model lies in the fact that a typology can be constructed with any two or more concepts. The overuse of typological models in sociology has probably impeded the progress of theory construction.

The typological model is not theory-like, as it presents no tendency relations among the concepts or variables. That is, given a dimension or value of one concept, no prediction can be made as to which dimension of the other concept is likely to occur. Rather, a typological model should be evaluated in terms of its usefulness in bringing the researcher one step closer to a theory. The misconception that it is a theory in itself should be avoided. By cross-classifying the con-

[17] Robert K. Merton, *Social Theory and Social Structure,* Free Press, Glencoe, Ill., 1957, chap. IV.

Table 3.2 Modes of Individual Adaptation

Institutionalized means	Cultural goals	
	Acceptance	Rejection
Acceptance	Conformity	Ritualism
Rejection	Innovation	Retreatism

Source: Robert K. Merton, *Social Theory and Social Structure*, Free Press, Glencoe, Ill., 1957, chap. IV.

cepts in a theory, a typological model aids the theorist in understanding its general framework. As soon as one has been constructed, however, the theorist should proceed to the next step in the modeling process of theory construction.

Contingency Model

A contingency model specifies the likelihood of the occurrence of one category of one concept, given the occurrence of one category of another concept. A contingency model not only specifies the cross-distribution of two or more concepts but also suggests that, for a given value or category of one concept, the likelihood of occurrence differs among the possible categories of another concept. For example, in Merton's typology of the modes of individual adaptation, a contingency model would specify that, if an individual accepts cultural goals, the likelihood that he will accept institutionalized means is much *greater* than the likelihood that he will reject them. Or, if an individual rejects cultural goals, the likelihood that he will accept institutionalized means is much *less* than the likelihood that he will reject them. In other words, the contingency model specifies different joint-occurrence likelihood among the categories of two or more concepts. It allows predictions.

However, the predictions allowed by the contingency model do not have to be complete. That is, a contingency model may not specify different joint-occurrence likelihood for *all* categories of two or more concepts. For example, in a comparison of occupational changes in the United States between 1870 and 1954 (see Table 3.3), Mayer found that the pattern changed drastically over this period. In 1870, about half of the people were wage workers, and 40 percent were self-employed; whereas in 1954 only 13 percent were self-employed and 31 percent were salaried employees. Over this period, the percentage of wage workers was not changed, but the percentage of self-employed decreased and that of salaried employees increased. From the standpoint of each time period, thus, the likelihood of occurrence of two or three occupational categories has changed significantly. It allows differential predictions about the distribution of occupational categories, given the time period.

A study of the male and female teachers in public schools for each age category also constitutes a contingency model. The data (see Table 3.4) show that for the 26–35 age category, there were more male teachers than females but, for all

Table 3.3   Changes in Occupational Structure in the United States 1870–1954, percent

Occupational category	1870	1954
Self-employed	40.4	13.3
Salaried employees	6.6	30.8
Wage workers	52.8	55.8

Source: K. Mayer, *Recent Changes in the Class Structure of the United States,* Transactions of the 3d World Congress of Sociology, 1956, vol. 3, p. 70, table I.

Table 3.4   Distribution of Teachers by Age, Percent

Age category	Men	Women
Under 26	19.6	80.4
26–35	51.4	48.6
36–45	26.7	73.3
46–55	15.8	84.2
56 and over	17.4	82.6

Source: National Education Association, *The Status of the American Public School Teacher,* Washington, D.C., 1957.

other age categories, there were overwhelmingly more female teachers than male teachers. Thus, it is possible to make predictions as to the likelihood of having a female teacher for all age categories except for teachers in the age bracket 26–35, where a prediction would be difficult (it is almost equally likely that a teacher be male or female). Thus, the contingency model only makes partial predictions.

Partial predictability characterizes the contingency model. It is considered to be the initial form of a theoretical proposition in that a certain relationship (a contingent relation) is specified for the two or more concepts involved. Thus, the contingency model is a theory-like model.

Associative Model

An associative model specifies the linear tendency of relationship among the categories of two or more concepts. An associative model not only specifies the cross-distribution of two or more concepts, but also indicates the likelihood of observing *each* category of a concept under each possible condition of the categories of another.

This associative model specifies a *covariational* relation between concept A and concept B. Further, the categories of each concept are assumed to be *ordered*

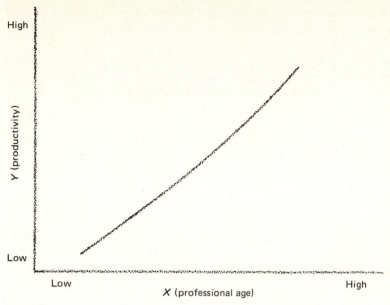

Figure 3.1   An associative model for "professional age" and "productivity."

(each category can be compared and rank-ordered with any other category of the same concept). Under these conditions, an associative model might resemble Figure 3.1.

Suppose a researcher is interested in the relationship between professional age (the number of years a person has been active in a scientific discipline) and productivity (the number of scientific publications per year) among a group of scientists. His associative model may indicate that, as professional age increases, productivity also increases.

The diagonal line in Figure 3.1 indicates the predicted association between concepts. The associative model allows the theorist to make covariational statements about two or more concepts in a simple, direct form.

The term *association* is used here in a limited sense. The relation specified is a *linear* one. That is, the associative model is restricted to the description of situations in which "The greater (less) the *A*, the greater (less) the *B*," or "The greater (less) the *A*, the less (greater) the *B*." This restriction is consistent with current usage of the term *association* among sociologists.[18]

Ideally, the construction of an associative model requires that all conditions for both the classificatory and typological models first be met. That is, the mutual exclusivity and joint exhaustiveness of the classifications of each concept should be verified and their cross-distribution explored. However, in practice, the exhaustiveness criterion need not be fulfilled for all concepts involved. Many social researchers have pursued associative models while lacking full knowledge

[18] Homans, op. cit., p. 952; Walter L. Wallace, *The Logic of Science in Sociology,* Aldine, Chicago, 1971, pp. 55 and 65.

of the ranges of potentially observable values. This procedure is justified as long as the theorist recognizes that his model may not apply to the heretofore unknown values.

The causal model is one variant of the associative model. The causal model is an associative model constrained by the three criteria of a causal relationship: change dependence, nonspuriousness, and temporal sequence.

Functional Model

A functional model specifies a one-to-one relationship between the categories of two or more concepts. In mathematics, a function specifies a relationship such that, for each given value of one variable, there is one and only one corresponding value of another variable. If variable Y is a function of variable X, for each given value of X, there is one and only one corresponding value of Y. The variable whose value is given (variable X above) is usually called the *independent* or predictor variable, and the one with the unique corresponding value (variable Y) the *dependent* or predicted variable. A functional model differs from an associative model in that, while the latter is restricted to a linear relationship between two or more concepts, the former is exclusively used to specify a curvilinear relationship.

Using the relationship between professional age and productivity again, a researcher may point out that, after a scientist reaches a certain professional age, his productivity in fact decreases. This researcher may propose a model stating that, before a scientist reaches the professional age of 25, as his professional age increases, his productivity also increases; but that after the professional age of 25, as professional age increases, productivity decreases. This nonlinear relationship appears in Figure 3.2.

This model is a functional one. It allows one to predict, for each value of the independent variable (professional age), one and only one corresponding value of the dependent variable (productivity). Productivity is a function of professional age, with the function changing at the 25-year limit.

If productivity is a function of professional age, then is professional age a function of productivity? Logically, it could be. Perhaps low productivity, up to a certain limit, discourages a scientist from continuing activity in a discipline, while high productivity encourages him. However, mathematically, the statement generally does not hold. If professional age were a function of productivity, then for each given value of productivity there would be one and only one corresponding value of professional age. However, looking again at Figure 3.2, we see that for almost every value of productivity there are two corresponding values of professional age (the exception, of course, occurs at the value of productivity where the scientist is exactly 25 years old professionally). For a given value of productivity (say, moderately low productivity), one could predict either that professional age would be relatively low (point *a*) or that it would be relatively high (point *b*). This constitutes poor prediction.

One might argue that the theorist could again impose a condition on the function by stating that prediction differs for scientists above and below 25 years

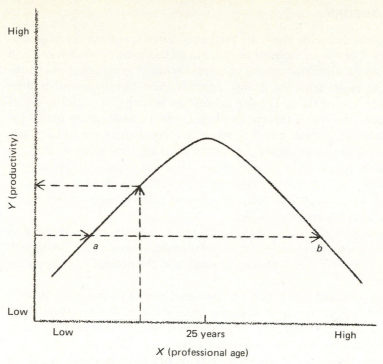

Figure 3.2   A functional model for "professional age" and "productivity."

of professional age. However, professional age here is the dependent variable being predicted from the independent variable, productivity. While values for productivity would be known to the theorist, values for professional age would not (otherwise he would not be predicting). Therefore, he could not impose such a condition.

When one variable Y is a function of another variable X, and X is also a function of Y, then it is said that Y has an inverse function. The most primitive type of functional model which also has an inverse function is actually an associative model involving a covariational linear relationship. In order to distinguish between the functional and associative models, the term *functional model* is reserved for nonlinear relationships.[19]

A functional model should fulfill all the requirements for the classificatory, typological, and associative models. Furthermore, the conditions under which the function holds and those under which the inverse function also applies should be specified.

[19] In the strictest sense, the associative model should be subsumed under the functional model, as the former is a special and restricted case of the latter dealing with linear relations. However, as noted earlier, the word *associative* is generally used in sociology to indicate a linear relationship. As a large portion of sociological analysis and theoretical writings is restricted to the linear relations among concepts, it seems appropriate to distinguish the two models as clearly as possible, for both theory construction and evaluation purposes.

MODELS AND THEORY

The first two models discussed above are pretheory models, lacking the basic elements of a theory. Only one concept is involved in a classificatory model, so there is no possibility of relationships among concepts. While a typological model incorporates two or more concepts, it only matches their categories rather than specifying relations among them. The two models are nonetheless useful as initial steps in theory construction. A theorist can begin with a classificatory model for each of his concepts of interest, and then move to a typological model to tie the concepts together. Each stage should aid him in thinking clearly about his concepts, and possible relationships among them. However, these models can be termed theoretical only insofar as they contribute to this process of theory construction. Unless conceptualization continues at least through a contingent model, it cannot be considered theory-like.

The contingency model, then, introduces a theory-like structure. It contains two or more concepts and it specifies certain relationships among them. Although the specification is incomplete, prediction is made and the process of proposition construction begun.

The associative model is the first propositional model in the sense that all categories of the concepts are involved in the specified linear relationship. From multiple associative models relating a set of concepts may emerge the basic logically deduced propositions in a theoretical structure.

The functional model is a more rigorous theory-like structure in that it allows the theorist to specify the conditions under which one or more functions, inverse functions, or both exist among his concepts. Such an elaborate theoretical structure represents the ultimate in the use of models in theory construction.

There are many classificatory and typological models in the social sciences today. Some of these have been mistakenly called theoretical structures. There are also numerous contingency and associative models, and most existing theories take these forms. However, there are very few functional models. Functional models become more feasible in the social sciences after numerous studies have been conducted on a particular topic and many initial theoretical structures in the form of associative models have been investigated. It is important for the beginning social theorist to start with a classificatory model and work his way up to an associative model. After gaining insight from empirical research into associative models, he may then advance to functional modeling. Plunging into functional modeling without sufficient theoretical and empirical examination usually brings confusion and frustration to the theorist.

What has been discussed here is not a substitute for theory. Rather, models are considered in relation to their potential contributions to theory construction and evaluation. Too often debates about the requirements of a theoretical structure are abstract and difficult to apply when a specific statement is being evaluated as to whether it is a theoretical one. The various models clearly call for theories to specify the relative stage of a theory being constructed as well as what future routes should be taken to advance a theory. Critical evaluation of theoretical structures can now be made tangible and, hopefully, more constructive. When an "implicit" theory is at hand, it should become possible to make it explicit by way of the modeling process.

The use of models should also aid in the training of social researchers in theory construction. A step-by-step procedure can now be presented in the attempt at modeling toward the construction of a theory.

ELABORATING COMPLEX THEORETICAL STRUCTURES

A theorist interested in a particular concept can formulate several types of theoretical structure focusing on it. He can analyze the relationships between the concept of interest and (1) its *antecedent* concepts, (2) its *consequent* concepts, or (3) both. In the first instance, he attempts to link the concept of interest to others which *precede* it either in theory or in time. These relationships may eventually prove to be causal. If so, the theoretical structure will hopefully explain the concept of interest in terms of its *causes*. Such a *convergent* structure is represented in Figure 3.3a.

For example, a theorist studying educational achievement might postulate that its major antecedents are (1) native intelligence and (2) parental socioeconomic status. His rationale could be that, while performing well in school requires a certain amount of intelligence, sufficient economic support at home is also necessary if this performance is to be consistent. Associative models may be constructed stating that, the higher the native intelligence, the higher the educational achievement and that, the higher the parental economic status, the higher also the educational achievement. The relative importance of the two antecedent concepts may also be detailed, for instance, by postulating that parental socioeconomic status has a stronger influence on educational achievement than does native intelligence. This structure is called a *convergent* or *causal* structure with regard to educational achievement.

The second analytical strategy connects the concept of interest with those which *follow* it in theory or in time, and which may eventually be found to be its *effects*. The resulting *divergent* structure is shown in Figure 3.3b.

Our theorist may wish to continue his study of educational achievement by examining its consequences. He may include among these the respondents' eventual socioeconomic status (occupational status and income) and marital stability. His associative models may posit that, the higher one's educational achievement, the higher his eventual socioeconomic status, while the higher one's educational achievement, the lower his marital stability. Higher educational achievement provides one with knowledge about the structure of socioeconomic status, which along with a degree or certificate enables him better to manipulate social channels in order to attain higher status. However, it may also increase his awareness of the rigidity of social norms, thus diminishing his respect for traditional institutions and lowering his marital stability. Again, the theorist may

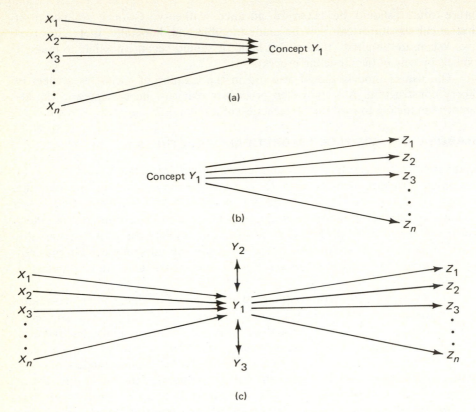

Figure 3.3 Types of complex theoretical structures. (*a*) Convergent (causal) structure for concept Y_1. (*b*) Divergent (effectual) structure for concept Y_1. (*c*) Causal-effectual structure for concept Y_1.

weigh the effects of educational achievement on socioeconomic status and on marital stability and predict that the effects on the former will be more pronounced.

A third analytical strategy is that of combining the first two. Here the theorist links the concept of interest to a number of potential causal as well as effectual concepts. This is the *causal-effectual* structure which is presented in Figure 3.3*c*.

In our example, the theorist may wish to study both the antecedents and the consequences of educational achievement. His theoretical structure would then include both potential causes of educational achievement such as native intelligence and parental economic status, and likely effects such as socioeconomic status and marital stability.

While the divergent and the causal-effectual theoretical structures are as important logically as the convergent structure, a survey of existing social science literature would probably show that the convergent structure is employed in over

90 percent of the cases. It would be interesting to investigate the historical reasons for this distorted focus.[20]

Two issues remain to be mentioned here. First, it should be noted that a concept may appear as either the antecedent or the consequence of itself. This occurs when the concepts are mapped along a time dimension. In Figure 3.3c, the X's temporally precede the Y's and the Z's, while the Y's precede the Z's. The theorist might wish to take into account changes in his concept of interest over time. He would then simply insert the concept as it operates during different time segments into his analytical scheme. For example, if early educational achievement were to be considered as one of the antecedents of later educational achievement, it could be included as one of the X's while later educational achievement remained as Y_1. This strategy involves what are usually known as *lagged* variables.[21]

The last issue concerns concepts which covary with the concept of interest, but present uncertainty as to whether they precede or follow it temporally and theoretically. They may, however, play a crucial role in the theory under construction and so should be incorporated into the analytical structure. As presented in Figure 3.3c, these covarying concepts are identified as Y_2 and Y_3. Their covariation with Y_1, the concept of interest, is indicated by the two-way arrows linking them with it. One-way arrows are used where temporal sequence is known, as between the X's, Y's, and Z's.

SUMMARY

This chapter has dealt with the construction of social theories, especially the use of models in theory construction and evaluation, and the elaboration of complex theoretical structures.

The utilization of models can be effective in the construction and evaluation of potential theories. A model is defined as a representation of some aspect of a theory. Five levels of modeling are differentiated, ranging from the most primitive classificatory model through the typological, contingency, and associative models to the sophisticated functional model.

A classificatory model specifies the categories or values of a concept; these

---

[20] One explanation may be that certain constraints were imposed on the social scientists of the past by the analytical and statistical methods available to them. Theories have traditionally had several independent variables but only one dependent variable, so that the analysis of variance and regressional analysis could be applied to the data. Anderson and Zelditch (Theodore R. Anderson and Morris Zelditch, *A Basic Course in Statistics*, Holt, New York, p. 102) go so far as to say that the dependent variable is "the variable in which the researcher is most interested." However, techniques [see Arthur S. Goldberger and Otis Dudley Duncan (eds.), *Structural Equation Models in the Social Sciences*, Seminar Press, New York, 1973] such as canonical analysis allow the incorporation of many effectual concepts into theoretical structures. It is now up to the present generation of social researchers to construct theories free of the traditional biases.

[21] See, for example, N. Kirshnan Namboodiri, Lewis F. Carter, and Hubert M. Blalock, Jr., *Applied Multivariate Analysis and Experimental Design*, McGraw-Hill, New York, 1975.

must be mutually exclusive and exhaustive. A typological model cross-classifies the specified dimensions of two or more concepts and labels each resulting "type" as to the characteristics associated with its particular combination of dimensions. A contingency model specifies certain differential tendencies of occurrences for a number of categories on a concept, given the occurrences of certain categories on another. An associative model expresses a linear tendency or predicts a linear relationship among the categories of two or more concepts. Here the researcher predicts the likelihood of occurrence, given each category of one concept, of each category of the other concept. The functional model extends the predictive power of the associative model to nonlinear relationships and indicates a one-to-one correspondence between the values of the concepts.

The classificatory and typological models are pretheoretical, the former dealing with only one concept and the latter specifying no tendency or relationship. However, they are important initial steps in theory construction. The contingent, associative, and functional models are theory-like in that they fulfill the definitions of theoretical propositions. To proceed to actual theory construction, the researcher need only specify the interrelationships among such propositions by way of logical deduction, empirical deduction, or both. Models also help a researcher evaluate theories proposed by others by enabling him to distinguish between pretheoretical classificatory and typological models and potential or existing theories.

Several types of complex theoretical structure may be formulated. A convergent (causal) structure focuses on the antecedents or potential causes of a concept; a divergent (effectual) structure on its consequents or potential effects; while a causal-effectual structure deals with both antecedents and consequents. All these structures are theoretically sound and deserve consideration.

Chapter 4

Verification and Modification of Social Theories

After a researcher has formulated a theoretical structure, he is ready to turn his attention to verifying and modifying it. *Verification* is the process of examining theoretical propositions using empirical observations. *Modification* is the process of reformulating theoretical propositions as informed by empirical observations. The connections between the propositions and the observations may occur either through *induction* (moving from observations to the construction of theory) or *deduction* (proceeding from theory to its testing with observations).

This chapter will deal with induction and deduction, their integration in the verification of theory, operationalization, theoretical and null hypotheses, falsification and modification of theory, and the relevance of theory construction to social research.

INDUCTION AND DEDUCTION

Induction involves the use of observations in theoretical formulations. Theory and observations may be envisioned as two points along a continuum which ranges from abstract theoretical structures to ongoing activities. Ideally, ongoing activities themselves should be used in theory formulation. But, in fact, the researcher has available only observations of ongoing activities. And human perceptions of ongoing activities never correspond perfectly to the actual activities. For example, if two different people observed and reported on a speech by a political candidate, it is likely that they would agree on some of the content of what they had heard and disagree on some of it. Until mechanisms are devised which can make observations corresponding perfectly to ongoing activities, social researchers will always be faced with the problem of minimizing discrepancies between observations and ongoing activities. The ways in which such discrepancies can be minimized will be discussed in Chapter 10, Measurement. It is sufficient here to note that observations, the starting point in inductive theory formulation, are not identical with ongoing activities.

How are observations used in theoretical formulations? One of their major contributions is to provide the empirical bases for new theories. This occurs when a researcher has no theory in mind before making observations. His or her analysis of the data from the specific observations made may suggest concepts, propositions, and a theoretical structure that seems to provide a plausible explanation for the observed relations.

Induction also comes into play when observations are used to test proposed or existing theories. The analyzed observations may reveal that part or all of a theory should undergo changes. When they actually contradict it, an empirical crisis is generated. Thus, observations can be used in the modification or even the discrediting of existing theories.

A third way in which induction contributes to theory formulation is through the serendipity function[1] of social research. Accidental and unexpected patterns which sometimes appear in analyzed observations may shed light on theoretical issues or provide insight for future theory construction. Serendipitous discoveries of relationships among variables are common in the social sciences.

Deduction was discussed extensively in Chapter 2. Contrary to induction, it begins with an abstract theoretical structure and culminates in observations which may be used to test empirical propositions. Whether a researcher starts with observations or with a theoretical structure, deduction must be utilized to construct empirical propositions and obtain observations to test them. Deduction is the ultimate route to the empirical verification required of a theory by our definition.

PROCESS OF THEORY VERIFICATION

Induction and deduction are combined in the process of theory construction. Figure 4.1 illustrates inductive and deductive connections between theoretical propositions and empirical observations.

To illustrate the inductive and deductive processes in theory construction we shall consider a hypothetical study which begins in the empirical world of ongoing social activities. A researcher may be interested in the ongoing activities in

[1] Robert K. Merton, *Social Theory and Social Structure,* Free Press, Glencoe, Ill., 1957, pp. 102–117.

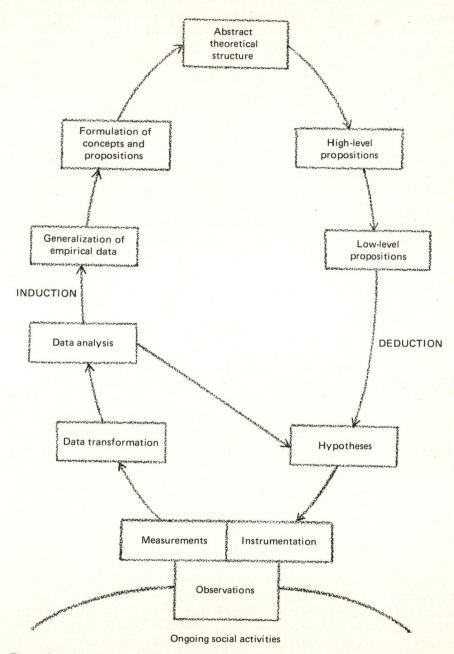

Figure 4.1 Induction and deduction in the process of theory verification.

classroom situations, specifically, patterns of interaction between teachers and students. Lacking preset notions or theoretical guidance as to what patterns are likely to occur, he goes to several classrooms and observes the interactions. (Remember that observations of interactions are not identical with the interactions themselves. An observer is necessarily selective, and his interpretations may be influenced by his cultural, social, and educational background.)

One type of interaction noticed by the researcher could be students nodding at the teacher. Once this activity has caught the researcher's eye, he undertakes more systematic observation. Two features might become evident: (1) the frequency of nodding varies from student to student, from almost no nodding by some students to almost constant nodding by others; and (2) students who nod more frequently seem to receive higher grades on tests.

The researcher has not only observed a particular activity, but has systematically measured its frequency among different individuals and recognized a potential relationship between two activities (nodding at the teacher more often and receiving higher grades on tests). He must measure these activities in a number of classrooms and ascertain that his data support the tendency for students who nod more frequently to receive higher grades as more than just a freak happening in one classroom. He next seeks possible explanations for the observed relationship by asking himself, "Why should nodding at the teacher more often be connected with receiving higher grades?" Here he is generalizing from empirical data to a theoretical structure whose concepts are represented by the observed activities.

Two plausible explanations may occur to the researcher. First, students may nod at the teacher when they understand the material being presented. Better comprehension should be associated with better performance on tests, which of course is indicated by higher grades. Thus the observed relationship between more frequent nodding at the teacher and receiving higher grades is explained by the theoretical proposition "Better comprehension leads to better performance."

An alternative explanation suggests that nodding at the teacher indicates performance of the student role as expected by the teacher. Students who nod frequently provide the teacher with positive reinforcement for his own role performance. And positive reinforcement induces positive response. The teacher reacts with more of a positive response (higher grades on tests) to those students who supply him with more positive reinforcement. Here the observed relationship between nodding more frequently and receiving higher grades is explained by the theoretical proposition "Furnishing more positive reinforcement to a role performer induces more positive response from him."

Since either of these theories could conceivably explain his observations, the researcher must find some means of discriminating between them. He hopes to verify one and discredit the other; or, if both theories are at least partially valid, to establish their relative credibility. There is also the possibility that still other propositions could be developed to explain his observations. However, for the time being, he is willing to restrict the verification process to these two.

The researcher has so far been involved with *inducing* theoretical structures from observations, as depicted on the left-hand side of Figure 4.1. He is now ready to *deduce* some empirical propositions from these two tentative theories so as to test them. The lowest-level propositions drawn up will in fact be hypotheses which can be verified using empirical observations. Empirical verification of a hypothesis lends credence to the theory from which it originated, and verification of multiple hypotheses deriving from the same theory supports it even further.

A theoretical structure containing empirical propositions deduced from the theory that better comprehension leads to better performance might look like this:

Postulates:

1   Better comprehension leads to better performance.

2a   Comprehension varies directly with the frequency with which a student nods at the teacher.

2b   Comprehension varies directly with the frequency with which a student responds correctly to the teacher's questions in class.

3   Performance varies directly with the test grades a student receives.

Deductions:

4a   More frequent nodding at the teacher by a student leads to his or her receiving better test grades.

4b   More frequent correct response by a student to the teacher's questions in class leads to his or her receiving better test grades.

The theory that positive reinforcement induces positive response could be examined using the following theoretical structure:

Postulates:

1   More positive reinforcement induces more positive response.

2c   Positive reinforcement varies directly with the frequency with which a student nods at the teacher.

2d   Positive reinforcement varies directly with the frequency with which a student volunteers to do some task for the teacher.

3   Positive response varies directly with the test grades a student receives.

Deductions:

4c   More frequent nodding at the teacher by a student leads to his or her receiving better test grades.

4d   More frequent volunteering by a student to do some task for the teacher leads to his or her receiving better test grades.

Note that in each case the deductions are actually hypotheses containing only empirical propositions. The first hypothesis deduced from each theory is identical to the researcher's previous observation. Its inclusion here allows him once more to demonstrate this pattern of interaction empirically, and thereby to accumulate evidence that it did not occur by chance.

The researcher also presents two new and dissimilar hypotheses. In proposition 2*b*, the concept of comprehension is operationalized using the variable "frequency of correct response to the teacher's questions in class." Proposition 2*d* contains the variable "frequency of volunteering to do some task for the teacher" as an operationalization of positive reinforcement. These operationalizations are then utilized in hypotheses 4*b* and 4*d*. It is essential that the concept of comprehension not overlap with the variable chosen to represent positive reinforcement (frequency of volunteering for tasks), while positive reinforcement should not be tapped by the operationalization of comprehension (frequency of correct response).

The theoretical structures of the two alternative explanations are shown in Figure 4.2. The next step for the researcher is the construction of questions, items, or both, and a coding scheme that will allow systematic observation of the variables in his hypotheses (frequency of nodding, test grades, frequency of correct response in class, and frequency of volunteering for tasks). This is known as *instrumentation* and will be discussed at length in Chapter 6.

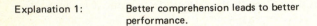

Explanation 1:   Better comprehension leads to better performance.

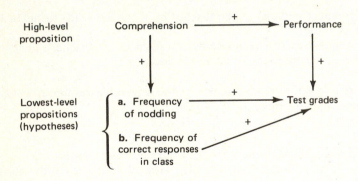

Explanation 2:   More positive reinforcement induces more positive response.

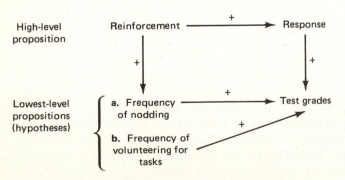

Figure 4.2   Theoretical structures of two alternative explanations.

The process of *deducing* empirical propositions from theory illustrated on the right-hand side of Figure 4.1 is now complete. However, there are still several vital procedures to be enacted before the researcher can actually collect the data which will provide the tests of his hypotheses. These are sampling (which involves, among other issues, judgments about what classrooms in what schools should be observed and whether these are representative of all those situations to which the researcher wants to generalize his findings) and selection of the appropriate type of study and method of data collection. They will be covered in later chapters.

Once he has accomplished these tasks and gathered his data, the researcher organizes them so that the hypothesized relationships among variables may be investigated. He then carries out the data analysis. This may confirm the first hypothesis deduced from both theories, thus validating his earlier observations. However, the data may tend also to support hypothesis 4*b* but not hypothesis 4*d*. This result suggests that the first theoretical explanation is more credible than the second. The theory that better comprehension leads to better performance has been verified, while the idea that more positive reinforcement induces more positive response has been at least partially discredited as an explanation for the relationship between frequency of nodding and test grades.

The researcher has now traveled the full cycle of the theory verification process depicted in Figure 4.1.

Several aspects of theory verification deserve elaboration here. They are operationalization, and the testing and falsification of theory.

Operationalization

The empirical testing of a theoretical structure actually begins within the structure itself. Consider the structures presented in Figure 4.2. The translation of the abstract terms (concepts) in the high-level propositions into the empirical terms (variables) in the lowest-level propositions makes possible the empirical testing of the high-level propositions, as the propositions containing variables can be tested with observations. The process of translating abstract terms (concepts) into empirical terms (variables) is called *operationalization.*

Postulates 2*a*, 2*b*, 3, 4*a*, and 4*b* in the first theoretical structure, and postulates 2*c*, 2*d*, 3, 4*c*, and 4*d* in the second, represent the process of operationalization. Thus, operationalization begins with the linkage of concepts with variables and culminates in propositions stating relations among variables. Without it, abstract propositions cannot be verified empirically. When operationalization is complete, the researcher has at hand propositions which contain only variables. These are called *theoretical hypotheses*. Theoretical hypotheses are the lowest-level propositions in a theoretical structure and provide the connection between high-level propositions and observations. They allow the realization of empirical testing of theory.

Theoretical and Null Hypotheses

The hypotheses discussed so far all fall under the general heading "theoretical hypotheses." They are deduced from high-level propositions and take the propositional form, "The greater the *A*, the greater (or the less) the *B*." They propose relationships, whether covariational or causal. In our extended example, hypotheses 4*a* and 4*c* posit a causal relation between the frequency of nodding and test grades, namely, more frequent nodding leads to better grades.

However, in order for a hypothesis to be tested, it must be capable of being falsified or discredited. If there were no way to "fail" the test of verification, then "passing" it would be meaningless. Two strategies for testing a hypothesis may be conceived. A *direct* test would consist of amassing empirical observations which allowed a statement of the probability that the hypothesis was *not* true. If this probability were high, we would know that the hypothesis was likely to be false.

The *indirect* testing strategy uses a null hypothesis which directly *contradicts* the theoretical one. For example, if the theoretical hypothesis proposes a positive linear relationship, the null hypothesis can propose *no relationship*. Empirical observations are then used to provide a statement of the probability that the hypothesis of *no* relationship is true. When the data show a positive relationship pattern which would occur only, say, 5 times out of 100 if the hypothesis of no relationship were true, the researcher usually feels justified in *rejecting* this null hypothesis. Since the null hypothesis contradicts the theoretical hypothesis, if one rejects the null hypothesis, one confirms the theoretical hypothesis. If, however, the researcher fails to reject the null hypothesis, he fails to confirm the theoretical hypothesis. Therefore the indirect strategy also constitutes a test which can be "failed."

In practice, *the indirect strategy is used*. Why is the complicated indirect test preferred to the simpler-sounding direct one? This is mainly due to the nature of available statistical procedures. Many of these procedures compare empirical observations with those that would be "expected" in case a null hypothesis is true. The more different the observed data are from what would be expected on the basis of the null hypothesis, the less likely it is that the null hypothesis is true. In the empirical test, then, one maximizes the chance for confirmation of the null hypothesis. Only when the null hypothesis is rejected will the theoretical hypothesis be given more credibility. Thus, it is a conservative strategy in theory construction—only relationships strong enough in empirical tests shall have a chance of being accepted as part of a theory.

There is still another objection to the direct strategy. What does it mean to the researcher when given the probability that the theoretical hypothesis is false? If there is a 95 percent chance that it is false, this does not necessarily mean that there is no relationship between the variables. It could also mean that there is a different kind of relationship than the one postulated. Such an inconclusive statement is not much help to a researcher. With the indirect strategy, once the null hypothesis is falsified, one knows that there is at least some credibility to the relationship between the variables as theorized. The range of alternative conclusions narrows. An indirect test can even be so structured that, if one rejects the null hypothesis, one knows the range within which the theoretically hypothesized relation may lie. This topic will be elaborated in Chapter 7.

Let us illustrate with our example. The theoretical hypothesis, which is usually symbolized as H_1, states that more frequent nodding at the teacher by a student leads to his or her receiving better test grades. A direct test of this hypothesis would give us a statement of the likelihood that it was false. If there were a very high likelihood of its being false, the researcher would know that the frequency of nodding was not positively related to test grades. However, he would not know whether the variables were in fact related in some other manner, or not related at all.

To use the indirect strategy, on the other hand, the researcher first formulates the null hypothesis, which is symbolized H_0. The null hypothesis in this case states that the frequency with which a student nods at the teacher is *not related* to the test grades he or she receives. The statistical analysis tells the researcher the extent to which the patterns in the data are different from those that would be expected to occur on the basis of chance (that is, if there were no relationship between the variables). If they are drastically different, the researcher knows that there is probably a real relationship between the frequency of nodding and test grades.

Thus, there are two types of hypotheses. Theoretical hypotheses are deduced from high-level propositions, contain variables, and specify the relations between them. Null hypotheses specify relations when the theoretical hypotheses *cannot* be true. Using the letters A and B to represent variables, a theoretical and a null hypothesis might read:

$$H_1: A \xrightarrow{+} B$$
$$H_0: A \xrightarrow{+}\!\!\!\!\!/\ \ B$$

The empirical verification of H_1 involves a statistical test for the validity of H_0. Two outcomes are possible: the rejection of H_0, which occurs when it is highly improbable that the null hypothesis is true; and the failure to reject H_0, when it is probable that the null hypothesis is true. When H_0 is rejected, H_1 is confirmed with a certain degree of significance. The level of significance depends on just how improbable it would be for the patterns in the data to occur if H_0 were true. When H_0 is not rejected, H_1 is not confirmed.

Note that one *does not* conclude from the failure to reject the null hypothesis that one should reject the theoretical hypothesis. The failure to reject the null hypothesis only informs the researcher that the particular set of observations gathered does not deviate from the expectation of the null hypothesis significantly. This does not mean that the theory is wrong. The data could be faulty, or operationalizations of the concepts could be poor.

If a theoretical hypothesis cannot be statistically rejected, can any theoretical proposition be rejected? And if not, can a theory ever be falsified?

FALSIFICATION AND MODIFICATION OF THEORY

Strictly speaking, a theory cannot be falsified, as is apparent in the above discussion. While the researcher may confirm or fail to confirm a theoretical hypothesis, he cannot reject it. However, to discriminate among proposed explanations, it is important to construct testing situations which at least promote one's confidence in discrediting certain theoretical explanations in favor of another explanation. The process of cumulated discredibility is then used as evidence that a theoretical explanation may be false. The discrediting process thus constitutes an important element in the falsification of a theory.

How does one go about discrediting a theory? There are three methodological possibilities. The first one involves the testing of multiple explanations.

In our example, two theoretical structures offered differing explanations for the observed relationship between frequency of nodding and test grades. Empirical examination of hypotheses deduced from each theory suggested that one of these was more tenable than the other. That is, the data revealed a stronger relationship between frequency of correct response in class and test grades than between frequency of volunteering for tasks and test grades.

When one theoretical explanation consistently receives more confirmative evidence than others in a series of empirical tests, the other explanations are further and further discredited. Although they cannot be falsified directly, cumulated discredit demonstrates their relative uselessness in explaining the relationship or relationships of interest to the researcher. Thus, the process of theory verification is important not only in supporting or confirming a theoretical explanation, but also in accumulating evidence which discredits alternatives.

A second method in the process of falsification involves the gathering of negative information about the theoretical hypothesis. That is, not only should the researcher look for positive evidence to verify the hypothesis, he should also be on the lookout for negative evidence, namely, any empirical evidence which not only demonstrates that the theoretical hypothesis is not confirmed in the expected direction, but also that the empirical evidence shows a reversed direction. Thus, when a researcher is testing the H_1 that A positively leads to B, he should not only ascertain the extent to which the empirical evidence deviates from the null hypothesis that A is not related to B, but also the extent to which A may negatively lead to B.

In the extended example, one theoretical hypothesis states, "The frequency of correct response in class is positively related to test grades" (see Figure 4.2). The null hypothesis for a statistical test of observations is, "The frequency of correct response in class is not positively related to test grades." The null hypothesis is statistically tested to decide the extent to which the theoretical hypothesis can be confirmed. However, if the data show not only that the theoretical hypothesis cannot be confirmed but also that the statement "The frequency of correct response in class negatively induces test grades" might be a more credible description of the observations gathered, this information is valuable. While it is impossible to falsify the original theoretical hypothesis with this one set of observations, the evidence raises stronger suspicion about the credibility of the theoretical hypothesis than the mere failure to confirm the theoretical hypothesis.

This method can be called the simple method of falsification, as it merely allows the researcher to pay attention to a greater range of statistical outcomes in the testing of specific theoretical hypotheses. Still a third method in the process of falsification involves a more extensive and critical examination of the credibility of a theoretical explanation. This is the critical method of falsification.

In the critical method of falsification, not only multiple alternative explanations are involved and examination of relations in the reverse directions as specified in the theoretical hypothesis is made, but secondary relationships derived from the theoretical explanations are examined also. For a theoretical explanation that A positively induces B, the critical method of falsification would enumerate not only that A does not negatively induce B but also that A and B show positive and causal relations with a number of other concepts which are logically related to them. Thus, if logically deducible relationships exist between A, B, and C, then empirical observations should also confirm the positive relationships among the variables tapping the concepts A, B, and C.

The three methods of cumulating credibility or discredibility for the falsification of a theoretical explanation are presented in Figure 4.3. In this example, the basic theoretical structure focuses on the causal relationship between A and B. Thus, the methods of verification simply examine if a null hypothesis about their indicators (X and Y) is true. In this case, the null hypothesis is that X does not cause Y. The rejection of the null hypothesis then leads to the verification of the theoretical hypothesis ($A \xrightarrow{+} B$). In the simple method of falsification, not only the null hypothesis, "X does not positively lead to Y," is examined, but also another alternative hypothesis, "X negatively leads to Y," is also examined. Only when both the null hypothesis and the other alternative hypothesis are rejected can one give more credibility to the theoretical hypothesis. Finally, in the critical method of falsification, in addition to the testing of the null hypothesis and of the other alternative hypothesis, examinations are extended to logically deduced relations between A and C and between B and C. That is, if logically B leads to C positively, then falsification must be carried to the relationships between X_1 and Y_1 and between Y_1 and Z_1. Only when the logically deduced relations as well as the original hypothesis ($X_1 \xrightarrow{+} Y_1$) are given credibility can one conclude that there is indeed a positive causal relationship between A and B. In summary, the process of theoretical verification only demonstrates the extent to which a particular hypothesized relationship is confirmed. The simple method of falsification goes further to examine potential negative or "damaging" evidence for the theoretical hypothesis. And finally, the critical method of falsification examines potential negative or damaging evidence not only for the hypothesized relationships but also for logically deduced relationships.

As indicated earlier, these methods help in cumulating evidence rendering credibility or discredibility to the various theoretical explanations. Any single set of observations cannot falsify a theoretical explanation. But cumulated sets of observations indicating unexpected relationships can discredit the explanation to the extent that alternative explanations must be given more weight.

When alternative explanations have gained credibility, then the process of modification of theory begins. This task requires the reformulation of theoretical concepts and propositions and their testing with further empirical evidence. Thus,

Theoretical structure:

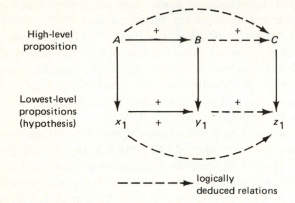

(a) Theoretical verification of H_1 ($A \xrightarrow{+} B$):

Must examine: $X_1 \dashrightarrow\!\!\!|\!|\!\!\!\rightarrow Y_1$

(b) Simple method of falsification of H_1 ($A \xrightarrow{+} B$):

Must examine: $X_1 \dashrightarrow\!\!\!|\!|\!\!\!\rightarrow Y_1$

and

$$X_1 \xrightarrow{-} Y_1$$

(c) Critical method of falsification of H_1 ($A \xrightarrow{+} B$):

Must examine $X_1 \dashrightarrow\!\!\!|\!|\!\!\!\rightarrow Y_1$

$$X_1 \xrightarrow{-} Y_1$$

and simple falsification of H_2 ($A \xrightarrow{+} C$) and H_3 ($B \xrightarrow{+} C$):

$$X_1 \dashrightarrow\!\!\!|\!|\!\!\!\rightarrow Z_1$$

$$X_1 \xrightarrow{-} Z_1$$

$$Y_1 \dashrightarrow\!\!\!|\!|\!\!\!\rightarrow Z_1$$

and

$$Y_1 \xrightarrow{-} Z_1$$

Figure 4.3 Methods of falsification.

because of the interaction among theory verification, theory falsification, and theory modification, there is no definite beginning or end point in the process of theory construction. Existing theories must be verified, falsified, and modified, and new ones suggested. A researcher's work is never done.

THEORY CONSTRUCTION IN SOCIAL RESEARCH

There is no intrinsic need for social research to be carried out in conjunction with theory construction, verification, or modification. Some research projects are directed solely toward practical objectives such as evaluating ongoing social activities, projecting or planning future social activities, and manipulating social activities. They may begin with a definition of the problem, proceed through instrumentation and data collection, and arrive at data analysis and interpretation. The generalization of findings is then from a specific study to a general population, and does not follow the inductive route to any theory.

However, some theory is usually involved in social research. A theory does not have to be elegant or very abstract. It presents, in summary form, ideas that are potentially important in the explanation of observed relationships among social activities. A researcher trained in theory construction should always do some theorizing in connection with his research, even when this is not its prime objective. Theory construction involving verification and modification are integral parts of social research.

SUMMARY

Verification of theory requires the examination of theoretical propositions using empirical observations and involves both induction and deduction. Induction, in which observations lead to the formulation of theoretical propositions, has several important functions relating to theory verification. It (1) provides the empirical bases for new theories, (2) suggests changes where needed in existing theories, and (3) contributes the serendipity function in which accidental and unexpected patterns in observations lead to the revision or construction of theories.

Deduction allows substitution for abstract, high-level propositions by empirical propositions which can be tested using observations. The process of translating abstract terms (concepts) into empirical terms (variables) is called operationalization. The lowest-level proposition in a deductive system of theory is the theoretical hypothesis. Because the theoretical hypothesis cannot be tested directly using available statistical methods, the null hypothesis, which states that no relationship exists between the variables, is tested in its stead. When the null hypothesis is rejected, the theoretical hypothesis is confirmed, and the credibility of the theoretical structure is enhanced. Failure to reject the null hypothesis indicates that the empirical evidence gathered does not support the theoretical hypothesis and thus diminishes the credibility of the theoretical structure. However, failure to reject the null hypothesis does not falsify the theoretical structure.

In fact, no single set of observations can falsify a theoretical structure. However, the process of falsification of a theory utilizes various discrediting methods and permits modification of the theoretical structure. In addition to the process of theory verification by empirically confirming the predicted relationships among variables, the simple method of falsification involves the examination of relationships among variables which are in opposite directions as predicted by the theoretical hypotheses. Further, the critical method of falsification examines the relationships among variables for concepts linked in logically deduced propositions to ascertain if any reversed directions from the predicted have occurred. Cumulation of evidence of relationships in the direction opposite that predicted by theoretical hypotheses over different sets of observations discredits the proposed theoretical structure and provides the impetus and guidance for modifications of the theoretical structure.

Part Two

Use of Statistics in Social Research

Chapter 5

Describing One Variable

Before one may proceed to explore phases of social research, a review of the use of statistics in social research is in order. This is not to say that all social research is quantitative in nature, thus requiring a knowledge of statistics. Rather, in social research, many decisions which have to be made are statistical in nature. For example, in selecting a sample of respondents from a population (Chapter 9), statistics helps one decide how many respondents are needed in a sample and how precise the information one obtains from a sample can become. In constructing a research form with which a researcher obtains information (the instrument), it is essential that a researcher know statistically how to ascertain the reliability and validity of the information obtained (Chapter 10).

In this and the next chapter, statistics is introduced as a tool to describe the information at hand—the descriptive statistics. In Chapter 7, statistics will be introduced as a tool to generalize findings from a sample of respondents to a larger population and to the theoretical structure—the inferential statistics. The discussion will be simple and straightforward, so that a reader with minimal or no statistical background may acquire the necessary understanding to proceed to other phases of social research.

DEFINITIONS

The information gathered in social research constitutes the basis for decisions as to whether certain null hypotheses should be rejected or not, and whether certain theoretical hypotheses should be confirmed. The term *data* is used to represent the recorded response patterns of the respondents to an instrument used in the study. The data usually can be represented in a matrix. A matrix is a grid which has intersecting rows and columns. For example, if a researcher has gathered information on sex and race from five respondents, the data matrix may look like the following:

Respondent	Sex	Race
001	1	1
002	2	1
003	1	2
004	1	1
005	2	2

Here, the matrix has five rows, each row representing a respondent. The respondent is identified in each row by the number in the first column (001, 002, etc.). The sex information is coded, following the respondent identification code, with "1" for "female" and "2" for "male." Finally, the last column of each row indicates the race information for each respondent, with "1" for "white" and "2" for "nonwhite." Thus, from the data matrix above, one knows that the first respondent, 001, is female and white; the second respondent, 002, is male and white; etc.

The data matrix contains information about each respondent on variables—each row representing a respondent and the columns representing the variables. A *variable* is defined as a characteristic which can take on two or more different categories. For example, both sex and race are variables, since they both can take on two or more categories (sex has two values, "male" and "female"; and race has also two values, "white" and "nonwhite"). In the data matrix, each respondent can assume only one particular category on a variable. Thus, a respondent cannot be both male and female at the same time, nor white and nonwhite simultaneously. A respondent's response to a particular category on a variable is called an *observation*.

SCALES OF VARIABLES

While some variables have fixed categories, such as sex, other variables, such as race, can assume different sets of categories. In the example given above, the race variable takes on "white" and "nonwhite" categories, But it may conceivably take on "white," "black," "Oriental," etc. Thus, the response categories of a variable may vary. The ideal categories tap both the qualitative (presence or absence of a characteristic) and the quantitative (how many, how much) aspects of the variable. In many cases in social research, finding and constructing the appropriate categories for the variables constitute a most crucial operation. This is crucial since in social research, unlike physical sciences, the correspondence between the response categories of a variable and the variation in a concept is not at all agreed on. Unless rational decisions on the categories can be made for all variables used, social researchers might just construct their own response categories for each variable studied and the result would be continuous confusion. This, in fact, has happened to varying degrees in social research. Thus, it is important to identify different types of response categories, so that evaluation of their adequacy can be made. In general, four scales can be constructed for a variable: nominal, ordinal, interval, and ratio.

Nominal Scale

A nominal scale consists of two or more categories distinguishing the presence or absence of a characteristic or several categories of the characteristic. These categories are exhaustive and mutually exclusive; that is, each and every observation can and must be placed in only one of the categories. No statement of comparison using "more" or "less" can be made across the categories. Typical examples of nominal variables in social research are sex, race, and religious affiliation. Statements summarizing such data might read: "There are more males than females at college A," "12 percent of the population of city B is black," and "The Catholic Church has more members in the United States than any other single religious denomination." A typical nominal scale has the form:

Scale value	Variable X (sex) response category
1	Female
2	Male

Ordinal Scale

An ordinal scale allows comparison among the values or categories of a variable with statements indicating "more" or "less." The values of an ordinal variable are ranked on a certain criterion. However, they cannot be compared in terms of *how much* "more" or "less." A typical ordinal scale has the form:

Scale value	Variable X ("Are we spending too much, too little, or about the right amount on improving the condition of blacks?") response category
1	Too little
2	About right
3	Too much

A respondent who checks response category "1" is assumed to feel more should be spent than one who checks category "2"; the latter, in turn, indicates more should be spent than someone who checks category "3," and so on. In symbolic form, the statement made by the scale is that "1" > "2" > "3." However, while the categories are ordered in terms of a certain criterion (in this case, amount spent to improve the condition of blacks), an ordinal scale does not enable the researcher to determine the extent (how much more or less) to which category "1," for example, is greater than category "2" or "3."

Interval Scale

An interval scale not only allows rank ordering of the categories of a variable, but also specifies the relative distance between each pair of categories. The distance between each contiguous pair of categories is the same as that between any other contiguous pair. A typical interval scale is a person's age. Thus, it can be said that the difference (in years) between a person 20 years of age and another, 15 years of age, is the same as that between a person 42 years old and a person 37 years old.

Ratio Scale

A ratio scale, in addition to all the features of the nominal, ordinal, and interval scales, has a meaningful zero point. Zero takes on significance as a category of the variable. With an interval scale, where the distance between each pair of categories is known, the points representing the categories can be added to or subtracted from one another. In the case of the ratio scale, because zero is meaningful, the points representing the categories can also be multiplied and divided by one another. The ratio between any pair of categories is known. A typical ratio scale is weight or height. In social research, for all practical purposes, interval and ratio scales are combined.

SCALES AND STATISTICS

The scales of variables have important consequences for a researcher in describing the data matrix. For the more sophisticated the scale is (moving away from the nominal scale and toward the interval scale), the more categories and values can be used to describe a variable. The more categories and values used to describe a variable, the more likely that the observation made for each respondent will approach the "exact value" for the respondent on the variable. In reality, measurement of a variable can never be so precise as to tap the "exact value." But, the closer the "exact value" is approached or estimated, the greater confidence a researcher has in describing the data matrix and making general statements estimating the activities in a larger population. This is so because more precise statistics are available for analyzing interval and ratio variables. *Statistics* can be defined as the theories and techniques with which the data matrix can be systematically reduced for summarization and inference.

USE OF NATIONAL OPINION RESEARCH CENTER DATA

Since 1972, the National Opinion Research Center (NORC) in Chicago has conducted an annual survey of a United States national sample of men and women, asking a large number of social, economic, political, demographic, and other questions. The data from these surveys are available on cards or tapes with codebooks to all researchers at a nominal cost.[1] These data undoubtedly will be used by many social researchers. To acquaint the reader with these data, we will use many questions and data from these surveys throughout the book, and include a selected set of questions (Appendix A) and occupational prestige scales (Appendix B) at the end of the book. The reader is encouraged to use these questions and data.

DESCRIPTIVE STATISTICS AND VARIABLES

To describe and summarize the data matrix, the researcher must consider (1) on what scale the variable is measured, and (2) how many variables are being analyzed simultaneously. In the following, the discussion will focus on single-variable analysis. The next chapter will discuss multiple-variable analysis. Single-variable analysis is also known as univariate analysis, and multiple-variable analysis as multivariate analysis.[2]

SINGLE-VARIABLE DESCRIPTIONS

For variables measured on nominal or ordinal scales, the frequency table, the ratio, the percentages, and the mode can be computed for graphic and table presentations.

Frequency Table

The data in the data matrix are called the *ungrouped data*. The simplest way of summarizing the data for a single variable is to group all the observations for each code for the variable. The result of the grouped data can be a simple table as in Table 5.1. This table is usually called the frequency table or the marginal table. Note that a category "unspecified" is used to keep track of data which have been either left unanswered by the respondent or miscoded by the coders. The codes which should not appear (in our example, anything other than "1" or "2") are called the illegal codes. All illegal codes can be grouped into the "unspecified" category.

In data analysis, responses with illegal codes are considered data with "missing values" and usually deleted for consideration. Thus, from this point on, the

---

[1] Inquiries should be sent to: Roper Public Opinion Research Center, Williams College, Williamstown, Massachusetts 01267; telephone 413 GL 8-5500.

[2] Strictly speaking, the term *multivariate* is reserved for an analysis in which two or more dependent variables are present (see discussion on the divergent structure in Chapter 3). However, the distinction is not maintained in the literature.

**Table 5.1   Frequency Table
for Sex of Respondents**

Category	Frequency
1. Female	803
2. Male	701
9. Unspecified	10
Total	1,514

Source: NORC 1973 General Social Survey.

discussion assumes that all missing data are deleted. When a variable draws a substantial number of missing data (say, over 20 percent of all respondents), the researcher should use the remaining data with caution, as perhaps the item used was too sensitive or incomprehensible to a good portion of the respondents. As a consequence, the validity and reliability of the measure can be questioned.

For simplicity, symbolic notations can be used to represent the frequency in a frequency table. For example, we may use "n" to represent the total number of observations, "n_1" to represent the number of observations in the first category, "n_2" observations in the second category, and so forth. Thus, the sex frequency table can be refined as in Table 5.2. Such grouped data can also be presented in graphs, such as in Figure 5.1.

Ratio

For grouped data, the frequencies of two or more categories can be compared. The result may be a ratio between two or more categories.

For example, in Table 5.2, the ratio between females and males in the data can be computed:

$$\text{Sex ratio} = \frac{\text{number of males}}{\text{number of females}} = \frac{701}{803} = 0.87$$

This means there is about one female for each male in the sample. To reduce the confusion, the ratio can be multiplied by 100:

$$\text{Sex ratio} = (100)\frac{\text{number of males}}{\text{number of females}} = (100)(0.87) = 87$$

Thus, there are 87 males for every 100 females in the sample.

**Table 5.2   Sex Distribution
of Respondents**

Category	Frequency
Female (n_1)	803
Male (n_2)	701
n	1,504

Source: NORC 1973 General Social Survey.

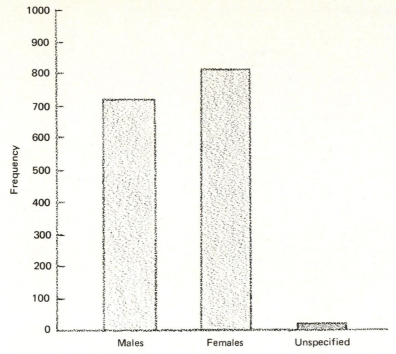

Figure 5.1 Sex distribution of respondents.

Percentage

Another way of comparing categories is to compare the number of observations in each category with the total number of observations having *legal* codes. In Table 5.1 there are 1,504 observations with legal codes. Thus, the percentage of "female" observations can be found.

$$\text{Percentage of females} = (100)\frac{803}{1,504} = 53$$

In other words, of all the observations, about 53 percent of them are females. Note that the percentage was calculated relative to 100 percent.

Usually, the frequencies and percentages of a variable are presented in a single table, as in Table 5.3.

Note that "*f*" is used to represent frequencies, and that in calculating the percentages the "unspecified" category was eliminated.

Mode

The mode is simply the category (with a legal code) in a frequency table which has the largest number of observations. For example, the modal category of the sex distribution in Table 5.1 is "female." However, it is possible that a distribution has more than one modal category. For example, an analysis of "number of children in the family" may result in the frequencies and percentages in Table 5.4.

Table 5.3   Distribution of Respondents by Sex

Category	f	Percent
Female	803	53
Male	701	47
Total	1,504	100

Source: NORC 1973 General Social Survey.

Thus, there are two modal categories ("two children" and "three children").

The ratio, the percentage, and the mode can also be displayed in graphs as in Figure 5.1, by changing the labels and measurements on the axes.

Central Tendency Measures

These are measures used to describe a set of data in terms of a single representative or typical value. For example, "What is the typical family income in this neighborhood?" "How much television does a typical 3-year-old watch in the United States?" These measures are appropriate for ordinal or interval data.

Median   When the categories are ordinal, the data are called an *ordered set.* Then, the *median* is defined as the value of a category which has equal numbers of observations lower and higher than that value.

For example, in Table 5.4, the data can be considered as an ordered set ranging from "one child" to "seven or more children." The counting proceeds from one extreme until it reaches the observation which represents the midpoint of the data distribution. Since there are 250 observations, the midpoint observation must be observation 125. When the counting starts from "one child," the number (125) is reached and exceeded in the "third" category. Thus, the median is 3.

There are times when the counting leads to a midpoint in between two values, for example, in a set of observations with values = 1, 1, 2, 3, 4, 4, 5, 5, 5, 6, 6, 7. For these twelve observations, the midpoint is the sixth observation ($^{12}/_2 = 6$). However, when we count from the lowest number, the midpoint is 4 and, when we

Table 5.4   Number of Children in the Family

Number of children	f	Percent
1	10	4
2	70	28
3	70	28
4	30	12
5	20	8
6	50	20
7 or more	0	0
Total	250	100

count from the highest number, it is 5. The median, then, is the average of these two values [median = (4 + 5)/2 = 4.5].

In general, when there is an odd number of observations, the median is simply the value of the observation which exceeds the midpoint value. When there is an even number of observations, the median is the average of the two midpoint values.

However, when the data are grouped so that each category contains a range of values, a different method must be used to find the median.

For example, in an analysis of "family income," the distribution shown in Table 5.5 is found.

The second column in Table 5.4 shows the cumulative frequency (cn) of the observations, starting the count from the first category.

The formula for finding the median for the grouped data is:

$$\text{Median} = l + \frac{(N/2) - cn}{n}(w) \tag{5.1}$$

where
l = lower limit of category containing the midpoint
N = total number of observations with legal codes
cn = cumulative number of observations in category immediately preceding the midpoint category
n = number of observations in category containing the midpoint
w = width of the category containing the midpoint

Thus, for the "family income" variable, the midpoint category is "$10,000–14,999," since the midpoint (half of 1,395 observations = 698) falls in this category.

l = 10,000 (the lower limit of "$10,000–14,999")
N = 1,395

Table 5.5   Family Income

Income category	f	cn
Under $1,000	36	36
$1,000–2,999	107	142
$3,000–3,999	85	227
$4,000–4,999	83	310
$5,000–5,999	69	379
$6,000–6,999	54	433
$7,000–7,999	90	523
$8,000–9,999	153	676
$10,000–14,999	348	1,024
$15,000–19,999	176	1,200
$20,000–24,999	103	1,303
$25,000 or over	92	1,395

Source: NORC 1973 General Social Survey, excluding illegal categories ("refused," "don't know," and "no answer").

$$cn = 676$$
$$n = 348$$
$$w = 4,999 \ (14,999 - 10,000 = 4,999)$$

Therefore,

$$\text{Median} = 10,000 \quad \frac{(1,395/2) - 676}{348} (4,999)$$

$$= 10,000 + \frac{21.5}{348} (4,999)$$

$$= 10,000 + (.06)(4,999)$$
$$= 10,000 + 308.85$$
$$= 10,308$$

We conclude that the median family income for this set of data is $10,308.

Mean (Arithmetic Mean)   The mean of a variable is defined as the sum of the values of a set of observations divided by the number of observations in the set. It is a central tendency measure for interval or ratio data.

Let X_i represent the observed value of respondent i, and X the mean. Then, the mean is defined as:

$$\bar{X} = \frac{1}{n} \sum_{i=1}^{n} X_i \tag{5.2}$$

where $\sum_{i=1}^{n}$ indicates the summation of the values for all (n) observations.

Suppose the IQs among eleven observations are 75, 85, 87, 95, 99, 100, 101, 105, 113, 115, and 125, then the mean IQ for this group is

$$\bar{X} = \frac{75 + 85 + 87 + 95 + 99 + 100 + 101 + 105 + 113 + 115 + 125}{11}$$

$$= 1100/11 = 100$$

If data are grouped, a simplified formula can be used to calculate the mean. For example, data of student ratings of the food service in a college dormitory may result in the grouped data presented in Table 5.6. The formula is:

$$\bar{X} = \frac{\sum_{i=1}^{m} (X_i f_i)}{n} \tag{5.3}$$

where X_i = rating value of category i
$\quad\quad\quad f_i$ = frequency of observations for category i
$\quad\quad\quad m$ = number of categories
$\quad\quad\quad n$ = number of observations

Table 5.6 College Food Service

Rating (X_i)	f_i
1 (good)	0
2	3
3	1
4 (average)	6
5	6
6	5
7 (bad)	2

Since three observations had a value of 2, the summation for these observations becomes $2 \times 3 = 6$. Similarly, for the value of 3, the summation is $3 \times 1 = 3$, etc. Thus, the mean is:

$$\bar{X} = \frac{(2 \times 3) + (3 \times 1) + (4 \times 6) + (5 \times 6) + (6 \times 5) + (7 \times 2)}{23} = 4.65$$

Thus, the mean attitude toward the college food services is 4.65—on the negative side.

Choice among Mode, Median, and Mean   Since the mode, the median, and the mean are all single values representing a set of data, how does a researcher decide which statistic to use? The mode is appropriate when the variable is nominal. But, when the variable is ordinal, interval, or ratio, the decision is more complicated. First, by simple observation of the grouped data, the researcher can determine whether there is a central tendency among the observations. When there is a central tendency, categories in the middle of the scale should have many more frequencies than those toward the two extremes. When there is no central tendency, then the mode should be the choice. When there is a central tendency, the purpose of the analysis becomes important. Note that the mean is affected by every value, since every observation is taken into account in the computation (see equation 5.2), while the median is not (see equation 5.1). Thus, extreme scores affect the mean, but not the median.

For example, for the "number of siblings" variable in Table 5.7, the mean is 4.47 and the median is 4. The mean is "inflated" because there is one observation claiming twenty-seven siblings. Similarly, for the income variable, if one or two observations had $70,000 or more, the mean would be inflated, while the median would remain the same. Thus, when the purpose of the analysis is to describe the typical value, without inflation or deflation by a few extreme scores present, the median should be used. When the purpose of the analysis is to describe the typical value, taking all scores into account or where extreme scores are absent, the mean should be the choice. For reasons to be discussed in Chapter 7, the mean is

Table 5.7   Number of Siblings in the Family

Number of Siblings	f_i
0	86
1	221
2	231
3	197
4	159
5	129
6	112
7	81
8	65
9	78
10	36
11	44
12	25
13	14
14	10
15	7
16	2
18	2
20	1
27	1

$\bar{X} = 6,702/1,501 = 4.47$

Source: NORC 1973 General Social Survey, excluding illegal category ("don't know").

preferred to the median when more powerful statistics is used in inferring the data from a group of respondents to a larger population.

Measures of Dispersion

The median and the mean indicate the central tendency of the data distribution—they attempt to identify the single typical value of the data.

However, description of the data is incomplete if we fail to summarize the distribution or the dispersion of the data—the extent to which the observations are spread out or dispersed. For instance, for the following two groups of IQ,

Group I = 75, 85, 87, 96, 99, 100, 101, 105, 113, 115, and 125
Group II = 97, 98, 99, 99, 100, 100, 100, 101, 101, 102, and 103

The mean IQ for both groups is 100. However, it is unfair to state that the respondents of the two groups have similar IQs. The dispersion of the IQ scores in the first group is much greater than that in the second group—the discrepancy between the lowest and the highest scores in the first group is 50 points, whereas it is only 6 points in the second group.

There are many measures of dispersion, among them the variance, the standard deviation, the interquartile range, the range, the skewness (asymmetry of distribution), and the kurtosis (peakedness of distribution).[3] The discussion here will deal with the variance and the standard deviation, since they are the most important and popular measures of dispersion of interval or ratio data.

Variance and Standard Deviation The discrepancy between a particular score and the mean is called a *deviation* from the mean, $X_i - \bar{X}$. For instance, for observation 1 in the first group, the deviation is -25. In other words:

$$X_1 - \bar{X}_1 = 75 - 100 = -25$$

where $\bar{X}_1$ = mean of group I

The deviation seems a reasonable measure of the dispersion of the data, since greater dispersions would also give greater deviations. What should be done next is to obtain an average of all deviations for the scores for the group. Thus, the sum of all deviations (from each observation value to the mean) for group I is:

$$\sum_{i=1}^{11} (X_i - \bar{X}) = (75 - 100) + (85 - 100) + (87 - 100) + (95 - 100)$$
$$+ (99 - 100) + (100 - 100) + (101 - 100) + (105 - 100)$$
$$+ (113 - 100) + (115 - 100) + (125 - 100) = 0$$

As can be seen, because the mean is the measure of the central tendency, deviations of scores are equally spread on both sides of the mean (positive and negative values). When the deviations are summed, they inevitably equal zero. In order to avoid the problem of getting the zero every time we calculate the sum of the deviations, we must make all deviations *positive*. One way to do this is to square the deviations from the mean. For example, for group I, we obtain the following table:

X_i	$X_i - \bar{X}$	$(X_i - \bar{X})^2$
75	−25	625
85	−15	225
87	−13	164
95	− 5	25
99	− 1	1
100	0	0
101	1	1
105	5	25
113	13	169
115	15	225
125	25	625
$\bar{X} = 100$	$X_i = 0$	$\sum_{i=1}^{11} (X_i - \bar{X}) = 2{,}090$

[3] Readers interested in the other measures are referred to Gene V. Glass and Julian C. Stanley, *Statistical Methods in Education and Psychology*. Prentice-Hall, Englewood Cliffs, N.J., 1970, chap. 5.

The average of the sum of the squared deviations can be expressed as the variance s^2:

$$s^2 = \frac{\sum_{i=1}^{n} (X_i - \bar{X})^2}{n - 1} \tag{5.4}$$

where n = number of observations

We shall postpone until Chapter 7 the discussion of why the average is taken over $n - 1$ rather than simply n, as this involves issues to be discussed in Chapter 7 (see "Estimation of Parameters").

For group I data:

$$s^2 = \frac{2,090}{10} = 209$$

The squared root of the variance is called the *standard deviation s*. It is simply:

$$s = \sqrt{s^2} = \sqrt{\frac{\sum_{i=1}^{n} (X_i - \bar{X})^2}{n - 1}} \tag{5.5}$$

To simplify matters, the i's are eliminated from $\sum_{i=1}^{n}$. From now on, unless otherwise noted, the summation sign indicates the sum over all observations n.

Instead of calculating the deviations from the mean, we can find s^2 and s by directly calculating $\sum X^2$ and $(\sum X)^2$:

$$s^2 = \frac{\sum X^2 - (\sum X)^2/n}{n - 1} \tag{5.6}$$

$$s = \sqrt{\frac{\sum X^2 - (\sum X)^2/n}{n - 1}} \tag{5.7}$$

For example, returning to our IQ group I again, the variance and the standard deviations can be computed directly from the observations:

X	X^2
75	5,625
85	7,225
87	7,569
95	9,025
99	9,801
100	10,000
101	10,201
105	11,025
113	12,769
115	13,225
125	15,625
$\sum X = 1,100$	$\sum X^2 = 112,090$

$$s_1^2 = \frac{\Sigma X^2 - \frac{(\Sigma X)^2}{n}}{n - 1} = \frac{112{,}090 - \frac{(1{,}100)^2}{11}}{11 - 1}$$

$$= \frac{112{,}090 - 110{,}000}{10} = \frac{2{,}090}{10} = 209$$

$$s_1 = \sqrt{209} = 14.46$$

where s_1^2 = variance for group I (the subscript 1)
  s_1 = standard deviation for group I

Similarly for group II data:

$$s_2^2 = \frac{\Sigma X^2 - \frac{(\Sigma X)^2}{n}}{n - 1} = \frac{110{,}030 - \frac{(1{,}100)^2}{11}}{10}$$

$$= \frac{110{,}030 - 110{,}000}{10} = \frac{30}{10} = 3$$

$$s_2 = \sqrt{3} = 1.73$$

Thus, it can be seen that the dispersion of data in group I is much greater than that in group II. *For grouped data* we may use the following formulas to find the variance and the standard deviation:

$$s^2 = \frac{\Sigma X_i^2 f_i - (\Sigma X_i \, f_i)^2/n}{n - 1} \tag{5.8}$$

$$s = \sqrt{s^2} = \sqrt{\frac{\Sigma X_i^2 f_i - (\Sigma X_i \, f_i)^2/n}{n - 1}} \tag{5.9}$$

where X_i = value of each category
  f_i = frequency of observations having given that specific value as the response category

For example, to compute the s^2 and s for the number of siblings (Table 5.7),

$\Sigma X_i^2 = 2{,}949$
$\Sigma X_i f_i = 6{,}702$
$n = 1{,}501$

Therefore,

$$s^2 = \frac{2{,}949 - (6{,}702)^2/1{,}501}{1{,}500} = \frac{2{,}949 - 29{,}924.59}{1{,}500}$$

$$= \frac{-26{,}975.59}{1{,}500} = 17.98$$

$$s = 4.24$$

Standard scores (z scores)   When the mean and the standard deviation of a set of data are known, individual scores can be represented relative to the mean and the standard deviation. For example, in the IQ group I data, the observation 87 can be seen as 13 units below the mean (100). Converting the 13 units in terms of the standard deviation ($13/14.46 = 0.90$) gives the distance between the score and the mean in standard deviation units. Thus, observation 87 is 0.90 standard deviations below the mean. This transformed score is called the *standard score* or *z score* for the observation. In general, for observation i, its standard score is:

$$z_i = \frac{X_i - \bar{X}}{s} \tag{5.10}$$

There is an important reason why standard scores are used. When all scores are transformed into standard scores, the new scores have a mean of 0 and a standard deviation of 1. (The reader should verify this fact by computing the z scores for group I and group II IQ data and calculating the mean and the standard deviation for each group of the transformed data). Thus, regardless of the central tendency and dispersion appearing in a set of data, the data can be standardized, by way of the z scores, so that the central tendency and dispersion for all variables under study will have a mean of 0 and a standard deviation of 1. In other words, the variables, after being standardized relative to their means and standard deviations, can be compared on "equal footing." When variables are in their natural units (such as age in years, income in dollars, and education in years of schooling), standardization of data is not critical. However, when variables are scaled arbitrarily with certain response categories (such as attitude toward blacks, status or prestige of an occupation, and degree of intelligence), standardization of data helps eliminate any possibility that an original score is mistakenly understood as the *real* or *true* amount of a property or activity a person possesses.

SUMMARY

This chapter has introduced the reader to the use of statistics in social research. Statistics is used in social research not only for analysis of data (Chapters 15–17), but also in other phases of social research, such as sampling (Chapter 9) and measurement (Chapter 10). Thus, a preliminary acquaintance with statistics before proceeding to these other topics helps one's ability to comprehend them and to make appropriate decisions during these phases of social research.

Focusing on the description of a single variable at a time, this chapter first introduced important concepts such as data, the data matrix, the variable, and the observation, and then discussed how a variable can be scaled at the nominal, ordinal, interval, or ratio level. To promote standardization of scaling variables and use of available data, the data and questions from NORC are and will continue to be used extensively in the examples provided in the discussion. Appendixed to the book are some standard questions and response categories (Appendix A) and the occupational prestige scales (Appendix B) used in the annual General Social Survey conducted by the NORC since 1972.

For describing single variables, various statistics have been discussed in terms of the scales of variables involved. For variables measured on nominal or ordinal scales, the frequency table, the ratio and percentage, and the mode can be used.

To describe the central tendency of data, the median (equation 5.1) can be used for ordinal, interval, or ratio data, and the mean (equations 5.2 and 5.3) can be used for interval or ratio data.

To describe the dispersion of interval or ratio data, the variance (equation 5.4, 5.6, or 5.8) and the standard deviation (equation 5.5, 5.7, or 5.9) can be used.

To describe individual observations (scores) relative to the mean and the standard deviation, the standard score, or z score (equation 5.10) can be used. By standardizing the data so that each variable has a mean of 0 and standard deviation of 1, the standard (z) scores eliminate the arbitrariness involved in the original response categories constructed for the variables.

The next chapter will show how statistics can be used to describe the relationships among two or more variables.

Chapter 6

Describing Relations among Variables

When a researcher attempts to describe two or more variables simultaneously, he is trying to ascertain if there is any relationship among the variables. For example, "Do Catholic families have more children than Protestants?" "Do females have different jobs from males, even when they have the same educational background?" In each of the questions, two or more variables are involved (e.g., religious affiliation versus number of siblings; sex versus occupation, given the same educational level) and a particular relation among the variables is postulated or questioned. All propositions in a theory are relational statements. On the empirical level, the theoretical hypotheses are statements about relations among variables. This chapter will introduce some of the ways these relationships can be described.

The specific way a researcher can describe a relationship is, to a large extent, determined by the scales of the variables involved, for the scales of the variables determine the types of models a researcher can construct. A discussion of the relevance of the scales of the variables and the models will precede the discussion of the specific ways relations among variables can be described.

SCALES OF VARIABLES AND THE MODELS

In Chapter 5, the four scales of variables were identified: the nominal, the ordinal, the interval, and the ratio. Also, it was shown that ways of describing single variables differ for variables measured with different scales. Similarly, relations among variables of different scales are described in different ways.

As mentioned in Chapter 3, there are three theory-like models: the contingency model, the associative model, and the functional model. Translated from the theoretical level to the empirical level, a contingency model specifies the likelihood of the occurrence of one category or value of one variable, given the occurrence of one category of another variable. The associative model specifies the linear tendency of relationship among the categories of two or more variables. And the functional model specifies a one-to-one relationship (in nonlinear fashion) between the categories of two or more variables.

There is an important relationship between the scales of the variables and the model a researcher can construct. The contingency model can be constructed with nominal or higher scales, since all that is required is that the categories of the variables involved in the model be mutually exclusive—a requirement met by the nominal scale. The associative model, on the other hand, can be constructed only when the variables are ordinal or higher, since a linear statement can be made only when the categories of each variable are an ordered set. Finally, the functional model, reserved for nonlinear one-to-one relationships, requires variables on the interval or ratio level, since precise distance among categories is required for each variable involved. The relationship between the scales of variables and the models is presented in Table 6.1.

The implication of Table 6.1 is that, for nominal variables, only the contingency model can be constructed; for ordinal variables, contingency and associative models can be constructed; and for interval and ratio variables, contingency, associative, and functional models can be constructed.

In this chapter, we shall only treat the contingency and the associative models. The functional model, for nonlinear, one-to-one relations, is beyond the scope of this book.

There is also the model which links variables of mixed scales (e.g., one variable is ordinal or interval and the other variable is nominal). This will be considered as a "difference between groups."

In the discussion to follow, *all notations refer to a sample* rather than to a population. Thus, the effort is to describe the data matrix in a sample.

Table 6.1 Compatibility of Scales of Variables and Theoretical Models

Scale of variable	Model		
	Contingency	Associative	Functional
Nominal	v		
Ordinal	v	v	
Interval	v	v	v
Ratio	v	v	v

CONTINGENCY TABLE

The usual way to describe a contingency model is to construct a contingency table. The contingency table is also a matrix, like the data matrix. However, while the data matrix has rows representing respondents and columns representing variables, in the contingency table both rows and columns represent variables. The simplest form of a contingency table represents the cross-tabulation of the response categories of two variables, a row variable and a column variable. For example, a contingency table cross-tabulating race by sex looks like the one in Table 6.2.

The table, first of all, presents the frequency counts for each response category of each variable as a row total (for race categories) and as a column total (for sex categories). These frequencies are called *marginals*. The total number of observations appears in the lower right corner of the table ($n = 1,504$). Note that the sum of the row totals ($1,308+183+13$) as well as the column totals ($701+803$) should be identical to the total number of observations ($n = 1,504$).

In the table, there are six *cells*, each of which represents a specific combination of one response category of race and one response category of sex. For example, in the cell for white and male (the upper left corner) there are 610 observations. This means that, out of the total 1,504 respondents in this NORC 1973 national survey, 610 of them are white males. Similarly, there are 698 white females, 84 black males, 99 black females, 7 males of other races (American Indians, Puerto Ricans, etc.) and 6 females of other races. Note that the sum of the observations in the cells for each row should add up to the corresponding row total, and that the sum of the observations in the cells for each column should add up to the corresponding column total. For example, for the white race, observations in the male cell (610) and in the female cell (698) add up to the row total of 1,308. Similarly, for the male category, observations in the white cell (610), in the black cell (84), and in the other cell (7) add up to the column total of 701.

Symbols can be used to represent the frequencies of observations in the cells, the marginals, and the total in a contingency table. For example, as shown in Table 6.3, for a column variable with two response categories and a row variable

Table 6.2   Race by Sex

| | Sex | | |
Race	1 (Male)	2 (Female)	Row total
White	610	698	1,308
Black	84	99	183
Other	7	6	13
Column total	701	803	1,504

Source: NORC 1973 General Social Survey.

Table 6.3 Symbolic Representations of Frequencies in a Table

Row variable category	Column variable category		Row total
	1	2	
1	f_{11}	f_{12}	$f_{1.}$
2	f_{21}	f_{22}	$f_{2.}$
3	f_{31}	f_{32}	$f_{3.}$
Column total	$f_{.1}$	$f_{.2}$	n

with three response categories, f is used to represent the frequency. Two subscripts are used for each f in each cell. The first subscript immediately to the lower right of the f symbol represents the row, and the second subscript represents the column. Thus, f_{11} represents the frequency of observations in the cell of the first row and the first column, f_{12} the frequency of observations in the cell of the first row and the second column, f_{21} the frequency of observations in the cell of the second row and the first column, etc. Going back to Table 6.2, we see that f_{11} is equal to 610, f_{12} is equal to 698, f_{21} is equal to 84, etc.

For the marginals, the subscripts consist of a number and a dot. The dot represents "the sum of all columns or rows." Thus, for the marginal of the first response category of the row variable, $f_{1.}$ represents the sum of the observations in all columns for the first row. Similarly, $f_{2.}$ represents the sum of the observations in all columns for the second row; $f_{3.}$, the sum of the observations in all columns for the third row; $f_{.1}$, the sum of the observations in all rows for the first column; and $f_{.2}$, the sum of the observations in all rows for the second column. In Table 6.2, $f_{1.}$ is 1,308, $f_{2.}$ is 183, etc.

Finally, the total number of observations is represented by n; n is 1,504 in Table 6.2.

Describing the Contingency Table with Percentages

Just as for single variables, the relations between two or more variables in a contingency table can be described by computing the percentages. There are three ways percentages can be computed for a contingency table: (1) in terms of row totals (row marginals), (2) in terms of column totals (column marginals), and (3) in terms of the total number of observations (n).

For percentages relative to each row marginal, the f in a cell is divided by the corresponding f in the row total. For example, to find the percentage of f_{11} relative to $f_{1.}$, we simply divide f_{11} by $f_{1.}$. For example, in Table 6.2,

$$\frac{f_{11}}{f_{1.}} = \frac{610}{1,308} = 0.466$$

Similarly, percentages relative to each column marginal and to the total n can be computed:

$$\frac{f_{11}}{f_{.1}} = \frac{610}{701} = 0.870$$

$$\frac{f_{11}}{n} = \frac{610}{1504} = 0.406$$

The interpretations are, then: (1) about 47 percent of the white respondents (the first row of "race") are males; (2) 87 percent of the male respondents (the first column of "sex") are whites; and (3) about 41 percent of all respondents (the total) are white males.

Similarly, percentages of each row or column total relative to the total (n) can be computed. These marginal percentages are identical to the percentages for single variables.

Usually, the percentages are multiplied by 100. In Table 6.4, the percentages relative to each row, each column, and the total are computed for the data presented in Table 6.2. For each cell, three percentages are computed. The first percentage is relative to the row total, the second percentage is relative to the column total, and the third percentage is relative to the total. Thus, one can describe the data in a number of ways:

1 Among the white respondents, about 47 percent are males and 53 percent are females. Among the black respondents, about 46 percent are males and 54 percent are females. On the other hand, among the respondents of other races, 54 percent are males and 46 percent are females.

2 Among the male respondents, 87 percent are white, 12 percent are

Table 6.4   Race by Sex, Percent

Race	Sex		Row percent
	Male (n = 701)	Female (n = 803)	
White (n = 1308)	46.6	53.4	87.0
	87.0	86.9	
	40.6	46.4	
Black (n = 183)	45.9	54.1	12.2
	12.0	12.3	
	5.6	6.6	
Other (n = 183)	53.8	46.2	0.9
	1.0	0.7	
	0.5	0.4	
Column percent	46.6	53.4	100.0

Source: NORC 1973 General Social Survey.

black, and 1 percent are of other races. Among the female respondents, about 87 percent are white, 12 percent are black, and less than 1 percent are of other races.

    3 Of all respondents in the survey, 41 percent are white males, 46 percent white females, 6 percent black males, 7 percent black females, 0.5 percent males of other races, and 0.4 percent females of other races.

Note that the frequencies of the row and column totals are presented under each response category label for each variable, so that a reader of the table can convert the percentages back to frequencies for the cells if he or she wishes.

Describing the Contingency Table in Terms of the Independent Variables

Usually, the contingency table is presented in a simpler form, with as few numbers or percentages as possible, for too many percentages in a table, such as in Table 6.4, may be confusing for untrained readers. One way to simplify a table is to identify the independent and the dependent variables in the table. Recall that in Chapter 2 two types of variables were identified: the independent and the dependent variable. The independent variable, also called the explaining or exogenous variable, precedes the dependent variable, also called the explained or endogenous variable, in the theoretical structure. When the proposition involved is a covariational one, the distinction is not very meaningful. For example, for the contingency table of race by sex, it is impossible to state that one variable precedes, in either temporal or other order, the other. However, in many propositions, the sequence of the variables is possible either on a logical basis, a temporal basis, or both. For example, in the hypothesis, "Catholic families have more children than Protestant families," the two variables involved are "religious affiliation" and "number of children in the family." Because of certain theoretical considerations of the religious doctrines and beliefs, a researcher can be quite confident that "religious affiliation," as a variable, *precedes* "number of children," the other variable, rather than vice versa.

    When the variables in a contingency table can be identified in terms of the independent and dependent variables, the percentages of each cell can simply be computed in terms of each response category of the independent variable.

    For example, for a contingency table for religious affiliation by number of siblings, percentages for the cells can be computed in terms of each category of religious groups. Table 6.5 is such a contingency table.

    The percentages of the response categories of the row variable, "number of siblings," are computed in terms of each of the response categories of the column variable, "religious affiliation." The data are thus described in terms of the independent variable for the dependent variable. As can be seen, the data do not show that Catholic families have more children than Protestant families. In fact, there is a tendency for Protestant families to have more children than Catholic families.

Describing the Contingency Table of Three or More Variables

There are situations in which more than two variables are involved in a relational statement. It may be that multiple independent variables are involved, or that ad-

Table 6.5   Number of Siblings by Religious Affiliation

Number of siblings	Religious affiliation, percent			
	Protestant (n = 939)	Catholic (n = 386)	Jewish (n = 42)	None (n = 16)
0	5.3	7.5	4.8	5.2
1	12.4	14.8	35.7	28.1
2	15.8	14.5	16.7	18.8
3	12.2	15.8	14.3	9.4
4	11.2	9.6	11.9	10.4
5	8.4	8.8	7.1	8.3
6	7.3	8.0	7.1	5.2
7 or more	27.4	21.0	2.4	14.6

* The item for "religious affiliation" was, "In what religion were you raised?" and the item for "number of siblings" was, "How many brothers and sisters did you have?" (including those born alive but no longer living, stepbrothers, stepsisters, and adopted by parents).
   Source: NORC 1973 General Social Survey.

ditional variables are "partialed out" when the relationship between two variables is described. In a description of a relationship between two variables, there is always the possibility that the relationship is spurious, in that it is due to some other factors. Thus, it is important to partial out the effect of the other factors in the analysis. If the relationship between the two variables remains after partialing out the other factors, then the researcher is more confident that the relationship found is not spurious. However, when the relationship between the two variables disappears after the effect of the other factors has been partialed out, then the relationship is considered spurious.

For example, in describing the relationship between occupation and sex, the sex variable is taken as the independent variable and the occupation as the dependent variable. A contingency table with percentages computed relative to each sex category is constructed as shown in Table 6.6. The occupation categories are

Table 6.6   Occupation by Sex, Percent

Occupation	Sex	
	Male (n = 663)	Female (n = 669)
Professional, technical, and kindred workers	15.1	13.3
Managers, administrators, sales workers	19.0	11.7
Clerical and kindred workers	5.4	34.8
Craftsmen and kindred workers	21.7	2.2
Operatives	12.7	14.1
Transport equipment operatives, laborers	12.2	1.6
Farmers, farm managers, farm laborers, and farm foremen	5.0	0.4
Service workers	9.0	21.8

Source: NORC 1973 General Social Survey, excluding those who did not hold regular jobs at the time of survey.

abbreviated from the U.S. Bureau of the Census classifications for 1970. Note that the table contains only the observations of respondents who held regular jobs at the time of the 1973 NORC survey.

As can be seen, males tend to hold down professional, technical, managerial, and craftsmen jobs, whereas females have clerical and service jobs. The description may raise the suspicion that there is job discrimination against females. However, the researcher may wonder whether the relationship is spurious in the sense that perhaps occupations are more contingent on educational background than on sex. Since it may be that females are less likely to have the same level of educational achievement as males, perhaps the relationship between occupation and sex would become spurious when the effect of educational background is partialed out.

To partial out the education variable, the researcher needs to construct a series of contingency tables for each level of education. Such a table is presented in Table 6.7.

In this table, the relationship between occupation and sex is analyzed for three educational levels: (1) less than high school, (2) high school diploma holders, and (3) some college and higher. Thus, the relationship between occupation and sex is analyzed for respondents having a similar level of education.

For simplicity, the occupational categories have further been reduced to five. The percentages are computed, in terms of the sex categories, for each educational level. As can be seen, for each educational level, males still tend to hold

Table 6.7 Occupation by Sex and Education, Percent

	Sex	
Occupation by education level	Male	Female
Less than high school	(n = 256)	(n = 212)
Professional, technical, and managerial workers	11.0	9.9
Clerical workers	2.7	16.0
Craftsmen and kindred workers	24.6	3.3
Operatives and farm workers	50.4	33.9
Service workers	11.3	36.8
High school diploma	(n = 286)	(n = 365)
Professional, technical, and managerial workers	35.3	25.0
Clerical workers	8.7	47.1
Craftsmen and kindred workers	24.1	1.9
Operatives and farm workers	21.3	9.9
Service workers	10.5	16.2
Some college or higher	(n = 116)	(n = 86)
Professional, technical, and managerial workers	81.9	64.0
Clerical workers	3.4	29.1
Craftsmen and kindred workers	8.6	1.2
Operatives and farm workers	5.2	0.0
Service workers	0.9	5.8

Source: NORC 1973 General Social Survey.

jobs in professional, technical, managerial, and craftsmen categories, and females in clerical and service categories. The discrepancies also tend to increase as the educational level increases. For example, while 11 percent of males and 10 percent in the "less than high school" category hold professional, technical, and managerial jobs, as do 35 percent of males and 25 percent of females among high school graduates, in the "some college or higher" category, 82 percent of the males as compared to 64 percent of the females hold such jobs. Thus, the data show for the group of respondents interviewed in the survey:

1 The relationship between occupation and sex still holds, even when the effect of education is partialed out.
2 Education does show some effect on the relationship between occupation and sex; the higher the educational level, the greater the discrepancy of job differences between the sex categories.

Thus, by incorporating the education variable, the researcher is able to show that occupation is contingent on sex. While education also contributes to the difference, it does not eliminate the relationship between occupation and sex.

It is possible to incorporate additional variables in a contingency table. However, as each additional variable is incorporated, the number of cells in the table is increased by as manyfold as there are response categories for the new variable.

DIFFERENCE BETWEEN GROUPS

When a proposition involves two or more variables of different scales, another way of describing the data can be used. The discussion here will be restricted to the case in which the independent variables are nominal or ordinal and the dependent variables are interval or ratio.

Similar to the analysis of single variables, relationships between a nominal or ordinal independent variable and an interval or ratio dependent variable can be described in terms of the central tendency (the mean in equation 5.3), and the dispersion (the variance and the standard deviation in equations 5.8 and 5.9) of the observations on the dependent variable for each of the independent variable categories. Thus, each response category of the independent variable is considered as a group. The mean and the variance (or the standard deviation) of the data on the dependent variable in each group are computed. Then, the means and the variances between groups are compared. Differences of the means and the variances can be used to describe the relationship between the independent and the dependent variables.

For example, in the study of the relationship between occupation and sex, the researcher may wish to further explore whether the jobs held by males and females are not different in kind but also different in prestige. Since there is an occupational prestige scale and it is an interval variable, the researcher may compare the male and female groups in terms of the mean and the variance (and the standard deviation) of their occupational prestige.

The occupation prestige scale to be used here was constructed by Siegel.[1] It is a two-digit scale, ranging from 10 to 90, with the higher the scale the greater the prestige.

The result of the analysis is presented here. Group 1, male respondents ($n = 663$):

$$\bar{X}_1 = 39.6$$
$$s_1^2 = 203.4$$
$$s_1 = 14.3$$

Group 2, female respondents ($n = 669$):

$$\bar{X}_2 = 37.7$$
$$s_2^2 = 176.0$$
$$s_2 = 13.1$$

The data show that male respondents, on the average, have higher occupational prestige than female respondents. Further, the dispersion of occupational prestige scores is greater among male respondents than among female respondents. In other words, females tend to concentrate on jobs having a limited range of prestige, as compared with males.

Groups can also be constructed on two or more independent variables. For example, one may define groups in terms of both sex and education categories: (1) males with less than high school education, (2) males with high school education, (3) males with college or higher education, (4) females with less than high school education, (5) females with high school education, and (6) females with college or higher education. Then, the mean, the variance, and the standard deviation can be computed for the occupational prestige scores for each group. Comparisons among the groups will again indicate whether any relationships are spurious or not, and whether the two independent variables both contribute to "explain" the differences of the occupational prestige scores.

LINEAR RELATIONS (ASSOCIATIONS)

When the variables are all measured in the interval or ratio scale the associative model can be constructed. Here, two common statistical techniques in describing associative (linear) relationships are discussed: regression and correlation.

The regression statistic, called the *regression coefficient* β_{yx}, is used to make predictions from the independent variable X to the dependent variable Y. The *correlation coefficient r* is used to describe the covariation between two variables X and Y, without stating which of the variables is causal to the other.

[1] Paul M. Siegel, "Prestige in the American Occupational Structure," unpublished Ph.D. dissertation, Department of Sociology, University of Chicago, March, 1971. The listing is available in NORC General Social Survey Codebooks and in Appendix B.

Regression: The Prediction Equation

Suppose that a researcher wishes to examine the immigration flow into the United States during 1940–1965. He compiles the data for the relationship between the years (X) and the number of immigrants (in thousands, Y) in a table (see Table 6.8). A cursory look at the table suggests that perhaps the relationship can be described as an associative model—the immigration flow increased over the years. It may be possible, then, to predict the number of immigrants if one knows the year. To further examine this potential trend, the researcher may draw a scatter diagram. A scatter diagram is a diagram in which the horizontal axis represents the values of the independent variable X and the vertical axis

Table 6.8   Immigration Flow to United States, 1940–1965

Year (last two digits)	Number of immigrants (thousands)
40	77
41	60
42	83
43	148
44	202
45	162
46	151
47	238
48	280
49	323
50	299
51	335
52	242
53	261
54	287
55	337
56	387
57	272
58	292
59	292
60	340
61	391
62	373
63	384
64	340
65	368

Source: U.S. Bureau of the Census, *Current Population Reports: Estimates of the Population of the United States and Components of Change: 1940 to 1966,* ser. P-25, no. 331, March 22, 1966, as reported in Donald J. Bogue, *Principles of Demography,* Wiley, New York, 1969, p. 140, table 6-4.

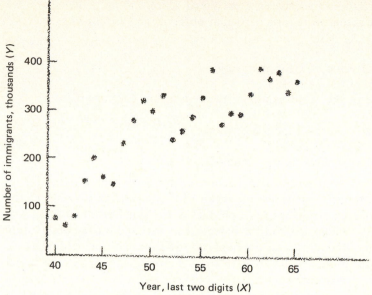

Figure 6.1   Scatter diagram of immigration flow to the United States, 1940–1965.

represents the values of the dependent variable Y, as in Figure 6.1. Each paired observation of the year and the number of immigrants constitutes a single dot in the diagram.

To describe the predictive relationship, a linear (straight) line can be used to represent the model. In this example, the line should start from the lower left side of the diagram and move toward the upper right side, since the association between the two variables seems to be a positive one. The task at hand, then, is to find one straight line which somehow can be considered as more representative of the relationship than any other possible straight line—the best-fit line. If such a line can be found, then it will help the researcher make the prediction, "For year X_i, Y_i number of immigrants should have come to the United States."

There is, of course, no ideal line that can completely and everywhere represent every dot in the diagram. Any straight line will generate a discrepancy between the predicted (based on the straight line) score and the actual score (each dot). In other words, using a straight line to make predictions will generate errors. The question becomes one of finding a straight line, among many possible lines, which will make the least amount of error in the prediction of Y from X. Thus, if one computes the distance between a position along the straight line (the predicted) and an actual dot, one may find an average distance between the predicted and the actual scores. When this average distance is minimal (the error is minimal), one has found the most representative (best-fit) straight line. The technique for finding such a straight line which commits the least amount of error in prediction from one variable to another is called *least squaring*. The line is called the *regression line*.

To see the relationship between a predicted score and an actual score, we may represent the actual score for a particular observation i as follows:[2]

$$Y_i = \bar{Y} + \beta_{yx}(X_i - \bar{X}) + e_i \tag{6.1}$$

where Y_i = actual value of Y for observation i
$\bar{Y}$ = mean of the variable Y
β_{yx} = slope of the regression line, the regression coefficient for Y on X
X_i = actual value of X for observation i
$\bar{X}$ = mean of the variable X
e_i = error or residual of the prediction

Equation 6.1 shows that the actual score on the dependent variable for an observation i has three components: the mean of the dependent variable $\bar{Y}$; the prediction from the regression line (as a product of the slope of that line β_{yx} and the deviation of the actual score of the independent variable for the observation X_i from the mean of the independent variable $\bar{X}$); and the error or residual of the prediction e_i for the particular observation from the regression line to the actual observation on the dependent variable.

The means of the independent and the dependent variables can be computed from the data. For example, for the data in Table 6.8, the mean year and the mean number of immigrants can be found with equation 5.2. Also, the particular score of the independent variable for an observation is available. The only statistics to be computed for equation 6.1 are the regression coefficient β_{yx} and the residual e_i.

The regression coefficient β_{yx} can be computed by means of the following formula:

$$\beta_{yx} = \frac{\Sigma(X_i - \bar{X})(Y_i - \bar{Y})}{\Sigma(X_i - \bar{X})^2} \tag{6.2}$$

where the numerator is the sum of the products of the deviations for both the independent variable and the dependent variable scores over all observations, and the denominator is the sum of the squared deviation scores for the independent variable for all observations.

The residual e_i can then be computed from

$$e_i = Y_i - \bar{Y} - \beta_{yx}(X_i - \bar{X})$$

The portion $\bar{Y} + \beta_{yx}(X_i - \bar{X})$ of equation 6.1 can be seen as the predicted score of the dependent variable from the regression line for observation i:

$$\hat{Y}_i = \bar{Y} + \beta_{yx}(X_i - \bar{X}) \tag{6.3}$$

[2] For those familiar with statistical notations, this equation is expressed for a sample rather than a population.

where $\hat{Y}_i$ = the predicted value of Y from the regression line
Then,

$$e_i = Y_i - \hat{Y}_i \tag{6.4}$$

As an example, the data on the immigration flow in Table 6.8 are used to calculate the regression coefficient and the regression line. The procedure of regression analysis is presented in Table 6.9.

Table 6.9 Regression Analysis of Immigration Flow to the United States, 1940–1965

Year (X_i)	Number of Immigrants (Y_i)	$X_i - \bar{X}$	$Y_i - \bar{Y}$	$(X_i - \bar{X})^2$	$(X_i - \bar{X})(Y_i - \bar{Y})$
40	77	−12.5	−189.3	156.25	2,366.25
41	60	−11.5	−206.3	132.25	2,372.45
42	83	−10.5	−183.3	110.25	1,924.65
43	148	− 9.5	−118.3	90.25	1,123.85
44	202	− 8.5	− 64.3	72.25	546.55
45	162	− 7.5	−104.3	56.25	782.25
46	151	− 6.5	−115.3	42.25	749.45
47	238	− 5.5	− 28.3	30.25	155.65
48	280	− 4.5	13.7	20.25	− 61.65
49	323	− 3.5	56.7	12.25	−198.45
50	299	− 2.5	32.7	6.25	− 81.75
51	235	− 1.5	68.7	2.25	−103.05
52	242	− 0.5	− 24.3	0.25	12.15
53	261	0.5	− 5.3	0.25	− 2.65
54	287	1.5	20.7	2.25	31.05
55	337	2.5	70.7	6.25	176.75
56	387	3.5	120.7	12.25	422.45
57	272	4.5	5.7	20.25	25.65
58	292	5.5	25.7	30.25	141.35
59	292	6.5	25.7	42.25	167.05
60	340	7.5	73.7	56.25	552.75
61	391	8.5	124.7	72.25	1,059.95
62	373	9.5	106.7	90.25	1,013.65
63	384	10.5	117.7	110.25	1,235.85
64	340	11.5	73.7	132.25	847.55
65	368	12.5	101.7	156.25	1,271.25

$\bar{X} = 52.5 \quad \bar{Y} = 266.30$

$\Sigma(X_i - \bar{X})^2 = 1,462.50$

$\Sigma(X_i - \bar{X})(Y_i - \bar{Y}) = 16,531.00$

$\beta_{yx} = \dfrac{(X_i - \bar{X})(Y_i - \bar{Y})}{(X_i - \bar{X})^2} = \dfrac{16,531.00}{1,462.50} = 11.30$

$Y_i = \bar{Y} + \beta_{yx}(X_i - \bar{X}) + e_i$

$\quad = 266.30 + (11.30)(X_i - \bar{X}) + e_i$

The regression coefficient β_{yx} is found to be 11.30, and the regression line

$$Y_i = \bar{Y} + \beta_{yx}(X_i - \bar{X}) + e_i$$
$$= 266.30 + (11.30)(X_i - \bar{X}) + e_i$$

To show the regression line in a scatter diagram of the data, one may use any pair of observations in the data. If we use the first and last observations,

$$\hat{Y}_1 = 266.30 + (11.30)(40 - 52.5) = 125.05$$

and

$$\hat{Y}_{26} = 266.30 + (11.30)(65 - 52.5) = 407.55$$

We may plot the two predicted values of Y for the years 1940 and 1965 (the first and twenty-sixth observations, respectively) in the diagram and draw a line connecting the two points. This line is the regression line, as shown in Figure 6.2. To calculate the residual for an observation, the predicted value Y_i is first calculated and then subtracted from the actual value. For example, for the year 1957,

$$\hat{Y}_i = 266.30 + (11.30)(4.5) = 317.15$$

Then, from equation 6.4,

$$e_i = Y_i - \hat{Y}_i = 272 - 317.15 = -45.15$$

Thus, the prediction is 45.15 units more than the actual number of immigrants for that year. This residual is also plotted in Figure 6.2.

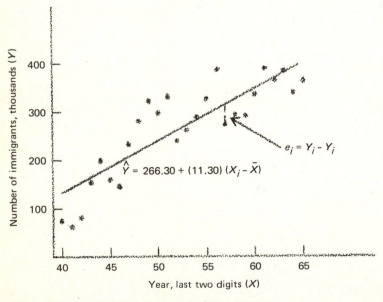

Figure 6.2   Regression of immigration flow on year.

In summary, to predict a dependent variable from an independent variable in a linear line, it is possible to find a regression line which makes the minimal error for the prediction. The slope of the regression line also helps determine the error (residual) of the prediction for each observation.

Correlation: The Covariation Equation

While regression predicts the variation of the dependent variable from the independent variable, there is another technique which indicates the *covariation* between the two variables. The technique is called *correlation* and the resulting quantity r is called the *correlation coefficient*. The correlation coefficient for two variables X and Y can be computed from:

$$r_{xy} = r_{yx} = \frac{\Sigma(X_i - \bar{X})(Y_i - \bar{Y})}{\sqrt{\Sigma(X_i - \bar{X})^2 \Sigma(Y_i - \bar{Y})^2}} \tag{6.5}$$

The coefficient r varies from -1 to $+1$. The more the coefficient deviates from 0, the greater the linear association between the two variables. When the coefficient is a positive one, the relation is a positive one, "The greater the one, the greater the other." When the coefficient is a negative one, the relation is a negative one, "The greater the one, the less the other." Also, the correlation coefficient reflects the linear *mutual* association between X and Y, regardless of which of the variables is the independent or dependent variable. Thus, the relationship between X and Y as expressed in r is a covariational one, $r_{yx} = r_{xy}$.

As an example, the data on immigration flow from Table 6.8 are again used to compute a correlation coefficient between the years and the number of immigrants. The procedure of the correlation analysis is presented in Table 6.10.

The result shows that there is a positive correlation between the progression of years and the number of immigrants arriving in the United States. In other words, there is an increasing trend of more and more immigrants arriving in the United States during the 1940–1965 period.

When the correlation coefficient is squared, r^2, it indicates the magnitude or extent of the covariation between the two variables. r^2 indicates the amount of overlap between the variations of the two variables, and varies from 0 to $+1$ (always positive). The greater the number (approaching 1), the greater the overlap is between the two variables. Usually, it is called the *proportion of variance* explained jointly for variables X and Y, or the *coefficient of determination*. The statistic $1 - r^2$ is the unexplained (residual error) variance of the variables.

For our example, r^2 is $(0.87)(0.87) = 0.76$. That is, the progression of years and the inflow of immigrants are highly correlated. The unexplained variance $(1 - 0.76 = 0.24)$ is relatively small.

Relationship between r and

It may be noted from comparing equations 6.6 and 6.2 that the difference between r and β_{yx} lies in the denominator, where the r takes into account the

Table 6.10 Correlation Analysis of Immigration Flow to the United States, 1940–1965

Year (X_i)	Number of immigrants (Y_i)	$X_i - \bar{X}$	$(X_i - \bar{X})^2$	$Y_i - \bar{Y}$	$(Y_i - \bar{Y})^2$	$(X_i - \bar{X})(Y_i - \bar{Y})$
40	77	−12.5	156.25	−189.3	35,834.49	2,366.25
41	60	−11.5	132.25	−206.3	42,559.69	2,372.45
42	83	−10.5	110.25	−183.3	33,598.89	1,924.65
43	148	− 9.5	90.25	−118.3	13,994.89	1,123.85
44	202	− 8.5	72.25	− 64.3	4,134.49	546.55
45	162	− 7.5	56.25	−104.3	10,878.49	782.25
46	151	− 6.5	42.25	−115.3	13,294.09	749.45
47	238	− 5.5	30.25	− 28.3	800.09	155.65
48	280	− 4.5	20.25	13.7	187.69	− 61.65
49	323	− 3.5	12.25	56.7	3,214.89	−198.45
50	299	− 2.5	6.25	32.7	1,069.29	− 81.75
51	335	− 1.5	2.25	68.7	4,719.69	−103.05
52	242	− 0.5	0.25	− 24.3	590.49	12.15
53	261	0.5	0.25	− 5.3	28.09	− 2.65
54	287	1.5	2.25	20.7	428.49	31.05

Table 6.10 (Continued)

Year (X_i)	Number of immigrants (Y_i)	$X_i - \bar{X}$	$(X_i - \bar{X})^2$	$Y_i - \bar{Y}$	$(Y_i - \bar{Y})^2$	$(X_i - \bar{X})(Y_i - \bar{Y})$
55	337	2.5	6.25	70.7	4,998.49	176.75
56	387	3.5	12.25	120.7	14,568.49	422.45
57	272	4.5	20.25	5.7	32.49	25.65
58	292	5.5	30.25	25.7	660.49	141.35
59	292	6.5	42.25	25.7	660.49	167.05
60	340	7.5	56.25	73.7	5,431.69	552.75
61	391	8.5	72.25	124.7	15,550.09	1,059.95
62	373	9.5	90.25	106.7	11,384.89	1,013.65
63	384	10.5	110.25	117.7	13,853.29	1,235.85
64	340	11.5	132.25	73.7	5,431.69	847.55
65	368	12.5	156.25	101.7	10,342.89	1,271.25

$\bar{X} = 52.5$

$\bar{Y} = 266.30$

$\Sigma(X_i - \bar{X})^2 = 1,462.50$

$\Sigma(Y_i - \bar{Y})^2 = 248,249.54$

$\Sigma(X_i - \bar{X})(Y_i - \bar{Y}) = 16,531.00$

$$r = \frac{\Sigma(X_i - \bar{X})(Y_i - \bar{Y})}{\sqrt{\Sigma(X_i - \bar{X})^2\Sigma(Y_i - \bar{Y})^2}} = \frac{16,531.00}{\sqrt{(1,462.50)(248,249.54)}}$$

$= 0.87$

variation of the dependent variable Y as well as that of the independent variable X. The relationship between r and β_{yx} can be found:

$$r_{xy} = r_{yx} = \frac{\Sigma(X_i - \bar{X})(Y_i - \bar{Y})}{\sqrt{\Sigma(X_i - \bar{X})^2 \; \Sigma(Y_i - \bar{Y})^2}} \qquad \text{from equation 6.5}$$

$$= \frac{\Sigma(X_i - \bar{X})(Y_i - \bar{Y})}{\sqrt{\Sigma(X_i - \bar{X})^2 \Sigma(Y_i - \bar{Y})^2}} \cdot \frac{\sqrt{\Sigma(X_i - \bar{X})^2}}{\sqrt{\Sigma(X_i - \bar{X})^2}}$$

$$= \frac{\Sigma(X_i - \bar{X})(Y_i - \bar{Y})}{\Sigma(X_i - \bar{X})^2} \cdot \frac{\sqrt{\Sigma(X_i - \bar{X})^2}}{\sqrt{\Sigma(Y_i - \bar{Y})^2}}$$

$$= \frac{\Sigma(X_i - \bar{X})(Y_i - \bar{Y})}{\Sigma(X_i - \bar{X})^2} \cdot \frac{\sqrt{\Sigma(X_i - \bar{X})^2/(n-1)}}{\sqrt{\Sigma(Y_i - \bar{Y})^2/(n-1)}}$$

$$= \beta_{yx} \cdot \frac{s_x}{s_y} \tag{6.6}$$

where s_x and s_y are the standard deviations of X and Y, respectively (see equation 5.5). Thus, as far as the dependent variable Y is concerned, β_{yx} is the prediction from X when Y is unstandardized in that the standard deviation of Y is not taken into account; and r is the prediction from X when Y is standardized in that the standard deviation of Y is taken into account. The regression coefficient is also known as the unstandardized coefficient, and the correlation coefficient as the standardized coefficient.

Also note that β_{yx} and β_{xy} are usually different. β_{yx} gives the coefficient when Y is predicted from X (or Y is regressed on X), and β_{xy} gives the coefficient when X is predicted from Y (or X is regressed on Y). The correlation coefficient, on the other hand, is the same for both variables ($r_{xy} = r_{yx}$), since it indicates a covariational relationship.

It is possible to incorporate more than two variables in the regression and correlation analysis (multiple regression and multiple correlation), the discussion of which will appear in Chapter 16.

SUMMARY

This chapter has introduced several ways of describing relationships among variables. Consideration of the scales of the variables guide a researcher to determine which model to construct (contingency, associative, or functional). Each model makes certain assumptions about the scales of the variables involved. For example, the contingency model can be constructed for nominal, ordinal, interval, or ratio variables; associative models can be constructed for ordinal, interval, or ratio variables; and functional models for interval or ratio data only. Only descriptions of the contingency model and the associative model have been attempted in this book.

For the contingency model, a contingency table can be constructed for the data, expressing the joint occurrences of observations for the response categories of the variables.

When the independent variable is nominal and the dependent variable is interval or ratio, differences between groups (categories of the independent variable) can be computed in terms of the central tendency (the mean) and the dispersion (the variance and the standard deviation) of the dependent variable.

For the associative model, regression and correlation coefficients can be computed for either prediction or association.

Since the more sophisticated models can be constructed with statistics which are more precise (taking more precise values of the variables into account), every effort should be made so that variables are measured on ordinal or interval scales. This issue will be further discussed in Chapter 10, Measurement.

Statistical Inference: An Introduction

In Chapters 5 and 6, a description of data relative to a group of respondents was made. The statistics used are considered descriptive because the description applies only to the respondents whose responses are recorded in the data matrix. Suppose a researcher wishes to study the men and women of the United States. In order to describe them, he would have to obtain responses from all men and women, no matter how they are defined, in the United States. Such a task, of course, is prohibitive, because of cost, time, personnel, and other factors. There are other situations in which the data matrix does not contain information about all the potential cases and responses one wishes to describe. For example, it is possible that such potential cases and responses are infinite, such as all automobiles or light bulbs (the production continues infinitely). In other instances, studies of the cases and responses may involve physical or mental damage—the test of the strength of glass and the breakage of certain housewares, etc. In still other cases, prompt information is demanded for action—a political candidate may wish to know what his constituents think and believe so that his campaign strategy can be planned quickly and relevantly. In any event, in most cases in social research, study of a population, defined as all cases sharing certain predetermined characteristics, is impossible. The researcher only has the opportunity and the ability to study a sample (a subgroup of the cases). Yet, he still wishes to provide some information about the population as a result of his analysis of the data matrix from the sample. The process by which findings from "some" cases are generalized to all cases is called *inference*.

In this chapter, some fundamental issues and procedures involving inference and the use of statistics in inference (statistical inference) are introduced. One important assumption made in the discussion to follow is that the sample drawn from the population is a *simple random sample*. A simple random sample is one in which each case and combination of cases in the population has an equal chance of being selected for inclusion in the sample. A detailed discussion of population, sampling, and simple random sampling, along with other sampling issues, appears in Chapter 9, Sampling.

STATISTICS AND PARAMETERS

When descriptive measures about variables in the data matrix are used, one is using statistics. The discussion in Chapters 5 and 6 deals with *statistics* of variables, such as the percentage p, the mean $\bar{X}$, the variance s^2, the standard deviation s, and the correlation coefficient r. When one is concerned with descriptive measures of variables in a population, one is dealing with *parameters*. For example, the parameter for the mean is symbolized as μ, the standard deviation σ, the variance σ^2, the correlation coefficient ρ, and the percentage P. The process of making inferences with statistics is called *statistical inference*. The reader should be aware that the term *statistics* is used in two semantic ways in social research. It is loosely used to denote the theories and techniques with which the collected data can be systematically reduced for summarization and inference (see Chapter 5) and, more restrictively, it is used to denote the descriptive measures of variables observed in a sample, in contrast with the parameters (the descriptive measures for a population). In this chapter, *statistics* is used in the second, more restrictive sense.

The reader should also be clear about the differences between variables, on the one hand, and parameters and statistics, on the other hand. Both parameters and statistics are descriptive measures involving variables. Parameters are descriptive measures of variables for all cases and responses in a population, whereas statistics are descriptive measures of variables for the cases and response categories in a sample as exhibited in a data matrix.

The task of statistical inference is twofold: (1) to make estimations about the values of parameters in the population, and (2) to test relationships among variables in the population.

Estimation of parameters involves questions like "What percentage of the population is black?"; "What is the mean income of the population?"; "Does the population in general favor laws against abortion?" Such estimations must be made without information from all the cases in the population.

Also, the researcher is interested in testing the relationships among variables in the population. For example, "Is it true that women tend to have different jobs, and often less prestigious jobs, than men do in the population?" and "Is it true that belonging to a religious group tends to be associated with less inclination to commit suicide?" For a researcher interested in theory construction, such questions are essential, for they constitute the basis for confirmation of theoretical propositions or inductive modifications of theoretical propositions.

Unfortunately, there is no technique which enables one to make completely accurate estimations and testing of the relationships among variables in the population, with the information available in the data matrix of a sample. The estimations and testing are made with a certain risk that they are wrong. There is no way to eliminate the risk completely. Rather, *statistical inference merely makes such a risk explicit and known,* so that researchers can assess how much confidence one should place on the estimations and the relationships among certain variables, given the known degree of risk involved. Thus, no researcher dealing with statistics is able to answer questions raised about a population's average income or attitude toward legalized abortion, or about the relationship between sex and occupations or between religious affiliation and inclination to commit suicide, with "true" answers. A researcher can only suggest the possibilities of the values of the parameters, with a certain degree of risk of being wrong.

To make such a risk explicit and known, and preferably to reduce such risk, we need, in addition to the sample statistics, the help of a theoretical mathematical curve, the normal curve. Thus, we will have to set aside the problems of statistical inference for a while in order to describe and understand what a normal curve is and what its properties are.

NORMAL CURVE

The normal curve, a mathematical and theoretical curve, as shown in Figure 7.1, has several characteristics: (1) it is symmetric (both halves of the area between the curve and the baseline partitioned in the middle cover the same amount of space); (2) it has an identical mean, median, and mode (in the middle); (3) the area

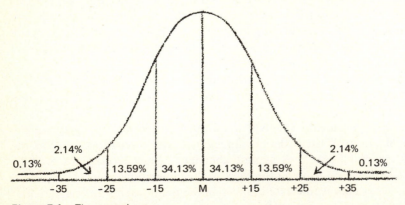

Figure 7.1   The normal curve.

(space) covered between the curve and the baseline extends to infinity on both sides of the curve (the curve never touches the baseline); and (4) it has a standard deviation σ which earmarks the distances on the baseline from the center point, the mean μ, in such a manner that the area between the curve and the baseline, expressed in percentages, is partitioned so that:

1 About 68 percent of the area lies within one σ from each side of μ (i.e., $\mu \pm \sigma$).
2 95 percent of the area lies within two σ's of μ ($\mu \pm 2\sigma$).
3 99.7 percent of the area lies within three σ's of μ ($\mu \pm 3\sigma$).

The reader should verify these percentages in Figure 7.1.

There are many normal curves, since each pair of values of μ and σ will provide a different normal curve in terms of the height of the curve and the width of extension. However, the above-stated characteristics apply to all normal curves.

It is possible to standardize these normal curves. Recall that Chapter 5 showed that, when we compute z scores (standard scores) for a set of data, we may obtain a mean of 0 and a standard deviation of 1 (equation 5.10). When a normal curve is standardized so that it has a mean of 0 and a standard deviation of 1, it is called the *standard (or unit) normal curve* (see Figure 7.2). The standard normal curve has all the characteristics of other normal curves, as well as the property that the area between the curve and the baseline is 1. We are particularly interested in the unit area.

Discussion of the area can be expressed in terms of the distance from any

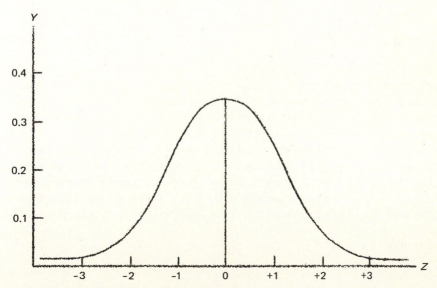

Figure 7.2 The standard (unit) normal curve ($\mu = 0$ and $\sigma = 1$).

point to the mean, the z score. Relative to the standard normal curve, it is expressed as:

$$z_i = \frac{X_i - \mu}{\sigma} \tag{7.1}$$

and is called the *standard normal deviate*. Each z_i expresses a particular height of the curve at that point. For example, when z_i is equal to the mean (0), the height Y of the area is 0.3989; when z_i is equal to 1 standard deviation to the right of the mean ($z_i = +1\sigma$), the height Y of the area is 0.2420.

Further, the area between two z's can be found. For example, we know that the area between the mean (0) and 1 standard deviation (standard normal deviate) to the right of the mean ($+1\sigma$) is 0.3413 (see Figure 7.1).

Table 2 in Appendix C presents the ordinates (the height Y) and the areas (from the mean) for standard normal deviates of up to 3.00. Since we know that 3 standard deviations (standard normal deviates) from each side of the mean cover 99.7 percent of the area, almost all the areas under the curve can be calculated with the knowledge of the standard normal deviates and Table 2, Appendix C. For example:

z	Area	Ordinate (Y)
0.00	0.0000	0.3989
0.50	0.1915	0.3521
1.00	0.3413	0.2420
1.65	0.4505	0.1023
1.96	0.4750	0.0584
2.58	0.4951	0.0143

When z is 0, its height is 0.3989, and the area covered between it and the mean is 0, since it overlaps completely with the mean (0). When z is 0.50, its height is 0.3521 and the area covered between it and the mean is 0.1915. The negative z's, on the left side of the mean, have the same values of areas covered and ordinates (heights), since the normal curve is symmetric about the mean.

Since the total area under the standard normal curve is equal to 1, we may express the areas covered as percentages of the total area. One usual way of expressing the area covered is "the area to the left of the z." Since the mean partitions the two halves of the curve, each side has 0.50 of the total area. Thus, when z is equal to 0.00, the area to the left of it is 0.50—half of the area. It is expressed as:

$$z_{0.50} = 0.00$$

Thus:

$$z_{0.6915} = 0.50$$

where 0.6915 is the summed area of 0.50 (to the left of the mean) and 0.1915 (between the mean and $z = 0.50$).

$$z_{0.8413} = 1.00$$
$$z_{0.9505} = 1.65$$
$$z_{0.9750} = 1.96$$
$$z_{0.9951} = 2.58$$

and

$$-z_{0.1587} = 1.00 = +z_{0.8413}$$

where $z_{0.1587} = -1.00$ and, therefore, $-z_{0.1587} = 1.00$.

$$-z_{0.0495} = 1.65 = +z_{0.9505}$$
$$-z_{0.0250} = 1.96 = +z_{0.9750}$$
$$-z_{0.0049} = 2.58 = +z_{0.9951}$$

If the normal curve represents the distribution of values of a parameter, then it is possible to compare the values of a statistic (say, a sample mean) with this distribution. By using the standard normal deviate, one can compute the distance between the parameter (say, the population mean) and the statistic (the sample mean) to determine how far away the statistic is from the parameter. Such a comparison helps a researcher estimate the parameter and test relationships among variables. However, before we proceed to discuss these issues, we must know if the distribution of values of a parameter resembles a normal distribution. For many variables, we know that parameter values distribute normally but, for others, they do not. Since usually the knowledge about the parameters is absent in social research, one should not simply make the assumption that they are normally distributed in the population. Here we are confronted with a problem. Fortunately, statisticians have provided the help we need.

SAMPLING DISTRIBUTION

One basic finding about many parameters is that, if one draws a sample of a sufficiently large size from the population, the distribution of the statistic will become similar to the distribution of the parameter. This is not difficult to see. If the population has 50 men and 50 women and we wish to estimate the 50-50 split of the sexes among the population cases, we probably would not make too much of a mistake if we drew a sample of 75 or 80 persons from the population, and certainly make little mistake if we drew 99 of the 100 persons in the population into the sample. The relationship between the sample size and the likelihood of better estimation is called the *law of large numbers*. What concerns us here is that the *population parameter*, say percentage of men $P(\text{men})$, *can be better estimated from the sample statistic p as the size of the sample increases*.

A second important finding about the parameter is that, if one draws samples of size n repeatedly from a population, one may compute a sample statistic, say the mean, for each of such samples. When the sample size n is sufficiently large, then all the sample means can be plotted in a graph. What is fascinating is that this *sampling distribution of the means* will almost always be approximately normal. Furthermore, the mean of this distribution (the sampling distribution of the means) will equal the population mean—the parameter. These empirical facts are expressed as *the central limit theorem*.

It is not necessary to know how these findings were constructed. What we are concerned with here are the consequences of the law of large numbers and the central limit theorem. First, let us demonstrate these facts.

Walker and Lev (1969) used scores on the Cooperative Service English Test of 447 college students as the population.[1] The scores were normally distributed. Then they drew twenty samples each for sample sizes of 1, 5, and 25, respectively. In other words, twenty 1-score samples were drawn, twenty 5-score samples were drawn, and twenty 25-score samples were drawn. The means of all samples were computed. The sampling distributions of the means for the three groups (sample sizes of 1, 5, and 25) are presented in Table 7.1. For each sampling distribution, the mean and the standard deviation were computed.

As can be seen, the facts of the law of large numbers and the central limit theorem are supported. According to the law of large numbers, the larger the sample size, the better the estimates of the parameter. For samples of size 25, all the sample means are less than 15 points from the population mean of 121.7 (100–114 to 130–134). For samples of size 5, the sample means spread from 80–84 to 140–144, some of which deviate as much as 30 points or more from the population mean. Finally, for samples of size 1, the sample means range all the way from 35–39 to 165–169. This difference in the ability of estimations relative to the sample size is also reflected in the standard deviations computed for the three groups. The sampling distribution of the means for the samples of size 25 has a standard deviation of 6.1, while it is 18.0 for samples of size 5, and 39.5 for samples of size 1.

The central limit theorem informs us that (1) the sampling distribution of the means should approach normality, and that (2) the mean of the sampling distribution will approach the population mean—if the sample size is sufficiently large. As can be seen in Table 7.1, the sampling distribution of the means for samples of size 25 resembles a normal distribution, whereas those for samples of sizes 1 and 5 do not.[2] Further, the mean of the sampling distribution of the means for samples of size 25 (121.7) is almost identical to the population mean (121.6), whereas the means of the other two sampling distributions do not fare so well.

While the above example demonstrated the application of the law of large numbers and the central limit theorem for samples from a normally distributed population, *the same principles about the sampling distribution hold for samples*

---

[1] Helen M. Walker and Joseph Lev, *Elementary Statistical Methods,* 3d ed., Holt, New York, 1969, pp. 140–143.

[2] The reader is encouraged to construct curves for the three sampling distributions by using the score intervals as the values for the baseline and the frequencies of the means as the heights for the ordinates (Y).

Table 7.1 Distributions of Means of Twenty Samples Drawn from a Normal Population with $\mu = 121.6$ and $\sigma = 37.15$, when $n = 1$, $n = 5$, and $n = 25$

Score interval	Number of samples		
	$n = 1$	$n = 5$	$n = 25$
165–169	2		
160–164	1		
155–159	1		
150–154	3		
145–149	1		
140–144	2	3	
135–139		1	
130–134	1	2	1
125–129		2	5
120–124	1	1	6
115–119		2	5
110–114	1	1	3
105–109	1	4	
100–104	2	2	
95–99			
90–94			
85–89		1	
80–84		1	
75–79			
70–74	1		
65–69	1		
60–64			
55–59	1		
50–54			
45–49			
40–44			
35–39	1		
Total	20	20	20
Mean of twenty means*	122.5	119.0	121.7
Standard deviation of twenty means*	39.5	18.0	6.1

* Computed from ungrouped values.
Source: Helen M. Walker and Joseph Lev, *Elementary Statistical Methods*, 3d ed., Holt, New York, 1969, p. 141.

of a sufficiently large size, regardless of how the population is distributed. While it is too difficult to specify how large a sample size is "sufficiently" large, samples of size 100 or more usually are large enough to yield nearly normally distributed sampling distribution of the means.[3]

[3] Gene V. Glass and Julian C. Stanley, *Statistical Methods in Education and Psychology,* Prentice-Hall, Englewood Cliffs, N.J., 1970, p. 245.

Standard Error of the Mean

Returning briefly to the standard deviations of the sampling distributions of the means in Table 7.1, we note that each is called the *standard error of the mean* for the corresponding distribution. It is expressed as:

$$\sigma_{\bar{x}} = \frac{\sigma}{\sqrt{n}} \tag{7.2}$$

where σ = standard deviation of the population

n = sample size

Thus, the standard errors of the mean for samples of sizes 1, 5, and 25 are 37.15 $(37.15/\sqrt{1})$, 16.6 $(37.15/\sqrt{5})$, and 7.4 $(37.15/\sqrt{25})$, respectively. Compared to the actual standard deviations of the sampling distributions, which are 39.5, 18.0, and 6.1, respectively, we can see the estimations are not far off, even when each distribution is constructed on the basis of only twenty samples. This relationship has enormous significance when one attempts to estimate parameters from statistics.

Since we know the mean (121.6) and the standard deviation (37.15) of the population from which the distributions in Table 7.1 were derived, the information of the standard error of the mean can be used to assess how accurately the sample means in each size group would estimate the population mean. Recall that, earlier in the discussion of the standard normal deviate z, we calculated the area under the curve between the mean and z_i. For $z = 1.96$, for example, the area covered between that point and the mean constitutes 0.4750 of the area of 1, or 47.5 percent of the probabilities of the observations. Similarly, $z = 1.96$ gives the area covered between that point and the mean to be 47.5 percent. Thus, the area covered from $z = -1.96$ to $z = 1.96$ constitutes about 95 percent (47.5 + 47.5) of the entire area, or about 95 percent of the observations should fall within this range. If the samples are randomly drawn from the population, then 95 percent of the sample means should fall within this range. The standard error of the mean, $\sigma_{\bar{x}}$, can be used as the standard normal deviate in the sampling distribution of the means. Thus, we should expect 95 percent of the sample means to fall within the range $\mu \pm 1.96\sigma_{\bar{x}}$. When these expected ranges for the three sampling distributions in Table 7.1 are computed, we obtain:[4]

Size of sample	Value of $1.96\sigma_x$	Range of $\mu \pm 1.96\sigma_x$	Observed means outside range	
			Number	Percent
$n = 1$	72.8	48.8 to 198.4	1	5
$n = 5$	32.5	89.1 to 154.1	2	10
$n = 25$	14.5	107.1 to 136.1	0	0

[4] Walker and Lev, op. cit., p. 144.

Conversely, if one has only the information from the sample, one could conceivably construct a range around the sample mean by using the standard error of the mean. This information would tell us how much confidence we have that the range would cover the population mean. This strategy has to be modified in reality, since the standard deviation of the population is not known, and thus the standard error of the mean cannot be computed. However, with some slight modification to be discussed in the next section, we know that it is possible to draw inferences from statistics to parameters, because the nature of the sampling distribution is now understood.

Now we return to the topics central to inference, namely, making estimations of parameters and testing relationships of variables in the population.

ESTIMATION OF PARAMETERS

There are two ways to estimate parameters: (1) the point estimate and (2) the interval estimate.

Point Estimates

The point estimate singles out a particular value of a statistic, as informed by the sample data matrix, for which it is considered to be a good bet that it approximates the parameter value. Since there are many types of statistics and parameters, a researcher needs some guidelines as to which statistics are better estimators than others. An estimate is considered a good one if it fulfills three criteria: (1) unbiasedness, (2) consistency, and (3) efficiency.[5]

An estimate is unbiased if the mean of the sampling distribution of the statistic equals the value of the parameter being estimated. From preceding discussions, we know that *the mean of a sample is an unbiased estimate of the population mean*, since the mean of the sampling distribution of the means equals the mean of the parameter, given a sufficiently large sample size. When the population is symmetrically (for example, normally) distributed, then the median of a sample is also an unbiased estimate of the population mean, since the mean of the sampling distribution of the medians also equals the population mean. Similarly, the mean of the sampling distribution of the variances s^2 also equals the population variance σ^2; thus the sample variance (s^2) is an unbiased estimate of the population variance. Recall that the formula for s^2 in equation 5.4 is:

$$s^2 = \frac{\Sigma(X_i - \bar{X})^2}{n - 1}$$

where the denominator is $n - 1$ rather than n. Now this choice of $n - 1$ can be explained. For if the variance were computed with n as the denominator, then the mean of the sampling distribution of these statistics will not equal the population variance. Rather, that estimate will always be smaller than the population

⁵ Gene V. Glass and Julian C. Stanley, op. cit., pp. 250–256.

variance, unless and until the sample size n approaches the population size. In other words, while the variance s^2 is unbiased, the statistic with n as the denominator is a biased estimate, on the negative side.

On the other hand, *the sample standard deviation s is a biased estimate of the population standard deviation*. The mean of the sampling distribution of the standard deviations is consistently smaller than the population standard deviation, unless and until the sample size n approaches the population size.

The sample correlation coefficient r is a biased estimate of the population correlation coefficient ρ, except when ρ = 0. When the population correlation coefficient ρ equals 0, then the sample correlation coefficient r is an unbiased estimate. Otherwise, the mean of the sampling distribution of the r's will be smaller than ρ, unless and until the sample size approaches the population size.

An estimate is consistent when it gets closer and closer to the parameter value as the sample size becomes larger and larger. As mentioned above, some of the biased estimates, such as the standard deviation and the correlation coefficient, are consistent estimates, since they approximate the parameter values as the sample size increases.

Finally, *an estimate is efficient when the value of the statistic has a relatively smaller range of variability from sample to sample*. The standard error of the statistic for the sampling distribution can be used to determine the relative efficiency of a statistic. Since the standard error of the mean is always smaller than that of the median, the sample mean thus is a relatively more efficient estimate of the population mean than the sample median. This is why, even though when both the sample mean and the sample median are unbiased estimates of the population mean, *the sample mean is inevitably used as the estimate because of its relative efficiency over the median*.

Interval Estimates

While the point estimate gives the single best possible bet as to what the value of the parameter is, there is no guarantee that any estimate equals the parameter value, and there is no information as to how probable it is that a particular estimate from a sample data matrix approaches the parameter value. The point estimate may be right or simply wrong. Suppose a researcher needs to know the probability that the parameter value lies within a certain range of values of the statistic, then the interval estimate is called for. The interval estimate is an extremely useful inferential strategy, for it spells out explicitly how probable it is that a parameter value will be "caught" within a range of statistic values, with a known degree of risk. It allows researchers to make statements such as, "With .95 confidence, I think the Democratic party will end up with 290 seats in the House, give or take 15 seats, after this upcoming election," and "The probability is .99 that 50 percent to 52 percent of the population are females."

An *interval estimate* is a range of contiguous values of a statistic, called the interval, within which probably lies the true parameter value, with a known degree of risk or uncertainty. It was pointed out that the standard error of the mean can be used as the standard normal deviate in the sampling distribution of the means. By using the range $\mu \pm z\sigma_{\bar{x}}$ (for example, $\mu \pm 1.96\sigma_{\bar{x}}$), then 95 percent of the sample means should fall within this range.

Conversely, if one constructs a range, say $\bar{X} \pm 1.96\sigma_{\bar{x}}$, around the sample mean $\bar{X}$ rather than around the population μ, one should expect that there is a .95 chance that the population mean would fall within this range.

However, as mentioned earlier, the standard error of the mean $\sigma_{\bar{x}}$ is usually not known; thus it also has to be estimated. The point estimate of the standard error of the mean is:

$$s_{\bar{x}} = \frac{s}{\sqrt{n}} \tag{7.3}$$

where s = standard deviation in the sample
$\quad\quad n$ = sample size

Thus, we may now construct a range, called the *confidence interval*, around the sample mean with the estimated standard error of the mean $s_{\bar{x}}$.

For example, in the NORC 1973 survey question on siblings, it was found that the mean is 4.47 and the standard deviation is 3.46, for the data matrix of 1,501 respondents. Assuming that the sample was a random one for the adults in the United States,[6] then we may estimate the mean number of children in the families in the country. Suppose we wish to be certain that 95 out of 100 times the sample estimate will cover the population mean, we choose to take the risk when the area under the curve on *each* extreme end of the normal curve is 0.025 or less. In other words, we choose $z_{0.975} = 1.96$ and $z_{0.025} = -1.96$. This was found in Table 2, Appendix C. Then:

$$\bar{X} + z_{0.975}s_{\bar{x}} = 4.47 + (1.96)\left(\frac{3.46}{\sqrt{1501}}\right)$$

$$= 4.64$$

and

$$\bar{X} + z_{0.025}s_{\bar{x}} = 4.47 - (1.96)\left(\frac{3.46}{\sqrt{1501}}\right)$$

$$= 4.30$$

Thus, the probability is .95 that the confidence interval, 4.30 to 4.64, will cover the mean number of siblings in the population families. If we wish to add the respondent to the number of siblings to estimate the mean number of children, then the confidence interval would simply become $5.30 - 5.64$.

In general, the probability of risk is called the *confidence coefficient c* or $1 - \alpha$. In the example above, the confidence coefficient chosen was .95. Then, the two extreme areas under the normal curve are located with the z's in Table 2,

---

[6] The NORC General Social Survey uses a modified multistage random sample, where the quota sampling is used on the block level. Thus the actual estimates should be modified. But for the purpose of illustration here, it was considered a simple random sample.

Appendix C, and the confidence intervals are computed:

$$\bar{X} + z_{(1+c)/2} \frac{s}{\sqrt{n}} \quad \text{and} \quad \bar{X} + z_{(1-c)/2} \frac{s}{\sqrt{n}} \tag{7.4}$$

It is also possible to provide an interval estimate for the correlation coefficient ρ. The point estimate for the correlation coefficient is biased, except when $\rho = 0$. However, the bias decreases as the sample size increases. In practice, r is frequently used to estimate ρ. To construct an interval estimate for ρ, we need the standard error of r, which is unknown. Fisher's z transformation helps solve the problem. It transforms the r's into z's, so that the area under the normal curve can be used to construct the confidence interval for r, as it is for the mean $\bar{X}$. In Table 6, Appendix C, one may find the correspondence between each r value and z_r value by Fisher's z transformation. The standard error for the distribution is $1/\sqrt{n - 3}$. Thus, a researcher may find the confidence interval for r:

$$z_r + z_{(1+c)/2} \frac{1}{\sqrt{n - 3}} \quad \text{and} \quad z_r + z_{(1-c)/2} \frac{1}{\sqrt{n - 3}} \tag{7.5}$$

Then, the interval values can be transformed back to r's by again using the z transformation in Table 6, Appendix C.

HYPOTHESIS TESTING

Statistical inference is also useful for the purpose of hypothesis testing. Recall from Chapters 2, 3, and 4 that empirical propositions are deduced from theoretical propositions. Empirical propositions, consisting of variables, are the theoretical hypotheses to be tested with data. However, the empirical data in the data matrix are sampled data. To test the extent to which the relationship observed in the data matrix may hold up in the population is the goal of hypothesis testing. Again, the reader must realize that such inference always involves risk. The best one can do is to make explicit the degree of risk involved by specifying the level of significance (α, or $1 -$ confidence coefficient). We shall return to this issue shortly.

However, the procedure of hypothesis testing is not as straightforward as estimating parameters. For, to a greater degree, the researcher has to make a binary (two-choice) decision—either the theoretical hypothesis is confirmed or it is not, even though the decision always involves risk. To be conservative and to minimize the risk, an indirect approach to hypothesis testing is used. A statistical hypothesis is constructed, and a sampling distribution of the statistic (say, the mean) is constructed for the statistical hypothesis. The test involves comparison of the data mean from the sample (the observed value) with the mean of the sampling distribution (the expected value). When the sample mean deviates substantially from the mean of the sampling distribution, say, so that the observed value would only occur in 5 out of 100 times in the sampling distribution constructed from the statistical hypothesis, then one may be willing to think that, since this event is so rare if the statistical hypothesis is true, one feels rather confident that the statistical hypothesis is false and can be rejected. The observed value would then lead one to an alternative sampling distribution. If somehow the theoretical hypothesis is one such likely distribution, then rejection of the statistical hypothesis lends more confidence to the credibility of the theoretical hypothesis.

The simplest example is to use a problem studied in Chapter 6. If a researcher wishes to test the hypothesis that males are more likely to hold prestigious jobs than females, he may set up a statistical hypothesis which states that females are just as likely as males to hold prestigious jobs. Based on this statistical hypothesis, then a male or a female has an equal chance of obtaining any prestigious job. In other words, the mean difference in job prestige between males and females randomly matched would approach zero. A sampling distribution of the mean difference can be constructed, which will have a mean of zero ($\mu = 0$). Using the knowledge about the sampling distribution, one may construct a confidence interval around the sample mean difference $\bar{X}$ to determine how likely the interval would be to span the population mean difference of zero, given a confidence coefficient $C = 1 - \alpha$ of .95 or .99. If the computation shows that such an interval around the sample mean difference does not cover the population mean difference, then one concludes that, if the statistical hypothesis on which the sampling distribution was constructed is true, the probability is less than .05 or .01 (level of significance, α) that an interval constructed of similar samples would span the population mean difference. Since the chances are so small for a sample to show such a difference, then perhaps the statistical hypothesis is not true after all. If the statistical hypothesis, that females and males are equally likely to obtain prestigious jobs, is false, then the alternative hypothesis (the theoretical hypothesis), that males are more likely to hold prestigious jobs than females, may be true. Note that there is another alternative hypothesis, that females are more likely to hold prestigious jobs than males. Mere rejection of the statistical hypothesis could also lend credence to this second alternative hypothesis. Thus, this alternative hypothesis should also be examined, unless the researcher has greater confidence that such a second alternative hypothesis can be ruled out. In fact, it is possible to do so, to be discussed in a later section, "One-Tailed Test versus Two-Tailed Test."

To summarize the discussion so far on hypothesis testing, the following procedure may be outlined:

Step 1: The formulation of a theoretical hypothesis. This hypothesis is also known as H_1. The subscript indicates that it is the first alternative hypothesis. It is possible that a second alternative hypothesis (H_2) can also be constructed. The theoretical hypothesis is deduced from either a theoretical structure or other considerations.

Step 2: The formulation of a statistical hypothesis. This hypothesis is also known as the null hypothesis, H_0, since the purpose of setting it up is to provide an opportunity to nullify it. A statistical hypothesis does not have to state a no-difference relationship between the variables. In fact, *a statistical hypothesis may specify the difference to be any value, the falsification of which would lend more support to the theoretical hypothesis.*

Step 3: The construction of a sampling distribution for the statistic based on the statistical hypothesis. With the data matrix of a sample, we have shown in the preceding section the procedure for constructing the standard error of the statistic (for example, the mean or the correlation coefficient) for the distribution.

Step 4: Specification of the degree of risk in concluding that the statistical hypothesis is false. In *interval estimates,* a confidence coefficient ($c = 1 - \alpha$) is set up. However, for *hypothesis testing,* the attention is given to α, called *the level of significance.* In essence, the level of significance is set up as the probability that a particular sample value may be observed if the null hypothesis is true. Thus, if the designated level of significance is small, say .05 or .01, and such a value is in fact observed in a sample, then it is considered a "rare" event. A rare event is an event that can still occur in the sampling distribution based on the null hypothesis. However, since its probability of actual occurrence is so small and yet it is observed, then the researcher may be willing to take the risk of being wrong by saying that he would rather believe that the observed value comes from a sampling distribution based on another hypothesis than from the one based on the null hypothesis. Since he has reasons to believe that the theoretical hypothesis is one such alternative hypothesis, he is now inclined to give the theoretical hypothesis more credibility.

Once the level of significance is specified, one must decide whether both extreme tails of the sampling distribution should be considered. If only one tail is considered, it means that the researcher is confident that the theoretical hypothesis H_1 is the only alternative hypothesis under consideration. Two tails should be considered, when the researcher also wishes to examine the second alternative. The one-tailed or two-tailed decision, to be discussed in greater detail later in the chapter, leads to specification of *the region or regions of rejection* (or, critical regions). A region of rejection is an extreme area under the normal curve. When the sample value of the statistic falls in this region, then the researcher is willing to take the risk of rejecting the statistical hypothesis. These areas are specified in terms of z's in Table 2, Appendix C.

Step 5: Analysis and examination of sample data and decision making. The researcher gathers data, computes the value of the statistic, compares the observed value with the expected value when the statistical hypothesis is true, and decides, with the given level of significance, whether the statistical hypothesis should be rejected and the theoretical hypothesis given more credibility.

The decision and its ramifications need to be elaborated. One can never overemphasize the tentativeness of the confirmation of a theoretical hypothesis, even when the decision is to reject the null hypothesis. This tentativeness will be discussed in terms of the relationship between the theoretical hypothesis and the null hypothesis, the one-tailed versus the two-tailed test, and types of errors in decision making.

Relationship between the Null Hypothesis and the Theoretical Hypothesis

Hypothesis testing is in fact a direct examination of the null hypothesis. The decision with the probability of risk also spelled out concerns only the likelihood of the null hypothesis being false. Statistically, it does not state anything directly about the theoretical hypothesis. Thus, the *degree of relevance* of the null hypothesis to the theoretical hypothesis is crucial. The usual procedure of stating a null hypothesis is to specify a null relationship between the variables, such as, "The average prestige of jobs held by working men is the same as that of jobs held by working women." Rejection of such a null hypothesis leaves room for many alternative hypotheses, such as, "The average prestige of jobs held by working men is higher than that of jobs held by working women," "The average prestige of jobs held by working men is 5 points, on the Hodge-Siegel-Rossi occupational scale, greater than that of jobs held by working women," and "The average prestige of jobs held by working men is 15 points, on the Hodge-Siegel-Rossi occupational prestige scale, below that of jobs held by working women," etc. While two alternative hypotheses can be set up so that a positive or negative relationship between sex and job prestige can be discerned, rejection of the null hypothesis still leaves a wide range of values, any one of which may be the true parameter value. *The level of significance α has been mistakenly thought to provide some information as to where the parameter value may lie. This is entirely false.* The level of significance only suggests the probability that certain values will appear in the sampling distribution *if the null hypothesis is true.* It gives no information as to where the parameter value may lie. We may illustrate the relationship between a null hypothesis and the theoretical hypothesis with a graph.

Suppose there is reason to believe that the true relationship between two variables, say, as expressed by a correlation coefficient, is a positive one, as shown in Figure 7.3, and that null hypothesis I states that there is no relation, or $\rho = 0$. Then, rejection of the null hypothesis, when an observed value is positive, leads only to the exclusion of the 0 value as improbable, but leaves all other positive values up to 1 (the maximal value for a correlation coefficient) still likely as the parameter value. On the other hand, if null hypothesis II is used, which states that the correlation coefficient should be the fraction w, then rejection of the null hypothesis and presumably with an observed value greater than w, can lead to the elimination of all positive values from 0 to almost w. Further, if null hypothesis III states that the correlation coefficient should be the fraction x, then rejection of the null hypothesis when an observed value is less than x can lead to the elimination of all positive values from 1.00 (the maximal) to almost x from the above. Thus, for the parameter value l, null hypotheses II and III are much more relevant than null hypothesis I.

In reality, of course, the parameter value is not known. The best one may hope for is that repeated studies drawing samples from the same population will enable one to construct null hypotheses more and more relevant to the theoretical

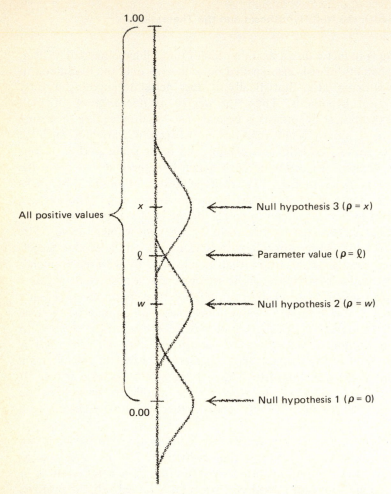

Figure 7.3 Relevance of null hypothesis to parameter value for a correlation coefficient, ρ.

hypothesis, so that a narrow range can eventually be identified within which the parameter value may be "caught" with a high degree of probability. One may never be able to pinpoint the parameter value, as samples always involve errors. Further, as the null hypothesis gets closer and closer to the parameter value, the power of a statistical test to reject the null hypothesis becomes weaker and weaker. The *power of a test* is defined as the ability of a test to reject the null hypothesis when the alternative hypothesis is in fact true. It will be discussed in greater detail in the section dealing with types of errors in decision making. Suffice it to mention that to overcome the loss of power of a test, one has to increase the sample size. But it eventually will reach a point where the cost becomes prohibitive. Thus, we should, with a specified degree of risk, reach an optimal range built around relevant null hypotheses that make explicit the narrow range within which the parameter value may lie.

The reader must readily be warned that the discussion so far in this section on the relevance of null hypotheses to the theoretical hypothesis deviates from the conventional discussion on hypothesis testing. In the literature, a social researcher will inevitably find hypothesis testing to be restricted to the testing of the null hypothesis of no difference or no relationship between variables. The test nearly always seeks a relationship "significantly different from 0." This convention is built on two factors.

For one thing, in many cases, research is conducted on an exploratory basis. The researcher has no prior knowledge as to what direction or magnitude the relationship should assume. Thus, one is reluctant to make any commitment until the null hypothesis of no relationship is rejected. In the initial state of theory construction in which inductive explorations are attempted, it is entirely justified to start with the null hypothesis of no relationship.

The second factor concerns the state of the art of theory construction. Most of the propositions constructed are associative models; they merely state the direction of relationship postulated. No magnitude of relationship is specified. Thus, a researcher is left with no alternative but to test the null hypothesis of no relationship, so that the associative relation, in a specified direction, may be confirmed.

As social research moves more and more toward deductive rather than inductive reasoning, and as more and more initial empirical observations are cumulated, we should expect that the propositions will become more and more precise in stating the magnitude as well as the direction of relations, and that the demand for and contribution of more relevant null hypotheses will increase in the continuous task of inferring the relationship of the variables in the population.

One-Tailed Test versus Two-Tailed Test

The tails describe the two extreme areas of the sampling distribution, to the left and right tails of the curve. The mean of the sampling distribution is the expected value for the null hypothesis in hypothesis testing. For example, in the typical null hypothesis of no relationship, the mean of the sampling distribution is 0. Then, the area under the curve is divided into two halves, the left half indicating deviations from the mean toward the negative (a potential negative relationship), and the right half indicating deviations from the mean toward the positive (a potential positive relationship). A two-tailed test involves two alternative hypotheses—a positive relationship and a negative relationship. A one-tailed test involves only one alternative hypothesis—a positive *or* a negative relationship to the null hypothesis as specified in the theoretical hypothesis.

In the one-tailed test, the region of rejection lies only in one extreme area of the sampling distribution. In the two-tailed test, the region of rejection lies in both extreme areas of the sampling distribution. For example, if the level of significance is set at .05, the region of rejection for the one-tailed test involves $z_c = z_{0.95} = 1.65$. But, for the two-tailed test, the region of rejection on each side will be $z_{(1+c)/2} = z_{0.975} = 1.96$ and $z_{(1-c)/2} = z_{0.025} = -1.96$ respectively. Thus, for the same level of significance, it is much more difficult to reject the null hypothesis with a two-tailed test than with a one-tailed test.

The decision as to which test to make depends on the degree of confidence the researcher has in the relationship tested. If the researcher has no confidence or prior evidence that the relationship should deviate only in one direction from the null hypothesis, then the two-tailed test should be used. On the other hand, if the researcher has evidence from past research of similar relationships that the expectation is toward one particular direction, then the one-tailed test should be used. In general, the two-tailed test is favored, as most social research is a preliminary attempt at theory construction and a conservative stance (more difficult to accept a theoretical hypothesis) should be taken.

Types of Errors in Decision Making

Since statistical inference can be made only on probabilistic grounds, there is always the chance that an error can be made in the decision. The types of errors which may occur can be described in a typology for the null hypothesis and the decision. As presented in Table 7.2, the null hypothesis can either be true or false, and the decision can be either to reject it (thereby accepting the alternative hypothesis) or to accept it (thereby not accepting the alternative hypothesis). Thus, in combination, three results may occur:

1   When H_0 is true and the decision is to reject it, it is called a type I error, with a given probability of α, which of course is the degree of risk (level of significance) involved in rejecting the null hypothesis.

2   When H_0 is false and the decision is to accept it, it is called a *type II error,* with a given probability of β, which is the degree of risk involved in failing to reject the null hypothesis.

3   When H_0 is true and the decision is to accept it, or when H_0 is false and the decision is to reject it, then the correct decision is made—no error is involved.

In hypothesis testing, it is desirable to minimize both type I and type II errors. To minimize type I error, it is necessary to keep α as small as possible. As mentioned earlier, α is the level of significance. The smaller the level of significance, the smaller the regions of rejection, and thus the less the likelihood that the null hypothesis will be rejected.

Table 7.2   Types of Errors in Hypothesis Testing

Decision	Null hypothesis (H_0)	
	True	**False**
Reject H_0	Type I error (probability = α)	Correct decision (probability = $1 - \beta$)
Accept H_0	Correct decision (probability = $1 - \alpha$)	Type II error (probability = β)

To minimize type II error, it is necessary to increase the power of the test. One way to increase the power of the test is to increase the level of significance. For the greater the level of significance, the greater the regions of rejection, and thus the greater the likelihood that the null hypothesis will be rejected. However, as one realizes, the increase in the power of the test, and thus the minimization of type II error may be at the expense of increased type I error. The only way to minimize type II error while also retaining a low level of type I error is to increase the sample size. Thus, it is important that a researcher draw as large a sample as financially feasible so that the power of the test can be maximized.

DISTRIBUTIONS DERIVED FROM THE NORMAL CURVE

So far, the normal curve has been utilized for the purpose of statistical inference. The normal curve also contributes to social research in another way—other types of distributions can be derived from it which are not normal. Thus, when the data violate certain assumptions about the normal sampling distribution, such as when the sample size is small, the variables are not measured on interval or ratio scales, the population standard deviation is not known, and so forth, other derived distributions will come in handy. In fact, in most studies, derived distributions are used to make statistical inferences rather than the normal curve itself.

For example, when variables are measured on the nominal or ordinal level, such as in a contingency table, inference has to use chi-square (χ^2) distributions. Inference for differences between groups may use F distributions, when the independent variables are nominal or ordinal and the dependent variable interval or ratio; or it may use t distributions, when the sample size is small and the population standard deviation is unknown. Details of the use of these distributions will be discussed in Chapter 16. Suffice it to say here that these are very useful distributions, and they are all related to the normal distribution.

SUMMARY

This chapter introduced the concept and procedures of statistical inference. As social research usually involves samples rather than populations, statistical inference helps make generalizations from specific findings to the large population. Statistical inference performs two important tasks: (1) estimates the values of parameters in the population, and (2) tests relationships among variables in the population. Since only a sample is involved, there is inevitably risk and error involved in inference. What is important is to make the risk explicit and known, so that one may decide how much confidence should be placed on the estimations and the relationships estimated.

Statistical inference relies on our knowledge about the normal curve, a theoretical and mathematical curve, which is determined by two parameters: (1) a mean, and (2) a standard deviation. The areas under the curve, when standardized, constitute the probabilities of occurrence of values. As it happens, when repeated samples of a fixed size are drawn randomly from a population, whether it is normally distributed or not, the sample statistic, say the means of the samples, will form a sampling distribution which approximates a normal curve, with the mean equal to the population parameter value. Thus, when standardized, the area of the sampling distribution of the statistic becomes the probability of the occurrence of values of the statistic to be observed in any sample. Since it is possible to estimate the standard deviation of the sampling distribution (the standard error) from the sample data, the sampling distribution can be used to examine the closeness of a particular statistic value observed to the mean of the sampling distribution, which equals the parameter value.

In making the estimation, the parameter value is never known. However, it allows one to make a statement such as, "With a .95 probability, the average family income in the population will fall within the range of $10,000 to $12,000."

Hypothesis testing involves the construction of theoretical and null (statistical) hypotheses. The theoretical hypothesis constitutes an alternative hypothesis (H_1) to the null hypothesis (H_0). The null hypothesis is set up so that it can be nullified. When a null hypothesis is nullified, the theoretical hypothesis gains credibility. It is important to set up the null hypothesis to be as relevant to the theoretical hypothesis as possible, so that only a limited range of values remains as plausible parameter values. Similarly, hypothesis testing also involves risk. When the null hypothesis is true and the decision is to reject it in favor of the theoretical hypothesis, a type I error is committed. When the null hypothesis is false and the decision is to accept it, a type II error is made. Type II error is also known as the power of the test. It is important to minimize both types of errors. One way to increase the power of the test while still retaining the minimal type I error is to increase the size of the sample as much as is feasible.

Part Three

Research Initiation, Sampling, and Measurement

Chapter 8

Initiating Social Research

Previous chapters have dealt with the elements and structure of a theory, the relationship between theory and research, theory construction and verification, and the use of statistics in social research. The focus will now shift to the sequence of events which occurs in the actual conduct of a research study. This chapter covers the initial phases of social research: the formulation of a research problem and the selection of the appropriate type of study.

FORMULATION OF A RESEARCH PROBLEM

The crucial first step in conducting a research project is the formulation of a research problem. It is probably the least systematic phase. As mentioned in Chapter 1, research issues may arise from theoretical considerations, pragmatic considerations, or both. However, there are always many such considerations and therefore many research ideas available to a researcher. There are no set guidelines for selecting a particular research issue, and some of the reasons for doing so have little to do with its intrinsic scientific value.

The formulation of a research problem may be broken down into five areas of consideration. While these need not follow in the same sequence in every research project, the researcher may find them helpful in arriving at a researchable problem.

Discovery of a Research Issue

There is no definitive answer to the question as to where a researcher finds an issue for research, whether it be theoretical or pragmatic in nature. Prime sources include personal experience, materials read, conversations, exposure to the mass media, theory, beliefs, and values. In fact, anything that happens to a researcher may provide the inspiration for a research project.[1]

With sources of possible research issues so numerous, how does a social researcher settle on one issue? There are a number of factors which may influence him. Some of the more prominent are as follows.

Colleagues' Respect and Recognition   One of the major rewards of being a researcher is receiving recognition from fellow researchers and scientists. Research in "hot" areas, those defined as important by other scientists in one's discipline, is likely to win such recognition.

Available Financial and Personnel Support   Financial and personnel support are required for most research projects of substantial scope. Since such resources are limited, a researcher may choose a topic for which they are easier to obtain. Areas of inquiry which today seem to receive federal funding readily include drug use, public health (e.g., cancer), race relations, women's roles in society, urban problems, and social indicators of community structure.

Practical Needs   Questions which relate directly to ongoing activities may interest a researcher. What are the viable alternatives to the way the educational system is presently organized? Can couples make family-planning decisions that are beneficial both to themselves and to society? How can interaction among urban residents be improved? What constitutes an effective social welfare program? Have current policies succeeded in reducing smoking? Research which evaluates or suggests change in ongoing activities can be rewarding.

Imagination and Curiosity   The researcher may attempt research on a topic to satisfy his own intellectual curiosity.

Thus, there is a variety of reasons for picking a particular research issue.[2] The decision involves a value judgment, so no researcher should feel defensive about a topic he wants to study.

Reduction of a Research Issue to a Research Problem

Usually, the research issue chosen is too broad and vague to be examined in a single study. The researcher must reduce its scope to that of a researchable problem. A research problem differs from a research issue in that an issue may involve only one concept. Research issues could be expressed by saying, "I am

---

[1] Sanford Labovitz and Robert Hagedorn, *Introduction to Social Research,* McGraw-Hill, New York, 1971, pp. 14–16.

[2] Russell L. Ackoff, *The Design of Social Research,* University of Chicago Press, Chicago, 1953, pp. 14–48.

interested in interracial conflict," "I am curious about drug users," and "I wonder what happens to kids whose mothers work." However, research problems deal with the *whats, hows,* and *whys* of social activities. Statements of research problems might read, "The intensity of interracial conflict is probably related to the proportion of the population belonging to a single race," "Perhaps drug users tend to be socially isolated," and "Children with working mothers must be more highly motivated to achieve than those whose mothers do not work." Such speculation serves the useful function of leading the researcher to think about his concept of interest in terms of other concepts that may be related to it. The postulated relations may or may not be valid, but they provide a researchable problem or a series of them.

Frequently a research issue is reduced to a series of research statements or questions which together form the core of a research problem. The most rigorous transformation of a research issue into such a set of statements occurs by means of theory construction. In this process propositions are formulated and organized both logically and empirically into a theoretical structure.

Operationalization of Terms in the Research Problem

After specifying his research problem in the form of propositions, the researcher translates the concepts they contain into terms which correspond directly to observable social activities (see Chapter 2). Such terms are said to possess *empirical correspondence,* and the translation process is called *operationalization* (see Chapter 4). Statements containing empirical terms (variables) are called *hypotheses.*

In order to study the relationship between working by the mother and the offspring's motivation to achieve, the researcher must define what constitutes "working." Does it have to be full-time work (forty hours a week), or does part-time work count? He must also decide how to measure achievement motivation. He might utilize questionnaire items devised for this purpose by other researchers, such as McClelland's scale.[3] All the abstract concepts in a research problem must be represented by empirical terms (variables), so that observations can be used in their measurement.

Envisioning Empirical Evidence

The researcher next must envision just what results in his observations would constitute confirmation of the relationship in his research statement (or hypothesis). Will statistical tests be employed? If so, are their data assumptions met by the observations he plans to collect?

Some decisions involving probabilities are necessary. Many statistical tests tell the researcher how likely it would be for the patterns in his data to occur if there were no relationship between the variables (the statistical or null hypotheses). In our example, it may develop that the observed difference between the achievement motivations of the offspring of working and nonworking mothers

[3] David C. McClelland, *The Achieving Society,* Van Nostrand, Princeton, N.J., 1961.

would appear only 5 times out of 100 if achievement motivation were distributed among children by chance. (Chance, in this context, would indicate that whether mothers work or not makes no difference in the degree of achievement motivation among children.) Is the research justified in concluding that this event would occur rarely by chance and thus that it signifies a "real" relationship? These decisions must be made in advance, so that the researcher will not be tempted to engage in "data snooping" and, once he knows the results his data contain, structure the test so as to confirm his research statement.

Envisioning Research Consequences

As a member of the scientific community, a social researcher has the responsibility of conducting work that will contribute to the accumulation of knowledge. It is helpful for him to envision ahead of time the potential contributions of his research findings. They may be generalizable to other activities within the same subject matter area. If the offspring of working mothers are found indeed to have higher achievement motivation than those of nonworking mothers, this conclusion might lead inductively to the theoretical proposition that the degree of positive orientation toward achievement is directly related to the achievement level of significant others. Other research problems flow from this proposition by deduction. One might conjecture that the offspring of higher-income parents aspire to higher income for themselves, that persons whose friends have better jobs aim for better jobs, and that wives whose fathers held more prestigious occupations are eager for their husbands to attain more prestigious jobs. Thus envisioning the integration of possible research conclusions with developing theoretical explanations through induction, with other empirically observable relations through deduction, or both enables the researcher to sharpen his research statements, enhances their probable contribution to scientific knowledge, and in general promotes a better study.

The researcher should also envision the potential consequences of his research findings as regards ongoing social activities. If the offspring of working mothers tend to have higher achievement motivation than those of nonworking mothers, should all mothers be encouraged to work so that their children will be highly motivated to achieve? The way this question is answered will affect policy making and have ramifications in the family structure, the employment situation, and the interaction between parents and children. A researcher should think through such potential implications as thoroughly as possible. The process of envisioning research consequences becomes more critical, since the findings may affect a larger number of people in society.

There is yet a third area of possible research consequences. This is the generalization of findings to different groups of people. The researcher should consider how he will find out whether and to what extent his conclusions indeed apply to one or more other groups. There are analytical techniques which can aid him in this endeavor if the selection of respondents follows certain rules (see Chapter 9, Sampling).

SELECTION OF THE APPROPRIATE TYPE OF STUDY

After formulating a research problem, the social researcher must select the type of study most appropriate for its investigation. There are four main types: (1) exploratory, (2) descriptive, (3) hypothesis-generating, and (4) hypothesis-testing studies. Which type is appropriate depends on the nature of the research problem, the availability of data sources, and how much is known about the subject matter.

Exploratory Studies

Exploratory studies provide the most general information about a research problem. They usually supply the researcher with his first exposure to the existing information in his area of interest, and provide the basis for later, more rigorous studies. Exploratory studies include literature review, consultation with experts, and case exploration.

Literature Review Probably the best initial approach to any research project is literature review. This consists of several activities: locating relevant literature, browsing through and reading publications, and abstracting and summarizing information.

Locating relevant literature As scientific information has increased exponentially, one researcher cannot possibly locate all the literature relevant to any but an esoteric topic. However, he can generally still identify much of the information pertaining to a specific research problem. The major sources of such information are journals, books, and documents, most of which can usually be located quickly. Local librarians and experts in the subject matter area may be approached for help in identifying the most recent publications. But even if such local consultation is not available, a literature search in sociology can be conducted without much difficulty, because the number of journals in the field is still relatively limited.

For general sociological work, the following United States journals are well-known and cover a wide range of research topics: the *American Sociological Review*, the *American Journal of Sociology*, *Social Forces*, *Sociometry*, the *Journal of Personality and Social Psychology*, *Sociology of Education*, the *Journal of Health and Social Behavior*, *Demography*, the *Journal of Marriage and the Family*, *Social Problems*, the *American Sociologist*, the *Administrative Science Quarterly*, the *Public Opinion Quarterly*, *Sociological Methods and Research*, *Social Science Research*, and *Rural Sociology*. In addition, there are international journals such as the *British Journal of Sociology* and the *International Social Science Journal*.

A social researcher is assisted by secondary sources which furnish guides to relevant literature. These include *Sociological Abstracts*, *Psychological Abstracts*, the *Social Science Citation Index,* and *Contemporary Sociology*. Abstracts provide the author, topic, journal issue, and a short summary for each recently published article. The *Citation Index* lists the major cited contributors in a research area and the journals in which their reports have been published. *Contempo-*

rary Sociology contains reviews of books in sociology and related fields. These sources lead the researcher to the most applicable recent publications. He can then consult the references and bibliographies of the latter for additional relevant materials.

A thorough search of the literature should also pay heed to journals in other disciplines such as psychology, economics, anthropology, political science, history, and even psychiatry. Articles bearing on the research problem may have been written by scientists in these areas.

There are also computer data available to the social researcher. In the biomedical area a computerized retrieval system has been developed which catalogs health-related publications in many fields, including the social sciences. Extensive data are stored at the National Opinion Research Center in Chicago, the Institute for Social Research at the University of Michigan, the Roper Public Opinion Research Center, and the U.S. Bureau of the Census. All these data may be acquired, some at a nominal cost, for secondary analysis.

Initial reading   After locating potentially relevant literature, the researcher browses through each publication and makes an initial determination as to whether and to what extent it applies to his research problem. He reads the abstracts (when available) or conclusions and summaries of journal articles, usually covering the past three to five years. The tables of contents of books and possibly their author and subject indexes are perused.

Initial reading familiarizes the researcher with the existing literature, and usually allows him to eliminate a large volume of the publications browsed. Those remaining may be roughly classified into three groups, according to whether they (1) bear on the research idea but not on the envisioned research problem and statements; (2) relate to the research idea and some research statements generally; or (3) apply directly to the research idea, problem, and study strategy. Their consideration requires further effort.

Abstracting and summarizing information   The publications in the first group should be abstracted onto reference cards. A *reference card* is an index card containing on one side the name or names of the author or authors of the publication, its title, year published, and source; and on the other side general information about the publication and the researcher's comments. (The *source* of a publication consists of the volume, issue, and page numbers for a journal article, and the name and location of the publisher for a book, monograph, or other document.) Figure 8.1 shows an example of a reference card.

The researcher's reference cards constitute a bibliography of all the publications he has found relevant to his work. Sometimes items initially considered peripheral become more important as one further acquaints himself with the literature and expert opinion on a problem. Reference cards allow him to locate these materials easily for more examination.

The publications in the second group, those which relate to the research idea and some research statements generally, should also be abstracted onto reference cards. But they merit additional, more detailed treatment in the form of summary sheets like the one in Figure 8.2. A *summary sheet* gives the author and source of

```
┌─────────────────────────────────────────────┐
│  Coleman, James S., Elihu Katz, and Herbert  │
│        Menzel                                 │
│                                               │
│  1966         Medical Innovation              │
│               Bobbs-Merrill, Indianapolis     │
│                                               │
│                                               │
│                                               │
└─────────────────────────────────────────────┘
```

Side A

```
┌─────────────────────────────────────────────┐
│                                               │
│  An empirical study of the diffusion          │
│                                               │
│  of a new drug among physicians in three      │
│                                               │
│  communities.                                 │
│                                               │
│                                               │
│                                               │
│                                               │
└─────────────────────────────────────────────┘
```

Side B

Figure 8.1   Reference card for literature review.

a publication; indicates whether it is a survey, a theoretical discussion, a review and synthesis of literature, or an experimental study; and specifies the major concepts utilized, including the independent and dependent variables. Sampling information, such as whether the units sampled were individuals or communities and how they were chosen for the sample (for example, by a random method, by volunteering for an experiment, or by being part of a saturation sample consisting of every member of the population), is provided for an empirical study. The summary sheet lists the relationships the authors set out to explain, their postulates and hypotheses, and their conclusions. Its reverse side may be used for a description of the unique features of the publication and any additional comments by the researcher.

The third group of publications assembled by the researcher is composed of those with research ideas and problems directly relevant to his own and procedures similar to the ones he plans to follow. A reference card and a summary sheet should be constructed for each of these materials, and the researcher should also attempt to obtain a *copy for his own file*. Photocopy machines are often available in libraries and academic buildings, so journal articles and short papers may be copied readily. Books, monographs, and other publications too long to be duplicated in their entirety may be procured by writing to the publishers or authors. Commercial publishing firms sometimes allow a discount to researchers affiliated with academic or nonprofit organizations. Some important publications in the social sciences are published by the U.S. Government Printing Office or nonprofit sponsors, and copies may be acquired at nominal cost. The author of any publication is usually knowledgeable as to how it is most easily obtained.

Author (last name, initials):

Journal (or book) title (issue, volume):

Date of publication (publisher):

1. Nature of report: _____ Survey   _____ Theoretical
   _____ Review   _____ Other (specify)
   _____ Experimental _____
   _____ Observational _____
   _____ Documentary _____

2. Central concepts:
   Dependent variable(s):
   a.
   b.
   c.

   Independent variables:
   a.
   b.
   c.

3. Sampling technique:

   Unit of analysis:

   _____ Individual   _____ Community
   _____ Other (Specify)

   Nature of samples:

   _____ Random   _____ Stratified
   _____ Clustering   _____ Multistage
   _____ Nonrandom (specify)

4. Postulates, hypotheses, relationships:
   a.
   b.
   c.

5. Conclusions:

6. Remarks (see other side)

Figure 8.2 Summary sheet for literature review.

It is useful for a researcher to indicate on the appropriate reference card, summary sheet, or both that additional information on a publication is available in his file. An "S" might be placed in the upper right-hand corner of a reference card when a summary sheet for the same item has been prepared, and a "C" on the reference card, summary sheet, or both when a copy has been filed.

Consultation with Experts A second variety of exploratory study involves consulting with experts in the area of interest. These experts need not be social

scientists, but they must have a first-hand knowledge of the activities being investigated. For a study of drug use on a university campus, probable "experts" include psychological counselors, residence supervisors, students who know drug
users or who have used drugs themselves, and even the parents of students.
Observations made by such experts can enhance the researcher's insight into real-
life situations involving his research topic.

Experts are interviewed in informal, face-to-face situations. The researcher
talks to them individually or as a group, and in whatever environment they find
most congenial. However, he should prepare himself in advance so that the conversations are more than just "rap sessions." While he may not yet know enough
about the activities to ask scientific questions, he should be prepared to direct the
discussion toward several issues: *who, how, what,* and *why.*

Who are the participants in the activities? *What* are their salient characteristics? In studying drug use, the researcher tries to find out which students tend to
use drugs. He is interested in their age, sex, type of residence (dormitory, off-
campus apartment, fraternity house, or other arrangement), social background
(Is there a tendency for students from certain social classes to engage in drug
use?), and academic interests and performance (Are drug users better or worse
students than nonusers? Do they tend to major in the arts and humanities or in
the sciences?). The experts are encouraged to characterize drug users by utilizing
any descriptions with which they feel comfortable.

How did the current state of the activities being studied come about? For the
drug use study, this issue concerns the historical development of drug use on
campus, including the correspondence of events on the university, community,
and national levels to this development. It also relates to the process by which
students become drug users. Attention to individual cases is fruitful here.

What is the current state of the activities? Interest might focus on the kinds
of drugs being used, student attitudes toward various drugs, the attitudes and behaviors of the university administration and the community toward drug use on
campus, police involvement, sources of drugs, etc.

Why are the activities the way they are today? The researcher probes the
experts for explanations of the present drug use situation. Their projections and
predictions as to campus drug use in the future may also be included.

While consultation with experts can supply the researcher with invaluable
insight, information so gathered is preliminary and tentative. Descriptions offered
by experts are subject to the accuracy of their observations, while interpretations
may be colored by their own relations to the activities being examined, their
values and beliefs, and the unsystematic nature of their contracts with participants in the activities. Therefore, consultation with experts is used only to
provide a general outline of the research topic and to suggest variables which
should be taken into account. The information it yields should not be treated as
precise or even reliable.

Case Exploration Case exploration represents a third variety of exploratory
study. It consists of the detailed examination of individual cases of involvement
with the activities being studied. In investigating drug use on campus, the re-

searcher might seek out several student drug users and delve into their case histories. A representative sample is not attempted for case exploration; in fact,
extreme cases are preferred. It is often impractical to draw a representative
sample or to work with more than a handful of cases, and the characteristics
associated with the activities are likely to be most salient among extreme cases.
This salience should prevent even the researcher unfamiliar with the activities
from neglecting crucial variables. As in consultation with experts, conversations
in a case exploration study should be unstructured, so that the output is
minimally affected by the researcher's own perceptions and interpretations of the
activities.

After these exploratory studies (literature review, consultation with experts,
and case exploration) have been conducted, either by himself or by others, the researcher proceeds to more systematic studies.

Descriptive Studies

The purpose of a descriptive study is, as the name implies, to obtain a description
of the activities of interest. Like the exploratory study, it focuses on the issues of
who, how, what, and *why*. However, a descriptive study is more structured than
an exploratory one, and differs also in that it requires a representative sample.

A descriptive study may be the ultimate or an intermediate objective in a
research program. The former applies when the researcher attempts merely to
describe the activities as fully as possible, and poses no theoretical questions. This
situation is illustrated by the various public opinion polls, as well as by studies of
population (birthrates and mortality rates, population stability, and change), occupational structure (the relative growth or decline of each occupational group in
a society over time), industrialization (the rate of industrial growth in a given
area or country), and public health (the incidence of various diseases). These
studies are important both for the information they contain and for their
contributions to policy making and planning for the future.

But the descriptive study may also serve as a stepping stone to more refined
hypothesis-generating and hypothesis-testing studies. Its functions in this regard
are to try out the sampling procedure, establish data-collection methods, identify
crucial variables, determine appropriate operationalizations, assemble data
analysis techniques, formulate potential hypotheses, and so on.

For whichever purpose it is intended, the descriptive study must be
systematic in design and execution. Although it does not attempt explanation, it
must be as comprehensive as possible in description, and thus tends to be the
lengthiest type of study. The researcher is guided by the information gleaned from
previous literature reviews, consultations with experts, and case explorations. But
this information requires qualification where it is incomplete, biased, or both. As
a result of such considerations, descriptive studies tend to be elaborate and often
expensive.

Hypothesis-Generating Studies

The hypothesis-generating study is used by the researcher who has some ideas
about potential relationships, which he wishes to sort out and formulate into a

precise research problem. For example, a researcher interested in the causes of crime may review the literature and find that a number of causes have been proposed: parental rigidity, low parental socioeconomic status, low educational attainment, sexual frustration, genetic traits, drug use, suicidal tendency, etc. He also discovers that several indicants of criminal behavior have been used, including arrest records, conviction records, and severity of punishment. He may be at a loss as to how to construct meaningful research statements when confronted with this plethora of potential causes and indicants of criminal behavior. Instead of testing specific hypotheses, he should conduct a hypothesis-generating study.

In such a study the researcher confines his attention to that set of variables which the literature, consultation with experts, etc., suggest as most fruitful. He examines the relationships among various combinations of independent and dependent variables and chooses the one (or more) which empirically seems to merit further consideration in a hypothesis-testing study. If he finds, for instance, that the frequency of arrest is most strongly related to suicidal tendency, he may proceed inductively to a theory postulating a psychological basis for criminal behavior (rather than a sociological explanation such as the idea that persons of lower parental socioeconomic status are more likely to be arrested).

The hypothesis-generating study shares with the descriptive study the function of providing a testing ground for the sampling, data-collection, operationalizing, and data analysis techniques to be used later in a hypothesis-testing study. However, it is still more structured than the descriptive study, involves fewer variables, and requires that they be measured more rigorously.

Hypothesis-Testing Studies

The ultimate form of study for theory verification is the hypothesis-testing study, in which a specific hypothesis derived from theoretical propositions is tested empirically. The hypothesis-testing study is the most severely structured, controlled, and limited empirical study in social research. Few variables are included, and the questions are tightly structured. The researcher controls for external influences on the study situation, such as the sequence of events, changes over time, and the influence of other variables on those under consideration.

Hypothesis-testing studies share many research procedures with descriptive and hypothesis-generating studies. But each type is characterized by its distinctive purposes, scope, rigor, control, and firmness of conclusions. The details of the latter differentiations will be covered in subsequent chapters which deal with sampling, measurement, data collection, data analysis, and the interpretation of results.

SUMMARY

The initial phases of social research are the formulation of a research problem and the selection of the type of study most appropriate for its investigation. There are no set guidelines for the discovery of a research issue, which may be suggested by personal experience, materials read, conversations, exposure to the mass media, theory, beliefs, and values. But the researcher's choice is likely to be influenced by factors such as his colleagues' respect and recognition, available financial and personnel support, practical needs, and his own imagination and curiosity.

A research issue, once selected, must be reduced to a research problem. While a research issue represents a general interest, a research problem relates two or more concepts. The researcher translates the concepts contained in the research problem into variables which can be measured using observations, in the process of operationalization. He also envisions what results in his observations would constitute confirmation of the relationship in his research statement, and tries to foresee the consequences of the study in terms of its contributions to theoretical explanations and ongoing activities.

The decision as to what type of study is conducted hinges on the nature of the research problem, the availability of data sources, and how much is known about the subject matter. The four main types are exploratory, descriptive, hypothesis-generating, and hypothesis-testing studies. These are arrayed from the broadest in scope and least rigorous (exploratory studies) to the narrowest in scope and most rigorous (hypothesis-testing studies).

Exploratory studies include literature review, consultation with experts, and case exploration. Literature review utilizes abstracting and summarizing devices such as the reference card and the summary sheet. A descriptive study is more structured than an exploratory one and requires a representative sample. However, it still serves merely to describe activities rather than to explain them.

To explain activities in terms of their relationships with other activities, the researcher may first conduct a hypothesis-generating study. This enables him to try out his sampling procedure, improve the measurement of variables, test his data-collection and analysis techniques, and formulate a precise hypothesis for testing. The hypothesis-testing study is the most rigorous empirical study in social research, and therefore the one used for theory verification. It consists of an empirical test of a specific hypothesis derived from theory.

Chapter 9

Sampling

After the researcher has formulated the research problem and selected the most appropriate type of study, he or she must decide just which cases (people) are to be included as subjects in the study. Ideally, every case to which the research applies would be included. However, the cost and effort involved in so doing are usually prohibitive. Therefore, a subset of cases is chosen to represent the total group. Choosing such a subset is called *sampling*.

To see how important the procedure of selecting a sample is in social research, a historical incident in the public opinion polls of presidential elections may be enlightening. Since the late nineteenth century, newspapers and magazines in the United States had polled people's voting intentions before elections. The procedure of selecting respondents was usually the street-corner variety, in which an inquirer would ask anyone who happened to pass by his or her voting intention. Gradually, the selection procedure was "improved" with the use of telephone directories, automobile registration lists, magazine subscription rosters, and voter registration lists. The strategy was to distribute a brief questionnaire through the mail, by newspaper delivery, or through retail stores to generate as many responses as possible. The belief was that, the larger the sample, the more valid the result in predicting the actual election outcome. *Literary Digest,* a popular magazine in the 1920s, developed a poll from telephone directories and automobile registration lists. The sampling procedure seemed rather valid in predicting the election results in the 1920, 1924, 1928, and

1932 presidential elections. In 1936, Franklin D. Roosevelt, seeking his second term as president, was opposed by the Republican candidate Alfred M. Landon. With massive mailings and massive responses (over 2 million "ballots" returned), *Literary Digest* confidently predicted that Landon would beat Roosevelt by about 15 percentage points. Roosevelt, of course, won the race.

The failure of the prediction was attributed mainly to the sampling plan of the *Literary Digest* poll in that it left out those voters who did not own telephones or automobiles. The result was that the lower socioeconomic group was under-represented in the sample. While in earlier elections, the lower socioeconomic group had not participated in voting substantially, the depression had realigned voters along the socioeconomic dimension—more lower-class, working voters went out to vote for the Democratic party. The disastrous failure of the *Literary Digest* 1936 prediction has taught pollsters two lessons: (1) the accuracy of prediction is not necessarily determined by the sample size, and (2) the sample must be representative of the population if it is to predict from the sampled characteristics to the population characteristics. It also shows how important it is to develop a sample which is least biased in making inferences about the population.

This chapter will discuss several aspects of sampling: basic definitions, probability and nonprobability sampling, combinations of probability and non-probability sampling, determination of sample size, and some special techniques.

BASIC DEFINITIONS

The total group of people which meet certain criteria of interest to the researcher is called the *population*. If a researcher wants to study female voters in the United States, the population consists of all those individuals who are citizens of the United States, who are female, and who vote. Thus, the population is the total group of cases which conform to a certain designated set of specifications. The list of all cases or groups of cases in the population is called a sampling frame.

A subset of cases from the population chosen to represent it is called a *sample*. The researcher wants to be able to generalize the results obtained by studying the sample to statements about the population. This may be done, with the help of statistics, if the selection of the sample is based on a probabilistic strategy. Such generalization involves errors, since it is practically impossible to select a sample which represents completely all the behaviors and relationships in the population. However, the extent of probable error is known to the researcher, and guides him in interpreting his results with regard to the population with a known degree of confidence. The process of generalizing results from a sample to the population is called *inference*. A sample then is a subset of the elements in a population, the characteristics of which may be used to infer characteristics of the population.

If a researcher does not want to generalize his findings to a larger population, he need not worry about sampling. His results are assumed to apply only to the group which was directly studied.

A *sampling plan* is simply the method of choosing a sample. There are two main classes of sampling plans: probabilistic and nonprobabilistic.

PROBABILITY SAMPLING

Sampling according to a *probabilistic* (or *representative*) plan is called *probability sampling.* A representative sample is one for which inference to the population is guided by a known probability of accuracy. The researcher can specify the probability that any particular element of the population will be included in the sample.

The most commonly used types of probability sampling are simple random sampling, stratified random sampling, cluster sampling, and a combination of two or more of the above in multistage sampling.

Simple Random Sampling

The most basic type of probability sampling is simple random sampling. In simple random sampling each case has an equal chance of appearing in the sample, as does every combination of cases. That is, every case not only has an equal chance of being selected to be in the sample, but also has an equal chance of being selected after one or more other cases have been selected. For example, in a simple random sample of houses in an urban area, not only has each house an equal chance of being selected, but each house's chance of being selected after a neighboring house has already been selected is still as good as that of any of the remaining houses. In order to select a simple random sample, the researcher assigns a number to every case in the population and then chooses numbers at random until the desired sample size is reached. If the population were small, it would be possible simply to write all the numbers on equal-sized pieces of paper, put them into a hat, mix them thoroughly, and draw the sample. However, this method is not practical for most sociological work, for such a procedure involves substantial preparation and also the danger of having the pieces not well mixed in the hat. Thus, some pieces would tend to stay at the bottom and have less chance than the pieces at the top of being selected. A device commonly used to select simple random samples is the *random number table* (see Table 1, Appendix C). By assigning each case in the population a number, the researcher can go through the random number table with a random start (any column or row, left to right, right to left, upward, downward, or diagonally) to pick up the numbers which match any of the cases, until all cases needed for the sample are selected.

Simple random samples may be chosen in two ways: with or without replacement. In *sampling with replacement* each case is returned to the population after being chosen to be in the sample. Thus, a population case can appear more than once in the same sample. In *sampling without replacement,* on the other hand, cases chosen to be in the sample are not returned to the population and a population case can appear only once in the same sample. Strictly speaking, sampling with replacement is the ideal sampling plan according to sampling theory.

However, sampling without replacement poses no statistical problem as long as the population is sufficiently large, and is the more prevalent method of simple random sampling in social research.

Simple random sampling is the ideal form of probability sampling. There is a well-developed body of rules governing inference from simple random samples to the population; however, simple random sampling is often impractical or too expensive for many research purposes. Other types of probability sampling have been developed which provide adequate substitutes. The statistical procedures designed for simple random sampling are also applicable to these types with certain statistical adjustments.

A simple variation of simple random sampling is systematic sampling. Systematic sampling draws one random number from a range of numbers, the nth number, and selects the nth number, the $2n$th number, $3n$th number, and so on, as the sample. For example, to draw a sample of 200 students from a student directory of 1,000, 1 in every 5 students (200/1,000) must be included in the sample. In systematic sampling, all the students listed in the directory are numbered consecutively. Then, a random number is drawn between 1 and 5 to determine the first student to be sampled. Suppose the random number is 4, then the students listed fourth, ninth, fourteenth, nineteenth, etc., are selected to be in the sample. The difference between simple random sampling and systematic sampling is that only one random number, rather than 200 random numbers, is drawn in the selection of the student sample. However, if the initial list of the population cases is random (i.e., not arranged in any systematic manner) and does not present any systematic bias, then the results of the two sampling plans are almost always identical. Both allow every case and combination of cases to have an equal chance of being selected—in the case of systematic sampling, it is the initial random listing which guarantees such equal probabilities.

In practice, systematic sampling is preferred to the simple random sampling, since it only draws one random number rather than as many as the number of cases to be included in the sample. Systematic sampling can be used however only when the researcher is certain that there is no systemic bias in the listing of cases in the initial roster of cases. For example, some lists provide names in alphabetical order. Many ethnic names tend to cluster in several places on the list. If a study's variables are related to ethnic characteristics of the respondents, then the systematic sampling of the alphabetical roster may either overrepresent or underrepresent certain ethnic groups, thus biasing the results. Other lists tend to be periodical or cyclical in nature. In apartment buildings, dormitories, and certain street blocks, every nth house or room may be a corner unit, a unit near the stairway, etc. Systematic sampling of the nth house or room creates a biased sample. In these cases, in which the list is not random, one way to safeguard representativeness of the systematic sampling is to utilize multiple random starts. Instead of using a single random number, several are used. For example, instead of one random number for each five consecutive numbers, the researcher can draw four random numbers for each twenty consecutive names.

Stratified Random Sampling

In stratified random sampling, the researcher *stratifies* the population, or breaks it down into groups, according to the categories of one or more variables, and then randomly selects samples from each group (stratum). Stratified random sampling has two important advantages over simple random sampling: (1) it makes possible disproportionate sample sizes from different strata, and (2) it takes into account crucial variables by using them to define the strata. A researcher sometimes wants to study a group which represents a relatively small proportion of the population, like blacks, Puerto Ricans, Asian-Americans, and native Americans (American Indians), in a college. Simple random sampling would yield similarly small proportions of these groups and perhaps too small a number to permit any definitive statements about their characteristics. For example, in a college of 10,000 students where 10 percent (1,000), 5 percent (500), 2 percent (200), and 1 percent (100), are blacks, Puerto Ricans, Asian-Americans, and native Americans, respectively, a simple random sample of 500 students would yield approximately 50 blacks, 25 Puerto Ricans, 10 Asian-Americans, and 5 native Americans. Most of these sampled groups are so small in number that they are statistically unstable and do not allow the researcher to make any precise projections about these groups in the college from the sample. If the variable of ethnicity is important in the study, the small sizes of these sampled groups would render the study a total loss. One way to incorporate such important variables into sampling consideration involves stratification of the population *before* simple random sampling. Using stratified random sampling, the researcher might divide the student population into whites, blacks, Puerto Ricans, Asian-Americans, and native Americans. Simple random samples would then be drawn, one from among each of these ethnic groups. The sample could incorporate 1 percent (82 of the 8,200) of the white students, 10 percent (100 of the 1,000) of the black students, 20 percent (100 of the 500) of the Puerto Rican students, 50 percent (100 of the 200) of the Asian-Americans, and all (100) the native Americans. While the total sample size is about the same as that of the simple random sample (482 versus 500), all the ethnic groups are now adequately represented in the sample. The researcher thus ensures that an important variable (ethnicity) will have sufficient distribution over the variations for study.

Another advantage of stratified random sampling is that it takes into account the effect of one or more particular variables in the stratification process. When a researcher is reasonably sure that the population cases can be identified by one or more variables such as sex, religion, age, etc., and furthermore, that the cases in each have similar views or behavioral patterns in terms of the variables to be studied, the stratification process allows him to take advantage of such *homogeneous* behavior in the sampling. If the cases in a stratum show homogeneous behaviors, relatively few sampled cases would be required to represent the stratum. In contrast, a stratum showing heterogeneous or diversified behavioral patterns would require a relatively large number of sampled cases in order to represent all the heterogeneous behavioral patterns in the sample.

To take advantage of the stratified random sampling then requires *selection of stratification variables which will provide homogeneous strata so that relatively small sample sizes are required from each stratum.*

Disproportionate Sampling One important consequence of selecting a different number of cases from different strata is that it becomes necessary to adjust the findings before inference to the population can be made. For example, the results of a stratified random sampling on religious affiliation and the distribution of favorable attitudes toward the death penalty for persons convicted of murder are shown in Table 9.1. As can be seen in the table, the number of cases in each sample from each stratum was 100 for all strata (see row *c*). If the study found the percentages of each group having favorable attitudes toward the death penalty varied from 50 percent of the Protestant sample to 70 percent of the Jewish sample (row *d* in Table 9.1), it would be erroneous for the researcher to estimate the percentage of the population in favor of the death penalty by simply dividing the number of cases in the sample in favor of the death penalty (300) by the total number of cases in the sample (500). This would lead to the estimation that three-fifths (60 percent) of the population are in favor of the death penalty. The estimation is wrong because the researcher failed to take into account that different weights were given to different strata in the selection of samples. That is, the relative sample size for each stratum did not correspond to its population size (row *b*). In order to make the correct point estimate, it is necessary to multiply the percentage favoring the death penalty for each stratum (row *d*) by the weights (row *b*) first. The correct point estimate as presented in rows *e* and *f* were quite different from the initially unadjusted erroneous estimations. In fact, only slightly over half (53.9 percent) of the population were in favor of the death penalty.

Ideally, stratification variables should be among the factors most influencing the variables to be studied. However, in many situations, the researcher does not have the specific information about each population case for these factors. Therefore, the actual selection of stratification variables is determined by the availability of the factors considered important. In most social research, depending on what population is being studied, such important and generally available factors include sex, age, education, race, and religion.

Cluster Sampling

Cluster sampling is another probabilistic sampling method. It is often more economical than either simple or stratified random sampling. Like the latter, it involves dividing the population into groups. Unlike the latter, the population is broken down into clusters (groups) according to some specific criterion (often geographic in nature). A number of clusters is randomly selected and from these selected clusters the eventual respondents are chosen, usually by a combination of sampling techniques.

Cluster sampling is especially appropriate when the study population is scattered over a large geographic area, as are the citizens of the United States. It is more economical to contact a number of people in each of several restricted areas

Table 9.1 Inference from Weighted Stratified Random Samples to the Population

	Religious affiliation					
	Protestant	Catholic	Jewish	None	Other	Total
Population						
a. Absolute size	6,500	2,500	350	300	350	10,000
b. Relative size, percent	65	25	3.5	3	3.5	100
Stratified sampling						
c. Absolute size	100	100	100	100	100	500
d. Percent in favor of death penalty for persons convicted of murder (number of cases)	50	60	70	50	70	
Inference from sample to population—point estimate (in favor of death penalty)	(50)	(60)	(70)	(50)	(70)	(300)
e. Absolute size (d × a)	3,250	1,500	245	150	245	5,390
f. Relative size (d × b), percent	32.5	15.0	2.45	1.5	2.45	53.9

of the country than to contact a large number of people scattered throughout the country, as would be necessary with a simple or stratified random sample.

In many situations, natural groupings can be used as clusters, such as schools, hospitals, and census blocks for many urban areas in the United States. In other cases, such natural groupings are not available. Then the researcher can use any arbitrary groupings of the population. For example, in sampling residents of a rural area, the researcher can draw grids to define the clusters. The use of arbitrary clusters, in fact, provides an advantage to cluster sampling not available to simple random sampling or stratified random sampling. Namely, it becomes possible to define clusters without having first to identify all the population cases. When a set of clusters is selected to be in the sample, enumeration of all the cases need only be done within the sampled clusters. This represents a major savings in cost and effort, since all the cases in clusters not selected no longer need to be enumerated.

Since sampling of individual cases is done only in clusters selected to be included in the sample, the question arises how to ensure that these sampled clusters are representative of the population. The question becomes especially crucial when natural groupings are used as clusters. The likelihood of similarity of characteristics for people belonging to the same group is potentially great. Neighborhoods usually show similar socioeconomic characteristics, courses in colleges attract students sharing certain common academic interests, and people working at the same firm or institution share certain skills or behavioral patterns. If only an extremely limited number of such clusters is sampled, the chances of obtaining an unrepresentative sample increase. In general, cluster sampling deviates from simple random sampling, since (1) homogeneity of cases within each cluster is great, and (2) the number of sampled clusters is small. These two issues will now be discussed.

The first issue concerning the homogeneity of cases within clusters can be handled by carefully constructing clusters composed of heterogeneous cases. In fact, the greater heterogeneity there is among the cases in each cluster, the better the chances are for the cluster sampling to resemble simple random sampling. When each cluster is composed of cases as heterogeneous as all the cases in the population, cluster sampling should result in a sample essentially identical to that obtained in simple random sampling. Thus, the researcher should pay attention to the compositions of the clusters. If possible, the variations of case characteristics in each cluster should be maximized. This procedure is essentially the opposite of the one used in defining strata in stratified random sampling, in which variations of case characteristics within each stratum are to be minimized. What usually happens is that different clusters have varying degrees of heterogeneity among the cases. When this occurs, the researcher should then use the *disproportionate sampling procedure,* as mentioned in the section "Stratified Random Sampling." For clusters with great heterogeneity only a limited number of cases needs to be selected, whereas for clusters of less heterogeneity a greater number of cases needs to be selected. *There is a direct relationship between variations among cases (in terms of the variables to be studied) and the required sample size,* for a given degree of precision in the eventual inference from the sample to the population. At one extreme, if every case in the population had an identical behavioral pattern regarding the variable to be studied, then one case would be sufficient as a representative sample of the population. At the other extreme, if every case differed in the behavioral pattern, then it would take a lot of cases in the sample to even begin to describe the population from the sample results. Thus, for clusters of varying degrees of heterogeneity, different numbers of cases (relative to the total number of cases in each cluster) need to be drawn into the sample. Again, when inference is made from the sample to the population, adjustments must be made in estimating the population characteristics (see Table 9.1).

The second issue, the number of sampled clusters, ideally could be resolved by merely increasing the number of sampled clusters. However, this strategy would eventually defeat the purpose of clustering, since the number of sampled clusters would approach the total number of clusters and if sampling of cases came from all clusters, it would be similar to either simple random sampling or stratified random sampling. An alternative strategy to resolve this difficulty is to reduce the number of cases in each cluster. Since the population contains a fixed number of cases, as the number of cases in each cluster decreases, the number of clusters increases. As a result of reducing the number of cases in clusters, more clusters are available for selection. Since, as more clusters are sampled, the sample more accurately represents the population, this strategy seems viable. However, increased clusters and a greater number of clusters mean wider scattering of the sampled clusters. The economic savings of using cluster sampling rather than simple random sampling or stratified random sampling would be nullified.

In summary, while it is desirable to approximate the simple random sampling plan by increasing the heterogeneity of cases in each cluster and increasing the number of clusters to be included in the sample, overdoing either would substantially reduce the advantage of cluster sampling over other sampling plans. Thus, in the final analysis, the researcher should recognize that in general cluster sampling seldom, if ever, achieves the degree of precision in its inference as is provided by simple random sampling. On the other hand, with discriminating clustering and proper balance between the number of clusters and cases in each cluster, the precision lost in the sampling is almost always compensated for by the simplicity and economical procedural gains involved in cluster sampling. Therefore, in many social research situations in which a large number of cases is scattered over a wide geographic area in the population, cluster sampling is a superior sampling plan when compared with others.

In order to further clarify the process of cluster sampling, let us consider a specific example. A researcher wanting to study attitudes toward drug use in a particular city might first divide the city into geographic clusters. The clusters should be as heterogeneous as possible; that is, they should contain a cross-section of people with regard to characteristics (such as age, sex, race, socioeconomic status, and perhaps political orientation) that seem likely to affect attitudes toward drug use. A random sample of these clusters would be taken, and the smaller number of clusters which appeared in the random sample would be studied. If there were fifteen clusters to begin with, three or four might be selected for study. Since each cluster is heterogeneous, a valid cross-section of population responses would hopefully be obtained by interviewing people within the randomly selected clusters.

Note that cluster sampling is usually used in combination with at least one other type of sampling (in the instance discussed above, simple random sampling). The combination of various sampling plans falls under the general heading of multistage sampling.

Multistage cluster sampling consists of a series of clusterings based on like or different criteria. For the study of attitudes toward drug use, after dividing the city into fifteen clusters and selecting four at random, the four selected clusters might be broken down into yet smaller clusters, perhaps city blocks. Each original cluster might contain approximately fifty city blocks, and fifteen blocks in each of the four clusters could be selected to represent the clusters. Finally, random sampling of households and respondents in each selected block could be carried out.

As mentioned earlier, clusters usually are disproportionate, there being varying numbers of cases in each cluster. Thus, in multistage cluster sampling, when a disproportionate number of clusters and cases is selected, *adjustments for each and every stage where disproportions occur* must be made before inference of the sample data back to the population.

Multistage Sampling and an Illustrative Example

Probability sampling for social research is often *multistage* in nature, combining two or more of the types of sampling discussed above. The sampling plan for a study of attitudes toward drug use in a particular city was introduced in the previous section to illustrate how cluster sampling could be altered to incorporate multistage sampling. For example, after selecting the four clusters, each cluster might then be stratified according to a characteristic such as sex, and then a random sample taken from within *each* of the sex groups in each cluster. Or, if it was impossible to construct clusters in different parts of the city with approximately similar distributions on socioeconomic status, the clusters could be grouped according to whether they represent low, middle, or high socioeconomic status and a subset of clusters selected from each class. The researcher would then be utilizing the principle of stratification across, rather than within, clusters. Finally, in the examples of both single and multistage cluster sampling given above, multistage sampling in the broader sense occurs because the researcher takes a simple random sample of the residents of each selected cluster or block.

To illustrate the multistage, multimethod sampling plan, a study consisting of a sample of persons 18 years of age and older who were not full-time students in an urbanized area (Albany, New York) will be used. To define accurately the area and estimate the population and number of housing units in the area, the 1970 U.S. Bureau of the Census Block Statistics for this urbanized metropolitan area was obtained. The Block Statistics divide the area into 16 blocks and provide detailed information such as population size, number of housing units, house ownership, and a map locating all the streets and housing units on each block.

The total number of housing units in the area, determined from the Block Statistics, was 178,409 in 1970. In order to obtain the desired inferential accuracy from the sample to the population, the study needed approximately 250 respondents.[1] In the first stage, the clustering sampling plan was used. Each cluster designated three consecutive housing units within a block, and all three housing units in each sampled cluster were included in the sample. This meant that the sample size of 250 was divided by 3 to obtain the number of clusters (83) the study would need. Then, systematic sampling was used. To arrive at the first housing unit to be included in the sample, the total number of housing units (178,409) was divided by the number of clusters (83) to determine the skip interval constant. This number turned out to be 2,149. In other words, we needed to find a cluster in each group of 2,149 housing units. Since the Block Statistics listed all the housing units consecutively in each block, it was simply a matter of following the listed housing units in the selection of the clusters. The first cluster was chosen by drawing a random number between 1 and 2,149. It happened to be the number 1,501. Starting from the first housing unit in the first listed block, we proceeded to find the 1,501th housing unit. Thus, the first sampled cluster included housing units numbered 1,501, 1,502, and 1,503. To find the second sampled cluster, we simply added the skip interval constant (2,149) to the first sampled housing unit (1,501). Thus, the sampled second cluster included housing units numbered 3,650, 3,651, and 3,652. The systematic sampling procedure continued until the eighty-third cluster was selected.[2]

In order to keep track of the housing units in the Block Statistics we used a calculator to cumulate the number of housing units for each block consecutively listed in the Block Statistics.

Resulting from a cluster, systematic sampling was a list of 83 clusters with 249 sampled housing units. In this sampling, the cluster is very small and all housing units in a sampled cluster were included in the sample. This has the advantage of saving interview costs—an interviewer could be responsible for and conduct interviews for the entire cluster of three housing units. However, since residents in a neighborhood tend to have similar socioeconomic backgrounds, any large cluster unit (say, with 5 or 6 housing units) would increase the risk of having too many homogeneous housing units in the sample.

The final step in the cluster, systematic sampling was the selection of a random sample of respondents in the sampled housing units.[3] Since there might be more than one eligible respondent in each sampled household (persons 18

---

[1] Statistical tables determine the needed sample size in order to predict a population characteristic from a sample within ±3% accuracy in 95 out of 100 similar samples for the given population size.

[2] For details of this sampling method, see Charles H. Backstrom and Gerald D. Hursh, *Survey Research,* Northwestern University Press, Evanston, Ill., 1963.

[3] The random selection of respondents in sampled households is applicable to any sampling plan in which the initial unit of sampling is not a person (i.e., a household). It is not restricted to the cluster sampling plan.

years of age and older who were not full-time students), the specific person to be sampled was predetermined for the interviewer. That is, for each sampled housing unit a random number ("1" for female and "2" for male) was used to determine whether it should be a male or female respondent. Furthermore, another random number was drawn to determine whether the first or second person of the appropriate sex whom the interviewer met should be sampled. For example, if the second-appearing or -mentioned female person was to be sampled, the interviewer, on coming to the house, asked for another qualified female in the house if a female answered the door, and asked for the names of two females who might qualify in the house if a male answered the door so that the second female mentioned could be requested to respond. The only time this procedure was not followed was when only one qualified person lived in the house. Then, regardless of the order of appearance or mention desired, the qualified person was interviewed. If a sampled housing unit did not have a qualified person, then the interviewer proceeded to the next housing unit on the same side of the street beyond the sampled housing unit in the cluster.

When the unit of analysis is the household itself, the interviewer should be instructed to interview the specific person(s) in the sampled household who has the knowledge or information about the household the researcher is interested in, such as the head of the house or the provider of the house. Instructions should be specific so that the interviewer is directed toward the identifying and interviewing of a particular type of person in the household.

While the abovementioned sampling procedure is desirable and efficient in an urbanized area where detailed block statistics are available, it must be modified when dealing with a rural area for which such detailed information is not readily available. Identifications of housing units must come from local sources. One way to sample a rural area is to first divide the area into grids 4 by 5 miles, as the census divides urban areas (blocks), and to number the grids consecutively. Then a randomly selected sample of grids can be used. Or, when drastic differences in population density are found among the grids, the stratified sampling plan can be used. The number of grids sampled for each county can be proportional to the population of that county relative to the population of the area. It is possible, for example, that one county should be represented by $3\frac{1}{2}$ grids and another 5 grids, and so forth. In counties where a fraction of 1 grid is needed, 1 grid is randomly sampled and the fraction of a randomly selected adjacent grid is sampled.

Since rural areas are generally more homogeneous than urban areas, the likelihood of bias in such a sample would be greater than the cluster, systematic sampling. However, it is usually economically unfavorable to have sampled houses in scattered rural areas. To avoid such bias, the sample size for such a sampling plan in a rural area should be expanded. However, such a strategy may increase the study cost drastically. In general then, sampling rural areas is more expensive than urban areas.

After the sampled grids are determined, the researcher should consult local offices for enumeration of housing units. The police, the transportation department, local chamber of commerce, and the local government may provide such information or leads to such information. In some cases, the military or the government may have aerial shots which can be readily used to identify houses. When such information is not available, the researcher must canvass the sampled areas and draw maps to identify the houses.

Once the houses in the sampled grids have been identified, either cluster, systematic sampling, or simple random sampling can be used to select the sampled houses and respondents. Again, the decision depends on the scale of the area and economic factors. Usually, cluster sampling can be effectively used.

NONPROBABILITY SAMPLING

In some research situations the generalization of results to a larger population is not desired. For example, probability samples are virtually unobtainable for certain studies because the boundaries of the population are unknown. Such is the case with studies of narcotics users, street gangs, or the mentally ill. There is no sampling frame or complete list of narcotics users which would allow the selection of a probabilistic or representative sample of users and nonusers. When none of the probabilistic methods are usable, nonprobabilistic ones must suffice.

Nonprobability sampling poses statistical problems because it is impossible to tell the magnitude of error made in making inference to the whole population. Therefore, any inferences drawn are extremely risky. Nonprobability samples may be useful in providing the researcher with insight or a general idea of what is happening in the population, but they are not scientific reflections of the population itself. This will become evident as we describe the various types of nonprobability sampling.

Accidental Sampling

The most blatantly nonprobabilistic type of sampling is *accidental* or *haphazard sampling*. A researcher takes an accidental sample when he selects any case he happens to run across for inclusion in the sample. For example, if he stands outside the student union at a community college and asks the first 10 students who leave the building their opinions on a political issue, he is taking an accidental sample. He has no way of knowing whether these students are representative of the entire student population (although he can be pretty sure that they are not) or how they deviate from it (whether they are more liberal or more conservative than the student body as a whole). A well-known breed of accidental sampling consists of the "man-on-the-street" interviews sometimes conducted by television, radio, and newspaper reporters as an informal meter of public opinion. This practice fails to take into account the likelihood that persons that frequent different streets represent different spectra of opinion.

Quota Sampling

Slightly more sophisticated than accidental sampling is *quota sampling*. Here the researcher attempts to obtain a cross-section of the population by selecting cases from each of the major categories of one or more variable believed to influence the dependent variable. That is, he sets a "quota" for each category. Instead of talking to the first ten students who come out of the student union, he might select the first two freshmen, sophomores, juniors, seniors, and graduate students. Quota sampling may be refined by *weighting* the category quotas according to the proportion of the population comprised by each category. Thus, if freshmen comprise 30 percent of the campus population and graduate students only 10 percent, the researcher would include three freshmen and one graduate student in his ten-person sample.

Similarly, a quota sample can be based on a combination of variables. For example, combining sex and race may result in a two-by-two table of four categories: (1) male and white, (2) female and white, (3) male and nonwhite, and (4) female and nonwhite. Then, a designated number of respondents for each category is selected from the population. Again, this final selection of respondents is on an ad hoc basis rather than on a random sampling basis.

Naturally, quota sampling makes sense only if the variable used to determine the quotas has something to do with the dependent variable (in this case, if class year affects the opinions of students on a political issue). But even when this condition is met, quota sampling in no way allows one to ascertain the magnitude of error in making inference to all the persons in the categories they belong to. If students who frequent the student union tend to be somewhat more liberal than the student population as a whole, the results obtained by the researcher will be biased even if he uses quotas or weighted quotas and thereby ensures the inclusion of liberal freshman, sophomores, and so on. The fallacy of quota sampling is the notion that membership in a category automatically qualifies a person to represent all members of that category.

Purposive and Theoretical Sampling

Purposive sampling involves the use of judgment on the part of the researcher. He forms his sample by selecting cases *he* thinks are representative of the population. If he is very knowledgeable in his field, he may obtain a reasonably accurate cross-section of the population. Purposive sampling is a viable alternative if the boundaries of a study population are impossible to define (as would be the case, for example, with a study of homosexuals), or if the time and facilities available to a researcher are too limited to allow probability sampling. However, it is always risky because of the degree of arbitrariness and the fact that there is no way to establish the magnitude of error being made.

A variation of purposive sampling is *theoretical sampling*. The objective of theoretical sampling is to construct meaningful categories and dimensions for variables under study.[4] This sampling plan is desirable for the construction of classificatory models (see Chapter 3). The intention is not to find the proportions of cases in the population belonging to each category of a variable as the statis-

---

[4] Barney G. Glaser and Anselm L. Strauss, *The Discovery of Grounded Theory*, Aldine, Chicago, 1967.

tical inference would allow; rather it attempts to identify, exhaustively and exclusively if possible, all the meaningful categories a variable can take. The results of successful theoretical sampling constitute models of one or more dimension and provide the basic information about variables so that propositions and hypotheses can be formulated.

The process of theoretical sampling, then, involves continuous collection, coding, and analysis of data which the researcher feels would lead to discovery of the categories and relationships among variables. The process does not verify the magnitude of the categories or the relationships in the population, but merely acknowledges the presence and existence of such phenomena. Theoretical sampling thus serves well in a research study to explore and generate hypotheses.

Combinations of Probability and Nonprobability Sampling

Probability and nonprobability sampling are sometimes combined for reasons of economy and prediction. Nonprobability samples are more economical, but probability samples allow for better prediction.

For instance, a researcher studying the use of hospital emergency rooms might confine his attention to the hospitals in three neighboring cities. This is a form of purposive sampling in that the researcher is making the judgment that these cities are at least to some extent typical of all cities in regard to the use of their hospital emergency rooms. He might then randomly select a number of emergency room patients from each hospital. Strictly speaking, the results of his study would apply only to those hospitals and not to hospitals elsewhere. However, insights so obtained very often prove fruitful in suggesting valid generalizations.

Another procedure of combining probability and nonprobability sampling frequently used in large-scale cross-section surveys first goes through multistage sampling down to the city block level and then selects respondents using quota sampling based on sex and age. This sampling procedure is used by the NORC in its annual general social survey. This procedure may include sampling biases, mainly due to the "not at homes" which are not controlled for by the quotas. Thus, it is appropriate only when the past experience and judgment of a researcher indicate that such sample biases are likely to be small, relative to the precision of the measuring instrument, to the saving of the cost, and to the decisions to be made as a result of the study.[5]

DETERMINATION OF SAMPLE SIZE

There are rules a researcher can use to determine the sample size necessary to ensure a given probability of accuracy for the various statistics he intends to compute. The four main factors influencing the requisite sample size are the population size, the confidence interval for the estimation, the confidence coefficient c, and the variance in the population.

[5] NORC, *Codebook for the Spring 1972 General Social Survey*. Distributed by Roper Public Opinion Research Center, Williams College, Williamstown, Mass. 01267.

The general assumption that the larger the population from which the sample is drawn and to which inferences are to be made, the larger the sample must be to ensure a sufficient probability of accuracy, is true only to a limited extent. As the population size increases, the necessary sample size does not keep pace with it.

As shown in Figure 9.1, for a given set of conditions (the confidence level, the confidence interval, and the variance of the characteristic in the population), there is a rise in the required sample size as the population size increases from 1,000 to 500,000 or more. However, the sample sizes required for a population size beyond 10,000 are so similar that it is claimed that *the sample size is minimally affected by the population size when the population size is reasonably large.* Inferences to populations numbering in the millions may be made from samples of several hundred.

The second and third factors in the determination of a sample size concern the desired confidence interval or level of prediction, and the confidence coefficient ($c = 1 - \alpha$). If a researcher wishes to infer from a sample to a population characteristic with a set of given conditions (the population size and the variance of the population characteristic), then the sample size required varies positively with the confidence coefficient (see discussion of $c = 1 - \alpha$ in Chapter 7); the greater the confidence coefficient desired, the greater the sample size required. The sample size is also affected by the confidence interval desired (say, the population percentage would fall within a range of $\pm$ 3 percent from the sampling

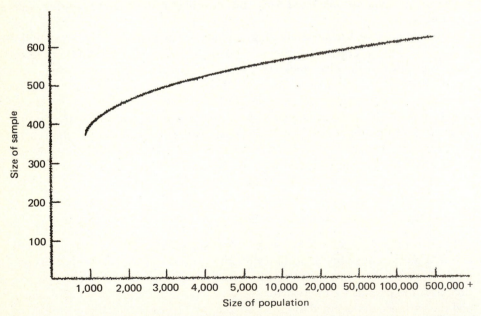

Figure 9.1 Required sample sizes for different population sizes (for 95 percent confidence level and ± 3 percent confidence interval and with the assumption of 50–50 percent split of the percentages for the characteristic in the population).

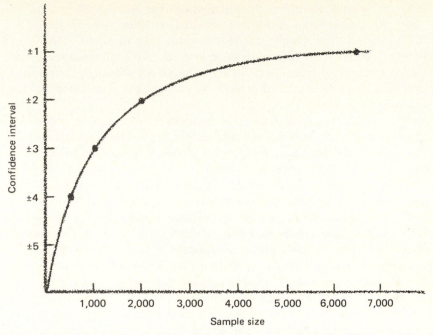

Figure 9.2 Sample size required to calculate the percentage of a finite population (20,000) falling into one of the two categories of a dichotomous variable with a confidence coefficient of 95 percent when the range in the population is assumed to be 50 percent. (*Adapted from Herbert Arkin and Raymond R. Colton,* Tables for Statisticians, *2d ed., Barnes and Noble, New York, 1963, p. 145.*)

percentage, an interval estimate, see Chapter 7). This is equivalent to the extent of the standard error $s_{\bar{x}}$ of the sampling distribution discussed in Chapter 7.

For example, Figure 9.2 shows, for a population of 20,000 and a confidence coefficient of 95 percent, the relationships between the sample size required for each desired confidence interval of the prediction (width of the interval estimate). To achieve the prediction that the population percentage is within plus or minus 5 percent of the sample percentage would require 377 respondents in the simple random sample. To achieve the prediction that the population percentage is within plus or minus 4 percent from the sample percentage would require 583 respondents in the sample. However, to achieve the prediction that the population percentage is within plus or minus 1 percent of the sample percentage would require 6,489 respondents, or about a third of the entire population.

The *variance* or *heterogeneity* of the population characteristic (how much its members differ from one another on the variable being measured) also affects the requisite sample size. More heterogeneous population distributions require larger samples. For example, in predicting a winner in a presidential election, if candidate A is in fact leading candidate B by a 75 percent–25 percent split among the voter population, the sample size required would be much smaller than if candidate A and candidate B were running "neck to neck" (close to the 50 percent–50 percent split). In general, the closer the distribution approaches a 50 percent–50 percent split, the greater the sample size required. If there were in fact a 50 percent–50 percent split, the sample size required would be maximal, if the other conditions remained constant (the confidence interval, the confidence level, and the population size). Thus, when a researcher is uncertain about the distribution of the population characteristic, a 50 percent–50 percent split is assumed and the maximal sample size is used.

Given the conditions of his study (the confidence interval, the confidence coefficient, the variance of the population characteristic, and the population size), a researcher can calculate precisely how large a sample is necessary. Tables 8*a* to 8*f* in Appendix C will help the researcher determine the sample size in a study.

As an illustration of the use of these factors in actual research, one may cite the fact that most of the national polls in the United States today seldom exceed a sample of 2,000 respondents in their voting prediction studies for the population of 70 million to 80 million American voters. From such a sample a poll may be able to predict that in a national election candidate X is favored by 64–56 percent (confidence interval) of the voters and candidate Y by 36–44 percent of the voters, say, for a confidence coefficient of .95. The poll can then predict that candidate X would win the election if it were held on the day of the study. If two candidates are running very closely and the poll shows that candidate X is favored by 54–48 percent of the voters and candidate Y by 46–52 percent of the voters, then the poll would not be able to predict which candidate would win. Since the two confidence intervals overlap, each has a chance to go ahead of the other. If the poll wishes to make a prediction of the winner, it will have to increase the sample size in another study. The increased sample size could reduce the confidence interval of the predictions and increase the probability of accuracy. However, as shown in Figure 9.2, in order to increase the accuracy to the point at which the two predicted intervals do not overlap with one another, the sample size would have to be substantially increased. The curvilinear relationship between the sample size and the probability of accuracy approaches a straight line as the demand for accuracy increases. Thus, it may become too costly and impractical for the poll to draw such a sample size (as it may indeed be approaching the population size separating the two predicted ranges). The poll would simply state, then, that the race is "too close to call."

OTHER SAMPLING PLANS

Other sampling plans have been developed for use in some of the research situations in which traditional probabilistic methods are impractical or impossible. Among these are snowball sampling, spatial sampling, and saturation sampling.

Snowball Sampling

Snowball sampling is useful when information about the cases in the population is lacking. This might be the case if a researcher wanted to study the members of a particular national or ethnic group in a specified area, such as the Chinese Americans in Washington, D.C. Snowball sampling for this study would involve interviewing all the Chinese who could be located by ordinary means (immigration and census records, membership lists of Chinese-American organizations, etc.). These subjects would be asked for the names of other Chinese with whom they are acquainted but who might not be known to the researcher. By repeating this process over several stages, most of the Chinese in the city would hopefully be identified and contacted. For reasons of economy, a simple random sample would probably then be drawn from among this group.

Up to 90 percent of all cases of a phenomenon of interest can be generated through the use of snowball sampling. However, the researcher should be aware that the cases which cannot be located may have unique properties, the omission of which may bias the study.

Snowball sampling is useful only if the members of the target group maintain some kind of formal or informal communication network among themselves. The mentally ill represent a population which could not be reached successfully through snowball sampling, although its boundaries are indeed unknown. Also, the effectiveness of snowball sampling is hindered if members of the group have something to lose by revealing the names of other members. For instance, a drug user might not want to name other users for fear of exposing them to the police and possibly bringing retaliation on himself.

Within these limitations, snowball sampling can often aid a researcher in overcoming the difficulty faced by traditional probabilistic sampling plans in situations in which not all the cases in the population can be identified.

Spatial Sampling

Some populations are not static, but exist only while an event is taking place. This situation is exemplified by a political demonstration. There is no defined population, participants may move from one place to another, subgroups form and dissolve, people leave and others arrive. However, the physical space in which the event takes place may be finite, so that systematic sampling of participants over the space is feasible. It is important that the whole population be sampled simultaneously so that its composition does not have time to change significantly.

Spatial sampling was used to study a right-wing, pro-Vietnam war march and rally organized by the Reverend Carl McIntire, which took place in Washington, D.C., on October 3, 1970. After a march down Pennsylvania Avenue, the group congregated within a roughly delineated physical space for the rally. A description of the spatial sampling technique follows.

> The fifteen trained and conservatively dressed interviewers line up before the speaker's platform facing the audience. They spaced themselves evenly to reach both ends of the high platform. As soon as the march columns arrived and began to form a crowd in front of the speaker's stand, each interviewer began interviewing the person closest to him. From there, moving away from the platform, the interviewer attempted to interview the next person alternately to his right or left at every tenth step he walked. If he encountered a refusal, the interviewer was to record the distance from the platform and to identify the refuser by approximate age, race, and sex. Then

he would attempt to interview the person in the other direction (right or left) facing him, if he was not in the midst of an apparent group. If he *was* in the midst of such a group, he would proceed ten more steps before interviewing the next person. When the interviewer reached the end of the crowd he would turn to his right or left (alternately) and walk five steps, then walk back in toward the speaker's platform continuing his sampling and interviewing.[6]

Spatial sampling thus is used when the social situation itself defines a population. Participants in many social movements and demonstrations can best be sampled this way.

Saturation Sampling

Saturation sampling is a special technique used when the researcher needs a picture of the population that includes some of the activities of all its members. It consists of studying every member of the population. Obviously, this method is more feasible when the population is small and confined to one area, but it is also used with larger groups. (The United States census, for example, involves a saturation sample.)

Certain research situations require saturation sampling. The most prominent of these is *structural analysis,* in which the network of relationships (sociometrics) among a group of people is investigated (Chapter 17). If any person is left out, the network is distorted.

A relational study of the teachers in a school might consist of asking the teachers who their best friends are within the school and to whom they most often go for advice.[7] Sociometric "stars," those group members whom many others consider a best friend, to whom many go for advice, or both, could then be identified. So could the "isolates," those whom no one considers a best friend and to whom no one goes for advice.

As more and more social researchers realize the importance of informal social structures in effecting social activities, saturation sampling will also gain in importance. The increasing capacity of the computer has also contributed to the feasibility of analyzing such data.

While it is desirable to study populations of unmanageable sizes, it is also desirable to retain generalizability of the research results. Thus, in saturation sampling, a researcher should first select the populations to be studied with care. Preferably, the studied populations are representative samples of a large population. It then becomes possible to generalize the research results to the larger population.

In a series of studies conducted in El Salvador, Costa Rica, and Haiti, dealing with the effects of the local informal social structure on receptivity to health services such as nutrition, family planning, and mass immunization, a sample of

[6] Nan Lin, "The McIntire March: A Study of Recruitment and Commitment," *Public Opinion Quarterly,* vol. 38, no. 4, pp. 562–573, Winter 1974–1975.
[7] Nan Lin, "Innovative Methods for Studying Innovation in Education," in *Research Implications for Educational Diffusion,* Michigan State Department of Education, Lansing, 1968, pp. 105–161.

communities was selected to approximate the "average" villages in each country and to control on different levels of socioeconomic development. Then, saturation sampling involving the lady of every occupied household in each sampled community was utilized in the study. Thus, a structural analysis for each sampled community was made, and the results still generalized to the "average" communities in these and other countries on similar developing levels.

SUMMARY

Sampling involves the selection of cases from a defined population. When inference can be made from a sample to a population with a known probability of accuracy, the sample is called a representative or probabilistic sample. Otherwise, it is a nonrepresentative or nonprobabilistic sample.

Representative samples can be drawn with simple random sampling, stratified random sampling, and cluster sampling plans. The simple random sampling plan gives each case and each combination of cases in the population an equal chance to be selected. The stratified random sampling plan first stratifies the population cases into strata according to some defined criteria, and then randomly selects a subsample from each stratum. It is most effective when the cases in each stratum are maximally homogeneous. The cluster sampling plan also divides the population cases into clusters. However, only a selected number of clusters are used to draw subsamples from. The plan is most effective when cases in each cluster are maximally heterogeneous.

In actual research, multiple-sampling plans and multistages are sometimes utilized in the selection of the sample. A sample may also include disproportionate numbers of respondents from different strata or clusters. When disproportionate sampling is involved, adjustments can be made for sample statistics in making inferences to the cases in the population.

Occasions may call for the use of nonrepresentative samples. Theoretical sampling, for example, constructs categories for variables rather than a representation of cases in the population.

While there is a general positive relationship between the sample size and the accuracy of prediction, the payoff of increasing sample size for more accurate prediction decreases quickly. Beyond a certain sample size, any increment in accuracy would require a prohibitively large sample size.

Several recently developed sampling plans have unique features. Snowball sampling can be useful when not all cases of the population are identifiable. Spatial sampling draws a representative sample in a defined geographic area rather than a population of cases. It is most useful in studies dealing with dynamic group situations in social movements. When relations among the cases in the population are to be studied, saturation sampling, involving all cases in the population, can be utilized.

Each sampling plan has advantages and disadvantages. A researcher should weigh these factors and select the best plan or combination of plans to achieve maximal representation of the population within his capability and resources.

Chapter 10

Measurement

The deductive process begins with a theoretical structure made up of propositions which contain concepts. The propositions are operationalized into hypotheses which provide empirically testable statements of relationships among variables. The testability of the hypotheses depends on the actual items and response categories which can be constructed to tap these variables. Without adequate items and response categories the testing of hypotheses becomes problematic; and without viable hypothesis testing the verification of theoretical propositions is impossible. Even when a researcher has no particular theory to test, poor items and response categories lead to untrustworthy and even incorrect conclusions, which in turn hinder effective application of research results to policy decisions or valid induction for the purpose of theory construction.

The process of constructing items and response categories to tap variables is called *instrumentation*. The items and response categories constitute the *instrument* for the variable. Instrumentation may be simple and straightforward or difficult and indirect, depending on the nature of the variable and how the researcher intends to analyze the resultant data. For variables such as sex, age, and race, the instrument may consist of a single item with a number of response categories such as "male" and "female" for sex; "age in years" or "date of birth" for age; and "white," "black," "Puerto Rican," "Oriental," and "native American" for race in the United States.

However, some variables complicate instrumentation. Education, seemingly a simple variable, could be variously measured by asking, "How many years of schooling have you completed?"; "What was the last grade you completed?"; and "What was the last degree or diploma you received?" Each item would yield a different response from someone who had spent 14 years in school and quit after completing the junior year of high school. His responses would be "14," "eleventh," and "junior high," which do not directly correspond to one another. Variables dealing with opinions, attitudes, and feelings, which cannot be observed directly, pose even greater problems for instrumentation. The construction of items is difficult enough, but the construction of response categories is even more difficult. There are no "empirical" guidelines to follow in the construction of response categories for these variables, as there are for such variables as sex, age, and race.

The assignment of numerals to the response categories of a variable is called *measurement*. It is the most critical component of instrumentation, as it is the only link between the conceptual work of a researcher and the ongoing activities he is studying. Measurement in fact determines the variations in observations made by the researcher and how closely these correspond to ongoing activities. Because of the importance of measurement in instrumentation, *instrument* and *measure* are sometimes used interchangeably to designate the set of items and the response categories with their appropriate numerical labels.

The numerals assigned to the variations represented by the response categories may be either qualitative (e.g., when they are applied to the presence or absence of a characteristic such as citizenship, or to different religious or racial groupings) or quantitative (e.g., indicating the magnitude of income, education, or intensity of activities and attitudes). The choice of qualitative or quantitative numerals is vital for the researcher.

The sociological literature shows confusion as to whether there should be one or more measures for a variable. The convention adopted here is that *each variable can only have one measure. Each concept,* on the other hand, *can be indicated by multiple variables and,* therefore, *multiple measures.*

The relationships among concepts, variables, instrumentation, measurement, hypotheses, and ongoing activities are presented in Figure 10.1.

What constitutes a good measure? There are two basic criteria. First, the measure must reflect accurately the actual social activity it purports to measure. As mentioned in previous chapters, the observations made by a researcher are not actual social activities but simply the results of measurement. Thus, it is crucial that these measured responses reflect actual social activities as accurately as possible. The extent to which they do so is called their *validity*. For measures of some social activities and characteristics (sex; amount of education; purchasing behaviors—types of cars, brands of food; daily and public behaviors—when last visit to a bank took place, number of restaurants patronized during the last month), validity can be easily verified. The validity of measures of others (voting behavior, income, racial prejudice) is more difficult to determine, either because the information is considered private by many people or because the activities are

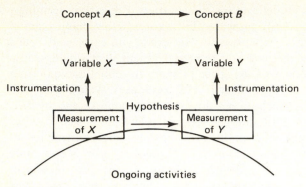

Figure 10.1 Relationships among concepts, variables, instrumentation, measurement, hypothesis, and ongoing activities.

psychological in nature and present problems in social measurement. Nevertheless, the researcher should make certain that the measurement used is the best one possible for gauging actual social activities.

The second major criterion for a good measure is the extent to which it generates similar responses every time it is used and in various situations. This is called its *reliability*. A measure of racial prejudice which shows 30 percent of the target population to be prejudiced every time the same group is studied is more reliable than another measure which indicates that 30 percent of the population is prejudiced in one study and that 40 percent of the same population is prejudiced in the next. A reliable measure produces consistent results even for different researchers.

Besides validity and reliability, a good measure also has a built-in ability to sort out responses which do not meet the assumptions of the variables. In a study of residents' needs for a new road, a good measure sorts out respondents who do not live in the area being studied. Results obtained using a measure which does not do so are in error.

SOURCES OF MEASUREMENT ERROR

An understanding of the sources of possible measurement errors, either validity or reliability errors, is essential. Such an understanding helps the researcher to avoid common measurement errors and thus to increase the validity and reliability of his measures.

Generally, there are two kinds of measurement errors: study-related errors and study-unrelated errors. Study-related errors occur because certain activities involved in the study interact with the measures, whereas study-unrelated errors occur because certain ongoing activities in the environment affect the respondents.

Study-related Sources of Errors

Campbell, in a discussion of experimental designs, singled out a number of factors in the test situation which may generate errors in responses to the measures.

While his discussion primarily focused on a particular method of data collection, experiment, the factors mentioned can occur in almost any research situation.[1]

The first factor is associated with the *testing* situation as perceived by the respondents in a study. Interactions with and exposures to the researcher, his associates (such as the interviewer, observer, etc.), and the instrument itself may sensitize the respondents to provide biased responses. The second factor concerns *instrument decay*. The respondents may be tired and bored, or angered, toward the end of an instrument, so that the responses provided to the measures appearing in the latter part of the instrument may be more error-prone. A third factor is concerned with a test-retest situation, in which respondents were divided into different groups. If the respondents were assigned to different groups, on the basis of differences in their initial responses to one or more measures (e.g., IQ, attitudes), there might be a tendency for their later responses on the same measures to regress toward the averaged response (e.g., the arithmetic mean). This *regression toward the mean* phenomenon would reduce or eliminate the difference of the scores on the basis of which they were assigned to different groups. In other words, when the respondents were initially assigned to different groups in the study based on their differential responses to a measure, the regression toward the mean phenomenon introduced errors in data which were intended to utilize the group difference as a variable.

Another factor also concerns the formation of respondent groups. If the assignment of respondents to different groups is based not on the difference of responses to a measure, but rather on the assumption that the respondents in each group are similar to those in other groups, say, for the purpose of administrating alternative forms of a measure, then the problem of constructing *equivalent groups,* if unrealized, can create errors in the measurement. When groups differ on some characteristics, the different response patterns on the alternative forms may be due to these differences rather than to differences on the forms.

In using respondents in a study over a period of time (a longitudinal study or experiment), it is important that most if not all respondents remain with the study. Losing respondents during the study (mortality) could introduce errors in the measurement, as those who drop out may possess different characteristics from those who remain.

Other personal, situational, mechanical, or processing variation in the study situation can also introduce measurement errors. On the day a study is conducted, the respondent or the researcher may be in a bad mood, fatigued, or sick. Such unplanned personal factors easily affect normal performance and lead to invalid or unreliable responses or recording of responses. The situation in which the study takes place may also induce measurement errors. The temperature in the room, the noise of an airplane overhead, music from a loudspeaker, and numerous other unplanned or unanticipated factors can all interfere with measurement. Small mechanical failures such as a pencil breaking while the respondent is answering questions, forgotten glasses, or a page missing from a

---

[1] Donald T. Campbell, "Factors Relevant to the Validity of Experiments in Social Settings," *Psychological Bulletin,* vol. 54, pp. 297–312, July 1957.

questionnaire also contribute to measurement error. Even after the information has been safely measured, errors can still occur in the handling and processing of the data. Use of the wrong code, incorrect numbers being punched on computer cards, and many other accidents associated with data analysis constitute measurement errors. Errors can occur in the coding and organization of the data. For example, if a coder misreads a "0" as a "6" so that all zeroes are incorrectly coded as sixes, the resulting error is systematic indeed.

Errors of measurement can also result from the selection of particular questions in a study. For example, in a study of students' attitudes toward their college, a researcher might use a set of questions concerning various specific attributes of the college: the library, food service, the bookstore, and the city where the campus is located. But systematic error can occur if he attempts to project the students' overall attitude toward their college from these specifics. Suppose the percentages of students evincing favorable attitudes on the specific items are as follows:

Toward the library:	19 percent
Toward the food service:	10 percent
Toward the bookstore:	20 percent
Toward the city:	18 percent

He is mistaken if he concludes that the students' general attitude toward their college must lie somewhere near the average of their attitudes toward these specifics. If he decides that about 17 percent of the students probably have favorable general attitudes toward the college, he might find to his surprise that, when they are asked to express their general attitudes, 41 percent of these are favorable. This does not mean that the students lied in their responses; the discrepancy follows rather from the nature of the specific questions selected. The most important factor in the students' general attitudes toward their college may be the quality of the teaching faculty, which was not among those attributes chosen for study. The questions selected may draw systematically biased responses and result in measurement error.

Another source of study-related measurement error is lack of clarity of questions. Responses to the item, "Some people think that human beings are basically unselfish. Do you agree?" would be difficult to interpret. A negative answer indicates that the respondent does not agree with the statement. But the researcher cannot tell whether the respondent disagrees because he or she feels that human beings are not basically unselfish or because he or she believes that "most people" or "few people," rather than "some people," think they are unselfish. Similar problems arise with a positive response.

Finally, mechanical factors also contribute to errors of measurement. If questionnaires are unreadable because there was not enough ink in the mimeograph machine, respondents reply not to the intended questions but to their own interpretations of the unreadable questions.

Study-unrelated Sources of Errors

There are factors which have little to do with a specific study, yet can introduce errors in the measurement of the study. Four types of events can be identified in this group. One is *social history,* events which have occurred during the span of the study. For example, during the study of a community's attitude toward integrated schools, a bomb exploded in an integrated school. Then, an expected influence of this event on the attitudinal measure would introduce errors into the study. Another type of event is *personal history*. During the study, for example, a particular event may happen to a respondent (a death in the family, a wedding, or loss of a job) and could affect the respondent's response to the measure.

A third type of study-unrelated error is introduced by the natural *maturation* of the respondents during the time span of the study. This type of error is especially pronounced in a study spanning months or even years. Many experimental and longitudinal studies, attempting to ascertain the long-term effects of certain variables on other variables, must take into account the possibility that the physical and mental changes of the respondents may contribute to responses to the measures over time. For example, in a longitudinal study of the effect on behavior of viewing violent television programs, an investigation beginning with a group of respondents in their preschool or early school years and tracing their behaviors into early or later adult years must ascertain the physical and mental changes of the respondents over time, so that these effects on their behaviors may be taken into account, instead of attributing behavioral patterns entirely to their earlier television-viewing patterns.

A fourth type of error is related to *cultural* factors. For example, in the United States, there is a tendency for people to overreport education and the achievement of their children, but to underreport income and marital problems. In a study in Central America, it was found that physical illness was overreported, and Jesus appeared regularly as a best friend in answers to sociometric questions.

All these sources, unrelated to a study, may contribute to errors of measurement.

Systematic Errors versus Random Errors

Sources of errors, whether or not they are study-related, lead to two types of errors in measurement. Systematic error occurs when the effect biases all responses in a systematic pattern. For example, if in a culture everyone tends to underreport age, then systematic error occurs in the measurement of the variable "age." Random error occurs when the effect biases some responses, or all responses in a nonsystematic pattern. For example, an interview conducted early in the morning or late in the evening may have different effects on different respondents—some will be alert and accurate in reporting, while others will be drowsy and inaccurate in reporting.

When the measurement error is random, then the resulting biases are random—some responses may overreport while others underreport. If enough respondents are studied, chances are that the random errors in both directions will cancel each other out. Thus, the predicted averaged response for the group of respondents will remain unbiased, and the result will still be valid. What is affected is the reliability of the responses. Thus, *random error affects the reliability rather than the validity of the measurement*.

On the other hand, if the measurement is systematic, then the response pattern will be invalid. For example, in a culture where age is systematically underreported, the predicted averaged age for a group would be lower than the actual averaged age. This would be true in any studies conducted in the same culture. Thus, in repeated studies, the responses may be reliable, but consistently invalid. Thus, *systematic error affects the validity rather than the reliability of the measurement*.[2]

The discussion on measurement error, thus, leads directly to the issues of validity and reliability of measurement.

VALIDITY OF MEASUREMENT

As defined earlier, the validity of a measure is the extent to which it accurately reflects what it purports to measure. More specifically, it is the extent to which differences in scores on an instrument (the items and response categories tapping a specific variable) reflect true differences among individuals, groups, or situations in the characteristic (variable) it seeks to measure. To ask the validity of a measurement is to ask the question, "Does it measure what it is intended to measure?"

Suppose that in a study of the distribution of sex in the United States, a researcher finds that 52 percent of the sample is female and 48 percent male. The validity of the measure depends on whether 52 percent of the United States population is indeed female and 48 percent male.

A measure can be validated by either empirical or conceptual confirmation. Empirical confirmation, also known as pragmatic validity, compares the information obtained from the measure with facts and outcomes found in reality. To ascertain the validity of the sex distribution above, the researcher can compare the percentages of females and males with the data gathered by the U.S. Bureau of the Census (assuming that these data are accurate). If the most recent census data also show that the distribution of males and females in the United States is 48 and 52 percent, then the measure used by the researcher is validated empirically. A public opinion poll prediction of the outcome of a presidential election can also be empirically confirmed. Suppose a poll conducted during the last week before the election shows that 54 percent of the qualified voters who intend to vote are for candidate X, 41 percent are for candidate Y, and the rest are undecided. In the actual balloting, candidate X receives 56 percent of the votes and candidate Y 44

---

[2] Gene F. Summers, "Introduction," in Gene F. Summers (ed.), *Attitude Measurement*, Rand McNally, Chicago, 1970, pp. 14–15.

percent. Assuming that the election is conducted fairly, the poll is to a large extent validated by the election results.

However, for many social variables there are no obvious facts or outcomes with which measures may be compared. Measures of attitudes, for example, are difficult to confirm empirically. Attitudes toward busing school children or legalized abortion may bear somewhat on behaviors such as signing petitions or participating in demonstrations, and even more directly on actions such as transferring children to a nonbusing school or having an abortion. However, there is not usually a one-to-one correspondence between an attitude toward something and a behavioral pattern regarding it.[3] Thus, direct empirical confirmation is impossible for measures of such variables. The researcher must resort to the conceptual confirmation method.

Conceptual confirmation is also known as *inferred,* or *construct,* validity. It is used when empirical confirmation of validity is difficult or impossible. Validity is instead inferred from the conceptual evidence—the extent to which the variables' relationships are consistent with the deduction of the theoretical structure. For example, the validity of political ideology can be assessed from the selection of political candidates in elections. Rebellion against social and political institutions may be inferred from rebellion against parents. *Conceptual confirmation may be inferred either from internal validity or external validity.*[4] Internal validity occurs when a measure has some significance within the study situation and can be analyzed from (1) the expected relationships among different measures of the same concept (convergent validity), and (2) the expected relationship of the variables measured with other variables as expressed in a theory (discriminant validity).[5] External validity refers to the generalizability of the relationships to the larger population or theoretical structure. We shall now discuss each type of validity in detail.

Internal Validity

Convergent validity is examined when we devise several different measures for a concept which is impossible to validate directly. The validity of the measures is assessed according to the similarity of their results. For example, in a study of attitudes toward busing school children, the respondents may be asked their attitudes toward busing; their neighbors may be asked to describe the respondents' attitudes toward busing; they may be given a petition for or against busing and asked if they would sign it; and the schools their children attend may be classified according to whether or not children are bussed to them. The results of these

---

[3] The rare occurrences of "single-criterion" validity in attitude research are discussed by William A. Scott, "Attitude Measurement," in Gardner Lindzey and Elliot Aronson (eds.), *The Handbook of Social Psychology,* Addison-Wesley, Reading, Mass., vol. 2, chap. 11, especially p. 204.

[4] D. T. Campbell, loc. cit.

[5] The terms convergent and discriminant validations are originally proposed in D. T. Campbell and D. W. Fiske, "Convergent and Discriminant Validation by the Multitrait-Multimethod Matrix," *Psychological Bulletin,* vol. 56, pp. 81–105, 1959.

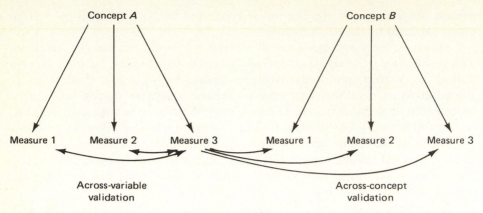

Figure 10.2   Two types of internal validity for measure 3 of concept *A*.

measures are then compared. Measures which show similar distributions of attitudes for and against busing among the respondents are considered more likely
to be valid than those which do not. Thus, the greater the number of measures
designed for a concept which cannot be empirically confirmed, the more likely it
is that their validity can be established conceptually. Further, the greater the
number of *different* methods of data gathering (survey, experiment, observations,
and documents), the more likely it is that the measures' validity can be established conceptually.

Inference across concepts (discriminant validity) is another way of confirming internal validity. A researcher might expect occupational prestige to be related to educational achievement and income. In other words, the three variables
are conceptually related. In order to validate his measure of occupational prestige
indirectly, the researcher investigates whether it is positively related to both
educational achievement and income. That is, he checks to see whether, the
higher the occupational prestige of a respondent according to the measure, the
higher the educational achievement and income observed for that respondent.
When such correspondence occurs, the measure of occupational prestige is validated by the inference of its relationship to other variables as expressed in
theory.[6]

The two types of internal validity are illustrated in Figure 10.2. Convergent
validity (across-variable validation) is used to confirm measure 3 as a valid
measure of concept A when measure 3 is compared with other measures (1 and 2)
of the same concept. Discriminant validity (across-concept validation) examines
the relations of measure 3 to measures of another concept (concept B) to which
concept A is theoretically related.

[6] The validation of occupational status in terms of education and income was originally
proposed in Otis Dudley Duncan and Robert W. Hodge, "Education and Occupational Mobility,"
American Journal of Sociology, vol. 68, pp. 629–644, 1963.

External Validity

External validity relies, to a large extent, on (1) the operationalization process, and (2) the sampling process. A sound operationalization process, discussed in Chapter 4, ensures the correspondence between concepts and variables, so that significant relationships among variables can be considered indications of the significance of propositions linking the concepts in the theoretical structure. A sound sampling process, discussed in Chapter 9, provides a linkage between a particular set of data used in a study and a larger population, whereby the significance of results found in the study can be used to estimate certain characteristics and relations in the larger population with a known probability. However, external validity of a measure also implies the extent to which its relationship with other variables in a given theoretical structure can be generalized beyond the population or theoretical structure from which the current study was directly deduced. The greater the variety of populations involved and the greater the variety of theoretical structures brought to bear, the more likely it is to ascertain the external validity of a measure.[7]

Conceptual confirmation must be used with caution. The validity of a measure can be inferred only from other measures or variables selected before carrying out the research. Otherwise the temptations of ex post facto analysis may mislead the researcher. Many measures and variables may show correspondence in the analysis. Relying on such empirical correspondence rather than prechosen measures and theoretical considerations involves the researcher in too many questionable decisions. His assessment of validity is entirely ad hoc and unacceptable.

Suppose that the researcher mentioned above was not guided by the theoretical proposition that occupational prestige is related to educational achievement and income, but proceeded to gather data using his measure of occupational prestige. Then, in order to validate the measure, he analyzes his data and finds that occupational prestige is related to sex and race (males tend to have greater occupational prestige than females, and whites greater occupational prestige than nonwhites). Speculating that, because of social discrimination these results are to be expected, he concludes that his measure is valid. This ex post facto interpretation can be challenged by alternative interpretations. For example, it can be argued that the researcher's measure of occupational prestige is in fact a measure of occupational opportunity. Since the researcher and the challenger are both speculating after the data has been gathered, it is impossible to determine which interpretation is better. Validation of the measure is jeopardized.

Also, to be able to validate a measure, it is important that (1) there are three or more measures for each concept involved, (2) the methods of data gathering in which the various measures are used are as independent as possible, and (3) the

---

[7] The term *cross-validation* sometimes appears in the literature instead of *external validity*. See, for example, C. I. Mosier, "Problems and Designs of Cross-validation," *Educational and Psychological Measurement,* vol. 11, pp. 5–11, 1951.

relationship among the concepts is indeed substantial.[8] The third condition is difficult to verify. Thus, any validity test must be used and interpreted with caution.

RELIABILITY OF MEASUREMENT

The reliability of a measure is defined as the degree to which the measure generates similar responses over time and across situations. The relevant question regarding the reliability of a measure is, "Does it give the same results every time it is used on the same or similar respondents?" The usual procedure for ascertaining the reliability of a measure is to study the correspondence of the results of its repeated use on the same or similar respondents. If this correspondence is high, the measure is reliable.

In the study of attitudes toward busing, the researcher may use the same measure—for instance, asking the respondents whether or not they would sign a petition in favor of busing—on the same group of respondents at several different times. Suppose that, at time 1, 30 percent of the respondents say they would sign and 60 percent say they would not sign (with 10 percent undecided). At time 2, the same distribution appears, and likewise at time 3. The researcher concludes that his measure of attitudes toward busing is reliable. However, if he finds 30 percent willing to sign and 60 percent unwilling at time 1, but 40 percent willing and 50 percent unwilling at time 2, then the measure is relatively unreliable.

Two issues must be clarified. One concerns the relationship between reliability and validity, and the other the effect of real change over time on the reliability of measurement.

Reliability is independent of validity. It is possible for a measure to be very reliable but totally invalid. For example, a measure of the sex distribution may give the same result (53 percent female versus 47 percent male) every time it is used on the the same group of respondents. Thus it is reliable. However, it is invalid if census data show the actual distribution of females versus males to be 51 to 49 percent. The invalid result might have been caused by certain respondents deliberately writing down the wrong sex every time they were studied, or by the responses of individuals who were undergoing sexual identity crises. Regardless of the cause, the measure is reliable in that the same error is made consistently, and yet invalid in that the result is incongruent with facts or other, valid measures.

[8] For discussions on these conditions, see Herbert L. Costner, "Theory Deduction, and Rules of Correspondence," *American Journal of Sociology,* vol. 75, pp. 245–263, 1969; Robert P. Althauser and Thomas Heberlein, "Validation and the Multitrait-Multimethod Matrix," in Edgar F. Borgatta and George W. Bohrnstedt (eds.), *Sociological Methodology 1970,* Jossey-Bass, San Francisco, 1970, chap. 9, pp. 151–169; Gene F. Summers, Lauren H. Seiler, and Glenn Wiley, "Validation of Reputational Leadership by the Multitrait-Multimethod Matrix," in Edgar F. Borgatta and George W. Bohrnstedt, op. cit., chap. 10, pp. 170–181; Robert P. Althauser, Thomas A. Heberlein, and Robert A. Scott, "A Causal Assessment of Validity: The Augmented Multitrait-Multimethod Matrix," in Hubert M. Blalock, Jr. (ed.), *Causal Models in the Social Sciences,* Aldine, Chicago, chap. 22, pp. 374–399; Duane F. Alwin, "Approaches to the Interpretation of Relationships in the Multitrait-Multimethod Matrix," chap. 4 pp. 79–105; and Robert P. Althauser, "Inferring Validity from the Multitrait-Multimethod Matrix: Another Assessment," in Herbert L. Costner (ed.), *Sociological Methodology 1973–1974,* Jossey-Bass, San Francisco, 1974, chap. 5, pp. 106–127. The general consensus on the multitrait-multimethod matrix is that, unless the conditions stated in the text are assumed, there are too many unknowns in the equations to make precise estimates of the various validations.

Change over time often creates a serious problem in the measurement of reliability. Many social and psychological activities in which researchers are interested change over time for a number of reasons. One reason is that people's opinions and attitudes change. Even though individual changes may be slight, the cumulative effect can be significant when a researcher looks at a group. Also, the maturation process molds and remolds behavioral patterns and thought processes. Changes due to maturation appear when individuals are studied over time. Environmental events also change individual behaviors and opinions. An energy crisis inevitably changes driving behavior. It also alters working, dressing, purchasing, and recreational patterns; and the use of heating, television, stoves, washing machines, etc. Opinions and attitudes about the government, oil companies, gas stations, and so on are affected in their turn. If the researcher's interests relate to any of these factors, the measurements he obtains over time will certainly show marked change.

Thus, a researcher must carefully assess over-time measurements before he can decide whether or not a measure is reliable. The indices of reliability now to be discussed help him to determine whether the low correspondence of repeated measurements is due to the effects mentioned above or to unreliability of the measure itself.

The three major methods of the reliability of a measure available to social researchers are (1) the test-retest method, (2) the alternative-form method, and (3) the subsample method.

In the test-retest method, the same measure is administered to the same group of respondents repeatedly over time. In the alternative-form method, the measure is presented in different forms, which presumably represent the same measure, to the same group of respondents. Or, the same measure is administered by different investigators to different groups of respondents. The subsample estimation procedure divides the group of respondents into subsamples, each of which presumably is similar to the other subsamples in composition. The measure is administered to all subsamples, and similar or different responses of the subsamples are used to assess the reliability of the measure.

Stability Coefficient

The stability coefficient is an index of the lack of fluctuation in the activity being measured or in personal and situational factors over time. For example, in a study of public opinion about the desirability of banning private cars in the downtown area of a city, the researcher may design two measures to indicate the proportions of the residents of the city and its suburbs who are for or against the innovation. A comparison of the patterns of response to the two measures over time is then made. As shown in Table 10.1, the overall change for measure A over the two time periods totals 6 percent, as opposed to 24 percent for measure B. If there has been no major social event that would be expected to affect residents' opinions about not using private cars downtown, the researcher concludes that measure A is relatively more stable than measure B.

However, before deciding that a measure is unstable, the researcher should make certain that the change it exhibits is not due either to (1) a "test effect"

Table 10.1 Relative Stability over Time of Two Measures of Opinion
(Public Opinion about the Desirability of Banning Private Cars Downtown)

	Measure A			Measure B		
	In favor	Against	Undecided	In favor	Against	Undecided
Time 1	32	60	8	45	47	8
Time 2	34	61	5	35	59	6
Changes	+2	+1	−3	−10	+12	−2

from the time 1 study, or (2) genuine individual, social, or maturational change. It is possible that responding to the measures at time 1 "cues in" the respondents as to what to expect in the second study. Respondents might formulate the idea that they "did all right" on measure A the first time but "not so well" on measure B. Therefore, when the second study is conducted, they try to "do better" on measure B. As a result of such considerations, their exposure to the first study biases their responses to measure B in the second study.

Also, the difference in public opinion shown by measure B may reflect genuine change which takes place between time 1 and time 2. Suppose that during the 3 months which elapse between the two studies there is a public transportation strike involving bus drivers and subway conductors. This suggests to many of the residents that, without the use of their own cars, they would have difficulty getting around in the city. Some of the respondents who originally favored the idea of banning private cars downtown now have second thoughts. Measure B is able to show this genuine shift in opinion, whereas measure A is not sensitive enough to do so. (In this case the validity of measure A is brought into question.)

Thus, the researcher must exercise extreme caution in the selection and testing of measures. He should attempt to ensure (1) that the measures give minimal and about equal senses of "testing" to the respondents, (2) that the second study is made after any "test effect" has worn off, but (3) that the second study is conducted before social events effect any genuine change. These conditions are rather difficult to fulfill. Thus, more and more attention has been paid to other estimation methods not affected by time.

Equivalence Coefficient

The equivalence coefficient is an index of the lack of fluctuation in the activity being measured by different investigators with the same measure or by the same investigator with different measures. Thus, it is an index of reliability across investigators for the same measure and across measures for an investigator.

A typical test of the equivalence of measures is the split-half reliability test. This is a special case of the alternative-form method discussed above. When a measure contains a sufficiently large number of test items, say twenty, it is possible to assign randomly the twenty items to two groups of ten items each. Responses to the ten items in each group are summed for each respondent, and he or she receives a score for each group. Thus the original measure of twenty items becomes two submeasures with ten items each. If the original measure is reliable,

Table 10.2   Combined Test of Equivalence and Stability

Respondent group	Time	
	1	2
A	Submeasure 1	Submeasure 2
B	Submeasure 2	Submeasure 1

the two submeasures will show similar patterns of response from each respondent. A respondent who scores high on one submeasure also scores high on the other. A simple test of the correspondence between two sets of scores is the correlation coefficient (see Chapter 6).[9] When correspondence is high, the two submeasures are said to be equivalent and the split-half reliability of the original measure high.

Combined Test of Stability and Equivalence

It is possible to test the stability and equivalence of a measure simultaneously. The test utilizes two submeasures administered alternately (at least once apiece). The simplest design for such a test is shown in Table 10.2. At time 1, half of the respondents (group A) receive submeasure 1 and the other half (group B) receive submeasure 2. At time 2, the first half is given submeasure 2 and the second half submeasure 1. Thus, for each time period, there is a test of the equivalence of the two submeasures. This is because the respondents are assigned to group A or B at random, so that overall their responses to similar items should be similar. The submeasures accrue two sets of responses over time, allowing a test of their stability. In its totality, this design enables the researcher to ascertain the stability of a measure (as decomposed into two submeasures) over time and its equivalence (as reflected by the correspondence between the submeasures).

Jacknife Estimation[10]

The alternative-form method, while having eliminated the time effect as present in the test-retest method, faces the problem of whether or not or to what extent the alternative forms are indeed for the same measure. To avoid this problem, a more recent method, using subsamples, promises to be a most effective procedure for estimating the reliability of a measure across respondents. The procedure first computes a standard deviation for responses to a measure for all respondents. Then, a specific number of respondents constituting a subsample is eliminated

---

[9] For an excellent discussion on the various coefficients of reliability for alternative forms, see George W. Bohrnstedt, "Reliability and Validity Assessment in Attitude Measurement," in Gene F. Summers (ed.), *Attitude Measurement*, Rand McNally, Chicago, 1970, pp. 80–99.

[10] J. W. Tukey, "Bias and Confidence in Not-quite Large Samples," *Annals of Mathematical Statistics*, vol. 29, p. 614, 1958; J. W. Tukey, "The Inevitable Collision between Computation and Data Analysis," in *Proceedings of the IBM Scientific Computing Symposium on Statistics, October 21–23, 1965*, IBM Data Processing Division; White Plains, N.Y., 1965, pp. 141–152; F. Mosteller and J. W. Tukey, "Data Analysis, Including Statistics," in G. Lindzey and E. Aronson (eds.), *The Handbook of Social Psychology*, Addison-Wesley, Reading, Mass., 1968, vol. 2, pp. 80–203; Bernard M. Finifter, "The Generation of Confidence: Evaluating Research Findings by Random Subsample Replication," in Herbert L. Costner (ed.), *Sociological Methodology 1972*, Jossey-Bass, San Francisco, 1972, chap. 4, pp. 112–115.

from the total sample. Say, there are 100 respondents in the total sample, and we create 100 subsamples of one respondent each. Then, 100 subsets of 99 respondents each are created for the 100 consecutive respondents eliminated. Thus, the first subset is constituted of the 99 respondents without the subsample of the first respondent; the second subset is constituted of the 99 respondents without the subsample of the second respondent; the third subset is constituted of the 99 respondents without the subsample of the third respondent, etc. An easy way to see this process is by envisioning the respondents as a deck of cards. Each card is considered a subsample, and the remaining cards are considered the subset for this subsample.

For each subset, a standard deviation for responses to the measure is computed for the remaining respondents in the set. A comparison between the standard deviation of the measure for the total sample and each subset generates a discrepancy which can be interpreted as the contribution of unreliable responses of the particular subsample (respondent-eliminated) to the measure. When all 100 comparisons are computed, a mean and a variance can be computed for the discrepancy scores. A test of significance can then be made (a t test, which will be discussed in Chapter 16, is a test for the difference between groups) to determine the extent of fluctuation of the subsample responses to the measure and can be used to indicate the extent of reliability of the measure for the respondents.

To illustrate the jacknife estimation procedure, the analysis made by Mosteller and Tukey can be used. They presented eleven scores on a measure for eleven respondents: 0.1, 0.1, 0.1, 0.4, 0.5, 1.0, 1.1, 1.3, 1.9, 1.9, 4.7. First, they computed the standard deviation for these eleven scores (see equation 5.5 in Chapter 5 for the formula of the standard deviation) which was $\theta_t = 1.3437$, where t represents the total sample. Then, they constructed eleven subsamples of one respondent each and computed the standard deviation of the scores for each subset of ten respondents, as presented in Table 10.3 as θ_i (i indicates the ith subset with the ith score eliminated). Then, a discrepancy (θ_{*i} for each ith subsample) between each standard deviation of a subsample and the standard deviation of the total sample was computed, with the following formula:

$$\theta_{*i} = k(\theta_t) - [(k - 1)(\theta_i)]$$

where k is the number of subsamples and in this case equals 11. The θ_{*i}'s are also called pseudovalues. Finally, the mean θ_* and the standard deviation s_* of the eleven pseudovalues were computed with the following formulas:

$$\theta_* = \frac{\Sigma \theta_{*i}}{k}$$

$$s^2 = \frac{\Sigma(\theta_{*i}^2) - \frac{(\Sigma \theta_{*i})^2}{k}}{k - 1}$$

$$s_*^2 = \frac{s^2}{k}$$

$$s_* = \sqrt{s_*^2}$$

Table 10.3 Jacknife Estimation for a Standard Deviation

i	X_i	Standard deviation of subset without $X_i = \theta_i$	Pseudovalues (θ_{*i})
1	0.1	1.36382	1.1400
2	0.1	1.36382	1.1400
3	0.1	1.36382	1.1400
4	0.4	1.38888	0.8894
5	0.5	1.39539	0.8243
6	1.0	1.41457	0.6325
7	1.1	1.41578	0.6204
8	1.3	1.41563	0.6219
9	1.9	1.39427	0.8355
10	1.9	1.39427	0.8355
11	4.7	0.70742	7.7040

$$\theta_t = 1.34347 \qquad\qquad \theta_* = 1.4894$$

Source: F. Mosteller and J. W. Tukey, "Data Analysis, Including Statistics," in G. Lindzey and E. Aronson (eds.), *The Handbook of Social Psychology,* Addison-Wesley, Reading, Mass., 1968, vol. 2, p. 139; and Bernard M. Finifter, "The Generation of Confidence: Evaluating Research Findings by Random Subsample Replication," in Herbert Costner (ed.), *Sociological Methodology 1972,* Jossey-Bass, San Francisco, 1972, chap. 4, p. 156.

For the set of eleven scores, the mean was 1.4894 and the standard deviation was 0.6244. The t value[11] with a .95 confidence coefficient for this set of data (eleven pseudovalues) was 2.23. This gives a confidence interval of 1.4894 $\pm$ (2.23) (0.6244). Thus, the variability of the measure as registered by the eleven respondents extends from 0.1 to 2.88. It indicates a potential reliability problem associated with the measure.

The jacknife estimation technique can be used for a variety of purposes and subsample sizes, thus the name, *jacknife.* For example, a subsample size may vary from 1, as in the above example, to any number smaller than the total sample size. Although relatively complicated, because of its potential application to the reliability problem as well as to other measurement problems, we should see increasing use of the method in social research.

SCALES OF MEASUREMENT

Besides providing valid and reliable information, a good measure is as specific as observation of the ongoing activity allows. It is sensitive to both qualitative and quantitative aspects of the activity. The qualitative aspect refers to the presence or absence of a value for a variable. For example, in a study of working women, a good measure detects whether or not a respondent has a job. The quantitative

[11] The t test, to be discussed in Chapter 16, is used rather than the z test for the normal distribution when the sample size is small.

aspect refers to degree, amount, or comparison across the values of a variable. A good measure for a study of working women indicates not only whether or not a respondent has a job, but also how much time (number of hours per week) she spends on the job.

A scale consists of the categories which indicate the values of a variable. In general, there are four types of measurement scales: nominal, ordinal, interval, and ratio, already mentioned in Chapter 5.

CONSTRUCTION OF SCALES

The four types of measurement scales yield different amounts of information. They can be rank-ordered (ascending from nominal through ordinal and interval to ratio) in terms of the amount of information provided and thus the number of statistical methods available for data analysis. The construction of a scale which yields the maximum in information about a variable is desirable. To maximize scaling possibilities, a researcher must be acquainted with scale construction at the various levels.

A *rating scale* is a scale containing response categories which vary in value according to a certain criterion, such as the extent to which a respondent agrees or disagrees with a statement or considers it to be likely or unlikely. The simplest type of rating scale involves one statement and a number of rating responses, as follows:

Legalized abortion will occur within the next year in this country.

Scale value	Response category
——— 1	Extremely likely
——— 2	Very likely
——— 3	Likely
——— 4	Not sure
——— 5	Unlikely
——— 6	Very unlikely
——— 7	Extremely unlikely

Each respondent is asked to select the one response category which most accurately describes his or her opinion about the statement. The resulting data are ordinal in nature.

Another variation of scale construction utilizes many statements. The response categories for each statement are either nominal (yes-no, agree-disagree) or ordinal (like the 7-point scale shown above). Responses for all items are then summed for each respondent. However, summated response scores can be computed only if the researcher is confident that the statements "hang together" or measure one underlying concept. Certain tests of interrelatedness among the items, such as coefficients of contingency and correlation, should be used. The resulting data may be ordinal in nature.

Many social variables are measured on such composite scales. Socioeconomic status (SES) is usually measured by using items on education, occupational prestige, and income. These items constitute an *index* of SES. (When items and response categories have direct empirical correspondence, the resulting measure is called an *index*. Otherwise it is simply referred to as a *scale*.)

A third variation of scale construction involves asking each respondent to choose the one statement in a set of statements with which he most strongly agrees. According to his choice, a scale value representing his attitude is assigned to him. If the researcher selects the statements with care, such a scale can be ordinal (or even interval or ratio) in nature.

The researcher faces a number of choices in scale construction. His decisions must take into account the original hypotheses and how they can best be tested. He must be fully aware of the statistical techniques appropriate for each type of scale. To provide some examples of how scales are constructed, several well-known scales used by social researchers will now be described.

Interval Scale: Summated Scale

A summated scale consists of a number of statements, with response categories usually indicating degrees of agreement or disagreement. The statements represent either positive or negative views on a certain issue, but not neutral or equivocal positions. The rationale is that a respondent who feels strongly about the issue will respond more extremely to such statements than will someone who feels less strongly about it. When responses to these items are matched with score values and added up for each respondent, the resulting score value constitutes the measured response value on the variable for that respondent. The respondents can be rank-ordered in terms of the summated value scores they register over the statements.

The best-known summated scale in social research is probably the type initially proposed by Likert[12] to measure respondents' attitudes toward certain issues. The method is general enough to apply to a wide range of variables. The original Likert scale involved a number of statements, each with five response categories such as strongly approve, approve, undecided, disapprove, and strongly disapprove. For example, the following statements and response categories might be used to measure attitudes toward legalized abortion:

1 Abortion should be performed for any woman requesting such a service.
　——— 1　Strongly agree
　——— 2　Agree
　——— 3　No opinion
　——— 4　Disagree
　——— 5　Strongly disagree

2 An unborn child has as many human rights as anybody else, so abortion should not be performed under any circumstances.
　——— 1　Strongly agree
　——— 2　Agree

---

[12] R. Likert, "A Technique for the Measurement of Attitudes," *Archives of Psychology*, no. 140, 1932; G. Murphy and R. Likert, *Public Opinion and the Individual*, Harper, New York, 1937.

———— 3 No opinion
———— 4 Disagree
———— 5 Strongly disagree

3 To achieve true equality, women must have the right to decide when they desire children. Therefore, abortion services should be provided for them.

———— 1 Strongly agree
———— 2 Agree
———— 3 No opinion
———— 4 Disagree
———— 5 Strongly disagree

4 A woman who does not desire children should take precautions (birth control) rather than rely on abortion.

———— 1 Strongly agree
———— 2 Agree
———— 3 No opinion
———— 4 Disagree
———— 5 Strongly disagree

Note that there are two statements favoring legalized abortion and two against it. It is desirable for a summated scale to contain positive and negative statements in equal numbers and presented at random. To compute response scores, the researcher first transforms the scores for either the positive or the negative statements. For example, in the scale shown above, the scores for responses 1, 2, 3, 4, and 5 to statements 1 and 3 can be transformed into 5, 4, 3, 2, and 1, respectively. Then all the statements yield higher scores for more favorable attitudes toward abortion. When the response values are summated for each respondent, those respondents with more favorable attitudes will receive higher scores. The researcher could equally well transform the response scores for statements 2 and 4, so that the less favorable a respondent's attitude toward legalized abortion, the higher his score.

Usually up to twenty statements are presented to the respondents. The researcher then examines each statement individually to determine whether it consistently elicits high response scores from those respondents who receive high total scores and low response scores from those who receive low total scores. The statements which show such consistency with the total scores of the respondents are retained. Those which register mixed response patterns are considered inadequate to distinguish high scorers from low scorers and are eliminated. This method of eliminating inconsistent items is called *item analysis*. The result of item analysis is a set of statements which show response patterns consistent with the total scores. These remaining statements constitute the final scale statements. The total scale score for each respondent is recomputed based on the selected statements.

In summation, the use of a Likert scale involves the following procedure: (1) initial construction and selection of positive and negative statements about an issue with five response categories for each statement, (2) collection of responses to these statements from a group of respondents, (3) computation of total scores for the respondents across all statements, (4) examination of the consistency of the response pattern for each statement relative to the total scores received, (5) elimination of inconsistent statements, (6) compilation of the final set of statements, and (7) recomputation of total scores for the respondents based on this final set.

Variations on the original Likert scale are also used. Response categories vary in wording (indicating agreement-disagreement, like-dislike, approval-disapproval, likelihood-unlikelihood, etc.), depending on the statement and the nature of the issue involved. The number of response categories varies from two (yes-no, agree-disagree, etc.) to seven (extremely likely, very likely, likely, undecided, unlikely, very unlikely, extremely unlikely).

Three major assumptions underlying the use of the Likert scale, or summated scales in general, should be made clear. One concerns the intensity of opinion. Summated scales do not provide the opportunity for a respondent to express the degree of intensity or relevance he attaches to each statement. Thus they contain the assumption that all statements are reacted to with equal intensity and relevancy.

Second, the scale assumes that different patterns of response to the items are unimportant. It is possible for respondents who registered different patterns of responses to the items to receive the same score. For example, in a four-item scale, a person who responded in the middle response category for all items, a person who responded to the opposite extreme categories on two items each, and a person who responded to opposite extreme categories on two items and in the middle for the remaining two items will all receive identical scores. The response variability, thus, is assumed unimportant. When this assumption is violated, then the scale cannot be used.

The third assumption is that the final selected set of statements taps the variable in which the researcher is interested. The accepted method of checking this assumption is to conduct an item analysis. However, item analysis only identifies a set of statements which "hang together." It does not prove that these statements actually tap the variable ostensibly being measured. As a safeguard against the misuse of summated scales, the researcher should include in his research report the specific statements used. Other researchers can then examine the scale and decide whether or not and to what extent they feel it measures the variable.

While summated scales are simple to use, the researcher must be fully aware of the assumptions involved and provide opportunities for others to investigate whether or not and how these have been met.

Ordinal Scale: Cumulative Scale

The cumulative scale, also known as the Bogardus-Guttman scale, differs from the summated scale in two of its important features. First, the Guttman scale employs statements with dichotomous response categories (yes-no, agree-disagree) rather than several categories. Second, it attempts to rank-order the degrees of intensity of the statements, rather than assuming that all of them have the same degree of intensity. The major assumption of the Guttman scale is that it is possible to find a set of statements which can be completely rank-ordered on a certain criterion. If statements can be rank-ordered, it is also possible to rank-order respondents in terms of their response patterns. If the following four statements were constructed as a Guttman scale of the attitude toward the legalized abortion:

1   Abortion should be legal for any pregnant woman who requests it.
———— Agree
———— Disagree
2   Abortion should be legal in cases in which continuation of pregnancy would cause sociopsychological damage to the woman.
———— Agree
———— Disagree
3   Abortion should be legal in cases in which pregnancy threatens the life of the woman.
———— Agree
-———— Disagree
4   Abortion should be legal in cases in which the baby has serious congenital defects.
———— Agree
———— Disagree

Then, these statements should be rank-ordered; they range from a very liberal opinion about legalized abortion to a very conservative opinion. Responses to the four statements should sort respondents into the five major response patterns shown in Table 10.4. The most liberal respondents (pattern A) agree with all the statements. The most conservative respondents disagree with all four statements, indicating that they feel abortion should not be legal under any of the circumstances described in the four statements (pattern E).

To construct such a scale, the researcher tabulates the responses in the form shown in Table 10.5. The response patterns are divided into two groups: the scale pattern group and the nonscale pattern group. The scale pattern group represents the response patterns expected if the statements do in fact constitute a cumulative scale. The nonscale patterns are "unexpected" response patterns, those in-

Table 10.4   Four Statements Forming a Cumulative Scale

+ = Agree; − = Disagree

Response pattern	Statement 1	2	3	4
A	+	+	+	+
B	−	+	+	+
C	−	−	+	+
D	−	−	−	+
E	−	−	−	−

Table 10.5   Analysis of the Scalability of Four Statements

+ = Agree; − = Disagree

Response pattern	Statement				Number of Respondents	
	1	2	3	4		
Scale pattern						
A	+	+	+	+	27	
B	−	+	+	+	34	
C	−	−	+	+	21	
D	−	−	−	+	19	
E	−	−	−	−	33	Subtotal = 134
Nonscale patterns						
F	+	−	+	+	3	
G	+	+	−	+	4	
H	+	+	+	−	5	
I	−	+	−	+	7	
J	−	+	+	−	4	
K	+	−	−	+	2	
L	+	−	+	−	3	
M	+	+	−	−	2	
N	−	−	+	−	6	
O	−	+	−	−	4	
P	+	−	−	−	1	Subtotal = 41
Marginal frequency for each statement	47	87	103	117		

$$\text{Error ratio} = \frac{\text{number of errors}}{\text{maximum number of errors}} = \frac{41}{96.78} = 0.42$$

consistent with the rank ordering of the statements into a cumulative scale. They are also called *error patterns*.

The researcher expects an overwhelming majority of the respondents to show scale patterns (A, B, C, D, or E in Table 10.5), and a minimal number to exhibit nonscale patterns. Respondents are assumed to fit nonscale patterns only as a result of error. Calculation of the error ratio aids the researcher here.

The error ratio, suggested by Borgatta, is "a ratio of errors in the scale to the maximum number of errors for a scale of the same marginal frequencies."[13] Thus,

$$\text{Error ratio} = \frac{\text{number of errors}}{\text{maximum number of errors}}$$

[13] Edgar F. Borgatta, "An Error Ratio for Scalogram Analysis," *Public Opinion Quarterly*, vol. 19, pp. 96–100, Spring 1955. The original error measurement, coefficient of reproducibility, introduced by Guttman is considered inferior; see discussion in Louis E. Dotson and Gene F. Summers, "Elaboration of Guttman Scaling Techniques," in Gene F. Summers (ed.), *Attitude Measurement*, Rand McNally, Chicago, 1970, pp. 203–213.

To calculate the error ratio, the marginal frequencies of positive responses to all the statements are first calculated. In Table 10.5, positive responses to statement 1 include patterns A, F, G, H, K, L, M, and P. Adding the frequencies in these patterns gives a frequency of 47 for the statement. Then, the expected frequency for each statement is computed by dividing the marginal frequency of each statement by the total number of respondents. Thus, the expected frequency of positive responses for statements 1, 2, 3, and 4 are 0.27 ($^{47}/_{175}$), 0.50 ($^{87}/_{175}$), 0.59 ($^{103}/_{175}$), and 0.67 ($^{117}/_{175}$), respectively.

Then, focusing on the nonscale patterns, the expected frequency for each is computed. For example, pattern F ($+-++$) has the expected frequency for statement 1, 0.27. However, statement 2 has a negative ($-$) response, thus its expected frequency should be $1 - 0.50 = 0.50$. Statements 3 and 4 are positive; thus their respective expected frequencies are 0.59 and 0.67. Thus, pattern F has the expected frequencies of 0.27, 0.50, 0.59, and 0.67, respectively, for the four statements. Multiplication of the four numbers results in:

$$(0.27)(0.50)(0.59)(0.67) = 0.053$$

This number is further multiplied by the total number of respondents and the number of "corrections" necessary to change it into a scale pattern. In this case, the total number of respondents is 175 and only one correction is required (to change statement 2 from $-$ to $+$ so that the pattern becomes $++++$):

$$(0.053)(175)(1) = 9.34$$

The same computations are made for all nonscale patterns:

F	$(0.27)(0.50)(0.59)(0.67)(175)(1) = 9.34$
G	$(0.27)(0.50)(0.41)(0.67)(175)(1) = 6.49$
H	$(0.27)(0.50)(0.59)(0.33)(175)(1) = 4.60$
I	$(0.73)(0.50)(0.41)(0.67)(175)(1) = 17.55$
J	$(0.73)(0.50)(0.59)(0.33)(175)(1) = 12.44$
K	$(0.27)(0.50)(0.41)(0.67)(175)(1) = 6.49$
L	$(0.27)(0.50)(0.59)(0.33)(175)(1) = 9.20$
M	$(0.27)(0.50)(0.41)(0.33)(175)(1) = 6.39$
N	$(0.73)(0.50)(0.59)(0.33)(175)(1) = 12.44$
O	$(0.73)(0.50)(0.41)(0.33)(175)(1) = 8.64$
P	$(0.27)(0.50)(0.41)(0.33)(175)(1) = 3.20$

The sum of the expected frequencies for the nonscale pattern responses (96.78) is used to indicate the maximum number of errors. The actual total of respondents in the nonscale patterns is the number of errors. Thus, for the data in Table 10.5, the error ratio is 0.42.

In general, the error ratio varies from 0.0 to 1.0; the lower the ratio, the greater the internal consistency of the scale.

If a set of statements is acceptable as a cumulative scale, the researcher proceeds to assign scale values to each respondent according to the latter's particular response pattern. For example, a respondent whose response pattern is

++++ on the four statements in Table 10.5 receives a scale value of 5, another whose response pattern is $-+++$ receives a 4, and so forth. Those in nonscale patterns receive the scale values of the patterns closest to their (presumably erroneous) responses. For example, a respondent with the pattern $++-+$ is assigned a 5, since this involves only one change of response (that to statement 3, from $-$ to $+$). However, assigning scale values to other nonscale patterns is more difficult. A respondent with the pattern $+-++$ could receive a scale value of 5 ($++++$) or 3 ($--++$). Either involves a change in the response to one statement. Since there is no way to tell exactly how the respondent erred in his response, the only solution is to draw either 5 or 3 at random. This is done for each respondent in the pattern $+-++$ to assign his scale value.

The Guttman scale has not gained popularity among social researchers for several reasons. First, the assumption that the scale items are unidimensional is difficult to prove. Recent developments in multidimensional scaling have tried to rank order statements in terms of a number of criteria or dimensions. These methods are beyond the scope of this text.[14]

Second, it has been questioned whether the items reflect popularity rather than magnitudes.

Third, the scale may have limited generalizability. The Guttman scale is constructed after the data have been collected. It is an ex post facto scale dictated by the set of data collected. Whether another group of respondents would react similarly to the statements, thus allowing the same rank ordering with an acceptable coefficient of reproducibility, is open to question. It is important for a researcher to analyze his data every time a Guttman scale is used to make certain that the statements "hang together" for the given set of respondents.

And, finally, empirically, it has been found that the summated scale, on which the responses to the items are simply added up, shows a result for the scale score and its relationship with other variables similar to that of the cumulative scale.[15] Since the summated scale is much simpler in procedure, it is usually preferred to the Guttman scale.

Interval Scale: Thurstone Scale

One type of interval scale was first suggested by Thurstone.[16] Combining statements, judges' ratings, and rating categories, Thurstone constructed a number of scales which he considered to be interval. Among the methods he used are paired comparisons, equal-appearing intervals, and successive intervals. The equal-appearing intervals method is the most commonly used.

The following hypothetical example illustrates the equal-appearing intervals

[14] Roger N. Shepard, A. Kimball Romney, and Sara Beth Nerlove, *Multidimensional Scaling: Theory and Applications in the Behavioral Sciences*, Seminar Press, New York, 1972, vols. 1 and 2.

[15] William Scott, "Attitude Measurement," in G. Lindzey and Elliot Aronson (eds.), *The Handbook of Social Psychology*, 2d ed., Addison-Wesley, Reading, Mass., vol. II, pp. 204–273.

[16] L. L. Thurstone, "Theory of Attitude Measurement," *Psychological Bulletin*, vol. 36, pp. 222–241, 1929; L. L. Thurstone, "The Measurement of Social Attitudes," *Journal of Abnormal and Social Psychology*, vol. 26, pp. 249–269, 1931; L. L. Thurstone, *The Measurement of Values*, University of Chicago Press, Chicago, 1959.

Table 10.6   Tabulation of 30 Judges' Sorting for a Thurstone Equal-Appearing Intervals Scale

Statement	Favorable						Unfavorable					Retain	Average value
	1	2	3	4	5	6	7	8	9	10	11		
1	5	7	12	6	0	0	0	0	0	0	0	Yes	2.63
2	7	19	3	0	1	0	0	0	0	0	0	Yes	1.96
3	1	7	0	4	1	3	2	4	0	5	3	No	
4	0	1	1	3	5	9	8	3	0	0	0	Yes	5.86
5	0	0	4	6	10	5	4	1	0	0	0	Yes	5.06
6	0	0	4	3	5	2	2	6	1	4	3	No	
7	0	0	0	0	0	2	1	4	9	7	7	Yes	9.30
8	0	0	0	0	0	0	0	5	14	9	2	Yes	9.26
9	1	3	0	4	2	7	8	4	0	1	0	No	
10	0	0	0	8	15	6	1	0	0	0	0	Yes	5.00

method. Suppose a researcher has thirty judges sort a large number of statements into eleven favorability-unfavorability piles. The results of the sorting are presented in Table 10.6. The number of judges placing each statement on each pile is tabulated. For example, five judges place statement 1 on the first pile, indicating that they feel it is one of the most favorable statements on the issue. Seven judges place it on the second pile, twelve on the third, and six on the fourth. A visual check determines which statements receive dispersed ratings.[17] Statements 3, 6, and 9 show great dispersion, while the other statements are rated on a limited number of piles. Thus, the decision is to retain statements 1, 2, 4, 5, 7, 8, 10, and so on.

An average value (the mean value) for each retained statement is calculated. Statements 5 and 10 have approximately the same mean value, as do statements 7 and 8. After all statements are so evaluated, the researcher selects subsets of statements representing various points on the favorability-unfavorability spectrum. One subset might contain statements 2 (with a mean value of 1.96), 1 (2.63), 10 (5.0), 4 (5.86), and 7 (9.30), and other retained statements with approximate mean values of 1.0, 4.0, 7.0, 8.0, 10.0, and 11.0. An alternative subset could include statements 5 and 8, and other statements with approximately the same mean values as those in the initial subset. The initial and alternative subsets are then used in the study.

Each respondent is asked to indicate the statements with which he or she agrees. The statements appear in random order, and their mean values are not presented. The mean values of the statements with which each respondent agrees are tabulated, and their average (usually the mean, calculated by dividing the sum of the mean values by the number of statements agreed to) is considered the respondent's degree of favorability or unfavorability toward the issue. The smaller the average, the more favorable the attitude.

[17] A more precise way of measuring dispersion is to calculate the standard deviation (see Chapter 5).

The Thurstone equal-appearing intervals scale is considered an interval scale. Since large numbers of statements, judges, and judgment categories are involved, the distance between contiguous categories or piles becomes extremely small, so small in fact that the distance between each pair of contiguous categories can be said to be approximately equal to that between any other pair. Thus the scale fulfills the assumption of an interval scale, namely, the distance between each pair of points is known.

While the Thurstone scale is widely used, several qualifications are in order. One problem concerns the selection of judges. Who is qualified as a judge? When the scale was first introduced, it was contended and supported by empirical evidence that it really did not matter who the judges were as long as a significant number was used. However, the early procedure threw out data from judges who placed more than four statements on a single pile, on the grounds that these judges were careless. Later studies showed that judges from varying social backgrounds (differing on variables such as race and political ideology) not only rated statements differently but also showed differential tendencies in placing certain numbers of statements on given piles. Thus, it is important to select judges who are representative of the eventual respondents in a study. A researcher who intends to utilize a scale constructed by someone else should examine the background characteristics of the judges used and decide whether they are similar to those of his respondents or whether another group of judges is needed to verify the scale values.

Another problem is the varying degrees of dispersion among the retained statements. For example, in Table 10.6, statements 5 and 10 received approximately the same mean value. But statement 5 was placed on six piles (ranging from 3 to 8), whereas statement 10 was placed on only four piles (4 to 7). The original procedure did not examine the different amounts of dispersion among the retained statements. However, less dispersion indicates greater consensus among the judges. When two statements have approximately the same value, the one with less dispersion is preferable.

Variation in the amounts of dispersion within the subsets of statements selected for the study is also problematic. It means that different degrees of consensus were given to the statements by the judges. In constructing a scale, therefore, the researcher selects statements which not only represent different scale values but which also have similar dispersions.

Different respondents agree with different numbers of statements. One respondent may agree with only two or three statements, while another agrees with five or more. Yet they may register the same average scale value. An indication of the "span of tolerance" in these respondents' attitudes toward the issue is missing. The researcher uses one of two strategies to combat this problem. Sometimes each respondent is simply asked to select the one statement which most closely represents his attitude toward the issue. The scale value of the single statement selected is assigned to the respondent. This strategy eliminates the flexibility of respondents' tendencies to select certain numbers of statements. The other strategy is to have the respondents rank-order the statements with which they agree. The single-response strategy simplifies scoring, but eliminates information which may be interesting and important. The rank-ordering strategy retains such information but complicates scoring. There is no ideal solution to this problem. However, the single-response strategy is adequate for most studies in which the primary interest is in attitudes toward an issue.

Again, the summated scale has empirically been found to be just as good as the Thurstone scale.

In sum, while many types of scaling are available to a researcher, most of them are only of historical interest. *The summated scale has been a most popular and effective scaling technique in social research.*

MEASUREMENT SCALES AND THEORETICAL MODELS

As the reader may recall, in the discussion of modeling theoretical structures in Chapter 3, five models were specified: the classificatory model, the typological model, the contingency model, the associative model, and the functional model. Of the five models, three are considered theory-like: the contingent model, the associative model, and the functional model. It was also pointed out that as modeling progresses from the contingent model toward the functional model, the rigor of the theoretical structure improves. Ideally, all models should be functional. However, realistically, most models are not. One basic reason why many hypotheses operationalizing the theoretical statements are contingent or associative rather than functional is related to the measurement scales used in social research. In strict terms, variables measured on the nominal scale can only be analyzed for contingency relationships, as no comparison of degree or amount can be made across categories in a nominal scale. Thus, the model being tested is a contingency one. With variables measured on the ordinal and interval scales, associative relations (in the linear sense) can be tested. For it is now possible to test statements such as, "The greater the A, the greater the B," or "The greater the C, the less the D," as the ranking orders or distances among the categories of the variables are known. Finally, when variables are measured on the ratio scale, functional relations among variables can be delineated. For the ratio scale allows the interpretation of the zero (0) as a meaningful value, and calculations of ratios for the variables become possible.

The implications of the relationship between the scales of measurement and the types of models to be tested are twofold. One, measurement, to a large extent, dictates the type of model which can be constructed and tested. Thus, the testing and generalization of a theoretical structure depend heavily on the kind of measurements which can be devised for the variables. The more precise the scale is, the more rigorous the model that can be constructed. Second, the selection of a model to be constructed and tested must take into account the scales used to measure the variables. Misuse of modeling can occur when the required precision of the measurement is absent. As an initial step toward the matching of the measurement and the modeling process, standardization (uniformity) of measurements of variables constitutes an important methodological problem in social research.

MEASURES COMMONLY USED IN SOCIAL RESEARCH

Results from different studies are comparable only when identical measures or measures which permit direct transformation by a certain calculus are used. Since the eventual goal of social research is the construction of general social theories, standardization of measures plays a most important role in social research today. To promote such standardization, a selected list of items and response categories used by the NORC in its annual national survey is presented in Appendix A. The items cover most of the basic variables interesting to social researchers. The response categories have been developed as optimal for the items through years of experience by prominent social researchers. The reader is encouraged to select items and response categories from Appendix A for any study to be conducted.

A list of selected occupational codes and classifications used by the U.S. Bureau of the Census in 1970 appears in Appendix B. Along with the census classifications and three-digit codes are scores from two occupational prestige scales. The NORC scale was developed at NORC in 1963–1965 by Hodge, Siegel, and Rossi[18] to measure the perceived social standing of occupations. It has been widely used in studies conducted in the United States and other industrialized societies. The Standard International Occupational Prestige Scale was constructed by Treiman.[19] Based on data from occupational prestige studies conducted in over 50 countries around the world, it provides prestige scores for each of 509 detailed occupations classified according to the International Standard Classification of Occupations (revised edition) developed by the International Labor Office in 1969. This scale is best suited for use in cross-cultural studies involving countries at different developmental levels. However, it should not be used in underdeveloped countries, as occupations in these countries may not have become sufficiently differentiated to establish a stable significance for the different degrees of prestige.

When any of the appendixed items or scales are used, it is appropriate to acknowledge the sources and scientists who originated them.

SUMMARY

Measurement, or the assignment of numerals to variations of a variable as represented by the response categories, is the vital link between conceptualization and ongoing activities. Valid, reliable, and precise measurement promotes

---

[18] Paul M. Siegel, "Prestige in the American Occupational Structure," unpublished Ph.D. dissertation, Department of Sociology, University of Chicago, 1971; Paul M. Siegel, P. H. Rossi, and R. W. Hodge, *Social Standings of Occupations,* Seminar Press, New York, in press.

[19] Donald J. Treiman, *Occupational Prestige in Comparative Perspective,* Seminar Press, New York, in press.

construction and verification of social theories and effective application of research to policy decisions. Validity indicates that the measured responses reflect as accurately as possible the actual social activities, and reliability defines the degree to which a measure generates similar responses over time and situations.

Measurement errors can result from (1) study-related sources and (2) study-unrelated sources. They can be minimized with various tests of validity and reliability.

A measure can be validated in terms of empirical evidence or conceptual evidence. Empirical confirmation compares the information obtained from the measure with facts and outcomes found in reality. When such facts and outcomes are difficult or impossible to observe, conceptual confirmation is used. The validity of the measure is inferred by (1) internal validity—significance within the study situation, or (2) external validity—generality to a larger population or theoretical structure.

Reliability is examined with (1) the test-retest method, (2) the alternative-form method, and (3) the subsample method. In the test-retest method, a stability coefficient reveals the extent to which a measure provides similar results over time. In the alternative-form method, the equivalence coefficient examines the extent to which a measure in alternative forms yields similar results. The jacknife estimation is used in the subsample method to assess the variability of response patterns across respondents. It should be noted that a reliable measure is not necessarily valid, but may provide consistently false results.

A researcher can construct different types of measurement scales to accommodate different types of variables and analyses: nominal, ordinal, interval, and ratio scales.

As the level of measurement ascends from nominal to ratio, more and more statistical techniques become available to the researcher for data analysis. Thus, it is desirable to construct a scale at the highest level of measurement that the variations of an ongoing activity allow. Many techniques have been developed to construct ordinal scales (e.g., the Guttman scale) and interval scales (e.g., the Likert scale and the Thurstone scale).

The advance of social theories depends to a great extent on precise measurement. To promote the use of uniform and tested measures of variables of general interest to social researchers, a list of items and response categories appears in Appendices A and B. The reader is encouraged to use these measures (with acknowledgment of the original sources).

Part Four

Data Collection

Chapter 11

Data Collection: An Introduction

Data collection is the process by which information is gathered from respondents. It may involve direct participation of the respondents (obtrusive method), or it may lack their participation (unobtrusive method). There are many methods of data collection and, more often than not, more than a single method is used in a research study. This chapter outlines the general procedures common to all data collection and introduces generally the major methods of data collection.

GENERAL PROCEDURE

Data collection is usually initiated with a review of the relevant literature and consultation with experts. In this first phase, the researcher tries to become familiar with the issue to be studied, concepts and variables used by other researchers in studying similar issues in the past, and hypotheses and speculations about the relationships among the variables suggested or found in the past. Furthermore, the literature review and consultation with experts should also be extended to familiarize the researcher with the social settings and characteristics of the persons and activities from which he will gather the data. This initial phase introduces the proper perspective into which the researcher is to put his study, the larger body of relevant knowledge and the specific social context in which the study is to take place.

The second phase of data collection is the gaining of entry into the social system in which the data are to be collected. The way a researcher approaches the social system may well decide to what extent he will be allowed to gather data and to what extent the persons in the system will cooperate with him either as respondents or as subjects of his observations. The researcher must receive permission from authorities of the social system to conduct the study. He also has to make a decision as to whether he should be introduced to respondents as an "insider" associated with the authorities in the formal structure, or as an independent "outsider" who has no association whatever with the authorities. A wrong decision can be costly; the worst possibility being that the researcher is denied cooperation by the persons in the system, or that a pretense is put up by these persons, which results in distorted or biased responses.

The advantages of identifying oneself as an independent outsider are many.[1] First, it reduces the amount of time required to gain acceptance by the persons involved, since the researcher does not have to go through the various formal channels to obtain approval for the identification. Second, it tends to stimulate more open and uninhibited responses from the respondents, since the researcher is not identified with the "establishment" and thus is less likely to leak confidential information back up the hierarchical ladder. Third, it reduces the likelihood of developing too much rapport between the researcher and the respondents. Too much rapport would hinder the study, since the researcher would be less free in asking emotional and penetrating questions. Finally, being an outsider provides the researcher a better opportunity to maintain his objectivity, for he does not have any emotional ties with the system itself through any identification.

On the other hand, without identification with the social system, the researcher may find several difficulties in his data-gathering process. First, it poses a threat to the respondents. Since they consider him "not one of us," the respondents are less sure about the objectives of the research and may decide to camouflage activities and behavior. Second, because of the objectivity associated with being an outsider the researcher may not be allowed to see and record activities which are intimate and informal in nature. Third, without identifying with the system, the researcher is less likely to receive support from the authorities in the system, which at times may become necessary to continue the study. In general, being an outsider has more advantages when the social system is a formal rather than an informal one. Since a formal system has a defined hierarchy of authority, identification with the system carries with it the values of the authority, which may inhibit the expression of certain activities and behaviors on the part of the respondents. An outsider role also should work better for the researcher if the respondents have socioeconomic characteristics similar to those of the researcher. Persons having similar characteristics develop rapport much easier and sooner than those having different characteristics. Too much rapport

---

[1] H. M. Trice, "The 'Outsider's' Role in Field Study," in William J. Filstead (ed.), *Qualitative Methodology*, Markham, Chicago, 1970, pp. 77–82.

should be avoided, and the outsider status may maintain such a gap between the researcher and his respondents.

On the other hand, when the respondents have socioeconomic characteristics different from those of the researcher, rapport is more difficult to develop, and one way to bridge the status gap is for the researcher to establish common identification with the respondents by taking on the role of an insider.

Finally, the activities and behaviors to be studied also help determine the role the researcher should assume in the system. When the activities and behaviors to be studied are considered normative in the system, identification with the system does not bias such activities and behavior. When, on the other hand, the activities are considered abnormal, as with homosexuals, drug users, and political demonstrators, being an outsider should be the role to take so that the researcher poses minimal threat to the respondents.

The third phase of data collection necessitates gaining familiarity with the respondents and their environment. Once the researcher has entered the system, he must "feel" his way around, getting to know the respondents and their environment, before any formal research activities can be initiated. The researcher must sensitize himself to the mannerisms and routines of the respondents—how they think, how they interact, how they behave, how they use language and gestures, etc. This process enables the researcher to better formulate the strategy of data collection and to plan ways in which the social environment can adequately be described and reflected in the study.

The fourth phase of data collection consists of a pilot study or pretest. A *pilot study* is a "dress rehearsal" for the study on a small scale. It proceeds as if the actual study is taking place and involves a limited number of respondents or persons who have characteristics similar to those of the respondents sampled for the main study. The respondents are not usually representative of the population, and a draft rather than the final form of the instrument is used. It is used to examine the feasibility and efficiency of all operating procedures to be used in the study. It involves not only data collection, but also improvements in the instrument and in the execution of data analysis.

The *pretest* is a restricted pilot study focusing mainly on the draft of the instrument. The pilot study is superior to the pretest in general, unless the researcher is thoroughly familiar with the social context of his study. In that case, an intensive examination of the instrument and the training of his collaborators (e.g., interviewers, stooges, and observers) is sufficient. As a rule, however, if the researcher has any doubts about procedures for data collection and data analysis, a pilot study should be conducted.

The pilot study has many advantages. First, it provides an occasion for a final test and modification of the instruments to be used. Second, the pilot study represents an initial firsthand involvement of the researcher with the social environment in which the study will be conducted. He has an opportunity to understand the complexity and dynamics of the environment of the social activities.

A third advantage of the pilot study is the opportunity it affords the researcher to conduct trial analyses of the data. Many unforeseeable problems can come up in the analysis, some of which may be unsolvable because of the nature of the data. Thus, it is wise for the researcher to conduct some analyses of the pilot study data. Should any data collected turn out not to be suitable for testing the hypotheses the researcher has formulated, he will still have time to make the necessary changes in the instrument for the main study, thus avoiding problems which may occur in the subsequent analysis.

Still another advantage of the pilot study is that it allows the researcher to take a hard look at the variables, hypotheses, and theories formulated and used. The pilot study can provide information and insight as to the viability and usefulness of these variables, hypotheses, and theories. The researcher has an opportunity to make a final selection of variables and to consider reformulation or refinement of hypotheses and theory.

Finally, the pilot study provides a last-minute evaluation of the study before it is launched in full. It may turn up information which suggests that the triviality or fruitlessness of the study does not warrant investment. Thus, the researcher, basing his decision on the information gathered, may decide to abandon the study and move into a different area of research.

In short, the pilot study or the pretest provides many advantages to the researcher with minimal cost and effort. Such a "dress rehearsal" of the main study is imperative. In fact, the researcher must justify why a pilot study is not being undertaken should he decide not to conduct one.

The fifth phase of data collection is the formulating and posing of the right questions. After becoming familiar with the study environment, the researcher should formulate and pose for himself as well as for his respondents the kinds of questions which would be meaningful to his research interest as well as to the respondents. It is not an easy task. The right questions must be both scientifically (theoretically) and substantively (empirically) meaningful. Many times, the questions the researcher initially had in mind, while scientifically meaningful, have no meaning in the symbolic system of the study environment (among the respondents). At other times, the questions the researcher formulates, after he becomes familiar with the study environment, have substantive meaning (in the symbolic system of the study environment) but have no direct correspondence in the scientific structure to which the data will ultimately have to be linked. The result of formulating the wrong questions in either case is what is called *measurement by fiat*—the correspondence between the empirical world and the theoretical structure is made arbitrarily.[2]

The sixth phase of data collection is the recording and coding of information. This step consists of actual recording and coding of information. The researcher decides what particular technique should be used. The recording involves several parties: (1) the instrument, (2) the respondent, and (3) the recorder. In certain techniques (e.g., the questionnaire survey), the recording takes place in the direct contact between the respondent and the instrument. The respondent writes out responses on the questionnaire. In other techniques, the recording is conducted by

---

[2] Warren Torgerson, *Theory and Method of Scaling*, Wiley, New York, 1958; Aaron V. Cicourel, *Method and Measurement in Sociology*, Free Press, New York, 1964, pp. 7–72.

a third party such as the observer, the experimenter, or the interviewer. When a third party intervenes in the contact between the instrument and the respondent, the interaction of the third party with the instrument, and between him and the respondent, creates a possibility of biases being introduced into the data. Such biases are called the *observer's effect,* the *experimenter's effect,* or the *interviewer's effect,* and will be discussed in the chapters dealing with each specific method of data collection. If the third party is involved in the recording, the training, instructing, or supervising of the recording activity is important.

The seventh phase of data collection is cross-checking, validating, and reliability-testing of the coded information. For the first few interviews or observations made, the researcher should go over the information collected carefully and thoroughly with his collaborators who collected the information. Missing or incorrect data must be rectified by sending the collaborators back to the respondents for verification. For all subsequent interviews and observations, spot checks should be conducted. When all the interviews and observations have been completed, the researcher should verify a portion of the information by direct contact (usually by telephone) with 5 percent of the sampled respondents, including both those who responded and those who did not participate in the study.

The eighth phase of data collection involves the organization and recoding of the data gathered so that data analysis can be performed. In this last phase, data collected should be cleaned up—all incorrect and inconsistent information should be eliminated by careful checking and recoding.

In summary, the process of data collection involves (1) reviewing the literature and consulting experts, (2) conducting a pilot study or pretest, (3) gaining entry into the study system, (4) becoming acquainted with the respondents and their environment, (5) formulating and posing the "right" questions, (6) recording and coding information (data), (7) cross-checking, validating, and reliability-testing data, and (8) organizing and recoding data.

While most studies share the procedures of data collection mentioned so far, there are distinctive methods of data collection, each of which emphasizes different aspects of the data collection process to obtain the kind of data best suited for a certain research purpose. What follows is a discussion of the major methods of data collection. In describing each method, some of the most relevant aspects of the data collection process particular to that method will be described.

METHODS

There are many variations in the methods for collecting data, and more than a single method is usually involved in a study. However, there are four commonly used methods of data collection in social research; all other methods are variations and combinations of these four methods. They are as follows: the observational method, the documentary-historical method, the survey method, and the experimental method. The differences among the four methods are more a matter of emphasis on a particular data-collection strategy to obtain observable data for a particular research purpose than a clear-cut "either-or" distinction. For example, in the observational method, while the emphasis is on the researcher's observing and recording social activities as they occur, the researcher does interview the participants—a technique associated with the survey and experimental methods. Similarly, in the experimental method, the subjects (participants) are usually under the observation of the researcher and his collaborators. The information gained in such observations also plays a crucial role in the final analysis and interpretation of the data. Moreover, documents and historical evidence are almost always used in observational, survey, and experimental studies.

The selection of data-collection method is to a large extent dependent on the type of information desired.[3]

To study a sequence of events, the events which precede and follow them, and explanations of the meanings of the events by the participants and other observers before, during, and after their occurrence, observation (especially participant observation) seems to be the best method of data collection.[4] The researcher directly observes and participates in the study system with which he has established a meaningful and durable relationship. While he may or may not play an active role in the events, he observes them firsthand and can record the events and the participants' experiences as they unfold. No other data-collection method can provide such a detailed description of social events. Thus, observation is best suited for studies intended to understand a particular group or substantive social problem. When these events are not available for observation as they occurred in the past, the documentary-historical approach is the logical choice of method for collecting data.

If the researcher wishes to study norms, rules, and status in a particular group (especially communities and formal organizations), intensive interviewing of "key" persons and informants in or outside the group is the best method of data collection. Those who set and enforce norms, rules, and status, because of their positions in the group or relations with persons in the group, are the ones who are the most knowledgeable about the information the researcher wishes to obtain. Intensive interviews (especially with open-ended questioning) with these persons allow the researcher to probe for such information.

The methods so far mentioned, observation, documentary, and intensive interviews, are better for generating hypotheses and propositions. Thus, they are mainly used for theoretical induction, in addition to their utility in describing particular and substantive groups and events. For theoretical deduction, to test specific hypotheses derived from a theoretical structure, systematic survey and experiment are better suited as the methods of data collection.

When the researcher wants to determine numbers, proportions, ratios, and other quantitative information about the persons in the study system possessing certain characteristics, opinions, beliefs, and other categories of various variables, then the best method of data collection is the survey in which a representative

---

[3] Morris Zelditch, Jr., "Some Methodological Problems of Field Studies," *American Journal of Sociology,* vol. 67, pp. 566–576, March 1962.

[4] Howard S. Becker and Blanche Geer, "Participant Observation and Interviewing; A Comparison," *Human Organization,* vol. 16, pp. 28–34, 1957.

sample of the population cases can be drawn and in which a standardized instrument can be administered to all sampled cases. The survey also provides one way to analyze relationships among variables (such as a causal analysis).

Finally, the experiment is the best method of data collection when the researcher wants to measure the effect of certain independent variables on some dependent variables. The experimental situation provides control over the respondents and the variables and gives the researcher the opportunity to manipulate the independent variables.

MULTIMETHOD APPROACH

The primary goal of data collection is to generate data which, on the one hand, best reflect ongoing activities and, on the other hand, are most appropriate for the examination and evaluation of theories. Thus, a researcher should utilize the most appropriate method of data collection. In other words, *research objectives dictate the method of data collection rather than vice versa.*

More importantly, the researcher must consider the use of multiple methods of data collection to achieve research objectives. To generate data which are reliable and valid, it is crucial that the researcher have a certain degree of confidence that the data generated are not artifacts of a particular method of data collection used. A researcher's confidence in any pattern of relations to be tested or found is increased as more and more different methods of data collection yield a similar result. Thus, for example, if a relationship between two variables is found in both a questionnaire survey and an interview survey, then more confidence can be given to the theoretical structure from which the relationship derives.

Further, the more the multimethods differ, the more confidence a researcher has in the found relationship. For example, if a relationship appearing in data gathered in a questionnaire survey also appears in an observational study and a documentary study, the researcher will feel much more confident about its validity. This is so, because, if we assume that certain methods are similar to each other, say, the questionnaire survey and the interview survey, the chances of similar results being generated as artifacts of the methods remain relatively high. When drastically different methods are used instead, say observation, survey, and documentary methods, the chances of any consistent finding attributable to any similarities among these methods are substantially reduced.

Thus, to obtain precise and generalizable data, the multimethod approach to data collection is the most desirable.[5]

SUMMARY

Data collection involves a number of distinctive steps: (1) reviewing the literature and consulting the experts, (2) gaining entry into the study system, (3) becoming

[5] See footnotes 5 and 8 in Chapter 10 for discussions of the multimethod approach.

acquainted with the respondents and their environment, (4) conducting a pilot study, (5) formulating and posing the right questions, (6) recording and coding information (data), (7) cross-checking, validating, and reliability-testing data, and (8) organizing and recoding of data.

There are four major methods of data collection: (1) observation, (2) the documentary-historical method, (3) the survey, and (4) the experiment. Each method represents a set of information-gathering activities required of the researcher to obtain the kind of data best suited for the purpose of the study. Usually, the researcher should utilize any combination of these methods to obtain the type of information desired. In the following three chapters, the major methods of data collection are discussed in detail.

Chapter 12

Observations and Documentary-Historical Methods

Observation is a method of data collection in which the researcher or his collaborators record information as they witness events occurring in the study system. The witnessing recorders are the *observers*. There are many advantages in using the observational method. First, information is recorded as the event unfolds. Thus, the validity of the recorded information can be high. When instantaneous recording of an unfolding event is impossible, the recording should be done soon afterward while the observers still have a fresh memory of the event, thus minimizing any recall bias and distortion. Second, observations are made and information is recorded independently of the observed persons' abilities to report events. On occasions when direct verbal or written communication between the researcher and the respondents is difficult, for example, in studying Stone Age tribes, observation is the only method by which the researcher can obtain information. Third, the observer need not rely on the willingness of the observed persons to report events. In studies dealing with "abnormal" behaviors, behaviors which are socially unacceptable to the majority of the persons in the social system or which are illegal, there may be problems of obtaining a sufficient number of persons who engage in such behaviors and who are willing to cooperate fully with the researcher and his collaborators. Observations can bypass the required interaction between the observer and the observed. Fourth, observations can provide detailed information which may seem insignificant or nonconsequential at the time of recording, but which may eventually prove crucial in the sequence of events. Because recording can be done immediately following an event, detailed description is made possible, thereby reducing the chances of missing potentially significant information. In cases in which chains and sequences of events are important, observation provides the best coverage.

However, there are limitations to the observational method of data collection. First, it is impractical to use observations for unpredictable events. Riots, hijackings, earthquakes, and fires are some of the events that do not easily, if at all, lend themselves to planned observation. A second limitation occurs when the group is so large or the event so extensive that observations cannot adequately cover the group or the event as a whole. Limited observations of a few participants and segments of the event will most likely result in biased and distorted information. Third, although observation is a good method for collecting data to construct theoretical propositions, it usually proves inadequate when testing hypotheses derived from theory unless it is rigidly conducted, such as in a laboratory situation. While it remains possible to make inferences from observations of certain groups and events to similar groups and events, these inferences are primarily intended for constructing rather than verifying theoretical propositions.

To obtain the information and details desired, the observer must "stay" in the study system with the participants. This requirement brings up the question as to what particular role the observer should take in his interaction with the participants.

ROLES OF THE OBSERVER

The observer can assume a number of different roles in his relation with the participants in the group as he gathers data.[1] First, he can take the role of *complete participant,* while withholding his true identity from the other participants. He could act as if he were an alcoholic seeking help at an Alcoholics Anonymous meeting, a newly enlisted trainee in a military training program, a true believer in a religious group, or a homosexual sympathizer in a study of homosexual behaviors.[2] The reason for full participation without revealing the researcher's true identity is twofold. First, the researcher himself can experience what the participants experience, thereby sharing the emotional and behavioral involvement of being in the group; second, since the group members are not aware of any outsiders, he will tend not to disturb the ongoing activities of the group. However,

---

[1] Raymond L. Gold, "Roles in Sociological Field Observations," *Social Forces,* vol. 36, pp. 217–223, March 1958.

[2] John F. Lofland and Robert A. Lejeune, "Initial Interaction of Newcomers in Alcoholics Anonymous: A Field Experiment in Class Symbols and Socialization," *Social Problems,* vol. 8, pp. 102–111, 1960; Mortimer A. Sullivan, Stuart A. Queen, and Ralph C. Patrick, Jr., "Participant Observation as Employed in the Study of a Military Training Program," *American Sociological Review,* vol. 23, pp. 660–667, 1958; Leon Festinger, Henry W. Riecken, and Stanley Schacter, *When Prophecy Fails,* University of Minnesota Press, Minneapolis, 1956; and Laud Humphreys, *Tearoom Trade: Impersonal Sex in Public Places,* Aldine, Chicago, 1970.

the researcher who takes the role of full participant may be confronted with several serious problems. For example, how far and to what extent should he behave as the other participants do? To study drug users should he also use drugs? To study homosexuals, should he also participate in homosexual acts? To study demonstrators, should he also burn flags and throw rocks at the police? Furthermore, how far should the observer go in terms of initiating activities? Finally, there is the issue of ethics. The disguised researcher may in fact be taking advantage of the participants and violate the interpersonal trust so crucial to the functioning of their social group and to the interactions and participation of individuals in that group. While it is possible for the researcher to reveal his true identity to the participants after the data have been gathered, the danger of damage already done to the mental and physical well-being of the participants prevails. Thus, the full-participant role is the least desirable role for the observer to take.[3]

Second, the observer can take the role of *participant as observer.* In this role, while the observer still participates in the activities, both he and the participants are aware of his true identity as observer.[4] Under these circumstances it is possible for him to limit his activities in the group, so that he will not be expected to behave like everyone else. The participant-as-observer role has the advantage of firsthand participation and observation of activities, but it avoids the problems associated with disguised identity. However, because of the need to participate, there still may be a tendency for the observer as well as the other participants to involve the observer in the activities more intensively and extensively than is desired in order to maintain the objective stance of the observer and his recording behavior. It is important for the observer to remain conscious of his scientific role and to restrain the full expression of his emotions and his behavior. Last, he should prepare himself as well as the other participants for the forthcoming termination of their relationship.

A third role the observer can take is that of an *observer as participant.* In this role, the observer participates only to the extent that is required to make his observations. This role substantially reduces the possibility of the observer having to "go native," which may be necessary in the above two roles, and increases his objective stance. There are situations in which the observer-as-participant role can best serve the study purpose. In a study of identity crisis, Rokeach brought together three mental patients all of whom claimed to be Jesus Christ.[5] The researcher introduced himself as a social psychologist but restricted his participation to mostly observing and responding when the participants specifically sought his interaction. The study resulted in one of the most insightful descriptions of the process of identity crisis and resolution available in the sociopsychological litera-

---

[3] Kai T. Erikson, "A Comment on Disguised Observation in Sociology," *Social Problems,* vol. 14, no. 4, pp. 366–373, 1966.

[4] William F. Whyte, *Street Corner Society,* University of Chicago Press, Chicago, 1943; Herbert J. Gans, *The Levittowners,* Pantheon, New York, 1967; Gerald D. Suttles, *The Social Order of the Slum,* University of Chicago Press, Chicago, 1968; Howard S. Becker, Blanche Geer, Everett C. Hughes, and Anselm Strauss, *Boys in White,* University of Chicago Press, Chicago, 1961.

[5] Milton Rokeach, *The Three Christs of Ypsilanti,* Knopf, New York, 1964.

ture. Even with his limited participation, the researcher admitted feeling strained toward the end of the study.

On the other hand, because the contact between the observer and the observed is chiefly based on the necessity that the observer obtain the data and, because this objective is understood by the observed, the information obtained may be biased and distorted either because of the types of behaviors and opinions the observed are willing to express in front of the observer or because of the misunderstanding of the observer as a result of his limited understanding of the observed and their environment.

Finally, the observer can take the role of a *complete observer,* without any participation in the activities or interactions of the observed. In this role, the observer is entirely detached from the observed and therefore has no chance of "going native." While this approach virtually eliminates the subjective entanglement of the observer with the participants, it also leaves the observer with no real emotional experiences similar to those of the participants. The observer thus is in danger of misinterpreting activities and events. However, there are occasions when such misinterpretations are minimized and the complete-observer role provides the optimal method of collecting data on detailed and fast-moving activities. One such occasion is the structured observation, as it occurs in laboratory situations.[6] In studying the process of interaction in a task situation, Bales separated the observer from the participants. The observer viewed the activities of the participants through a one-way mirror and recorded each verbal and gestural expression of each participant according to a prearranged set of categories. Thus, the observer was not allowed to interpret the activities, other than recording them according to defined categories, and the participants engaged in the activities among themselves without the feeling of being closely watched. In this kind of structured observation, the crucial elements are that the categories be so well designed that they exhaustively and exclusively represent all verbal and gestural activities possible in such a situation, and that the observers be sufficiently trained so that their observations are reliable.

In summary, the observer can take one of four roles in defining his relationship with the participants whom he observes: as complete participant, as participant-as-observer, as observer-as-participant, or as complete observer. Because of ethical issues, social researchers tend not to take the complete-participant role. The other three roles have both advantages and disadvantages, depending on the need to share the participants' experiences and thus "go native," and on the need to maintain the objectivity required to record accurate information. The choice is a difficult one and must be made with care. The researcher must take into account the nature of the study, the kind of information needed, the type of group and participants involved, and the precision of the recording instrument. Should the researcher decide to participate in part or in full, he should train himself to be able to empathize (see things from the participants' viewpoint) with the par-

---

[6] Robert F. Bales, *Interaction Process Analysis: A Method for the Study of Small Groups,* Addison-Wesley, Reading, Mass., 1950.

ticipants and, at the same time, be able to maintain emotional detachment, terminating the relationship as soon as the observations have been completed.

PROCESS OF OBSERVATION

Observation as a data-collection method can be discussed as a process involving the following more-or-less sequential activities: (1) preparation and training, (2) entry into the study environment, (3) initial interaction, (4) observation and recording, and (5) termination of field work.

The initial step in observation is to decide what to observe and how to observe. The researcher and his collaborators should review the purpose of the study and familiarize themselves with the setting and characteristics of the group and the participants they are about to observe. They should also decide on strategies and options for making recordings. They should practice the procedures of observation and recording so that, if more than one observer is involved, interobserver reliability can be guaranteed.

Then, the researcher should clear the entry of the observer into the group by going through the proper channels and persons identified in the initial study of the group. The approval of the key persons in the group is most crucial in gaining proper entry and acceptance for the observer. Once the observer is in the group, and if he is to participate, he should immediately identify his role—either as an outsider or as an insider. The observer must take time to develop a normal relationship with the participants, as initial interactions are inevitably restrained and tense. The observer should demonstrate that he considers the participants the experts in the activities they are engaged in. He should convey the idea that he is sympathetic to their activities and that he must maintain a certain degree of detachment to do a fair job. Usually, the observer is able to guarantee the confidentiality of the identification of specific informants (participants providing information about other participants) and of the group in data analysis and reporting.

As the relationship and interaction between the observer and the participants become less restrained, the observer should note if the interactions among the participants have also relaxed in front of him. When such interactions seem to have returned to normal, the observer proceeds in full with his observation and recording. Recording may present a dilemma to the observer. While he should record information as soon as an event takes place, it may be disruptive to do the recording in front of the participants. Also, while recording is being done, significant events may occur and thus escape the attention of the observer. The general rule is to train the observer so that he can memorize details of activities for a period of time and then record the activities as a segment when there is a break in the action. Depending on the pace of events and the routine of activities, a segment may be short as minutes or as long as a day. The observer should determine whether recording should be done right in front of the participants or away from them. While pocket-sized tape recorders are easy to handle, oral statements, even in a whispered tone, may still draw too much attention and prove to be too distracting. Taking notes, while eliminating noise, may also draw attention. If recording proves to be too disruptive or distracting to the participants, the observer should do the recording away from them. This should not present too much of a problem, as reasonable excuses can be made to leave the group or the informants. Even if recording is done while away from the participants, the observer may still have to write down key words to keep the details from slipping from his memory. Such activity should be done as unobtrusively as possible.

One crucial element in the recording of information is the evaluation of the credibility of statements made by an informant. An informant is defined as either a participant or a nonparticipant who has acquainted himself with the participants, their activities, and their environment, and who provides the observer with information regarding the observed. The credibility of an informant can be verified by the extent to which his statements are consistent with other statements he makes (internal consistency), with actual behaviors and events observed (empirical consistency), and with the statements made by other informants about the same or similar events and behavior (external consistency). In addition, some informants tend to rationalize and justify events as they are inquired into by the observer. The observer must note whether the statement made by an informant is a voluntary one or a response to a question put to him by the observer. When it is a directed statement in response to the observer's inquiry, credibility of the statement must be carefully verified for its internal, external, and empirical consistency.

As the observation and recording approach an end, the observer should prepare himself as well as the participants for the forthcoming termination of their relationship. Emotional ties, if they exist, must now begin to be broken. Continuation of such ties beyond the formal termination of the observation simply adds to possible biased and distorted analysis and interpretation of data. After the termination, the observer is bound by the formal and/or informal ethical agreements and contracts made between him and any participants (especially the informants). Abiding by the agreements and contracts not only leaves room for the observer to reenter the study system in the future, but also promotes the chances for other researchers to enter the study system. Thus the ethical responsibility of the observer not only involves the well-being of the participants and of himself, but is also for other scientists and researchers.

STRUCTURED OBSERVATION

One particular form of observation involves observation under rigidly designed and controlled situations. The recording of activities can also be structured by the researcher in that specific events are defined and response categories of the respondents are provided by the researcher to the observers as they record the activities and interactions.

Structured observation can be used only when the researcher has specific activities and interactions in mind for observation, and when he is aware of the types of events which will occur and the response categories which will exhaustively and exclusively describe the events. Thus, the researcher is able to set up these events and response categories ahead of the time in the training of the observers. The observers record only the events specified and check-mark the response categories provided. They are given minimal freedom to select and interpret events for recording. Thus, structured observation is useful in testing hypotheses with observational data, since the rigidly constructed and recorded information provides easily quantifiable data for analysis.

Structured observation can be conducted in either the laboratory situation or the natural setting. For example. Bales studied group interactions in a laboratory situation in which the respondents were assigned a certain group task to perform.[7] Starting with more than fifty categories, Bales and his associates conducted a series of laboratory studies, with the assistance of a number of observer-coders. Eventually, as the intercoder coding reliability increased and his theory about group interactions sharpened, he was able to arrive at twelve categories, each with a careful definition. With these twelve categories (with the response categories of either "presence" or "absence" of the particular behavior tapped by a category), he attempted to map the process of group interactions.

Similarly, structured observaton can be conducted in natural settings, where observer-coders collect the data while the participants engage in their "normal" behaviors.

Structured observation, thus, broadens the use of observation as a technique in hypothesis-testing situations. However, because structured observation requires the specification of categories and responses, it may lose the advantage of the open-endedness in the formulation of data usually associated with the observation method. This is further compounded by the danger that the structured categories and responses may not describe the actual activities as they occur. Thus, a researcher is advised to engage in intensive pilot studies and coding reliability testing before conducting structured observations.

PROBLEMS OF OBSERVATION

Several problems are central to the successful acquisition and interpretation of observational data. These are as follows: accuracy of observation, the relationship between the observer and the observed, methods of interpretation, and inference from observational data.

Because the data are the results of the observer's observation and recording, the accuracy of the observation and recording constitutes one of the most crucial elements in the data-collection process. Several general guidelines aid in the collection of accurate data. First, the observer should record as much detail as possible. Audiovisual equipment such as tape recorders, cameras, and motion picture and videotape equipment should be used whenever the circumstances allow. The details reduce the possibility of the observer relying on his memory and mak-

[7] Robert F. Bales, ibid.

ing generalizations as he records. Second, if possible, the researcher should use as many observers as possible. The greater the number of observers, the easier it is to verify intercoder reliability, which contributes to a check on greater validity. Moreover, the researcher should try to select observers with heterogeneous socioeconomic backgrounds. People with similar socioeconomic backgrounds tend to perceive and interpret events similarly. Heterogeneous observers may be able to determine the extent to which data collected are objective recordings rather than interpretations influenced by the particular backgrounds of the observers. Third, the observer should clearly delineate between fact and interpretation in his recording. While the observer's own interpretation of the events helps in the eventual analysis and interpretation of the data, the practice of making clear which statement is a factual report and which is the observer's own interpretation of the event will reduce the possibility of unconsciously introducing bias and distortion into the data. The observer should always precede his own interpretations with a remark such as "I think," "I believe," "It seems to me," etc. Finally, the accuracy of the information recorded may be affected by the relationship between the observer and the observed. This brings up the second major problem in observing.

Unless the observer has no direct contact whatsoever with the observed, such as operating behind one-way mirrors, it is inevitable that interactions and emotional ties develop. Such interactions and ties may drag the observer into the group. He may then be expected by certain participants, such as informants, to show appreciation of their cooperation. Such expectations of the participants in turn induce them to enact atypical types of expression and behavior for the observer's benefit. The result is that the information provided by the participants is invalid and ungeneralizable to group life, that the observer is influenced by his involvement in the group or with certain participants, or both. The second result may affect the extent to which his recordings become partisan to certain participants and even biased (in most cases, in favor of) toward the group or participants. To obtain and record accurate information, the observer should be constantly aware of the relationship (1) between himself and the informants, (2) between himself and the rest of the group, and (3) between the informants and the rest of the group. These relationships must be taken into account in the recording and interpretation of information.

Finally, the problem of inference from observational data presents a crucial issue. While observations are not optimally suited to test hypotheses derived from theoretical propositions, they can be very useful in generating hypotheses through the inductive route to theory construction. But how valid can such generalized hypotheses be when observations are usually limited to a few observers and one or a few groups? Becker[8] suggested that observations can contribute in three ways in constructing models. First, observations can lead to statements about the necessary and sufficient conditions for the existence of some phenomena. In other words, the data can suggest the variables which are either causal or correlative to

---

[8] Howard S. Becker, "Problems of Inference and Proof in Participant Observations," *American Sociological Review,* vol. 23, pp. 652–660, December 1958.

the variables of interest. Second, observations can also lead to statements indicating the salient features of certain social systems. Finally, observations can serve as empirical referents for some process or phenomenon described more abstractly in sociological theory. In other words, observations may provide empirical evidence of abstract terms explicated in a theoretical structure.

Thus, observations can contribute to theory just as other methods of data collection—mapping dimensions of salient or crucial variables, constructing causal or correlational relations among variables, and empirically confirming theoretical properties. However, observation differs from other methods of data collection in an important way—it is best suited for the detailed description of a particular study system or particular events and for providing an empirical basis for theoretical induction, rather than for the empirical testing and verification of hypotheses deduced from some theoretical structure. Thus, it is a good method to use if the researcher wishes to describe thoroughly a particular sequence of events occurring in a particular type of social system. To make theoretical contributions, observations can generate hypotheses and contingent hypotheses which may inductively lead to some theoretical structure. These newly generated hypotheses and the theoretical structure underlying them must then be subjected to verification with the use of a method which utilizes a representative sample of the population, rigorous control and manipulation of variables and respondents, e.g., verification through some form of survey or experiment (to be discussed in Chapters 13 and 14), or both.

DOCUMENTARY-HISTORICAL METHOD

Often a researcher deals with a research topic which does not allow him to contact the originators or participants of the events for a variety of reasons, such as timing (e.g., public opinion on the eve of the French Revolution or the social organization of the Mayans in Central America), the extent of information required (the occupational structure of a country), or the cost involved (the criminal patterns in different countries). As a substitute for direct data from the participants and, more positively, in taking advantage of many voluminous and often insightful sources, contents from documents and historical materials are used as a method of data collection. These documents and materials can range from census data, archives of various types, official files, and archeological evidence, to personal diaries, witness accounts, propaganda literature, and numerous other personal and contemporary accounts. The researcher uses these available data sources to conduct what is generally referred to as secondary analysis, that is, the data were not originally generated or collected for the specific purpose of the study formulated by the researcher.

The usefulness of the documentary-historical method depends, to a large extent, on the accuracy and thoroughness of the documents and materials. With accurate and thorough data, the researcher may be able to gain insights, generate hypotheses, and even test hypotheses.

Four major types of documents can be identified for use in the documentary-historical method: (1) archival data, (2) personal documents (including life histories), (3) private documents (diaries, confessions, secret files, etc.), and (4) public documents (mass media, literature, etc.). We will now briefly discuss some uses of such documents by social researchers.

Archival data are becoming more and more important in social research for several reasons. First, more and more statistical census data are gathered by governments, offices, industries, and others. Second, more and more such data have become readily available, partly because of the increasing interest and demand shown by the public and by research communities, and because of computerization of the data. For example, in the United States, the census data, since 1960, have been released in whole or in part to many libraries, universities, and communities for a fee. Third, more and more such data are gathered with the participation of social scientists. The information gathered has become more relevant to the interests of social researchers. Also, the number of data banks making available data sets gathered by social researchers has increased. For a nominal fee, any social researcher can obtain a copy of a data set on computer cards or tapes for secondary analysis.

Two examples will demonstrate the usefulness of archival data.

Durkheim, for example, studied the suicide rates in various social systems and groups. He tested the hypothesis that suicide might be a consequence of lack of integration into the social groups of which the individual may form a part. The lack of integration, he suggested, leads to psychological stress, which in turn leads to the tendency to commit suicide. To test his hypothesis, he examined the suicide rates of various religious groups, family statuses, and countries of different political atmospheres in Western Europe. These characteristics were taken as indications of various degrees of social integration of groups. He found that suicide rates were higher for Protestants than for Catholics, for the unmarried than for the married, and for countries in which citizen participation in political activities was low than for countries in which such participation was high. These data were considered to confirm his hypothesis, since they tended to support the relationship between suicide and lack of social integration. The study has become a classical work of empirical social research, which had been accomplished entirely with available documents and materials.

Another example of the use of archival data is provided by Blau and Duncan.[9] They obtained the 1960 national census and then constructed questions which were incorporated in a Census Bureau survey in 1962 in a national sample of households. In this supplementary survey, questions relevant to occupational issues were asked of the sampled household heads. The result of the data analysis showed that both a person's social origin (father's occupation and education), as well as his own educational achievement, contribute to the degree of occupational success (occupational prestige) of the person. While both ascribed status (social origin) and achieved status (educational achievement) were significant factors, occupational achievement, at least in the United States, proved to rely more on

[9] Peter Blau and Otis D. Duncan, *The American Occupational Structure,* Wiley, New York, 1967.

achieved status than on ascribed status. This study is generally considered a pace-setting research project in the area of social stratification, and its model of the process of occupational achievement has been used as a paradigm for numerous subsequent studies.

In sum, the census data are fast becoming the most systematic and large-scale data available to social researchers. For example, the Census Bureau compiles one-hundredth and one-thousandth samples (drawing samples from the census data on a basis of one sample from each 100 or 1,000 respondents) on a number of items gathered and copies them on data tapes for secondary analysis. These sampled data are available in many universities and regional consortiums. Researchers can also request sampled data on specific census items on paying a fee to the Census Bureau. It is entirely possible that census data will become the greatest resource for social research in the United States in the next decade or so.

A second type of documentary-historical method is based on narrations of personal experiences generally known as the *life-histories* method; this technique requires that the researcher rely solely on a person's reporting of life experiences relevant to the research interest, with minimal commentary.[10] Such a narration consists of a detailed description of the development of a phase in a person's life (e.g., becoming a juvenile delinquent) or a detailed description of the typical behaviors and activities of a particular life-style (e.g., that of a hobo). It usually involves one person's experiences, and focuses on subjective experiences and interpretations, thus providing insights into a world usually overlooked by the objective methods of data collection. The narrator is simultaneously the central subject and the interpreter of the data.

The life-histories method serves several functions.[11] First, it provides empirical reflections (especially subjective views) of theoretical propositions which purport to deal with similar empirical phenomena. When the propositions are reflected in life histories, it does not indicate empirical confirmation of the propositions. On the other hand, when the life-history data do not reflect the theoretical propositions, it indicates that the case deviates from prevailing theoretical expectation. Then, the researcher can make a decision as to whether or not the case provides sufficient clues for proposing conditions under which the propositions may not hold or for suggesting the reexamination of the credibility of the propositions. In either case, such evidence may dictate directions for future research.

Second, life histories can serve as the basis for making assumptions necessary for more systematic data collection. In more systematic investigations, many assumptions are made. These assumptions are crucial background, adding

---

[10] Some examples are: W. I. Thomas and Florian Znaniecki, *The Polish Peasant in Europe and America*, Knopf, New York, 1927; Clifford R. Shaw, *The Natural History of a Delinquent Career*, University of Chicago Press, Chicago, 1931, and *Brothers in Crime*, University of Chicago Press, Chicago, 1936; Chic Conwell and Edwin H. Sutherland, *The Professional Thief*, University of Chicago Press, Chicago, 1937; Helen MacGill Hughes (ed.), *The Fantastic Lodge*, Houghton Mifflin, Boston, 1961; Henry Williamson, *Hustler*, edited by R. Lincoln Keiser, Doubleday, Garden City, N.Y., 1965; Clifford R. Shaw, *The Jack Roller*, University of Chicago Press, Chicago, 1966.

[11] Howard S. Becker, "Introduction," in Clifford R. Shaw, ibid.

to the credibility of any findings. However, the validity of these assumptions may not receive appropriate attention in large-scale studies. Life histories provide clues as to the kinds of assumptions a researcher can make realistically.

Third, life histories, because of their details, provide insights into new or different perspectives for research. When an area has been studied extensively and has grown "sterile," life histories may break new grounds for research studies.

Finally, life histories offer an opportunity to view and study the dynamic process of social interactions and events, not available with many other kinds of data.

Because they are subjective interpretations and limited in number, life histories cannot by themselves provide the empirical basis for theoretical construction or empirical generalization. However, their richness of detail helps stimulate ideas which may be examined more systematically and may provide further verification of generalizations derived from systematic studies. In conjunction with more systematic studies, life histories contribute details, vividness, and insights to make the findings more lifelike.

While the documentary-historical method may be effective and insightful, its major difficulty lies in the limited accuracy and thoroughness of the documents and materials involved. As the data are "compiled" by others with no supervision or control by the researcher, the researcher is in fact at the mercy of those who record the information. Systematic and random errors are more likely to occur in such uncontrolled and unsupervised activities. The recorders use their own definitions of situations, define and select events as important for recording, and introduce subjective perceptions, interpretations, and hindsights into their recordings. For example, how do the recorders define a suicide?[12] What evidence is used to judge whether a death resulted from suicide, murder, an accident, or natural causes? What assumptions are made when the recorder documents the case? Furthermore, when more than one recorder is involved in the documentation, it is likely that each recorder's own definitions, perceptions, and assumptions will differentially affect his recording behavior. For example, in the 1960s, the official criminal records showed that several cities, including New York City, had the highest number of recorded criminal acts per 100,000 persons in the United States. However, the police officials in these cities claimed that the statistics were distorted, because they kept better records than other cities. In 1974, a national survey was conducted in the major American cities in which random samples of the population were interviewed. Respondents were questioned about criminal acts that had been committed against them during a recent period of time and asked how many such acts had been reported to the police. The results showed that, in fact, New York City had a lower crime rate than a dozen other cities. The police records in Philadelphia reflected less than half of all the criminal acts committed. Because either the citizens in some cities were more reluctant than those in others to report crimes, or the official criminal classifications were not

[12] Jack D. Douglas, *The Social Meanings of Suicide*, Princeton University Press, Princeton, N.J., 1967.

recorded uniformly, the resulting documents presented serious problems for comparative analysis and interpretation.

A researcher must assess the reliability and validity of documents. Again, the documents should be verified for internal consistency (consistency between each portion of the document and other portions) and external consistency (consistency with empirical evidence, other documents, or both). The documentary-historical method provides details and, in certain cases, presents a processual view of events often unmatched by any other method of data collection. It is extremely desirable to combine the documentary-historical method with another data-collection method.

CONTENT ANALYSIS

One particular issue concerning nonstatistical materials in observational and documentary-historical research is the process of transformation of such materials into sets of data which can be manipulated statistically. *Content analysis,* representing this process, is defined as "any methodical measurement applied to text for social science purposes. Or, any systematic reduction of a flow of text, that is, recorded language, to a standard set of statistically manipulable symbols representing the presence, the intensity, or the frequency of some characteristics relevant to social science."[13]

In content analysis, the symbols in the text are considered either programable or semantic units. *Programable units* are currently specified unambiguously and can be identified by a digital computer. Words are in most cases programable units. Semantic units cannot be rigorously defined at the present time, and they are usually called *themes.* Thus, the researcher can either study the appearances of certain words or themes in the text. While word counting may be simple and straightforward as far as coding is concerned, interpretation is more difficult, as words may have different meanings in different contexts of association with other words. Thematic coding, on the other hand, is more meaningful for interpretation, but presents a more serious problem for coding.

With the assistance of high-speed, large-memory computers, content analysis in terms of word counting and word association has advanced. A well-known computer program, called The General Inquirer, was developed by Phillip Stone and his associates and can be used to analyze not only the occurrences of particular words but combinations of words which do not have to appear contiguously.[14] The program has been used, for example, to code certain psychodynamics of the sources of certain documents (e.g., What were some of the

---

[13] John Markoff, Gilbert Shapiro, Sasha R. Weitman, "Toward the Integration of Content Analysis and General Methodology," in David R. Heise (ed.), *Sociological Methodology 1975,* Jossey-Bass, San Francisco, 1974, chap. 1, pp. 1–58. As pointed out by these authors, content analysis should be more appropriately called *content coding* or *textual coding.* However, the more conventional term *content analysis* is used here.

[14] P. J. Stone et al., *The General Inquirer: A Computer Approach to Content Analysis,* Cambridge, Mass.: M.I.T., 1966.

personality and psychological factors operating within the communication sources as reflected in the documents they formulated?).

However, on other occasions when the purpose is not to identify the appearance of word combinations considered symptomatic of certain psychological forces, but to ascertain what the source tried to convey to his intended audience, the use of coders is still extensively employed so that thematic units can be identified. As soon as coders become involved, interaction between the coders and the document occurs and must be taken into account in evaluating the results. Intercoder reliability must be determined (see Chapter 10, on reliability, and Chapter 13, on the use of interpreters in the cross-cultural equivalence of instruments) before data can be analyzed.

A specific example of content analysis applied to mass media content may illustrate the general process. In a study to determine the interaction patterns among different types of actors (a person, an agent of a person, a corporation, and a latent corporation) in the United States during the last century (1877–1972), Burt had two characteristics of the front page of selected issues of *The New York Times* coded for the various actors and combinations of actors: (1) the average percentage of space on the front page of *The New York Times* which discusses a certain type of actor, and (2) the average percentage of space on the front page of *The New York Times* which discusses two types of actors simultaneously.[15]

Instructions were provided for the coders in determining the type of actor involved. When a coder had trouble deciding on a label to apply to an actor in a news article, he was asked to proceed through a series of binary (yes-no) decisions: (1) All actors were assumed to be persons, unless one or more of the following conditions described the actor: (a) the actor was exchanging resources belonging to another actor, (b) the actor was representing the interests of another actor, (c) the actor was a collectivity of actors referenced with a single noun or phrase, (d) the actor was a representative of a collectivity of actors referenced with a single noun or phrase, or (e) the actor was a "king." (2) If the actor was not a person, then the actor was assumed to be an agent of an actor unless the actor was a collectivity of actors referenced with a single noun acting to realize collective interests. (3) If the actor was not a person, and was not an agent of a person, then the actor was assumed to be a corporate actor and was classified as a latent corporate actor if the collectivity had no formal organization; otherwise, the actor was classified as a type of corporate actor according to the Standard Industrial Classification.

Then, intercoder reliability was assessed for a given set of *New York Times* issues. On the basis of analyses of coded data, Burt concluded that (1) there has been an increase in the prominence of corporate actors, at the expense of person actors, as reflected in selected *New York Times* issues during the last century in the United States, and (2) latent corporations appeared on the scene in intensive interactions with persons and corporations, especially with government agents

[15] Ronald S. Burt, "Corporate Society: A Time Series Analysis of Network Structure," *Social Science Research,* 4 (September 1975).

and finance corporate actors, when either persons or corporate actors perceive that they are experiencing differential economic growth relative to the other. This second conclusion implies that the latent corporate actors serve as a medium of interaction between persons and corporate actors when one of the two types of actors experienced or perceived relative economic deprivation.

As can be seen, interesting and significant results can be obtained from content analysis of observational or documentary-historical information.[16]

SUMMARY

This chapter has discussed two methods of data collection: (1) observation and (2) the documentary-historical method.

Observations provide data on events as they occur. They provide a dynamic view of sequences of events, unmatched by data gathered by other methods of data collection. Moreover, the observer may participate in the activities in order to share the firsthand insights and feelings the participants experience. However, observers must be careful not to let their participation interfere with the participants' normal behaviors or with the observer's objective recording of the information.

Because of the limited scope of events which can be observed, observation is a useful method of generating data on substantive issues concerning specific social groups rather than for testing specific hypotheses. Structured observation, on the other hand, can be used for hypothesis testing under rigidly controlled situations.

When data cannot be generated from the respondents for the purpose of the study, the researcher may rely on documents and materials generated for other purposes. Documents and histories such as archival and statistical-census data, popular literature, mass media messages, life histories, and diaries can all be used. The usefulness of the documents depends largely on the accuracy and thoroughness of the recording. When the documents are accurate and systematic, such as census data, powerful quantitative and content analysis can be made to uncover and test theoretical structures.

---

[16] Discussions on content analysis, in addition to the citations in footnotes 13–15, can be found in: B. Berelson, "Content Analysis," in G. Lindzey (ed.), *Handbook of Social Psychology,* Addison-Wesley, Reading, Mass., 1954, vol. 1, p. 489; I. de Sola Pool (ed.), *Trends in Content Analysis,* University of Illinois Press, Urbana, Ill., 1959; G. Gerbner et al. (eds.), *The Analysis of Communication Content,* Wiley, New York, 1969; H. A. Simon and L. Siklossy, *Representation and Meaning: Experiments with Information Processing Systems,* Prentice-Hall, New York, 1972.

Chapter 13

The Survey

The *survey* is a data-collection method in which an instrument is used to solicit responses from a sample of respondents. Usually, it has the following characteristics:

1 It deals with a representative sample of a population. Thus, sampling, especially probabilistic sampling, is essential to survey studies.

2 It seeks responses directly from the respondents. The respondents either have to record the responses on the instrument themselves or provide the responses to interviewers sent by the researcher. In either case, there is a direct interaction between the respondents and the instrument. The success of a survey depends to a large extent on the ability of the instrument, the interviewers, or both to solicit unbiased and valid responses from the respondents.

3 Because surveys usually use a representative sample of a population, they are the preferred method of data collection when inference must be made from the sample to the population. Inference usually dictates a large size of the sample. Thus, surveys usually involve many respondents, as compared with other methods of data collection.

4 The survey is conducted in natural settings. Usually, responses are solicited in the offices and homes of the respondents. As a rule, respondents are not required to present themselves in settings unfamiliar to their daily routines.

Because of its ability to cover large areas and many respondents, the survey method has become the dominant method of data collection in social research.

There are basically two types of surveys: the *interview* survey, in which the replies from the respondents are recorded by the researcher's collaborators, the interviewers; and the *questionnaire* survey, in which the respondents themselves are asked to record their responses on the instrument or form provided.

COMPARISON OF THE INTERVIEW AND THE QUESTIONNAIRE SURVEY

Interviews are usually conducted in face-to-face situations in which the interviewers visit the respondent, read off questions, solicit responses, and record the responses. The instrument used in interviews is called the *schedule.*

The most common form of the questionnaire survey utilizes the mail questionnaire, which is sent directly to the respondent. Instructions are provided on the questionnaire to guide and explain the recording of responses by the respondent. The instrument used in the questionnaire survey is called the *questionnaire.*

Advantages of the questionnaire are mainly due to its standardization and low cost, whereas advantages of the interview survey are related to its flexibility and less dependence on the respondents. In deciding which method of survey to use, the economic factor may be the decisive factor. But if the economic factor does not enter into the picture, the general rules of selection are:

1 Response rate. If a high response rate, say 80 percent, is needed, the interview survey has a much greater chance of succeeding than the questionnaire. On the other hand, if a response rate of somewhat less than 65 percent is sufficient, then the questionnaire is adequate.

2 Sensitivity of the questions. If the information to be obtained deals mostly with facts which are public knowledge, such as sex, and activities considered "normal" in the social system, the questionnaire should be adequate, since in this case the respondents will not feel threatened. However, when the information sought concerns private information such as income, sexual behavior, racial attitudes, or activities considered "abnormal" in the social system, such as drug use in the United States, then the interview survey should be used, as the respondents would tend to refrain from recording such information for the researcher on a questionnaire.

Thus, for more private and accurate information, the interview survey is preferred to the questionnaire. The general trend in social research is that, when the economic situation allows, the interview survey is favored over the questionnaire. The savings in cost in a questionnaire survey are usually outweighed by the loss of precision of information.

PROCEDURE FOR THE QUESTIONNAIRE SURVEY

A questionnaire survey begins with the preparation of the instrument and the sample. In the preparation of the questionnaire, special attention must be given to a covering letter and instructions provided for the respondents to follow in formulating and recording their responses.

Covering Letter

The covering letter should identify the persons and organizations conducting the study. It should also briefly mention the objective of the study. In many instances, revelation of the precise objective of the study may provide respondents with cues so that they will respond in the direction of what they feel to be the expectation of the researcher. Therefore, the objectives must be described in general terms. Sometimes the objective stated is much broader than the specific objective intended by the researcher. For example, in a study of drug use among college students, the respondents can simply be informed that the study deals with the life-style of college students.

The covering letter should also tell the respondents why the study is important and to whom. While it would be helpful if the study could benefit the respondents directly, usually findings from a study do not have immediate and direct effects on the respondents. Thus, the covering letter should try to convince the respondent of the long-range and broader implications of the study for the social system or for an organization with which he can identify.

The respondents must also be shown in the covering letter how they were selected for study. The nature of the sampling procedure can be briefly described, and the importance of the respondent's returning the completed questionnaire should be stressed. The respondents must be made to understand that the study results can be applied to a large population only when the sampled respondents cooperate in the participation.

Finally, the covering letter should guarantee the anonymity of the respondent and the confidentiality of the information provided. It should indicate that only the researcher and his associates have access to the identification of the respondents and the responses. All information generated from the data should be in aggregate form and statistical numbers, so that no identification of the respondent or matching of the respondent and any information is possible.

The covering letter should bear the signature, name, and address of the research director. A telephone number through which the researcher can be reached can also be reassuring to the respondent.

The covering letter should be an integral part of the questionnaire. It can constitute the first page of the questionnaire or part of the first page. The best procedure is to print and bind the questionnaire as a booklet and to have the covering letter serve as the cover of the booklet.

The covering letter has the major purpose of providing sufficient information and guarantee in motivating the respondent to participate in the study. To personalize the covering letter, remarks (such as a postscript) written in longhand add a personal touch.

Instructions to Respondent

If the respondent is properly motivated by the covering letter, he probably will examine the questionnaire quickly for two things: how long it is and what it is all about. A long questionnaire will either be set aside if the respondent is busy or simply generate a negative response from the respondent who will refuse to fill in the questionnaire. The strategy to use is to print questions on both sides of each sheet when possible, and limit the length of the questionnaire to no more than four or five sheets.

To guide the respondent in understanding properly and responding to the questions, it is important that instructions be provided throughout the question-naire wherever the focus is shifted and different response patterns are called for. The instructions are especially crucial to guide the respondent in selecting and re-cording the appropriate response categories. For example, to ask the respondent to rank-order certain activities, the instruction should be specific as to how the rank ordering should be recorded. It should be worded as follows:

> Please rank-order the following activities in terms of the amount of time you usually spend weekly on each activity. Write "1" in front of the activity that takes the largest amount of time, "2" in front of the activity that takes the next largest amount of time, etc. Please rank-order all listed activities. If you spend no time on the activity, write "0" in front of the activity.
>
> _____ Teaching
> _____ Advising students
> _____ Conducting basic research
> _____ Writing reports
> _____ Writing proposals
> _____ Administering
> _____ Consulting within the institute
> _____ Consulting outside the institute
> _____ Conducting applied research
> _____ Committee work within the institute
> _____ Committee work outside the institute
> _____ Other (please specify _____)
> _____ Other (please specify _____)

In another case, in which the respondent is to pick only one of the response cate-gories, the instructions should make sure that the respondent will choose one and only one response category. For example:

> Please put a check mark in front of the response category which characterizes most closely your feeling about the issue. Make sure that you choose _one and only one_ response category for each question.

If the researcher is still uncertain whether or not the respondent understands the instructions, he can provide a sample question with a set of sample response categories with one of the categories checked. Whether or not there is a need to provide such sample questions and responses should become clear to the researcher after analysis of the pretest data.

While it is desirable that appropriate instructions be provided throughout the questionnaire, the researcher should avoid long, complicated, or hard-to-understand instructions. He should use simple words and short phrases and sentences, and be as succinct as possible. A respondent can easily be frustrated by instructions which make things complicated.

Arrangement of Questions

The arrangement of questions constitutes another important issue in a questionnaire survey. As a rule, the questionnaire should start with questions soliciting simple, broad, factual, public information and proceed to questions eliciting complicated, indirect, attitudinal, and private information. This is known as the *funnel* or *reversed-pyramid* procedure. The rationale behind this arrangement is to induce the respondent to provide responses in the beginning. When a respondent has committed himself to responding, the chances of his completing the questionnaire are improved. Further, even if a respondent decides not to provide responses to some later questions which may be too sensitive and private to him, he can still return the questionnaire, and the questions to which he responded can be used for analysis. On the other hand, if the questionnaire starts with sensitive questions or uses a mixed format in which nonsensitive and sensitive questions are interwoven, the respondent may immediately decide not to continue with the questions and discard the questionnaire entirely.

In addition to the formal arrangement of the questions, the researcher should evaluate the extent to which the questions will be of interest to the respondents. If most of the questions are laborious or repetitive, the researcher may wish to ask some *padding questions*. Padding questions are not central to the research objective but are of interest to the selected respondents. These questions are added to the questionnaire to generate and maintain the respondent's interest in completing the questionnaire. Padding questions should appear just before or after the more sensitive questions, to provide a "breather" for the respondent, and can appear in a number of places in the questionnaire.

Another crucial issue dealing with the questionnaire is the wording of the questions and the response categories. This usually presents a problem to a researcher. On the one hand, the researcher does not want to insult the respondents by using wording that is childish or elementary. On the other hand, sophisticated or complicated wording can result in misunderstanding. Besides, a group of respondents may be quite diversified in their educational backgrounds, so that wording considered insulting by some may be appropriate for others. The problem of cultural differences is also involved. Wording which makes perfect sense to blacks may be meaningless or may have a different meaning for whites.

When the researcher conducts a cross-cultural investigation, the problem of using terms that are equivalent in each culture can become extremely serious. The proper strategy is to aim toward the lowest level of all respondents in terms of their abilities. If a study involves both physicians and janitors, then the wording must be such that the janitors understand. This strategy may not please the physicians. However, at least every respondent in the sample will be on equal terms relative to understanding the questions and the response categories. Thus, the wording should favor the lowest level of sophistication among the respondents and sacrifice, if any, is toward the highest level of sophistication.

Cross-Cultural Translation of the Instrument

When a cross-cultural study is being conducted, the researcher must make sure that the wordings are equivalent for all questions and response categories for all languages involved. The procedure to use here is the double-translation technique. First, two or three bilingual translators are used to translate the questionnaire from one language (A) to another language (B). The translators should work together so that some consensus can be achieved in the translations. The translated questionnaire in language B should then be translated by another group of two or three bilingual translators into language A. These translators should work independently and be encouraged to translate the wording on a first-impression basis. The results of the double-translation process are compared to the original wording of the questionnaire in language A. The researcher should then work with the first group of bilingual translators to discuss discrepancies found in the two versions. The researcher should clarify the meanings of the questions and the response categories in doubt and have them translated into language B once again. Then, a third group of bilingual translators independently translates the second version of the questionnaire in language B back into language A. This process continues until the last translated version in language A is almost identical to the original version in language A. The last version of the questionnaire in language B can then be used as an equivalent instrument. This process is diagramed as shown in Figure 13.1. The translators should (1) be proficient in both languages, and (2) have backgrounds similar to those of the intended

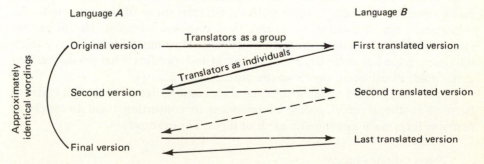

Figure 13.1

respondents. The rationale behind the translators working as a group in translating from language A to language B is for the researcher to consult with them closely in reaching wording which is by consensus the optimal version of the questionnaire in language B. When the translators translate the questionnaire back into language A, they are in fact simulating the respondents, so that individual interpretations of the wording are valuable in helping to assess intertranslator (simulating interrespondent) reliability in the wording of the questionnaire. In some situations, it becomes difficult to obtain proficient bilingual translators with backgrounds similar to those of the respondents. For example, the study may concern farmers in different cultures. In certain cultures almost all the farmers may not have knowledge of a second language. In this case, the researcher should employ a proficient bilingual translator to work with two or three persons who have characteristics similar to those of the respondents and who know the same language as the respondents. The translator first translates each question or set of response categories, and the simulated respondents work together to come up with proper wording understandable to them, which also has the same meaning as the original version as far as the translator can determine. A second group of simulated respondents should be asked to interpret the meanings of the questions and response categories in the second language to a bilingual translator who translates them back into the first language. This process can be repeated as before.

Construction of Response Categories and Precoding

A final issue in the preparation of the instrument deals with response categories and precoding. The researcher must decide for which questions response categories must be provided and how many categories should be used. As a rule, response categories must be provided if the questions deal with attitudes and opinions or with simple, straightforward questions such as sex, education, income, etc. Response categories should also be used if responses to the question can be formulated differently in terms of measurement units. For example, in asking what television shows a respondent has viewed in the past week, the researcher should specify whether the response should be in terms of specific shows or categories of shows (comedy, drama, detective, etc.) by providing the appropriate response categories, so that different interpretations of the question by the respondents can be avoided. In general, then, response categories should be provided unless the response is straightforward (e.g., How many hours did you watch television in the last three days? _____ hours) and specific (What job do you currently hold? Please be as specific as you can _____).

Precoding refers to the inclusion on the questionnaire of numerical codes to be used in the eventual coding of responses in converting them to machine-readable form, such as computer cards or tapes. For example,

Please indicate your sex:
_____ 1.   Female
_____ 2.   Male

The codes "1," for female, and "2," for male, appear beside the response categories. Furthermore, precoding can be done to specify the positions on the machine-readable form, such as computer cards, of each of the response items. For example:

Please indicate your birth date:
                                     Columns
_____ year, _____ month   18–19 _____

Thus, the response to the question about birth date can be converted to actual age by the coder when the completed questionnaire is returned. The age information, to be coded in columns 18 and 19 on a certain computer card, for example, can be entered by the coder immediately in the space provided on the right-hand side. Such precoding can save a lot of coding time when questionnaires are to be processed into machine-readable form. Precoding on the questionnaire can substantially reduce efforts later required in the processing of responses for data analysis.

Processing of Returned Instruments

When the questionnaire is to be sent to each respondent, a stamped return envelope should be enclosed. Such an enclosure encourages the participation of the respondent and a speedy return of the questionnaire. The added cost is usually more than compensated for by earlier returns and a higher response rate.

When a questionnaire is returned, the researcher should examine it to identify any inconsistencies and missing information. If a significant number of inconsistencies or amount of missing information occurs, the researcher may be forced to eliminate the questionnaire from further processing. Otherwise, the returned questionnaire should be properly identified and coded. The researcher may have to make decisions to eliminate minor inconsistencies. When in doubt, the particular response can be eliminated as missing data, or a random decision can be made by flipping a coin. The rule is not to allow subjective interpretation of the data on the part of the researcher or the coder.

Follow-ups

Follow-ups are important in conducting this type of survey, because questionnaire surveys tend to have lower response rates than interview surveys. The actual time gap between the initial mailing and the first follow-up depends on several factors, such as the speed of the mail service and the distance between the original location and the respondent location. As a rule of thumb, the time gap should be equal to the estimated mail traveling time for the two-way mailing plus three days, counting only weekdays. The first follow-up should contain a simple reminder to bring the respondent's attention to the fact that the researcher is anxiously waiting for the completed questionnaire. It should also state that, if the questionnaire has been returned, then the note should be disregarded, and if the respondent has misplaced the questionnaire, another copy of the questionnaire will be sent on request.

A second follow-up should be sent to those respondents whose questionnaires still have not arrived after another two weeks or after a similar time gap following the first follow-up. The second follow-up should contain a copy of the questionnaire and the covering letter, along with a note again reviewing the purpose and importance of the study and the respondent's participation. On the assumption that the previous questionnaire was either lost in the mail or misplaced, another copy of the questionnaire is enclosed. To demonstrate the urgency of the request, the enclosed return envelope should contain an airmail stamp, if the economic situation allows.

Usually, the original mailing and the two follow-ups result in a return of questionnaires from the overwhelming majority of those respondents who can be reached and who care to respond. Subsequent follow-ups usually cannot be justified by the additional cost involved for the additional percentage of responses.

PROCEDURE FOR THE INTERVIEW SURVEY

There are many similarities in conducting the questionnaire survey and the interview survey. In discussing the procedure for the interview survey, we will stress the points which will maximize the advantages of using interviewers in a survey and minimize the disadvantages and errors usually associated with this type of survey.

The interview survey takes many forms, ranging from the strict formal interview in which the interviewer follows instructions provided by the researcher and in no way varies the procedure or helps the respondent in formulating and verbalizing his responses, to the completely open-ended, in-depth interview in which the interviewer actively engages the respondent in conversation in the hope that a deeper understanding of certain opinions, attitudes, and behaviors can be obtained.

The discussion in this section will focus on the most popular form of the interview survey—dealing with a structured instrument, a large number of interviewers, and a large sample of respondents.

Selection of Interviewers

Assuming the interview instrument is prepared as discussed in Chapter 10, Measurement, and in the section "Procedure for the Questionnaire Survey" in this chapter, the researcher has the added responsibility of selecting interviewers. Several traits are desirable for all interviewers.[1] First, they must be *honest*. Honesty is not easy to detect in the selection process, but as soon as dishonesty is discovered in an interviewer in the training, the pretest, or the main study, he must be immediately dismissed. Second, interviewers must be *interested in the work and in the topics*. After several interviews, the work usually becomes routine, repetitive, and rather boring. Unless the interviewer is genuinely

---

[1] C. A. Moser and G. Kalton, *Survey Methods in Social Investigation,* 2d ed., Basic Books, New York, 1972, pp. 282–287.

interested in the work, the chances of making errors increase. Third, they must be *accurate* in following instructions, understanding responses, and recording responses. Fourth, interviewers must be *adaptable* in working with different topics and respondents. Many personal adjustments must be made to accommodate necessary questioning techniques in dealing with different topics and ways of establishing a comfortable relationship with a respondent. Fifth, they must have the appropriate *personality and temperament*. Ideally, they should be neither overaggressive nor oversociable. Pleasantness and a businesslike manner are required. Other factors to be considered in selecting interviewers are age (between 25 and 45), sex (women are usually preferred since they are perceived as being less aggressive, less competitive, and less hostile by potential respondents of both sexes), personal appearance, and verbal ability (to make statements clearly and with a regional accent to establish closer identity with the respondent).

While the desirable traits are known to the researcher, the selection of interviewers is not a straightforward matter. The general procedure involves the following steps. The researcher first advertises in the local mass media (usually newspapers) for interviewers. The advertisement usually generates many responses. The researcher may send a brochure describing the nature of the study, what is required of the interviewers, and how they will be paid. The brochure asks only those who are interested, willing, and capable to telephone to make a personal appointment. This simple screening usually eliminates more than 80 percent of the initial applicants. At the meeting, the applicant is again briefed on what the study is about, the interviewer's responsibilities and activities, etc. Then, the applicant is asked to conduct a brief interview of the researcher or one of his collaborators (usually a two- or three-page interview schedule which contains a variety of questions and response categories). This mock interview will provide an opportunity for the researcher to examine the mannerisms, ability, and personality of the applicant as he handles an interview situation. The simulating interviewee can provide incorrect, irrelevant, and complicated responses to test the persistence and patience of the applicant. Then, an evaluation is made for each applicant, and an invitation to a training session is sent to those who seem qualified. By the time the training session begins, usually about 10 to 15 percent of the original applicants have survived and are still sufficiently interested to care to appear.

How many interviewers should a study employ? The general rule is that each interviewer should be responsible for less than 20 completed interviews. A limited number of interviews for each interviewer results in less pressure on the interviewer to rush through interviews in a limited time span and, thus, less chance for low morale and inaccuracies. It also allows the researcher to complete the field work in a short period of time.

An interviewer should be paid on an hourly basis (the actual amount of time consumed in conducting interviews, traveling, and follow-up trips when previous trips have failed to reach the respondents) rather than on a per-interview or per-trip basis. Per-interview and per-trip pay schedules encourage interviewers to rush through interviews or to make a minimal effort to identify the respondents. To prevent abuse of the hourly pay schedule, interviewers should be informed, before the field work, that the amount of time spent per case will be analyzed for each interviewer periodically, and that the services of extremely slow workers will be terminated.

Are college students good interviewers? Because many researchers are affiliated with universities and colleges, the temptation is strong to employ students. However, there is evidence that students, as compared with trained recruits, are less likely to complete interviews successfully and more likely to experience refusals. It is not clear whether intensive training of students can eliminate this difference, or whether students are ineffective because they differ basically (e.g., in age, education, and intelligence) from the members of the general public usually involved in large-scale surveys. In any case, college students should be used only if (1) there is no other recourse (because of lack of response from applicants or lack of adequate pay for general interviewers), or (2) when the interviewees are also students or have socioeducational backgrounds similar to those of the students.

Training of Interviewers

If possible, an interview manual should be provided for each interviewer; or, at least, the instructions for an interview should be mimeographed and given to each interviewer. The interviewer must then familiarize himself with the final draft of the instrument. Also, it is desirable to involve the interviewers from the very beginning of the field work, including any pilot study or pretest, so that they may gain additional field experience; this also provides the researcher with suggestions for the improvement of the instrument or other field techniques.

After the interviewers have read the interview schedule with care, the researcher should go over the schedule slowly and thoroughly with them, providing instructions and explanations as he goes along. Interviewers should be encouraged to raise questions. The researcher should make clear the specific tasks required of the interviewer, how each item and its response categories should be presented, and how the responses should be recorded.

After the explanations the interviewers are asked to practice interviewing in pairs. Each interview must be fully recorded as in an actual field situation. Then, several interviewers are randomly selected to conduct demonstration interviews in which they take turns interviewing the researcher and his collaborators or each other in front of other interviewers. The demonstration interviews should be conducted in a very informal fashion, so that they can be interrupted by anyone present for clarifications, suggestions, or questions. Again, the interviewer must behave as he would in an actual interview situation. Demonstration interviews should bring out and resolve most potential interviewing problems. The researcher should encourage criticism and suggestions. If warranted, changes should be made in the instructions provided to the interviewers.

Next, the interviewer is asked to go out and conduct three or four practice interviews—interviews with strangers or acquaintances who fit the description of the respondents. The interviews should be conducted as if they were actual interviews. In the final session of interviewing training, the results of these practice interviews are discussed among the researcher and the interviewers. The completed schedules are examined carefully by the researcher, as a final assessment of the competence and carefulness of each interviewer. The interviewers should be reminded that any omissions and abbreviations on the schedule must be completely filled in immediately after the interview. The interviewers are also encouraged to record personal comments and reactions to the interview situation.

Interviewers should be trained so that they are able to perform interviews that require: (1) being accepted by the respondent; (2) providing clear statements, including explanations of questions, without leading the respondent or biasing the responses; (3) probing to obtain the proper responses; and (4) recording responses accurately. The interviewer must gain the respondent's confidence in an extremely short period of time—usually less than five minutes. For different types of persons, different approaches should be used. Usually the interviewer should adopt the respondent's behavior. For an outgoing, outspoken respondent, a timid and quiet interviewer would not be a match. Similarly, a quiet and introverted respondent needs a quiet and understanding interviewer. Interviewers should be trained to play different roles as interviewers. They are warned against "overrapport" with the respondent. Overfriendliness tends to encourage the respondent to formulate responses he thinks may suit the interviewer's expectations.

While the interviewer should be skillful in presenting questions clearly, the neutrality of his own stand on the issues must be strictly maintained. Cooperating respondents tend to seek cues from the interviewers as to whether they are "on the right track," and try not to offend the interviewer. The interviewer should maintain an understanding but noncommittal posture. This can be achieved by looking into the eyes of the respondent, nodding his head slightly, making a verbal acknowledgment such as "Hm . . . ," "I see," or "I understand," and continuously writing down the responses. On the other hand, any overt remarks or body gestures suggesting agreement or opposition to the views expressed should be avoided. Sometimes a respondent seeks reinforcement by asking the interviewer, "Don't you think so?" or "Wouldn't you agree?" The interviewer must refrain from expressing his opinion. Rather, he should simply respond, "It's your views that count in this interview and I understand your point," and proceed.

When the respondent does not provide the appropriate responses, he has either misunderstood the question or tried to skirt the issue. The interviewer should be trained to probe for the appropriate response. An inappropriate response is one the meaning of which is unclear in terms of the question. For example, if a respondent responds to the question, "Do you prefer watching television or reading books," with "Yes," it is an inappropriate response. The interviewer should then clarify the question. Usually, repeating the same question is sufficient.

Finally, recording must be accurate—to the word, if possible. Not only should responses to open-ended questions be verbatim, but those to structured questions should also be recorded with extreme care. Simple checking errors (e.g., a male respondent checked as female) can easily occur.

While the formal training of the interviewers may be conducted and completed in one or two weeks, informal interviewer training continues through the pilot study and the main study. Problems with each interviewer must be dealt with individually.

Preparation of Interview Schedule and Materials

While the general strategy of instrumentation for an interview schedule is similar to that for a questionnaire, there are variations.

Instead of a covering letter, the interview schedule should begin with a statement with which the interviewer introduces himself to the respondent or the person who answers the door. The statement, containing information similar to that in the covering letter, is less formal and uses shorter sentences. It usually starts like this, "Hello, I am _____ from _____. We are doing a study on [the general topic]. [The name of the respondent] has been selected in a scientific sampling procedure to participate in the study. It will only take _____ minutes. . . ." To help reduce suspicion, an identification card bearing the interviewer's name and the sponsoring organization can be helpful.

In the schedule itself, instructions for the interviewer and the respondent should be made clear to both the interviewer and the respondent. To avoid confusion, any instructions to the interviewer should be identified by using a set of specific symbols, for example, brackets or blocks. (E.g., "What is your religious affiliation? [Hand the card listing religious groups to the respondent.])

Instructions should be provided for locating and identifying the respondent. In some sampling plans, only a description of the potential respondent is provided, such as "married, 18 to 44 years old, woman." In this case, it is important that the schedule begins with specific instructions to the interviewer to ask a series of questions such as "I have to interview a lady who is married and is between 18 and 44 years of age. Are there persons in the house who fit this description?" Further instructions must be provided in case there is more than one person in the household who fits the description. Usually, the rule is for the interviewer to alternatively choose the first or second name mentioned (to take the first person fitting the description in the first household which has more than one person fitting the description, and the second person fitting the description in the next household which has more than one person fitting the description, and then the first person fitting the description again). The interviewer must fully understand and follow the instructions.

One device that can be used to help respondents when questions contain many or hard-to-formulate response categories is a response card which is an index card listing all the response categories. This device is most helpful when the information to be obtained from the respondent is private (e.g., income) or complicated (attitudes). Reading of the response categories by the interviewer may sound too complicated or be embarrassing. For example, in the NORC annual social survey, a response card is used in conjunction with a question regarding the household income of the respondent.[2] (See Appendix A for the use of response cards.)

> In which of these groups did your total family income, from all sources, fall last year, before taxes, that is. Just tell me the letter. [Hand respondent card J.]

As soon as the interviewer reads off the question, he hands the respondent a response card (card J) which contains the following categories:

A. Under $1,000
B. $1,000 to $2,999
C. $3,000 to $3,999
D. $4,000 to $4,999
E. $5,000 to $5,999
F. $6,000 to $7,499
G. $7,500 to $8,999
H. $9,000 to $11,499
I. $11,500 to $14,999
J. $15,000 to $19,999
K. $20,000 to $24,999
L. $25,000 or over

The response card method usually improves the response rate for questions of a similar type.

Toward the end of the schedule, additional information about the respondent and the household can be gathered by using the interviewer as an observer. The interviewer can be asked to rate the verbal ability of the respondent and the extent of his willingness and his attitude toward participation in the interview, and to identify particular questions with which the respondent experienced difficulty either in understanding or in providing appropriate responses. Such information helps in assessing the adequacy of the schedule relative to the respondent's personality and ability to provide the responses obtained in the study.

Other observations the interviewer may report may include a description of the house (type of house or apartment—single, duplex, row, apartment building, trailer, etc.) and of the neighborhood (general maintenance of houses on the street and types of houses on the street). Such information provides an environmental view of the living conditions of the respondent.

At the end of the schedule, items must be provided asking the interviewer to indicate the time and date of the interview, length of the interview, name of the interviewer, and name, address, and telephone number (if obtained) of the respondent. Such information can be used to assess any systematic differences among the interviewers in terms of response patterns, and to reach respondents in subsequent selective verifications of the interview and information obtained.

[2] National Opinion Research Center, University of Chicago. *General Social Survey Codebook for Spring 1973.*

Sampled interview items and response categories commonly used in interview surveys appear in Appendix A. Most of these have been used in national surveys. The researcher is encouraged to use them, so that data from different studies can be compared.

Organization and Supervision of Field Work

Before any actual field work is conducted, it may be necessary to inform local agencies such as the police or the city government. This action will become more and more essential as more and more institutes, government offices, commercial firms, and other organizations utilize the door-to-door technique to either gain information from the population or sell products. The public may be sufficiently harassed to react suspiciously or even violently. The tendency of the public to seek verification or register complaint at local agencies is on the increase.

A final briefing of the interviewers preceding the field work should remind them that participation of any respondent must be voluntary and that no force or pressure should be exerted on any respondent to participate. The increasing concern on the part of the federal government (especially the National Institutes of Health) for the mental and physical health of human subjects used in all forms of research encourages the researcher to guarantee the mental and physical well-being of participating respondents in a survey as well. Interviewers should also be reminded that their dress and appearance must be in conformity with community norms. Suits and dresses do not help interviewers in slums, just as jeans and sandals do not help interviewers in executive suites.

A headquarters should be established while field work is being carried out. The researcher or a collaborator should be stationed and available to the interviewers, so that an interviewer encountering any difficult or unexpected situation can telephone in quickly and receive advice or aid.

The researcher should be aware of the activities and progress of the interviewers at all times. The interviewers can be asked to report either in person or over the telephone periodically and be required to return completed schedules on certain dates. The researcher should also have periodic meetings with the interviewers if the field work extends into weeks.

As soon as the completed schedules have been returned, the researcher or his collaborators should go over them quickly but carefully. Should any inconsistencies or inadequacies be uncovered, clarifications must be sought from the interviewer immediately. And, if necessary, the interviewer may be asked to return to the respondent to seek clarifications.

While the field work is in progress, the researcher should also keep a record on the progress of each interviewer and interview success in each area. Adjustments of assignments of interviewers should be made to increase the speed of field work, reduce or eliminate the workload of unreliable or slow interviewers, and send more experienced interviewers to areas where resistance (the refusal rate) to the survey is strong.

In short, the field work in an interview survey demands decisions and adjustments from the researcher not unlike those required of a general conducting a military campaign. Unless detailed planning and careful execution are carried out, the results may be disastrous—rendering the data useless because they have all sorts of biases and errors.

Verification and Organization of Data   To determine the validity of the information as recorded by the interviewers, the researcher can select a subsample of respondents, contact them on the telephone or by mail, and ascertain that (1) the interview indeed took place, and (2) information was correctly recorded (by asking the respondent a selected question from the schedule).

Schuman has suggested a random probe technique to evaluate the validity of structured questions.[3] In each interview, a number of randomly preselected items is probed. As each question is asked in the interview, the interviewer immediately follows with a simple probe, "Can you explain a little why you say that?" "Could you tell me a little more about that?" or "Could you give me an example of that?" The response or lack of response to the probe is then recorded accurately by the interviewer. The results of such randomly selected probes are a set of explanations for each respondent, each question, and each interviewer. An independent group of coders is then asked to read the explanations without seeing the actual responses. Then they try to predict the respondent's responses and evaluate the "fit" between each explanation and the actual response recorded. Using a simple 5-point "fitness" scale ("1," excellent explanation for prediction; "2," adequate explanation for prediction; "4," inadequate explanation for prediction; and "5," no fit), and probing failure (when the explanation is a literal repetition of the response), the researcher can evaluate the extent of validity of questions, respondents' responses, and each interviewer's probing. A question with a high score indicates a comprehension problem involving the wording of the question, and is an indication of poor instrumentation. A respondent with a high score probably had a problem understanding the question, and this is an indication of invalid responses from the respondent. An interviewer with a high rate of probing failure probably did not probe adequately, and this is an indication of invalid responses induced by improper interviewing.

Thus, the random probe can be used in both the pilot study and the main study to ascertain the extent of invalidity of responses which results from distortions introduced by a respondent, a question, or an interviewer. The evaluation then helps the researcher make decisions as to whether or not the data are valid enough to warrant further analysis.

The verified data constitute the raw and original data. They are also the basis for any further activities the researcher may conduct in terms of the respondents. The researcher should take necessary steps to safeguard the identity of the respondents and the linkage between specific information and specific respondents. Each respondent should be designated by a number. The researcher

---

[3] Howard Schuman, "The Random Probe: A Technique for Evaluating the Validity of Closed Questions," *American Sociological Review,* vol. 31, pp. 218–222, 1966.

should be sure that only a few research personnel know the actual names and addresses of the respondents. All other research personnel should know only numbers.

When the interviewers are discharged, they should be reminded again of their ethical responsibility not to reveal any respondent's identity or any information. They may be asked to sign a statement promising not to reveal the respondents' identities or information obtained in the interview.

OTHER SURVEY METHODS

While the mail questionnaire and the personal interview are the standard survey methods, other methods which are variations of these techniques provide advantages in certain research plans.

Telephone Interview

A simple variation of the personal interview is the telephone interview. The procedure is similar to that for the personal interview, except for two things. First, the interviewer has to rely completely on his audio ability and that of the respondent in obtaining information. Facial and body gestures on the part of the interviewer cannot serve as cues to bias the respondent's answers. At the same time, however, the interviewer has more problems in assessing the validity of the information being provided by the respondent. Second, the telephone interview differs from the personal interview in that it represents a substantial saving in cost. Telephone interviews can be effective for brief interviews. Interviews with professionals (e.g., architects, physicians) are easier to obtain on the telephone, as such respondents tend to maintain schedules too busy to accommodate an interviewer's visit. Telephone interviews have also been used to study the impact of a major news event, such as the assassination of a president. The respondents can be reached quickly, and information can be gathered while recall of the news is still fresh.

Telephone interviews can be useful only when the respondents can be located through telephone directories. This constraint usually eliminates its use in surveys dealing with the general public, since not all persons or households have telephones or listed telephone numbers.

To provide the respondents with more accurate information about the interview schedule, a researcher can use a more elaborate procedure in telephone interviews. First, the interviewer or the researcher calls the respondent and briefs him about the purpose of the study and solicits his participation. If the respondent agrees to participate, an appointment is made for a second telephone call. A copy of the interview schedule is immediately sent to the respondent. So, when the actual interview takes place at the appointed time, the respondent has the schedule in front of him. This procedure can reduce any misunderstanding caused by restricted audio cues in the telephone conversation. In some cases, in order to not let the respondent see the instructions provided on the schedule for the interviewer, a questionnaire rather than a schedule is sent to the respondent. Thus, the telephone survey combines questionnaire and interview techniques.

The Group Survey

Another alternative method of survey also involves characteristics of both the questionnaire survey and the interview survey. The *group survey* can take place when a group of respondents, such as all the teachers in a school, all the employees in an office, or all the prisoners in a prison, is gathered together. Then, either a questionnaire or an interview strategy is employed. In the *group interview survey,* an interviewer reads off the questions and provides each respondent with an answer form on which to record his responses. The interviewer can indicate to the respondent how to record the responses ("If you agree with the statement, put a check mark in box 12a, and if you disagree with the statement, put a check mark in box 12b"). This method can be effective for a number of reasons. First, it is more economical than personal interviews. Second, it eliminates biases introduced by using interviewers. Third, it facilitates obtaining information from less educated respondents. However, in using the group interview survey with less educated respondents, it is important that the answer forms contain simple-to-understand symbols and that the interviewer repeat the question and the response categories as frequently as the respondents request. Also, additional research personnel should be stationed throughout the room, so that individual questions or problems can be handled quickly and effectively.

In the *group questionnaire survey,* questionnaires are passed out to the respondents and no interviewer is involved. The respondents proceed as in the mail questionnaire situation. However, they are allowed to ask questions of the research personnel, which usually includes the researcher and several associates all of whom are trained to handle questions and problems relating to the questionnaire. The group questionnaire survey also has several advantages. First, it provides opportunities for respondents to raise questions and interact with the researchers, so that misunderstanding about the questionnaire can be minimized. Second, it is economical and time-saving. When the respondents tend to have the same working schedule, as in the case of teachers, the group questionnaire technique provides a fast and efficient way of administering a questionnaire to a large number of respondents.

While group surveys have important advantages, they also have limitations. The major drawback is the potential that the group situation will bias the responses. This is especially true if the questions concern abnormal behaviors and interpersonal relationships. These issues may prove too sensitive for the respondents in an essentially "public" situation. The implicit "group pressure" as defined by the group situation may encourage noncommittal responses (many "no," "don't know," and "so-so" responses) or responses toward the ideals as perceived by each respondent for the group. A second problem with group surveys is control over the respondents. If not handled properly, some respondents may initiate hostile or joking remarks and set the tone for the whole group. Thus, the introductory remarks made by the researcher are crucial yet difficult, because of the diversified personalities in the group. Also, the group situation affords an opportunity for interaction among respondents, which results in an additional control problem for the researcher. A third difficulty in a group survey is the probability that the study will be perceived as sanctioned by and therefore available to some authority. The respondent's perception of fear, threat, or anger can result in any number of systematic errors being introduced into the data. The further concern for potential lack of confidentiality of the information will tend to introduce a bias in the data toward the group or organizational norms and ideals.

Despite these difficulties, group survey methods can be useful alternatives to the mail questionnaire and personal interview methods. The economical factor as well as the combined features of both questionnaire and survey techniques provides opportunities for the researcher to reach large numbers of respondents quickly and systematically. However, if the nature of the study and the situation tend to induce any of the major difficulties mentioned, the group survey may lose all its merits.

Panel Survey

Another method of survey is the *panel survey*. The panel survey is a direct extension of a questionnaire or interview survey over time. The basic strategy is to survey the same group of respondents repeatedly over time. There are several important advantages in using the panel survey. First it allows the researcher to observe and assess any changes which take place among the respondents over time. It thus presents a dynamic view of the activities the researcher is interested in. Questionnaire and interview surveys are usually considered one-shot methods which present a view of activities for a single slice of time. Thus, the view is that of a "frozen" piece of the ongoing activities. The panel survey provides data from several slices of time.

A second advantage of the panel survey is that it provides an opportunity for a researcher to ascertain causal orders among different variables.[4] One problem associated with the questionnaire and interview surveys is that, because the data are gathered at one point in time, all variables are measured simultaneously. Thus, any relationships found among the variables can only be considered covariational rather than causal. Only when the nature of the variables is such that they can be naturally sequenced over time can survey data be analyzed for causal relations. For example, a person's educational attainment usually precedes his occupational attainment; therefore, a causal linkage from educational attainment to occupational attainment can be analyzed in the data. When the variables themselves do not appear in temporal sequence, then any statements concerning their causal relations are only conjectural. However, the panel survey measures the variables over time. Thus, if there is a distinctive causal influence of variable X on variable Y rather than of Y on X, such a relation can be detected. This can

[4] Donald C. Pelz and Frank M. Andrews, "Detecting Causal Priorities in Panel Study Data," *American Sociological Review*, vol. 29, pp. 836–848, December 1964.

Time 1   Time 2

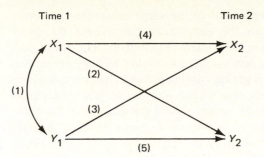

Figure 13.2 Relations between two variables measured at two points in time (1 and 2) in a panel survey.

be demonstrated with a simple example involving two variables (X and Y) measured at two different time points in a panel survey. The resulting relations are shown in Figure 13.2.

The relations between X_1 and Y_2 (X measured at time 1 and Y measured at time 2), and between Y_1 and X_2, are crucial in the causal analysis. For if there is a causal effect from X to Y, then it is expected that the relationship between X_1 and Y_2 would be stronger than that between Y_1 and X_2. In other words, if X has a causal influence on Y, rather than vice versa, then the effect of X on Y over time should be greater than the effect of Y on X over the same period of time. Thus, a simple comparison of relations 2 and 3 in Figure 13.2, taking into account the initial relation between X_1 and Y_1 at time 1, called *cross-lagged coefficients,* should reveal whether or not the causal influence of X on Y indeed exists.[5]

These two assets make the panel survey a most desirable alternative method of survey. However, it has some drawbacks as well. First, it is more costly than one-shot survey methods. It may cost more than twice as much, as the problem of tracking down the same respondents and obtaining their cooperation repeatedly can become most time-consuming. Second, there is the problem of exposing respondents to the same instrument repeatedly. The multiple exposure may result in sensitization of the respondents to the instrument and introduce biases in their subsequent responses to the same instrument. This problem can be countered by introducing additional (and also representative) respondents from the same population into subsequent surveys as control respondents. The data from these respondents, who participate in only one of the subsequent surveys, can be com-

[5] For detailed discussion of this analytical model, see David R. Heise, "Causal Inference from Panel Data," in Edgar F. Borgatta and George W. Bohrnstedt (eds.), *Sociological Methodology 1970,* Jossey-Bass, San Francisco, 1970, chap. 1, pp. 3–27. More complicated analytical models for panel data involving unobserved concepts (factors) are discussed in: Otis D. Duncan, "Unmeasured Variables in Linear Models for Panel Analysis," in Herbert L. Costner (ed.), *Sociological Methodology 1972,* Jossey-Bass, San Francisco, 1972, chap. 2, pp. 36–82; Douglas A. Hibbs, Jr., "Problems of Statistical Estimation and Causal Inference in Time-series Regression Models," in Herbert L. Costner (ed.), *Sociological Methodology 1973–1974,* Jossey-Bass, San Francisco, 1974, chap. 10, pp. 252–308; and David A. Kenny, "Cross-lagged and Synchronous Common Factors in Panel Data," in Arthur S. Goldberger and Otis D. Duncan (eds.), *Structural Equation Models in the Social Sciences,* Seminar Press, New York, 1973, chap. 8, pp. 153–167.

pared to the data from the panel respondents in the same subsequent survey to determine whether prior exposure to the instrument has caused the panel respondents to respond differently from the control respondents. The use of control respondents in the panel survey is demonstrated in Figure 13.3. For point 3 in time, for example, data from the panel group, control group 2, and control group 4 can be compared. If any prior exposure to the instrument has affected the responses, then the data from the panel group should be different from those from control group 2. Further, if multiple exposures increase the bias, the data from the panel group should be different from the data from control group 4. If the data are similar, then the researcher may conclude that sensitization may not be a problem for the particular panel survey. Should the data show differences, indicating that sensitization does affect the response pattern, the researcher can make necessary adjustments in the analysis of the data to take such effects into account.

A third potential drawback of the panel survey, concerning measurement errors and fluctuations, also should be taken into account. Measurement errors and fluctuations, rather than the genuine influence of one variable over another, may also induce changes in response patterns. However, this problem can be detected and resolved by the use of control respondents. For if measurement errors and fluctuations have occurred, the data from the panel group and from different control groups for the same point in time should also show different response patterns, and they can be taken into account in the analysis by the researcher.

Still another potential difficulty with the panel survey is the correspondence between the points of measurement and the intervals of causation. That is, the interval between points of measurement may not correspond to the interval in which the causation or change takes effect. The intervals of measurement may either be too short or too long. The result is that the causal priorities cannot be detected with ease. For if the interval of measurement is too short, then the causal influence may not have already occurred and, if it is too long, the causal influence may have already waned. One way to take this possibility into account is to vary the intervals of measurement over time. If the interval from time 1 to time 2 is four units (weeks, months, etc.), then the researcher can vary the interval from time 2 to time 3 to six units, etc.

		TIME		
GROUP	1	2	3	4
Panel	✓	✓	✓	✓
Control 1		✓		
Control 2			✓	
Control 3				✓
Control 4	✓		✓	
Control 5	✓			✓

Figure 13.3 Use of control respondents in panel survey.

The countermeasures in the abovementioned two drawbacks, involving addition of control respondents and manipulation of time intervals, introduce additional costs. Thus, they are generally not used. However, when the economic situation allows, the panel survey is a most desirable alternative to one-shot surveys, because of the unusual opportunities it provides for a researcher to study the dynamic and causal relations among variables.

PROBLEMS OF SURVEYS

Response Rate

Several problems are common to most of the survey methods discussed and deserve careful consideration by any researcher before a survey is conducted. Probably foremost among the problems is the response rate, or the nonresponse rate. Since one of the most important reasons for conducting a survey is that it deals with a large representative sample from a population and thus permits inference from the sampled data to the population, it is imperative that the sample maintain its representativeness which may be affected severely or even fatally when a substantial portion of the respondents fail to participate in the study. There is no fixed rule as to what constitutes a good response rate, and there are also different opinions about how a response should be calculated.

In general, a *response rate* is a ratio between the number of returned usable questionnaires or schedules and the number of reachable sampled respondents. A respondent is not reachable if he has died, moved out of the defined population area, has lost the characteristics of the population (e.g., in a study of active persons in a profession, a person who has retired, resigned, or for other reasons is no longer associated with the profession), or is physically incapable, mentally incapable, or both, of participation (unless the study focuses on such persons). For example, if a sample of 1,000 respondents is drawn from the population, of which 100 are not reachable and 500 have actually participated in the survey, then the response rate is approximately 56 percent (500/900).

Most social researchers feel that, for a survey of the general public in the United States, a response rate of 50 percent or higher in a questionnaire survey is adequate, 60 percent or higher is good, and more than 70 percent is very good. However, these are simply rough guides formulated by past experiences dealing with questionnaire surveys. For the interview survey, the expected response rate is higher than that of the questionnaire survey. An interview survey should have a 15 to 20 percent better response rate than a comparable questionnaire survey. But the actual response rates vary greatly from survey to survey, depending on the respondents involved, the training of the interviewers, the construction and pretest of the instrument, and the pursuit of follow-ups. It is not unusual for mail questionnaire surveys to reach response rates better than 85 percent or even 90 percent. For example, for a series of mail questionnaire surveys conducted of groups of 30,000 scientists, engineers, and technologists in the United States, the

Johns Hopkins Center for Research in Scientific Communication attained response rates never less than 80 percent and averaging in the 90th percentile.[6]

Regardless of how good the response rate, the researcher is responsible for examining any possible biases in response patterns. Were female respondents more likely to respond than male respondents? Were older respondents more likely to respond than younger respondents? Were white respondents more likely to respond than nonwhite respondents? Any significant lack of response from a particular group weakens the precision of the inference from the data to the population. Thus, the researcher should always attempt to gather information from other sources about the sampled respondents who did not respond, so that comparisons between them and those who did respond can be made to ascertain the existence and extent of bias introduced into the data because of the underrepresentation of certain types of respondents. If such a bias is uncovered, the researcher could either make additional and concerted efforts to obtain data from the underrepresented respondents, or make necessary analytical adjustments. The analytical adjustments required are similar to those used in dealing with disproportionate samples (see Chapter 9, pages 150–151). Bias introduced by low response rates can have a drastic effect on the usefulness of the data in making inferences to the population. Thus, the researcher must warn the reader in reports dealing with the data of restrictions on inferences made from unrepresentative response patterns.

Interactions among Instrument, Respondent, and Interviewer

A second problem in survey studies concerns the interactions among the instrument, the respondent, and the interviewer (if used). Such interactions generally induce the respondents to respond toward neutrality or toward perceived ideals. Similarly, untrained or inexperienced interviewers tend to record responses in the direction of their own perceptions and judgments. It has been found that in interviews (1) questions posing threats to the respondents and (2) interviewers who lack experience and lack knowledge of the respondents and their social environment or who come from social backgrounds different from those of the respondents tend to induce response biases.[7] Thus, interviewers should be selected from those having backgrounds similar to those of the respondents. In training the interviewers, stress should be placed on the need for maintaining *objectivity and empathy* in interviewing. Empathy is the ability to "stand in the shoes of the other person." It is a role-playing activity in which the interviewer attempts to understand and record opinions expressed by a respondent from his standpoint. However, no standardized empathy training kit is available to researchers.

Interactions between the respondents and the instrument and the interviewer also create potential bias from the arousal of suspicion of the auspices of the study. If a respondent suspects that the study will serve a police, administrative,

[6] Johns Hopkins Center for Research in Scientific Communication, *The Role of the National Meeting in Scientific and Technical Communication,* Baltimore, vol. 1, June 1970.

[7] J. Allen Williams, Jr., "Interviewer Role Performance: A Further Note on Bias in the Information Interview," *Public Opinion Quarterly,* vol. 32, pp. 287–294, 1968.

or service function for a certain organization, he may bias his responses by withholding negative information or opinions, or by providing distorted responses to protect himself from possible use of the data by the organization against his well-being. This type of biasing behavior intensifies when the questions deal with what the respondents perceive as abnormal (relative to the sponsoring organization or organizations which may obtain the data) or deviant activities.

Lack of Dynamics

A third major problem of the survey is that it presents a "frozen" slice of reality. With the exception of the panel survey, the data are collected at one point in time. It is true that the data may be collected from geographic cross-sections and from different cohorts composed of different groups of persons defined according to age, sex, race, education, and other characteristics, thus allowing the researcher to conduct a comparative analysis, e.g., young versus old, less educated versus more educated, black versus white, and South versus North. But such comparisons make sense only in terms of one point in time and do not provide a view of how things became what they are and how things will be in the future. In essence, the data do not consider time as an intrinsic variable relating to the "frozen" slice of reality. For example, the difference between older people and younger people today cannot be used to predict how the younger people will become when they grow old, simply because the behaviors and opinions of the older people today have been influenced by events and experiences tied to their past, and such events and experiences may not occur or affect today's younger people as they grow old.

This valid criticism reminds all social researchers of a fundamental limitation of survey data and increases their consideration of combining the survey method with other types of methods to compensate for the lack of dynamic view of the activities studied. The use of the panel survey is a move in this direction. The incorporation of life histories into the data is another step in this direction. Respondents, thus, are asked not only about their current activities, such as their current job, but also their job history, educational history, family history, etc., so that a mapping can be made to link the past to the present and to sequence events as they occurred in the person's life and as they might have influenced subsequent events. While recall may present a problem in the collection of such data, with proper interviewer training, structuring of the questions, and analytical techniques, life histories have been successfully gathered in social research.[8] The main strategy of structuring the questions is to lead the respondent back to a significant event early in his life (such as when he quit school or when he graduated from an elementary school) and let him recall all the events relating to the variables of interest to the researcher in each time segment (say, four years)

---

[8] Jorge Balan et al., "A Computerized Approach to the Processing and Analysis of Life Histories Obtained in Sample Surveys," *Behavioral Science,* vol. 14, no. 2, pp. 105–120, March 1969; Zahava D. Blum, Nancy L., Karweit, and Aage B. Sorensen, *A Method for the Collection and Analysis of Retrospective Life Histories,* Center for Social Organization of Schools, report no. 48, Johns Hopkins University, Baltimore, July 1969.

following the event. However, life histories are possible only for events and behaviors perceived as significant to the respondent. Their use remains untested for opinions, attitudes, and other psychological types of information.

Other methods which can help provide some dynamic views of survey data include observations and documentary-historical data, discussed in Chapter 12.

SUMMARY

The survey is by far the most commonly used method of data collection in social research. Because of its ability to deal with large numbers of respondents and to handle elaborate instruments, it is best for studies intending to make inferences from a sample to a population. The survey takes many forms, ranging from the mail questionnaire to in-depth personal interviews. While the questionnaire method is less costly, the interview method usually yields more valid and reliable data—when the interviewers are properly trained.

A successful survey depends on the many activities the researcher carries out and supervises. Among them are the preparation of the instrument (including instructions, questions, and response categories), training of interviewers, determination of the response rate, and validation of data obtained.

Different types of research situations, respondents, and research purposes call for alternative survey methods such as the telephone interview, the group survey, and the panel survey. The panel survey is especially useful in obtaining a dynamic view of social phenomena and in ascertaining causal priorities among variables.

The survey, like many other obtrusive methods of data collection, can be affected by biases introduced in the interactions among the instrument, the respondents, and the interviewers. But with proper planning and execution, the survey remains the most powerful method of data collection available to the social researcher to infer results from a sample to a population.

Chapter 14

The Experiment

In the methods of data collection so far discussed, it is usually difficult for the researcher to assess causal relations among variables. The panel survey helps, as well as some recently developed methods of data analysis. But the prevailing method for testing causal relations used by social scientists, especially psychologists, is the experiment. Discussion of the causal analysis of nonexperimental data will be deferred to Chapter 16. In this chapter, the experiment as a method of data collection will be considered.

The best way to illustrate the usefulness of the experiment is to give an example. Suppose a researcher is interested in assessing the effect of housing arrangement on the residents' racial prejudice. More specifically, if he wishes to find out whether or not integrated housing, as contrasted to segregated housing, reduces the residents' prejudice toward a minority group, the simplest method of data collection would be to conduct a survey of sampled respondents from two different types of housing developments—integrated and segregated. Suppose the researcher obtained from such a survey the results shown in Table 14.1. Among the respondents residing in segregated housing developments 75 percent showed strong racial prejudice (on a certain attitudinal scale), as compared to only 25 percent of those residing in integrated housing developments. Assuming that sampling was random in both housing groups, can the researcher conclude that

Table 14.1   Racial Prejudice by Housing

Racial prejudice	Integrated housing	Segregated housing
Strong	25	75
Weak	75	25
Total	100	100

housing arrangement did have an effect on the extent of racial prejudice among the residents?

The answer to the question is necessarily negative, because the researcher does not really know whether the racial attitudes of the residents were influenced after they moved into a housing development, or whether the residents chose to live in a certain housing development because of their prior racial attitudes. The first possibility supports the researcher's hypothesis that housing arrangement influenced the racial attitudes of the residents.[1] But the second possibility, which is also consistent with the findings presented above, supports just the reverse of the first possibility, namely, that racial attitudes affected the selection of housing arrangement. It might be possible that housing arrangement and racial attitudes are interdependent, affecting each other; people with less racial prejudice may have tended to move into integrated housing developments, which in turn further reduced their racial prejudice. In any case, the researcher needs more evidence before any causal statement can be made.

One way to obtain better evidence to support the statement that housing arrangement had an effect on the racial attitudes of the residents is to utilize the following strategy. First, the researcher surveyed residents as they were moving into the different housing arrangements. Then, he resurveyed the same respondents after they had resided in the housing development over a period of time. If he obtained the results shown in Table 14.2, the researcher might have a stronger basis for believing that housing arrangement made a difference in terms of racial prejudice. For the data indicated that when people moved into different housing arrangements their initial racial attitudes showed no difference. Over a period of time, residents living in integrated housing showed a reduction in racial prejudice, while those in segregated housing showed no significant change.

One problem remains in considering the results in this design. The residents might actually have had different racial attitudes when they moved in, but did not feel sufficiently at ease with their neighbors and the researcher to confide their true feelings. Over a period of time, their interactions with their neighbors had reduced such anxiety, and thus at time 2 they revealed their true racial attitudes. The reverse could also be true, that the residents revealed their true attitudes at

---

[1] This statement may be valid even if the housing arrangement per se did not have a direct effect on the racial attitudes of the residents; the housing arrangement might have simply provided an initial structural proximity which in turn promoted social interactions among the residents which in turn affected their racial attitudes.

Table 14.2 Racial Prejudice by Housing in Two Time Periods

Racial prejudice	T_1 (time of moving in)		T_2 (after a period of time)	
	Integrated	Segregated	Integrated	Segregated
Strong	50	50	25	55
Weak	50	50	75	45
Total	100	100	100	100

time 1 but found it necessary to hide their true attitudes at time 2, as they felt their true feelings might offend their neighbors. The problem, then, concerns the possibility of unwillingness of respondents to provide true responses in surveys because they have committed themselves to certain activities and behaviors (e.g., moving into an integrated neighborhood) and they have to guard against offending others.

An even better strategy could be used if the researcher could assign people to different housing arrangements. Then, he could randomly assign respondents to two groups for the two housing developments with different housing arrangements. The randomization would guarantee that the people moving into the two different housing developments have similar racial attitudes. However, the researcher does not have to take this assumption for granted. He should conduct a survey before the people are assigned and before they move into the different housing developments to verify the fact that the two groups of residents have a similar distribution of racial attitudes. Finally, after the residents move in and have lived in the developments for a period of time, the researcher can conduct another survey to ascertain their racial prejudice again. Should he obtain the results shown in Table 14.3, then, the researcher would have more confidence in stating that for group 1, which was assigned to the integrated housing development, racial prejudice had been reduced over time, and that for group 2, which was assigned to the segregated housing development, racial prejudice had remained about the same. For at least he knows that the responses provided at time 1 were either true or similar between the two groups for any concealed attitudes, since at that time the residents did not know which housing development they would reside in. What remains is the probability that the respondents concealed their true responses at time 2. To reduce that probability, the researcher should construct the instrument with care so that

Table 14.3 Racial Prejudice by Housing before and after Housing Assignment

Racial prejudice	T_1 (before housing assignment)		T_2 (after a period of time)	
	Group 1	Group 2	Integrated	Segregated
Strong	50	50	25	55
Weak	50	50	75	45

the respondents are not aware of the purpose of the study at the times of the surveys. The questions dealing with racial attitudes should be disbursed throughout the questionnaire or the schedule and intermixed with other questions.

This hypothetical illustration in fact has provided the rationale as well as the basic design of the experiment. The last-mentioned strategy is the basic, although incomplete, experimental design. We may now discuss the rationale and basic design of the experiment more systematically.

RATIONALE AND BASIC DESIGN OF THE EXPERIMENT

The main reason for conducting an experiment is to try to determine the potential effect of one variable (the independent variable) on another (the dependent variable), while eliminating or controlling all other variables which may confound such a relationship. Thus, a "good" experiment should have three basic elements: random assignment of respondents to experimental groups, control over extraneous variables, and manipulation of the independent variable. The researcher uses randomization to ensure that the effects of other variables which may affect the independent and the dependent variables are evenly distributed in each and every experimental group, so that if they have any effect on the respondents they will affect all experimental groups similarly.

Other extraneous variables which are known or expected to have an effect on the independent variable, the dependent variable, or both, may be used as control variables and incorporated into the experimental design. For example, in a study of the effect of housing arrangement (integrated versus segregated) on racial prejudice, if the researcher expected that females tend to be less prejudiced than males, he could further analyze his findings for females and males separately in each housing arrangement. As most of the social activities and behaviors have multiple interlocking relationships, the more control variables brought into the design, the more chances the researcher has to demonstrate the effect of the independent variable on the dependent variable. For if in spite of the effects of the control variables on the dependent variable, either directly and independently or jointly with the independent variable, the independent variable still shows a significant effect on the dependent variable, the researcher then has greater confidence in the causal relation between the independent and the dependent variables.

Manipulation of the independent variable represents the most distinctive characteristic of the experiment, as compared to other methods of data collection. In the abovementioned example, the housing arrangement was the independent variable which was manipulated by the researcher—the residents were assigned to different housing developments. In reality, such manipulation may present many problems, but other variables are much easier to manipulate. For example, to assess the effect of source credibility on the believability of a message, the researcher can manipulate the identification of the sources who present the same message to two groups of subjects (as respondents are usually called in an experiment, because they are subjected to manipulation by the researcher). In delivering a message about how to feed young children, to one group of young mothers, the source person may identify herself as a nutritionist affiliated with a medical college and, to another, the same source may identify herself as a housewife with two young children. Many other variables can be manipulated in a similar fashion. The manipulation of the independent variable provides the researcher with an opportunity to vary the kind and the intensity of the values of the independent variable and to assess the effect of such variations on the dependent variable.

These three characteristics, randomization, control, and manipulation, make the experiment a desirable method to use in testing specific hypotheses, because of its ability to single out the independent and dependent variables while eliminating and controlling the effects of other variables. The manipulation aspect becomes more attractive to a researcher for testing a causal relation between two variables.

The basic design of an experiment involves the following steps: (1) selection and random assignment of subjects to experimental groups, (2) pretest measurement of the dependent variable, (3) differential treatment (manipulation), and (4) posttest measurement of the dependent variable. Figure 14.1 shows such a design.

Strictly speaking, the selection of the subjects should also use a representative sampling plan. But in most experiments conducted by social scientists, voluntary subjects are recruited. The researcher then screens the volunteers for competence in receiving, understanding, and responding to the type of manipulation to be performed. Hopefully, any bias introduced by this voluntary recruitment procedure will be eliminated by randomly assigning the subjects to different experimental groups.

Then the subjects are interviewed or required to complete a questionnaire in which measurement of the dependent variable is made. In order to not sensitize the subjects to the purpose of the study, the actual instrument used contains many

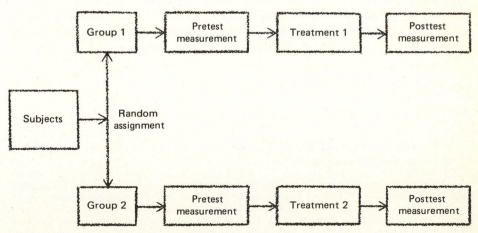

Figure 14.1   Basic design of an experiment.

more questions than those dealing with the dependent variable. In fact, successful manipulation depends to a large extent on the ability of the researcher to camouflage the measurement of the dependent variable in the pretest measurement.

Usually, there is a time lag between the pretest measurement and the treatment (manipulation of the independent variable); should there be any lingering suspicion about the purpose of the study among some subjects, the time lag hopefully will diminish it to a minimum. The variations of the treatment can be either different values or categories of the independent variable, such as the integrated housing versus the segregated housing in our illustration. Or, they could represent the presence and the absence of the independent variable (e.g., one group is exposed to a message while the other is not).

Finally, after another time gap, the instrument administered in the pretest measurement is again administered to the subjects.

To measure the effect of the independent variable on the dependent variable, a *difference score* is computed between the pretest measurement and the posttest measurement of the dependent variable for each subject in each group. For example, in an experiment to test the differential effects of source credibility on attitude change toward racial prejudice, if a subject in the high-credibility source group registered a "2" response on a racial prejudice scale of 7 points ("1," most prejudice; "7," least prejudice) in the pretest measurement and a "5" response on the same scale in the posttest measurement, he receives a difference score of positive 3 ($5 - 2 = +3$). We may then compute the averaged difference score for each group, say, the high-credibility source group and the low-credibility source group. From now on, the term *difference score* is used to indicate the averaged difference score for each group. Ideally, the difference score should be interpreted as the change in the value of the dependent variable (e.g., attitude change toward racial prejudice) resulting from the treatment (manipulation of the values of the independent variable, e.g., high- and low-credibility sources). But, in reality, such an interpretation is faulty, for the difference score may actually represent the effects of a number of other factors involved in the experiment, in addition to the effect of the independent variable. In the following sections, the various factors affecting the difference score, and elaborations of the basic design, will be discussed.

FACTORS AFFECTING THE DIFFERENCE SCORE[2]

There are at least seven factors which may contribute to the difference score:

    1   The treatment effect *T*. The effect of the treatment (the independent variable) on the difference score.

   [2] Further discussion of topics in this and the following sections appear in: Donald T. Campbell, "Factors Relevant to the Validity of Experiments in Social Settings," *Psychological Bulletin,* vol. 54, pp. 297–311, July 1957; Donald T. Campbell and Julian C. Stanley, *Experimental and Quasi-Experimental Designs for Research,* Rand McNally, Chicago, 1967; John Ross and Perry Smith, "Orthodox Experimental Designs," in Hubert M. Blalock, Jr., and Ann B. Blalock (eds.), *Methodology in Social Research,* McGraw-Hill, New York, 1968, pp. 333–389. This section is an abbreviated summary of the discussion by Ross and Smith.

2   The pretest measurement effect X. The pretest measurement may sensitize the subjects to the manipulation and the subsequent posttest measurement, thus affecting the difference score.

3   The time effect U. Since the experiment is conducted over a period of time, time-related events and maturation may influence a subject's exposure to the treatment and his responses on the posttest measurement. Time-related factors cannot be controlled by the researcher; thus, they are also known as *uncontrolled factors*.

4   The interaction effect between the pretest measurement and the uncontrolled factors I_{XU}. Sensitization to the pretest measurement and factors related to time may jointly affect the posttest measurement scores of a respondent. Here, the symbol I is used to indicate interaction effects, X the pretest measurement effect, and U the time effect. For example, sensitization to the pretest measurement may not by itself affect the posttest measurement. But should some event occur between the pretest measurement and the posttest measurement, it may cause the respondent to recall the pretest measurement, resulting in a certain pattern of response which otherwise would not have been formulated. An illustration might be a study focusing on attitudes toward blacks among whites. After the pretest measurement of such attitudes, along with a number of other attitude measurements, and preceding the posttest measurement, civil rights legislation has been passed into law by Congress. This event triggers the respondents' recall of the pretest measurement items and may result in more positive attitudes toward blacks in the posttest measurement than would be the case if the legislation had not occurred.

5   The interaction effect between the pretest measurement and the treatment I_{XT}. Sensitization to the pretest measurement and the exposure to the manipulation may jointly affect a subject's posttest measurement score.

6   The interaction effect between the treatment and the uncontrolled factors I_{TU}. Exposure to the treatment and the time-related uncontrolled factors may jointly affect the posttest score of a subject.

7   The interaction effect among the pretest measurement, the treatment, and the uncontrolled factors I_{XTU}. Finally, activities associated with the pretest measurement, the treatment, and the time-related uncontrolled factors may all jointly affect a subject's posttest score.

All the subjects in the basic experimental design discussed in the last section are subject to the influence of these factors. Further, these seven factors may independently affect the difference score. Thus, the difference score may represent the added effect of all seven factors. Using the symbol d to represent the difference score, a simple equation may be constructed to represent the relationship between d and the seven factors; namely, d is equal to the sum of the seven factors:

$$d = X + T + U + I_{XT} + I_{TU} + I_{XU} + I_{XTU} \tag{14.1}$$

Equation 14.1 shows that, for the basic experimental design in Figure 14.1, the averaged difference score for all the subjects in each experimental group in fact represents the consequences of the effects of the seven factors on the subjects over the period during which the experiment takes place.

The problem then becomes whether it is possible to identify each of the effects so that the difference score d can be decomposed and interpreted adequately and the effect of the treatment T on the difference score identified. For the researcher, equation 14.1 contains only one known score—the difference score computed from the change between the pretest measurement and the posttest measurement. In general, this type of equation (called a nonhomogeneous equation) can be solved for only one unknown. But equation 14.1 has seven unknowns, and therefore we cannot determine the effects individually.

The strategy, then, is to construct different experimental groups, so that different equations can be formulated containing these effects. Theoretically, if seven different equations, or seven different experimental groups, could be constructed, then all seven effects could be identified. This is possible because seven equations would provide solutions for seven unknowns. Unfortunately, it is impossible to construct seven different experimental groups. In other words, there is no perfect experimental design.

However, the knowledge that there is no perfect experimental design should not prevent a researcher from becoming familiar with various alternative experimental designs, so that optimal decisions can be made in making a selection. In the following section, various available experimental groups will be introduced; alternative experimental designs constructed from the various groups will be discussed; and the utilities of the various research designs in helping the researcher identify certain effects in the experiment will be considered.

AVAILABLE EXPERIMENTAL GROUPS AND ALTERNATIVE EXPERIMENTAL DESIGNS

Experimental Groups

There are four different experimental groups a researcher can utilize in an experiment. These groups are presented in Table 14.4. Group 1 is the basic experimental group discussed previously. The subjects in this group are exposed to the pretest measurement, the treatment, the uncontrolled factors, and the posttest measurement. In group 2, the subjects are administered the pretest measurement but do not participate in the treatment.[3] They are, however, subjected to the effects of the uncontrolled factors.

Group 3 subjects are not administered the pretest measurement, but are exposed to the treatment; therefore they are affected by $T, U,$ and P. Finally, group 4 subjects do not participate in the pretest measurement and do not receive the treatment; they are administered only the posttest measurement.

There are other possible but useless groups which can be constructed. For example, groups could be constructed which participate in the pretest measure-

---

[3] Groups 2 and 4 are usually referred to as *control groups* in the literature. However, as they are integral to any experimental design, they are considered experimental groups here and labeled as such.

Table 14.4 Possible Experimental Groups

Group	Pretest measurement	Treatment	Uncontrolled factors	Posttest measurement
1	X	T	U	P
2	X		U	P
3		T	U	P
4			U	P

ment only, the treatment only, or the pretest measurement and the treatment only. But the lack of posttest measurement would prevent the computation of the difference scores for the subjects in these groups. Thus, they cannot be considered.

For each of the four available groups, we may now discuss the computation of the difference score. For clarity, d_1 will represent the difference score computed for group 1, d_2 for group 2, etc.

Group 1   As represented in equation 14.1, the group 1 difference score d is composed of: (1) the effect of the pretest measurement X, (2) the effect of the treatment T, (3) the effect of uncontrolled events U, (4) the effect of the interaction of the pretest measurement and the treatment I_{XT}, (5) the effect of the interaction of the pretest measurement and the uncontrolled events I_{XU}, (6) the effect of the interaction of the treatment and the uncontrolled events I_{TU}, and (7) the effect of the interaction among the pretest measurement, the treatment, and the uncontrolled events I_{XTU}.

Thus,

$$d_1 = X + T + U + I_{XT} + I_{XU} + I_{TU} + I_{XTU} \tag{14.1}$$

This equation has one known score (d_1) and seven unknowns. Thus, there is no way to identify each individual effect.

Group 2   In the same way, the difference score d_2 between the posttest and the pretest measurements can be shown as follows:

$$d_2 = X + U + I_{XU} \tag{14.2}$$

There is one equation but three unknowns.

Group 3   The equation for the effects in group 3 is:

$$d_3 = T + U + I_{TU} \tag{14.3}$$

Since this group does not have a pretest measurement, d_3 is not known. Therefore, equation 14.3 (or group 3) is meaningful *only* if the pretest score can be estimated from another group (either group 1 or group 2). In that case, and if it can be assumed that the groups are relatively large (therefore that the estimated pretest score is stable) and randomized (therefore that there are no prearranged differences between the groups), then the averaged pretest score of another group can be used to find d_3. This estimation method will be demonstrated later in the chapter.

Equation 14.3, then, also has three unknowns (T, U, and I_{TU}).

Group 4   Group 4 does not have a pretest measurement. The discussion for group 3 also applies here to obtain d_4 for the following equation:

$$d_4 = U \tag{14.4}$$

In summary, there can be up to four groups, and their equations are:

$$d_1 = X + T \quad + U + I_{XT} \ + I_{XU} + I_{TU} + I_{XTU}$$
$$d_2 = X \qquad\quad + U \qquad\quad + I_{XU}$$
$$d_3 = \qquad\quad T + U \qquad\qquad\qquad + I_{TU}$$
$$d_4 = \qquad\qquad\quad U$$

Since four equations can be solved only for four unknowns, no matter which groups are used, no experiment design can identify all the effects.

One solution to this problem of lack of information from the data is for the researcher to make necessary assumptions about certain unknowns. For example, if a researcher chooses a one-group design (group 1), he has one equation and seven unknowns. In order for him to solve for the effect of one factor, say the effect of the treatment T, he would have to make assumptions about the other six unknowns in equation 14.1. Three types of assumptions can be made. An easy way out is simply to assume that all the other unknowns are equal to zero. In other words, all other factors have no effect on the difference score. Or, a researcher can assume that these factors have effects on the difference score but that effects canceled each other out. Third, he can assign numbers to the various factors to represent the extent of the effects they have on the difference score. These numbers can be based on evidence from past research. How realistic these assumptions are depends on the experimental situation, the nature of the study, the activities which have taken place during the experiment, and past evidence reported in the literature. The fewer assumptions a researcher has to make, the less likely it is that he will distort the data.

In general, two criteria help the researcher to select a particular design: (1) to minimize the number of assumptions, and (2) to assume effects which either have been determined in previous studies or are less consequential in relation to other alternative effects.

Thus, a research design which requires two assumptions is in general preferred to a design requiring three assumptions. A research design assuming effects determined in the past is preferred to a design assuming effects without such previously determined values. A research design assuming effects which intuitively have no important consequences on the crucial variables is preferred to one which has to assume values for effects affecting the crucial variables.

Experimental Designs

In the following, we will discuss several popular experimental designs and assess their relative merits in terms of the two criteria just mentioned.

Two-Group Design 1   In this design, groups 1 and 2 are used. Thus, equations 14.1 and 14.2 are employed:

$$d_1 = X + T + U + I_{XT} + I_{TU} + I_{XU} + I_{XTU} \tag{14.1}$$
$$d_2 = X + U + I_{XU} \tag{14.2}$$

This is the most commonly used experimental design, in which one experimental group receives the treatment and the other does not. Since two equations are involved, and there are seven unknowns, the researcher must make assumptions about five unknowns in order to find solutions for the other two unknowns. To illustrate the solutions, an example is provided in Table 14.5. In this example, the pretest measurement of the dependent variable shows an average of 20 points on the scale for both groups, indicating that randomization was effective in the assignment of subjects to the two groups. The posttest measurement scores are 100 and 60 points, respectively, for the two groups. Thus, the averaged difference scores can be computed for the two groups. The researcher decided that he would assume that all the interaction effects and the uncontrolled factors did not appreciably affect the posttest scores of the subjects. After eliminating the terms assumed to vanish in the equations, the researcher obtained two equations containing only two unknowns. The two unknowns were then solved. The researcher concluded that the treatment induced a change of 40 points from the

Table 14.5   Example of Solving Two Unknowns in Two-Group Design 1

Group	Pretest measurement	Treatment	Uncontrolled factors	Posttest measurement	d
XTUP	20	Yes	Yes	100	80
XUP	20	No	Yes	60	40

$$d_1 = 80 = X + T + U + I_{XT} + X_{TU} + X_{XU} + I_{XTU}$$
$$d_2 = 40 = X + U + X_{XU}$$

Assumptions (for five unknowns):
$$U = I_{XT} = I_{TU} = I_{XU} = I_{XTU} = 0$$
Then, $d_1 = 80 = X + T$
     $d_2 = 40 = X$
Therefore, $X = 40$ and $T = 80 - X = 40$

pretest measurement to the posttest measurement, and that the pretest measurement effected a change of 40 points also.[4]

Instead of assuming that the uncontrolled factors U had no effect on the difference score, the researcher could alternatively make a similar assumption about the pretest measurement effect X or the interaction effect between the pretest measurement and the uncontrolled factors I_{XU}. The decision would not affect the solution for the treatment T, but would drastically change the effect of X, U, or I_{XU}, depending on which one was selected for solution.

Thus, it can be concluded that the experimental design utilizing groups 1 and 2 requires the researcher to make many assumptions and that the solutions are extremely unreliable.

Two-Group Design 2   An alternative two-group design utilizes groups 3 and 4. The equations involved are:

$$d_3 = T + U + I \tag{14.3}$$
$$d_4 = U \tag{14.4}$$

Thus, there are two equations and three unknowns. The researcher needs to make only one assumption to solve for two unknowns. However, since neither group received a pretest measurement, how can the difference score be computed? If we denote the pretest measurement score for group 3 as b_3, and the posttest measurement score as a_3, and likewise for group 4 as b_4 and a_4, then the difference scores for the two groups are:

$$d_3 = a_3 - b_3$$
$$d_4 = a_4 - b_4$$

Thus,

$$d_3 - d_4 = a_3 - b_3 - (a_4 - b_4)$$
$$= (a_3 - a_4) - (b_3 - b_4)$$

However, if randomization was in effect in the assignment of subjects to the two experimental groups, then the pretest measurement scores for the two groups should be approximately the same. In order words, b_3 and b_4 should be approximately the same and cancel each other out in the last equation. Then,

$$d_3 - d_4 = a_3 - a_4$$

Thus, the difference between the two difference scores for the two groups can be computed from the difference between the two posttest measurement scores

---

[4] Note that in Table 14.5, if the researcher was merely interested in finding the effect of the treatment T on the difference score, and not in the effect of the pretest measurement, he would only need to make assumptions about I_{XT}, I_{TU}, and I_{XTU}, as X, U, and I_{XU} canceled each other out.

Table 14.6 Example of Solving One Unknown (T) in Two-Group Design 2

Group	Pretest measurement	Treatment	Uncontrolled factors	Pretest measurement	d
TUP	No	Yes	Yes	100	?
UP	No	No	Yes	60	?

$d_3 = T + U + I_{TU}$
$d_4 = \quad U$

Therefore,

$d_3 - d_4 = 100 - 60 = 40$
$\quad\quad\quad = T + I_{TU}$

Assumption: $I_{TU} = 0$
Then, $T = 40$

alone. From equations 14.3 and 14.4, we know that:

$$d_3 - d_4 = a_3 - a_4 = T + I_{TU}$$

Thus, we only need to make an assumption about I_{TU} to solve for T. An example of this design is presented in Table 14.6.

A comparison between this design and the two-group design 1 discussed earlier (Table 14.5) shows that this design needs only one assumption as contrasted to three assumptions for the other design to solve for the effect of the treatment T (see footnote 4). Further, no pretest measurement represents savings for the researcher. Thus, we may conclude that in general the two-group design utilizing groups 3 and 4 is superior to the two-group design utilizing groups 1 and 2 in finding the effect of the treatment. This conclusion is valid only if the assignment of the subjects to the groups is completely random, so that the pretest measurement scores can be assumed to have been similar for the two groups if a pretest measurement was administered.

The only advantage of the two-group design 1 over the two-group design 2 is the fact that the former permits determination of the effect of another factor (for example, in Table 14.5 the effect of the pretest measurement), whereas the latter does not (it is impossible to find U, because the difference score for each group is unknown). However, this advantage is based on the heavy price a researcher has to pay for making assumptions about the effects of five factors.

Three-group design 1   The best known three-group design uses groups 1, 2, and 3. The system of equations involved is:

$$d_1 = X + T + U + I_{XT} + I_{TU} + I_{XU} + I_{XTU} \quad\quad (14.1)$$
$$d_2 = X + U + I_{XU} \quad\quad (14.2)$$
$$d_3 = T + U + I_{TU} \quad\quad (14.3)$$

Thus, this design has three equations and seven unknowns. To solve for three unknowns, assumptions must be made for the other four unknowns. In general, the researcher is interested in finding T, so no assumption should be made for it. Further, assumptions can be made for only two of the unknowns X, U, and I_{XU}, since the third value would automatically be derived from equation 14.2. Thus, the researcher can make assumptions about the four factors selected from the combination of two or three of the three interactions I_{XT}, I_{XU}, and I_{XTU}, and one or two from among X, U, and I_{XU}. An example of such a design is presented in Table 14.7. In this example, the researcher assumed that the effects of I_{XT}, I_{TU}, I_{XU}, and I_{XTU} were minimal, so that solutions were found for T, X, and U.

Note that in this example the third group (TUP) did not take the pretest measurement. In order to compute d_3, an estimate of the pretest measurement score was computed by taking the average of the pretest measurement scores from the first two groups. This could be done because, again, it was assumed that the random assignment of subjects to the three groups ensured similar pretest scores for all groups. However, when taking the average from the pretest scores

Table 14.7 Example of Solving Three Unknowns in Three-Group Design 1

Group	Pretest measurement	Treatment	Uncontrolled factors	Posttest measurement	d
$XTUP$	245	Yes	Yes	765	520
XUP	255	No	Yes	295	40
TUP	250 ± 20	Yes	Yes	650	400 ± 20

$$d_1 = X + T + U + I_{XT} + I_{XU} + I_{TU} + I_{XUT} = 520$$
$$d_2 = X + U + I_{XU} = 40$$
$$d_3 = T + U + I_{TU} = 400 \pm 20$$

Assumptions: $I_{XT} = I_{TU} = I_{XU} = I_{XTU} = 0$
Then,

$$d_1 = X + T + U = 520 \tag{1}$$
$$d_2 = X + U = 40 \tag{2}$$
$$d_3 = T + U = 400 \pm 20 \tag{3}$$

From (2),
$$X = 40 \times U \tag{4}$$
From (3),
$$T = 400 \pm 20 - U \tag{5}$$

Substituting (4) and (5) into (1),
$$(40 - U) + (400 \pm 20 - U) + U = 520$$
$$-U = (520 - 440) \pm 20 = 80 \pm 20$$
$$U = -80 \pm 20 \tag{6}$$

Substituting (6) into (4),
$$X = 40 - (-80 \pm 20) = 120 \pm 20$$

Substituting (6) into (5),
$$T = 400 \pm 20 - (80 \pm 20) = 480 \pm 20$$

Table 14.8 Example of Solving Three Unknowns in Three-Group Design 2

Group	Pretest measurement	Treatment	Uncontrolled factors	Posttest measurement	d
XUP	250	No	Yes	295	40
TUP	250 ± 20	Yes	Yes	650	400 ± 20
UP	250 ± 20	No	Yes	350	100 ± 20

$$d_2 = X + \quad + U + I_{XU} = 40$$
$$d_3 = \quad\quad T + U + I_{TU} = 400 \pm 20$$
$$d_4 = \quad\quad U \quad\quad = 100 \pm 20$$

Assumptions:

$$I_{XU} = I_{TU} = 0$$

Then,

$$d_2 = X + U = 40 \tag{1}$$
$$d_3 = T + U = 400 \pm 20 \tag{2}$$
$$d_4 = U = 100 \pm 20 \tag{3}$$

Substituting (3) into (1),

$$X = 40 - 100 \pm 20 = -60 \pm 20$$

Substituting (3) into (2),

$$T = 400 \pm 20 - 100 \pm 20 = 300 \pm 20$$

from the first two groups, the researcher should take into account the fact that the scores differed slightly from subject to subject. This variation indicates that there might be some random error involved in the estimate of the pretest score for group 3. Thus, the final estimate must include a point estimate (250) and an interval estimate[5] (± 20). The two estimates must be carried in all subsequent computations.

Three-Group Design 2 Another three-group design uses groups 2, 3, and 4 and involves the following equations:

$$d_2 = X + U + I_{XU} \tag{14.2}$$
$$d_3 = T + U + I_{TU} \tag{14.3}$$
$$d_4 = U \tag{14.4}$$

There are three equations and five unknowns, making it necessary to assume the effects of two factors. An example of this design is shown in Table 14.8. Note

---

[5] The meaning of *interval estimate* was discussed in detail in Chapter 7. The interpretation in this case is that, "With reasonable confidence, say, in 95 out of 100 similar samples, the actual average of the pretest scores for group 3 would have been between 230 and 270." It should be noted that, the narrower the interval estimate the more useful the estimate is to the researcher. To reduce the interval estimate involves an increase in the number of subjects in the groups exposed to the pretest measurement (see discussion on the relation between sample size and prediction precision in Chapter 9, Sampling).

that estimates for the pretest scores for groups 3 and 4 were computed from the pretest scores of group 2. The effect of the pretest measurement on the change score X was estimated as -60 ± 20, a negative score. It suggested that the subjects exposed to the pretest measurement tended to be affected negatively toward the dependent variable in the posttest measurement.

A comparison between the two three-group designs discussed shows that the three-group design 2 needs fewer assumptions (two versus four) and pretest measurements (one versus two) than the three-group design 1. Thus, in general, the three-group design utilizing groups 2, 3, and 4 is superior to the three-group design utilizing groups 1, 2, and 3. Again, this statement is valid only if complete random assignment of the subjects to the groups is assumed, so that the estimates of the pretest measurement scores for the groups not taking the pretest measurement are reliable and within a tolerable range.

Four-Group Design   The design utilizing all four groups is known as the Solomon four-group design and involves all four equations and seven unknowns. With assumptions made for the effects of three factors, solutions for the effects of four factors can be found. An example of the design and the solutions appears in Table 14.9.

Note several things in Table 14.9. First, the pretest and posttest measurement scores are not given; only the difference scores and the estimated change scores are presented. Second, the assumptions about the effects of the three factors X, I_{XT}, I_{TU} are actual scores rather than zeroes. This suggests that past research evidence has provided realistic estimates of the effects of the factors. Finally, the effect of the interaction between the pretest measurement and the uncontrolled factors is 15 ± 25, an interval including both positive and negative scores. This suggests that the effect of this factor was small, thus making the estimate unreliable.

FURTHER DISCUSSION OF EXPERIMENTAL DESIGNS

What has clearly been shown is that the two-group design using groups 3 and 4 is extremely useful in determining the effect of the treatment. The advantages of few assumptions and no pretest measurement of that design are unsurpassed by any other design involving any number of experimental groups. The question, then, arises as to why researchers pay attention to the more complex designs involving three or four groups. If more groups are involved, more equations are constructed, and therefore the effects of more factors can be identified. Thus, there are legitimate and useful occasions for the use of the more complex experimental designs. In general, the following statements are valid:

1   If a researcher is interested only in finding the effect of the independent variable on the dependent variable, then the two-group design involving TUP and UP is the most efficient.

2   The advantage of more complex designs over the two-group design does

Table 14.9   Example of Solving Four Unknowns in the Four-Group Design

Group	Pretest measurement	Treatment	Uncontrolled factors	Posttest measurement	d
XTUP	Yes	Yes	Yes	Yes	615
XUP	Yes	No	Yes	Yes	70
TUP	No	Yes	Yes	Yes	510 ± 25
UP	No	No	Yes	Yes	40 ± 25

$$d_1 = X + T + U + I_{XT} + I_{XU} + I_{TU} + I_{XTU} = 615$$
$$d_2 = X \qquad U + \qquad I_{XU} \qquad = 70$$
$$d_3 = \qquad T + U + \qquad I_{TU} \qquad = 510 \pm 25$$
$$d_4 = \qquad U \qquad = 40 \pm 25$$

Assumptions:
$$X = 15$$
$$I_{XT} = 20$$
$$I_{TU} = -25$$

Then,

$$d_1 = 15 + T + U + 20 + I_{XU} - 25 + I_{XTU} = 615 \qquad (1)$$
$$d_2 = 15 + \qquad U + \qquad I_{XU} \qquad = 70 \qquad (2)$$
$$d_3 = \qquad T + U \qquad - 25 \qquad = 510 \pm 25 \qquad (3)$$
$$d_4 = \qquad U \qquad = 40 \pm 25 \qquad (4)$$

Substituting (4) into (2),
$$I_{XU} = 70 - 15 - 40 \pm 25 = 15 \pm 25 \qquad (5)$$

Substituting (4) into (3),

$$T = 510 \pm 25 - 40 \pm 25 - 25 = 445 \pm 25 \qquad (6)$$

Substituting (4), (5), and (6) into (1),

$$I_{XTU} = 615 - 15 - 445 \pm 25 - 40 \pm 25 - 20 - 15 \pm 25 + 25$$
$$= 105 \pm 25 \qquad (7)$$

not lie in providing better estimates of the effect of the independent variable on the dependent variable. Rather, it lies in the ability of these designs to allow estimates of the effects of other factors on the dependent variable.

However, the researcher must keep in mind that the use of complex designs and designs allowing estimates of the effect of pretest measurement depends on whether or not realistic assumptions regarding the effects of some factors can be made. In several examples provided in the preceding section, zero effects were assumed. They may be convenient, but not necessarily realistic. Blind assumptions may lead to totally biased results. Thus, unless past research evidence or the experimental situation allows the researcher a confident estimate of the effects of some factors, he should settle for the simple two-group design which uses only one assumption.

The researcher should also be alerted to the fact that, in the formulation of the equations for the various experimental designs, the effect of the uncontrolled factors is assumed to be similar for subjects in all groups. That is, the U for every group is assumed to be the same. Otherwise, each group should have a U composed of the effect of uncontrolled factors common to all groups and of the effect of uncontrolled factors unique to each group. For example, for group 1:

$$U_1 = U + u_1$$

That is, the composite U_1 contains the common U and the unique u_1. Similarly, U_2, U_3, and U_4 should be constructed. The result would create further complications in the assumptions and estimations. To avoid such complications, the researcher should strive to control stimuli acting on the subjects during the course of the experiment. He should make sure that the subjects in all groups involved are exposed to and experience similar or identical stimuli.

The above discussion underlines the importance of the three basic elements of the experiment: randomization, control, and manipulation. Unless rigor and precision are applied in the execution of the experiment regarding these three elements, the researcher will encounter difficulties rendering the collected data useless for analysis or interpretation.

MULTITREATMENT DESIGNS

In the discussion of experimental groups, it was assumed that the treatment involved only the presence or absence of the independent variable. For example, for groups 1 and 3 a treatment is administered (the independent variable is present), whereas for groups 2 and 4 no treatment is administered (the independent variable is absent). Thus, in the discussion, the independent variable was operationalized into a one-value variable. More realistically, of course, the independent variable must have two or more values. The example of the relationship between housing arrangement and racial prejudice demonstrates this fact. The independent variable, housing arrangement, has two values: integrated housing and segregated housing.

Further, an experiment can involve more than one independent or dependent variable. For example, in the study on housing arrangement and racial prejudice, the researcher could have introduced a second independent variable, the amount of social interactions allowed. Thus, within each housing arrangement, the residents would be allowed different amounts of interaction with their neighbors. Then, the researcher would try to assess the effect of each independent variable (housing arrangement and interaction) independently and jointly on the dependent variable (racial prejudice). The fact that an experiment can involve multivalues for an independent variable and multivariables complicates the basic designs as illustrated in Table 14.4. Each additional value of an independent variable or each additional independent variable requires additional subgroups for groups 1 and 3. For example, for a three-value independent variable, the original group 1 ($XTUP$) must be enlarged to three groups (XT_1UP, XT_2UP, and XT_3UP), with each group exposed to one value of the independent variable. Extensive discussion of the various multitreatment designs is outside the scope of this book. Here, we will only briefly identify the major multitreatment designs and point out the advantages and disadvantages of each.[6]

Single-Factor Design

This design is also known as the *simple randomized design,* and each factor represents one independent variable. Thus, this design involves the manipulation of various values of one independent variable. It represents a straightforward elaboration of the basic design. Each treatment is a manipulation of a particular value of the independent variable. In the example of the study on the effect of housing arrangement on racial prejudice, two values (treatments) were manipulated for the independent variable—integrated housing and segregated housing. The single-factor design remains the most commonly used design in experiments.

Single-Factor Design with Blocks

If a researcher suspects that subjects with different characteristics will respond differently to the manipulations, he can "block" the subjects into homogeneous groups, e.g., males versus females, levels of economic status, levels of education, black versus white, etc. Then, each block of subjects can be further randomly assigned to various experimental groups to receive different treatments under different experimental conditions. In other words, the single-factor design is used completely and repeatedly for each block of subjects. If the different blocks of subjects respond differently in the experiment, the single-factor design with blocks is superior to the single-factor design. This is because the single-factor design does not allow comparison of effects among different types of subjects. On the other hand, if the different blocks of subjects respond similarly, the single-factor design with blocks is inferior to the single-factor design. For it is costly to construct the various blocks and to repeat the same experiment for each block. Problems of randomization, control, and manipulation multiply in parallel to the number of blocks defined. The researcher has to rely on the evidence in the literature and his experiences in the past to decide whether or not it is worthwhile to set up blocks and make the necessary investment of effort and money.

One way to locate clues as to whether or not there is a block effect is for the researcher to analyze data gathered by himself or others in the past with the single-factor design. The secondary analysis divides the participating subjects into blocks and determines whether different types of subjects responded differently in the experiments. Since these studies were not designed to test block effects, randomization, control, and manipulation probably were not equally and precisely administered to or received by each block of subjects. Thus, the secondary analysis can only provide hunches as to whether or not blocks should be considered. Such hunches can lead to rational decisions in selection of the appropriate design for the experiment contemplated by the researcher.

---

[6] Readers interested in more extensive discussions on this topic should consult: E. F. Linquist, *Design and Analysis of Experiments in Psychology and Education,* Houghton Mifflin, Boston, 1953; William G. Cochran and Gertrude M. Cox, *Experimental Designs,* Wiley, New York, 1957.

Two issues relating to the single-factor design with blocks should be made clear. First, the blocks can be constructed on the basis of one or more characteristics. Thus, a quota method can be used to construct the blocks. For example, sex and race can be used to construct four blocks: (1) white males, (2) white females, (3) black males, and (4) black females. Second, it is possible to administer only some of the treatments to each block or to administer all the treatments to some blocks. In other words, the researcher can eliminate certain treatments or blocks or part of each in the single-factor design with blocks. The reduction is a saving for the researcher, but must be made with sufficient knowledge and confidence that differences in the response patterns will occur among the remaining treatments and blocks. Thus, this technique is applied only (1) when the researcher has sufficient confidence, backed by past evidence, or (2) as a desperate move when a sufficient number of subjects cannot be found to participate in the experiment (e.g., human twins).

Multifactor Design

Also called the *full-factorial design,* this design incorporates more variables than a single independent variable to be manipulated. The factors may include two or more variables to be manipulated, as well as variables to be explicitly controlled for. In the design, each value of a variable is combined with each and every value of another variable. For two treatment variables, each with three values and one control variable, with two values, they combine into $3 \times 3 \times 2 = 18$ cells. Thus, for the basic experimental group, *XTUP,* 18 subgroups must be constructed, each representing a unique combination of the values of the three variables (factors). This design may sound similar to the single-design with blocks. However, there are substantial differences.

First, the multifactor design allows the researcher to manipulate more than one variable, which the single-factor design does not. Second, while the control variable acts the same way as the block in classifying subjects into different groups, the control variable is represented by its values. The researcher is interested in the systematic differences in the response patterns from subjects belonging to different value categories of each control variable. In other words, the researcher is interested in the systematic relationship between each control variable and the dependent variable. This is not true with blocks. In the single-factor design, the researcher is merely interested in isolating different effects on the dependent variable of blocks constructed from one or more specific characteristics of the subjects. The researcher is not interested in any systematic differences in effects from block to block. For the single-factor design with blocks, analysis of data is performed for each block and then comparisons are made across block analyses. The block itself does not enter into the picture of analysis. For the multifactorial design, on the other hand, analysis of data is performed for all factors; the relation of each combination of factors with the dependent variable is equally important in the statistical analysis.

The multifactor design allows the researcher to examine the effects of the factors, independently and jointly (interactive), on the dependent variable. Thus, a researcher should utilize this design if (1) he wishes to identify the major factors affecting the dependent variable, in an exploratory study, or (2) he is especially interested in the effects of interactions among the factors on the dependent variable. However, these advantages must be considered in conjunction with the substantial investment of money and effort involved in the use of the full-factorial design.

Multifactor Design with Blocks

Like the single-factor design, the multifactor design can also incorporate blocks. First, blocks of subjects are identified. Then, the subjects in each block are randomly assigned to each of the cells containing a unique combination of values of all factors.

Latin-square Design

While designs using blocks and multifactors attempt to tease out effects on the dependent variable of various characteristics and variables, another design is also available to the researcher in which he makes sure that the effects of such confounding factors are balanced or canceled out for all treatments. The randomization assignment process in the single-factor design attempts to achieve such cancellation for all undefined confounding factors. The Latin-square and related designs, on the other hand, attempt to make such cancellation by first identifying the confounding factors. The Latin-square design, associated specifically with the identification of two confounding factors, is illustrated in Table 14.10.

In the Latin-square design, two confounding factors (A and B) are defined by the researcher. Then, for each confounding factor, three values (or categories) are identified. The combination of the values of the two confounding factors constitutes the nine cells presented in Table 14.10. For this combination, three treatments (or three values or categories of an independent variable) can be administered. The strategy is to administer the three treatments respectively and alternatively to subjects (or sometimes a single subject) in each of the three cells in each row or column.

Thus, each treatment is administered to only one value of a factor in

Table 14.10 Latin-square Design*

Confounding factor B	Confounding factor A		
	1	2	3
1	T_1	T_2	T_3
2	T_2	T_3	T_1
3	T_3	T_1	T_2

* T_1 = treatment 1; T_2 = treatment 2; T_3 = treatment 3.

combination of a unique value of another confounding factor. The purpose, then, is to administer each treatment under mixed conditions involving the two confounding factors. Hopefully, whatever effect there was from the two confounding factors is equally absorbed in each treatment. The equalizing process hopefully cancels any possible unique effect of each confounding factor on the dependent variable.

Similar designs can be used to incorporate three or more confounding factors.

The Latin-square and related designs have one advantage over the multifactor design and designs with blocks. In designs involving factors and blocks every combination of every value of each control factor and each block must receive all the treatments. In the Latin-square design, on the other hand, only one treatment is administered to each such combination. Take the example in Table 14.10: in the cell combining values 1 of both factors A and B, only one treatment (T_1) is administered in the Latin-square design. For the same cell in designs involving multifactors and blocks, all the treatments must be administered. Thus, as many groups of subjects as there are treatments must be constructed for the one cell to receive the treatments. For three treatments, instead of the nine groups of subjects involved in the nine cells in Table 14.10, three times that many (twenty-seven) groups would have to be constructed in the designs involving multifactors and blocks. Thus, the Latin-square design represents a substantial saving in terms of identification and assignment of subjects and in terms of the frequency of treatment administrations. The simplified procedure can improve the precision of experimentation.

However, there are two limitations associated with the Latin-square and related designs. First, the number of treatments and the number of values for each factor must be identical. In Table 14.10, for example, each factor has three values, and exactly three treatments are administered. Any variation will not fit into the design. Thus, unless the researcher can justify the equivalence of row numbers, column numbers, and the number of treatments, the Latin-square design cannot be used. Second, this design is superior to designs involving multifactors and blocks, because it eliminates a substantial number of groups. Such elimination assumes, however, that the factors involved do not have any interactive effect on the treatment and on the subjects' responses to the dependent variable. Each factor is assumed to have the same effect on the treatment and the dependent variable, regardless of what value independent of another factor is present. For if there were an interactive effect, then it would become necessary to administer all treatments to every combination of the values of all factors. This, of course, represents the multifactor and block designs. Thus, the Latin-square design can be used only when the researcher is positive that the confounding factors have independent (additive) effects on the treatments and on the dependent variable. In many cases, such assumptions cannot and should not be made.

In summary, the researcher has almost an infinite number of multitreatment designs to choose from. Each design offers him certain advantages and certain limitations. The researcher must examine the purpose of his study and be guided by past evidence and experiences in his selection of an appropriate experimental design.

FIELD EXPERIMENT

The experiment is usually conducted in a laboratory situation. Subjects are isolated from the outside and from their "natural lives." The laboratory experiment has been criticized for its unnaturalness and questioned as to its generalizability. The common question is, "How can experiments conducted with college students in laboratories be generalized to the general population living in natural day-to-day settings, with all the extraneous variables not considered in the laboratory situations impinging on their activities and behaviors?" The generalizability problem of experimentation will be discussed in more detail later in the chapter. For now, one answer to this question is to conduct experiments utilizing natural groupings in their natural environments. This method of data collection is called a *field experiment*. Instead of randomly assigning subjects to different experimental groups, individuals or groups in natural settings such as city blocks, villages, and schools are used. In the selection of subjects or groups, the researcher must make sure that they are comparable, so that their initial responses to the dependent variable can be assumed to be similar, if not identical. Further, the researcher must also make sure that the subjects are in similar environments, so that whatever extraneous factors are operating on them will have similar effects and interact similarly with treatments and the dependent variable.

In general, the field experiment increases the generalizability of the data, because of its natural groupings and settings, at the expense of loss of precision and control as compared to the laboratory experiment. It usually is difficult to find sufficient comparable groups to assign to the various experimental groups. It is also unrealistic to assume that all these groups are exposed to similar extraneous factors or are affected similarly by these factors. The field experiment also costs more than the laboratory experiment.

Despite these problems, the field experiment probably will become the type of experiment most suitable and meaningful for social research, as many researchers are committed to the generalizability of data to a large social grouping. Further, there are ways which can help the researcher estimate and, therefore, take into account the effects of different extraneous factors for different experimental groups in the analysis of data. The potential use of the field experiment in the test of causal relations in natural settings should not be underestimated. To provide an illustration of the use of the field experiment, a recent study on the effect of messages on improving the baby-feeding habits of mothers in Haiti can be cited.

In this study, eight villages were selected in a triangular region northwest of Port-au-Prince, the capital of Haiti. The villages were selected after a general survey of the region, because they were representative of the villages in Haiti in

**Table 14.11   A Field Experiment
Design in Haiti***

Informal structure	Socioeconomic status	
	High	Low
Strong	V_1, V_2	V_3, V_4
Weak	V_5, V_6	V_7, V_8

* V = Village.

terms of size and socioeconomic variation. Then, a typology on SES and on the informal social structure was constructed. As shown in Table 14.11, the eight villages were paired into four cells as defined by the two control variables. The SES of the villages was measured by an index composed of items on roof construction, floor construction, land ownership, education, occupation, and radio ownership; the informal structure of the villages was based on the analysis of sociometric data (choices of friends in the village) which provided indices on how integrated the villagers were to one another. All these data were gathered in a pretest measurement.

One independent variable was manipulated. A message instructing how mothers can provide nutritious food for their babies was prepared and delivered by personal messengers to the villages. For each pair of villages, the messages were delivered to different persons in the village. In one village, the message was delivered to two opinion leaders, also defined from the sociometric data. In the other paired villages, the message was sent to two social isolates, defined as those who did not name any friends in the village nor were named as friends directly or indirectly by other villagers. The isolates and opinion leaders selected were in similar geographic locations in their respective villages.

The purpose of the field experiment was to test the effects of the treatments on the improvement of knowledge and behavior of feeding habits. It was hypothesized that the personal message would be more effective when delivered to the opinion leaders rather than to the social isolates, because the opinion leaders were expected to be more effective in disseminating the message among the villagers through their informal networks. The difference was expected to increase from villages in cells of low SES and weak informal structure to those in cells of high SES and strong informal structure.

In addition to the eight villages which were administered treatments, three other villages were involved in the field experiment. Two of the three villages were outside the region. One of them was administered the pretest measurement and the posttest measurement, while the other was administered only the posttest measurement. The third village in the region was administered only the posttest measurement. These three villages provided additional equations in the estimation of the effect of other factors not controlled for in the experiment.

This illustration demonstrates the viability of the field experiment in social research. When well executed, the field experiment has the precision and control of the laboratory experiment and the generalizability of the survey. The implications of a field experiment for a well-designed survey should also be stressed. Even in survey research, where manipulation is not used, control over extraneous variables and variability among respondents, as used in field experiments, can strengthen the measurement and, therefore, the validity and reliability of the data.

PROBLEMS OF THE EXPERIMENT

While the experiment has the precision, control, and manipulation most desirable for the identification of causal relations, it has a number of limitations.

One limitation, discussed in the section dealing with the effects of various factors in experimental groups, relates to the impossibility of constructing a sufficient number of different groups to isolate all the effects of seven types of factors. Thus, assumptions about some effects must be made. How realistic the assumptions are affects drastically the validity of the results. The researcher should always try to use a design which requires the fewest number of assumptions or which allows realistic assumptions.

A second limitation results from any changes in research procedures taking place during the period of the experiment. For example, any variations in the instrument, the instructions given to the subjects, the coding procedure, or the observation procedures used in the pretest and posttest measurements can introduce changes in the responses, adding another type of factor uncontrolled for by the researcher. Thus, the researcher should carry out the same procedures throughout the experiment to avoid such added complications in the difference scores. Another change which may occur during the process of experimentation is the loss of subjects after they have been assigned to groups. For various reasons, some subjects may withdraw or be unable to continue after the groups have been set up. Such attrition of subjects can have a drastic effect on the experimental results. If unreplaced, some groups may end up being much smaller in size than other groups, making comparability among groups a problem. Further, if the loss of subjects concentrates in one or more categories of a characteristic which may interact with the treatments and the difference scores, the whole experiment can be completely invalidated. For example, if the researcher anticipates some interaction between sex and racial prejudice, the loss of a substantial number of male subjects during the experiment would effectively bias the results to make the experiment an invalid one. On the other hand, if the lost subjects are replaced, the effect of randomization in the assignment of subjects to groups may be violated. Thus, it is important that, when the researcher recruits subjects, a sufficient number of subjects is used and they are not allowed to participate unless they can commit themselves for the entire anticipated period of the experiment. In experiments involving a substantial period of time, say several months, it is almost inevitable that loss of subjects will occur. But appropriate planning and selection can reduce the effect of the loss to a minimum.

Another element, called *regression toward the mean,* may invalidate the experiment if certain types of subjects are used. When subjects are selected because they register extreme (either highest or lowest) scores on some scale relevant to the measurement of the dependent variable, it has been found that the natural tendency over time is for their scores to regress toward the average. For example, one variable used may be the racial attitudes of the subjects, and two blocks of subjects may be constructed for the extreme high- and extreme-low prejudice respondents. However, the tendency is that over time the extreme high and low scores will regress toward the middle. The result is that the clear distinction between the extreme high and low groups and the medium group will substantially be reduced over the period of the experiment. Statistical regression can be minimized by careful scale construction and by testing the scale with a number of respondents over time to determine whether or not the scale is stable enough so that the regression does not take place.

Another limitation of the experiment is the problem of generating a sufficient effect in the treatments so that the dependent variable, the difference scores, will reflect the impact. Because the experiment is usually conducted during a limited period of time, say a few weeks or months, it is difficult for certain types of variables to generate effects of the treatments significant enough to be noticeable in the posttest measurement. One solution to this problem is to provide a sufficient amount of time between the treatment and the posttest measurement. But the longer the time gap, the more the time-related uncontrolled factors U will have an effect on the posttest measurement. The hope is that the uncontrolled factors will have identical or similar effects on all experimental groups over the time gap between the treatment and the posttest measurement.

The interaction of the experimenters (the researcher and his associates) with the subjects can also have an effect on the response patterns of the subjects; this is known as the *experimenter effect.* The subjects may attempt to rationalize their responses, to be deceptive in their responses, or to formulate responses consistent with their speculations on the objective of the study based on the way the experimenter conducts the study. To reduce such effects, the researcher may use several procedures. One is to ask the subjects about their perceptions of the activities and behaviors of the experimenters after each treatment or measurement is administered, so that an estimate can be made as to what extent the subjects may formulate responses in accordance with their perceptions of the demand for "correct" responses on the part of the experimenters. A second procedure is to minimize cues to the subjects by the standardization of presentations in measurements and in treatments. The procedure is similar to the one in dealing with standardization of the instrument and interviewing techniques associated with surveys (see Chapter 13). A third procedure is for the researcher to use persons who do not know the purpose of the study to administer measurements and treatments. These collaborators are thoroughly trained only for the administration of the tasks at hand. While they are efficient administrators in the experiment, their activities and behaviors are not affected by knowledge of the study purpose and thus they do not provide any cues to the subjects.[7] A fourth procedure involves the confederates (stooges) the researcher uses in the experiment. Their true identity is concealed from the subjects. However, their activities and behaviors may provide cues to the subjects which bias their responses. The researcher should train the confederates by placing them in the same experimental situations as the subjects, so that they become sensitized to the cues that the subjects look for. This experience hopefully will minimize their providing such cues when they serve as collaborators in the experiment.

Still another potential limitation of the experiment is misinterpretation of the significance of the independent variables for the dependent variable. The researcher should realize that the fact that the independent variables show a statistically significant influence on the dependent variables in an experiment does not necessarily indicate that they are the most important causal variables as far as the dependent variable is concerned. The researcher should not confuse statistically significant relations with theoretically or substantively significant relations. Many phenomena are related to each other. Given the proper control and measurement, experiments can demonstrate that such relations may exist; however, this does not necessarily imply that the relations are important. For example, variations in housing arrangement may lead to different racial attitudes, but this does not mean that housing arrangement is the most important factor in inducing certain racial attitudes. It may well be that the social interactions afforded by housing arrangement or prior experiences in interaction with multiracial groups are much more important in determining racial attitudes. Confusing significant results with important results should be especially avoided in experiments, since usually a limited number of independent variables is involved. Unless the researcher has supportive evidence from past research, or constructs a multifactor design into which all factors found to be significantly related to the dependent variable are incorporated, there is no basis for the researcher to claim, based on significant findings, that any single independent variable manipulated is the most important independent variable for the dependent variable. While no method of data collection can claim discovery of the most important variables for a research issue, the temptation should be strictly avoided in an experiment because of the in-depth but narrow approach to the number of variables involved. Again, this problem reflects the need for a multimethod approach to data collection. If the researcher conducts a survey study first to determine the relatively more important variables, then the experiment can be extremely useful in testing specific hypotheses derived from the formulation of a theoretical structure incorporating all the potential important variables.

[7] Readers interested in the experimenter effect should consult: Robert Rosenthal, "The Effect of the Experimenter on the Results of Psychological Research," in B. A. Maher (ed.), *Progress in Experimental Personality Research,* Academic, New York, 1964, pp. 79–114, and *Experimental Effects in Behavioral Research* (Appleton-Century-Crofts, New York, 1966); James A. Wiggins, "Hypothesis Validity and Experimental Laboratory Methods," in Hubert M. Blalock, Jr., and Ann B. Blalock, *Methodology in Social Research,* McGraw-Hill, New York, 1968, pp. 390–427.

A last but not least limitation of the experiment concerns its *generalizability*. The usual experiments utilizing homogeneous subjects present a serious problem for inference—as one psychologist remarked, "College sophomores are not people." The inferential problem is further accentuated by the fact that most experiments utilize volunteers as subjects. It is likely that only people with certain characteristics are attracted by the incentives to volunteer for participation in social experiments. However, the issue of generalizability must be clarified. As Aronson and Carlsmith pointed out,[8] two types of realism are involved in research. *Experimental realism* is achieved in an experiment "if the situation is realistic to the subject, if it involves him, if he is forced to take it seriously, if it has impact on him." On the other hand, *mundane realism* refers "to the extent to which events occurring in a laboratory setting are likely to occur in the 'real world.'" They argued that mundane realism cannot be equated to importance: "Many events that occur in the real world are boring and uninvolving." In other words, in certain studies, internal validity rather than external validity (discussed in Chapter 10) is more important, and experimental realism outweighs mundane realism in the experiment.

When external validity is crucial, the importance of using natural groupings in experiments and the use of field experiments in general should be emphasized. With more and more powerful analytical procedures available to improve identification of extraneous factors statistically, field experiments seem destined to become a most powerful method of data collection for social research. Potentially, as a cross-breed of survey and experiment, it provides the researcher with both precision and generalizability, the most desirable characteristics of data for a researcher.

SUMMARY

The experiment is a method of data collection in which the researcher randomly assigns subjects to different experimental groups, controls for extraneous variables, and manipulates the independent variable or variables so that the effect of the independent variable or variables on the dependent variable can be assessed over time. However, there are seven identifiable factors operating in the experiment which may affect the measurements of the dependent variable. Since no more than four different kinds of experimental groups can be constructed, it is impossible to identify the effects of all seven factors. Thus, the researcher always has to make assumptions in order to identify the effect of the independent variable or variables on the dependent variable. The selection of a particular experimental design composed of certain experimental groups should be guided by two criteria: (1) the minimal number of assumptions to be made, and (2) assump-

---

[8] Elliot Aronson and J. Merrill Carlsmith, "Experimentation in Social Psychology," in Gardner Lindzey and Elliot Aronson (eds.), *The Handbook of Social Psychology,* 2d ed., Addison-Wesley, Reading, Mass., vol. II, 1968, chap. 9, pp. 1–79, especially pp. 22–26.

tions to be realistically made with knowledge from past research and for factors known not to operate substantially in the proposed design.

The basic experimental design can be varied to incorporate multiple values of an independent variable, to control for blocks of subjects, to incorporate multiple independent and control variables, and to balance the effects of confounding factors.

The laboratory experiment is superior in precision and control but lacks generalizability. The field experiment, utilizing natural groups in natural settings, can become a most desirable method of data collection when precisely executed and controlled.

While the experiment is the most precise and controllable method of data collection, the researcher must be fully aware of its limitations relating to assumptions to be made, procedural changes, statistical regression, insufficient time to generate substantial effect, the experimenter effect, selection of significant but not necessarily important independent variables, and generalizability of results, all of which may affect the validity of the data.

Part Five

Data Analysis

Chapter 15

Univariate Analysis

The information gathered from respondents in a research project constitutes the basis for analysis. The term *data* is used to represent the recorded response patterns of the respondents to an instrument used in the study. Data analysis has two objectives: (1) to summarize and describe the data, and (2) to make inferences from the data to the population from which the sample was drawn. Chapters 5 and 6 dealt with descriptive statistics; readers interested only in describing the data matrix may skip this chapter and the next. Chapter 7 introduced statistical inference; this chapter and the next will elaborate the procedures of parameter estimation and hypothesis testing in inference. Readers interested in statistical inference may find it helpful to review Chapters 5, 6, and 7 before proceeding further.

In statistical inference, a researcher has many choices of techniques. The selection of an appropriate technique is guided by: (1) whether one or more variables are involved, (2) what level of measurement was used for the variables, and (3) how large the sample size is.

When the focus is on a single variable at a time, *univariate analysis* is required. When two or more variables are examined simultaneously, *multivariate analysis* should be used. For statisticians the term *multivariate* is reserved for a situation in which two or more dependent variables are involved. However, the term is more loosely used here to denote any analysis involving two or more variables simultaneously. Thus, bivariate analysis is a multivariate analysis which involves two variables. This chapter discusses univariate analysis, and the next chapter multivariate analysis.

Recall that in Chapter 7 it was mentioned that the normal distribution can be utilized for inference when the variables are interval or ratio and when the sample size is sufficiently large. If some variables are measured on a nominal or ordinal scale, the sample size is small, or both, other distributions derived from the normal curve must be used instead. In other words, when certain assumptions of the normal curve are not met, alternative ways must be used to analyze the data.

Before statistical analysis can be performed on the data, they must be well organized and prepared for such analyses. Especially with the use of statistical routines for computer analysis, preparation of the data becomes an important, and sometimes time-consuming, task for the researcher.

PREPARATION OF DATA[1]

The field work gathers data on forms such as the questionnaire and the interview schedule. The completed questionnaires and schedules are the raw data. To simplify and organize the data for subsequent analysis, the raw data must be transformed into some other form. The transfer is necessary for two reasons. First, the raw data are the original materials, and the researcher should make sure they are not misplaced or lost. Thus, after the transfer, the raw data are stored as permanent records and can be used to verify and clarify transferred data later on. Second, the potential use of machines, such as the computer, requires that all data be in a certain systematic form, such as computer cards or tapes, which is machine-readable.

The transfer of data involves coders and coding schemes, and opens the way for errors. Precoding on the instrument can help reduce such errors. But systematic checking between the raw data and the transferred data is necessary.

One issue in the coding and transferring of data concerns incomplete data. Data may be partially missing for respondents. For example, certain respondents may have refused to respond to a question about their annual income. It is not economical to throw out all the data for a respondent if certain data are missing. The usual practice is to use the extreme codes for missing or "illegal" responses such as "don't know" or "not applicable" (e.g., asking the college major of a respondent who attended only high school). For example, for the variable of sex, the codes "1" and "2" can be used for "male" and "female" and the code "9" for no response. This practice is important when computer analysis is utilized. The extreme codes can be easily deleted from a computer analysis.

In most analysis, data with illegal codes should be excluded, since interpretation of their substantive meaning is difficult (unless the objective of the study

[1] Details of the preparation of data are discussed in Nan Lin, Ronald S. Burt, and John Vaughn, *Conducting Social Research,* McGraw-Hill, New York, 1976.

focuses on certain social withdrawal phenomenon such as the characteristics of those who did not report income as compared to those who did). When the illegal codes are converted to extreme codes, deletions can easily be made by most statistical computer programs (e.g., Statistical Package for Social Sciences, SPSS) without having to throw out each respondent who has registered one or more illegal response.

The transferred data can be further organized before any analysis is made. Scales can be constructed and item analysis be made. Resulting from these transformations may be a set of new variables to be analyzed. For example, the occupational codes can be transformed to scores on an occupational status rating scale.[2] The occupational status scores then constitute a variable for analysis.

When the data have been transferred, transformed, and cleaned up, the researcher may then begin analysis.[3]

In the following, the discussion will review some univariate analytical techniques for statistics such as the proportion, the mean, and the variance. For each statistic, both the point estimate and the interval estimate will be discussed, as well as hypothesis testing. Special attention will be given to the case in which the sample size is relatively small, say, less than 100. Because of the limitation of the scope of this book, the treatment of the statistical analysis inevitably is brief and selective. Interested readers should consult texts addressed specifically to the statistical analysis of social data.[4]

In discussing each technique, a specific example will be used as an illustration. Many of the examples are drawn from NORC General Social Survey sample data. While all inferential statistics assume that the sample is a simple random sample of the population, the NORC sample is not (it is a modified multistage sample in which quota sampling is used at the block level). For purposes of illustration, however, we simply make the assumption that the data came from a simple random sample of United States adults.

TECHNIQUES OF UNIVARIATE ANALYSIS

For univariate analysis, we will focus on the proportion P, the mean μ, and the variance σ^2. The task in each case is to analyze the data gathered in a sample, so that inferences to the value of the population parameter can be made and a hypothesis can be tested.

---

[2] See Appendix B for such occupational status rating scales.

[3] Omitted here is the application of the computer programs for data analysis. Interested readers are referred to Nan Lin, op. cit.

[4] Some examples of such texts are (in ascending order from elementary to intermediary coverage and treatment): Jack Levin, *Elementary Statistics in Social Research,* Harper, New York, 1973; Theodore R. Anderson and Morris Zelditch, Jr., *A Basic Course in Statistics,* 2d ed., Holt, New York, 1968; Herman J. Loether and Donald G. McTavish, *Descriptive Statistics for Sociologists and Inferential Statistics for Sociologists,* Allyn and Bacon, Boston, 1974; John H. Mueller, Karl F. Schuessler, and Herbert L. Costner, *Statistical Reasoning in Sociology,* Houghton Mifflin, Boston, 1970; Hubert M. Blalock, Jr., *Social Statistics,* 2d ed., McGraw-Hill, New York, 1972; Gene V. Glass and Julian C. Stanley, *Statistical Methods in Education and Psychology,* Prentice-Hall, Englewood Cliffs, N.J., 1970.

Proportion

If one wishes to deal with the population proportion P for a *nominal variable,* say, proportion of females in the population, one may first compute the sample proportion for females p. For example, from the NORC 1973 General Social Survey sample, it was found that for the 1,504 respondents 53 percent ($n = 803$) were females (see Table 5.3). One is now prepared to make an inference about the proportion of females in the population. To make such an inference, it is important to note that the sample is assumed to be a simple random sample from the population.

Estimates of the Parameter   There are two estimates of the population P: (1) the point estimate, and (2) the interval estimate. For the point estimate, we mentioned in Chapter 7 that the sample p is an unbiased estimate. Therefore, one may claim that the best point estimate of the proportion of females in the population from which the NORC sample was drawn is 53 percent.

For the interval estimate, a confidence coefficient, $c = 1 - \alpha$, must first be specified. Suppose it is set at .99, then the interval estimate of P can be found:

$$p + \frac{1}{2n} + z_{(1+c)/2}\sqrt{\frac{p(1-p)}{n}} \qquad\qquad (15.1)$$

and

$$p - \frac{1}{2n} + z_{(1-c)/2}\sqrt{\frac{p(1-p)}{n}}$$

where $\frac{1}{2}n$ is a correction factor for the sample size n, and $\sqrt{p(1-p)/n}$ is the estimate of the standard deviation of the population. For our example, where $p = .53$ and $n = 1,504$, the z value can be found in Table 2, Appendix C. Since we set $c = 1 - \alpha = .99$, then $(1 + c)/2 = .995$, and $(1 - c)/2 = .005$. In Table 2, Appendix C, the value of z which covers .995 of the area to its left is 2.58, and the value of z which covers .005 of the area to its left is -2.58. Thus, the interval estimate for the proportion of females in the population is:

$$.53 + \frac{1}{2(1,504)} + (2.58)\sqrt{\frac{(.53)(1-.53)}{1,504}} = .5636$$

and

$$.53 - \frac{1}{2(1,504)} - (2.58)\sqrt{\frac{(.53)(1-.53)}{1,504}} = .4964$$

Thus, one may conclude that with .99 probability the proportion of females in the population is within the interval .5636 to .4964 (or approximately 56.4 to 49.6 percent).

Hypothesis Testing If the researcher wishes to test the theoretical hypothesis that more than 50 percent of the population are females, he may set up a null hypothesis which states, "Fifty percent of the population are females," the level of significance at .05, and proceed to determine if it can be rejected and the theoretical hypothesis can be accepted. To do so, a z test can be used, as follows:

$$H_0 : P = a$$
$$H_1 : P > a$$

$$z = \frac{p - a}{\sqrt{\dfrac{a(1 - a)}{n}}} \qquad\qquad (15.2)$$

Thus, for our example data,

$$H_0 : P = .50$$
$$H_1 : P > .50$$

$$z = \frac{.53 - .50}{\sqrt{\dfrac{(.50)(1 - .50)}{1,504}}} = \frac{.03}{.0129} = 2.33$$

Referring to Table 2, Appendix C, again, we find $z_c = z_{1-\alpha} = z_{.95} = 1.65$. Since the observed z (2.33) is greater than the expected z (± 1.65), the null hypothesis, "Fifty percent of the population are females," is rejected at the .05 level of significance, and the theoretical hypothesis, "More than 50 percent of the population are females," is accepted (or gains credibility).

Note that in this particular example we used a one-tailed test (we were interested only in the proportion being greater than 50 percent). This was because past United States censuses informed us that this should be expected.

If one does not have such an expectation, then a two-tailed test ($H_1 \neq .50$, or the proportion is not 50 percent) should be used. In that case, the level of significance for each side of the sampling distribution would be $z_{(1+c)/2} = z_{.975} = 1.96$ and $z_{(1-c)/2} = z_{.025} = -1.96$, rather than $z_{.95} = 1.65$ for only the positive side.

Mean

When the parameter is the mean of the population μ, sample data can be used to estimate the value of the parameter, as well as for hypothesis testing. It is assumed that the sample is a simple random sample from the population. Furthermore, it is assumed that the variable (its values) is normally distributed in the population. Thus, the variable must be measured at the interval level or ratio level.

Estimates of the Parameter   There are two estimates of the parameter: (1) the point estimate, and (2) the interval estimate.

As mentioned in Chapter 7, the sample mean $\bar{X}$ is an unbiased estimate of the population mean μ. Thus, the researcher may compute the sample mean and claim it to be the best single estimate of the population mean. For example, in the NORC 1973 data, there was an item involving the age of each respondent when he or she first married. Table 15.1 presents the frequency distribution of the data for the married respondents ($n = 1{,}310$).

The mean of the sample can be found with the formula for grouped data (from equation 5.3):

$$\bar{X} = \frac{\Sigma(X_i \cdot f_i)}{n} = \frac{\Sigma(X_i \cdot f_i)}{1{,}310} = 22.142$$

where X_i = value of each category (age)
f_i = frequency of observations in each category

The numerator is the sum for all 35 categories of the products of X_i and f_i. The denominator is the number of respondents. Thus, the sample mean is 22.142, the best point estimate of the mean age of first marriage in the population.

For an interval estimate of the population mean, when the sample size is suf-

Table 15.1   Frequency Distribution of Age at First Marriage

Age at first marriage (X_i)	Frequency (f_i)	Age at first marriage (X_i)	Frequency (f_i)
13	2	31	8
14	6	32	13
15	15	33	7
16	37	34	4
17	87	35	8
18	136	36	2
19	138	37	5
20	120	39	3
21	176	40	6
22	114	41	1
23	101	42	1
24	79	43	2
25	61	44	3
26	54	45	2
27	31	46	1
28	29	55	1
29	31	63	1
30	25		

Source: NORC 1973 General Social Survey, for married respondents only ($n = 1{,}310$).

ficiently large, say, over 100, the regular z formula can be used (see equation 7.3):

$$\bar{X} + z_{(1+c)/2}\frac{s}{\sqrt{n}} \quad \text{and} \quad \bar{X} + z_{(1-c)/2}\frac{s}{\sqrt{n}}$$

where z = expected value for the confidence coefficient, $c = 1 - \alpha$, both tails
$s/\sqrt{n}$ = estimate $s_{\bar{x}}$ of the standard error of the mean for the sampling distribution of the mean

The s, the standard deviation of the sample, can be obtained by using the formula for grouped data (equation 5.9):

$$s = \sqrt{\frac{\Sigma X_i^2 f_i - (\Sigma X_i f_i)^2/n}{n-1}} = 4.956$$

If we set the confidence coefficient c at .99, then $z_{(1+c)/2} = z_{.995} = 2.58$, and $z_{(1-c)/2} = z_{.005} = -2.58$ (from Table 2, Appendix C). Thus, the interval estimate of the population mean age at first marriage is:

$$22.142 + 2.58\frac{4.956}{1,310} = 22.495$$

and

$$22.142 - 2.58\frac{4.956}{1,310} = 21.789$$

The researcher, then, concludes that, with .99 confidence, the mean age of the population at first marriage is caught somewhere between 22.495 and 21.789 years of age.

When the sample size is not sufficiently large, say, less than 100, the interval estimate of the population mean cannot be made with the normally distributed sampling distribution and the z value. Instead, a family of distributions derived from the normal curve, *t distributions* (Student's distributions) must be used. For the t distribution, each score is converted to a standard score relative to the population mean:

$$t = \frac{\bar{X} - \mu}{s/\sqrt{n}}$$

The distribution for repeated samples is a symmetric distribution with a mean of zero. However, since it is contingent on the sample size (in the denominator), there is a t distribution for each sample size. The t distributions are presented in

Table 4, Appendix C. The formulas for finding the interval estimate of the population mean for a small sample are:

$$\bar{X} + t_{(1+c)/2} \frac{s}{\sqrt{n}} \quad \text{and} \quad \bar{X} + t_{(1-c)/2} \frac{s}{\sqrt{n}} \tag{15.3}$$

For example, from the NORC 1973 data, if one wishes to estimate the population mean age at first marriage for black males only, the sample size for married black male respondents is $n = 69$. With a sample mean $\bar{X}$ of 23.855 and a sample standard deviation of 6.049, the researcher sets a confidence coefficient of .99. He may then go to Table 4, Appendix C, where he finds the column for $t_{(1+c)/2} = t_{.995} = t_{(1-c)/2} = -t_{.005}$. To find the appropriate value in the column, the degrees of freedom ν, or d.f., must be calculated. The degrees of freedom is $n - 1$, or 68 in our example. The reason why the degrees of freedom is $n - 1$ rather than n is that with the knowledge of the sample mean $\bar{X}$ we need only $n - 1$ scores to know what the other score must be. For instance, if we know that the mean is 4 for a group of five scores, we only need to know any four scores (e.g., 1, 2, 7, 5) to predict the fifth score (1 in this case).

One looks down the ν column. Since there is no value 68, the next lower value must be used, 60. Thus, for $\nu = 60$ and $t_{.995}$, the expected t percentile value equals 2.66. The interval estimate may now be calculated for equation 15.3:

$$23.855 + 2.66 \frac{6.049}{\sqrt{69}} = 25.792$$

and

$$23.855 - 2.66 \frac{6.049}{\sqrt{69}} = 21.918$$

The researcher concludes that with .99 probability the interval 25.792 to 21.918 will cover the population mean age at first marriage for black males. Comparing this interval with the one computed for all respondents (22.495 to 21.789), one notes that the interval is wider for the smaller sample size. Thus, there is a decrease in estimation precision as the sample size decreases.

Hypothesis Testing   To test a hypothesis about the mean in the population, the t distribution should again be used. The researcher sets up the null hypothesis and the theoretical hypothesis, and a t test can be made:

$$H_0: \mu = a$$
$$H_1: \mu \neq a$$

$$t = \frac{\bar{X} - a}{s/\sqrt{n}} \qquad \text{d.f.} = n - 1$$

For example, we wish to test the null hypothesis that white females tend to marry for the first time when they are 20 years of age. Thus, the H_0 is $\mu = 20$. The theoretical hypothesis is that they tend to marry for the first time when they are older than 20 years of age. Since there is always the possibility that they may tend to marry for the first time when they are less than 20 years old, a two-tailed test is used. Thus, the alternative hypothesis H_1 is $\mu \neq 20$. From the NORC 1973 sample, we find for married white female respondents the following statistics:

$$\bar{X} = 20.751$$
$$n = 634$$
$$s = 4.008$$

Thus,

$$t = \frac{20.751 - 20.000}{4.008/\sqrt{634}} = \frac{.751}{.159} = 4.72$$

We set the level of significance α at .01. For 633 degrees of freedom ($n - 1$), we go to the t distributions in Table 4, Appendix C, and find that the next lower available ν is 120. For $t_{(1+c)/2}$, $t_{.995}$, and $-t_{(1+c)/2}$, $-t_{.005}$, it equals 2.62 for 120 degrees of freedom.

The observed t (4.72) is much greater than the expected t (2.62); thus the null hypothesis can be rejected at the .01 level of significance, and the theoretical hypothesis can be accepted. We conclude that white females in the population, on the average, marry for the first time when they are over 20 years of age.

A remark on the use of the t distribution for hypothesis testing of the population mean is in order. When the sample size is sufficiently large, such as in our example in which $n = 634$, one may use the standard normal curve, the z test, in Table 2, Appendix C. However, as the sample size increases toward infinity (∞), the t values correspond closely to the z values for the same level of significance. For example, $t_{.95} = 1.645$ in Table 4, Appendix C, is almost the same as $z_{.95} = 1.65$ in Table 2, Appendix C. In fact, $t_{.95} = 1.66$ for 120 degrees of freedom deviates only about .01 from the z value. Thus, for simplicity, the t test can be used without losing generality for all sample sizes.

Variance

If one wishes to make inferences about the population variance σ^2, two assumptions must be met. First, the sample must be a simple random sample from the population; and second, the variable must be distributed normally in the population. Again, like the mean, the variable must be measured on the interval or ratio level.

Estimates of the Parameter   There are two estimates of the population variance of a variable: (1) the point estimate, and (2) the interval estimate. As mentioned in Chapter 7, the sample variance s^2 is an unbiased estimate of the population variance σ^2. For example, to make an inference about the variance of age at first marriage among white males in the population, one may examine the NORC 1973 sample data for married white male respondents. The sample variance, 27.421, constitutes the best point estimate of the population variance.

To construct an interval estimate for the population variance when the sample size is greater than 100, a formula with the use of the normal curve is available:

$$\frac{s^2(2n-2)}{(z_{(1+c)/2} + \sqrt{2n-2})^2} \quad \text{and} \quad \frac{s^2(2n-2)}{(z_{(1-c)/2} + \sqrt{2n-1})^2} \quad\quad (15.4)$$

where s^2 = sample variance

n = sample size

When a confidence coefficient c is specified, $z_{(1+c)/2}$ and $z_{(1-c)/2}$ can be found in Table 2, Appendix C.

For example, if one wishes to construct an interval estimate for the variance of age of first marriage among white males in the population, one may obtain the following statistics from the NORC 1973 sample:

$s^2 = 27.421$

$n = 506$

and, setting the confidence coefficient at .95, one finds from Table 2, Appendix C:

$z_{(1+c)/2} = z_{.975} = 1.96$

$z_{(1-c)/2} = z_{.025} = -1.96$

Then, the interval is:

$$\frac{(27.421)(506-2)}{(1.96 + \sqrt{506-2})^2} = \frac{13820.184}{595.845} = 23.194$$

and

$$\frac{(27.421)(506-2)}{(-1.96 + \sqrt{506-2})^2} = \frac{13820.184}{419.84} = 32.918$$

Thus, one estimates that with .95 probability the interval 32.918 to 23.194 will cover the population variance of age of first marriage among white males.

To construct an interval estimate for the population variance σ^2, when the sample size is less than 100, another family of distributions must be introduced.

Chi-square (χ^2) distributions are derived from the normal distribution in that each score is converted to a distance score to the mean and standardized over the population variance:

$$\chi^2 = \frac{\Sigma(X_i - \bar{X})^2}{\sigma^2}$$

$$= \frac{(n-1)\dfrac{\Sigma(X_i - \bar{X})^2}{n-1}}{\sigma^2}$$

$$= \frac{(n-1)s^2}{\sigma^2}$$

Again, it can be seen that χ^2 is affected by the sample size n. Thus, there is a family of chi-square distributions for different sample sizes. Table 3, Appendix C, presents the percentile values of the chi-square distributions. To find the appropriate χ^2 value in the table, a confidence coefficient c must be specified, and the degrees of freedom ν is $n-1$.

The interval estimate of the population variance is given by:

$$\frac{(n-1)s^2}{\chi^2_{(1+c)/2}} \quad \text{and} \quad \frac{(n-1)s^2}{\chi^2_{(1-c)/2}}$$

For example, if one wishes to construct the interval estimate of the population variance of age at first marriage for persons who have gone to graduate school, the following statistics for age at first marriage are calculated from the NORC data for 41 married respondents who have done graduate work:

$$s^2 = 30.845$$
$$n = 41$$

If the confidence coefficient is set at .95, the χ^2 value for 40 degrees of freedom at $\chi^2_{(1+c)/2}$ and $\chi^2_{(1-c)/2}$ can be found in Table 3, Appendix C:

$$\chi^2_{.975} = 59.3 \qquad \chi^2_{.025} = 24.2 \qquad \text{d.f.} = 40$$

Thus, the interval estimate is:

$$\frac{(40)(30,845)}{59.3} = 20.81 \quad \text{and} \quad \frac{(40)(30.845)}{24.2} = 50.98$$

One concludes that with .95 probability the interval 50.98 to 20.81 will span the population variance.

It should be noted that both the normal curve and the t distribution are symmetric; therefore, $z_{(1+c)/2}$ and $z_{(1-c)/2}$ give the same value, although with different signs, as do $t_{(1+c)/2}$ and $t_{(1-c)/2}$. However, χ^2 is not distributed symmetrically; thus the values for $\chi^2_{(1+c)/2}$ and $\chi^2_{(1-c)/2}$ are different, although always positive.

Since the standard deviation σ is the square root of the variance σ^2, the interval estimate of the population standard deviation can be obtained by taking the square roots of the two estimated values of the variance.

Hypothesis Testing.   For testing a hypothesis, chi-square distributions are again used. More specifically,

$$H_0 : \sigma^2 = a$$
$$H_1 : \sigma^2 \neq a$$

$$\chi^2 = \frac{(n-1)s^2}{a} \qquad \text{d.f.} = n - 1$$

For example, if we wish to test the theoretical hypothesis that the population variance of age at first marriage for persons who have gone to graduate school is less than 35, for a two-tailed test at .01 level of significance, then,

$$H_0 : \sigma^2 = 35.00$$
$$H_1 : \sigma^2 \neq 35.00$$
$$s^2 = 30.845$$
$$n = 41$$

$$\chi^2 = \frac{(41-1)(30.845)}{35.00} = 35.25$$

For a level of significance at .01 for two tails ($\chi^2_{.995}$) and 40 degrees of freedom, the χ^2 value is 66.8. Since the observed value (35.25) is less than the expected value (66.8), the null hypothesis cannot be rejected at a .01 level of significance. Thus, we have failed to confirm that the population variance for age at first marriage among those who have gone to graduate school is less than 35.

SUMMARY

This chapter has dealt with some techniques of univariate analysis. Several commonly used statistics (the proposition, the mean, and the variance) are used to infer to parameter values as well as to test hypotheses. For the estimation of parameters, both the point estimate and the interval estimate are discussed. For hypothesis testing, *when the sample size is sufficiently large ($n > 100$), formulas utilizing the sampling distribution of the standard normal curve can be used.*

When the sample size is small ($n \leq 100$), other distributions must be used in *testing the hypothesis. For a hypothesis involving the population mean, t* distributions can be used. For a hypothesis involving the population variance, chi-square (χ^2) distributions are used.

The t distribution and the chi-square distribution, along with the F distribution, are used frequently in multivariate analysis, to be discussed in the next chapter.

Chapter 16

Multivariate Analysis

In Chapter 6, the relationships between two or more variables in a data matrix were described in a variety of ways. The choice of the descriptive technique is to a large extent determined by the scales of the variables involved and by the models to be constructed. More specifically, three types of models are identified. The *contingency model* is used to describe variables measured on any level of measurement (nominal, ordinal, interval, or ratio). The *difference-between-groups model* is used when the independent variable is measured at any level of scale but the dependent variable is measured at the interval or ratio level. Finally, the *regression and correlation model* is used when both the independent and the dependent variables are measured at the interval or ratio level and the relationship described is an associative (linear) one.

This chapter will take up statistical inference for the three types of models. The task of multivariate analysis, for each model, is to use the information contained in the data matrix of a sample, along with the properties of several theoretical distributions (such as the normal curve, the *t* distribution, and the chi-square distribution), to estimate whether or not certain relationships among the variables hold true in the population. To begin such a task, it must be assumed that the data matrix represents the response patterns of a simple random sample drawn from the population to which the inference is being attempted. Other assumptions also will be made in terms of each group of models. These assumptions are necessary for hypothesis testing. When statistical techniques are used for description of the data matrix, then most of the assumptions can be relaxed or ignored (see Chapter 6).

The data sets to be used in this chapter to illustrate the various techniques either are hypothetical or may not necessarily come from such simple random samples. The reader is cautioned that the use of the data sets in this chapter is necessarily for illustration purposes. Even when the data comes from a NORC survey, necessary adjustments are made to suit the purpose of illustration. Thus, no substantive interpretations about the data are warranted.

CONTINGENCY HYPOTHESIS

In a contingency table, two or more variables are cross-tabulated by their categories. The frequencies in the marginals for each category of each variable, as well as each cell in the table, can be expressed symbolically, as in Table 6.3. For example, a contingency table for religious affiliation (Protestant or Catholic) and race (white or black) from an NORC sample is presented in Table 16.1.

$$
\begin{aligned}
f_{11} &= 782 & f_{12} &= 152 & f_{1.} &= 934 \\
f_{21} &= 369 & f_{22} &= 15 & f_{2.} &= 384 \\
f_{.1} &= 1{,}151 & f_{.2} &= 167 & n &= 1{,}318
\end{aligned}
$$

While percentages can be computed for each cell relative either to the total n, or each row or cell total for describing the data, a researcher may wish to ask whether or not there is any relationship between religion and race (e.g., Are whites less likely than blacks to be Protestants?) in the population from which the sample was drawn. Assuming that the sample is a simple random sample from that population, the researcher in effect has formulated a theoretical hypothesis to be tested. To test such a hypothesis, a statistical hypothesis must be constructed.

There are two ways to construct a statistical hypothesis for a contingency table; it can either assume total randomness or take into account the marginals ($f_{1.}$, $f_{2.}$, $f_{.1}$, $f_{.2}$). If one assumes total randomness, then every cell should be ex-

Table 16.1   Religion by Race

Religion	Race		Total
	White	Black	
Protestant	782	152	934
Catholic	369	15	384
Total	1,151	167	1,318

Source: NORC 1973 General Social Survey, for selected categories only.

pected to have the same number of observations or percentages (probability) of occurrence. For example, the statistical (null) hypothesis, assuming total randomness for the table in Table 16.1, will be:

$$H_0: f_{11} = f_{12} = f_{21} = f_{22} = \frac{n}{m}$$

$$p_{11} = p_{12} = p_{21} = p_{22} = \frac{1}{m}$$

where n = grand total of respondents
$\quad\quad m$ = number of cells

Or, one may use the information of the marginals. The distribution of observations or percentages of occurrence in each cell should be contingent on the number of observations belonging to the specific categories (the marginals) relative to the grand total. For example, f_{11} should be contingent on $f_{1.}$ (the first row total) and $f_{.1}$ (the first column total) relative to n (the grand total). For if there are more whites than blacks and more Protestants than Catholics in the population, then expectation of the occurrence of white Protestants in the sample should certainly be greater than any other combination in the table. In the analysis to follow, the second type of null hypothesis will be constructed, since usually the marginals are available in the data. As long as the sample is a simple random one from the population, the use of marginal information will improve the precision of our expectations—the null hypothesis will become more relevant to the theoretical hypothesis (see Chapter 7 for a discussion of the relevancy of the null hypothesis to the theoretical hypothesis).

Based on the information in the marginals and the grand total, distributions of expected occurrences of observations can be constructed. These are expected distributions for the null hypothesis. That is, if the null hypothesis is true, then the actual distribution of frequencies in the cells should be approximately the same as the expected distribution. Then, a statistical test is administered to determine the extent to which the actual distributions deviate from the expected distributions. With a preset level of significance, one will be led to either accept the null hypothesis or to reject it. When the null hypothesis is rejected, one gives more credibility to the theoretical hypothesis.

For the test of a contingency hypothesis, the χ^2 distribution can be used. First, however, the expected distributions must be constructed. The expected frequency of a cell in the ith row and the jth column is:

$$F_{ij} = \frac{f_{i.}f_{.j}}{n}$$

where $f_{i.}$ = marginal for the ith row (the ith row total)
$\quad\quad f_{.j}$ = marginal for the jth column (the jth column total)
$\quad\quad n$ = grand total

Then the χ^2 test is:

$$\chi^2 = \sum\sum \frac{(f_{ij} - F_{ij})^2}{F_{ij}}$$

or   (16.1)

$$= n\left(\sum\sum \frac{f_{ij}^2}{f_{i.} f_{.j}} - 1\right) \quad \text{d.f.} = (r - 1)(c - 1)$$

There are two alternative and equivalent formulas for the χ^2 test. In the first formula in equation 16.1, the expected frequency is computed for each cell. Then, the expected frequency is subtracted from the observed frequency. This result is squared and divided by the expected frequency.

The operation is repeated for each cell and summed over all cells (as indicated by the double summation signs). Or, one may square the observed frequency for each cell and divide it by the product of the two marginals. Then, such ratios from all the cells are summed. Subtract 1 from this sum, multiply the result by n, and this will give χ^2. The second formula is usually easier to use, since it avoids computation of the expected frequencies.

The degrees of freedom needs explanation. r designates the number of rows and c the number of columns in the table. For example, in Table 16.1, there are two rows and two columns; thus, the degrees of freedom is $(2 - 1)(2 - 1) = 1$. Again, the reasoning has to do with the pieces of information required. Since we know the marginals for each row and column, when the frequency in any one cell is known, we can figure out the frequencies for the other three cells. Thus, there is only 1 degree of freedom.

We may now calculate χ^2 for the data in Table 16.1:

$$
\begin{aligned}
f_{11}^2 &= (782)^2 = 611,524 & f_1.f_{.1} &= (934)(1,151) = 1,075,034 \\
f_{12}^2 &= (152)^2 = 23,104 & f_1.f_{.2} &= (934)(167) = 155,978 \\
f_{21}^2 &= (369)^2 = 136,161 & f_2.f_{.1} &= (384)(1,151) = 441,984 \\
f_{22}^2 &= (15)^2 = 225 & f_2.f_{.2} &= (384)(167) = 64,128
\end{aligned}
$$

$$
\begin{aligned}
\therefore \quad \chi^2 &= (1,318)(611,524/1,075,034 + 23,104/155,978 + 136,161/441,984 + \\
&\qquad 225/64,128 - 1) \\
&= (1,318)(.5688 + .1481 + .3081 + .0035 - 1) \\
&= (1,318)(.0285) \\
&= 37.56
\end{aligned}
$$

If the level of significance is set at .05, we find in Table 3, Appendix C, for 1 degree of freedom, $\chi_{.975}^2 = 5.0$. The observed χ^2 (37.56) in fact is significant beyond $\chi_{.999}^2$ (10.8). Thus, the null hypothesis can be rejected, and the theoretical hypothesis can be accepted. Blacks are more likely to belong to the Protestant church than are whites in the population.

The reader is reminded that the χ^2 test is affected by the sample size n, as it plays a prominent role in equation 16.1. As the sample size increases, the likeli-hood of rejecting the null hypothesis also increases.

HYPOTHESIS ABOUT THE DIFFERENCE BETWEEN GROUPS

When a researcher suspects that several groups, defined over a variable such as sex, race, student classification, etc., hold different attitudes or show different be-havioral patterns, and when such attitudes and behaviors can be measured at the interval or ratio level, he is faced with a difference-between-groups problem. In this problem, the population can be classified into categories of a variable, the in-dependent variable, and differences should be observed in terms of the dependent variable. The classification of the population may be according to a number of in-dependent variables (race and sex, for example, would give the four major groups: "white males," "white females," "black males," and "black females"). When simple random samples are drawn from each of the groups in the population, the data provide the basis for the testing of the hypothesis.

As discussed in Chapter 6, a difference between groups can be described in terms of the central tendency (such as the mean) or the dispersion (the variance and the standard deviation). Testing a hypothesis about a difference between groups can also be done in terms of the discrepancy of the central tendencies between groups or of the dispersions between groups for the dependent variable. In this section, we will focus on the case in which the defining independent variables are measured on nominal or higher scales and the dependent variable is measured on the interval or ratio level.

The first technique, testing the hypothesis in terms of the difference of the means between groups, uses the t distribution; and the second technique, testing the hypothesis in terms of the difference of the variances between groups, uses the F distribution. The reader is not yet familiar with the F distribution; it will be in-troduced later in this section. Suffice it to say here that each F distribution is a ratio of two χ^2's and a direct variation of the t distribution.

The first technique is called the t *test* or the *difference of the means test,* and the second technique is called the F *test* or, more specifically in this case, the *analysis of variance* (ANOVA). The two tests can be interconverted rather easily ($F = t^2$ for the appropriate degrees of freedom). The t test is easy to use when a comparison is made for two groups. For three or more groups, the t test becomes much more complicated, and the F test should be used. We shall return to this issue later.

t Test for the Difference of the Means

The t test can be applied to an independent variable measured on a nominal or higher scale and a dependent variable measured on an interval or ratio scale. To use the test, three assumptions must be made: (1) that the samples are simple random samples from the groups defined by the categories of the independent variables in the population, (2) that the dependent variable is normally distributed in each of the groups in the population, and (3) that the variances of the dependent variable in the groups are the same (equal population variances for all groups, $\sigma_1^2 = \sigma_2^2 = \sigma_3^2 = \sigma_4^2 = \ldots$, or homoscedasticity).

There are a number of t tests applicable to different data sets.[1] Here the discussion will focus on the t test for data fulfilling the three assumptions mentioned above and will be illustrated with a data set which has two groups.

The specific null hypothesis to be tested is that the groups do not differ, on the average, on the dependent variable; $\mu_1 = \mu_2$ or $\mu_1 - \mu_2 = 0$. When the difference obtained in the samples ($\overline{X}_1 - \overline{X}_2$) is compared with the expected difference, zero in this case, it can be determined whether or not for a specified level of significance the observed difference can be considered a rare event. When it can, the null hypothesis is rejected and the theoretical hypothesis is accepted. When it cannot, the null hypothesis cannot be rejected and the theoretical hypothesis cannot be accepted.

The formula for the t test when there are two categories of the independent variable is:

$$t = \frac{\overline{X}_1 - \overline{X}_2}{s_{\overline{X}_1 - \overline{X}_2}} \tag{16.2}$$

where $s_{\overline{X}_1 - \overline{X}_2}$ is the point estimate of the standard error of the sampling distribution of the statistic $\overline{X}_1 - \overline{X}_2$ (called the standard error of the mean difference) and can be found by:

$$s_{\overline{X}_1 - \overline{X}_2} = \sqrt{\left(\frac{(n_1 - 1)s_1^2 + (n_2 - 1)s_2^2}{n_1 + n_2 - 2}\right)\left(\frac{1}{n_1} + \frac{1}{n_2}\right)} \tag{16.3}$$

where s_1^2 and s_2^2 = variance of the two samples

n_1 and n_2 = size of the two samples

An illustration of the t test appears in Table 16.2. Hypothetical data are constructed for two groups of the independent variable, sex (female and male students), on the dependent variable, attitude toward the college the respondents attend. If it is assumed that the attitude scale is an interval variable and the two samples, for females and males, are simple random samples of the two groups attending the college, the data can be tested against the null hypothesis that there is no difference, on the average, between the two groups in their attitude toward the college. The theoretical hypothesis is that female students tend to be more favorable toward the college than male students. The hypothesis testing is set at a

---

[1] There are five models for which the Student's t distribution is applicable; see, for example, discussions in Helen M. Walker and Joseph Lev, *Statistical Inference,* Holt, New York, 1953, chap. 7, especially pp. 144–160. The model discussed in the text here deals with the difference of two means between two groups of respondents with independent samples when the population variances are unknown but presumed equal.

Table 16.2 A t Test of Difference of the Means (Hypothetical Data)

Attitude toward college (X_i)	Female			Male		
	f_i	$X_i f_i$	$X_i^2 f_i$	f_i	$X_i f_i$	$X_i^2 f_i$
1 (most favorable)	1	1	1	0	0	0
2	4	8	16	0	0	0
3	6	18	54	1	3	9
4	10	40	160	4	16	64
5	2	10	50	8	40	200
6	0	0	0	6	36	216
7 (most unfavorable)	0	0	0	3	21	147

Formulas:

$$t = \frac{\bar{X}_1 - \bar{X}_2}{s_{\bar{X}_1 - \bar{X}_2}} \quad \text{where } s_{\bar{X}_1 - \bar{X}_2} = \sqrt{\left[\frac{(n_1 - 1)s_1^2 + (n_2 - 1)s_2^2}{n_1 + n_2 - 2}\right]\left(\frac{1}{n_1} + \frac{1}{n_2}\right)}$$

Computations:

Females:

$$\Sigma(X_i f_i) = 77 \qquad \Sigma(X_i^2 f_i) = 281$$

$$\bar{X}_1 = \frac{\Sigma(X_i f_i)}{n_1} = \frac{77}{23} = 3.3478$$

Males:

$$\Sigma(X_i f_i) = 116 \qquad \Sigma(X_i^2 f_i) = 636$$

$$\bar{X}_2 = \frac{\Sigma(X_i f_i)}{n_2} = \frac{116}{22} = 5.2727$$

$$s_1^2 = \frac{\Sigma(X_i^2 f_i) - [\Sigma(X_i f_i)]^2/n_1}{n_1 - 1} = \frac{281 - \dfrac{(77)^2}{23}}{22} = 1.0556$$

$$s_2^2 = \frac{636 - (116)^2/22}{21} = 1.1602$$

$$s_{\bar{X}_1 - \bar{X}_2} = \sqrt{\left[\frac{(22)(1.0556) + (21)(1.1602)}{43}\right]\left(\frac{1}{23} + \frac{1}{22}\right)} = 0.3138$$

$$t = \frac{3.3478 - 5.2727}{0.3138} = \frac{1.9249}{0.3138} = 6.1342$$

0.5 level of significance and for a two-tailed test. To use Table 4, Appendix C, for the t values, the degrees of freedom v must be determined. The appropriate degrees of freedom are:

$$\text{d.f.} = n - k$$

where $n = n_1 + n_2$
k = number of groups

For the example in Table 16.2, it is 43. Since Table 4, Appendix C, does not contain $v = 43$, the next lower value, 40, should be used. For the .05 level of significance ($1 - c$), $t_{(1+c)/2} = t_{.975} = -t_{(1-c)/2} = -t_{.025} = 2.02$ at $v = 40$. Since the observed t (6.13 from Table 16.2) is much greater than the expected t (2.02), the null hypothesis that there is no attitudinal difference between the two groups of students is rejected at the .05 level of significance, and the theoretical hypothesis that female students are more favorable toward the college than male students is accepted.

Analysis of Variance (ANOVA)

When three or more groups are involved in the comparison, the t test becomes complicated, as the estimate of the standard error of the sampling distribution involving pooling of the individual sample variances (equation 16.3) expands quickly for more groups. An alternative testing procedure, using the F distribution, is commonly used. It is known as *analysis of variance* (ANOVA). It requires the same assumptions as the t test: independent and random samples, normal distribution of the dependent variable in each population group, and homoscedasticity of the variances.

Suppose four simple random samples of ten respondents each are drawn from four groups in a population defined over sex and race (for married persons only) and the age at first marriage for all respondents. The hypothetical data are presented in Table 16.3. If we assume that the variable, age at first marriage, is normally distributed in each group in the population and the variance of the variable is identical, $\sigma_1^2 = \sigma_2^2 = \sigma_3^2 = \sigma_4^2$, the task is to ascertain whether the theoretical hypothesis that different groups, on the average, tend to differ on age at first marriage is valid.

To test the theoretical hypothesis a null hypothesis, that all groups on the average tend to marry for the first time at about the same age, is set up. ANOVA tests the null hypothesis with information about the variances of the dependent variable in the population groups. Its rationale is that, if the theoretical hypothesis is right, that is, if the independent variable (groups defined by sex and race, for example) does make a difference for the dependent variable (age at first marriage), we should observe that variations (variance) among the persons on the

Table 16.3 Hypothetical Data on Age at First Marriage for Four Sample Groups

Group I, white males (Y_{i1})	Group II, white females (Y_{i2})	Group III, black males (Y_{i3})	Group IV, black females (Y_{i4})
30	26	25	20
17	17	17	15
19	22	33	17
20	17	20	19
24	18	23	17
25	19	24	23
27	21	24	21
23	20	25	21
23	20	21	19
42	30	28	18
$\sum_{i=1}^{10} Y_{i1} = 250$	$\sum_{i=1}^{10} Y_{i2} = 210$	$\sum_{i=1}^{10} Y_{i3} = 240$	$\sum_{i=1}^{10} Y_{i4} = 190$

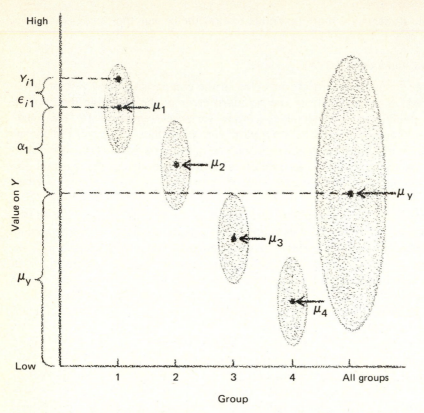

Figure 16.1   Hypothetical dispersion of values on the dependent variable (Y) for four groups and the combined group (the population).

dependent variable (age at first marriage) are less than variations (variances) among all persons. In other words, persons belonging to the same group should show greater similarity (less variance) on age at first marriage than all persons from all groups combined. This rationale can be seen in Figure 16.1. Thus, for example, for a person belonging to the first group Y_{i1}, the distance from his value on the dependent variable Y to the group mean μ_1 should, on the average, be less than that from his group mean μ_1 to the grand mean for all groups combined[2] μ_y.

On the other hand, the null hypothesis suggests that there should not be such a difference, because the independent variable does not make any difference for the dependent variable. In other words, the distance from each observation to the group mean, on the average, should be about the same as that from each group mean to the grand mean.

To determine which hypothesis is more credible, ANOVA computes the average distance from each observation to the group mean, called the *variance*

---

[2] In Figure 16.1, the dispersion of observations is represented as an olive-shaped cluster of dots. Within each group, the observations may only differ on the dependent variable Y, and have an identical value on the independent variable (a group). The clustering is used only to show the normal distribution of the values on the dependent variable within each group.

within each independent variable category V_w, and the average distance from each group mean to the grand mean, called the *variance between means* V_b.

From the researcher's point of view, the independent variable should make a difference in terms of the dependent variable. Therefore, the variance between means V_b represents the usefulness of the independent variable for the dependent variable. The variance between means is then interpreted as the power of the independent variable to "explain" the dependent variable. The greater the variance between means, the greater the explaining power the independent variable has as far as the dependent variable is concerned. Thus, the variance between means is also called the *explained variance*. The variance within each independent category, on the other hand, represents the residual variations between each observation and the group mean, which cannot be explained by the independent variable. Thus, the variance within each independent variable category is also called the *unexplained variance*, the *residual variance*, or the *error variance*.

A ratio between the two variances is set up:

$$\text{Variance ratio} = \frac{V_b}{V_w}$$

If the theoretical hypothesis is more credible, we should expect a relatively greater V_b than V_w; and the variance ratio should be significantly greater than one. If the null hypothesis is more credible, we should expect V_b to be approximately the same as V_w; and the variance ratio should not be significantly different from one.

In the following section, we will justify the variance ratio with further mathematical elaboration. The reader who has no interest in learning further mathematical justification may skip the next section.

Further Elaboration of the ANOVA Model

The basic ANOVA model suggests that a person's score on a dependent variable Y in the population can be represented by three linear components: (1) the population mean of the dependent variable over all persons, (2) the deviation from the population mean to the mean of the group to which the person belongs, and (3) the deviation from the group mean to the person's actual score:

$$Y_{ij} = \mu_y + \alpha_j + \epsilon_{ij} \tag{16.4}$$

where y_{ij} = score of the ith person in the jth group on the variable Y
μ_y = population mean on variable Y
α_j = difference between the population mean and the mean of group j on variable Y
ϵ_{ij} = difference between the mean of group j and the score of person i on variable Y

This relationship can be seen in Figure 16.1. For example, for a person belonging to group 1, his score on Y, Y_{i1}, can be expressed as consisting of three parts on the Y axis. The first part is the score on Y for all persons, as represented by the population mean μ_y. The second part is the deviation between the population mean and the mean for persons in group 1, α_1. And the third part is the deviation from the group mean to what is left of the ith person's score on Y, ϵ_{i1}. When the three parts are added up, the ith person's score on Y is obtained, Y_{i1}. Thus, the ANOVA model is an additive model.

To construct a deviation score between the actual score Y_{ij} and the population mean μ_y, we simply move μ_y from the right-hand side of equation 16.4 to the left-hand side:

$$Y_{ij} - \mu_y = \alpha_j + \epsilon_{ij} \tag{16.5}$$

Now, the equation has three deviation terms. On the left-hand side, it is the deviation from the individual score to the population mean. On the right-hand side, the first term is a deviation score from the group mean to the population mean, and the second term is the deviation from the individual score to the group mean. These deviations can be estimated from the samples:

$\hat{\mu}_y = \bar{Y}_{..} =$ the mean on Y for all respondents in all groups $=$ the grand mean

$\hat{\alpha}_j = \bar{Y}_{.j} - \bar{Y}_{..} =$ the deviation from the mean of group j to the grand mean

$\hat{\epsilon}_{ij} = Y_{ij} - \bar{Y}_{.j} =$ the deviation from the individual score of the ith person to the mean of group j

Thus, equation 16.5 can be estimated from:

$$Y_{ij} - \bar{Y}_{..} = (\bar{Y}_{.j} - \bar{Y}_{..}) + (Y_{ij} - \bar{Y}_{.j}) \tag{16.6}$$

To obtain the average of all deviations for all respondents, two operations must be added to equation 16.6 which represents only the deviation from the grand mean for one respondent i in group j. First, a double summation sign ($\Sigma\Sigma$) must be used. The first summation sign indicates the summation over all groups, and the second summation sign indicates the summation over all respondents in each group. Second, both sides of the equation must be squared; otherwise, the sum of the deviations will always equal zero (see discussion on the variance and the standard deviation in Chapter 5). Thus, for J groups and n_j respondents in each group,

$$\sum_{j=1}^{J} \sum_{i=1}^{n_j} (Y_{ij} - \bar{Y}_{..})^2 = \sum_{j=1}^{J} \sum_{i=1}^{n_j} [(\bar{Y}_{.j} - \bar{Y}_{..}) + (Y_{ij} - \bar{Y}_{.j})]^2$$

$$= \sum_{j=1}^{J} \sum_{i=1}^{n_j} [(\bar{Y}_{.j} - \bar{Y}_{..})^2 + 2(\bar{Y}_{.j} - \bar{Y}_{..})(Y_{ij} - \bar{Y}_{.j}) + (Y_{ij} - \bar{Y}_{.j})^2]$$

$$= \sum_{j=1}^{J} \sum_{i=1}^{n_j} (\bar{Y}_{.j} - \bar{Y}_{..})^2 + 2\sum_{j=1}^{J} \sum_{i=1}^{n_j} (\bar{Y}_{.j} - \bar{Y}_{..})(Y_{ij} - \bar{Y}_{.j}) + \sum\sum (Y_{ij} - \bar{Y}_{.j})^2$$

The second term on the right-hand side of the equation drops out, since the sum of each of the deviation terms will equal zero:

$$\sum_{i=1}^{n_j} (Y_{ij} - \bar{Y}_{.j}) = \sum_{j=1}^{J} (\bar{Y}_{.j} - \bar{Y}_{..}) = 0$$

Further, the first term on the right-hand side is the sum of the squared deviations from each group mean to the grand mean. Since the group mean is the same for all n_j respondents in the jth group, the term becomes $\Sigma n_j (\bar{Y}_{.j} - \bar{Y}_{..})^2$. Thus, the equation is simplified:

$$\sum \sum (Y_{ij} - \bar{Y}_{..})^2 = \sum n_j (\bar{Y}_{.j} - \bar{Y}_{..})^2 + \sum \sum (Y_{ij} - \bar{Y}_{.j})^2 \qquad (16.7)$$

This equation is known as the *sum-of-squares equation*. The sum of squares on the left-hand side of the equation is for deviations from every respondent to the grand mean; it is called the *total sum of squares SS_t*. The first term on the right-hand side is the sum of squares for the deviations from all group means to the grand mean; it is called the *sum of squares between groups SS_b*. And, the second term on the right-hand side is the sum of deviations for each respondent to the group mean; it is called the *sum of squares within groups SS_w*.

Equation 16.7 indicates that the total sum of squares can be broken down into two additive sums of squares—the sum of squares between groups and the sum of squares within groups:

$$SS_t = SS_b + SS_w \qquad (16.8)$$

Finally, to convert these components to variance terms, we have to take the average of each sum-of-squares term. To take the average, the appropriate degrees of freedom for each term are used. If there are n respondents and J groups, then:

    d.f. for $SS_b = J - 1$
    d.f. for $SS_w = n - 1$

and

    d.f. for $SS_t = n - 1$

These variance terms are called the *means of squares MS*:

$$MS_w = \frac{SS_w}{\text{d.f.}} = \frac{\sum \sum (Y_{ij} - Y_{.j})^2}{n - J}$$

$$MS_b = \frac{SS_b}{\text{d.f.}} = \frac{\sum n_j (Y_{.j} - Y_{..})^2}{J - 1}$$

Also,

$$MS_t = \frac{SS_t}{\text{d.f.}} = \frac{\sum \sum (Y_{ij} - Y_{..})^2}{n - 1}$$

Recall that the task at hand is to construct a ratio between the between-group variance and the within-group variance. So, the ratio between MS_b and MS_w can be used. The ratio between two variances constitutes an F distribution. Thus:

$$F = \frac{MS_b}{MS_w}$$

Each F test is based on two sets of degrees of freedom, one for the numerator and another for the denominator. In ANOVA they are $J - 1$ and $n - J$, respectively.

Analysis of Variance (ANOVA) Continued

From the preceding section, it can be seen the F test can be administered to a ratio of two variances, the mean squares of deviations between groups MS_b and the mean squares of deviations within groups MS_w, for the respective $J - 1$ and $n - J$ degrees of freedom:

$$F = \frac{MS_b}{MS_w} \qquad \text{for } J - 1 \text{ and } n - J \text{ degrees of freedom} \tag{16.9}$$

where J = number of groups
n = total number of respondents in all groups

To compute the MS_b and MS_w from data such as those in Table 16.3 directly without first calculating the deviations, the following equivalent formulas can be used:

$$MS_b = \frac{\sum\limits_{j=1}^{J} \dfrac{(\sum\limits_{i=1}^{n_j} Y_{ij})^2}{n_j} - \dfrac{(\sum\limits_{j=1}^{J} \sum\limits_{i=1}^{n_j} Y_{ij})^2}{n}}{J - 1} \tag{16.10a}$$

$$MS_w = \frac{\sum\limits_{j=1}^{J} \sum\limits_{i=1}^{n_j} Y_{ij}^2 - \sum\limits_{j=1}^{J} \dfrac{(\sum\limits_{i=1}^{n_j} Y_{ij})^2}{n_j}}{n - J} \tag{16.10b}$$

where Y_{ij} = score on the dependent variable Y of the ith respondent in group j
n_j = number of respondents in group j
J = number of groups
n = total number of respondents in all groups

$$\sum_{i=1}^{n_j} = \text{sum of all scores for all respondents } (n_j) \text{ in group } j$$

$$\sum_{j=1}^{J} = \text{sum of all scores for all } J \text{ groups}$$

Now we may illustrate the use of ANOVA in testing a hypothesis for the data in Table 16.3. Our theoretical hypothesis is that different groups composed of race and sex classifications tend to marry for the first time at different ages. The null hypothesis is then that the groups, on the average, do not marry for the first time at different ages.

$$H_0: \mu_1 = \mu_2 = \mu_3 = \mu_4$$

The procedure of computing MS_b and MS_w with equations 16.10a and 16.10b is presented in Table 16.4.

If it is decided that the level of significance (α) be set at .05, the expected F value ($F_{.95}$) for the null hypothesis can be found in Table 5, Appendix C. To use this table, we need the two sets of degrees of freedom for MS_b and MS_w; they are

Table 16.4   Analysis of Variance of Data in Table 16.3

Group	Group size (n_j)	Sum of scores $\left(\sum_{i=1}^{n_j} \mathbf{Y}_{ij}\right)$	Sum of squared scores $\left(\sum_{i=1}^{n_j} \mathbf{Y}_{ij}^2\right)$	Squared sum of scores $\left[\left(\sum_{i=1}^{n_j} \mathbf{Y}_{ij}\right)^2\right]$
I	10	250	6,702	62,500
II	10	210	4,564	44,100
III	10	240	5,934	57,600
IV	10	190	3,660	36,100

J (number of groups) $= 4$

n (total number of respondents) $= \sum_{j=1}^{J} n_j = 40$

$\sum_{j=1}^{J} \sum_{i=1}^{n_j} Y_{ij}$ (sum of all scores) $= 890$

$\left(\sum_{j=1}^{J} \sum_{i=1}^{n_j} Y_{ij}\right)^2$ (squared sum of all scores) $= 792,100$

$$MS_b = \frac{62,500/10 + 44,100/10 + 57,600/10 + 36,100/10 - 792,100/10}{4 - 1}$$

$$= \frac{227.5}{3} = 75.83$$

$$MS_w = \frac{6,702 + 4,564 + 5,934 + 3,660 - 62,500/10 - 44,100/10 - 57,600/10 - 36,100/10}{40 - 4}$$

$$= \frac{830}{36} = 23.06$$

Table 16.5   Summary of ANOVA from Table 16.4

Source of variation	Sum of squares (SS)	Degrees of freedom (d.f.)	Mean squares (MS)	Observed value (F)	Expected value ($F_{.95}$)
Between means	227.5	3	75.83	3.29	2.86
Within groups	830.0	36	23.06		
Total	1,057.5	39			

$J - 1$ and $n - J$, respectively. In the example, there are 3 and 36 degrees of freedom. The degrees of freedom (3) for the numerator (MS_b) corresponds to the values of the columns in Table 5, Appendix C (ν_1); and the degrees of freedom (36) for the denominator (MS_w) correspond to the values of the rows in Table 5, Appendix C (ν_2). Thus, we find two values in the third column and the thirty-sixth row; 2.86 in lightface type and 4.38 in boldface type. The lightface value is for $F_{.95}$ (confidence coefficient .95), and the boldface value is for $F_{.99}$ (confidence coefficient .99). Since the preassigned level of significance for the problem at hand is at .05, the value of the lightface type for $F_{.95}$ is the expected value (2.86).

The observed F value is found by dividing MS_b into MS_w (equation 16.9), 3.29. Since the observed F value is greater than the expected F value at the preset .05 level of significance, the null hypothesis is rejected. The theoretical hypothesis that different groups composed of sex and race classifications differ in age at first marriage is confirmed at .05 level of significance. These comparisons are summarized in Table 16.5.

It should be noted that for the F test, usually the one-tailed test is used. This is so, because one has no interest in the other tail, when MS_b is smaller than MS_w or the observed F value is less than 1.

Also note that $F = t^2$, for similar degrees of freedom. Thus, for testing a difference between groups, the F test can always be used. The t test is frequently used, because it is the easier of the two tests to compute when there are only two groups involved. When there are three or more groups, the standard error for the t test becomes complicated; thus the F test is preferred to the t test.

Analysis of Variance and Experiments

ANOVA is most frequently used in conjunction with experiments, because an experiment usually involves a nominal or ordinal independent variable in the limited number of treatments the researcher can manipulate. Also, some interval or ratio scales can be constructed as a measure of the dependent variable. The ANOVA method can also be extended to accommodate multitreatment designs. There is a variety of factorial designs in ANOVA.[3]

[3] Interested readers should consult: E. F. Lindquist, *Design and Analysis of Experiments in Psychology and Education,* Houghton Mifflin, Boston, 1953; B. J. Winer, *Statistical Principles in Experimental Design,* McGraw-Hill, New York, 1962.

The popular use of ANOVA by experimenters, however, should not lead a researcher to perceive ANOVA experiments as the only match. Two clarifications are necessary. First, an experiment should not be designed to suit any particular method of ANOVA. The researcher must be guided by theoretical, practical, and observational demands. Whatever data are generated should be analyzed by the optimal method of analysis the researcher can find. A method of analysis should never dictate the measurement, design, and collection of data. This applies to any one of the methods of data analysis, but is emphasized here because of the dominant use of ANOVA by experimental researchers.

Second, ANOVA can be used for nonexperimental as well as experimental data. There is nothing in ANOVA that intrinsically prevents its use for analyzing nonexperimental data. In fact, it has been demonstrated to be one of a variety of methods utilizing deviation or covariance patterns of data, which are commonly used in nonexperimental studies.[4] Any data fulfilling the three assumptions of the ANOVA model can be analyzed with this test.

HYPOTHESIS OF ASSOCIATION

For hypotheses about associative (linear) relationships between variables, we will treat (1) the regression coefficient β_{yx} and (2) the correlation coefficient ρ. For convenience, we will first discuss the correlation coefficient, as the treatment of the regression coefficient is more lengthy and complicated.

Inferences from the sample data to the population, for both correlation and regression, require two assumptions: (1) that the sample is a simple random sample from the population, and (2) that the variables involved are jointly (multivariate) and normally distributed in the population. The second assumption states that the probability of joint occurrence of all values for all variables involved is distributed as in a normal curve. The variables, of course, must all be measured on the interval or ratio level.

Correlation: Covariation Equation

In Chapter 6, the correlation coefficient r was introduced as a measure of covariation between two variables. The population parameter for the correlation coefficient is designated ρ. In Chapter 7, it was mentioned that, while r is a biased estimate of ρ, the interval estimate of ρ can be found by converting r to a z score, using Fisher's Z transformation in Table 6, Appendix C. Then, the interval estimate for ρ is:

$$z_r + z_{(1+c)/2}\frac{1}{\sqrt{n-3}} \quad \text{and} \quad z_r + z_{(1-c)/2}\frac{1}{\sqrt{n-3}}$$

for a confidence coefficient of c. The z values can be found in Table 2, Appendix

[4] James Fennessey, "The General Linear Model: A New Perspective on Some Familiar Topics," *American Journal of Sociology*, vol. 74, pp. 1–27, 1968.

C. Then the scores can be converted, via Fisher's Z transformation, back to r values.

For hypothesis testing, two cases can be distinguished: (1) when the null hypothesis is that the parameter value equals zero, and (2) when the null hypothesis is that the parameter value does not equal zero.

When $H_0: \rho = 0$, a t test is used:

$$t = \frac{r}{\sqrt{(1 - r^2)/(n - 2)}} \qquad \text{d.f.} = n - 2 \tag{16.11}$$

For the specified degrees of freedom and level of significance, the expected t value can be found in Table 4, Appendix C, for the null hypothesis, and a decision can be made as to whether or not the null hypothesis should be rejected. Or, one may use Table 7, Appendix C, which gives the expected value for specified degrees of freedom.

For example, from the NORC 1973 survey data, it was found, among full-time working male respondents ($n = 380$) that the correlation between the respondent's father's job prestige and the respondent's own job prestige was .1567. The prestige of a job was rated on the Hodge-Siegel-Rossi scale (see Appendix B). To test whether this correlation in the population is significantly different from zero, we compute t:

$$t = \frac{.1567}{\sqrt{(1 - .0246)/(378)}} = 3.09$$

For a significance level of .01, and 120 degrees of freedom (the next lower available value to $n - 2 = 378$), the expected t value is $t_{.995} = 2.58$ in Table 4, Appendix C. Since the observed value (3.09) is greater than the expected value (2.58), the null hypothesis is rejected at a .01 level of significance and the theoretical hypothesis that the correlation between father's job prestige and son's job prestige is significantly different from zero is confirmed. Similarly, for 300 degrees of freedom, Table 7, Appendix C, gives $r_{.995} = .148$. Again, the null hypothesis can be rejected.

When $H_0: \rho = a$, a z test should be used, with the Z transformation of r:

$$z = \frac{z_r - z_a}{1/\sqrt{n - 3}} \tag{16.12}$$

For example, if we wish to test whether the correlation between father's job prestige and son's job prestige is significantly greater than .10 in the population, we set $H_0: \rho = .10$. Referring to Table 5, Appendix C, we find the entry for .0997 (the closest to .10), for which the row value is .1 and the column value is .00, thus $z_{a=.10} = .10$. For $r = .1567$, the next lower value entry is .1489; its row value is .1, and its column value is .05. Thus, $z_{r=.1567} = .15$, by adding the two values.

$$a = .10 \qquad z_a = .10$$
$$r = .1567 \qquad z_r = .15$$
$$z = \frac{.15 - .10}{1/\sqrt{377}} = .97$$

For a .05 level of significance, we find, in Table 2, Appendix C, for a one-tailed test, $z_{.95} = 1.65$. Since the observed value (.97) is less than the expected value (1.65), the null hypothesis cannot be rejected and we have failed to confirm the theoretical hypothesis at the .05 level. In other words, we cannot state for sure that the correlation coefficient in the population would be greater than .10 at a .05 level of significance.

Regression: Prediction Equation

In Chapter 6, the regression equation was introduced. The purpose there, however, was simply to describe the predictability from one variable X to another Y for a sample. For the population, the equation should be:

$$Y_i = \mu + \beta_{yx}(X_i - \bar{X}) + \epsilon_i \tag{16.13}$$

where $\quad \mu$ = population mean for Y
$\qquad \beta_{yx}$ = slope of Y on X
$\qquad \epsilon_i$ = residual on Y for the ith person

To estimate this equation in the population with data from a sample, the estimation (sample) regression equation is:

$$Y_i = \bar{Y} + \hat{\beta}_{yx}(X_i - \bar{X}) + e_i \tag{16.14}$$

where $\quad \bar{Y}$ = sample mean of Y
$\qquad \hat{\beta}_{yx}$ = sample regression slope
$\qquad e_i$ = sample residual on Y for the ith respondent

In this equation, $\bar{Y}$ and $\hat{\beta}_{yx}$ are the estimates of μ and β_{yx}. The last term, e_i, indicates the error of prediction. In other words, there are two components of each observed value of Y in the sample data: (1) the score predicted with the regression line, $\hat{Y}_i = \bar{Y} + \hat{\beta}_{yx}(X_i - \bar{X})$; and (2) the residual score e_i. In other words,

$$Y_i = \hat{Y} + e_i \tag{16.15}$$
$$\hat{Y}_i = \bar{Y} + \hat{\beta}_{yx}(X_i - \bar{X}) \tag{16.16}$$

and

$$e_i = Y_i - \hat{Y}_i \tag{16.17}$$

Before proceeding to a discussion on hypothesis testing, we will first examine the interval estimate for β_{yx}. From now on, for simplicity, we will use β to designate β_{yx} exclusively. That is, β is the regression slope of Y (the dependent variable) on X (the independent variable).

To construct the interval estimate of β, one needs an estimate of the standard error of the regression coefficient s_β. First, the standard deviation of Y_i from the predicted line in the sample (called the *standard error of the estimate or prediction*) is constructed:

$$s_{y.x} = \sqrt{\frac{\Sigma(Y_i - \hat{Y}_i)^2}{n - 2}} \tag{16.18}$$

Then, the standard error of the regression slope is:

$$s_\beta = \frac{s_{y.x}}{s_x\sqrt{n - 1}} \tag{16.19}$$

where s_x = standard deviation of X in the sample

         n = the sample size

The interval estimate of β can be found with the following formulas and the t distribution in Table 4, Appendix C:

$$\hat{\beta} + t_{(1+c)/2}s_\beta \quad \text{and} \quad \hat{\beta} + t_{(1-c)/2}s_\beta$$

For example, in Chapter 6, a regression equation was computed for the flow of immigrants into the United States during 1940–1965. By using information from Table 6.9 and with additional computations in Table 16.6, the standard error of the regression coefficient is found to be 1.32.

If the confidence coefficient is set at .99, for 25 degrees of freedom, Table 4, Appendix C, shows $t_{(1+c)/2} = t_{.995} = -t_{(1-c)/2} = -t_{.005} = 2.79$.

Thus,

$$11.30 + (2.79)(1.32) = 14.98$$

and

$$11.30 - (2.79)(1.32) = 7.62$$

One concludes that with .99 probability the interval 14.98 to 7.62 will span the regression coefficient in the population.

Now we may proceed to discuss hypothesis testing for the regression equation. In the next section, a mathematical derivation will be provided for testing a null hypothesis about the population regression coefficient. Readers not interested in the discussion may go on to the following section. Suffice it to say that the same strategy for the ANOVA test applies—the variance of the regression is decomposed into two components: (1) the variance explained by the regression line,

Table 16.6 Standard Error of the Regression Coefficient for the Data in Table 6.9

Year (X_i)	Number of Immigrants (Y_i)	$X_i - \bar{X}$	$\bar{Y} + \hat{\beta}(X_i - \bar{X})$	$Y_i - \hat{Y}_i$	$Y_i - \hat{Y}_i$
40	77	−12.5	125.05	−48.05	2,308.80
41	60	−11.5	136.35	−75.35	5,677.62
42	83	−10.5	147.65	−64.65	4,179.62
43	148	− 9.5	158.95	−10.95	119.90
44	202	− 8.5	170.25	31.75	1,008.06
45	162	− 7.5	181.55	−19.55	383.20
46	151	− 6.6	192.85	−41.85	1,751.42
47	238	− 5.5	204.15	33.85	1,145.82
48	280	− 4.5	215.45	64.55	4,166.70
49	323	− 3.5	226.75	96.25	9,264.06
50	299	− 2.5	238.05	60.95	3,714.90
51	325	− 1.5	249.35	85.65	7,335.92
52	242	− 0.5	260.65	−18.65	347.82
53	261	0.5	271.95	−10.95	119.90
54	287	1.5	283.25	3.75	14.06
55	337	2.5	294.55	42.45	1,802.00
56	387	3.5	305.85	81.15	6,585.32
57	272	4.5	317.15	−45.15	2,038.52
58	292	5.5	328.45	−36.45	1,328.60
59	292	6.5	339.75	−47.75	2,280.06
60	340	7.5	351.05	−11.05	122.10
61	391	8.5	362.35	28.65	820.82
62	373	9.5	373.65	− 0.65	0.42
63	384	10.5	384.95	− 0.95	0.90
64	340	11.5	396.25	−52.25	2,730.06
65	368	12.5	407.55	−39.55	1,564.20

$$s = \sqrt{\frac{\Sigma(X_i - \bar{X})^2}{n - 1}} = \sqrt{\frac{1{,}462.50}{25}} = 7.65 \qquad \text{from Table 6.9}$$

$$\hat{Y} = 266.30 \qquad \text{from Table 6.9} \qquad \hat{\beta} = 11.30 \qquad \text{from Table 6.9}$$

$$s_{y.x} = \sqrt{\frac{\Sigma(Y_i - Y_i)^2}{n - 2}} = \sqrt{\frac{60{,}809.8}{24}} = 50.34$$

$$s_{\beta} = \frac{50.34}{(7.65)(25)} = \frac{50.34}{38.25} = 1.32$$

and (2) the residual variance. In other words, the total sum of squares of deviations SS_t has two components, the sum of squares of deviations attributable to the regression line SS_r, and the sum of squares of deviations not attributable to the regression line SS_e:

$$SS_t = SS_r + SS_e$$

Analysis of Regression Components

Recall equation 16.15 which shows that the score of the ith respondent on Y consists of two parts: (1) the score predicted with the regression line $\hat{Y}_i$, and (2) the residual score e_i.

$$Y_i = \hat{Y}_i + e_i$$

e_i is also called the *unique* part of the score for respondent i. Two assumptions are made for the e_i's. First, the sum of the unique scores for all respondents equals zero:

$$\sum_{i=1}^{n} e_i = 0 \tag{16.20}$$

That is, it is assumed that the "errors" are randomly distributed; thus, when added up, they should cancel each other out. Second, the sum of the product between each unique score and the independent variable value equals zero:

$$\sum_{i=1}^{n} (X_i - \bar{X})e_i = 0 \tag{16.21}$$

Since the independent variable cannot predict these parts of the scores, it is therefore assumed that the sum of the interaction between each unique score and the variable value adds up to zero.

Now we subtract $\bar{Y}$, the sample mean, from each side of equation 16.15:

$$Y_i - \bar{Y} = (\hat{Y}_i - \bar{Y}) + e_i$$

Then, we square both sides and sum over all respondents:

$$\Sigma(Y_i - \bar{Y})^2 = \Sigma[(\hat{Y}_i - \bar{Y}) + e_i]^2$$
$$= \Sigma(\hat{Y}_i - \bar{Y})^2 + 2\Sigma(\hat{Y}_i - \bar{Y})e_i + \Sigma e_i^2$$

The second term on the right-hand side, with $\bar{Y} + \hat{\beta}(X_i - \bar{X})$ substituting for $\hat{Y}_i$ (from equation 16.16), becomes:

$$2\Sigma(\hat{Y}_i - \bar{Y})e_i = 2\Sigma[\bar{Y} + \hat{\beta}(X_i - \bar{X}) - \bar{Y}]e_i$$
$$= 2\Sigma\hat{\beta}(X_i - \bar{X})e_i$$
$$= 2\hat{\beta}\Sigma(X_i - \bar{X})e_i$$

However, from equation 16.21, we know $\Sigma(X_i - \bar{X})e_i = 0$; thus the term equals zero. Therefore, the equation is reduced to

$$\Sigma(Y_i - \bar{Y})^2 = \Sigma(\hat{Y}_i - \bar{Y})^2 + \Sigma e_i^2$$

These three terms are called the total sum of squares SS_t, the regression sum of squares SS_r, and the error sum of squares SS_e, respectively. The total sum equals the regression sum plus the error sum:

$$SS_t = SS_r + SS_e$$

Substituting $\hat{Y}_i$ in SS_r with $\bar{Y} + \hat{\beta}(X_i - \bar{X})$ (from equation 16.16),

$$
\begin{aligned}
SS_r &= \Sigma(\hat{Y}_i - \bar{Y})^2 = [\bar{Y} + \hat{\beta}(X_i - \bar{X}) - \bar{Y}]^2 \\
&= \Sigma[\hat{\beta}(X_i - \bar{X})]^2 \\
&= \hat{\beta}\Sigma(X_i - \bar{X})^2
\end{aligned}
\tag{16.22}
$$

and, from equation 16.17,

$$SS_e = \Sigma e_i^2 = \Sigma(Y_i - \hat{Y}_i)^2 \tag{16.23}$$

From $SS_t = SS_r + SS_e$, we divide each side by SS_t:

$$1 = \frac{SS_r}{SS_t} + \frac{SS_e}{SS_t}$$

The first term on the right-hand side of the equation is called the *coefficient of determination R^2*:

$$R^2 = \frac{SS_r}{SS_t} = 1 - \frac{SS_e}{SS_t} \tag{16.24}$$

R^2 is the portion of the variance explained by the regression line. When there is one independent variable and one dependent variable, R^2 equals r^2. It varies from 0 to 1, and is always positive. The greater R^2, it is said that the more variance of the dependent variable is explained by the regression line, and that the less the error (residual) variance SS_e/SS_t becomes.

An F test can now be used to test the relative magnitudes of SS_r and SS_r, with their appropriate degrees of freedom:

$$F = \frac{(SS_r)/(K - 1)}{(SS_e)/(n - K)} \tag{16.25}$$

where K = number of variables
             n = number of respondents

For a given level of significance and the degrees of freedom, the F distributions that are shown in Table 5, Appendix C, give the expected F value for the null hypothesis that the independent variable does not predict the dependent variable. Comparison between the observed F and the expected F leads to a decision about the null hypothesis and the theoretical hypothesis, that the independent variable does predict the dependent variable in a linear fashion at the specified level of significance.

The formula in equation 16.25 can be simplified by the use of R^2 in equation 16.24, when the null hypothesis is $\beta = 0$:

$$F = \frac{SS_r/(K-1)}{SS_e/(n-K)} = \frac{(SS_r/SS_t)/(K-1)}{(SS_e/SS_t)/(n-K)}$$

$$= \frac{R^2/(K-1)}{(1-R^2)/(n-K)} \qquad\qquad (16.26)$$

Thus, once R^2 is computed, the F test can be made with the appropriate degrees of freedom specified.

Hypothesis Testing about the Regression Coefficient

To recap briefly, when the null hypothesis is that the population regression coefficient is zero ($\beta = 0$) the F test, with either equation 16.25 or 16.26, can be used.

For example, for the data on flow of immigrants presented in Table 16.6, the estimated regression coefficient was found to be 11.30 and the correlation coefficient r was found to be .88 (from Table 6.10). Thus,

$$H_0{:}\beta = 0 \qquad \text{for } K = 2, n = 26, \text{ and } r^2 = R^2 = .77$$

$$F = \frac{R^2/(K-1)}{(1-R^2)/(n-K)}$$

$$= \frac{.77/(2-1)}{(1-.77)/(26-2)}$$

$$= 80.35 \qquad\qquad \text{d.f. (numerator)} = K - 1 = 1$$
$$\text{d.f. (denominator)} = n - K = 24$$

If the level of significance is set at .01, then with 1 degree of freedom for the numerator and 24 degrees of freedom for the denominator, Table 5, Appendix C, gives the expected F value as $F_{.99} = 7.82$. Thus, the null hypothesis is rejected and the theoretical hypothesis is supported at the .01 level of significance. The population regression coefficient is highly likely to be different from zero.

When the null hypothesis is that the regression coefficient in the population equals a nonzero fraction, $\beta = a$, then a t test should be used—for example, if the theoretical hypothesis is that the regression slope in the population should be greater than 10.00 for the sample data in Table 16.6, in which the estimated regression coefficient is 11.30. With the standard error s_β and the $n - 2$ degrees of freedom, the t test can be made:

$$H_0{:}\beta = 10.00$$
$$\hat{\beta} = 11.30$$
$$s_\beta = 1.32$$
$$n = 26$$

$$t = \frac{\hat{\beta} - \beta}{s_\beta} = \frac{11.30 - 10.00}{1.32} = .98 \qquad \text{d.f.} = 24$$

If the level of significance is set at .05, for a two-tailed test and with 24 degrees of freedom, Table 4, Appendix C, gives the expected t value as $t_{.995} = 2.80$. Thus, the null hypothesis cannot be rejected, and we have failed to confirmed the theoretical hypothesis at a .05 level of significance. In other words, at the .05 level of significance, we cannot eliminate the possibility that the population regression coefficient is equal to or less than 10.00.

We have now concluded the discussion on hypothesis testing for associative relationships. The remainder of this chapter will introduce the reader to three multivariate techniques commonly used when the association involves three or more variables: partial correlation, multiple regression and correlation, and path analysis. Each of these techniques is used for either controlling the effects of additional variables or mapping the causal order of variables, two of the most important tasks for data analysis in social research.

OTHER MULTIVARIATE TECHNIQUES

Just as the contingency table and the difference between groups can take into account more than two variables in an analysis, association among three or more variables can be analyzed. Here, three such techniques will be introduced. The first technique, partial correlation, computes the correlation between two or more variables after the correlation between these variables and other variables has been eliminated. For example, it may be found that father's occupational prestige is highly related to son's education. The researcher may wonder how much of this correlation is due to the effect of father's education. Thus, a partial correlation can be computed between father's occupational prestige and son's education, while taking out any effect father's education may have on both father's occupational prestige and son's education.

Another technique, multiple regression (or correlation), also considers three or more variables simultaneously. But, instead of eliminating the effect of certain variables from the correlations as partial correlation does, multiple regression seeks to ascertain the relative contributions (effects) a number of independent variables have on a dependent variable. For example, in the study of father's education, father's occupational prestige, and son's education, instead of partialing out the correlations between father's education and father's occupational prestige, and between father's education and son's education, in the computation of the correlation between father's occupational prestige and son's education, one may seek the relative contributions of father's education, his occupational prestige on son's education (multiple regression), and the joint contribution of father's education and father's occupational prestige on son's education (multiple correlation).

A third technique, path analysis, extends the idea of multiple regression to situations in which two or more dependent variables are involved. For example, if one wishes to ascertain the relative contributions of father's education and father's occupational prestige on son's education, and the relative contributions of father's education, father's occupational prestige, and son's education on son's occupational prestige, then two dependent variables (son's education and son's occupational prestige) must be sequentially analyzed in terms of a number of independent variables. Path analysis is the technique to use for such a complex structure.

Partial Correlation

Without elaboration, the formula for the partial correlation between variables 1 and 2, partialing out the effect of variable 3 is:

$$r_{12.3} = \frac{r_{12} - r_{13}r_{23}}{\sqrt{1 - r_{13}^2}\sqrt{1 - r_{23}^2}} \tag{16.27}$$

Thus, when the correlations between each pair of the variables are computed, the partial correlation coefficient for any two variables can readily be computed.

For example, if father's occupational prestige is variable 1, son's education is variable 2, and father's education is variable 3, the NORC 1973 survey data for full-time working male respondents show:

$$r_{12} = .246$$
$$r_{13} = .416$$
$$r_{23} = .409$$

For $n = 380$, $r_{12} = .246$ is significant beyond a .001 level of significance for rejecting the null hypothesis that there is no relationship between father's occupational prestige and son's education, $\rho = 0$ (see Table 7, Appendix C). However, if one suspects that part of the relationship is due to father's education, then one may compute the partial correlation coefficient for the two variables, partially out the effect of father's education:

$$r_{12.3} = \frac{.246 - (.416)(.409)}{\sqrt{1 - (.416)^2}\sqrt{1 - (.409)^2}}$$

$$= \frac{.076}{\sqrt{.827}\sqrt{.833}}$$

$$= \frac{.076}{.830} = .092$$

To test this observed value against the expected value of the null hypothesis $\rho = 0$, an F test can be used:

$$F = \frac{r_{12.3}^2(n - 3)}{1 - (r_{12.3}^2)}$$

$$= \frac{(.092)^2(377)}{1 - (.092)^2}$$

$$= 3.22$$

$$\text{d.f. (numerator)} = 1$$
$$\text{d.f. (denominator)} = n - K$$
$$= 380 - 3$$
$$= 377$$

where K = total number of variables

In Table 5, Appendix C, the entry for column 1 and row $\nu_2 = 400$ (the next lower value to 377), for a .01 level of significance $F_{.99} = 6.70$, shows a greater value than the observed value (3.22). Thus, we conclude that the null hypothesis cannot be rejected at a .01 level of significance.

By using the partial correlation technique, it was found that the correlation between father's occupational prestige and son's education is not significantly different from zero when father's education was partialed out from the analysis. In other words, the relationship between father's occupational prestige and son's education is a spurious one, due mainly to the effect of father's education on both father's occupational prestige and son's education.

It is possible to partial out two or more variables. However, the computation becomes complicated for hand calculations. Usually, a computer program, such as the SPSS, can be used to compute the more complicated coefficients.[5]

Interval estimates for partial correlation coefficients can also be calculated with the following formulas:

$$z_r + z_{(1+c)/2} \frac{1}{\sqrt{n - K - 1}} \quad \text{and} \quad z_r + z_{(1-c)/2} \frac{1}{\sqrt{n - K - 1}}$$

where k = total number of variables

By using the Z transformation in Table 6, Appendix C, the interval values of z can be found in Table 2, Appendix C, for a specified confidence coefficient c.

Multiple Regression and Multiple Correlation

When a number of independent variables is involved, two statistics are useful. The multiple-regression model specifies the relative predictive contributions of the independent variables to the explanation of the dependent variable. The multiple-correlation coefficient gives an indication of the joint association between all the independent variables and the dependent variable or, by using the multiple correlation squared R^2, it indicates the proportion of the variance of the dependent variable explained by the independent variables combined. For discussion, the simple case involving two independent variables will be used. The more general case, involving any number of independent variables, is too complicated for hand computations, and the reader is again referred to the use of computer routines (see footnote 5).

---

[5] Norman H. Nie, et al., *Statistical Package for Social Scientists*, 2d ed., McGraw-Hill, New York, 1975. For an introduction to SPSS, see Nan Lin, Ronald S. Burt, and John Vaughn, *Conducting Social Research*, McGraw-Hill, New York, 1976.

Multiple-Regression Model The multiple-regression model is an extension of the basic model in equation 16.13. For example, the population multiple-regression model for two independent variables X_1 and X_2 is:

$$Y_i = \mu + \beta_{y1}(X_{i1} - \bar{X}_1) + \beta_{y2}(X_{i2} - \bar{X}_2) + \epsilon_i \qquad (16.28)$$

where μ = population mean of Y
       β_{y1} = regression slope of Y on X_1 (the partial regression coefficient of Y on X_1)
       X_{i1} = score of person i on X_i

The corresponding sample multiple-regression equation is:

$$Y_i = \bar{Y}_i + \hat{\beta}_{y1}(X_{i1} - \bar{X}_1) + \hat{\beta}_{y2}(X_{i2} - \bar{X}_2) + e_i \qquad (16.29)$$

where the $\hat{\beta}$'s are estimates of the β's.

To compute the $\hat{\beta}$'s, we need a set of symbols (m's) to represent the various sums and products of deviations:

$$m_{yy} = \Sigma(Y_i - \bar{Y})^2$$
$$m_{11} = \Sigma(X_{i1} - \bar{X}_1)^2$$
$$m_{22} = \Sigma(X_{i2} - \bar{X}_2)^2$$
$$m_{y1} = \Sigma(X_{i1} - \bar{X}_1)(Y_i - \bar{Y})$$
$$m_{y2} = \Sigma(X_{i2} - \bar{X}_1)(Y_i - \bar{Y})$$
$$m_{12} = \Sigma(X_{i1} - \bar{X}_1)(X_{i2} - \bar{X}_2)$$

Then, the $\hat{\beta}$'s can be expressed as:

$$\hat{\beta}_{y1} = \frac{m_{y1}m_{22} - m_{y2}m_{12}}{m_{11}m_{22} - m_{12}m_{12}} \qquad (16.30a)$$

$$\hat{\beta}_{y2} = \frac{m_{y2}m_{11} - m_{y1}m_{12}}{m_{11}m_{22} - m_{12}m_{12}} \qquad (16.30b)$$

and the predicted Y score for respondent i, $\hat{Y}_i$, as:

$$\hat{Y}_i = \bar{Y}_i + \hat{\beta}_{y1}(X_{i1} - \bar{X}_1) + \hat{\beta}_{y2}(X_{i2} - \bar{X}_2)$$

and the error score for respondent i, e_i, as:

$$e_i = Y_i - \hat{Y}_i$$

These estimates can be computed only when certain assumptions are made about the population and sample conditions. The basic conditions of simple random samples and normal distributions in the population, as well as equations 16.20 and 16.21 about the normal distribution of the error component and the independence between the error term and the independent variables, must be met. Further, each observed value of each independent variable is a fixed one and does not involve any error. Also, the number of respondents must exceed the number of regression coefficients to be estimated. Finally, no exact linear relation between any of the independent variables exists (no multicollinearity). These concepts are too complex to be explained here. However, if a researcher has any doubt about whether any of these assumptions are fulfilled, consultation with experts and advanced texts must be made before carrying out the analysis, as violations of these assumptions, to various degrees (from slight to severe), may render the resulting estimates meaningless.

For example, if one wishes to estimate the relative contributions of father's education and father's occupational prestige on son's education, one could compute the m's from the data. In reality, the computations are quite time-consuming, even when some simplified formulas involving no deviations are used. The actual task of computations is usually performed on the computer with existing statistical routines such as the SPSS. Here, only the results of such computer analysis, using the SPSS, on the NORC 1973 survey data on full-time working male respondents are presented:

$$\hat{\beta}_{y1} = .279$$
$$\hat{\beta}_{y2} = .025$$
$$\bar{Y} = 12.31$$

where X_1 = father's education
X_2 = father's occupational prestige
Y = son's education

Thus, the predicted Y score for respondent i, Y_i, is:

$$\hat{Y}_i = 12.31 + .279(X_{i1} - \bar{X}_1) + .025(X_{i2} - \bar{X}_2)$$

where education is measured in units of years and occupational prestige in units on the Hodge-Siegel-Rossi scale (Appendix B).

Standardized Regression Model There are occasions when it is desirable to standardize the units of measurement for all variables involved. For example, in the construction of a theoretical structure, the influence of empirical units may substantially determine the regression coefficients; the greater variance a variable has, the greater its partial regression coefficient is relative to other coefficients. To estimate the relative contributions of the variables in a theoretical scheme thus requires standardization of the variance for every variable. The idea of standardization was introduced in Chapter 5 (z scores) and in Chapter 7 (the standard error of the statistic, such as the mean, in the sampling distribution). It was mentioned, for example, that when a variable is standardized it has a mean of 0 and standard deviation of 1, regardless of what these statistics originally were for each variable.

Transformation of the partial regression coefficient $\hat{\beta}$ into the standardized regression coefficient $\hat{\beta}^*$ in fact is an extension of equation 6.6 in which it was demonstrated that the regression coefficent, an unstandardized coefficient, can be transformed into a standardized coefficient r by taking into account the standard deviations of the variables.[6]

$$\hat{\beta}_{y1}^* = \hat{\beta}_{y1} \frac{s_1}{s_y} \tag{16.31}$$

and

$$\hat{\beta}_{y2}^* = \hat{\beta}_{y2} \frac{s_2}{s_y}$$

where s_1 = sample standard deviation of variable 1
  s_y = sample standard deviation of variable y

The regression estimation equation then is simplified to:

$$Y_i^* = \hat{\beta}_{y1}^* X_{i1}^* + \hat{\beta}_{y2} X_{i1}^* + \hat{\beta}_{ye}^* e_i \tag{16.32}$$

where Y_i^*, X_{i1}^*, and X_{i2}^* = standard scores of Y, X_1, and X_2 for respondent i for two independent variables. Note that $\overline{Y}$ has vanished from the equation, as the standard score of the mean to itself is zero, and $\hat{\beta}_{ye}^*$ is the coefficient from the residual (or error) variable X_e.

The standardized regression coefficients allow one to draw a diagram to specify the relationships among the variables:

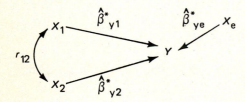

The solid lines and the arrows specify that standardized regression coefficients are assigned between each independent variable as it predicts or leads to the dependent variable. The curved line with double arrows indicates the correlation coefficient between the two independent variables. The arrowed line from X_e to Y indicates the residual coefficient from a residual (error) variable to the dependent variable which is $\hat{\beta}_{ye}^*$.

---

[6] Various labels and notations are used for $\hat{\beta}$ and $\hat{\beta}^*$. The terms and notations used here are consistent with econometric references. In social research, they usually are called *unstandardized regression coefficient* and *standardized regression coefficient*, or *beta coefficient* and *beta weight*.

The standardized regression coefficients can be directly calculated from correlation coefficients among the variables:

$$\hat{\beta}_{y1}^* = \frac{r_{y1} - r_{12}r_{y2}}{1 - r_{12}^2} \tag{16.33}$$

$$\hat{\beta}_{y2}^* = \frac{r_{y2} - r_{12}r_{y1}}{1 - r_{12}^2}$$

For example, to compute the standardized regression coefficients for father's education and son's education, and for father's education and son's education for the NORC 1973 survey data on full-time working male respondents:

X_1 = father's education
X_2 = father's occupational prestige
Y = son's education
r_{y1} = .409
r_{y2} = .246
r_{12} = .416

$$\hat{\beta}_{y1}^* = \frac{.409 - (.416)(.246)}{1 - (.416)^2}$$
$$= .371$$
$$\hat{\beta}_{y2}^* = \frac{.246 - (.416)(.409)}{1 - (.416)^2 \cdot}$$
$$= .093$$

The standardized regression coefficient from the residual variable X_e to the dependent variable β_{ye}^* can be estimated from:

$$\hat{\beta}_{ye}^* = \sqrt{1 - \hat{\beta}_{y1}^* r_{y1} - \hat{\beta}_{y2}^* r_{y2}}$$

Thus, for our example:

X_e = residual variable for Y

$$\hat{\beta}_{ye}^* = \sqrt{1 - (.371)(.409) - (.093)(.246)}$$
$$= .908$$

We may now draw a diagram expressing these relationships:

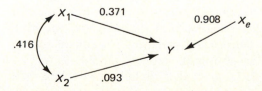

One sees that, when the variables are standardized, the relative contribution from father's education to son's education increased from .279 (the unstandardized coefficient) to .371, while that from father's occupational prestige to son's education remained low, .093. Thus, for son's education as the dependent variable, father's education is a much more important contributing factor than father's occupation.

The reader should also note that the diagram just presented bears a strong similarity to the theoretical structures presented in diagrams in Chapters 2 and 3, especially Figure 3.3*a*. In fact, the multiple regression model is the technique for constructing the convergent theoretical structure. Because of the popularity of the multiple-regression model among social researchers, the convergent theoretical structure has also become the dominant theoretical structure in social theories.

To test a hypothesis for the regression coefficient, the same F test and t test used for the simple regression model (see the section "Hypothesis Testing about the Regression Coefficient," pages 312–313) apply.

Multiple Correlation   If one wishes to ascertain the extent to which the independent variables have jointly explained or predicted the dependent variable, the multiple correlation coefficient can be used as an indicator. More specifically, the multiple correlation squared R^2 is considered the portion of the variance of the dependent variable explained by all the independent variables taken into account. R^2, also known as the coefficient of determination, was introduced earlier in the section, "Analysis of Regression Components" (see equation 16.24). It can be estimated directly from correlation coefficients and regression coefficients.

When the variables are not standardized, R^2 is:

$$R^2_{y.12} = \frac{\hat{\beta}_{y1}m_{y1} + \hat{\beta}_{y2}m_{y2}}{m_{yy}} \tag{16.34}$$

where the m's are sums and products of deviations as defined earlier when the multiple-regression model was introduced.

When the variables are standardized, R^2 is:

$$R^2_{y.12} = \hat{\beta}^*_{y1}r_{y1} + \hat{\beta}^*_{y2}r_{y2} \tag{16.35}$$

Note that the square root of $1 - R^2$ ($\sqrt{1 - R^2}$) is the regression coefficient from the residual variable to the dependent variable $\hat{\beta}^*_{ye}$. This is expected; for since R^2 represents the variance explained, what remains from the total variance of Y ($s_y^2 = 1$ when Y is standardized) is the residual variance. The square root of that variance gives the regression coefficient from the residual variable X_e to Y.

As an example, from the NORC 1973 survey data on full-time working male respondents, the correlation coefficients and regression coefficients have been calculated earlier. Thus, by using equation 16.35 for standardized variables,

$$R^2_{y.12} = (.371)(.409) + (.093)(.246)$$
$$= .175$$

In other words, father's education and father's occupational prestige combined explain about 18 percent of the variance of son's education. The reader may be disheartened by the relatively low explaining power of the two independent variables on the dependent variable. It is therefore important to point out two issues.

First, because of all the potential measurement errors involved in social research, a low R^2 is a common occurrence in research findings. But, more importantly, there is no theoretical reason why the independent variables must be expected to make overwhelming contributions to the dependent variable. The goal of theory construction is not necessarily to identify the independent variables which explain "completely" or "nearly completely" the variance of a dependent variable. For, in reality, as well as in theory, the more important task is to identify the relationship as it exists. Thus, if an independent variable contributes only so much, say 10 percent, of the variance to the dependent variable, any estimate, higher as well as lower, than 10 percent from sample data is in error. The closer the estimate is to the 10 percent mark, the more confidence we have in the estimate.

Desirability of a high R^2 has meaning only when one is making predictive statements (e.g., the estimation of number of immigrants to the United States) which have practical implications, or when theory construction has arrived at a point where most of the *important* independent variables have been identified for a dependent variable and the remaining task is to draw a closure to a theoretical structure with precise propositions. However, social research is far from that stage. These issues will be discussed in more detail in Chapter 19, when we consider the use of social research.

The multiple correlation squared R^2 can also be subjected to interval estimation and hypothesis-testing procedures mentioned earlier for simple β by using the t test and the F test.

Path Analysis

A simple extension of the regression model is to incorporate two or more dependent variables. To continue with the example used so far, suppose one wishes to estimate the contributions of father's education and father's occupational prestige to son's education, and the contributions of these three variables to son's occupational prestige, shown in the following path diagram:

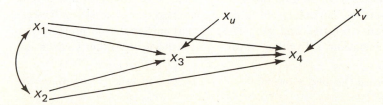

where X_1 = father's education
              X_2 = father's occupational prestige
              X_3 = son's education
              X_4 = son's occupational prestige
              X_u = residual variable for X_3
              X_v = residual variable for X_4

For those readers familiar with the literature on social stratification and social mobility, this diagram is readily identifiable as the basic model of occupational mobility proposed by Blau and Duncan.[7] This model attempts to ascertain, at the first stage, the relative contributions of ascribed status (father's education and father's occupational prestige) to son's education; and, at the second stage, to compare the relative contributions of the ascribed status and the achieved status (son's education) to son's occupational prestige.

Thus, in the first phase, there are two independent variables (X_1 and X_2) for the dependent variable (X_3); and, in the second phase of modeling, there are three independent variables (X_1, X_2, and X_3) for the dependent variable (X_4). Note that in path analysis, dependent as well as independent variables are designated X's, because at different phases a variable can be an independent as well as a dependent variable (for example, X_3).

Path analysis is frequently identified with causal analysis. Recall from Chapter 2 that a causal relation is characterized by three properties: (1) there is a covariational relation between the variables, (2) the independent variable temporally precedes the dependent variable, and (3) the relation is not spurious. With appropriate selection of variables and consideration given to the above requirements, it can be seen that path analysis can fulfill these requirements. *This does not mean that the use of path analysis automatically guarantees a causal relation.* Many path analysis results have not fulfilled the three requirements of the causal relationship and have been misinterpreted by authors as well as readers. Only when the variables are mapped in temporal sequence (either in actual time sequence or logically meaningful sequence) can one begin to consider a causal analysis. For example, education temporally precedes occupation, at least in the majority of cases and when occupation is defined as a full-time activity (37.5 hours per week). Logical sequence also helps. For example, religiosity logically precedes voting behavior, even though the time sequence of the two variables may be difficult to map. This is so, because logically a person's religious conviction can affect his voting decisions, whereas it is less likely that his voting decisions influence his religious conviction.

Also, it is important that the researcher has confidence that the model incorporates other variables so that potential spuriousness of relationships can be tested. For example, by partialing out father's education, the correlation between father's occupational prestige and son's education is minimal (see previous section, "Partial Correlation"). In other words, by incorporating father's education,

[7] Peter M. Blau and Otis Dudley Duncan, *The American Occupational Structure,* Wiley, New York, 1967.

it was demonstrated that the relationship between father's occupational prestige and son's education is to a large extent spurious.

These considerations must be made in causal analysis. When a causal analysis is called for, then path analysis is simply one technique, among others, which the researcher can use to test the causal relations. There is no doubt that, with recent advances in the use of structural equations, various path models have become powerful tools for causal analysis.[8] But there is no magic in path analysis itself that will produce a causal relationship. Such relationships are informed by theoretical considerations.

When all the dependent variables in the path model are connected with one-way arrowed lines, (e.g., from X_3 to X_4 but not from X_4 to X_3), then the path model is a recursive one. Further, when all the independent variables preceding each dependent variable in the model have one-way arrowed lines leading to the dependent variable (e.g., X_1 and X_2 to X_3, and X_1, X_2, and X_3 to X_4), then the path model is a complete model. Thus, the path diagram just shown is a complete recursive model.

For a complete recursive path model, the computations for the path coefficients are identical to those for regression coefficients. For a path diagram, the usual procedure is to compute the standardized regression coefficients. Thus, in our example, the regression coefficients previously calculated for X_1 and X_3, and X_2 and X_3 ($\hat{\beta}_{y1}^*$ and $\hat{\beta}_{y2}^*$ in "Standardized Regression Model" on page 319, are the path coefficients:

$$\hat{\beta}_{31}^* = p_{31} = .371$$
$$\hat{\beta}_{32}^* = p_{32} = .093$$
$$\hat{\beta}_{3u}^* = p_{3u} = .908$$

where p_{31} = path coefficient from variable 1 to variable 3
  p_{32} = path coefficient from variable 2 to variable 3

Similarly, by using the multiple regression technique, the path coefficients from X_1, X_2, and X_3 to X_4 can be obtained. However, we must consider a possible source for violating one of the assumptions for the regression model. On page 317, it was stated that one of the assumptions of the model is that no exact linear relation between any of the independent variables exists (no multicollinearity). But the correlation coefficient for X_1 and X_2 is rather substantial (r_{12} = .416; see the section on the standardized regression model) and the path coefficient p_{31} is also high, .371. If we proceeded to construct the path coefficients for X_4, the multicollinearity effect might occur. Indeed, it would occur; one of the path coefficients would be negative (p_{41} = −.111). This was an artifact resulting from the violation of the no multicollinearity assumption of the model and does not make any logical sense.

One way to eliminate the multicollinearity problem is to select from among the independent variables so that the source of the multicollinearity problem can

[8] See, for example, Arthur S. Goldberger and Otis Dudley Duncan (eds), *Structural Equation Models in the Social Sciences,* Seminar Press, New York, 1973.

be deleted from further calculations. In our example, father's education certainly should have a direct effect on son's education. However, we may consider the possibility that father's education has only an indirect effect on son's occupational prestige—the effect is mediated through son's education. This possibility seems logically sound. The implication is that the path from X_1 to X_4, p_{41}, should be eliminated in the path model, resulting in the following incomplete recursive path diagram:

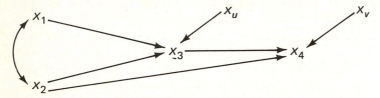

In this diagram, the coefficients p_{31}, p_{32}, and p_{3u} are unaffected. To estimate p_{42}, p_{43}, and p_{4v} poses a problem. Now three variables precede the dependent variable (X_1, X_2, and X_3), but only two paths lead to it. When there are more independent variables than there are paths for a dependent variable, it is mathematically called an *overidentification* problem. There is no exact solution to the problem or, in our terms, the exact path coefficients p_{42} and p_{43} cannot be found. There are various methods of approximating a solution. Without elaboration, it can be simply stated here that one of the better estimation procedures is regression analysis, deleting the independent variable whose path to the dependent variable is missing from the consideration.[9] In our example, this means that regression coefficients $\hat{\beta}_{42}^*$ and $\hat{\beta}_{43}^*$ can be used as estimates of p_{42} and p_{43}:

$$r_{23} = .246$$
$$r_{24} = .157$$
$$r_{34} = .548$$
$$p_{42} = \frac{r_{42} - r_{23}r_{34}}{1 - r_{23}^2}$$
$$= \frac{.157 - (.246)(.548)}{1 - (.246)^2}$$
$$= .023$$
$$p_{43} = \frac{r_{43} - r_{23}r_{24}}{1 - r_{23}^2}$$
$$= \frac{.548 - (.246)(.157)}{1 - (.246)^2}$$
$$= .542$$

[9] For example, another estimation procedure, incorporating the information of r_{14}, r_{12}, and r_{13}, is dependence analysis, proposed by Raymond Boudon in "A Method of Linear Causal Analysis: Dependence Analysis," *American Sociological Review*, vol. 30, pp. 365–374, 1965. The argument for the efficiency of the regular regression procedure for the estimations is made by Kenneth C. Land, "Identification, Parameter Estimation, and Hypothesis Testing in Recursive Sociological Models," in A. S. Goldberger and O. D. Duncan, *Structural Equation Models in the Social Sciences*, Seminar Press, New York, 1973.

$$p_{4v} = \sqrt{1 - r_{42}p_{42} - r_{43}p_{43}}$$
$$= \sqrt{1 - (.157)(.023) - (.548)(.542)}$$
$$= .836$$

Thus, the final solution of the path coefficients for the path model can now be presented in a path diagram:

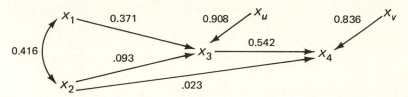

Again, multiple correlation squared R^2 can be calculated for X_3 and X_4 to determine how much of the variance of each dependent variable is accounted for by the independent variables:

$$R^2_{3.12} = r_{31}p_{31} + r_{32}p_{32}$$
$$= (.409)(.371) + (.246)(.093)$$
$$= .175$$
$$R^2_{4.23} = r_{42}p_{42} + r_{43}p_{43}$$
$$= (.157)(.023) + (.548)(.542)$$
$$= .301$$

As can be seen, about 18 percent of the variance of son's education is explained by his ascribed status, as indicated by father's education and father's occupational prestige. And about 30 percent of the variance of son's occupational prestige is accounted for by father's occupational prestige (ascribed status) and son's education (achieved status). Of the two types of status, achieved status (son's education) by far outweighs ascribed status (father's occupational prestige) in explaining or causing the son's occupational prestige. It is not the purpose here to comment on the theoretical interpretation of this analysis. But the reader, considering its substantive interest, should bear in mind that, in different societies, ascribed status may play a more important role than achieved status in affecting the education and occupational achievement of a person.[10]

Interval estimates and hypothesis testing can be obtained for the path coefficients by procedures similar to those used in the simple regression model. The usual procedure is that, when a path coefficient is insignificantly different from zero, then the path should be deleted and the model estimated again without the deleted path, as we did for X_4. For example, if carrying further, it may be necessary to recalculate the model in the example if p_{32} and p_{42} were found to be insignificant. Because the significance of a path coefficient is affected by the

[10] Nan Lin and Daniel Yauger, "The Process of Occupational Status Achievement: A Preliminary Cross-national Comparison," *American Journal of Sociology*, November 1975.

sample size—the larger the sample size, the more likely the path coefficient will be significantly different from zero—some minimal coefficients, for example, $p_{32} = .093$, may be statistically different from zero, with the large sample size. To eliminate the statistical effect of the sample size in the construction of a theoretical model, the rule of thumb is that, when the path coefficient is less than .10, the path should be eliminated and the estimations recalculated. There are procedures to make sure that elimination of any particular path does not distort the data. What is done is to reconstruct the original correlation coefficients from the estimated path coefficients; the topic is beyond the scope of this book. However, the making .10 the cutting point for deciding whether to keep a path or not inevitably ensures a close fit between the estimated coefficients and the observed correlation coefficients.[11]

A final note on the estimation of correlation and regression coefficients. The procedure outlined in this chapter is the usual least-squares procedure which finds the solution minimizing the average distance between the predicted score and the observed score $(Y_i - \hat{Y})$. There are other estimation procedures. Readers interested in the other potential useful procedures are advised to consult more advanced texts.[12]

LINEARITY AND ROBUSTNESS OF LINEAR MODELS

Two important issues involving the correlation and regression models deserve a further reminder. First, all these models assume linearity of the relationships—an associative (linear) assumption. The reader is reminded that the linear relationship is merely one of several possible relationships between variables. For example, two variables may have the relationship shown in Figure 16.2. If one uses the correlation or regression technique, R^2 would be low or near zero. The relationship, a curvilinear one, obviously does not fit with the assumption of the correlation and regression models. The reader is cautioned, therefore, that no linear relationship or a low linear relationship does not necessarily indicate that there is no relationship or that the relationship is low. It merely indicates that the relationship, if there is one, can be poorly described by a linear line. Advanced texts should be consulted for curvilinear techniques of analysis.

Second, while the correlation and regression models require a number of assumptions, the effect of any violation of the assumptions on the estimates varies depending on the nature of the violation and the degree of the violation. For example, we know that when the independent variables are highly correlated, the estimates will be incorrect. On the other hand, the assumption of variables being measured on interval or ratio scales is less severe. It has been found empirically that variables measured on ordinal scales do not bias the estimates substantially,

[11] For reconstruction of the correlation matrix from estimated coefficients, see John P. Van de Geer, *Introduction to Multivariate Analysis for the Social Sciences,* Freeman, San Francisco, 1971, especially chap. 7, pp. 70–71.

[12] For example, Jan Kmenta, *Elements of Econometrics,* Macmillan, New York, 1971; or Arthur S. Goldberger, *Econometric Theory,* Wiley, New York, 1964.

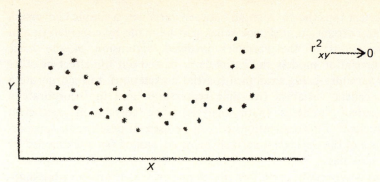

Figure 16.2

as long as a sufficiently large number of categories or values is involved (minimally five or six will do). When an assumption is violated and yet the estimates remain stable, the statistical model is said to be *robust*. For example, it has been found that violations of the assumption of normality of distribution of the variables in the population and of equal variance (homoscedasticity) of the variables do not significantly distort estimates of the regression coefficients. On the other hand, when the measurement is unreliable, especially when it involves systematic measurement errors, the estimates become unstable.[13]

In general, the correlation and regression models are very robust. However, when the independent variables are highly correlated or measurements of the variables are not very reliable (uncovered in reliability tests), or the relationship is suspected to be nonlinear, correlation and regression models should not be used.

SUMMARY

Multivariate analysis is introduced in this chapter for three groups of models: the contingency model, the difference-between-groups model, and the associative model. The contingency hypothesis testing relationships between two or more nominal or higher variables is made with the chi-square (χ^2) distribution. Hypotheses about differences between groups are tested with either the *t* distribution (when there are two groups) or the *F* distribution (when there are three or more groups). The independent variable or variables defining the groups are assumed to be nominal or high levels, whereas the dependent variable is measured on the interval or ratio level. ANOVA utilizing the *F* test can be used for either experimental or nonexperimental data.

Hypotheses about associations between variables measured at interval or ratio levels are tested with correlation and regression models. Linear and additive models can estimate the correlation and regression coefficients in the population with the least-squares technique. While regression is a predictive model and the

[13] George W. Bohrnstedt and T. Michael Carter, "Robustness in Regression Analysis," in Herbert L. Costner (ed.), *Sociological Methodology 1971*, Jossey-Bass, San Francisco, 1971, pp. 118–146.

correlation coefficient taps the covariation between variables, a simple conversion from regression to correlation, and vice versa, can be made by consideration of the standard deviations of the variables involved. Extension of the basic regression and correlation models can be made to partial out the effect of other variables on the variables being examined (partial correlation), to incorporate a number of independent variables (multiple regression), and to incorporate a number of dependent variables (path analysis). The correlation coefficient squared (or coefficient of determination) R^2 can be used to describe the proportion of the variance of the dependent variable being accounted for or explained by the independent variables.

Path analysis is especially useful for causal analysis, as it provides the mapping of temporal or logical sequences of variables and tests of the nonspuriousness of causal relations.

Each of these models makes certain assumptions about the distributions of the variables individually and jointly in the population, the sampling procedure, and certain conditions of the data. Violations of these assumptions may or may not affect the resulting estimates. To be safe, a user of any of these techniques is advised to consult experts or advanced texts, if a violation of one or more of the assumptions of an analytical model to be used is suspected.

Chapter 17

Structural (Sociometric) Analysis

Aside from statistical analysis, there are data in social research which require other analytical solutions. One type of such data is sociometric data. These data concern interpersonal and interorganizational relations. The instrument usually contains questions such as "Who are your three best friends?" "Who do you go to for advice on financial problems?" "Who are the teachers in the school you respect the most?" "Who in this office do you mix with socially most often?" and "Who do you consult about a new drug that comes on the market?" These questions result in a list of names of persons or offices, showing each respondent's structural linkage to the social system. The analysis applied to this type of data is known as *sociometric analysis, structural analysis,* or *relational analysis.* For consistency, the term *sociometric* will be used to describe the data, and the term *structural* to describe the analysis applied to the data. Many techniques have been developed for such analysis. Here, the discussion will selectively focus on a few, with emphasis on techniques applicable to the large-scale data often available in social research. Readers interested in the theoretical development of the techniques are advised to consult other publications.[1]

Two basic approaches have been used in the analysis of sociometric data: *graphic* and *matrical.* In the graphic approach, the data are analyzed in a socio-

[1] See, for example, C. Flament, *Applications of Graph Theory to Group Structure,* Prentice-Hall, Englewood Cliffs, N.J., 1963; F. Harary, R. Norman, and D. Cartwright, *Structural Models,* John Wiley, New York, 1965.

gram. A sociogram consists of nodes (dots) representing the persons or offices involved and lines connecting the nodes representing the nominating and nominated persons and offices. For example, in a three-person group, if person 1 cites person 2, person 2 cites person 3, and person 3 cites person 1, the sociogram representing the group structure is:

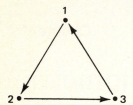

The relationship represented can be of two kinds. When the relationship is reciprocal or mutual, the relationship is *symmetric*. When the relationship is not reciprocal or mutual, the relationship is *asymmetric*. The above sociogram shows an asymmetric structure. However, sometimes the researcher may wish to assume that a symmetric relationship exists for a pair of nodes, even when the data are asymmetric. For example, in studying a kinship structure, when a person names another as his uncle on his mother's side, the researcher may assume such a relationship would be evident if the second person is also interviewed. This assumption is made so that any measurement errors (e.g., recall, attitude) causing asymmetric data can be eliminated. In our example, the uncle may detest his nephew and refuse to recognize the relationship. If the symmetric relationship must be verified by the pair of nodes involved, the data would be biased. Other researchers may wish to assume symmetric data for a variable such as a communication network. The assumption is that communication is always two-way. Thus, when person 1 names person 2 as a communication partner, then it is assumed that person 1 is the communication partner of person 2. The researcher must provide justification for the conversion of asymmetric data to symmetric data with theoretical or practical reasons.

While the graphic approach is visually attractive, it cannot adequately handle a large number of nodes. If there were, say, fifty or more nodes involved, the number of lines would make the sociogram difficult to analyze. The second approach, then, is the use of matrices to represent the data. A matrix consists of rows and columns. Each row and column can be designated as a node or a person. Then, for each cell in the matrix, we may use two numbers to represent the presence or absence of a relationship. For example, in the three-person group, the matrix representing the relationships is:

$$
\begin{array}{c}
\phantom{\text{Nominating}}\quad\text{Nominated} \\
\phantom{\text{Nominating}}\quad 1\quad 2\quad 3 \\
\text{Nominating}\quad
\begin{array}{c} 1 \\ 2 \\ 3 \end{array}
\left(
\begin{array}{ccc}
0 & 1 & 0 \\
0 & 0 & 1 \\
1 & 0 & 0
\end{array}
\right)
\end{array}
$$

Note that all persons appear both as rows and columns in the matrix, and that the convention is to use the rows to identify the nominating persons and the columns the nominated persons. For example, for person 1, it can be seen in row 1 that she nominated 2.

Also note that a value of 0 is assigned to all diagonal cells, not allowing any self-nominations (self-loops). When a matrix consists of cells of 1 and 0 values only, it is called an *incidence matrix*. Sociometric data, then, can be represented by a square incidence matrix in which the number of rows and the number of columns are equal. Call this matrix A; then, a_{ij} (representing the cell in row i and column j) is assigned a value of 1 if person i nominates person j and is assigned a value of 0 if person i does not nominate person j.

Conceptually, matrix A can be as large as one wishes it to be, involving any number of persons. Thus, it makes the sociogram less cumbersome. Further, as computer facilities become more readily available and capabilities expand, sociometric data in matrix forms can easily be adapted for computer analysis.

In many instances, both the graphic and matrical approaches are used in order to utilize the advantages of both in the analysis and presentation of data.

The objectives of structural analysis are twofold: (1) to describe and compare different social systems as reflected in sociometric data, and (2) to describe and compare individuals relative to each other in the social system. The first objective is to identify group properties and the second the relational properties.

IDENTIFICATION OF GROUP PROPERTIES

In the following discussion, a set of study data will be used for illustration. The study was to determine the extent to which group and relational properties were related to the extent to which high schools were receptive to educational innovations such as flexible scheduling and team teaching.[2] In the questionnaire distributed among teachers in three high schools, a sociometric item asked that each teacher nominate three fellow teachers within the school whose opinions she most frequently sought with regard to problems related to her teaching performance. The resulting sociograms for the three schools are shown in Figure 17.1.

In the analysis of group properties, it is sometimes advantageous to ignore the specific directions of the relationships. Conversion to symmetric relationships simplifies the overview of the group structures, especially when visual analysis is applied. In the following, the data are considered symmetric. A visual check of these sociograms indicates that the group structures in the three schools are of three different types. School-3 structure is tightly connected in a wired-wheel pattern in which each teacher is connected with other teachers directly or indirectly.

School 1 has a satellite structure, consisting primarily of a dominant group and two satellite groups together with three small groups and three isolated teachers. School 2 has many isolated teachers and predominantly a star-shaped

[2] Nan Lin, "Innovative Methods for Studying Innovation in Education," in *Research Implications for Educational Diffusion,* Michigan Department of Education, Lansing, Michigan, pp. 105–151, 1968; "Analysis of Communication Relations," in G. J. Hanneman and W. J. McEwen (ed.), *Communication and Behavior,* Addison-Wesley, Reading, Mass., pp. 237–252, 1975.

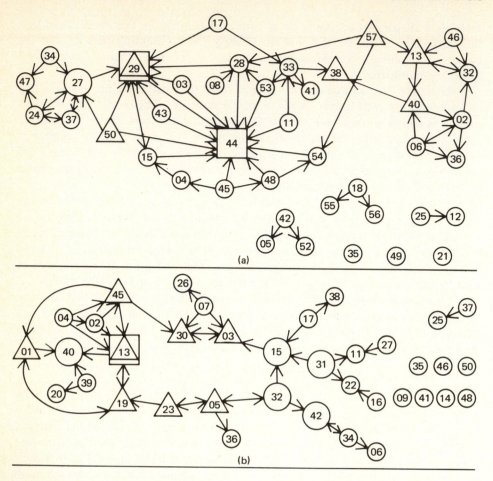

(a)

(b)

structure, with a circle-like network and a number of independent lines extending outward from the periphery of the circle. These casual observations can be reinforced with more specific properties:

Number of isolates. An *isolate* is defined as a person who neither nominates nor is nominated by any other person in the group. In the school study, there were no isolates in school 3, three (7 percent) in school 1, and seven (19 percent) in school 2.

Number of cliques. A *clique* is defined as a subgroup of persons having no connection with the dominant group. Thus, school 3 has no cliques, school 1 has 3, and school 2 has one.

Number of opinion leaders. An *opinion leader* is defined as a person nominated by more than 10 percent of the others in the group. School 3 has seven opinion leaders (teachers 33, 07, 03, 17, 14, 13, and 26 in Figure 17.1). Two appear in school 1 (teachers 44 and 29), and one in school 2 (teacher 13).

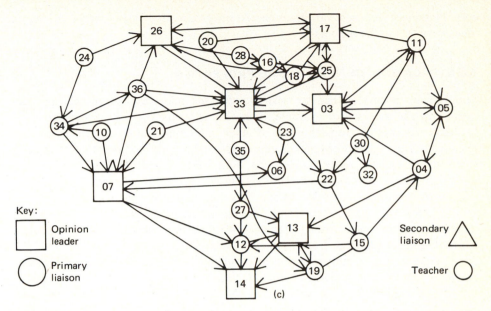

Figure 17.1 Sociograms of (teaching) advice communication network among teachers in three schools. *Opposite page:* (a) school 1 (n = 42); (b) school 2 (n = 37); *above:* (c) school 3 (n = 30).

Number of primary and secondary liaisons. A *primary liaison* is defined as a person whose absence from the group structure would separate one connected group into at least two groups, each consisting of at least two persons. A *secondary liaison* is defined as a person whose absence, together with the absence of another person, would separate one connected group into at least two groups, each consisting of at least two persons. A primary liaison cannot count as a secondary liaison, and secondary liaisons must exist at least in pairs. Thus, school 3 has no liaisons, either primary or secondary. In School 1, teacher 27 is a primary liaison, and teachers 29, 50, 57, 40, and 38 are secondary liaisons. In school 2, teachers 15, 31, 32, 40, and 42 are primary liaisons, and teachers 45, 19, 23, 30, 05, 03, 13, and 01 are secondary liaisons.

While these properties, overall form, isolates, cliques, opinion leaders, and primary and secondary liaisons, do not have any intrinsic meaning, studies have shown that groups function more efficiently when the structure is that of a star rather than that of a satellite or the spokes of a wheel, that members in a group are happier when the structure is wired-wheel-shaped rather than star-shaped or satellite, and that the presence of liaisons and isolates increases the communication cost. Identification and description of the opinion leaders help analyze the group as a whole.

Thus, sociological meanings can be developed for group properties. For example, the school study showed that school 3 was the most innovative school, school 1 second, and school 2 the least innovative. There was, therefore, a direct correspondence between variations in certain group properties and variations in innovativeness in the schools.[3]

IDENTIFICATION OF RELATIONAL PROPERTIES

Some group properties can be used to index the relative positions of the individuals in the group. For example, opinion leadership can be constructed as a variable in terms of the proportion of other individuals nominating a particular person. A square incidence matrix representing the sociometric data can be used to construct such an index. Tables 17.1, 17.2, and 17.3 present the matrices for the school data mentioned above. The sum of each column indicates the frequency with which a particular teacher was nominated by others and can be used as an index of opinion leadership. For example, for school 1, the opinion leadership scores range from 11 (teacher 44) to 0; for school 2, from 4 (teacher 13) to 0; and for school 3, from 9 (teacher 33) to 0.

The sum of each row indicates the frequency of the nominations each person has made. In the school data, variation is limited because each teacher was asked to nominate up to three other teachers. In cases in which each respondent can make as many nominations as he wishes, variation can be extensive. Again, it can be used to index the nominating behavior. Further, a ratio between the nominated frequency (the column sum) and the nominating frequency (the row sum) for each person can be used as an index of input or output propensity for each individual in the group.

While such indices may be sufficient in a gross analysis, their inadequacy is evident if indirect as well as direct linkages are considered. For example, in school 3, teacher 33 has the highest score on the opinion leadership index. However, teacher 03, who received only five direct nominations, served as an advisor to teacher 33. Thus, conceptually, the advice received by teachers who went to teacher 33 was indirectly influenced by teacher 03, who therefore should have or share the credit. This indirect influence is not reflected in opinion leadership scores computed on the basis of direct nominations.

To take the indirect linkages into account, the square incidence matrix can be manipulated to construct a distance matrix D in which all linkages, both direct and indirect, for each pair of nodes are obtained. To demonstrate the matrix manipulation, the three-person group described on page 330 will be used.

---

[3] Other techniques of analyzing group properties, such as cluster and liaison identifications, can be found in: James S. Coleman, *Introduction to Mathematical Sociology,* Free Press, New York, 1964, Chap. 14; Leo Katz, "A New Status Index Derived from Sociometric Analysis," *Psychometrika,* vol. 18, no. 1, pp. 39–43, March 1953; W. D. Richards, "A Conceptually Based Method for the Analysis of Communication Networks in Large Complex Organizations," paper presented at the meetings of the International Communication Association, 1971; C. H. Hubbell, "An Input-output Approach to Clique Identification," *Sociometry,* vol. 28, pp. 377–399, 1965; Phillip Bonacich, "Factoring and Weighting Approaches to Status Scores and Clique Identification," *Journal of Mathematical Sociology,* vol. 2, pp. 113–120, 1972; Richard D. Alba, "A Graph-theoretical Definition of a Sociometric Clique," *Journal of Mathematical Sociology,* vol. 3, pp. 113–126, 1973; Richard C. Roistacher, "A Review of Mathematical Methods in Sociometry," *Sociological Methods and Research,* vol. 3, no. 2, pp. 123–171, November 1974.

Table 17.1 Communication Matrix for Teachers in School 1

Nominated teachers

Nominating teachers

	44	41	18	12	02	40	28	25	52	38	42	15	24	36	56	11	54	06	04	47	27	53	03	49	08	34	46	57	43	35	05	33	45	29	32	48	50	17	37	55	21	13	
44	0	0	0	0	0	0	0	0	0	0	0	0	0	0	0	0	0	0	0	0	0	0	0	0	0	0	0	0	0	0	0	0	0	0	0	0	0	0	0	0	0	0	0
41	0	0	0	0	0	0	0	0	0	0	0	0	0	0	0	0	0	0	0	0	0	0	0	0	0	0	0	0	0	0	0	0	0	0	0	0	0	0	0	0	0	0	0
18	0	0	0	0	0	0	0	0	0	0	0	0	0	0	1	0	0	0	0	0	0	0	0	0	0	0	0	0	0	0	0	0	0	0	1	0	0	0	0	0	0	0	2
12	0	0	0	0	0	0	0	0	0	0	0	0	0	0	0	0	0	0	0	0	0	0	0	0	0	0	0	0	0	0	0	0	0	0	0	0	0	0	0	0	0	0	0
02	0	0	0	1	0	0	1	0	0	0	0	0	0	0	0	0	0	1	0	0	0	0	0	0	0	0	0	0	0	0	0	0	0	0	0	0	0	0	0	0	0	0	3
40	0	0	0	0	0	0	1	0	0	0	0	0	0	0	0	0	0	0	0	0	0	0	0	0	0	0	0	0	0	0	0	0	0	1	0	0	0	0	0	0	0	0	2
28	1	0	0	0	0	0	0	0	0	0	0	0	0	0	0	0	0	0	0	0	0	0	0	0	0	0	0	0	0	0	0	0	0	1	0	0	0	0	0	0	0	0	2
25	0	0	0	0	0	0	0	0	0	0	0	0	0	0	0	0	0	0	0	0	0	0	0	0	0	0	0	0	0	0	0	0	0	0	1	0	0	0	0	0	0	0	1
52	0	0	0	0	0	0	0	0	0	0	0	0	0	0	0	0	0	0	0	0	0	0	0	0	0	0	0	0	0	0	0	0	0	0	0	0	0	0	0	0	0	0	0
38	0	0	0	0	0	0	0	0	0	0	0	0	0	0	0	0	0	0	0	0	0	0	0	0	0	0	0	0	0	0	0	0	0	0	0	0	0	0	0	0	0	0	0
42	0	0	0	0	0	0	0	1	0	0	0	0	0	0	0	0	0	0	0	0	0	0	0	0	0	0	0	0	0	1	0	0	0	0	0	0	0	0	0	0	0	0	2
15	1	0	0	0	0	0	0	0	0	0	0	0	0	0	0	0	1	0	0	0	0	0	0	0	0	0	0	0	0	0	0	0	0	0	0	0	0	0	0	0	0	0	2
24	0	0	0	0	0	0	0	0	0	0	0	0	0	0	0	1	0	0	0	0	0	0	0	0	0	1	0	0	0	0	0	0	0	1	0	0	0	0	0	0	0	0	3
36	0	0	0	0	0	0	0	0	0	0	0	0	0	0	0	0	0	0	0	0	0	0	0	0	0	0	0	0	0	0	0	0	0	0	0	0	0	0	0	0	0	0	0
56	1	0	0	0	0	0	0	0	0	0	0	0	0	0	0	0	0	0	0	0	0	0	0	0	0	0	0	0	0	1	0	0	0	0	0	0	0	0	0	0	0	0	2
11	1	0	0	0	0	0	0	0	0	0	0	0	0	0	0	0	0	0	0	0	0	0	0	0	0	0	0	0	0	0	0	0	0	1	0	0	0	0	0	0	0	0	2
54	1	0	0	0	0	0	0	0	0	0	0	0	0	0	0	0	0	0	0	0	0	0	0	0	0	0	0	0	0	0	0	0	0	0	0	0	0	0	0	0	0	0	1
06	0	0	0	0	1	0	0	0	0	0	0	0	0	1	0	0	0	0	0	0	0	0	0	0	0	0	0	0	0	1	0	0	0	0	0	0	0	0	0	0	0	0	3
04	0	0	0	0	0	0	0	0	0	0	0	0	0	0	0	0	0	0	0	0	0	0	0	0	0	0	0	0	0	1	0	0	0	0	0	0	0	0	0	0	0	0	1
47	0	0	0	0	0	0	0	0	0	0	0	0	0	0	0	0	0	0	0	0	1	0	0	0	0	0	0	0	0	0	0	0	0	0	0	0	0	0	0	0	0	0	0
27	0	0	0	0	0	0	1	0	0	0	0	0	0	0	0	0	0	0	0	0	0	0	0	0	0	1	0	0	0	0	0	0	0	1	0	0	0	0	0	0	0	0	3
53	0	0	0	0	0	0	0	0	0	0	0	0	0	0	0	0	0	0	0	0	0	0	0	0	0	0	0	0	0	0	0	0	0	0	0	0	0	0	0	0	0	0	0
03	0	0	0	0	0	0	0	0	0	0	0	0	0	0	0	0	0	0	0	1	1	0	0	0	0	0	0	0	0	0	0	0	0	0	0	0	0	0	1	0	0	0	3
49	0	0	0	0	0	0	0	0	0	0	0	0	0	0	0	0	0	0	0	0	0	0	0	0	0	0	0	0	0	1	0	1	0	0	0	0	0	0	0	0	0	0	2
08	0	0	0	0	0	0	0	0	0	0	0	0	0	0	0	0	0	0	1	0	0	0	0	0	0	0	0	0	0	0	0	0	0	1	0	0	0	0	0	0	0	0	2
34	0	0	0	0	0	0	0	0	0	0	0	0	0	0	0	0	0	0	0	0	0	0	0	0	0	0	0	0	0	0	0	0	0	0	0	0	0	0	0	0	0	0	0
46	0	0	0	0	0	0	0	0	0	0	0	0	0	0	0	0	0	0	0	0	0	0	0	0	0	0	0	0	0	0	0	0	1	0	0	0	0	0	0	0	0	0	1
57	0	0	0	0	0	0	0	0	0	0	0	0	0	0	0	0	1	0	0	0	0	0	0	0	0	0	0	0	0	0	0	0	1	0	0	0	0	0	0	0	0	0	2
43	1	0	0	0	0	0	0	0	0	0	0	0	0	0	0	0	0	0	0	0	0	0	0	0	0	0	0	0	0	0	0	0	0	1	0	0	0	0	0	0	0	0	2
35	0	0	0	0	0	0	0	0	0	0	0	0	0	0	0	0	0	0	0	0	0	0	0	0	0	0	0	0	0	0	0	0	0	1	0	0	0	1	1	0	0	0	3
05	0	0	1	0	0	0	0	0	0	0	0	0	0	0	0	0	0	0	0	0	0	0	0	0	0	0	0	0	0	0	0	0	0	1	0	0	0	0	0	0	0	0	2
33	0	0	0	0	0	0	0	0	0	0	0	0	0	0	0	0	0	0	0	0	0	0	0	0	0	0	0	0	0	0	0	0	0	0	0	0	0	0	0	0	0	0	0
45	0	0	0	0	0	0	0	0	0	0	0	0	0	0	0	0	0	0	0	0	0	0	0	0	0	0	0	0	0	0	0	0	0	0	0	0	0	0	0	0	0	0	0
29	1	0	0	0	0	0	0	0	0	0	0	0	0	0	0	0	0	0	0	0	0	0	0	0	0	0	0	0	0	1	0	0	0	0	0	0	1	0	0	0	0	0	3
32	1	0	0	0	0	0	1	0	0	0	0	0	0	0	0	0	0	0	0	0	0	0	0	0	0	0	0	0	0	0	0	0	1	0	0	0	0	0	0	0	0	0	3
48	1	0	0	0	0	0	0	0	0	0	0	0	0	0	0	0	0	0	0	0	0	0	0	0	0	0	0	0	0	1	0	0	0	0	0	0	0	0	0	0	0	0	2
50	1	0	0	0	0	0	0	0	0	0	0	0	0	0	0	0	0	0	0	0	0	0	0	0	0	0	0	0	0	0	0	0	0	0	0	0	0	0	0	0	0	0	1
17	0	0	0	0	0	0	0	0	0	0	0	0	0	0	0	0	0	0	0	0	1	0	0	0	0	0	0	0	0	0	1	0	0	0	0	0	0	0	0	0	0	0	2
37	0	0	0	0	0	0	0	0	0	0	0	0	0	0	0	0	0	0	0	0	1	0	0	0	0	0	0	0	0	0	1	0	0	1	0	0	0	0	0	0	0	0	3
55	0	0	0	0	0	0	0	0	0	0	0	0	0	0	0	0	0	0	0	0	0	0	0	0	0	0	0	0	0	0	0	0	0	0	0	0	0	1	1	0	0	0	2
21	0	0	0	0	0	0	0	0	0	0	0	0	0	0	0	0	0	0	0	0	0	0	0	0	0	0	0	0	0	0	0	0	0	0	0	0	0	0	0	0	0	0	0
13	0	0	0	0	0	0	0	0	0	0	0	0	0	0	0	0	0	0	0	0	0	0	0	0	0	0	0	0	0	0	0	0	0	0	0	0	0	0	0	0	0	0	2
	11	1	0	1	2	2	3	0	1	2	0	2	2	2	1	1	0	2	1	1	2	4	1	0	0	0	0	0	0	1	2	2	7	3	1	0	0	2	1	0	3		

Table 17.2 Communication Matrix for Teachers in School 2

Nominated teachers

Nom.	06	09	31	46	04	25	41	40	22	45	07	20	35	30	03	32	50	36	01	19	13	23	14	38	15	37	11	26	27	17	02	05	16	34	42	48	39	Σ
06	0	0	0	0	0	0	0	0	0	0	0	0	0	0	0	0	0	0	0	0	0	0	0	0	0	0	0	0	0	0	0	0	0	0	0	0	0	0
09	0	0	0	0	0	0	0	0	0	0	0	0	0	0	0	0	0	0	0	0	0	0	0	0	0	0	0	0	0	0	0	0	0	0	0	0	0	0
31	0	0	0	0	0	0	0	0	0	1	0	0	0	0	0	0	0	0	0	0	0	0	0	1	0	1	0	0	0	0	0	0	0	0	0	0	3	3
46	0	0	0	0	0	0	0	0	0	0	0	0	0	0	0	0	0	0	0	0	0	0	0	0	0	0	0	0	0	0	0	0	0	0	0	0	0	0
04	0	0	0	0	0	0	0	0	0	0	0	0	0	0	0	0	0	0	0	0	0	1	0	0	0	0	0	0	0	1	0	0	0	0	1	0	0	3
25	0	0	0	0	0	0	0	0	0	0	0	0	0	0	0	0	0	0	0	0	0	0	0	0	0	0	0	0	0	0	0	0	0	0	0	0	0	0
41	0	0	0	0	0	0	0	0	0	0	0	0	0	0	0	0	0	0	0	0	0	0	0	0	0	0	0	0	0	0	0	0	0	0	0	0	0	0
40	0	0	0	0	0	0	0	0	0	0	0	0	0	0	0	0	0	0	0	0	0	0	0	0	0	0	0	0	0	0	0	0	0	0	0	0	0	0
22	0	0	0	0	0	0	0	0	0	1	0	0	0	0	0	0	0	0	0	0	0	0	0	0	0	0	0	1	0	0	1	0	0	0	0	0	0	3
45	0	0	0	0	0	0	0	0	0	0	0	0	0	0	0	0	0	0	0	0	0	0	0	0	0	0	0	0	0	0	0	0	0	0	0	0	0	0
07	0	0	0	0	0	0	0	0	0	0	0	0	0	0	0	0	0	0	0	0	0	1	0	0	1	0	0	0	0	1	0	0	0	0	0	0	0	3
20	0	0	0	0	0	0	0	0	0	0	0	0	0	0	0	0	0	0	0	0	0	0	0	0	0	0	0	0	0	0	0	0	0	0	0	0	0	0
35	0	0	0	0	0	0	0	0	0	0	0	1	0	1	0	0	0	0	0	0	0	0	0	0	0	0	0	0	0	0	0	0	0	0	0	0	1	1
30	0	0	0	0	0	0	0	0	0	0	0	0	1	0	0	0	0	1	1	0	0	0	0	0	0	0	0	0	0	0	0	0	0	0	0	0	1	1
03	0	0	0	0	0	0	0	0	0	0	0	0	0	1	1	0	0	1	0	0	1	0	0	0	0	0	0	0	0	0	0	0	0	0	0	0	3	3
32	0	0	0	0	0	0	0	0	0	0	0	0	0	0	0	0	1	0	0	0	0	0	0	0	1	0	0	0	0	0	0	0	0	0	0	0	0	0
50	0	0	0	0	0	0	0	0	0	0	0	0	0	0	0	0	0	0	0	0	0	0	0	0	0	0	0	0	0	0	0	0	0	0	0	0	0	0
36	0	0	0	0	0	0	0	0	0	0	0	0	0	0	0	0	0	0	0	0	0	0	0	0	0	0	1	0	0	0	0	0	0	0	0	0	1	2
01	0	0	0	0	0	0	0	0	1	0	0	0	0	0	0	0	0	0	0	1	0	0	0	0	0	0	0	0	0	0	0	0	0	0	0	0	0	2
19	0	0	0	0	0	0	0	0	0	1	0	1	0	1	0	0	0	0	0	0	0	0	0	0	0	0	0	0	0	0	0	0	0	0	0	0	2	2
13	0	0	0	0	0	0	0	0	0	0	0	0	0	0	0	0	0	0	1	0	0	0	0	0	0	0	0	0	0	0	0	0	0	0	0	0	2	2
23	0	0	0	0	0	0	0	0	0	0	0	0	0	0	0	0	0	0	0	0	1	0	0	0	1	0	0	0	0	0	0	0	0	0	0	0	2	2
14	0	0	0	0	0	0	0	0	0	0	0	0	0	0	0	0	0	0	0	0	0	0	0	0	0	0	0	0	0	0	0	0	0	0	0	0	0	0
38	0	0	0	0	0	0	0	0	0	0	0	0	0	0	0	0	0	0	0	0	0	0	0	0	0	0	0	0	0	0	0	0	0	0	0	0	0	0
15	0	0	0	0	0	0	0	0	0	0	0	0	0	0	0	0	0	0	1	0	0	0	0	0	0	0	0	0	0	0	0	0	0	0	0	0	1	1
37	0	0	0	0	0	0	0	0	0	0	0	0	0	0	0	0	0	0	0	0	0	0	0	0	0	0	1	0	0	0	0	0	0	0	0	0	1	1
11	0	0	0	0	0	0	0	0	0	0	0	0	0	0	0	0	0	0	0	0	0	0	0	0	0	0	0	0	0	0	0	0	0	0	0	0	0	0
26	0	0	0	0	0	0	0	0	0	0	0	0	0	0	0	0	0	0	0	0	0	0	0	0	0	0	0	0	0	0	0	0	0	0	0	0	0	0
27	0	0	0	0	0	0	0	0	0	0	0	0	0	0	0	0	0	0	0	0	0	1	0	0	0	0	0	0	0	0	0	0	0	0	0	0	1	1
17	0	0	0	0	0	0	0	0	0	0	0	0	0	0	0	1	0	0	0	0	0	0	0	0	1	0	0	0	0	0	0	0	0	0	0	0	2	2
02	0	0	0	0	0	0	0	0	0	0	0	0	0	0	0	0	0	0	0	0	0	0	0	0	0	0	0	1	0	0	0	0	0	0	1	0	0	2
05	0	0	0	0	0	0	0	1	0	0	0	0	0	0	0	1	0	1	0	0	0	0	0	0	0	0	0	0	0	0	0	0	0	0	0	0	3	3
16	0	0	0	0	0	0	1	0	0	0	0	0	0	0	0	0	0	0	0	0	0	0	0	0	0	0	0	0	0	0	0	0	0	0	0	0	1	1
34	0	0	0	0	0	0	0	0	0	0	0	0	0	0	0	0	0	0	0	0	0	0	0	0	0	0	0	0	0	0	0	0	0	0	1	0	1	1
42	0	0	0	0	0	0	0	0	0	0	0	0	0	0	0	0	0	0	0	0	0	0	0	0	0	0	0	0	0	0	0	0	0	0	0	0	0	0
48	0	0	0	0	0	0	0	0	0	0	0	0	0	0	0	0	0	0	0	0	0	0	0	0	0	0	0	0	0	0	0	0	0	0	0	0	0	0
39	1	0	0	0	0	0	0	0	0	0	0	0	0	0	0	0	0	0	0	0	0	0	0	0	0	0	0	0	0	0	0	0	0	0	0	0	1	2
Σ	1	0	0	0	0	0	0	3	2	2	0	1	3	3	1	3	0	1	2	3	4	1	0	1	3	0	2	2	0	0	1	2	0	1	2	0	2	

Nominating teachers

Table 17.3 Communication Matrix for Teachers in School 3

Nominated teachers

Nom.	17	03	27	18	25	33	34	05	19	06	04	15	20	14	11	35	22	21	07	12	24	36	23	28	32	10	26	13	16	30	Σ
17	0	0	0	1	1	0	0	0	0	0	1	0	1	1	0	0	0	0	0	0	0	0	0	0	0	0	1	0	0	0	3
03	0	0	0	0	1	1	0	1	0	0	0	1	0	0	1	0	0	0	0	1	0	1	0	0	0	0	0	1	0	0	2
27	0	0	0	0	0	1	0	1	0	1	0	0	1	0	1	0	0	0	0	0	0	0	0	0	0	0	0	0	0	0	3
18	1	0	0	0	0	0	1	0	0	0	0	0	0	0	0	0	0	0	0	0	0	0	0	0	0	0	0	0	0	0	3
25	1	1	0	0	0	1	1	0	0	0	0	0	0	0	0	0	0	0	0	0	0	0	0	0	0	0	0	0	0	0	1
33	0	1	0	1	1	0	1	0	0	0	0	0	0	0	0	0	0	0	0	0	0	0	0	0	0	0	0	0	0	0	3
34	0	0	1	0	1	1	0	0	0	0	0	0	0	0	0	0	0	0	0	0	0	0	0	0	0	0	0	0	0	0	2
05	0	1	0	0	0	1	0	0	0	1	0	1	0	0	0	0	0	0	0	0	0	0	0	0	0	0	0	0	0	0	3
19	0	0	1	0	0	0	0	0	0	0	0	0	0	0	0	0	0	0	0	0	0	0	0	0	0	0	0	0	0	0	0
06	0	1	0	0	0	0	1	1	0	0	1	0	0	0	0	0	0	0	0	0	0	0	0	0	0	0	0	0	0	0	3
04	0	0	1	0	0	0	0	0	0	1	0	1	0	0	0	0	0	0	0	0	0	0	0	0	0	0	0	0	0	0	0
15	0	0	1	0	0	0	0	0	0	0	1	0	1	0	0	0	0	0	0	0	0	0	0	0	0	0	0	0	0	0	3
20	1	0	0	0	0	0	0	0	0	0	0	1	0	0	0	0	0	0	0	0	0	0	0	0	0	0	0	0	0	0	2
14	0	0	0	0	0	0	0	0	0	0	0	0	0	0	0	0	0	0	0	0	0	0	0	0	0	0	0	0	0	0	0
11	1	0	0	0	0	0	0	0	0	0	0	0	0	0	0	1	1	0	0	0	0	0	0	0	0	0	0	0	0	0	3
35	0	0	0	0	0	0	0	0	0	0	0	0	0	0	0	0	1	0	0	0	0	0	0	0	0	0	0	0	0	0	1
22	0	0	0	0	0	0	0	0	0	0	0	0	0	0	0	0	0	1	1	0	0	1	0	0	0	0	0	0	0	0	2
21	0	0	0	0	0	0	0	0	0	0	0	0	0	0	0	0	0	0	0	0	0	0	0	0	0	0	0	0	0	0	3
07	0	0	0	0	0	0	0	0	0	0	0	1	1	0	0	1	1	0	0	1	0	0	1	0	0	0	0	0	0	0	0
12	0	1	0	0	0	0	0	0	0	0	0	1	0	0	0	0	0	1	0	0	1	0	0	0	0	0	0	0	0	0	3
24	0	0	0	0	0	0	0	0	0	0	0	0	0	0	0	0	0	0	0	0	0	0	0	0	0	0	0	0	0	0	3
36	0	0	0	0	0	0	0	0	0	1	0	0	0	0	0	0	0	0	0	0	0	0	0	1	0	0	0	0	0	0	2
23	0	0	0	0	0	0	0	0	0	0	0	0	0	0	0	0	0	0	0	0	0	0	0	0	0	0	0	0	0	0	0
28	0	0	0	0	0	0	0	0	0	1	0	0	0	0	0	0	0	0	1	0	0	0	0	0	0	0	1	0	0	0	2
32	0	0	0	0	0	0	0	1	0	0	0	0	0	0	0	0	0	0	1	0	0	0	0	1	0	0	0	0	0	0	3
10	0	0	0	0	0	0	0	0	0	0	0	0	0	0	0	0	0	0	0	0	0	0	0	0	0	0	0	0	0	0	2
26	1	0	0	0	1	0	0	0	0	0	0	0	0	1	0	0	0	0	1	0	0	0	0	0	0	0	0	1	0	0	3
13	0	0	0	0	0	0	0	0	0	0	1	0	0	1	1	0	1	0	0	0	0	0	0	0	0	1	1	0	0	0	3
16	0	0	0	1	0	0	0	0	0	0	0	0	0	0	0	0	0	0	0	0	0	0	0	0	0	1	0	0	0	0	2
30	0	0	0	0	0	0	0	0	0	0	0	0	0	0	0	0	0	0	0	0	0	0	0	0	0	0	0	0	0	0	0
Σ	5	5	0	3	1	2	3	3	0	3	2	3	3	0	2	4	1	2	1	2	0	5	3	0	1	0	1	4	4	2	0

Nominating teachers

Let us call the square incidence matrix reflecting the direct linkages A^1. A^1 is the matrix indicating the linkages among the nodes involving one step (direct nomination):

$$A^1 = \begin{array}{c} \\ 1 \\ 2 \\ 3 \end{array} \begin{array}{ccc} 1 & 2 & 3 \\ \begin{pmatrix} 0 & 1 & 0 \\ 0 & 0 & 1 \\ 1 & 0 & 0 \end{pmatrix} \end{array}$$

The initial distance matrix D can be constructed. The ultimate distance matrix should reflect the minimal number of steps necessary for all reachable points. A linkage between two points involving the minimal number of steps is called a *path*. If there is no reachable path between the members of a pair then there is no direct or indirect linkage between them. When there is no path, the distance between the members of the pair can be said to be infinite. Thus, the initial distance matrix D assumes an infinite distance between the members of all pairs:

$$D = \begin{array}{c} \\ 1 \\ 2 \\ 3 \end{array} \begin{array}{ccc} 1 & 2 & 3 \\ \begin{pmatrix} \infty & \infty & \infty \\ \infty & \infty & \infty \\ \infty & \infty & \infty \end{pmatrix} \end{array}$$

If A^1 is compared with D, it is seen that person 1 reaches person 2, person 2 reaches person 3, and person 3 reaches person 1, each linkage requiring one step. Thus, we assign a value of 1, indicating a one-step linkage, to the corresponding cells d_{12}, d_{23}, and d_{31} in the distance matrix:

$$D = \begin{array}{c} \\ 1 \\ 2 \\ 3 \end{array} \begin{array}{ccc} 1 & 2 & 3 \\ \begin{pmatrix} \infty & 1 & \infty \\ \infty & \infty & 1 \\ 1 & \infty & \infty \end{pmatrix} \end{array}$$

In order to determine linkages which require two steps, we square the A^1 matrix to obtain matrix $A^{(2)}$; $A^{(2)} = A^1 * A^1$. The operation of this matrix multiplication to obtain the value of each cell for $A^{(2)}$ is:

$$a_{ij}^{(2)} = (a_{i1}^1 \cdot a_{1j}^1) + (a_{i2}^1 \cdot a_{2j}^1) + \cdots (a_{in}^1 \cdot a_{nj}^1)$$
$$= \sum_{k=1}^{n} (a_{ik}^1 \cdot a_{kj}^1)$$

where $a_{ij}^{(2)}$ = cell of the ith row and jth column in the $A^{(2)}$ matrix
In the three-person group, to find the value of $a_{13}^{(2)}$,

$$a_{13}^{(2)} = (a_{11}^1 \cdot a_{13}^1) + (a_{12}^1 \cdot a_{23}^1) + (a_{13}^1 \cdot a_{33}^1)$$
$$= (0 \times 0) + (1 \times 1) + (0 \times 0)$$
$$= 1$$

It indicates that person 1 can reach person 3 in two steps (through person 2). In general, $a_{ij}^{(2)}$ can take values of 0 (no path linking i to j in two steps), 1 (one path linking i to j in two steps), 2 (two paths linking i to j in two steps), up to $n - 2$ (i linked to j in two steps through each and every other person in the group). We may then summarize the information by constructing an A^2 matrix which contains only two values, 1 and 0. A cell of A^2 has a value of 1 when the corresponding $a_{ij}^{(2)}$ has a value greater than 0, or 0 when the corresponding $a_{ij}^{(2)}$ has a value equal to 0. Thus, A^2 represents the incidence matrix in two steps, regardless of how many paths are involved in each linkage.

$$a_{ij}^{2} = \begin{cases} 1 & \text{if } a_{ij}^{(2)} > 0 \\ 0 & \text{if } a_{ij}^{(2)} = 0 \end{cases}$$

Operating on the original matrix A^1 with the above formulas, we obtain matrix A^2:

$$A^2 = \begin{array}{c} \\ 1 \\ 2 \\ 3 \end{array} \begin{array}{ccc} 1 & 2 & 3 \\ \begin{pmatrix} 0 & 0 & 1 \\ 1 & 0 & 0 \\ 0 & 1 & 0 \end{pmatrix} \end{array}$$

which indicates that, after two steps, person 1 reaches person 3 (via person 2), 2 reaches 1 (via 3), and 3 reaches 2 (via 1). Comparing the distance matrix D to A^2, we find that the cells d_{13}, d_{21}, and d_{32} still have a value of infinity (∞). Thus, a value of 2 (number of steps) is placed in these cells. The distance matrix D is now:

$$D = \begin{array}{c} \\ 1 \\ 2 \\ 3 \end{array} \begin{array}{ccc} 1 & 2 & 3 \\ \begin{pmatrix} \infty & 1 & 2 \\ 2 & \infty & 1 \\ 1 & 2 & \infty \end{pmatrix} \end{array}$$

Repeating the same procedure, we find that:

$$A^{(3)} = A^1 \cdot A^2$$

and

$$a_{ij}^{3} = \begin{cases} 1 & \text{if } a_{ij}^{(3)} > 0 \\ 0 & \text{if } a_{ij}^{(3)} = 0 \end{cases}$$

$$A^3 = \begin{array}{c} \\ 1 \\ 2 \\ 3 \end{array} \begin{array}{ccc} 1 & 2 & 3 \\ \begin{pmatrix} 1 & 0 & 0 \\ 0 & 1 & 0 \\ 0 & 0 & 1 \end{pmatrix} \end{array}$$

and the distance matrix D becomes:

$$
D = \begin{matrix} & 1 & 2 & 3 \\ 1 \\ 2 \\ 3 \end{matrix} \begin{pmatrix} 3 & 1 & 2 \\ 2 & 3 & 1 \\ 1 & 2 & 3 \end{pmatrix}
$$

Since self-loops are not allowed, the final distance matrix is:

$$
D = \begin{matrix} & 1 & 2 & 3 \\ 1 \\ 2 \\ 3 \end{matrix} \begin{pmatrix} 0 & 1 & 2 \\ 2 & 0 & 1 \\ 1 & 2 & 0 \end{pmatrix}
$$

Now that all the off-diagonal cells contain noninfinity numbers, the operation is complete. In general, the maximal number of multiplications to be performed is $n - 1$. Once a noninfinity number is present in a cell in the distance matrix D, no other number can replace that number in subsequent operations, since it represents the minimal distance between the pair of points. The operations can now be summarized more systematically.

FORMAL MATHEMATICS OF MATRIX MANIPULATIONS

We begin with an incidence matrix $A_1 = a_{ij}{}^1$, where $a_{ij}{}^1 = 1$ if a_i chooses a_j, and $a_{ij}{}^1 = 0$ if a_i does not choose a_j. By using the matrix multiplication method, we obtain matrix A^m:

$$
A^m = A^1 \cdot A^{m-1}
$$

$$
\text{where } a_{ij}{}^m = \begin{cases} 1 & \text{if } a_{ij}{}^{(m)} = \sum_{k=1}^{n} (a_{ik}{}^1 \cdot a_{kj}{}^{m-1}) > 0, \text{ and } i \neq j \\ \\ 0 & \text{otherwise} \end{cases}
$$

This matrix simply indicates the linkage of any pair of persons at the mth step.
    We then define a distance matrix D, in which

$$
D = d_{ij} = \begin{cases} n & \text{if } a_{ij}{}^m = 1, a_{ij}{}^k = 0 \text{ for all } k < m, \text{ and } i \neq j \\ \\ 0 & \text{if } i = j \\ \\ \infty & \text{otherwise} \end{cases}
$$

Matrix D establishes, first, whether or not a linkage between any pair of persons exists and, if it does, indicates how many steps corresponding to the shortest path between the two persons are involved in the chain. The maximal number of m is $n - 1$, where n is the number of persons in the group, since self-loops are not allowed.

The distance matrices for the three schools appear in Tables 17.4, 17.5, and 17.6. For example, in school 3, teacher 19 (row 19) is six steps away from teacher 33 (column 33). To trace the teachers linking teacher 19 to teacher 33, we can work backward by first finding out whom teacher 19 reached in five steps. It is teacher 17. In four steps, teacher 19 reached teacher 11. In three steps, teacher 19 reached both teachers 03 and 05. To verify which of these two teachers was involved in this particular path, we go to rows 03 and 05 to see whether they reached teacher 11 in one step. We find teacher 03 did, but not teacher 05 (who needed three steps). Then, we see teacher 19 reached teachers 04 and 11 in two steps. But, only teacher 04 reached teacher 03 in one step (see row 04 and column 03), and it took teacher 12 three steps to reach teacher 03 (see row 12 and column 03). Repeating the same procedure, we find teacher 15 served as the one-step linkage for teacher 19 in the path, but not teacher 14. Thus, the path from teacher 19 to teacher 33 is:

$$19 \rightarrow 15 \rightarrow 04 \rightarrow 03 \rightarrow 11 \rightarrow 17 \rightarrow 33$$

This path can be verified in Table 17.6 for school-3 data.

Once the final distance matrix D is obtained, several indices of relational properties can be constructed.[4]

Influence Domain

The influence domain of a person I_i is defined as the extent to which the opinion of the person is sought, both directly and indirectly, by other persons in the group. Operationally, it is measured by the number of other persons in the group who are affected, directly or indirectly, by the other person's opinions.

When person j seeks advice from person i, we may say that person i exerts some influence on person j. In the sociograms in Figure 12.5, influence is indicated by the directions of the lines (note the arrow pointing toward the "influential" person). Indirect influence is reflected in the paths where other persons seek advice from person j, thus indirectly being influenced by person i from whom person j seeks advice. Succinct information about the influence domain for all persons can be obtained from the final distance matrix:

$$I_i = \sum_{k=1}^{n} d_{ki}^{1}$$

where $d_{ki}^{1} = \begin{cases} 1 & \text{if } d_{ki} > 0 \\ 0 & \text{otherwise} \end{cases}$

Thus, the influence domain of person i is the frequency of cells in column i in the distance matrix D which have noninfinity values, or the number of persons who

[4] Other and related indices are suggested in: Leo Katz, op. cit.; Michael Taylor, "Influence Structures," *Sociometry,* vol. 32, pp. 490–502, 1969; William R. Arney, "A Refined Status Index for Sociometric Data," *Sociological Methods and Research,* vol. 1, no. 3, pp. 329–346; Phillip Bonacich, op. cit.

Table 17.4 Distance Matrix for Teachers in School 1

Nominated teachers

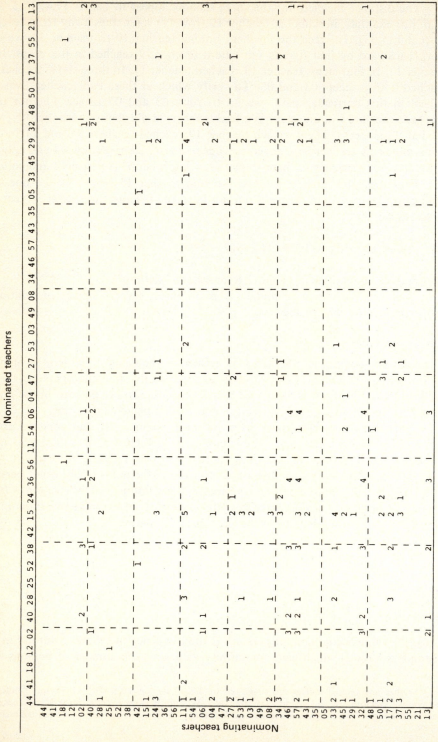

Nominating teachers

Table 17.5 Distance Matrix for Teachers in School 2

Nominated teachers

Nominating teachers	06	09	31	46	04	25	41	40	22	45	07	20	35	30	03	32	50	36	01	19	13	23	14	38	15	37	11	26	27	17	02	05	16	34	42	48	39
06																																					
09																											1										
31										1				3	2			2	2	2					1		1				1						
46																																					
04								2						2	3				1	2									1			1					
25																																					
41																																					
40																																					
22														1	2													1									
45														1	1						1																
07																																					
20																																					
35																																					
30															1					1																	
03																																					
32								5						3	2	2		2	4	3	4		2		1							1		1	2	1	
50																					2																
36																			1	1	1																
01								1											2	2	2	1															
19																			2	1																	
13								1						5	4	2																1		4	3		
23										1																											
14																																					
38														2	1										3							1	1				
15						1																															
37																																					
11																																					
26																																					
27																																					
17																																					
02								2		1				3	2	1		1	3	2	1		1		1									3	2		
05							1	4						2	3						3		1		2				1					1		1	
16																				2				1													
34																																					
42																																					
48																																					
39												1																									

343

Table 17.6 Distance Matrix for Teachers in School 3

Nominated teachers →

Nominating teachers ↓

Nom↓＼→	17	03	27	18	25	33	34	05	19	06	04	15	20	14	11	35	22	21	07	12	24	36	23	28	32	10	26	13	16	30
17		2	5	1	1	3	3	3	5	3	3	4	1	1	1	4	5	4	6	5	2	2	4	2		4	1	6	2	2
03	2		3	5	3	1	2	3	3		4	2	4	3	2	3	6		3	3	3	2	2	3		3	3	5	4	3
27	5	3		8	6	3		4	3	2	2	5	1	2	4	1	8		1	1	4		8	8		6	3	1	8	4
18	1	5	8		4	1	1			4	4	7	2	6	3	6	7		4	8	6		4	7		5	2	1	8	7
25	1	3	6	4		1		3	3		3	6	2	5	2	5	9		5	6	3		2	9		3	5	5	1	3
33	3	1	2	1	1		1	2	2		3	6	1	5	2	1	7		7	6	2		3	7		7	7	2		3
34	3	2		1		1		3	3	2	4	3	2	2	3		8	1		2	1	1		4		6	2	3	5	
05	3	2	4		3	2	3		2	2	1	3	1	2	2	3	7		5	5	4		6	6		5	4	3	3	
19	5	3	2		3	2	3	2		2	4	2	1	6	3	4	9		3	2	3		7	8		6	6	5	3	
06	3	1	3						2		2	1	1	1	1		8		1	1						2		1	1	3
04	3	4	4	4	3	4	1	4	4	2		4	2	6	4	1	4		2	4	5		5	4		4	4	3	3	3
15	4	2	2	2	4	5		3	1	2	1		7	2	3	3	7	1	3	1	2	1	4	7		3	7	2	5	
20	1	2	1		2	1		4	3	1	4	7		6	3	8	4		4	8	3		2	4		2	2	5	3	7
14	1	4		6	5	2	2	2	3	1	2	2	6		4	6	2	1		1	3		3	7		2	6	1	6	3
11	1	2	4		2	2		2			4	3	3	4					4	4	4		3	4		4	3	5	3	1
35	4	3	1	5	2						2								1	8				4						
22	5	6	8	6	5		8			2	2	7		2						2				7						
21	4						1					1		1																
07	6		4			1		1		1	4	3	4		5	1	2			1	2	1	2	9		1		3	8	2
12	5	3	3	8	6	2		2	5	1	2	1	8	1	4	8	2	2	1		3		3	8	3	2	8	3	8	3
24	2	3	4	6	3	2		4	3		5	4	2	3	4		3	2	2	3				3	2	3	5	4	2	
36	2		2				1														2				2					
23	4	2	2	4	2	1		6	3	1	5	3	2	3	3		3	2	2	3				7		5	5	4	5	
28	2	3	8	7	6	2	4	6	3		3	3	2	3	4	4	7		9	9	3		7			2	7	6	6	5
32																														1
10	4	3	6	5	3	2		4	4		4	3	2	2	4		5		1	2	2	2		5				3	4	5
26	1	3	3	2	5					2	4	4		6	3		5			8	1			2				5	1	3
13	6	3	1	1	5	2	4	3	2	1	4	2	1	6	3		3	2		3	4		4	7		3	5		8	4
16	2	4		8	1		3	3	5	7	3	6	2	1	4	1	2		1	3			6	9		7	1	8		4
30	2	3	5	7	3						3	2	7	3	1		1		2	3				5	1	3	3	4	4	

344

directly or indirectly choose person i. For example, in school 2, the distance matrix shows (Table 17.5) that teacher 40 is chosen (column 40) both directly and indirectly by 10 other teachers in the school. Thus, the influence domain of teacher 40 is 10.

Centrality

The concept of centrality is introduced to index the communication cost implied in the length (number of steps or links) of the paths. The *centrality* of a person C_i in a social system is defined in terms of the average length of the paths involved in his influence domain. For a person who is directly chosen by four others, the centrality index score is 1. For a person directly chosen by two persons and by two others one step removed, the centrality is 1.5: $(1 + 1 + 2 + 2)/4 = 1.5$. Thus, centrality is the ratio between the number of steps involved in each and every path between those who directly or indirectly choose person i, and the number of persons so involved (the influence domain):

$$C_i = \begin{cases} \dfrac{\sum\limits_{k=1}^{n} d_{ki}}{I_i} & \text{if } d_{ki} > 0, k \neq i, \text{ and } I_i \neq 0 \\ 0 & \text{otherwise} \end{cases}$$

It is an average of the number of steps involved in person i's linkage with all other persons directly or indirectly choosing him. The smaller C_i is, the more central person i is in the network in which all other persons choose him (directly or indirectly).

Prestige

To measure the importance or prestige of a person in a group, an index taking into account both his influence domain and his centrality in the group can be constructed. The *prestige* of a person p_i is defined as the extent to which he enjoys a large following (high-influence domain) and is centrally located in the group (centrality). Operationally, the prestige p_i of a person is defined as his influence domain divided by the product of his centrality and the total size of the group excluding herself $(n - 1)$:

$$p_i = \begin{cases} \dfrac{I_i}{C_i(n - 1)} & \text{if } C_i \neq 0 \\ 0 & \text{otherwise} \end{cases}$$

Thus, the prestige of person i is defined as a function of (1) the number of persons in the group, (2) the number of persons directly or indirectly choosing him, and (3) the average length of the choosing paths. p_i varies from 0 to 1, equaling 0 when no other person chooses person i, and 1 when every other person chooses

Table 17.7   Influence Domain and Centrality
of Teachers in School 1

Teacher	Influence domain	Centrality*	Prestige
44	20	1.60	0.305
41	3	1.67	0.044
18	0	∞	0.000
12	1	1.00	0.024
02	6	2.17	0.068
40	6	1.67	0.088
28	6	1.83	0.080
25	0	∞	0.000
52	1	1.00	0.024
38	10	2.20	0.111
42	0	∞	0.000
15	17	2.53	0.164
24	4	1.50	0.065
36	7	2.71	0.063
56	1	1.00	0.024
11	0	∞	0.000
54	3	1.33	0.055
06	6	3.00	0.049
04	1	1.00	0.024
47	5	1.80	0.068
27	4	1.00	0.098
53	3	1.67	0.044
03	0	∞	0.000
49	0	∞	0.000
08	0	∞	0.000
34	0	∞	0.000
46	0	∞	0.000
57	0	∞	0.000
43	0	∞	0.000
35	0	∞	0.000
05	1	1.00	0.024
33	2	1.00	0.049
45	0	∞	0.000
29	17	1.82	0.227
32	6	1.50	0.098
48	1	1.00	0.024
50	0	∞	0.000
17	0	∞	0.000
37	4	1.50	0.065
55	1	1.00	0.024
21	0	∞	0.000
13	6	1.83	0.080

* The minimum centrality score is 1.

Table 17.8 Influence Domain and Centrality of Teachers in School 2

Teacher	Influence domain	Centrality*	Prestige
06	5	3.00	0.046
09	0	∞	0.000
31	0	∞	0.000
46	0	∞	0.000
04	0	∞	0.000
25	1	1.00	0.028
41	0	∞	0.000
40	10	2.30	0.121
22	2	1.00	0.056
45	2	1.00	0.056
07	0	∞	0.000
20	1	1.00	0.028
35	0	∞	0.000
30	11	2.45	0.124
03	11	2.18	0.140
32	2	1.50	0.037
50	0	∞	0.000
36	3	1.67	0.050
01	8	2.13	0.105
19	8	1.75	0.127
13	8	1.88	0.119
23	2	1.50	0.037
14	0	∞	0.000
38	1	1.00	0.028
15	5	1.60	0.087
37	0	∞	0.000
11	2	1.00	0.056
26	1	1.00	0.028
27	0	∞	0.000
17	0	∞	0.000
02	1	1.00	0.028
05	0	∞	0.000
16	0	∞	0.000
34	4	2.50	0.044
42	4	1.75	0.063
48	0	∞	0.000
39	0	∞	0.000

* The minimum centrality score is 1.

person i directly. A person's prestige in a group increases as others choose him directly or indirectly, the averaged distances in these paths are shorter, and there are fewer individuals in the group.

Tables 17.7, 17.8, and 17.9 present the influence domains, centrality, and prestige scores of the teachers in the three schools.

Once relational properties such as prestige are identified, it is possible to use

**Table 17.9   Influence Domain and Centrality
of Teachers in School 3**

Teacher	Influence domain	Centrality*	Prestige
17	26	3.12	0.288
03	26	2.70	0.395
27	0	∞	0.000
18	26	5.42	0.165
25	26	3.92	0.229
33	26	2.85	0.315
34	2	1.00	0.069
05	26	2.88	0.311
19	26	3.69	0.243
06	9	2.00	0.155
04	26	3.15	0.284
15	26	4.12	0.218
20	0	∞	0.000
14	27	3.44	0.270
11	26	3.15	0.284
35	1	1.00	0.034
22	2	1.00	0.069
21	0	∞	0.000
07	8	1.38	0.201
12	26	4.58	0.196
24	0	∞	0.000
36	3	1.67	0.062
23	0	∞	0.000
28	26	5.50	0.163
32	1	1.00	0.034
10	0	∞	0.000
26	26	3.65	0.245
13	26	3.31	0.271
16	26	4.54	0.198
30	0	∞	0.000

* The minimum centrality score is 1.

them as variables in the study. Many of them are measured in interval scales, and thus can be incorporated in regressional and correlational analysis. For example, in a series of studies in Central America and Haiti, prestige scores, used as index of social integration, were found to be highly related to the acceptance of and use of health services (e.g., inoculations, family planning, and proper feeding instructions for mothers of infants) among women in rural communities.[5]

Also, relational properties can be aggregated from individuals for group indices. For example, the mean, the variance, and the standard deviation of prestige

[5] Nan Lin and Ronald S. Burt, "Differential Roles of Information Channels in the Process of Innovation Diffusion," *Social Forces,* September 1975; Ronald S. Burt, "The Differential Impact of Social Integration on Participation in the Diffusion of Innovations," *Social Science Research,* vol. 2, pp. 125–144, 1973.

scores for each group can be used as variables to indicate a group's social cohesiveness, which can be compared with those of other groups.

As most structural computations can become complicated and cumbersome, the social researcher must rely on high-speed computers to perform the calculations. Many computer programs and packages are available to the social researcher for a nominal fee.[6]

SUMMARY

Structural analysis is used to examine sociometric data, data dealing with relational and interactional activities. To obtain a picture of the dynamics of a social system, simple aggregation of individual activities and characteristics is not sufficient. Sociometric data and structural analysis investigate the group and relational properties for a social group or system, be it a friendship or kinship network, a community, an institution, or relations and interactions that are very complex, implicit, or invisible to outside observations. By utilizing graphic and matrical approaches, the researcher may identify structural properties associated with each group, and relations among individuals within the group. Knowledge of these properties helps the researcher understand the dynamics of the interlocking of individuals or groups, which is inaccessible by aggregational analysis.

Results of structural analysis in the form of variables can then be integrated for statistical analysis at the inter- and intragroup levels.

[6] For example, a computer program for computing the influence domain, centrality, and prestige, as well as the distance matrix, can be purchased from the International Center for Social Research, c/o Department of Sociology, State University of New York at Albany, Albany, New York 12222.

Part Six

Presentation and Use
of Social Research

Chapter 18

Interpretation and Reporting

INTERPRETATION

When data analysis has been completed, the researcher interprets the data in terms of the theoretical and practical objectives of the study. In the interpretation of the analytical results, it is important to keep in mind the restrictions of the conditions under which the study was conducted and the assumptions of the statistical techniques used. For descriptive data, where no inferences are made to any population, interpretation is restricted to providing a comprehensive and accurate description of the data regarding the group of respondents studied. For multivariate analysis, different patterns existing among the respondents can be discussed.

Evaluation of Procedures and Data

While the interpretation of the results of a descriptive analysis is straightforward, interpretation of an inferential analysis can be very complex. First, the researcher must evaluate the extent to which measurement errors have occurred. Was the sampling successful? Was the response rate high enough? Were the interviewers or observers properly trained? Were the instruments properly pretested and the instructions followed by the respondent? Did anything unexpected happen during the study, which introduced errors or biases into the data? Even in a perfectly planned study, things will go wrong or things will happen that are beyond the researcher's expectation or control. The effects of unanticipated errors, anticipated errors, or both, or deviations in the course of the conduct of the study on the research results, must be objectively evaluated and reported. It is a better strategy to make such errors known to other scientists and potential users of the research results than to conceal them, thus biasing the appropriate interpretation and evaluation of the study results.

Any false or concealed information only deters the development of scientific knowledge and eventually discredits the researcher's work and reputation. The price would be too costly for both the scientific community and the individual researcher.

Second, the researcher should evaluate the extent to which the assumptions of the analytical techniques (e.g., statistics) used were supported by the data. Evidence should be presented to document any assertions made in this regard.

Evaluation of Relations

In addition, several other issues, involving the relationships among the variables, must be made clear in the interpretation: (1) contingency, group difference, associative, or functional; (2) covariational versus causal; and (3) significant versus important.

The first issue stresses the limitation or generality of the statistical technique used. When regressional or correlational techniques are used, interpretation must address itself to the evidence that the patterns of the observations have a linear relationship. Failure to find a linear relationship between two variables in correlational analysis does not imply that there is no nonlinear (functional) relationship between the variables. In other words, failure to verify an associative model does not eliminate the possibility of the existence of a functional model. The associative model is simply a particular case of the functional model. The researcher must be careful not to confuse the two different types of relations when a statistical technique applicable to only one type is used.

The second issue addresses the two types of associative relationships: (1) the covariational relationship, in which the variables have a concomitant and interdependent relationship (e.g., positive or negative), and (2) the causal relationship, in which one variable is concomitant with, temporally precedes, and is nonspuriously related to the second variable. A causal relationship, while desirable for a theoretical structure, cannot be assumed from the confirmation of a covariational relationship. The researcher must provide evidence that all three requirements for a causal relationship are present in the data before he asserts such a relationship in the interpretation.

Finally, the interpretation should differentiate between a *significant* relationship and an *important* relationship among variables. Significance of a relationship, in the statistical sense, indicates only that the relationship rarely occurs by chance. Thus, a significant relationship suggests that the variables involved are probably associated in a nonrandom pattern. Importance of a relationship, on the other hand, not only suggests that the relationship among the variables is nonrandom probabilistically, but also that the magnitude of the relationship is substantial. A significant relationship is not necessarily an important relationship. As discussed in Chapter 9, Sampling, and Chapter 16, Multivariate Analysis, given a sufficient sample size, many variables will be significantly related (the relationship is significantly different from zero) in the sense that these relationships are not random. However, few relationships are important in the sense that their magnitudes are substantial. The literature usually reflects a careless interpretation of significant relationships as if they were also important ones. A relationship is important to the extent that the correspondence of a change in one variable with the change in another is strong and systematic.

For example, in correlational analysis, r^2 is used to indicate the degree of overlap between the independent variables and the dependent variable (that is, the extent to which the variation of the independent variables contributes to the explanation of the variation of the dependent variable), whereas the correlation coefficient r can be used only to test whether or not the relationships are nonrandom (that is, the significance of the relationships). A significant r does not necessarily imply a large r^2. Again, given a sufficient sample size, most r's would be significant, although many of them would be low in magnitude (r^2).

When the issues regarding the relationships among the variables have been properly documented, the researcher faces a still larger and more difficult task, that of linking the data to a theoretical structure or public policy.

Theoretical Inference

As presented in Chapters 2 and 3, data in the form of observations are linked to theoretical propositions through epistemic correlations between the concepts and the variables. The empirical finding of a relationship (in Figure 18.1, a causal relationship) between variable a and variable b does not automatically indicate a relationship between concept A and concept B. In Figure 2.6, four of the eight variations ($b, c, e,$ and g) show a relationship between variables a and b. But only one variation (b) actually shows that the two concepts A and B are related, as well as that A and B are related to a and b, respectively. Thus, confirmation of a relationship between concepts in a theoretical structure depends on the following conditions:

1. The variables are empirically related.
2. The variables and concepts are related.
3. The concepts are, in fact, related.

The third condition can never be empirically verified. Thus, the best a researcher can do is to demonstrate the validity of the first two conditions and to guard against drawing any definite fool-proof statement about the relationship of the concepts even when the first two conditions are shown to be evident.

An empirical check on the adequacy of the relationship among variables

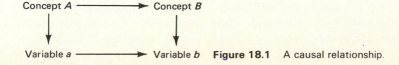

Concept A ⟶ Concept B

Variable a ⟶ Variable b   **Figure 18.1**   A causal relationship.

consists of an evaluation of the unexplained or residual variance of the dependent variable left after the effect of the independent variable or variables on the dependent variable has been taken into account. In correlational analysis, the unexplained variance is $1 - r^2$. When the unexplained variance is high, it suggests that the contribution of the independent variable to the explanation of the dependent variable is small. In other words, there may be other independent variables which are important in the explanation of the dependent variable, but which have not been accounted for by the researcher. A high unexplained variance may also suggest that the measurement of one or both of the variables was inadequate.

Even when empirical data confirm the relationship between variables, confirmation of the relationship between the concepts requires additional support. This support is provided by the demonstration of the relationships between the variables and the concepts (the epistemic correlation). The epistemic correlation relies on deductive strategy and measurement rigor. The researcher should utilize multiple variables for each concept. Multiple empirical deductive systems reduce the probability of concepts not being related while the variables are (see pages 39–40). Rigorous measurement increases the reliability of the results and the validity of the postulated relationship between the concepts (Chapter 10).

Thus, when the analysis shows the residual or unexplained variance to be high for the dependent variable, four issues are raised: (1) the likelihood that the measurement or operationalization of the concepts was inadequate, (2) the likelihood that some phases of the research were faulty, (3) the likelihood that the theoretical structure is inadequate in the sense that other important concepts have not been incorporated, and (4) the likelihood that the dependent variable has an intrinsic portion of randomness which cannot be explained by other variables.

In interpreting the results, then, the researcher should clearly delineate the procedures of measurement (operationalization) used and the research process (sampling, data collection, and data analysis), so that the reader can estimate the extent of adequacy or inadequacy of the epistemic correlation between the variables and the concepts.

As pointed out in Chapter 16, the task of a researcher in theory construction does not have to be strictly finding relationships which are important (substantial in R^2), for many relationships have interesting and meaningful roles in a theoretical structure and yet have relatively low magnitudes. As long as the magnitudes estimated are sufficiently precise, moderately low (say, standardized regression coefficients in the .10s or .20s) to medium (in the .30s to .40s), magnitudes of relationships usually provide the backbone propositions of a theoretical structure in its early stages.

Policy Inference

While it is tempting for a researcher to declare policy implications when certain relationships are found in the data analysis, the interpretation must be made with caution. Several major issues regarding this will be deferred to the next chapter which deals with the use of social research. Here, the researcher is simply alerted to the limitations of the generalizability of data collected in a study for policy decisions.

A research study may uncover relationships among variables, because the researcher is able to exercise control over many phases of the research. Thus, policy implications are restricted to the population from which the sample of respondents was representatively selected. Extension of the results to other populations runs the risk of having such relationships among the variables prove invalid.

Also, the observations are selective, and variables can be held constant or taken into account in the statistical analysis. In the natural course of events, activities and patterns cannot be held constant.

For example, a study may show that the use of local media, such as teachers, police, local officials and sound trucks, is effective in disseminating information and persuading peasants in an industrially less developed country to adopt certain appropriate health practices (e.g., feeding babies nutritious food, using birth control, and receiving inoculations against communicable diseases).[1] Moreover, this finding may hold for peasants of different socioeconomic status (SES) (holding the SES constant). However, there is no guarantee that an actual increase in the use of the local media in disseminating health information would benefit the different SES groups equally. One might assume that the local media were not functioning effectively at the time of the study. Thus, higher-SES groups would have been relying on other media for health information (e.g., mass media). The lower-SES groups, deprived of access to other media (newspapers, radios, etc.) would, therefore, seem to have benefited from the local media as much as the higher-SES groups. However, if the research finding were implemented in an accelerated campaign with extensive use of the local media, the higher-SES groups might well be quickly alerted through mass media and other sources much faster than the lower-SES groups. The result of such a policy implementation might be a parallel increase in benefit for the higher-SES groups who now utilize the effective local media fully while the lower-SES groups remain to be benefited marginally.

Further, manipulations of policies may affect activities and behaviors not studied, generating effects unpredictable or even undesirable. The ethical responsibility of a researcher in maintaining the well-being of human beings involved in the extension of research results cannot be avoided.

Thus, the researcher should interpret data with care, delineating all the restrictions and limitations. When suggesting policy implications, the researcher should always emphasize the need to conduct small-scale trials and to outline strategies for evaluation of the operations and results of such trials. Hopefully, any undesirable effects will be uncovered in the trials, and further trials can be designed to eliminate such effects before large-scale effects take care.

REPORTING

Before the writing of a report begins, the researcher must know clearly: (1) *who* the intended readers of the report (the audience) will be, (2) *what* the intended

---

[1] Nan Lin and Ronald S. Burt, "Differential Impacts of Information Channels in the Process of Innovation Diffusion," *Social Forces*, September 1975.

goal of the report (the purpose) is, (3) in *what* form the report should appear (the medium), (4) *what* style of writing should be employed (the writing style), (5) *how* the report should be organized (the content), and (6) *how* the report can be made in such a way so that the ethical responsibility of the researcher can be fulfilled (the ethical responsibility). All these questions are interrelated and, to a large extent, determine the effectiveness of the final product of social research—the report.

Audience

A research report can be addressed to a wide variety of audiences, ranging from scientists engaged in basic research to the general public. The audience can be classified into the following categories: (1) scientists engaged in basic research, (2) scientists engaged in applied research, (3) practitioners and service agents, (4) policy makers, (5) sponsors of research, and (6) the general public.

Scientists engaged in *basic research* are interested in information which contributes to the body of scientific knowledge. They are familiar with the concepts, theories, and procedures of research. Therefore, they expect the report to be precise, accurate, and tightly structured. Typically, they are associated with academic disciplines such as sociology, economics, psychology, etc., at colleges and research centers.

Scientists engaged in *applied research,* on the other hand, seek information which can be of use in their efforts in applying scientific methods and knowledge to the formulation of policies providing solutions to specific problems. They may not be as familiar with the concepts and theories as their colleagues engaged in basic research. The report they read must demonstrate the feasibility of the methods of knowledge in helping them to solve the problems at hand. Many of these scientists are affiliated with research centers, (e.g., the Center for Policy Research), research corporations, (e.g., the RAND corporation), public agencies (e.g., the National Institutes of Health), or private foundations (e.g., the Ford Foundation).

Practitioners and *service agents* utilize information in working for their clients. They are interested in information which has clear procedural instructions, implementational instructions, or both so that it can be incorporated in their practices and services. Librarians, teachers, physicians, social workers, and nurses are examples of this type of audience.

Policy makers are interested in information which suggests improvements in or alternatives to existing policies and administrations. They expect the report to have a minimum of scientific and disciplinary jargon and a maximum of information concerning solutions of problems associated with policies (or alternative policies).

Sponsors of research are interested in the technical details of the study and in information which demonstrates that the study has arrived at its findings as specified in the objectives and procedures of the proposal approved by the sponsors.

A research report should focus on a specific audience as the target audience.

While the report may also address other peripheral audiences, it must deliver information consistent with the normative practices and procedures expected by the target audience. Any uncertainty in the view of the researcher as to who the target audience is usually results in ineffective communication of the report to any audience.

Purpose

The report is also influenced by the researcher's purpose in preparing it. A report can summarize and synthesize all the research activities cumulated in an area—the *state-of-the-art* report. It compiles all significant existing research findings and organizes them into a body with a cohesive theoretical structure.

A report can describe a piece of information new to the existing body of knowledge. Such an addition can be either verification, replication, or extension of an existing body of concepts and theories—*normative information*; or proposed or verified new concepts and theories—*paradigmic* or *"revolutionary" information*.[2] One temptation is to report normative information as if it were paradigmic information. The temptation is great in social research, as little consensus exists regarding the correspondence between concepts and variables. Because of the primitive stage of measurement and the imprecise practices of social researchers, one variable may be used by different researchers to tap several concepts. Different variables, purportedly tapping the same concept, do not correspond to one another through a precise calculus. Imprecision in the epistemic correlation impedes the development of theoretical structures. A researcher must make a thorough search of the uses by other researchers of any variables and concepts he has examined. Chances are that epistemic correlations among these concepts and variables have previously been discussed, empirically examined, or both, by other researchers. Unless the researcher has valid justification, both theoretical and empirical, to refute the previous linkages, the researcher will do the scientific literature a great service by resisting the temptation to conjure up novel concepts in the interpretation of data. In scientific development, paradigmic information is infrequent.

A third purpose for writing a report is to demonstrate the practical utility of the information to practitioners and to the public. Essentially, no new information is reported. Rather, the researcher informs the reader of the implications of certain theories and methods in regard to their potential usefulness in the reader's professional work.

The purpose of the report dictates the form in which it appears, the writing style employed, and the details furnished.

Medium

The researcher has a choice of the form in which the report can appear. The selection is determined by the target audience, the purpose of the report, and the

---

[2] Thomas S. Kuhn, *The Structure of Scientific Revolutions,* 2d ed., University of Chicago Press, Chicago, 1970.

scientific and practical usefulness of the information to be presented. The media generally available to a reporting researcher include articles in journals, in-house technical reports, monographs, books, chapters in books, presentations at meetings or conferences, and news releases. Further, within each type of medium, different documents and forums are geared for specific target audiences. For example, different journals are identified with different segments of the audience. Some are addressed entirely to scientists conducting basic research, others to practitioners, still others to the general public.

However, there is a pattern of association between the media and the target audiences. Scientists in basic research tend to use journals and books as outlets for their work. Scientists in applied research tend to use technical reports and monographs. And scientists addressing themselves to the general public tend to use news releases or the mass media (magazines, television, etc.) available to the general public. The matching of a particular channel of communication on the one hand, with the intended audience and the purpose, on the other hand, determines to a large extent whether or not the report will receive attention.

There is no particular restriction as to the number of places a researcher can report the results of a study, as long as earlier reports are properly cited in subsequent reports. It is often the case that a study generates a series of publications and presentations. As a rule, the researcher first makes a report on an informal occasion such as a colloquium held in the department or institute with which he is affiliated, and sends drafts of the report to colleagues working with the same subject matter for informal review and comment. Then, he is likely to make a report at a conference or meeting attended by scientists from other institutions at the regional, national, or international level. Finally, he is ready to prepare a manuscript for a more formal channel such as a journal or a book. Subsequently, a news release may be issued to the mass media.[3] By using this sequence of reporting, the researcher benefits from comments and suggestions from colleagues before a report is finalized for publication.

Publication of a report in a journal can be a trying process. Because of a variety of reasons, such as relatively limited article space in social science journals and imprecise criteria for evaluation, the rejection rates of the recognized journals tend to be high—as high as 95 percent of submitted manuscripts. As a result, many manuscripts must be submitted to several journals before they are accepted. The ethical rule strongly suggests that a manuscript be submitted for consideration to only one journal at a given time. Thus, the time lost in the process of submissions and resubmissions is substantial. On the average it takes twenty-five months from the initiation of research work to journal publication of a report in physical sciences and thirty-two months in social sciences.[4]

---

[3] For detailed discussions on the process of dissemination of scientific information see: William D. Garvey, Nan Lin, and Carnot E. Nelson, "Communication in the Physical and Social Sciences," *Science,* vol. 170, pp. 1166–1173, Dec. 11, 1970; Nan Lin, William D. Garvey and Carnot E. Nelson, "A Study of the Communication Structure of Science," in C. E. Nelson and D. K. Pollock (ed.), *Communication among Scientists and Engineers,* Heath Lexington, Lexington, Mass., 1970.

[4] William D. Garvey, Nan Lin, and Carnot E. Nelson, "Some Comparisons of Communication Activities in the Physical and Social Sciences," in C. E. Nelson and D. K. Pollock, op. cit.

Contributing to the prolonged process of publication, there is the gentleman's agreement among scientists that any new information to be added to the body of knowledge must first be evaluated by qualified scientists in the subject matter area and published in a professionally recognized journal before the information is released to the mass media and the general public. This procedure safeguards the credibility of the body of knowledge, so that it will continue to represent the "consensus of universally accepted knowledge" of the scientists in the subject matter area.[5] However, it also prolongs the time period from the reporting to the scientific community to the awareness of practitioners, policy makers, and the public of new information useful in their work.

Shortcuts are used by researchers to reduce the various time lags. For example, technical reports and monographs, usually reviewed only by the researcher's colleagues elsewhere, are utilized as the media of publication. While inevitably suffering from the lack of and delay in professional evaluation and recognition, these media provide fast and efficient communication between the researcher and the target audience, especially practitioners, policy makers, and the general public. However, the dilemma remains as to how much credit should be given to information the evaluation of which has been limited or delayed, and as to how the target audience, without the competence to make such scientific evaluations, can use the information with any degree of confidence. The problem is reduced somewhat by the increasing use, by various agencies and institutions, of scientists as employees or consultants for the purpose of evaluating potentially useful scientific information. This brings up the issue of the involvement of scientists in goal-oriented institutions—whether scientists should involve themselves in value-laden activities. This issue will be further dealt with in Chapter 19.

Writing Style

Many writing styles have been used in research reporting, ranging from a straightforward style written in the first person ("I have discovered . . .") to an impersonal style written in the third person ("It was discovered . . ."). There is no consensus as to what style should be adopted. General usage favors the impersonal style. Moreover, there is a growing trend toward using the active ("The data suggest . . .") rather than the passive ("It is suggested . . .") tense. Also, there is a trend toward the use of simple rather than complex sentence structure. In the final analysis each researcher must choose the writing style with which he is the most comfortable and feels is the most effective in communicating his research to the target audience.

When a report contains visual presentations (e.g., tables and graphs) the text should flow independently of the visual presentations. In other words, while the visual presentations aid and clarify the discussion, the reader should be able to follow the discussion without having to read the visual presentations. Thus, while

---

[5] John Ziman, *Public Knowledges: The Social Dimension of Science.* Cambridge University Press, London, 1968.

the researcher may refer to the visual presentations in the text, the gist of the information contained therein should appear and be explained in the text. If at all possible, graphs and figures are preferred to tables, as the audience is more likely to grasp main ideas or findings presented in lines and circles rather than numbers.

A researcher should consult two sources in formulating a specific writing style: (1) the conventions adopted by researchers using the same medium (e.g., a specific meeting or journal) in the past, and (2) books on writing styles and scientific writing.[6]

Content

The content of a report should in general be organized in five major sections: (1) statement of the problem, (2) study design and procedure, (3) analysis and interpretation, (4) conclusions and discussion, and (5) bibliography.

The statement of the problem includes a general introduction to the subject matter area, a review of points and issues in past studies and discussions, a description of the specific topic to be studied, and a discussion of the justification and importance of the selected topic for research. The review of theoretical (or methodological) issues in an area should be short, precise, and focused. The researcher should then pinpoint the critical issues with which his study is concerned, present his position and argument on these issues, and elaborate potential contributions of the proposed effort to theoretical (or methodological) advance in the subject matter area. At the same time the researcher should point out the limitations of his effort, so as not to mislead the reader into expecting major "breakthroughs" when no such results are forthcoming in the report.

The report proceeds to describe the study design and procedures. Starting from deductions of theoretical propositions and operationalization of concepts into variables, the report states any proposed hypotheses to be tested. Then, it presents the sampling procedure (including a general and historical, if appropriate, description of the population and events to be studied), the instrumentation and measurement process, the method of data collection, and the data analysis plans. Unless the data set is well known (e.g., the United States census), details of sampling (e.g., the type, the procedure, and possible errors), measurement (with actual or selected items and numbers used), data collection (training of collaborators such as interviewers and observers, instructions for collaborators and respondents), and data analysis plans (introduction and justification of analytical techniques to be used) must be provided.

The next section of the report presents results of the data analysis and inferences from the results to the theoretical structure under consideration. This section should begin with a brief but sufficient description of the characteristics of the sampled respondents. If possible, the sampled characteristics should be compared with available information about the same characteristics of the population

[6] William Strunk, Jr., and E. B. White, *The Elements of Style,* Macmillan, New York, 1962; S. F. Trelease, *How to Write Scientific and Technical Papers,* M.I.T., Cambridge, Mass., 1969; F. Peter Woodford (ed.), *Scientific Writing for Graduate Students,* Rockefeller University Press, New York, 1968.

from which the sample was drawn, to demonstrate the extent of possible error in the sampling and measurement procedures. Findings should be presented in such a manner as to make it possible for the reader to independently derive or evaluate the final statistics from the basic data presented. For example, the means and standard deviations of variables should be presented when the regression or correlation coefficients are computed, so that the reader can determine whether or not the distributions of the variables warrant the use of regressional techniques.

Finally, the report can elaborate the findings relative to the verification or modification of the theoretical structure initially considered. The researcher should also state the shortcomings and limitations of the study, so that interpretations of and inferences from the findings will be made with caution. Future courses of research can be suggested.

The above-outlined organization varies, of course, depending on the audience, the purpose, the medium, and the writing style. For example, in a book or dissertation, the detailed review of the literature may be separated from the statement of the problem. Also, the final discussion section may lead to further analysis and interpretation of the reported data or other relevant data available to the researcher. However, a report must deal with all the issues outlined above, providing the audience with a comprehensive understanding and evaluation of the study involved.

Ethical Responsibility

The reporting researcher must maintain his ethical responsibility in the report. This responsibility includes: (1) protecting the respondents and collaborators in the study, and (2) providing accurate and complete information.

When confidentiality is promised to the respondents by the researcher, he should make sure such confidentiality is maintained. This is especially crucial when the data concern abnormal or illegal activities. The social researcher, like the journalist, must protect his sources of information. There are arguments as to the extent to which the ethical responsibility of the researcher must be recognized. For example, in a study of criminals, can a researcher protect the anonymity of murderers whose crimes have not been uncovered by law enforcement agencies? Or should a researcher studying sellers of illegal drugs conceal their identities? From the community's viewpoint, such protection seems unethical. However, if the researcher's data were obtained from the respondents with the promise that the identities would not be revealed, the researcher is obligated to keep his promise. In recent years, several researchers have risked convictions and jail terms in fulfilling their ethical responsibility to protect the identities of respondents.

Also, the researcher has the ethical responsibility to present accurate and complete information to the best of his ability and knowledge. Accurate information is information unbiased by deliberate distortion, "doctoring," or "fudging" of data on the part of the researcher and his associates. Presenting only partial information, although it may be accurate, does not reflect the fulfillment of the ethical responsibility of the researcher. The pressure of publishing should not be allowed to interfere with the researcher's presentation of accurate and complete information. Unfortunately, the temptation to present only positive results can be great. Most journals, for example, are reluctant to publish results which fail to support hypotheses outlined, because of the practical problem of distributing limited space. This practice indirectly discourages the documentation of findings unfavorable or even damaging to the existing body of knowledge on the one hand, and encourages the reporting of only positive results on the other hand. The shortcomings of editorial policies should be remedied as more journals and other forms of media in the relevant subject matter area become available to the researcher, and as more and more scientists involved in editorial decisions realize the positive contributions of negative results to the modification and, therefore, to the development of theoretical structures. In the meantime, the researcher should conduct his work according to the highest ethical standards. Any misrepresentation or incomplete presentation of information not only damages the development of scientific knowledge, but may bring discredibility to the researcher as other researchers attempt to replicate or extend his work. As more and more social scientists participate in pooling data, evident in the roles of several national data banks (the Roper Public Opinion Research Center at Williams College, the Inter-University Consortium of Political Research at the University of Michigan, etc.), the credibility of individual findings is becoming more easy to verify.

SUMMARY

Interpretation of data should be made within the limitations and shortcomings of a particular study. Relationships among variables should be classified as associative or functional, covariational or causal, and significant, important, or both.

When inferences are made from the data to a theoretical structure, correspondence of the relationships among variables and those among concepts is contingent on the empirical evidence of the relationship among the variables, as well as the epistemic correlation between each variable and its corresponding concept. Rigor of measurement and accounted variance help assess the adequacy of the proofs. When the empirical relationship among variables is found to be insignificant, the researcher cannot reject the theoretical proposition tested. Rather, he should merely state that no evidence has been found in support of the theoretical proposition (in the form of a hypothesis).

Inferences from data to policy decisions must be made with caution. The researcher should be aware at all times and make it clear to others that policy generalizations are restricted to the population from which the sample was representatively selected. Generalizations of empirical findings to other populations run the risk of producing invalid results. Also, data in a study are gathered with restrictions on the number of variables, observations, and social conditions under which they are collected. Implementation of recommendations guided by evidence from the data in ongoing natural settings may result in unanticipated effects on the participants and on the social system. Any implementation must, therefore, proceed with small-scale trials before a substantial number of people become involved in the process.

The reporting of a research study is guided by considerations of the intended audience, the purpose of the report, the medium used, the writing style, the content, and the ethical responsibility of the researcher to maintain the confidentiality of the sources of data and to provide accurate and complete information.

Chapter 19

Policy Contribution of Social Research

Research reports inform others of the findings of a particular research effort. If the research results are valid and reliable, they should have implications for the development of scientific knowledge, ongoing social policies, or both. The theoretical implications of research results have been discussed extensively in Chapters 2, 3, and 4. The policy implications of social research, on the other hand, deserve further elaboration. Before such elaboration is made, however, it is important to understand the process of social research in the larger social context.

SOCIAL CONTEXT OF SOCIAL RESEARCH

Social research does not exist in a vacuum. The research effort can in fact be viewed as one form of organized social activity. Thus, social research is intimately related to other organized social activities. Interaction and feedback take place continuously between social research and other social activities. For example, social research is becoming more and more dependent on the support of the larger society in providing the necessary financial resources to conduct studies. At the same time, the larger society is making more demands for useful information from social research for identifying and formulating solutions to social problems. These two factors, the financial support of social research and the expectation of useful research information by the larger society, thus deserve further examination here.

As social research becomes larger in scope and more costly, individual researchers no longer have the ability or capability to provide all the equipment, personnel, and materials required for research with their own resources. Support of research must come from other sources. In general, two types of sources provide such support. One type of source is mainly interested in the continuing development of scientific knowledge. For example, the National Science Foundation, a federal funding agency, provides funds for many research projects addressing fundamental issues in various scientific disciplines. Other private foundations, such as the National Endowment for the Humanities, the Social Science Research Council, and the Russell Sage Foundation, also support basic research in various fields.

Another type of source is primarily concerned with the generation of information which will have policy or applied implications. The interest of these sources is to provide support for research activities which will result in information relevant to specific ongoing activities. Such information is expected to help either in transferring the basic knowledge and techniques for use in policy decisions or in evaluating current policies or proposed policy alternatives. For example, the U.S. Agency for International Development and the Population Council are interested in supporting research which provides concrete suggestions for improved regulation of populations, such as family planning and birth control devices. Many sources support both types of research. For example, the U.S. National Institutes of Health support activities in the areas of health for the benefit of either theoretical or policy developments. In general, the support comes in two forms: as a grant or as a contract. A grant provides support for a research effort dealing with a research topic of interest to the proposing researcher. A contract provides support for a research effort dealing with a research topic of interest to the funding agency. Thus, the grant gives more flexibility to the researcher in terms of the implications of the research effort; whereas the contract demands fulfillment of specified objectives as outlined by the sponsoring agency. Usually, the contract format is used when the research deals with policy issues, and the grant format is used when basic research is involved.

Thus, funded social research must discharge its contractual or grant obligations to the sponsoring agency as well as to the scientific community.

In addition to the funding issue, in many cases research is conducted in an organized context. If one considers the research organization as a continuum from a one-man operation on the one extreme to a massive production-oriented firm on another, several reasons account for the increasing complexity of organized research efforts. Rossi (1971) suggested several gains from organized social research.[1] First, the traditional departments in colleges and universities prohibit interactions and relationships of research requiring the cross-cutting of disciplinary delineations. The formation of a research organization based on common interests in research facilitates such interactions and relationships. Second, organization of social research provides an opportunity for the pooling and sharing of

---

[1] Peter H. Rossi, "Observations on the Organization of Social Research," in R. O'Toole (ed.), *The Organization Management and Tactics of Social Research*. Schenkman, Cambridge, Mass., 1971.

resources, such as personnel, equipment, and administrative support. And third, and probably most importantly, research organizations allow division of labor in the conduct of research. As the task of social research becomes more complex, different talents are called for at different phases of research. Research organizations allow division of labor among competent administrators, research assistants, technical personnel (computer programmers, statisticians, machine operators, etc.), and field staff (observers, interviewers, etc.) to be repeatedly utilized in any number of projects. Finally, research organizations carry more weight than individual researchers in the view of funding agencies, university administrations, and respondents. Research organizations project a sense of permanence, stability, and competence unsurpassed by the mere aggregation of the researchers participating in it.

On the other hand, a research organization imposes certain constraints on individual researchers. The researcher loses a certain amount of autonomy; his research can be conducted only in compliance with the routines set up and the rules accepted by the organization. Further, a research organization may not be entirely compatible with the university with which it is affiliated. Arguments concerning the distribution of funds, allocation of faculty time, use of graduate students, research objectives, or overall responsibility can become heated. This in turn may pit researchers associated with the research organization against those affiliated solely with the departments of the university.

The most serious problem confronting university-affiliated research organizations concerns the traditional academic attitude toward policy research. Generally, universities and faculty members frown on applied research, considering it of little relevance to the main function of university research activities, namely, the production and transmission of scientific knowledge. University-affiliated research organizations and researchers tend to be considered second-class citizens by their colleagues. For example, few researchers in university-affiliated research centers hold permanent (tenured) positions. While such an attitude is changing, and the argument has been heard that these organizations provide the best opportunities for students to "get their hands dirty" in gaining invaluable research experiences which eventually make significant contributions to their careers, the presumably unequal status of basic researchers versus applied researchers in the university setting has spurred the development of other types of research organizations.

One alternative form of research organization is the nonprofit independent research organization. With the sole purpose of engaging in funded research, this type of organization provides maximal support for researchers engaging in, for example, policy research. It does not have to deal with the basic-applied controversy in a university setting, and still maintains the ideological goal of promoting research which contributes to either or both.

From the funding agency's point of view, the more efficient a research organization is in conducting and carrying out research objectives, the more justified it is in providing the funding. Thus, the nonprofit research organization presents a viable alternative form of research organization in which efficient and useful research can be supported.

However, the nonprofit research organization always has to struggle to survive financially. Relying solely on outside funds, the organization is vulnerable for continuity. Unless a rigorous leadership is present in the organization, continuously in pursuit of research funds, the organization rises and falls with the erratic pattern of fundings received. Unstable financial status tends to present the research organization with a serious problem in recruiting and maintaining a competent research staff.

As a result of the demand of funding agencies for efficiency in research administration and in carrying out research objectives, and of the financial vulnerability of nonprofit research organizations, another form of research organization has emerged—research firms. These research firms are similar to other profit-making commercial firms. They hire staff, maintain a formal organizational setup with hierarchically defined positions and roles, compete for research funds, and conduct contractual research, with the goal of making a profit. Because these firms are profit-oriented, they are more efficient in adhering to the required objectives of research contracts closely and to rigid time schedules. However, the primary goal of these firms is to achieve maximal profit, and they in fact become production machines. For the purpose of fulfilling objectives as outlined in a contract, the funding agency cannot find a more accommodating group.

However, as the research firm aims to please the funding agencies, its allegiance to the scientific community is substantially weakened. The question involves the extent to which the information produced by a research firm is of sufficiently high quality in both validity and reliability to constitute useful information for policy decisions. While such a problem has relatively little relevance in technological research, such as in building a plane or a submarine, where limited construction and demonstration of prototypes can be undertaken before large-scale production takes place, social research generally does not present itself to such immediate and reliable verification, nor does it have such opportunities for trials and demonstrations. The burden of scientific responsibility in social research conducted by the research firm falls squarely on the funding agency and on the firm itself.

Because of financial attractiveness and organizational efficiency, research firms present a most viable alternative to university-affiliated and independent research organizations. Their future contribution to policy research will, to a large extent, be determined by the rigor with which they recruit and maintain a scientifically qualified staff and with which the funding agencies employ qualified scientists to evaluate the end products and proposals they submit.

In summary, because of the funding sources and the expectations that they produce useful information for the funding agencies as well as the larger society, much social research involves complex organized endeavors with obligations to produce policy-relevant information as well as theoretical knowledge.

As presented in Figure 19.1, the theoretical contribution of social research involves the testing of hypotheses and the formulation and reformulation of concepts and propositions. The policy contribution of social research stems from policy implications derived from data analysis leading to policy recommendations and implementations. The theoretical contribution of social research culminates in the

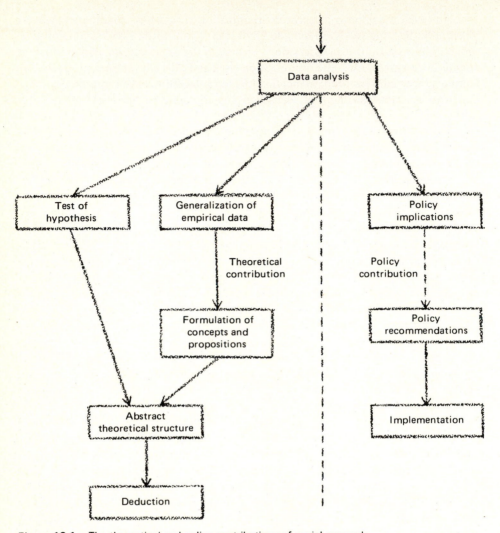

Figure 19.1 The theoretical and policy contributions of social research.

formation, verification, and modification of theoretical structures capable of explaining extensive empirical observations and social phenomena. The policy contribution begins with the analysis and interpretation of data for potential policy implications. However, whether or not the researcher should further participate in formulating policy recommendations and executing policy implementations constitutes a topic for debate and will be discussed in a later section.

DEVELOPMENTAL RESEARCH AND EVALUATION RESEARCH

In general, two types of social research which have policy implications can be identified according to the original intent of the social research. In one type, the research effort is based on a theoretical tradition and attempts to apply it to a specific policy problem at hand. This type of research is called *developmental research*. Developmental research is characterized by (1) the implicitness of policy implication of the original theoretical tradition, and (2) adaptation of the theoretical tradition in subsequent research to derive policy-related information for a given policy problem. An example of developmental research in social research is the use of scientific knowledge from the "diffusion of innovations" research tradition in a variety of policy areas such as marketing of new products, promotion of family planning, and incorporation of educational devices. The diffusion research tradition looks at the process by which a new practice (innovation) is spread in a social system and the process by which individuals become committed (adoption) behaviorally to such practices. While the propositions generated from such research have theoretical import,[2] the diffusion model has been widely utilized in generating and evaluating policies concerning a specific policy. Thus, developmental research applies an existing theoretical orientation or structure to a set of social phenomena, presumably with certain characteristics in the social phenomena corresponding to the concepts and variables in the structure or orientation.[3]

A second type of social research offering policy implications is one which is based on general sociological theory and methodology but aims specifically at providing information for policy decisions. This type of research is called *evaluation research* and is characterized by (1) explicitness of policy implications in the design and execution of the research plan, and (2) incorporation of variables specifically relevant to the problem at hand. Evaluative research is not guided or bound by any specific theoretical tradition and utilizes methodological knowledge as well as theoretical knowledge. It is problem-oriented.

Developmental research and evaluation research, while both attempting to provide information for policy decisions, are derived from different conceptual perspectives and therefore arrive at substantially divergent results. For developmental research, the researcher makes the important assumption that the informing research tradition is unchallenged in regard to its fundamental theoretical propositions and research strategies. In one sense, the primary objective of developmental research is to broaden the explanatory power of the particular theory involved to more and more social phenomena. Thus, the diffusion of innovative theoretical statements is applied to explain the process by which the use of birth control devices spreads in a social system or a particular brand of deodorant gains acceptance in a defined market.

On the other hand, evaluation research, having the aim of providing specific information for policy decisions regarding a particular social problem or activity, is not bound by specific theoretical statements existing in a discipline such as sociology. Rather, it utilizes the conceptual statements and methodological tools developed by academic disciplines, which have implications for policy develop-

---

[2] Everett M. Rogers and Floyd Shoemaker, *Communication of Innovations,* Free Press, New York, 1972.

[3] In a rigorous sense, only theoretical structures should be applied. However, in reality, much developmental research borrows a theoretical orientation which lacks specific propositions. For example, system analysis is a popular orientation applied extensively in developmental research.

ment, as well as variables seldom considered by previous researchers. The relevance of a variable in evaluation research is determined by two considerations:

1   Are the variables meaningful to the clientele system (the policy organization) as well as the target population (the people the policy affects or serves)?
2   Are the variables manipulatable by the policy organization?

These considerations are less prominent in developmental research, and we will return to the two considerations later. For the time being, it is important to point out that, as far as policy makers are concerned, evaluation research is much more meaningful than developmental research, as policy makers seek help in solving specific problems. However, many social researchers are either unaware of the difference or unwilling to sacrifice their "scientific theories" in policy research work. As a consequence, many social policy studies turn out results which, while confirming to a large extent the validity of a particular theoretical structure, do not provide immediate and concrete guidelines for policy decisions. In the remaining discussion, the term *policy research* will be used exclusively to indicate evaluation research.[4]

POLICY RESEARCH PROCEDURE

As pointed out in Figure 19.1, social research contributes to policy as well as theoretical issues. In the case of policy research, one may elaborate the process further, as presented in Figure 19.2. Lest the reader think that, up to the point of data analysis, social research goes through the identifying process for both theoretical and policy purposes, it is shown that policy research begins with (1) identification of needs, (2) specification of policy goals, or (3) both. These activities are outside the realm of scientific activities. It is the needs of the target population and the goals set out by the clientele system that guide the formulation of research objectives. These are organizational activities.[5] In many instances, goals may be formulated and specified without primary consideration being given to the needs of the target population. For example, a new brand of toothpaste may be marketed and promoted by a manufacturer, even though there is no evidence that there is a need among consumers for another brand of toothpaste with essentially the same ingredients as existing brands on the market. In other words, the goal of the policy organization (namely, profit-making in the above example, which may have no corresponding need) can dictate the policy. However, policy research should always address itself to the correspondence between the needs of the target population and the formulation of policies by the clientele. Thus, while it is quite legitimate for an

----

[4] It is possible that evaluation research may find a particular theoretical structure relevant to the problem at hand and thus employ the concepts and variables in that structure to guide the research. However, the overriding concern remains the specific problem at hand, and any "accidental fitting" of a theoretical structure must be considered serendipitous.

[5] For the distinction between organizational and scientific activities, see Robert K. Merton, *The Sociology of Science,* University of Chicago Press, Chicago, 1973, chap. 4, "Technical and Moral Dimensions of Policy Research," pp. 70–98, especially pp. 73–74.

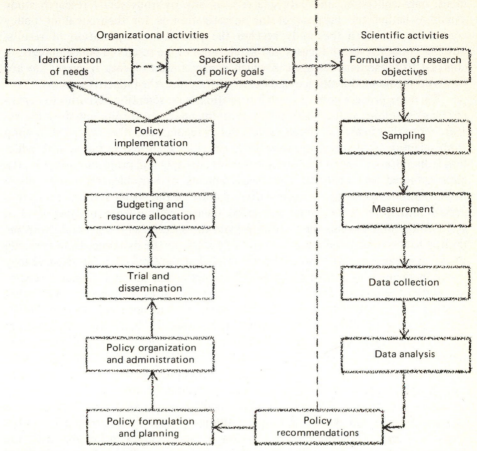

Figure 19.2   Process of policy research.

organization to initiate policy research to meet certain goals, it is equally legitimate for policy researchers to examine the extent to which any policies arising out of such considerations will meet the needs of the target population. Ideally, the policy researcher should have the option to challenge the existence of parts of or the whole of the clientele system, should the data show failure in the matching of organizational goals with the needs of the target population. But, in reality, with funding constraints and a profit-making orientation, policy research tends to refrain from incorporating such an option. This is an ideological and professional problem rather than a scientific problem. The process of social research, and policy research specifically, does not preclude such an option. We will return to this topic in the section, "Professional Responsibilities of Policy Research," pages 385–392.

The translation (operationalization) of policy goals, needs of the target population, or both to research objectives represents the initiation of scientific activities in policy research. Terms relevant to the organization and the population are operationalized into variables. The process then goes through sampling, measurement, data collection, and data analysis, as any rigorous social research study should, whether the purpose of the investigation is for theoretical or policy contributions. When the study reaches the point of interpretation of results, however, policy research focuses on the relevance of the results to policy makers, in contrast to theoretical research in which interpretation of data is geared toward verification and modification of a theoretical structure, the inductive process.

Then the process goes through a transition from scientific activities to organizational activities again, when policy recommendations are presented by the researcher to the clientele. The reason why policy recommendation represents a jump from scientific activities to organizational activities is similar to theoretical induction from observations to the formalization of concepts and propositions in that the data gathered and analyzed and measurements of variables represent only a partial, although perhaps representative, picture of the social system frozen in a certain limited amount of time and space. Generalization from analyzed data to systemwide policies risks the transition from the specific to the general, from the limited to the whole, and from the relatively static to the dynamic. Data can only show what happened as measured and sampled at the time of the study, and may prove inadequate in predicting what will happen when the new elements recommended in the policies are introduced into the system as they interact with other existing or unexpected elements in the system. Furthermore, while scientific activities are generally guided by accepted rules of scientific investigation, there are relatively few such rules for dealing with the clientele and the target population in the actual formulation and implementation of specific policies. Factors other than scientific, such as political and economic considerations and interpersonal relations, come into play in deliberation on and execution of policies.

Policy planning and formulation are usually made after there have been some "give-and-take" and some compromise among various interested parties in the clientele system. The resulting policies may in fact deviate considerably from the recommendations based on the data. Following the guidelines of the formulated policies, organizational and administrative units are formed for the execution of the policies. Ideally, new policies must be examined in small-scale trials in which possible ill effects as well as side effects can be uncovered before the policies affect the target population.

All policies involve investment of the economic resources of the clientele system. The final scrutiny of the results of policy research focuses to a large extent on the financial implications of the policies for the system in terms of procedure and amount of resource allocation. In the meantime, information must be disseminated to the target population to alert them about the forthcoming policies and their involvement in the activities of implementation. Finally, the policies are implemented.

The organization should never lose sight of the original goals of the policies, as reflected in the needs and goals set out before policy research was conducted. Thus, implementation of the policies should be paralleled by efforts to investigate the effects of the policies in regard to their fulfillment of the initial needs and goals. This organizational evaluation activity can be part of the new policies. That is, the policies must be implemented with the built-in element of self-continuous evaluation.

Any discrepancies between policy effects and the needs and goals, as well as unanticipated effects, must undergo careful evaluation. They may, again, constitute the initial point in another policy research effort, thus completing the cycle of policy research as represented in Figure 19.2.

RESEARCHERS AND PRACTITIONERS IN POLICY RESEARCH

One most significant problem in policy research is the extent to which the researcher and the practitioner (policy decision maker or administrator) participate in the process of social research. This is a topic of controversy in social research. Traditionally, researchers concern themselves mainly with scientific activities in the process of policy research (the right-hand side of Figure 19.2) and seldom intervene in the organizational activities of policy research (the left-hand side of Figure 19.2). Practitioners, on the other hand, are charged with the conduct of organizational activities and leave the scientific activities to the researchers. However, this traditional view is being challenged, by both researchers and practitioners. We will first examine the role of the researcher in the process of policy research.

The more traditional position is that the researcher should limit his activities to the sphere of scientific activities. This is where the strength of the researcher is, it is suggested, since these are activities guided by scientific principles and can be replicated and examined by other researchers. On the other hand, organizational activities involve value judgments on the part of the clientele system. A researcher's work should maintain scientific objectivity and therefore be value-free. The researcher can interpret the data and suggest implications for policies. But as soon as recommendations are made regarding specific policies, the researcher has immersed himself in the value system of the clientele. Not only does the researcher become involved in value judgments, but also, it is argued, he steps into the arena of activities concerning which his scientific competence does not equip him to provide advice. Thus, the legitimate terminal point of policy research, as far as researchers are concerned, is writing up the research report containing the policy implications of the data.

This view is not accepted by many policy researchers, and a more active role is argued. In this argument, it is felt that merely reporting and suggesting policy implications is not sufficient to guarantee that the policies will be formulated and implemented in line with the data, since the policy makers do not have a sufficient background in the social sciences to understand, translate, and execute the implicated policies appropriately. The resulting policies and their execution might become so inappropriate or inconsistent with the data that the effects would be unfortunate or even disastrous. Further, if the social researcher does not participate in the organizational activities of policy research, the clientele may tend to interpret the implications of the data in ways to justify the maintenance and even promotion of those in power. Changes which affect such status will not come about. It is thus argued that, without an active role of the researcher in organizational activities, impact of policy research is limited or even biased.[6]

As to the value judgment problem, activist policy researchers suggest that, while many social researchers maintain a "scientific-objective" posture, this is seldom possible or practiced. From the beginning of the selection and formulation of a research problem, the researcher has some ideological convictions on which he will take a stand. Thus, the difference is not between the absence or presence of values, it is argued; rather it is between the implicitness and the explicitness of such values. An open stand on the values involved increases the likelihood that the policies eventually formulated and executed will be consistent not only with the research evidence but also with the needs and goals of the social system, for now the researcher can take an active role in the design and execution of policies. Taking an active role in organizational activities does not in any way have to imply distortion of the data.

The debate is continuing among social researchers. However, as more and more clientele systems, including governments at various levels, demand precise and specific research applications to social problems at hand and channel their resources to support research which has such promise, it is inevitable that an active role of social researchers in both scientific and organizational activities in the process of policy research will continue to gain acceptance by both the research community and the general public.

The role of practitioners in policy research faces similar challenges and changes. While the traditional role restricts practitioners to outside the realm of scientific activity, the need for them to participate has become increasingly clear. Throughout the process of scientific activity, a familiarity with an understanding of the clientele system is crucial. In the formulation of research objectives, for example, the clientele system's goals and needs must be those expressed and understood by the policy organization and the target population. Misunderstanding and misinterpretation introduce discrepancies in the epistemic correspondence between goals and needs on the one hand and research objectives on the other. Such discrepancies result in research findings bearing little relevance to the clientele system. Similarly, an understanding of the clientele system is needed in the selection of samples, construction of measures, and analysis of data. The interpretation of data in terms of policy implications will make sense to the clientele system only if it is presented in a language familiar and understandable to the system. Thus, the participation of practitioners from the clientele system in the scientific activities of policy research only makes sense. However, in the past, there has been a fear

---

[6] For a discussion of the tendency of policy makers to interpret findings to fit their a priori opinions in certain policy research, see Margaret E. Boeckmann, "Policy Impacts of the New Jersey Income Maintenance Experiment," a paper presented at the American Sociological Association annual meetings, Montreal, August 1974.

among researchers that the participation of practitioners would interfere with the objectivity necessary to conduct the study. While it is generally allowed that practitioners may serve as consultants to the study, they are not permitted "to mess with the data." However, if mutual respect and understanding can be achieved and maintained, there is little reason to fear the inability of practitioners to maintain their objectivity while participating in scientific activities. Striving to achieve such mutual respect and understanding is a small price to pay for all the gains which can be made with the participation of practitioners.

In summary, both researchers and practitioners should expect and be expected to participate in both the organizational and scientific activities in policy research. While the talents and skills of each may require the leadership of the researchers in scientific activities and of the practitioners in organizational activities, full utilization of their understanding and competence in their respective spheres of expertise will greatly enhance the eventual success of policy research and policy implementation.

A TYPOLOGY OF POLICY RESEARCH

While policy research varies for organizations and situations, a typology of policy research can be constructed based on the *research focus* and on the *nature of the policy* under consideration. The research focus can be one of two kinds: (1) the means or (2) the ends. Research focusing on the means is guided by existing goals (ends) of the clientele system and attempts to identify potential defects and improvements in the organizational-managerial structure and process. Research focusing on the ends, on the other hand, assesses the outcome of existing organizational-managerial structure and process and tries to ascertain the extent to which the actual outcome (in terms of productivity, performance, or other effects on the target population) is consistent with the desired outcome.

The nature of the policy under consideration can be specified as being of two types: (1) existing policies, or (2) alternative or new policies. For existing policies, research is guided by variables already specified and defined by the clientele system; thus, it is variable-specified research. For alternative or new policies, research does not have to be bound by specified variables, although constraints (e.g., cost) may be set out by the clientele system. This can be defined as variable-unspecified research.

When the two factors, research focus and nature of policy, are jointly taken into consideration, a typology of policy research emerges, as presented in Table 19.1. When research deals with an existing policy and focuses on the means, it provides variable-specified and organizational-managerial analysis. That is, given the existing policy and the goals of the policy, the research attempts to evaluate the organizational-managerial structure and process activities in terms of their relative efficiency in achieving the predetermined goals of the policy. The research is guided by the component specifications of the clientele system; therefore, it is variable-specified. Although the variables are specified, it is for the researcher to

Table 19.1   A Typology of Policy Research

| | Research focus | |
Policy	Means	End (outcome)
Existing	Variable-specified organizational-managerial analysis	Variable-specified productivity-performance analysis (e.g., cost-benefit analysis)
Alternative	Variable-unspecified organizational-managerial analysis	Variable-unspecified productivity-performance analysis

ascertain the relative contributions of the variables in achieving the goals.[7] For example, in an information system geared to provide school teachers with information about new developments in the area of teaching methods, the clientele system may wish to find out to what extent its activities have fulfilled its goal—disseminating the information to school teachers. It hires a researcher to investigate its organizational setup to determine which aspects of the organization are doing a good or poor job. The researcher, thus, is limited in his focus to organizational aspects as defined and identified by the organization. These variables may include: (1) how the organization gathers information about new developments in teaching methods (Does it cover the research frontiers in this area? How fast is the information absorbed into the information system? etc.); (2) how the organization evaluates the gathered information (Does it have competent staff to evaluate the scientific quality of the information? Does it have anything to do with school teachers? etc.); (3) how the organization alerts school teachers to its information system (Does the organization disseminate information about its service? Does this information reach the target audience, school teachers at different levels? etc.); and (4) how efficient the system's service is (Does it respond quickly to any request made? Does it provide the information needed by the teachers making the requests? etc.) These variables are specified even before the researcher is hired to conduct the study. His task is to make precise measurements of the variables and identify their relative contributions (say, with the multiple-regression method) to the frequency of use of the information system by the teachers, and the teachers' evaluations of the system's usefulness in improving their teaching performance. The results of such a study should identify aspects of the organization which are doing a relatively good job and other aspects which need improvement.

[7] This is not to say that there are no unknowns in policy research dealing with existing policies. Rather, the research is directed more toward determining the relative contributions of known and identified variables in the organization to the achievement of its goals. It is entirely possible that the research results show that none or few of the existing variables make substantial contributions to the achievement of its goals, leading to the suggestion that perhaps the organization has overlooked or ignored other variables which are more important than those it has specified and identified. Research following through on such a suggestion, however, moves into alternative policies, which will be discussed shortly as another type of policy research.

When research deals with an existing policy and focuses on the ends (outcome), it is still bound by the defined and identified variables of the clientele system. But now the question raised concerns the extent to which organizational operations are justified by the outcome. In a procedure known as *cost-effect analysis,* the researcher attempts to determine the extent to which the outcome (benefits) can justify the existence and operations of the organization. For example, the federal government may decide to initiate a new training program for underprivileged young people, in order to facilitate their obtaining and keeping jobs. A research team may be called in, after the program has been in operation for a period of time, to determine whether or not and to what extent it has accomplished its goal. Research is guided by the variables defined and specified by the program, such as personnel structure, training methods, methods of recruiting underprivileged young people, etc. The question raised is, Under these conditions of recruitment and training, how many people have completed the training courses, how many have found jobs afterward, and how many have kept their jobs and for how long? The results of the study may help policy makers in deciding whether to continue such a program and, if so, what improvements may have to be made, both in terms of the means and ends of the program.

When research looks for an alternative policy and focuses on the potential variations in the means an organization uses in achieving certain goals, the research is not guided by specifically defined and identified variables, since there is no existing organizational-managerial structure associated with any policy being contemplated. The issue is to find either an alternative policy to the one currently in existence, or a new policy with certain organizational-managerial characteristics which would fulfill certain goals or needs of the clientele system. For example, when a state government decides that some kind of low-cost medical service should be organized to benefit the state population, since there is no existing organization to administer such a program, a research team may be called on to conduct studies to arrive at recommendations as to how a program should be organized in order to provide medical service to the population efficiently with minimal cost and maximal benefit. The research team, in this case, has to consider variables it feels will affect the delivery of such services to the population. It is up to the research team to identify and define in its recommendations variables which should be taken into account in the organizational-managerial structure and process.

Finally, when research deals with a new or alternative policy and focuses on the ends or outcomes of such a policy, it looks for potential ramifications, both positive and negative, of such a policy without any consideration of the specificity of organization-managerial aspects which may be related to the policy and affect variations of the outcome. For example, if an industrial firm decides to shorten the number of working days from five to four per week and wishes to consider the ramifications of such a policy change a research team may be called in to estimate such effects. Would the productivity of the workers increase or decrease? Would such a policy affect the use and cost of leisure time for workers? Would many workers seek a second job, and what effect would such actions have on the economic structure of the community and on commercial and recreational industries?

What would the organization gain, in addition to possible increased productivity? For example, would maintenance costs be reduced? By how much? Would such a policy attract more qualified recruits?

The research team is not concerned with organizational-managerial problems in executing such a program; rather, it tackles the problem of ramifications both for the organization and the community at large, should such a program be adopted by the organization. The research team is not bound by specified variables, since the variety of ramifications as well as their importance are to be defined, studied, and projected by the research.

Once a research effort is identified in terms of such a typology of policy research, defined by the nature of the policy involved and the research focus, a number of methodological issues can be enumerated. Each type of policy research has its own methodological emphasis and direction. Thus, such a typology helps clarify some methodological debates currently being discussed in policy research.

METHODOLOGICAL CONSEQUENCES OF THE TYPOLOGY OF POLICY RESEARCH

Some of the methodological issues having specific relevance to policy research include: (1) selection of variables, (2) selection of a theoretical structure, (3) use of field experiments, and (4) standardization of data. Each is an important issue and must be considered with care when policy research is conducted. The discussion of each issue will bring to bear the typology of policy research whenever appropriate.

Selection of Variables

Because policy research is geared toward applications for social action, it is important for the researcher to take into account variables in the research which not only can be identified in the specific organizational setting of the clientele system but also are accessible for possible manipulation.

In the usual procedure of selecting variables in social research, the focus is on variables which provide the best possible explanation for certain phenomena. Thus, consideration is given to the possible magnitude of contribution a variable may have in the explanatory structure. The extent to which the particular variable can be manipulated is of secondary importance in the consideration and subsequent analysis. For example, in the area of social stratification, prevailing theory suggests that the social status (e.g., father's occupation and education) of a person's origin, along with his educational achievement, accounts for a large portion of his eventual occupational status and level of income. Such a theoretical structure is geared to explain the variations of occupational status and, so long as such an explanation remains valid, the researcher is not concerned with the problem of the extent to which the variables involved can be manipulated from the social system's point of view.

However, the same topic examined in the framework of policy research presents a problem. For organizational purposes, the clientele system must ask the question, What can be done to equalize job opportunities and status for all who are qualified? The theoretical formulation suggests that providing educational opportunities for all may be one thing the clientele system may wish to manipulate. But the theoretical structure also informs us that the variable of educational achievement accounts for less than 30 percent of the variance of the dependent variable—job status. Further, the extent to which educational achievement can be manipulated is debatable. Such additional considerations about the manipulability of variables do not necessarily challenge the theoretical formulation suggested above. Rather, the consideration is a pragmatic one for the clientele system. Thus, one additional variable which may be considered may deal with the hiring and promotion practices of various firms, organizations, and corporations. Such information may lead to policy guidelines as to how to minimize social inequality rather than inequality of ability in the job structure in the clientele system.

Thus, for policy research, the selection of variables should take into account variables which can be manipulated and accounted for (e.g., cost). This is especially crucial for independent variables, for if the clientele system wants to manipulate for policy implementations or changes, it is usually the organizational-managerial aspects which can be manipulated to achieve the goals. In policy research, the means (organizational-managerial aspects) often constitute the independent variables used to account for the effects.

This is not to say that all independent variables in policy research must be manipulatable. If this is required, the data collected may ignore the basic variables in a credible theoretical structure, and make the results less explanatory even for the specific problem and clientele system at hand. What is suggested here is that, while maintaining the basic variables in a theoretical structure for the problem at hand, it is also important to incorporate as many manipulatable (independent) variables as pragmatically feasible and meaningful. The variables which are important in a theoretical sense but less susceptible for manipulation will still provide important descriptive information and serve as qualifying conditions in the application of research results to policy formulation and execution.

Selection of a Theoretical Structure

In Chapter 3, three different complex theoretical structures are discussed: (1) the convergent (causal) structure, (2) the divergent (effectual) structure, and (3) the causal-effectual structure. In the formulation of the convergent structure, the variable of focal interest is a dependent variable and the objective of the structure is to identify the relevant and important independent (causal) variables. The divergent structure, on the other hand, identifies a single or limited number of independent variables and enumerates the multiple consequent (effectual) variables. The causal-effectual structure is the most complex structure, in which the variable or variables of focal interest are studied in terms of both the independent and dependent variables. Selection from among the alternative theoretical structures is dictated by the type of policy research being undertaken.

For policy research focusing on the means (for existing or proposed policies), the convergent structure seems to be the most desirable. It allows the researcher to enumerate all the organizational-managerial aspects as multiple independent variables and to ascertain their relative contributions to productivity or performance (the outcome or dependent variable). The result of such analysis should allow the researcher to make interpretations of the relative importance of various organizational-managerial aspects for possible modifications or changes.

For policy research focusing on the ends, the divergent structure seems to be the most appropriate. The research question is, given the existing or proposed policies and means, what are the consequences? The researcher, with the given organizational and managerial characteristics, attempts to enumerate the kind and extent of their effects. The result of such a study should provide a description of the kind and magnitude of consequences and impacts deriving from the existing or proposed organizational-managerial characteristics.

Finally, the causal-effectual structure is applicable when the researcher is given certain predetermined or proposed organizational-managerial characteristics and asked to explore other desirable organizational-managerial characteristics to achieve certain optimal consequences for such predetermined or proposed organizational-managerial characteristics. In this formulation, the predetermined or proposed characteristics are the variables of focal interest, other organizational-managerial characteristics are to be examined as either causal or covariational variables, and the outcomes are examined as the dependent variables.

The correspondence of particular theoretical structure with a type of policy research helps a researcher locate the variables in the appropriate positions in the structure and apply appropriate analytical procedures to the data. Appropriate formulation of the theoretical structure in policy research also increases the likelihood that the results of the research will be useful for possible policy recommendations or implementations.

Use of a Field Experiment

One important methodological consideration in policy research is the use of a field experiment. Performing a field experiment serves as a critical test of any potential changes and their effects before these changes are fully implemented in the clientele system. A field experiment mainly involves manipulation of the means (organizational-managerial characteristics). Since such changes may bring unforeseeable ill effects to the clientele system, it is desirable to conduct a field experiment on a limited trial basis. In the field experiment, the proposed changes are administered to selective and representative subgroups (individuals or units) of the target population in the clientele system, while in the meantime data are also gathered from other individuals or units in the clientele system who are subjected to existing organizational-managerial characteristics. The various subgroups subjected to alternative changes serve as the experimental group, and the subgroup experiencing no changes as the control group. Following the procedures discussed in Chapters 13 and 14, the researcher can proceed to measure the relative effects of the various changes, as compared with existing procedures, on outcome variables such as productivity and performance.[8]

However, there are major problems in conducting field experiments in policy research. For example, the field experiment is less applicable when research focuses on outcome rather than on the means, as the outcome (effects and consequences) is less susceptible to manipulation. Also, the field experiment ideally involves experimental groups for variations of each characteristic or variable to be manipulated, as well as for different variables; thus the effects of such variations within each variable, as well as among variables, can be estimated on the outcome. However, in reality, economic and administrative considerations seldom permit such massive, intensive, and controlled design. As a result, the field experiment usually conducted in policy research involves only a limited number of experimental groups, and each group is exposed to one manipulation involving one or several organizational-managerial variables simultaneously. Such a confounding design creates a serious problem for the evaluation of the experiment, for it does not allow the researcher to single out the aspects of manipulation responsible for the positive or negative changes in the outcome (or no change in the outcome). The only conclusion that can be drawn from such data is whether the field experiment, involving all the manipulations, as a whole, has succeeded or failed. Such a conclusion tends to be costly for the clientele system. For if the field experiment was considered a success, all aspects manipulated must be incorporated for implementation and, if it was considered a failure, none of the aspects should be incorporated. In many cases of policy research, decision makers eventually have to make arbitrary choices among the aspects manipulated for implementation. Such choices are more often guided by economic, personal, social, administrative, or political considerations rather than scientific assessments. When such arbitrations are involved in the implementation of field experiment results, the rigor associated with the field experiment is completely lost.

Debate over Standardization of Data

Policy researchers have debated rigorously about the measurement of data. The debate focuses on two alternative ways of treating data measurement in statistical analysis: Should data be analyzed in their natural units (e.g., in dollars, number of hours, number of people, etc.) or in standardized units (converting the data to stan-

---

[8] An insightful discussion on the complexity and difficulties of conducting a field experiment in policy analysis appears in Katherine C. Lyall, "Some Observations on Design Issues in Large-Scale Social Experiments," *Sociological Methods and Research,* vol. 4, no. 1, pp. 54–76, 1975. Discussing the New Jersey Income Maintenance Experiment, "the only large-scale policy experiment completed to date with data and results analyzed," the author pointed out the restrictions of (1) numbers of factors (usually the single-factor design), (2) number of research sites (usually in sacrifice of generalizability), and (3) assumptions about the shape of the response surface and the values of the parameters (sampling of a limited number of values of the factor as treatments), which were imposed on the experiment. The experiment failed to "draw convincing policy conclusions, positive or negative," from the data because of these restrictions and assumptions, most of which are difficult to overcome in natural settings because of social, economic, and statistical considerations.

dardized scores)?[9] While the argument is seemingly a statistical one, the implications are much broader. The proponents of using natural units argue that, for policy decision makers, data are meaningful only in terms of units meaningful to them. Thus, it is logical to suggest, for example, that an increase of n persons to perform a certain task would increase the productivity by m units. Or, an increase of x dollars of investment in a certain activity would increase the profit by y dollars. Furthermore, when several possible variables all have certain effects on the outcome, a cost-benefit analysis may show differential costs involved in the implementation of the various variables. Thus, the policy makers can implement the ones within their economic ability. The proponents of standardized units, on the other hand, focus on the structural relations among the variables in the analysis. They argue that standardized units are meaningful units because they eliminate possible bias in the different natural units for explanatory purposes. For example, it is possible that one independent variable, in its natural unit, costs relatively less to implement than another independent variable (say, in dollars); however, the second independent variable explains much more variation of the dependent variable than the first independent variable. Should the first independent variable, for example, explain only 10 percent of the variance of the dependent variable, while the second independent variable explains 45 percent of the variance of the same dependent variable, even though the first independent variable is three times cheaper to implement per unit than the second independent variable, it would be still more efficient, per unit, to implement the second independent variable first, since its "pure" effect on the outcome is 4.5 times greater than that of the first independent variable. Thus, it is important, before any cost-benefit analysis is conducted, to ascertain the relative contribution of each independent variable to the explanation of the variance of the dependent variable. In other words, it is essential to determine the relative effects of the independent variables on the dependent variable. To uncover such relative magnitudes, the independent variables must be converted to similar units—standardized units.

As it should be apparent by now, both arguments are valid. It is important to utilize standardized units of variables to estimate the relative magnitudes of relations in the analytical structure. It is also important to analyze the natural units of variables to assess the cost-benefit equations for possible policy considerations. The use of natural units is meaningful only when the researcher is assured that the variables involved are important variables as far as the outcome is concerned. The use of standardized units of variables is necessary when such assurance is not available—when the researcher has no prior knowledge as to which variables have the greatest effects on the outcome variables. When these considerations are applied to the typology of policy research presented in Table 19.1, it can be seen that the use of natural or standardized units of data depends on the nature of the policy under consideration. When research involves an existing policy, the clientele system in fact imposes on the researcher the kinds of variables to be investigated.

---

[9] The standardization procedure for data is discussed in Chapter 5 and in Chapter 16 (the section "Standardized Regression Model").

Thus, there is an explanatory structure between the means and the outcome variables as specified by the ongoing policy. As long as the existing policy remains in force and is not to be challenged, the researcher must conduct the research using such variables as are given. The task of the research deals mainly with estimation of the relations between costs and benefits. Thus, the use of natural units in the measurement of data is called for.

On the other hand, when research is intended to explore new or alternative policies, there is no specific explanatory structure. The researcher has the freedom as well as the responsibility to identify the more important variables for such an explanatory structure. This is not to say that he is entirely free to construct such an explanatory structure, as there are constraints and conditions, such as the economy, manpower, etc., existing or available in the clientele system to be taken into account. However, within these constraints, the researcher should attempt to find the optimal explanatory structure. In doing so, he must identify the important variables which the clientele system must either take into account or manipulate to achieve certain goals in the new or alternative policy. These variables are important in the sense that they contribute substantially to the outcomes associated with the goals of the new or alternative policy. For this type of research, in search of an explanatory structure and with minimal imposition from the clientele system, data should be standardized, so that their relative contributions to the explanatory structure can be estimated. Once such an explanatory structure is identified, it is useful to conduct further research or analysis to estimate the costs and benefits involved in terms of the natural units of the variables. However, unless and until such an explanatory structure is identified, it is not meaningful to perform analysis on data in their natural units. Such analysis may present an inaccurate picture of the contributions of the variables for deliberations in policy decisions. For the policy makers' attention may be drawn largely and falsely to the cost factors of the new variables involved and away from the magnitude of their impact.

These methodological issues should sensitize researchers to the importance of identifying the appropriate type of policy research, as defined by the nature of the policy under study and the research focus. Also they should help the researcher to understand the importance of translating research results into interpretations useful but not misleading to policy decision makers.

Even when these methodological issues are properly resolved or taken into account, policy researchers still face many issues concerning their roles in the process of social research. These issues have already generated much interest as well as upheavals among social scientists, policy makers, and the general public. Any discussion on the policy contribution of social research would be incomplete without an exploration of these crucial issues.

PROFESSIONAL RESPONSIBILITIES OF POLICY RESEARCHERS

In policy research, researchers doing scientific work are confronted with problems and issues which have an impact on many people whose lives may be substantially altered or changed. Whether or not the researcher himself is involved in actual policy formulation and implementation, inevitably he will be identified with the policy and its related activities, and a disclaimer will not excuse him in the aftermath of any social manipulations. The greater the impact, or implied impact, of research-derived policies, the greater the association between the researcher and the policies. From the point of view of the profession of social research, many issues should not be left in the hands of individual researchers; for the profession as a whole must bear the consequences of the research-derived policy on the people. To begin exploring these issues it may be well to cite three studies in policy research which have generated much public attention and controversy.

In early 1965, the U.S. Army sponsored a project, with the code name Camelot, for measuring and forcasting the causes of revolution and insurgency in underdeveloped areas of the world.[10] The project also aimed to find ways of eliminating these causes, or of coping with revolutions and insurgencies. Intended for a project period of three to four years and with four to six million dollars committed, Camelot was to be carried out by the Special Operations Research Organization, a research agency specifically set up for the project and nominally affiliated with the American University in Washington, D.C. Specific activities planned included making analytical surveys of foreign areas, keeping up-to-date information on the military, political, and social complexes of these areas, and maintaining a rapid-response file for obtaining immediate information, on Army request, on any situation deemed militarily important. The first area selected for study was Latin America. While still at the planning and organizational stage, a small incident created alarming attention throughout Latin America as well as in Washington, D.C., and swiftly brought the project to its death.

A sociologist from the University of Pittsburgh, who had some peripheral relationship with the project, visited Chile in April on another academic business trip. He met with the vice-chancellor and a sociology professor at the University of Chile to discuss Project Camelot. The Chilean sociologist had earlier heard about the project and was infuriated with the idea that Chile might be considered as a study site. News quickly spread through the university and to the mass media and eventually was brought to the attention of the Chilean Senate. Accusations were made about the United States conducting espionage in the disguise of academic research. The American ambassador sent a cable to the State Department inquiring about Camelot and asked that it be stopped. Within a few weeks, Camelot generated much fury in Congress and at the White House. The State Department, feeling that the Defense Department had intruded into its jurisdiction, openly questioned the legitimacy of the Defense Department sponsoring such a project involving foreign countries.

On July 8, under the President's direction, Defense Secretary Robert McNamara's office vetoed the project's budget and killed the project.

In 1964, the U.S. Office of Education was authorized by the Civil Rights Act

[10] Irving Louis Horowitz, "The Life and Death of Project Camelot," *Trans-action*, vol. 3, no. 7, pp. 44–47. November-December, 1965.

to undertake a survey and "make a report to the President and Congress, within two years of the enactment of this title, concerning the lack of availability of equal educational opportunities for individuals by reason of race, color, religion, or national origin in public educational institutions at all levels in the United States, its territories and possessions, and the District of Columbia." Subsequently, a social survey on a massive scale was conducted by a social science team led by James S. Coleman, Ernest Q. Campbell, and five officials in the U.S. Office of Education. The survey included 570,000 school pupils, 60,000 teachers, and 4,000 schools. The final report, published in July 1966, is a 737-page document.[11]

Numerous analyses and reanalyses[12] have been conducted with the data, and the findings have also been numerous. The strongest inference coming out of the research is that

> the resources most important for a child's achievement in school are the cognitive skills in his social environment, including his fellow-students as well as his teachers, and that these effects are strongest for the children with the least educational resources outside school. . . . Other resources, on which school systems spend much money, appear unimportant; and lower-class students do better in absolute terms than worse (as one might have predicted) in schools where their relative achievement is low due to the presence of higher-performing middle-class students.[13]

Subsequent to this monumental study, efforts at the national and regional levels involving financial support and structural changes on a massive scale have been made for the purpose of achieving a better mix of students in schools and continuity of research activities in this area. One far-reaching policy outcome of the study was the decision of the federal government to implement busing for the purpose of achieving integrated schools. The issue of busing has remained a controversial policy and has generated many protests, counterprotests, and even violence. While the researchers involved in the original study may or may not agree with all the policies which have been formulated and implemented, the study's policy influence has been substantial.

A third illustration of policy research comes from the area of jury selection.[14] In 1971 and 1972, during the trial of eight Catholic radicals accused of, among other things, conspiring to kidnap Henry Kissinger, a sociologist, Jay Schulman, a social psychologist, Richard Christie, and some associates made use of the research methods used in the social sciences to attempt to help the defense attorneys pick ju-

[11] James S. Coleman, Ernest Q. Campbell, Carol J. Hobson, James McPartland, Alexander M. Mood, Frederic D. Weinfeld, and Robert L. York, *Equality of Educational Opportunity*, U.S. Government Printing Office, Washington, D.C., 1966.

[12] Frederick Mosteller and Daniel P. Moynihan (ed.), *On Equality of Educational Opportunity*, Vintage, New York, 1972.

[13] James S. Coleman, "Reply to Cain and Watts," *American Sociological Review*, vol. 35, no. 2, pp. 228–242, April 1970.

[14] Jay Schulman, Phillip Shaver, Robert Colman, Barbara Emrich, and Richard Christie, "Recipe for a Jury," *Psychology Today*, pp. 37–44, 77–84, May 1973; and Deborah Shapley, "Jury Selection: Social Scientists Gamble in an Already Loaded Game," *Science*, vol. 185, pp. 1033–1034, 1071, Sept. 20, 1974.

ries who might be more likely to be sympathetic to the defendants than a completely random, representative sample of local residents might be. In the several phases of survey, they determined the attitudes and characteristics of the types of people likely to show up in the jury pool. In these potential juror types, the researchers examined characteristics such as political affiliation, ethnic background, and newspaper habits, as well as attitudes toward the government and antiwar protests. When the selection of juries from the prospective jurors was made, the defense attorneys, with the knowledge of the characteristics of these prospective jurors, accepted only those who were more likely to sympathize with the defendants. While the two jurors who eventually held out for conviction and aborted the trial were in fact considered by the social scientists to be among those most likely to vote for the defense, the potential use of social research methods in the selection of sympathetic juries has caught on. Subsequently, similar research techniques were used in the trial and acquittal of Angela Davis, the trial and acquittal of 28 persons regarding a draft board raid in Camden, New Jersey, the trial of Daniel Ellsberg and Anthony Russo regarding the leaking of Pentagon documents, the trial and acquittal of John Mitchell and Maurice Stans, the trials of many Attica inmates, and the trial and acquittal of Joan Little regarding the death of a male guard in a prison. The techniques are still far from reliable and valid; however, conceivably more and more social research will be employed in legalistic and political (selection of candidates and issues) activities. In fact, any activities involving the participation of a significant number of the public can conceivably be affected by social research.

The above three illustrations involve policy research studies which have concerned different types of policies, met different fates, and affected different segments of the public. One thing is clear: Policy research can be significant and devastating in effect. Because of the interest of various policy-making groups in research evidence, the participation of social scientists in policy research will continue to increase, and their impact on policies and thus on the public will become greater. Professional issues, including (1) the ethical responsibility of researchers to the respondents from whom the data are collected, and to the target population affected by the policies derived from their studies, (2) the relationship between the researchers and the sponsors, (3) quality control of policy research, (4) the problem of the data-advocacy-decision gap, must be examined by social researchers. Unless the scientists themselves confront and examine these issues with care and determination, they may eventually be held responsible as a profession by the individuals and groups who may be injured either physically or socially by research-derived policies.

Ethical Responsibilities of Researchers

The policy researcher has the ethical responsibility to protect the confidentiality of the sources (informants) of data used in policy research, so that these individuals or units will not be subjected to legalistic or political persecution. Studies involving socially defined deviants, such as drug users, sexual deviants, and criminals, may require the researcher to conceal the identities of these respondents. However, the researcher is under political and legalistic pressure, as policing agents seek out these deviants. However, such cross-pressure is not unique among social researchers. In 1974, two lawyers defending an accused murderer in upstate New York were told by the defendant in confidence about two other murders and the locations where the bodies were buried. The two lawyers kept silent until the bodies were accidentally found by others. While the lawyers were bound by their professional responsibility not to reveal confidential information given by their clients, whether and to what extent such responsibility should be fulfilled remains a topic of controversy among the lawyers and law scholars as well as the general public. Similarly, social researchers are confronted with the cross-pressure of professional responsibility and social responsibility. At the present time, professional opinion is that professional responsibility overrides other considerations. Thus, researchers have risked convictions and jail terms by not revealing the identities of their respondents and informants.

On the other hand, the policy researcher also has an ethical responsibility for the well-being of his respondents. Data collection and experimental manipulation can conceivably affect respondents mentally and physically. The researcher is responsible for making every effort in taking such potential effects into account in the design and conduct of research. The federal government has mandated that any research sponsored by its agencies must be evaluated extensively for potential damage to the human subjects involved.

Less directly but equally important is the researcher's ethical responsibility to the individuals affected by policies derived from his research. As the effect of such policies can be devastating and long-lasting, the researcher should make as long-range and in-depth an examination as possible of such potential ramifications in the conduct and reporting of research.

Relationship between Researchers and Sponsors

Since the relationship between the researcher and the sponsor in policy research tends to be contractual, the researcher is obligated to perform the research as a service to the sponsor. Usually, the sponsor has vested interests to protect and tends to dictate minimally the directions the research should take. As a result, the researcher's allegiance to the scientific community and scientific principles may be compromised in his efforts to fulfill his contractual obligations to the sponsor. In cases in which contracts involve significant sums of money, competition is keen and tends to swing the contracted scientist's loyalty overwhelmingly toward the sponsor. Thus it is likely that the sponsor's wishes are given primary consideration in the research design and execution, while professional and academic rigor receive only secondary consideration. The use of consultants by the contracted researcher is intended to balance such bias. However, the selection of consultants is at the discretion of the researcher who may not recruit the best available scientists in the area of concern. More and more federal contracts are obtained by research firms rather than by academic institutions, for the simple reason that the firms tend to promise and deliver the kind of information the contracts specify and the sponsors desire. How to maintain the scientific rigor of such contractual research brings up the issue of quality control of policy research, which will be discussed in the next section.

More importantly, however, the relationship between the researcher and the sponsor may bias the research toward an organization orientation rather than a consumer orientation. That is, the researcher may attend more to the sponsors' and the policy makers' needs than to the needs of the target population. While the two groups' needs may coincide, the fact still remains that the researcher may identify with and be identified as part of the status quo, the "establishment." Thus, a researcher should explore a possible discrepancy in needs between the sponsors and the policy makers, on the one hand, and the target population on the other. This consideration must be kept in mind when policy implications or recommendations are formulated. The fact that the sponsors and policy makers have financial control over most policy research only accentuates the necessity for the researcher to be sensitive to the effects of research applications on the well-being and dignity of the target population.

Quality Control of Policy Research

The prevailing method of quality control practiced by federal agencies serving as sponsors involves the hiring of scientists to evaluate the research proposals submitted by bidding researchers and to appraise the progress of projects being considered for re-funding. While the preliminary selection of proposals may be guided by the scientific and methodological considerations of the peer review process, once a particular proposal has been accepted and funded, the review panel is seldom utilized any further. Thus, the actual planning, designing, executing, and reporting of the study are very much in the hands of the contracted researchers, with the guidance and advice of a monitoring official assigned by the funding agency to the task. The final report is usually read by the monitoring official and others in the funding agency, and the ultimate utilization of the data is in the hands of the policy decision makers who become aware of the study and the report.

The quality control of policy research becomes even more eclectic when the sponsors and policy makers represent a private rather than a public clientele system. The criteria of useful research are based solely on the empirical validity of the recommendations—how successful or profitable they are as far as fulfilling the interests of the sponsors and policy makers is concerned. The scientific rigor and ethical responsibilities involved can be easily bypassed and ignored.

In other words, quality control of policy research usually begins and ends at the stage where the sponsors are considering the funding of a project. The execution and use of policy research are usually under no specified professional and academic scrutiny. This problem, as pointed out by Noble, must be remedied so that quality control can be extended to the execution and use of policy research as well.[15] For example, sponsors should employ reputed scientists to spell out, in specific and unequivocal terms, the rigor and reproducibility of the methodological

---

[15] John H. Noble, "Peer Review: Quality Control of Applied Social Research," *Science,* vol. 185, pp. 916–921, Sept. 13, 1974.

procedure utilized and evaluation procedures used by the peer review panel, so that standardized criteria can be applied in the review process, as well as by policy researchers in the conduct of their studies. Also, the peer review process should be carried forward to assess and evaluate completed research to determine whether research being funded has answered specific questions. These procedures should help minimize the advantage of policy researchers and firms who tend to have "inside tracks" in receiving contracts because of their social relations with the sponsoring agency's personnel and acquaintance with scientists on the review panel. It should also minimize the overriding concern of policy researchers with the personality and personal views of the sponsoring officials. Also, the peer review structure, extended to the evaluation of completed research, should help discourage proposals which are less productive as far as policy implications are concerned.

Problem of the Data-Advocacy-Decision Gap

Even if all the precautions about the pitfalls of the quality control of policy research are taken into account, policy research remains confronted with a possible gap between data, advocacy, and policy decision.

Sound policy research must be based on empirical data which lead to certain policy implications and recommendations. A social researcher may choose to become the advocate of a policy when the data suggest the desirability of such a policy for the clientele system and the target population. Thus, in principle, there is a consistency between data and advocacy. However, a gap between data and advocacy occurs when a researcher advocates a policy not warranted or consistent with the data, or when a researcher becomes the advocate of a policy without any data. The first situation arises if the researcher, either by misinterpretation or arbitrarily, chooses to suggest and promote a policy not in any sense supported by the research evidence. This is a matter of the researcher's competence and integrity. The second situation poses a different problem. This is a case in which the policy advocate happens to be a social researcher. A researcher, like any other individual, can freely express opinions on policies based on his own insights, speculations, and judgment. However, while the policy being advocated has no empirical basis, the advocate is still identified as a social researcher because of his professional identification. It would be most unfortunate if the clientele system and the general public did not distinguish between a researcher who advocates a policy as a consequence of research evidence and a policy advocate who is affiliated with the social sciences profession. Data and policy advocacy should be directly linked in policy research. Should a social researcher decide to advocate a policy without the benefit of data, it is his obligation to inform the clientele system and the general public that his advocacy is based on his own ideology rather than on empirical evidence.

There is also a gap between data and policy decisions. In general, discrete decisions (to implement or not to implement a policy) must be made when data are usually continuous in nature (percentages, ratios, probabilities). Policy decision makers would like to have researchers suggest either "yes" or "no" in regard to a particular policy under consideration. Yet, the researcher is well aware that his data indicate only a "more" or "less" trend. For example, how expensive should implementation of a particular policy become when a decision is made that it is too costly to be implemented? At what point does a policy become too expensive when benefits continue to increase relative to the cost? In other words, while researchers are dealing with data which are essentially continuous, decision makers must make judgments whose outcomes are usually dichotomous (yes or no). For certain types of data, such a cutting-off point can be suggested (say, the marginal utility of a policy or organization); but in other cases decisions are not so clear-cut and easy. Many other factors come into play, and the decision is swayed by these other factors although the data may point other directions.

Such a dilemma makes the researcher cautious in making concrete suggestions and recommendations and thereby gives the policy makers the impression that the researcher is equivocal and the research is less helpful to their decision-making process than they would like. Consequently, cautious researchers alienate policy decision makers who expect clear-cut recommendations. As a result, either the researcher must make arbitrary decisions about the data and comply with the demands of the policy makers, or the policy makers will go to other less reluctant researchers, usually in research firms.

Most of these professional issues remain unresolved. However, as more and more funding goes to support policy research, social researchers as individual scientists and as a group must be sensitized to these issues and come to grips with the ramifications of policy research affecting fellow human beings.

SUMMARY AND DISCUSSION

Social research is conducted in a complex social context, with organizational, economic, professional, and political relationships linking it with other social activities. External financial support and expectation of socially useful information on the part of the larger society have substantial impact on the organization and use of social research. More and more research is conducted for the purpose of producing information useful for the formulation and implementation of social policies. And individual efforts have given way to large research centers and firms, some of which are profit-making, in meeting demands for large-scale, efficient policy research.

Two types of social research have policy implications: developmental research and evaluation research. In developmental research, components of a theoretical orientation or structure are transferred from an existing research tradition to a study for the purpose of determining the extent to which the theoretical formulation informs a given policy problem. Evaluation research, on the other hand, is informed by the general sociological, or other social science disciplinary, theory and methodology and aims specifically at providing information for policy decisions. It is problem-oriented. In the discussion, policy research is used exclusively to indicate evaluation research.

The process of policy research has two parts: organizational activities and scientific activities. Scientific activities begin with the formulation of research objectives in light of the needs and goals of the clientele system and end with data-derived policy implications. The transition from scientific activities to organizational activities occurs when policy recommendations are advanced. Subsequently, policies are formulated and necessary organization and administration take place. After initial trials, dissemination of policy information to the target population, budgetary consideration, and resource allocation, the policy is implemented. Policy research continues as evaluation is made of the effect of the implemented policy on the needs and goals the clientele system set out to meet. The comparison uncovers and defines further needs and goals for further scientific activities.

In policy research, it is important for practitioners and researchers to recognize the expertise and leadership of each in organizational and scientific activities, respectively. Also, both parties must participate in both organizational and scientific activities so that their talents and skills maximally enhance the eventual success of policy research and implementation.

Policy research can be classified into four types, according to the research focus and the nature of the policy under consideration. The research focus may be either on the means (organizational and administrative characteristics) or the ends (outcome characteristics such as productivity and performance), whereas the policy under consideration may either be existing policies or alternative or new policies. The type of policy research to be conducted affects methodological considerations, such as selection of variables, selection of a particular type of theoretical structure (convergent, divergent, or complete), use of a field experiment, and data standardization.

Scientific rigor constitutes only part of the social researcher's responsibility in policy research. There are also professional responsibilities to be discharged. The researcher has an ethical responsibility to protect the confidentiality and mental and physical well-being of sources of information, respondents, and the individuals affected by any policies derived from his research. He should also be sensitive to the relationship between himself and the research sponsor and the policy makers, and not let it cloud his vision of the effect of research applications on the well-being and dignity of the target population. Finally, he is responsible for differentiating between data, advocacy, and policy decisions. Advocacy of a policy without the benefit of data, while within the individual rights and freedom of each researcher, must be distinguished from advocacy following data for the policy makers and the general public, so that academic and professional criteria may be dissociated from the policy being advocated.

The potential policy contribution of social research is promising. Policy research in all probability will become the type of social research considered most desirable in the eyes of the public. The social researcher must be at his scientific and professional best if such potential is ever to be fulfilled.

Sample Items and Response Categories Frequently Used in Interview Survey*

1   Which of the categories on this card comes closest to the type of place you were living in when you were 16 years old? (HAND CARD A □.)

RESPONSE	CODE
In open country but not on a farm	1
On a farm	2
In a small city or town (under 50,000)	3
In a medium-size city (50,000–250,000)	4
In a suburb near a large city	5
In a large city (over 250,000)	6
Don't know	8
No answer	9

    * Unless otherwise indicated, the items and categories are drawn from the NORC 1973 General Social Survey Code Books. R = respondent; Bk = leave blank.

2   In what state or foreign country were you living when you were 16 years old? (REFER TO REGION CODES BELOW AND ENTER CODE NUMBER IN BOX ☐.)

RESPONSE	CODE
New England	1
Maine, Vermont, New Hampshire, Massachusetts, Connecticut, Rhode Island	
Middle Atlantic	2
New York, New Jersey, Pennsylvania	
East North Central	3
Wisconsin, Illinois, Indiana, Michigan, Ohio	
West North Central	4
Minnesota, Iowa, Missouri, North Dakota, South Dakota, Nebraska, Kansas	
South Atlantic	5
Delaware, Maryland, West Virginia, Virginia, Washington, D.C., North Carolina, South Carolina, Georgia, Florida	
East South Central	6
Kentucky, Tennessee, Alabama, Mississippi	
West South Central	7
Arkansas, Oklahoma, Louisiana, Texas	
Mountain	8
Montana, Idaho, Wyoming, Nevada, Utah, Colorado, Arizona, New Mexico	
Pacific	9
Washington, Oregon, California, Alaska, Hawaii	
Foreign-born	0

IF STATE NAMED IS SAME STATE R LIVES IN NOW, ASK A:

a   When you were 16 years old, were you living in this same (city/town/country)?

RESPONSE	CODE
Same state, same city	1
Same state, different city	2
Different state	3
Don't know; no answer	9

3   Were you living with both your own mother and father at the time you were 16? (IF NO: With whom were you living at that time?) (IF R MARRIED OR LEFT HOME BY AGE 16, PROBE FOR BEFORE THAT.)

RESPONSE	CODE
Both own mother and father (GO TO Q 4)	1
Father and stepmother (ASK A)	2
Mother and stepfather (ASK A)	3

RESPONSE	CODE
Father only (ASK A)	4
Mother only (ASK A)	5
Some other male *relative* (no female head) (SPECIFY AND ASK A)	6
Some other female *relative* (no male head) (SPECIFY AND ASK A)	7
Other arrangement with *both* male and female *relatives* (e.g., aunt and uncle, grandparents) (ASK A)	8
Other (SPECIFY AND ASK A)	0
No answer	9

a IF NOT LIVING WITH BOTH OWN MOTHER AND OWN FATHER: What happened?

RESPONSE	CODE
One or both parents died	1
Parents divorced or separated	2
Father absent in armed forces	3
One or both parents in institution	4
Other (SPECIFY)	5
No answer	9
Not applicable	BK

IF NOT LIVING WITH OWN FATHER: ASK Q 4, AND Q 21, IN TERMS OF STEP-FATHER OR OTHER MALE SPECIFIED ABOVE.

IF NO STEPFATHER OR OTHER MALE, SKIP Q 4 AND Q 21.

IF NOT LIVING WITH OWN MOTHER: ASK Q 22, IN TERMS OF STEPMOTHER, OR OTHER FEMALE SPECIFIED ABOVE.

IF NO STEPMOTHER OR OTHER FEMALE, SKIP Q 22.

NOTE SPECIAL INSTRUCTIONS BEFORE Q 5.

4 a What kind of work did your father (FATHER SUBSTITUTE) normally do? That is, what was his job called?

OCCUPATION: _____

b IF NOT ALREADY ANSWERED, ASK: What did he actually do on that job? Tell me, what were some of his main duties? _____

c What kind of place did he work for?

INDUSTRY: _____

d IF NOT ALREADY ANSWERED, ASK: What did they (make/do)? ____

FATHER'S OCCUPATION (see census codes in appendix B).☐☐☐

Not applicable; don't know   BK

PRESTIGE OF FATHER'S OCCUPATION (see prestige scale scores in Appendix B).☐☐

5   [ASK ONLY OF RESPONDENTS WHO LIVED WITH OWN MOTHER (IN Q 3); OTHERS SKIP TO Q 6.] Did your mother ever work for pay for as long as a year, after she was married?

RESPONSE	CODE
Yes (ASK A AND B)	1
No	2
Don't know	8
No answer	9
Not applicable	BK

IF YES:

a Did she work for as long as a year before you started first grade?

RESPONSE	CODE
Yes	1
No	2
Don't know	8
No answer	9
Not applicable	BK

b Did she work for as long as a year at about the time you were 16?

RESPONSE	CODE
Yes	1
No	2
Don't know	8
No answer	9
Not applicable	BK

6   Thinking about the time you were 16 years old, compared with American families in general then, would you say your family income was—far below average, below average, average, above average, or far above average? (PROBE: Just your best guess.)

RESPONSE	CODE
Far below average	1
Below average	2
Average	3
Above average	4

RESPONSE	CODE
Far above average	5
Don't know	8
No answer	9
Not applicable	BK

7 From what countries or part of the world did your ancestors come?
IF SINGLE COUNTRY IS NAMED, REFER TO NATIONAL CODES BELOW, AND ENTER CODE NUMBER IN BOXES.
IF MORE THAN ONE COUNTRY IS NAMED, ENTER CODE 88 AND ASK A.☐☐

a *IF MORE THAN ONE COUNTRY IS NAMED:* Which one of these countries do you feel closer to?
IF ONE COUNTRY IS NAMED, REFER TO CODES ☐☐ BELOW, AND ENTER NUMBER HERE.
IF CAN'T DECIDE ON ONE COUNTRY, ENTER CODE 88

COUNTRY	CODE	COUNTRY	CODE
Africa	01	Mexico	17
Austria	02	Netherlands (Dutch/	18
Canada (French)	03	Holland)	
Canada (other)	04	Norway	19
China	05	Philippines	20
Czechoslovakia	06	Poland	21
Denmark	07	Puerto Rico	22
England and Wales	08	Russia (U.S.S.R.)	23
Finland	09	Scotland	24
France	10	Spain	25
Germany	11	Sweden	26
Greece	12	Switzerland	27
Hungary	13	West Indies	28
Ireland	14	Other (SPECIFY)	29
Italy	15	No information	99
Japan	16	Not possible to code; see Q 7-B	BK

b (RECODE OF Q 7 AND Q 7-A)

RECODED RESPONSES	CODE
Names one country	1
Names two countries, chooses one	2
Names two countries, can't choose	3
Can't name any country	4
No information	5

8 How many brothers and sisters did you have? (Count those born alive, but no longer living, as well as those alive now. Also include stepbrothers and stepsisters, and children adopted by your parents.) (CODE EXACT NUM-BER ☐☐.)

9 Are you currently—married, widowed, divorced, or separated, or have you never been married?

RESPONSE	CODE
Married (ASK A AND B)	1
Widowed (ASK A AND B)	2
Divorced (ASK A)	3
Separated (ASK A)	4
Never married (GO TO Q 10)	5

IF EVER MARRIED:

a How old were you when you first married? (ENTER EXACT AGE: ☐☐.)

No answer	99
Not applicable	BK

b IF CURRENTLY MARRIED OR WIDOWED:
Have you ever been divorced or legally separated?

RESPONSE	CODE
Yes	1
No	2
No answer	9
Not applicable	BK

10 Last week were you working full time, part time, going to school, keeping house, or what? (CIRCLE ONE CODE ONLY. IF MORE THAN ONE RESPONSE, GIVE PREFERENCE TO SMALLEST CODE NUMBER THAT APPLIES.)

RESPONSE	CODE
Working full time (ASK A)	1
Working part time (ASK A)	2
With a job, but not at work because of temporary illness, vacation, strike (ASK B)	3
Unemployed, laid off, looking for work (GO TO Q 11)	4
Retired (ASK C)	5
In school (ASK C)	6
Keeping house (ASK C)	7
Other (SPECIFY AND ASK C)	8

a IF WORKING, FULL OR PART TIME: How many hours did you work last week, at all jobs? Hours: ☐☐

No answer	99
Not applicable	BK

b IF WITH A JOB, BUT NOT AT WORK: How many hours a week do you usually work, at all jobs? Hours: ☐☐

No answer	99
Not applicable	BK

c IF RETIRED, IN SCHOOL, KEEPING HOUSE, OR OTHER: Did you ever work for as long as one year?

RESPONSE	CODE
Yes (ASK Q 11)	1
No	2
No answer	9
Not applicable	BK

11 **a** What kind of work (do/did) you normally do? That is, what (is/was) your job called?

OCCUPATION: _____

b IF NOT ALREADY ANSWERED, ASK: What (do/did) you actually do on that job? Tell me, what (are/were) some of your main duties? _____

c What kind of place (do/did) you work for?

INDUSTRY: _____

d IF NOT ALREADY ANSWERED, ASK: What (do/did) they (make/do)?

RESPONDENT'S OCCUPATION (see Census codes in Appendix B). ☐☐☐

Not applicable; don't know	BK

PRESTIGE OF RESPONDENT'S OCCUPATION (see prestige scale scores in Appendix B). ☐☐

Not applicable; don't know	BK

IF R IS CURRENTLY MARRIED, ASK Q 12. OTHERS, SKIP TO INSTRUCTIONS BEFORE Q 14.

12 Last week was your (wife/husband) working full time, working part time, going to school, keeping house, or what? (CIRCLE ONE CODE ONLY. IF MORE THAN ONE RESPONSE, GIVE PREFERENCE TO CODE NUMBER THAT APPLIES.)

RESPONSE	CODE
Working full time (ASK A)	1
Working part time (ASK A)	2

RESPONSE	CODE
With a job, but not at work because of temporary illness, vacation, strike (ASK B)	3
Unemployed, laid off, looking for work (GO TO Q 13)	4
Retired (ASK C)	5
In school (ASK C)	6
Keeping house (ASK C)	7
Other (SPECIFY AND ASK C)	8
Not applicable	BK

a IF WORKING, FULL OR PART TIME: How many hours did (he/she) work last week, at all jobs? Hours: ☐☐

No answer	99
Not applicable	BK

b IF WITH A JOB, BUT NOT AT WORK: How many hours a week does (he/she) usually work, at all jobs? Hours: ☐☐

No answer	99
Not applicable	BK

c IF RETIRED, IN SCHOOL, KEEPING HOUSE, OR OTHER: Did (he/she) ever work for as long as one year?

RESPONSE	CODE
Yes (ASK Q 13)	1
No (SKIP TO INSTRUCTIONS BEFORE Q 14)	2
Don't know	8
No answer	9
Not applicable	BK

13 **a** What kind of work (does/did) SPOUSE normally do? That is, what (is/was) (his/her) job called?

OCCUPATION: _____

b IF NOT ALREADY ANSWERED, ASK: What (does/did) SPOUSE actually do on that job? Tell me, what (are/were) some of (his/her) main duties? _____

c What kind of place (does/did) (SPOUSE) work for?

INDUSTRY: _____

d IF NOT ALREADY ANSWERED, ASK: What (do/did) they (make/do)?

RESPONDENT'S SPOUSE'S OCCUPATION (see census codes in Appendix B). ☐☐☐

Not applicable; don't know   BK

PRESTIGE OF RESPONDENT'S SPOUSE'S OCCUPATION (see prestige scale scores in Appendix B). ☐☐
Not applicable; don't know   BK
IF R IS CURRENTLY WORKING (FULL OR PART TIME)—ASK Q 14 AND Q 15 ABOUT R. IF R IS MARRIED PERSON WHO IS NOT WORKING—ASK ABOUT SPOUSE IF SPOUSE IS WORKING. ALL OTHERS, SKIP TO Q 16.

14 Do you (does your SPOUSE) have a supervisor on your (his/her) job to whom you are (he/she is) directly responsible?

RESPONSE	CODE
Yes (ASK A)	1
No	2
Don't know	8
No answer (ASK A)	9
Not applicable (not working, not married, married—spouse not working)	BK

a IF YES OR NO ANSWER: Does that person have a supervisor on the job to whom (he/she) is directly responsible?

RESPONSE	CODE
Yes	3
No	4
Don't know	8
No answer	9
Not applicable	BK

15 In your (your spouse's) job, do you (does he/she) supervise anyone who is directly responsible to you (him/her)?

RESPONSE	CODE
Yes (ASK A)	1
No	2
Don't know	8
No answer (ASK A)	9
Not applicable (not working, not married, married—spouse not working)	BK

a IF YES OR NO ANSWER: Do any of those persons supervise anyone else?

RESPONSE	CODE
Yes	3
No	4
Don't know	8
No answer	9
Not applicable	BK

ASK EVERYONE

16   At any time during the last ten years, have you been unemployed and looking for work for as long as a month?

RESPONSE   CODE
Yes   2
No   2
No answer   9

17   Did you ever—because of sickness, unemployment, or any other reason—receive anything like welfare, unemployment insurance, or other aid from government agencies?

RESPONSE   CODE
Yes   1
No   2
Don't know   8

18   How many children have you ever had? Please count all that were born alive at any time (including those you have had from a previous marriage).

RESPONSE   CODE
None   0
One   1
Two   2
Three   3
Four   4
Five   5
Six   6
Seven   7
Eight or more   8
No answer   9

Now just a few more background questions.

19–22 ASK ALL PARTS OF QUESTION ABOUT RESPONDENT BEFORE GOING ON TO ASK R'S FATHER; THEN R'S MOTHER; THEN R'S SPOUSE, IF R IS CURRENTLY MARRIED.

a   What is the highest grade in elementary school or high school that [you/your father/your mother/your (husband/wife)] finished and got credit for? CODE EXACT GRADE.

RESPONDENT ☐☐; R'S FATHER (FATHER SUBSTITUTE) ☐☐; R'S MOTHER (MOTHER SUBSTITUTE) ☐☐; R'S SPOUSE ☐☐.

RESPONSE	CODE	RESPONSE	CODE
No formal schooling	00	7th grade	07
1st grade	01	8th grade	08
2d grade	02	9th grade	09
3d grade	03	10th grade	10
4th grade	04	11th grade	11
5th grade	05	12th grade	12
6th grade	06		

RESPONSE	CODE	RESPONSE	CODE
1 year of college	13	8 years	20
2 years	14	Don't know	98
3 years	15	No answer	99
4 years	16	Not applicable (no	
5 years	17	parental substi-	
6 years	18	tute and/or not	
7 years	19	married)	BK

b Did (you/he/she) ever get a high school diploma? (SEE D BELOW.)

c Did (you/he/she) complete one or more years of college for credit? IF YES: How many years did (you/he/she) complete—not including schooling such as business college, technical or vocational school?

d Do you [Does (he/she)] have any college degrees? IF YES: What degree?

23 In what year were you born? Month _____; year_____

24 CODE RESPONDENT'S SEX.

RESPONSE	CODE
Male	1
Female	2

25 CODE WITHOUT ASKING ONLY IF THERE IS NO DOUBT IN YOUR MIND. What race do you consider yourself? RECORD VERBATIM AND CODE.

RESPONSE	CODE
White	1
Black	2
Other (SPECIFY)	3

26 ASK THE "X" OR "Y" VERSION, DEPENDING ON THE LETTER ON THE COVER OF THIS QUESTIONNAIRE.

X If you were asked to use one of four names for your social class, which would you say you belong in: the lower class, the working class, the middle class, or the upper class?

RESPONSE	CODE
Lower class	1
Working class	2
Middle class	3
Upper class	4
No answer	9
Not applicable	BK

Y If you were asked to use one of five names for your social class, which would you say you belong in: the lower class, the working class, the middle class, the upper middle class, or the upper class?

RESPONSE	CODE
Lower class	1
Working class	2
Middle class	3
Upper middle class	4
Upper class	5
No answer	9
Not applicable	BK

27   What is your religious preference? Is it Protestant, Catholic, Jewish, some
     other religion, or no religion?

RESPONSE	CODE
Protestant (ASK A)	1
Catholic	2
Jewish	3
None	4
Other (SPECIFY RELIGION AND/OR CHURCH AND DENOMINA-TION)	5
No answer	9

   a   IF PROTESTANT: What specific denomination, if any?

RESPONSE	CODE
Baptist	1
Methodist	2
Lutheran	3
Presbyterian	4
Episcopalian	5
Other (SPECIFY)	6
No denomination given or nondenominational church	7
No answer	9
Not applicable	BK

28   In what religion were you raised?

RESPONSE	CODE
Protestant (ASK A)	1
Catholic	2
Jewish	3
None	4
Other (SPECIFY RELIGION AND/OR CHURCH AND DENOMINA-TION)	5
No answer	9

   a   IF PROTESTANT: What specific denomination, if any?

RESPONSE	CODE
Baptist	1
Methodist	2
Lutheran	3
Presbyterian	4
Episcopalian	5
Other (SPECIFY)	6
No denomination given or nondenominational church	7
No answer	9
Not applicable	BK

29 How often do you attend religious services? (USE CATEGORIES AS PROBES IF NECESSARY.)

RESPONSE	CODE
Never	0
Less than once a year	1
About once a year	2
Several times a year	3
About once a month	4
Two to three times a month	5
Nearly every week	6
Every week	7
Several times a week	8
Don't know; no answer	9

IF R IS CURRENTLY MARRIED, ASK Q 30 AND Q 31. (OTHERS, SKIP TO Q 32.)

30 What is your SPOUSE'S religious preference? Is it Protestant, Catholic, Jewish, some other religion, or no religion?

RESPONSE	CODE
Protestant (ASK A)	1
Catholic	2
Jewish	3
None	4
Other (SPECIFY RELIGION AND/OR CHURCH AND DENOMINA- TION)	5
No answer	9
Not applicable (not currently married)	BK

a IF PROTESTANT: What specific denomination, if any?

RESPONSE	CODE
Baptist	1
Methodist	2
Lutheran	3
Presbyterian	4
Episcopalian	5
Other (SPECIFY)	6
No denomination given or nondenominational church	7
No answer	9
Not applicable	BK

31 In what religion was your (husband/wife) raised?

RESPONSE	CODE
Protestant (ASK A)	1
Catholic	2
Jewish	3
None	4

RESPONSE	CODE
Other (SPECIFY RELIGION AND/OR CHURCH AND DENOMINA-TION)	5
No answer	9
Not applicable	BK

a IF PROTESTANT: What specific denomination is that, if any?

RESPONSE	CODE
Baptist	1
Methodist	2
Lutheran	3
Presbyterian	4
Episcopalian	5
Other (SPECIFY)	6
No denomination given or nondenominational church	7
No answer	9
Not applicable	BK

32 Generally speaking, do you usually think of yourself as a Republican, a Democrat, an Independent, or what?

RESPONSE	CODE
Republican (ASK A)	1
Democrat (ASK A)	2
Independent (ASK B)	3
Other (GO TO Q 33)	4
Refused	5
Does not vote owing to religious belief	6
No answer	9

a IF REPUBLICAN OR DEMOCRAT: Would you call yourself a strong (Republican/Democrat) or not a very strong (Republican/Democrat)?

RESPONSE	CODE
Strong	1
Not very strong	2
No answer	9
Not applicable	BK

b IF INDEPENDENT: Do you think of yourself as closer to the Republican or Democratic Party?

RESPONSE	CODE
Republican	3
Democrat	4
Neither	5
No answer	9
Not applicable	BK

33   In 1972, McGovern ran for President on the Democratic ticket against Nixon for the Republicans. Do you remember for sure whether or not you voted in that election?

RESPONSE	CODE
Voted (ASK A)	1
Did not vote (ASK B)	2
Ineligible (ASK B)	3
Refused	4
Does not vote owing to religious belief	6
Don't know/don't remember	8
No answer	9

    a   IF VOTED: Did you vote for McGovern or Nixon?

RESPONSE	CODE
McGovern	1
Nixon	2
Other	3
Refused	4
Don't know/don't remember	8
No answer	9
Not applicable	BK

    b   IF DID NOT VOTE: Who would you have voted for, for President, if you had voted?

RESPONSE	CODE
McGovern	1
Nixon	2
Other	3
Refused	4
Don't know/don't remember	8
No answer	9
Not applicable	BK

34   In 1968, Humphrey ran for President on the Democratic ticket against Nixon for the Republicans, and Wallace ran as an Independent. Do you remember for sure whether or not you voted in that election?

RESPONSE	CODE
Voted (ASK A)	1
Did not vote (ASK B)	2
Ineligible (ASK B)	3
Refused	4
Did not vote owing to religious belief	6
Don't know/don't remember	8
No answer	9

a IF VOTED: Did you vote for Humphrey, Nixon, or Wallace?

RESPONSE	CODE
Humphrey	1
Nixon	2
Wallace	3
Other	4
Refused to tell	5
Don't know/don't remember	8
No answer	9
Not applicable	BK

b IF DID NOT VOTE: Who would you have voted for, for President, if you had voted?

RESPONSE	CODE
Humphrey	1
Nixon	2
Wallace	3
Other	4
Don't know/don't remember	8
No answer	9
Not applicable	BK

ASK EVERYONE:

35 Now a few questions about this household.

a First, how many persons *altogether* live here, related to you or not? Please include any persons who usually live here but are away temporarily—on business, on vacation, or in a general hospital—and all babies and small children. Do *not* include college students who are living away at college, persons stationed away from here in the armed forces, or persons away in institutions. (Don't forget to include yourself in the total.)

No answer   99
TOTAL PERSONS ☐☐; IF TOTAL IS ONE PERSON, ENTER 01 AND SKIP TO Q 37.

b How many of these persons are babies or children *under* 6 years old? UNDER 6 YEARS: ☐

c How many are children age 6 through 12? 6–12 YEARS: ☐

d How many are teenagers 13 through 17? 13–17 YEARS: ☐

e And how many are persons 18 and over? 18+ YEARS: ☐ (B THROUGH E SHOULD TOTAL A; IF NOT, CHECK ANSWERS WITH RESPONDENT.)

36   Is everyone in the household related to you in some way? (IF NO, ASK A.)

    a   IF NO: How many persons in the household are *not* related to you in any way?

RESPONSE	CODE
1	1
2	2
3	3
4	4
5	5
6	6
Not applicable	BK

37   (Just thinking of your family now—those people in the household who *are* related to you . . .) How many persons in the family (including yourself) earned any money last year—1972—from any job or employment?

RESPONSE	CODE
None	0
One	1
Two	2
Three	3
Four	4
Five	5
Six	6
Seven	7
Eight or more	8
No answer	9

38   In which of these groups did your total *family* income, from all sources, fall last year—1972—before taxes, that is? Just tell me the letter. (HAND CARD J ☐.)

RESPONSE		CODE
a.	Under $1,000	01
b.	$1,000 to $2,999	02
c.	$3,000 to $3,999	03
d.	$4,000 to $4,999	04
e.	$5,000 to $5,999	05
f.	$6,000 to $6,999	06
g.	$7,000 to $7,999	07
h.	$8,000 to $9,999	08
i.	$10,000 to $14,999	09
j.	$15,000 to $19,999	10
k.	$20,000 to $24,999	11
l.	$25,000 or over	12
	Refused to answer	13
	Don't know	98
	No answer	99

39   Do you (does your SPOUSE) belong to a labor union?

RESPONSE   CODE
Yes, respondent belongs   1
Yes, spouse belongs   2
Yes, both belong   3
No, neither R (nor spouse) belongs   4
No answer   9

ASK EVERYONE:

40   For each area of life I am going to name, tell me the number that shows
how much satisfaction you get from that area. (READ ITEMS A THROUGH
E. CODE ONE FOR EACH. HAND CARD F ☐.)

   a   The city or place you live in.

RESPONSE   CODE
A very great deal   1
A great deal   2
Quite a bit   3
A fair amount   4
Some   5
A little   6
None   7
Don't know   8

   b   Your nonworking activities—hobbies and so on.

RESPONSE   CODE
A very great deal   1
A great deal   2
Quite a bit   3
A fair amount   4
Some   5
A little   6
None   7
Don't know   8
No answer   9

   c   Your family life.

RESPONSE   CODE
A very great deal   1
A great deal   2
Quite a bit   3
A fair amount   4
Some   5
A little   6
None   7
Don't know   8
No answer   9

d Your friendships.

RESPONSE	CODE
A very great deal	1
A great deal	2
Quite a bit	3
A fair amount	4
Some	5
A little	6
None	7
Don't know	8
No answer	9

e Your health and physical condition.

RESPONSE	CODE
A very great deal	1
A great deal	2
Quite a bit	3
A fair amount	4
Some	5
A little	6
None	7
Don't know	8
No answer	9

ASK ONLY IF CURRENTLY MARRIED:

41 Taking things altogether, how would you describe your marriage? Would you say that your marriage is very happy, pretty happy, or not too happy?

RESPONSE	CODE
Very happy	1
Pretty happy	2
Not too happy	3
Don't know	8
No answer	9
Not applicable	BK

42 In general, what was the respondent's attitude toward the interview?

RESPONSE	CODE
Friendly and eager	1
Cooperative but not particularly eager	2
Indifferent and bored	3
Hostile	4
No answer	9

43 Was the respondent's understanding of the questions . . . (CODE ONE.)

RESPONSE	CODE
Good	1
Fair	2
Poor	3
No answer	9

Occupational Categories and Occupational Prestige Scales*

Compiled by John Vaughn

Occupational classification	1970 Census code*	NORC prestige scale†	Inter-national scale‡
Professional and technical workers			
Accountants	001	57	55
Architects	002	71	72
Computer specialists			
Computer programmers	003	51	51
Computer analysts	004	51	51
Computer specialists, n.e.c.§	005	51	51

   * U.S. Bureau of the Census, "1970 Census of Population Alphabetical Index of Industries and Occupations," U.S. Government Printing Office, Washington, D.C., 1971.

   † Paul M. Siegel, "Prestige in the American Occupational Structure," unpublished Ph.D. dissertation, University of Chicago, 1971.

   ‡ Donald J. Treiman, "A Standard International Occupational Prestige Scale," in *Occupational Prestige in Comparative Perspective.* forthcoming. Certain categories were not available.

   § n.e.c. = not elsewhere classified.

   Source: Occupational titles, census codes, and prestige scores are from *National Data Program for the Social Sciences,* Codebook for the Spring 1972 General Social Survey, National Opinion Research Center, University of Chicago, Appendix F, pp. 88–102.

Occupational classification	1970 Census code*	NORC prestige scale†	Inter- national scale‡
Engineers			
Aeronautical and astronautical engineers	006	71	67
Chemical engineers	010	67	66
Civil engineers	011	68	70
Electrical and electronic engineers	012	69	65
Industrial engineers	013	54	54
Mechanical engineers	014	62	66
Metallurgical and materials engineers	015	56	60
Mining engineers	020	62	63
Petroleum engineers	021	67	—
Sales engineers	022	51	51
Engineers, n.e.c.	023	67	55
Farm management advisors	024	54	54
Foresters and conservationists	025	54	48
Home management advisors	026	54	—
Lawyers and judges			
Judges	030	76	76
Lawyers	031	76	73
Librarians, archivists, and curators			
Librarians	032	55	55
Archivists and curators	033	66	55
Mathematical specialists			
Actuaries	034	55	—
Mathematicians	035	65	67
Statisticians	036	55	55
Life and physical scientists			
Agricultural scientists	042	56	58
Atmospheric and space scientists	043	68	71
Biological scientists	044	68	69
Chemists	045	69	67
Geologists	051	67	67
Marine scientists	052	68	69
Physicists and astronomers	053	74	77
Life and physical scientists, n.e.c.	054	68	72
Operations and systems researchers and ana- lysts	055	51	51
Personnel and labor relations workers	056	56	57
Physicians, dentists, and related practitioners			
Chiropractors	061	60	63
Dentists	062	74	71
Optometrists	063	62	62
Pharmacists	064	61	64
Physicians, including osteopaths	065	82	78
Podiatrists	071	37	—
Veterinarians	072	60	61
Health practitioners, n.e.c.	073	51	50

Occupational classification	1970 Census code*	NORC prestige scale†	Inter-national scale‡
Nurses, dieticians and therapists			
Dieticians	074	52	52
Registered nurses	075	62	54
Therapists	076	37	52
Health technologists and technicians			
Clinical laboratory technologists and technicians	080	61	58
Dental hygienists	081	61	44
Health record technologists and technicians	082	61	—
Radiologic technologists and technicians	083	61	58
Therapy assistants	084	37	—
Health technologists and technicians, n.e.c.	085	47	—
Religious workers			
Clergymen	086	69	60
Religious workers, n.e.c.	090	56	39
Social scientists			
Economists	091	57	61
Political scientists	092	66	—
Psychologists	093	71	66
Sociologists	094	66	67
Urban and regional planners	095	66	—
Social scientists, n.e.c.	096	66	69
Social and recreation workers			
Social workers	100	52	56
Recreation workers	101	49	—
Teachers, college and university			
Agriculture teachers	102	78	78
Atmospheric, earth, marine, and space teachers	103	78	78
Biology teachers	104	78	78
Chemistry teachers	105	78	78
Physics teachers	110	78	78
Engineering teachers	111	78	78
Mathematics teachers	112	78	78
Health specialist teachers	113	78	78
Psychology teachers	114	78	78
Business and commerce teachers	115	78	78
Economics teachers	116	78	78
History teachers	120	78	78
Sociology teachers	121	78	78
Social science teachers, n.e.c.	122	78	78
Art, drama, and music teachers	123	78	78
Coaches and physical education teachers	124	78	78
Education teachers	125	78	78
English teachers	126	78	78
Foreign language teachers	130	78	78
Home economics teachers	131	78	78
Law teachers	132	78	78

Occupational classification	1970 Census code*	NORC prestige scale†	International scale‡
Theology teachers	133	78	78
Trade, industrial, and technical teachers	134	78	78
Miscellaneous teachers, college and university	135	78	78
Teachers, college and university, subject not specified	140	78	78
Teachers, except college and university			
Adult education teachers	141	43	—
Elementary school teachers	142	60	57
Prekindergarten and kindergarten teachers	143	60	49
Secondary-school teachers	144	63	61
Teachers, except college and university, n.e.c.	145	43	62
Engineering and science technicians			
Agriculture and biological technicians, except health	150	47	47
Chemical technicians	151	47	46
Draftsmen	152	56	55
Electrical and electronic engineering technicians	153	47	46
Industrial engineering technicians	154	47	—
Mechanical engineering technicians	155	47	46
Mathematical technicians	156	47	—
Surveyors	161	53	58
Engineering and science technicians, n.e.c.	162	47	46
Technicians, except health, engineering, and science			
Airplane pilots	163	70	67
Air traffic controllers	164	43	—
Embalmers	165	52	34
Flight engineers	170	47	67
Radio operators	171	43	49
Tool programers, numerical control	172	47	—
Technicians, n.e.c.	173	47	—
Vocational and educational counselors	174	51	55
Writers, artists, and entertainers			
Actors	175	55	52
Athletes and kindred workers	180	51	50
Authors	181	60	62
Dancers	182	38	45
Designers	183	58	56
Editors and reporters	184	51	56
Musicians and composers	185	46	45
Painters and sculptors	190	56	57
Photographers	191	41	45

Occupational classification	1970 Census code*	NORC prestige scale†	International scale‡
Public relations men and publicity writers	192	57	57
Radio and television announcers	193	51	50
Writers, artists, and entertainers, n.e.c.	194	51	—
Research workers, not specified	195	51	—
Professional, technical, and kindred workers—allocated	196	51	51
Managers and administrators, except farm			
Assessors, controllers, and treasurers, local public administration	201	61	—
Bank officers and financial managers	202	72	76
Buyers and shippers, farm products	203	41	39
Buyers, wholesale and retail trade	205	50	48
Credit men	210	49	49
Funeral directors	211	52	34
Health administrators	212	61	—
Construction inspectors, public administration	213	41	—
Inspectors, except construction, public administration	215	41	61
Managers and superintendents, building	216	38	47
Office managers, n.e.c.	220	50	59
Officers, pilots and pursers; ship	221	60	54
Officials and administrators; public administration, n.e.c.	222	61	65
Officials of lodges, societies, and unions	223	48	50
Postmasters and mail superintendents	224	58	58
Purchasing agents and buyers, n.e.c.	225	48	47
Railroad conductors	226	41	39
Restaurant, cafeteria, and bar managers	230	39	37
Sales managers and department heads, retail trade	231	50	47
Sales managers, except retail trade	233	50	—
School administrators, college	235	61	86
School administrators, elementary and secondary	240	60	68
Managers and administrators, n.e.c.	245	50	59
Managers and administrators, except farm—allocated	246	50	63
Sales workers			
Advertising agents and salesmen	260	42	42
Auctioneers	261	32	39
Demonstrators	262	28	28
Hucksters and peddlers	264	18	22

Occupational classification	1970 Census code*	NORC prestige scale†	Inter- national scale‡
Insurance agents, brokers, and underwriters	265	47	45
Newsboys	266	15	14
Real estate agents and brokers	270	44	49
Stock and bond salesmen	271	51	56
Salesmen and sales clerks, n.e.c.	280	34	28
Sales representatives, manufacturing industries	281	49	46
Sales representatives, wholesale trade	282	40	—
Sales clerks; retail trade	283	29	34
Salesmen, retail trade	284	29	32
Salesmen of services and construction	285	34	42
Sales workers—allocated	296	34	28
Clerical and kindred workers			
Bank tellers	301	50	48
Billing clerks	303	45	42
Bookkeepers	305	48	49
Cashiers	310	31	31
Clerical assistants, social welfare	311	36	—
Clerical supervisors, n.e.c.	312	36	55
Collectors, bill and account	313	26	27
Counter clerks, except food	314	36	—
Dispatchers and starters, vehicle	315	34	37
Enumerators and interviewers	320	36	—
Estimators and investigators, n.e.c.	321	36	—
Expediters and production controllers	323	36	44
File clerks	325	30	31
Insurance adjusters, examiners, and investigators	326	48	49
Library attendants and assistants	330	41	41
Mail carriers, post office	331	42	33
Mailhandlers, except post office	332	36	29
Messengers and office boys	333	19	26
Meter readers, utilities	334	36	21
Office machine operators			
Bookkeeping and billing machine operators	341	45	45
Calculating machine operators	342	45	45
Computer and peripheral equipment operators	343	45	53
Duplicating machine operators	344	45	—
Keypunch operators	345	45	45
Tabulating machine operators	350	45	—
Office machine operators, n.e.c.	355	45	—
Payroll and timekeeping clerks	360	41	42
Postal clerks	361	43	39
Proofreaders	362	36	41

Occupational classification	1970 Census code*	NORC prestige scale†	Inter-national scale‡
Real estate appraisers	363	43	48
Receptionists	364	39	38
Secretaries			
Secretaries, legal	370	46	59
Secretaries, medical	371	46	—
Secretaries, n.e.c.	372	46	—
Shipping and receiving clerks	374	29	29
Statistical clerks	375	36	—
Stenographers	376	43	42
Stock clerks and storekeepers	381	23	31
Teacher aides, except school monitors	382	36	50
Telegraph messengers	383	30	26
Telegraph operators	384	44	45
Telephone operators	385	40	38
Ticket, station, and express agents	390	35	37
Typists	391	41	42
Weighers	392	36	—
Miscellaneous clerical workers	394	36	38
Not specified clerical workers	395	36	37
Clerical and kindred workers—allocated	396	36	44
Craftsmen and kindred workers			
Automobile accessories installers	401	47	—
Bakers	402	34	33
Blacksmiths	403	36	35
Boilermakers	404	31	31
Bookbinders	405	31	33
Brickmasons and stonemasons	410	36	34
Brickmasons and stonemasons, apprentices	411	36	—
Bulldozer operators	412	33	32
Cabinetmakers	413	39	40
Carpenters	415	40	37
Carpenter apprentices	416	40	—
Carpet installers	420	47	—
Cement and concrete finishers	421	32	34
Compositors and typesetters	422	38	47
Printing trades apprentices, except pressmen	423	40	—
Cranemen, derrickmen, and hoistmen	424	39	34
Decorators and window dressers	425	37	—
Dental laboratory technicians	426	47	—
Electricians	430	49	45
Electrician apprentices	431	41	—
Electric power linemen and cablemen	433	39	36
Electrotypers and stereotypers	434	38	42
Engravers, except photoengravers	435	41	41
Excavating, grading, and road machine operators, except bulldozer	436	33	32

Occupational classification	1970 Census code*	NORC prestige scale†	Inter- national scale‡
Floor layers, except tile setters	440	40	—
Foremen, n.e.c.	441	45	46
Forgemen and hammermen	442	36	35
Furniture and wood finishers	443	29	28
Furriers	444	35	35
Glaziers	445	26	26
Heat treaters, annealers, and temperers	446	36	38
Inspectors, scalers, and graders; log and lumber	450	31	31
Inspectors, n.e.c.	452	31	—
Jewelers and watchmakers	453	37	40
Job and die setters, metal	454	48	—
Locomotive engineers	455	51	43
Locomotive firemen	456	36	33
Machinists	461	48	43
Machinist apprentices	462	41	—
Mechanics and repairmen			
Air conditioning, heating, and refrigeration	470	37	43
Aircraft	471	48	50
Automobile body repairmen	472	37	—
Automobile mechanics	473	37	43
Automobile mechanic apprentices	474	37	—
Data processing machine repairmen	475	34	—
Farm implements	480	33	—
Heavy equipment mechanics, including diesel	481	33	—
Household appliance and accessory installers and mechanics	482	33	—
Loom fixers	483	30	30
Office machines	484	34	—
Radio and television	485	35	42
Railroad and car shop	486	37	—
Mechanic, except automobile apprentices	491	41	—
Miscellaneous mechanics and repairmen	492	35	—
Not specified mechanics and repairmen	495	35	30
Millers: grain, flour, and feed	501	25	33
Millwrights	502	40	40
Molders, metal	503	39	38
Molders, apprentices	504	39	—
Motion picture projectionists	505	34	34
Opticians, and lens grinders and polishers	506	51	57
Painters, construction and maintenance	510	30	34
Painter apprentices	511	30	—
Paperhangers	512	24	24
Pattern and model makers, except paper	514	39	39
Photoengravers and lithographers	515	40	46
Piano and organ tuners and repairmen	516	32	33
Plasterers	520	33	31
Plasterer apprentices	521	33	—

Occupational classification	1970 Census code*	NORC prestige scale†	International scale‡
Plumber and pipe fitters	522	41	38
Plumber and pipe fitter apprentices	523	41	—
Power station operators	525	39	43
Pressmen and plate printers, printing	530	40	41
Pressmen apprentices	531	40	—
Rollers and finishers, metal	533	36	36
Roofers and slaters	534	31	31
Sheetmetal workers and tinsmiths	535	37	34
Sheetmetal apprentices	536	37	—
Shipfitters	540	36	—
Shoe repairmen	542	33	28
Sign painters and letterers	543	30	29
Stationary engineers	545	35	34
Stone cutters and stone carvers	546	33	39
Structural metal craftsmen	550	36	44
Tailors	551	41	40
Telephone installers and repairmen	552	39	35
Telephone linemen and splicers	554	39	36
Tile setters	560	36	—
Tool and die makers	561	42	40
Tool and die maker apprentices	562	41	—
Upholsterers	563	30	31
Specified craft apprentices, n.e.c.	571	41	—
Not specified apprentices	572	41	—
Craftsmen and kindred workers, n.e.c.	575	47	—
Former members of the armed forces	580	47	46
Craftsmen and kindred workers—allocated	586	47	—
Current members of the armed forces	590	47	46

Operatives, except transport

Asbestos and insulation workers	601	28	28
Assemblers	602	27	30
Blasters and powdermen	603	32	—
Bottling and canning operatives	604	23	35
Chairmen, rodmen, and axmen; surveying	605	39	—
Checkers, examiners, and inspectors, manufacturing	610	36	39
Clothing ironers and pressers	611	18	22
Cutting operatives, n.e.c.	612	26	34
Dressmakers and seamstresses, except factory	613	32	39
Drillers, earth	614	27	45
Dry wall installers and lathers	615	27	—
Dyers	620	25	25
Filers, polishers, sanders, and buffers	621	19	27
Furnacemen, smeltermen, and pourers	622	33	45
Garage workers and gas station attendants	623	22	18
Graders and sorters, manufacturing	624	33	—
Produce graders and packers, except factory and farm	625	19	22

Occupational classification	1970 Census code*	NORC prestige scale†	International scale‡
Heaters, metal	626	33	38
Laundry and dry cleaning operatives, n.e.c.	630	18	22
Meat cutters and butchers, except manufacturing	631	32	32
Meat cutters and butchers, manufacturing	633	28	18
Meat wrappers, retail trade	634	19	—
Metal platers	635	29	28
Milliners	636	33	32
Mine operatives, n.e.c.	640	26	34
Mixing operatives	641	29	—
Oilers and greasers, except automobile	642	24	—
Packers and wrappers, n.e.c.	643	19	—
Painters, manufactured articles	644	29	29
Photographic process workers	645	36	36
Precision machine operatives			
Drill press operatives	650	29	—
Grinding machine operatives	651	29	27
Lathe and milling machine operatives	652	29	36
Precision machine operatives, n.e.c.	653	29	40
Punch and stamping press operatives	656	29	—
Riveters and fasteners	660	29	—
Sailors and deckhands	661	34	35
Sawyers	662	28	31
Sewers and stitchers	663	25	26
Shoemaking machine operatives	664	32	28
Solderers	665	29	—
Stationary firemen	666	33	33
Textile operatives			
Carding, lapping, and combing operatives	670	29	29
Knitters, loopers, and toppers	671	29	29
Spinners, twisters, and winders	672	25	34
Weavers	673	25	30
Textile operatives, n.e.c.	674	29	26
Welders and flame cutters	680	40	39
Winding operatives, n.e.c.	681	29	—
Machine operatives, miscellaneous specified	690	32	38
Machine operatives, not specified	692	32	38
Miscellaneous operatives	694	32	35
Not specified operatives	695	32	35
Operatives, except transport—allocated	696	32	—
Transport equipment operatives			
Boatmen and canalmen	701	37	23
Bus drivers	703	32	32
Conductors and motormen, urban rail transit	704	28	28

Occupational classification	1970 Census code*	NORC prestige scale†	Inter-national scale‡
Deliverymen and routemen	705	28	28
Fork lift and tow motor operatives	706	29	29
Motormen: mine, factory, logging camp, etc.	710	27	27
Parking attendants	711	22	24
Railroad brakemen	712	35	29
Railroad switchmen	713	33	29
Taxicab drivers and chauffeurs	714	22	28
Truck drivers	715	32	33
Transport equipment operatives—allocated	726	29	28
Laborers, except farm			
Animal caretakers, except farm	740	29	—
Carpenters' helpers	750	23	23
Construction laborers, except carpenters' helpers	751	17	15
Fishermen and oystermen	752	30	28
Freight and material handlers	753	17	20
Garbage collectors	754	17	13
Gardeners and groundskeepers, except farm	755	23	21
Longshoremen and stevedores	760	24	21
Lumbermen, raftsmen, and woodchoppers	761	26	19
Stockhandlers	762	17	—
Teamsters	763	12	18
Vehicle washers and equipment cleaners	764	17	—
Warehousemen, n.e.c.	770	20	20
Miscellaneous laborers	780	17	19
Not specified laborers	785	17	18
Laborers, except farm—allocated	796	17	19
Farmers and farm managers			
Farmers (owners and tenants)	801	41	40
Farm managers	802	44	54
Farmers and farm managers—allocated	806	41	40
Farm laborers and farm foremen			
Farm foremen	821	35	41
Farm laborers, wage workers	822	18	21
Farm laborers, unpaid family workers	823	18	34
Farm service laborers, self-employed	824	27	30
Farm laborers, farm foremen, and kindred workers—allocated	846	19	22
Service workers, except private household			
Cleaning service workers			
Chambermaids and maid, except private household	901	14	14

Occupational classification	1970 Census code*	NORC prestige scale†	International scale‡
Cleaners and charwomen	902	12	17
Janitors and sextons	903	16	21
Food service workers			
Bartenders	910	20	23
Busboys	911	22	—
Cooks, except private household	912	26	31
Dishwashers	913	22	—
Food counter and fountain workers	914	15	16
Waiters	915	20	23
Food service workers, n.e.c., except private household	916	22	25
Health service workers			
Dental assistants	921	48	44
Health aides, except nursing	922	48	—
Health trainees	923	36	—
Midwives	924	23	47
Nursing aides, orderlies, and attendants	925	36	42
Practical nurses	926	42	44
Personal service workers			
Airline stewardesses	931	36	50
Attendants, recreation and amusement	932	15	20
Attendants, personal service, n.e.c.	933	14	—
Baggage porters and bell hops	934	14	17
Barbers	935	38	30
Boarding and lodging house keepers	940	22	22
Bootblacks	941	09	12
Child care workers, except private households	942	25	—
Elevator operators	943	21	24
Hairdressers and cosmetologists	944	33	35
Personal service apprentices	945	14	—
Housekeepers, except private households	950	36	33
School monitors	952	22	—
Ushers, recreation and amusement	953	15	—
Welfare service aides	954	14	—
Protective service workers			
Crossing guards and bridge tenders	960	24	25
Firemen, fire protection	961	44	35
Guards and watchmen	962	22	22
Marshals and constables	963	46	60
Policemen and detectives	964	48	40
Sheriffs and bailiffs	965	55	47
Service workers, except private household—allocated	976	25	31

Occupational classification	1970 Census code*	NORC prestige scale†	Inter- national scale‡
Private household workers			
Child care workers, private household	980	23	23
Cooks, private household	981	18	—
Housekeepers, private household	982	25	28
Laundresses, private household	983	18	—
Maids and servants, private household	984	18	17
Private household workers—allocated	986	18	22

Appendix C

Tables

Table 1 Random Numbers

10 09 73 25 33	76 52 01 35 86	34 67 35 48 76	80 95 90 91 17	39 29 27 49 45
37 54 20 48 05	64 89 47 42 96	24 80 52 40 37	20 63 61 04 02	00 82 29 16 65
08 42 26 89 53	19 64 50 93 03	23 20 90 25 60	15 95 33 47 64	35 08 03 36 06
99 01 90 25 29	09 37 67 07 15	38 31 13 11 65	88 67 67 43 97	04 43 62 76 59
12 80 79 99 70	80 15 73 61 47	64 03 23 66 53	98 95 11 68 77	12 17 17 68 33
66 06 57 47 17	34 07 27 68 50	36 69 73 61 70	65 81 33 98 85	11 19 92 91 70
31 06 01 08 05	45 57 18 24 06	35 30 34 26 14	86 79 90 74 39	23 40 30 97 32
85 26 97 76 02	02 05 16 56 92	68 66 57 48 18	73 05 38 52 47	18 62 38 85 79
63 57 33 21 35	05 32 54 70 48	90 55 35 75 48	28 46 82 87 09	83 49 12 56 24
73 79 64 57 53	03 52 96 47 78	35 80 83 42 82	60 93 52 03 44	35 27 38 84 35
98 52 01 77 67	14 90 56 86 07	22 10 94 05 58	60 97 09 34 33	50 50 07 39 98
11 80 50 54 31	39 80 82 77 32	50 72 56 82 48	29 40 52 42 01	52 77 56 78 51
83 45 29 96 34	06 28 89 80 83	13 74 67 00 78	18 47 54 06 10	68 71 17 78 17
88 68 54 02 00	86 50 75 84 01	36 76 66 79 51	90 36 47 64 93	29 60 91 10 62
99 59 46 73 48	87 51 76 49 69	91 82 60 89 28	93 78 56 13 68	23 47 83 41 13
65 48 11 76 74	17 46 85 09 50	58 04 77 69 74	73 03 95 71 86	40 21 81 65 44
80 12 43 56 35	17 72 70 80 15	45 31 82 23 74	21 11 57 82 53	14 38 55 37 63
74 35 09 98 17	77 40 27 72 14	43 23 60 02 10	45 52 16 42 37	96 28 60 26 55
69 91 62 68 03	66 25 22 91 48	36 93 68 72 03	76 62 11 39 90	94 40 05 64 18
09 89 32 05 05	14 22 56 85 14	46 42 75 67 88	96 29 77 88 22	54 38 21 45 98
91 49 91 45 23	68 47 92 76 86	46 16 28 35 54	94 75 08 99 23	37 08 92 00 48
80 33 69 45 98	26 94 03 68 58	70 29 73 41 35	53 14 03 33 40	42 05 08 23 41
44 10 48 19 49	85 15 74 79 54	32 97 92 65 75	57 60 04 08 81	22 22 20 64 13
12 55 07 37 42	11 10 00 20 40	12 86 07 46 97	96 64 48 94 39	28 70 72 58 15
63 60 64 93 29	16 50 53 44 84	40 21 95 25 63	43 65 17 70 82	07 20 73 17 90
61 19 69 04 46	26 45 74 77 74	51 92 43 37 29	65 39 45 95 93	42 58 26 05 27
15 47 44 52 66	95 27 07 99 53	59 36 78 38 48	82 39 61 01 18	33 21 15 94 66
94 55 72 85 73	67 89 75 43 87	54 62 24 44 31	91 19 04 25 92	92 92 74 59 73
42 48 11 62 13	97 34 40 87 21	16 86 84 87 67	03 07 11 20 59	25 70 14 66 70
23 52 37 83 17	73 20 88 98 37	68 93 59 14 16	26 25 22 96 63	05 52 28 25 62
04 49 35 24 94	75 24 63 38 24	45 86 25 10 25	61 96 27 93 35	65 33 71 24 72
00 54 99 76 54	64 05 18 81 59	96 11 96 38 96	54 69 28 23 91	23 28 72 95 29
35 96 31 53 07	26 89 80 93 54	33 35 13 54 62	77 97 45 00 24	90 10 33 93 33
59 80 80 83 91	45 42 72 68 42	83 60 94 97 00	13 02 12 48 92	78 56 52 01 06
46 05 88 52 36	01 39 09 22 86	77 28 14 40 77	93 91 08 36 47	70 61 74 29 41
32 17 90 05 97	87 37 92 52 41	05 56 70 70 07	86 74 31 71 57	85 39 41 18 38
69 23 46 14 06	20 11 74 52 04	15 95 66 00 00	18 74 39 24 23	97 11 89 63 38
19 56 54 14 30	01 75 87 53 79	40 41 92 15 85	66 67 43 68 06	84 96 28 52 07
45 15 51 49 38	19 47 60 72 46	43 66 79 45 43	59 04 79 00 33	20 82 66 95 41
94 86 43 19 94	36 16 81 08 51	34 88 88 15 53	01 54 03 54 56	05 01 45 11 76

Continued

Source: The RAND Corporation, *A Million Random Digits*, Free Press, Glencoe, Ill., 1955, pp. 1–3, by permission of the publisher.

Table 1   Random Numbers (Continued)

98 08 62 48 26	45 24 02 84 04	44 99 90 88 96	39 09 47 34 07	35 44 13 18 80
33 18 51 62 32	41 94 15 09 49	89 43 54 85 81	88 69 54 19 94	37 54 87 30 43
80 95 10 04 06	96 38 27 07 74	20 15 12 33 87	25 01 62 52 98	94 62 46 11 71
79 75 24 91 40	71 96 12 82 96	69 86 10 25 91	74 85 22 05 39	00 38 75 95 79
18 63 33 25 37	98 14 50 65 71	31 01 02 46 74	05 45 56 14 27	77 93 89 19 36
74 02 94 39 02	77 55 73 22 70	97 79 01 71 19	52 52 75 80 21	80 81 45 17 48
54 17 84 56 11	80 99 33 71 43	05 33 51 29 69	56 12 71 92 55	36 04 09 03 24
11 66 44 98 83	52 07 98 48 27	59 38 17 15 39	09 97 33 34 40	88 46 12 33 56
48 32 47 79 28	31 24 96 47 10	02 29 53 68 70	32 30 75 75 46	15 02 00 99 94
69 07 49 41 38	87 63 79 19 76	35 58 40 44 01	10 51 82 16 15	01 84 87 69 38
09 18 82 00 97	32 82 53 95 27	04 22 08 63 04	83 38 98 73 74	64 27 85 80 44
90 04 58 54 97	51 98 15 06 54	94 93 88 19 97	91 87 07 61 50	68 47 66 46 59
73 18 95 02 07	47 67 72 52 69	62 29 06 44 64	27 12 46 70 18	41 36 18 27 60
75 76 87 64 90	20 97 18 17 49	90 42 91 22 72	95 37 50 58 71	93 82 34 31 78
54 01 64 40 56	66 28 13 10 03	00 68 22 73 98	20 71 45 32 95	07 70 61 78 13
08 35 86 99 10	78 54 24 27 85	13 66 15 88 73	04 61 89 75 53	31 22 30 84 20
28 30 60 32 64	81 33 31 05 91	40 51 00 78 93	32 60 46 04 75	94 11 90 18 40
53 84 08 62 33	81 59 41 36 28	51 21 59 02 90	28 46 66 87 95	77 76 22 07 91
91 75 75 37 41	61 61 36 22 69	50 26 39 02 12	55 78 17 65 14	83 48 34 70 55
89 41 59 26 94	00 39 75 83 91	12 60 71 76 46	48 94 97 23 06	94 54 13 74 08
77 51 30 38 20	86 83 42 99 01	68 41 48 27 74	51 90 81 39 80	72 89 35 55 07
19 50 23 71 74	69 97 92 02 88	55 21 02 97 73	74 28 77 52 51	65 34 46 74 15
21 81 85 93 13	93 27 88 17 57	05 68 67 31 56	07 08 28 50 46	31 85 33 84 52
51 47 46 64 99	68 10 72 36 21	94 04 99 13 45	42 83 60 91 91	08 00 74 54 49
99 55 96 83 31	62 53 52 41 70	69 77 71 28 30	74 81 97 81 42	43 86 07 28 34
33 71 34 80 07	93 58 47 28 69	51 92 66 47 21	58 30 32 98 22	93 17 49 39 72
85 27 48 68 93	11 30 32 92 70	28 83 43 41 37	73 51 59 04 00	71 14 84 36 43
84 13 38 96 40	44 03 55 21 66	73 85 27 00 91	61 22 26 05 61	62 32 71 84 23
56 73 21 62 34	17 39 59 61 31	10 12 39 16 22	85 49 65 75 60	81 60 41 88 80
65 13 85 68 06	87 64 88 52 61	34 31 36 58 61	45 87 52 10 69	85 64 44 72 77
38 00 10 21 76	81 71 91 17 11	71 60 29 29 37	74 21 96 40 49	65 58 44 96 98
37 40 29 63 97	01 30 47 75 86	56 27 11 00 86	47 32 46 26 05	40 03 03 74 38
97 12 54 03 48	87 08 33 14 17	21 81 53 92 50	75 23 76 20 47	15 50 12 95 78
21 82 64 11 34	47 14 33 40 72	64 63 88 59 02	49 13 90 64 41	03 85 65 45 52
73 13 54 27 42	95 71 90 90 35	85 79 47 42 96	08 78 98 81 56	64 69 11 92 02
07 63 87 79 29	03 06 11 80 72	96 20 74 41 56	23 82 19 95 38	04 71 36 69 94
60 52 88 34 41	07 95 41 98 14	59 17 52 06 95	05 53 35 21 39	61 21 20 64 55
83 59 63 56 55	06 95 89 29 83	05 12 80 97 19	77 43 35 37 83	92 30 15 04 98
10 85 06 27 46	99 59 91 05 07	13 49 90 63 19	53 07 57 18 39	06 41 01 93 62
39 82 09 89 52	43 62 26 31 47	64 42 18 08 14	43 80 00 93 51	31 02 47 31 67

Table 1   Random Numbers (Continued)

```
59 58 00 64 78   75 56 97 88 00   88 83 55 44 86   23 76 80 61 56   04 11 10 84 08
38 50 80 73 41   23 79 34 87 63   90 82 29 70 22   17 71 90 42 07   95 95 44 99 53
30 69 27 06 68   94 68 81 61 27   56 19 68 00 91   82 06 76 34 00   05 46 26 92 00
65 44 39 56 59   18 28 82 74 37   49 63 22 40 41   08 33 76 56 76   96 29 99 08 36
27 26 75 02 64   13 19 27 22 94   07 47 74 46 06   17 98 54 89 11   97 34 13 03 58

91 30 70 69 91   19 07 22 42 10   36 69 95 37 28   28 82 53 57 93   28 97 66 62 52
68 43 49 46 88   84 47 31 36 22   62 12 69 84 08   12 84 38 25 90   09 81 59 31 46
48 90 81 58 77   54 74 52 45 91   35 70 00 47 54   83 82 45 26 92   54 13 05 51 60
06 91 34 51 97   42 67 27 86 01   11 88 30 95 28   63 01 19 89 01   14 97 44 03 44
10 45 51 60 19   14 21 03 37 12   91 34 23 78 21   88 32 58 08 51   43 66 77 08 83

12 88 39 73 43   65 02 76 11 84   04 28 50 13 92   17 97 41 50 77   90 71 22 67 69
21 77 83 09 76   38 80 73 69 61   31 64 94 20 96   63 28 10 20 23   08 81 64 74 49
19 52 35 95 15   65 12 25 96 59   86 28 36 82 58   69 57 21 37 98   16 43 59 15 29
67 24 55 26 70   35 58 31 65 63   79 24 68 66 86   76 46 33 42 22   26 65 59 08 02
60 58 44 73 77   07 50 03 79 92   45 13 42 65 29   26 76 08 36 37   41 32 64 43 44

53 85 34 13 77   36 06 69 48 50   58 83 87 38 59   49 36 47 33 31   96 24 04 36 42
24 63 73 87 36   74 38 48 93 42   52 62 30 79 92   12 36 91 86 01   03 74 28 38 73
83 08 01 24 51   38 99 22 28 15   07 75 95 17 77   97 37 72 75 85   51 97 23 78 67
16 44 42 43 34   36 15 19 90 73   27 49 37 09 39   85 13 03 25 52   54 84 65 47 59
60 79 01 81 57   57 17 86 57 62   11 16 17 85 76   45 81 95 29 79   65 13 00 48 60

03 99 11 04 61   93 71 61 68 94   66 08 32 46 53   84 60 95 82 32   88 61 81 91 61
38 55 59 55 54   32 88 65 97 80   08 35 56 08 60   29 73 54 77 62   71 29 92 38 53
17 54 67 37 04   92 05 24 62 15   55 12 12 92 81   59 07 60 79 36   27 95 45 89 09
32 64 35 28 61   95 81 90 68 31   00 91 19 89 36   76 35 59 37 79   80 86 30 05 14
69 57 26 87 77   39 51 03 59 05   14 06 04 06 19   29 54 96 96 16   33 56 46 07 80

24 12 26 65 91   27 69 90 64 94   14 84 54 66 72   61 95 87 71 00   90 89 97 57 54
61 19 63 02 31   92 96 26 17 73   41 83 95 53 82   17 26 77 09 43   78 03 87 02 67
30 53 22 17 04   10 27 41 22 02   39 68 52 33 09   10 06 16 88 29   55 98 66 64 85
03 78 89 75 99   75 86 72 07 17   74 41 65 31 66   35 20 83 33 74   87 53 90 88 23
48 22 86 33 79   85 78 34 76 19   53 15 26 74 33   35 66 35 29 72   16 81 86 03 11

60 36 59 46 53   35 07 53 39 49   42 61 42 92 97   01 91 82 83 16   98 95 37 32 31
83 79 94 24 02   56 62 33 44 42   34 99 44 13 74   70 07 11 47 36   09 95 81 80 65
32 96 00 74 05   36 40 98 32 32   99 38 54 16 00   11 13 30 75 86   15 91 70 62 53
19 32 25 38 45   57 62 05 26 06   66 49 76 86 46   78 13 86 65 59   19 64 09 94 13
11 22 09 47 47   07 39 93 74 08   48 50 92 39 29   27 48 24 54 76   85 24 43 51 59

31 75 15 72 60   68 98 00 53 39   15 47 04 83 55   88 65 12 25 96   03 15 21 92 21
88 49 29 93 82   14 45 40 45 04   20 09 49 89 77   74 84 39 34 13   22 10 97 85 08
30 93 44 77 44   07 48 18 38 28   73 78 80 65 33   28 59 72 04 05   94 20 52 03 80
22 88 84 88 93   27 49 99 87 48   60 53 04 51 28   74 02 28 46 17   82 03 71 02 68
78 21 21 69 93   35 90 29 13 86   44 37 21 54 86   65 74 11 40 14   87 48 13 72 20
```

Continued

Table 1   Random Numbers (Continued)

```
41 84 98 45 47    46 85 05 23 26    34 67 75 83 00    74 91 06 43 45    19 32 58 15 49
46 35 23 30 49    69 24 89 34 60    45 30 50 75 21    61 31 83 18 55    14 41 37 09 51
11 08 79 62 94    14 01 33 17 92    59 74 76 72 77    76 50 33 45 13    39 66 37 75 44
52 70 10 83 37    56 30 38 73 15    16 52 06 96 76    11 65 49 98 93    02 18 16 81 61
57 27 53 68 98    81 30 44 85 85    68 65 22 73 76    92 85 25 58 66    88 44 80 35 84

20 85 77 31 56    70 28 42 43 26    79 37 59 52 20    01 15 96 32 67    10 62 24 83 91
15 63 38 49 24    90 41 59 36 14    33 52 12 66 65    55 82 34 76 41    86 22 53 17 04
92 69 44 82 97    39 90 40 21 15    59 58 94 90 67    66 82 14 15 75    49 76 70 40 37
77 61 31 90 19    88 15 20 00 80    20 55 49 14 09    96 27 74 82 57    50 81 69 76 16
38 68 83 24 86    45 13 46 35 45    59 40 47 20 59    43 94 75 16 80    43 85 25 96 93

25 16 30 18 89    70 01 41 50 21    41 29 06 73 12    71 85 71 59 57    68 97 11 14 03
65 25 10 76 29    37 23 93 32 95    05 87 00 11 19    92 78 42 63 40    18 47 76 56 22
36 81 54 36 25    18 63 73 75 09    82 44 49 90 05    04 92 17 37 01    14 70 79 39 97
64 39 71 16 92    05 32 78 21 62    20 24 78 17 59    45 19 72 53 32    83 74 52 25 67
04 51 52 56 24    95 09 66 79 46    48 46 08 55 58    15 19 11 87 82    16 93 03 33 61

83 76 16 08 73    43 25 38 41 45    60 83 32 59 83    01 29 14 13 49    20 36 80 71 26
14 38 70 63 45    80 85 40 92 79    43 52 90 63 18    38 38 47 47 61    41 19 63 74 80
51 32 19 22 46    80 08 87 70 74    88 72 25 67 36    66 16 44 94 31    66 91 93 16 78
72 47 20 00 08    80 89 01 80 02    94 81 33 19 00    54 15 58 34 36    35 35 25 41 31
05 46 65 53 06    93 12 81 84 64    74 45 79 05 61    72 84 81 18 34    79 98 26 84 16

39 52 87 24 84    82 47 42 55 93    48 54 53 52 47    18 61 91 36 74    18 61 11 92 41
81 61 61 87 11    53 34 24 42 76    75 12 21 17 24    74 62 77 37 07    58 31 91 59 97
07 58 61 61 20    82 64 12 28 20    92 90 41 31 41    32 39 21 97 63    61 19 96 79 40
90 76 70 42 35    13 57 41 72 00    69 90 26 37 42    78 46 42 25 01    18 62 79 08 72
40 18 82 81 93    29 59 38 86 27    94 97 21 15 98    62 09 53 67 87    00 44 15 89 97

34 41 48 21 57    86 88 75 50 87    19 15 20 00 23    12 30 28 07 83    32 62 46 86 91
63 43 97 53 63    44 98 91 68 22    36 02 40 09 67    76 37 84 16 05    65 96 17 34 88
67 04 90 90 70    93 39 94 55 47    94 45 87 42 84    05 04 14 98 07    20 28 83 40 60
79 49 50 41 46    52 16 29 02 86    54 15 83 42 43    46 97 83 54 82    59 36 29 59 38
91 70 43 05 52    04 73 72 10 31    75 05 19 30 29    47 66 56 43 82    99 78 29 34 78
```

Table 2 Ordinates and Areas of the Standard Normal Curve

z	Area	Ordinate	z	Area	Ordinate	z	Area	Ordinate
.00	.0000	.3989	.50	.1915	.3521	1.00	.3413	.2420
.01	.0040	.3989	.51	.1950	.3503	1.01	.3438	.2396
.02	.0080	.3989	.52	.1985	.3485	1.02	.3461	.2371
.03	.0120	.3988	.53	.2019	.3467	1.03	.3485	.2347
.04	.0160	.3986	.54	.2054	.3448	1.04	.3508	.2323
.05	.0199	.3984	.55	.2088	.3429	1.05	.3531	.2299
.06	.0239	.3982	.56	.2123	.3410	1.06	.3554	.2275
.07	.0279	.3980	.57	.2157	.3391	1.07	.3577	.2251
.08	.0319	.3977	.58	.2190	.3372	1.08	.3599	.2227
.09	.0359	.3973	.59	.2224	.3352	1.09	.3621	.2203
.10	.0398	.3970	.60	.2257	.3332	1.10	.3643	.2179
.11	.0438	.3965	.61	.2291	.3312	1.11	.3665	.2155
.12	.0478	.3961	.62	.2324	.3292	1.12	.3686	.2131
.13	.0517	.3956	.63	.2357	.3271	1.13	.3708	.2107
.14	.0557	.3951	.64	.2389	.3251	1.14	.3729	.2083
.15	.0596	.3945	.65	.2422	.3230	1.15	.3749	.2059
.16	.0636	.3939	.66	.2454	.3209	1.16	.3770	.2036
.17	.0675	.3932	.67	.2486	.3187	1.17	.3790	.2012
.18	.0714	.3925	.68	.2517	.3166	1.18	.3810	.1989
.19	.0753	.3918	.69	.2549	.3144	1.19	.3830	.1965
.20	.0793	.3910	.70	.2580	.3123	1.20	.3849	.1942
.21	.0832	.3902	.71	.2611	.3101	1.21	.3869	.1919
.22	.0871	.3894	.72	.2642	.3079	1.22	.3888	.1895
.23	.0910	.3885	.73	.2673	.3056	1.23	.3907	.1872
.24	.0948	.3876	.74	.2703	.3034	1.24	.3925	.1849
.25	.0987	.3867	.75	.2734	.3011	1.25	.3944	.1826
.26	.1026	.3857	.76	.2764	.2989	1.26	.3962	.1804
.27	.1064	.3847	.77	.2794	.2966	1.27	.3980	.1781
.28	.1103	.3836	.78	.2823	.2943	1.28	.3997	.1758
.29	.1141	.3825	.79	.2852	.2920	1.29	.4015	.1736
.30	.1179	.3814	.80	.2881	.2897	1.30	.4032	.1714
.31	.1217	.3802	.81	.2910	.2874	1.31	.4049	.1691
.32	.1255	.3790	.82	.2939	.2850	1.32	.4066	.1669
.33	.1293	.3778	.83	.2967	.2827	1.33	.4082	.1647
.34	.1331	.3765	.84	.2995	.2803	1.34	.4099	.1626
.35	.1368	.3752	.85	.3023	.2780	1.35	.4115	.1604
.36	.1406	.3739	.86	.3051	.2756	1.36	.4131	.1582
.37	.1443	.3725	.87	.3078	.2732	1.37	.4147	.1561
.38	.1480	.3712	.88	.3106	.2709	1.38	.4162	.1539
.39	.1517	.3697	.89	.3133	.2685	1.39	.4177	.1518
.40	.1554	.3683	.90	.3159	.2661	1.40	.4192	.1497
.41	.1591	.3668	.91	.3186	.2637	1.41	.4207	.1476
.42	.1628	.3653	.92	.3212	.2613	1.42	.4222	.1456
.43	.1664	.3637	.93	.3238	.2589	1.43	.4236	.1435
.44	.1700	.3621	.94	.3264	.2565	1.44	.4251	.1415
.45	.1736	.3605	.95	.3289	.2541	1.45	.4265	.1394
.46	.1772	.3589	.96	.3315	.2516	1.46	.4279	.1374
.47	.1808	.3572	.97	.3340	.2492	1.47	.4292	.1354
.48	.1844	.3555	.98	.3365	.2468	1.48	.4306	.1334
.49	.1879	.3538	.99	.3389	.2444	1.49	.4319	.1315
.50	.1915	.3521	1.00	.3413	.2420	1.50	.4332	.1295

Continued

Table 2   Ordinates and Areas of the Standard Normal Curve (Continued)

z	Area	Ordinate	z	Area	Ordinate	z	Area	Ordinate
1.50	.4332	.1295	2.00	.4772	.0540	2.50	.4938	.0175
1.51	.4345	.1276	2.01	.4778	.0529	2.51	.4940	.0171
1.52	.4357	.1257	2.02	.4783	.0519	2.52	.4941	.0167
1.53	.4370	.1238	2.03	.4788	.0508	2.53	.4943	.0163
1.54	.4382	.1219	2.04	.4793	.0498	2.54	.4945	.0158
1.55	.4394	.1200	2.05	.4798	.0488	2.55	.4946	.0154
1.56	.4406	.1182	2.06	.4803	.0478	2.56	.4948	.0151
1.57	.4418	.1163	2.07	.4808	.0468	2.57	.4949	.0147
1.58	.4429	.1145	2.08	.4812	.0459	2.58	.4951	.0143
1.59	.4441	.1127	2.09	.4817	.0449	2.59	.4952	.0139
1.60	.4452	.1109	2.10	.4821	.0440	2.60	.4953	.0136
1.61	.4463	.1092	2.11	.4826	.0431	2.61	.4955	.0132
1.62	.4474	.1074	2.12	.4830	.0422	2.62	.4956	.0129
1.63	.4484	.1057	2.13	.4834	.0413	2.63	.4957	.0126
1.64	.4495	.1040	2.14	.4838	.0404	2.64	.4959	.0122
1.65	.4505	.1023	2.15	.4842	.0395	2.65	.4960	.0119
1.66	.4515	.1006	2.16	.4846	.0387	2.66	.4961	.0116
1.67	.4525	.0989	2.17	.4850	.0379	2.67	.4962	.0113
1.68	.4535	.0973	2.18	.4854	.0371	2.68	.4963	.0110
1.69	.4545	.0957	2.19	.4857	.0363	2.69	.4964	.0107
1.70	.4554	.0940	2.20	.4861	.0355	2.70	.4965	.0104
1.71	.4564	.0925	2.21	.4864	.0347	2.71	.4966	.0101
1.72	.4573	.0909	2.22	.4868	.0339	2.72	.4967	.0099
1.73	.4582	.0893	2.23	.4871	.0332	2.73	.4968	.0096
1.74	.4591	.0878	2.24	.4875	.0325	2.74	.4969	.0093
1.75	.4599	.0863	2.25	.4878	.0317	2.75	.4970	.0091
1.76	.4608	.0848	2.26	.4881	.0310	2.76	.4971	.0088
1.77	.4616	.0833	2.27	.4884	.0303	2.77	.4972	.0086
1.78	.4625	.0818	2.28	.4887	.0297	2.78	.4973	.0084
1.79	.4633	.0804	2.29	.4890	.0290	2.79	.4974	.0081
1.80	.4641	.0790	2.30	.4893	.0283	2.80	.4974	.0079
1.81	.4649	.0775	2.31	.4896	.0277	2.81	.4975	.0077
1.82	.4656	.0761	2.32	.4898	.0270	2.82	.4976	.0075
1.83	.4664	.0748	2.33	.4901	.0264	2.83	.4977	.0073
1.84	.4671	.0734	2.34	.4904	.0258	2.84	.4977	.0071
1.85	.4678	.0721	2.35	.4906	.0252	2.85	.4978	.0069
1.86	.4686	.0707	2.36	.4909	.0246	2.86	.4979	.0067
1.87	.4693	.0694	2.37	.4911	.0241	2.87	.4979	.0065
1.88	.4699	.0681	2.38	.4913	.0235	2.88	.4980	.0063
1.89	.4706	.0669	2.39	.4916	.0229	2.89	.4981	.0061
1.90	.4713	.0656	2.40	.4918	.0224	2.90	.4981	.0060
1.91	.4719	.0644	2.41	.4920	.0219	2.91	.4982	.0058
1.92	.4726	.0632	2.42	.4922	.0213	2.92	.4982	.0056
1.93	.4732	.0620	2.43	.4925	.0208	2.93	.4983	.0055
1.94	.4738	.0608	2.44	.4927	.0203	2.94	.4984	.0053
1.95	.4744	.0596	2.45	.4929	.0198	2.95	.4984	.0051
1.96	.4750	.0584	2.46	.4931	.0194	2.96	.4985	.0050
1.97	.4756	.0573	2.47	.4932	.0189	2.97	.4985	.0048
1.98	.4761	.0562	2.48	.4934	.0184	2.98	.4986	.0047
1.99	.4767	.0551	2.49	.4936	.0180	2.99	.4986	.0046
2.00	.4772	.0540	2.50	.4938	.0175	3.00	.4987	.0044

Table 3 Percentile Values of the Chi-square Distribution

ν	$\chi^2_{.005}$	$\chi^2_{.01}$	$\chi^2_{.02}$	$\chi^2_{.025}$	$\chi^2_{.05}$	$\chi^2_{.10}$	$\chi^2_{.25}$	$\chi^2_{.50}$	$\chi^2_{.75}$	$\chi^2_{.90}$	$\chi^2_{.95}$	$\chi^2_{.975}$	$\chi^2_{.98}$	$\chi^2_{.99}$	$\chi^2_{.995}$	$\chi^2_{.999}$
1	—	—	—	—	—	.02	.10	.46	1.3	2.7	3.8	5.0	5.4	6.6	7.9	10.8
2	.01	.02	.04	.05	.10	.21	.58	1.4	2.8	4.6	6.0	7.4	7.8	9.2	10.6	13.8
3	.07	.11	.18	.22	.35	.58	1.21	2.4	4.1	6.3	7.8	9.4	9.8	11.3	12.8	16.3
4	.21	.30	.43	.48	.71	1.1	1.92	3.4	5.4	7.8	9.5	11.1	11.7	13.3	14.9	18.5
5	.41	.55	.75	.83	1.1	1.6	2.7	4.4	6.6	9.2	11.1	12.8	13.4	15.1	16.7	20.5
6	.68	.87	1.13	1.2	1.6	2.2	3.5	5.4	7.8	10.6	12.6	14.4	15.0	16.8	18.5	22.5
7	.99	1.24	1.56	1.7	2.2	2.8	4.3	6.4	9.0	12.0	14.1	16.0	16.6	18.5	20.3	24.3
8	1.3	1.65	2.03	2.2	2.7	3.5	5.1	7.3	10.2	13.4	15.5	17.5	18.2	20.1	22.0	26.1
9	1.7	2.09	2.53	2.7	3.3	4.2	5.9	8.3	11.4	14.7	16.9	19.0	19.7	21.7	23.6	27.9
10	2.2	2.55	3.06	3.2	3.9	4.9	6.7	9.3	12.5	16.0	18.3	20.5	21.2	23.2	25.2	29.6
11	2.6	3.05	3.61	3.8	4.6	5.6	7.6	10.3	13.7	17.3	19.7	21.9	22.6	24.7	26.8	31.3
12	3.1	3.57	4.18	4.4	5.2	6.3	8.4	11.3	14.8	18.5	21.0	23.3	24.1	26.2	28.3	32.9
13	3.6	4.11	4.76	5.0	5.9	7.0	9.3	12.3	16.0	19.8	22.4	24.7	25.5	27.7	29.8	34.5
14	4.1	4.66	5.37	5.6	6.6	7.8	10.2	13.3	17.1	21.1	23.7	26.1	26.9	29.1	31.3	36.1
15	4.6	5.23	5.98	6.3	7.3	8.5	11.0	14.3	18.2	22.3	25.0	27.5	28.3	30.6	32.8	37.7
16	5.1	5.81	6.61	6.9	8.0	9.3	11.9	15.3	19.4	23.5	26.3	28.8	29.6	32.0	34.3	39.3
17	5.7	6.41	7.26	7.6	8.7	10.1	12.8	16.3	20.5	24.8	27.6	30.2	31.0	33.4	35.7	40.8
18	6.3	7.02	7.91	8.2	9.4	10.9	13.7	17.3	21.6	26.0	28.9	31.5	32.3	34.8	37.2	42.3
19	6.9	7.63	8.57	8.9	10.1	11.7	14.6	18.3	22.7	27.2	30.1	32.9	33.7	36.2	38.6	43.8
20	7.4	8.26	9.24	9.6	10.9	12.4	15.5	19.3	23.8	28.4	31.4	34.2	35.0	37.6	40.0	45.3
21	8.0	8.9	9.9	10.3	11.6	13.2	16.3	20.3	24.9	29.6	32.7	35.5	36.3	38.9	41.4	46.8
22	8.6	9.5	10.6	11.0	12.3	14.0	17.2	21.3	26.0	30.8	33.9	36.8	37.7	40.3	42.8	48.3
23	9.3	10.2	11.3	11.7	13.1	14.8	18.1	22.3	27.1	32.0	35.2	38.1	39.0	41.6	44.2	49.7
24	9.9	10.9	12.0	12.4	13.8	15.7	19.0	23.3	28.2	33.2	36.4	39.4	40.3	43.0	45.6	51.2
25	10.5	11.5	12.7	13.1	14.6	16.5	19.9	24.3	29.3	34.4	37.7	40.6	41.6	44.3	46.9	52.6
26	11.2	12.2	13.4	13.8	15.4	17.3	20.8	25.3	30.4	35.6	38.9	41.9	42.9	45.6	48.3	54.0
27	11.8	12.9	14.1	14.6	16.2	18.1	21.7	26.3	31.5	36.7	40.1	43.2	44.1	47.0	49.6	55.5
28	12.5	13.6	14.8	15.3	16.9	18.9	22.7	27.3	32.6	37.9	41.3	44.5	45.4	48.3	51.0	56.9
29	13.1	14.3	15.6	16.0	17.7	19.8	23.6	28.3	33.7	39.1	42.6	45.7	46.7	49.6	52.3	58.3
30	13.8	15.0	16.3	16.8	18.5	20.6	24.5	29.3	34.8	40.3	43.8	47.0	48.0	50.9	53.7	59.7
40	20.7	22.2	23.8	24.4	26.5	29.1	33.7	39.3	45.6	51.8	55.8	59.3	60.4	63.7	66.8	73.5
60	35.5	37.5	39.7	40.5	43.2	46.5	52.3	59.3	67.0	74.4	79.1	83.3	84.6	88.4	92.0	99.7
100	67.3	70.0	73.1	74.2	77.9	82.4	90.1	99.3	109.1	118.5	124.3	129.6	131.1	135.8	140.2	149.5

Source: Abridged from table in *Biometrika,* Vol. 32 (1941), and published with the permission of the author, Catherine M. Thompson, and the editor of *Biometrika.* Columns $\chi^2_{.02}$, $\chi^2_{.98}$, and $\chi^2_{.999}$ are reprinted abridged from R. A. Fisher and F. Yates, *Statistical Tables for Biological, Agricultural, and Medical Research,* published by Oliver & Boyd Ltd., Edinburgh, 1963, by permission of the publishers.

Table 4 Percentile Values of "Student's" Distribution

ν	$t_{.75}$	$t_{.80}$	$t_{.90}$	$t_{.95}$	$t_{.975}$	$t_{.99}$	$t_{.995}$	$t_{.9995}$	ν
1	1.00	1.38	3.08	6.31	12.71	31.82	63.66	636.62	1
2	.82	1.06	1.89	2.92	4.30	6.96	9.92	31.60	2
3	.76	.98	1.64	2.35	3.18	4.54	5.84	12.94	3
4	.74	.94	1.53	2.13	2.78	3.75	4.60	8.61	4
5	.73	.92	1.48	2.02	2.57	3.36	4.03	6.86	5
6	.72	.91	1.44	1.94	2.45	3.14	3.71	5.96	6
7	.71	.90	1.42	1.89	2.36	3.00	3.50	5.40	7
8	.71	.89	1.40	1.86	2.31	2.90	3.36	5.04	8
9	.70	.88	1.38	1.83	2.26	2.82	3.25	4.78	9
10	.70	.88	1.37	1.81	2.23	2.76	3.17	4.59	10
11	.70	.88	1.36	1.80	2.20	2.72	3.11	4.44	11
12	.70	.87	1.36	1.78	2.18	2.68	3.05	4.32	12
13	.69	.87	1.35	1.77	2.16	2.65	3.01	4.22	13
14	.69	.87	1.34	1.76	2.14	2.62	2.98	4.14	14
15	.69	.87	1.34	1.75	2.13	2.60	2.95	4.07	15
16	.69	.87	1.34	1.75	2.12	2.58	2.92	4.02	16
17	.69	.86	1.33	1.74	2.11	2.57	2.90	3.96	17
18	.69	.86	1.33	1.73	2.10	2.55	2.88	3.92	18
19	.69	.86	1.33	1.73	2.09	2.54	2.86	3.88	19
20	.69	.86	1.32	1.72	2.09	2.53	2.85	3.85	20
21	.69	.86	1.32	1.72	2.08	2.52	2.83	3.82	21
22	.69	.86	1.32	1.72	2.07	2.51	2.82	3.79	22
23	.69	.86	1.32	1.71	2.07	2.50	2.81	3.77	23
24	.68	.86	1.32	1.71	2.06	2.49	2.80	3.74	24
25	.68	.86	1.32	1.71	2.06	2.48	2.79	3.72	25
26	.68	.86	1.32	1.71	2.06	2.48	2.78	3.71	26
27	.68	.86	1.31	1.70	2.05	2.47	2.77	3.69	27
28	.68	.85	1.31	1.70	2.05	2.47	2.76	3.67	28
29	.68	.85	1.31	1.70	2.04	2.46	2.76	3.66	29
30	.68	.85	1.31	1.70	2.04	2.46	2.75	3.65	30
40	.68	.85	1.30	1.68	2.02	2.42	2.70	3.55	40
60	.68	.85	1.30	1.67	2.00	2.39	2.66	3.46	60
120	.68	.85	1.29	1.66	1.98	2.36	2.62	3.37	120
∞	.6745	.842	1.282	1.645	1.960	2.326	2.576	3.291	∞
	$-t_{.25}$	$-t_{.20}$	$-t_{.10}$	$-t_{.05}$	$-t_{.025}$	$-t_{.01}$	$-t_{.005}$	$-t_{.0005}$	

Source: Reprinted abridged from R. A. Fisher and F. Yates, *Statistical Tables for Biological, Agricultural, and Medical Research,* published by Oliver & Boyd Ltd., Edinburgh, 1963, by permission of the authors and publishers.

Table 5 99th and 95 Percentile Values of the *F* Distribution

95th Percentile in Lightface Type; 99th Percentile in Boldface Type;
ν_1 = Degrees of Freedom for Numerator

ν_2	1	2	3	4	5	6	7	8	9	10	11	12
1	161	200	216	225	230	234	237	239	241	242	243	244
	4,052	**4,999**	**5,403**	**5,625**	**5,764**	**5,859**	**5,928**	**5,981**	**6,022**	**6,056**	**6,082**	**6,106**
2	18.51	19.00	19.16	19.25	19.30	19.33	19.36	19.37	19.38	19.39	19.40	19.41
	98.49	**99.01**	**99.17**	**99.25**	**99.30**	**99.33**	**99.34**	**99.36**	**99.38**	**99.40**	**99.41**	**99.42**
3	10.13	9.55	9.28	9.12	9.01	8.94	8.88	8.84	8.81	8.78	8.76	8.74
	34.12	**30.81**	**29.46**	**28.71**	**28.24**	**27.91**	**27.67**	**27.49**	**27.34**	**27.23**	**27.13**	**27.05**
4	7.71	6.94	6.59	6.39	6.26	6.16	6.09	6.04	6.00	5.96	5.93	5.91
	21.20	**18.00**	**16.69**	**15.98**	**15.52**	**15.21**	**14.98**	**14.80**	**14.66**	**14.54**	**14.45**	**14.37**
5	6.61	5.79	5.41	5.19	5.05	4.95	4.88	4.82	4.78	4.74	4.70	4.68
	16.26	**13.27**	**12.06**	**11.39**	**10.97**	**10.67**	**10.45**	**10.27**	**10.15**	**10.05**	**9.96**	**9.89**
6	5.99	5.14	4.76	4.53	4.39	4.28	4.21	4.15	4.10	4.06	4.03	4.00
	13.74	**10.92**	**9.78**	**9.15**	**8.75**	**8.47**	**8.26**	**8.10**	**7.98**	**7.87**	**7.79**	**7.72**
7	5.59	4.74	4.35	4.12	3.97	3.87	3.79	3.73	3.68	3.63	3.60	3.57
	12.25	**9.55**	**8.45**	**7.85**	**7.46**	**7.19**	**7.00**	**6.84**	**6.71**	**6.62**	**6.54**	**6.47**
8	5.32	4.46	4.07	3.84	3.69	3.58	3.50	3.44	3.39	3.34	3.31	3.28
	11.26	**8.65**	**7.59**	**7.01**	**6.63**	**6.37**	**6.19**	**6.03**	**5.91**	**5.82**	**5.74**	**5.67**
9	5.12	4.26	3.86	3.63	3.48	3.37	3.29	3.23	3.18	3.13	3.10	3.07
	10.56	**8.02**	**6.99**	**6.42**	**6.06**	**5.80**	**5.62**	**5.47**	**5.35**	**5.26**	**5.18**	**5.11**
10	4.96	4.10	3.71	3.48	3.33	3.22	3.14	3.07	3.02	2.97	2.94	2.91
	10.04	**7.56**	**6.55**	**5.99**	**5.64**	**5.39**	**5.21**	**5.06**	**4.95**	**4.85**	**4.78**	**4.71**
11	4.84	3.98	3.59	3.36	3.20	3.09	3.01	2.95	2.90	2.86	2.82	2.79
	9.65	**7.20**	**6.22**	**5.67**	**5.32**	**5.07**	**4.88**	**4.74**	**4.63**	**4.54**	**4.46**	**4.40**
12	4.75	3.88	3.49	3.26	3.11	3.00	2.92	2.85	2.80	2.76	2.72	2.69
	9.33	**6.93**	**5.95**	**5.41**	**5.06**	**4.82**	**4.65**	**4.50**	**4.39**	**4.30**	**4.22**	**4.16**
13	4.67	3.80	3.41	3.18	3.02	2.92	2.84	2.77	2.72	2.67	2.63	2.60
	9.07	**6.70**	**5.74**	**5.20**	**4.86**	**4.62**	**4.44**	**4.30**	**4.19**	**4.10**	**4.02**	**3.96**
14	4.60	3.74	3.34	3.11	2.96	2.85	2.77	2.70	2.65	2.60	2.56	2.53
	8.86	**6.51**	**5.56**	**5.03**	**4.69**	**4.46**	**4.28**	**4.14**	**4.03**	**3.94**	**3.86**	**3.80**
15	4.54	3.68	3.29	3.06	2.90	2.79	2.70	2.64	2.59	2.55	2.51	2.48
	8.68	**6.36**	**5.42**	**4.89**	**4.56**	**4.32**	**4.14**	**4.00**	**3.89**	**3.80**	**3.73**	**3.67**
16	4.49	3.63	3.24	3.01	2.85	2.74	2.66	2.59	2.54	2.49	2.45	2.42
	8.53	**6.23**	**5.29**	**4.77**	**4.44**	**4.20**	**4.03**	**3.89**	**3.78**	**3.69**	**3.61**	**3.55**
17	4.45	3.59	3.20	2.96	2.81	2.70	2.62	2.55	2.50	2.45	2.41	2.38
	8.40	**6.11**	**5.18**	**4.67**	**4.34**	**4.10**	**3.93**	**3.79**	**3.68**	**3.59**	**3.52**	**3.45**
18	4.41	3.55	3.16	2.93	2.77	2.66	2.58	2.51	2.46	2.41	2.37	2.34
	8.28	**6.01**	**5.09**	**4.58**	**4.25**	**4.01**	**3.85**	**3.71**	**3.60**	**3.51**	**3.44**	**3.37**
19	4.38	3.52	3.13	2.90	2.74	2.63	2.55	2.48	2.43	2.38	2.34	2.31
	8.18	**5.93**	**5.01**	**4.50**	**4.17**	**3.94**	**3.77**	**3.63**	**3.52**	**3.43**	**3.36**	**3.30**
20	4.35	3.49	3.10	2.87	2.71	2.60	2.52	2.45	2.40	2.35	2.31	2.28
	8.10	**5.85**	**4.94**	**4.43**	**4.10**	**3.87**	**3.71**	**3.56**	**3.45**	**3.37**	**3.30**	**3.23**
21	4.32	3.47	3.07	2.84	2.68	2.57	2.49	2.42	2.37	2.32	2.28	2.25
	8.02	**5.78**	**4.87**	**4.37**	**4.04**	**3.81**	**3.65**	**3.51**	**3.40**	**3.31**	**3.24**	**3.17**
22	4.30	3.44	3.05	2.82	2.66	2.55	2.47	2.40	2.35	2.30	2.26	2.23
	7.94	**5.72**	**4.82**	**4.31**	**3.99**	**3.76**	**3.59**	**3.45**	**3.35**	**3.26**	**3.18**	**3.12**
23	4.28	3.42	3.03	2.80	2.64	2.53	2.45	2.38	2.32	2.28	2.24	2.20
	7.88	**5.66**	**4.76**	**4.26**	**3.94**	**3.71**	**3.54**	**3.41**	**3.30**	**3.21**	**3.14**	**3.07**
24	4.26	3.40	3.01	2.78	2.62	2.51	2.43	2.36	2.30	2.26	2.22	2.18
	7.82	**5.61**	**4.72**	**4.22**	**3.90**	**3.67**	**3.50**	**3.36**	**3.25**	**3.17**	**3.09**	**3.03**
25	4.24	3.38	2.99	2.76	2.60	2.49	2.41	2.34	2.28	2.24	2.20	2.16
	7.77	**5.57**	**4.68**	**4.18**	**3.86**	**3.63**	**3.46**	**3.32**	**3.21**	**3.13**	**3.05**	**2.99**
26	4.22	3.37	2.98	2.74	2.59	2.47	2.39	2.32	2.27	2.22	2.18	2.15
	7.72	**5.53**	**4.64**	**4.14**	**3.82**	**3.59**	**3.42**	**3.29**	**3.17**	**3.09**	**3.02**	**2.96**

ν_2 = degrees of freedom for denominator

Continued

Source: From *Statistical Methods,* 6th edition, by George W. Snedecor and William G. Cochran, © 1967, the Iowa State University Press, Ames, Iowa, by permission of the publisher.

Table 5 99th and 95 Percentile Values of the *F* Distribution (Continued)

95th Percentile in Lightface Type; 99th Percentile in Boldface Type;
ν_1 = Degrees of Freedom for Numerator

14	16	20	24	30	40	50	75	100	200	500	∞	ν_2
245	246	248	249	250	251	252	253	253	254	254	254	1
6,142	**6,169**	**6,208**	**6,234**	**6,258**	**6,286**	**6,302**	**6,323**	**6,334**	**6,352**	**6,361**	**6,366**	
19.42	19.43	19.44	19.45	19.46	19.47	19.47	19.48	19.49	19.49	19.50	19.50	2
99.43	**99.44**	**99.45**	**99.46**	**99.47**	**99.48**	**99.48**	**99.49**	**99.49**	**99.49**	**99.50**	**99.50**	
8.71	8.69	8.66	8.64	8.62	8.60	8.58	8.57	8.56	8.54	8.54	8.53	3
26.92	**26.83**	**26.69**	**26.60**	**26.50**	**26.41**	**26.35**	**26.27**	**26.23**	**26.18**	**26.14**	**26.12**	
5.87	5.84	5.80	5.77	5.74	5.71	5.70	5.68	5.66	5.65	5.64	5.63	4
14.24	**14.15**	**14.02**	**13.93**	**13.83**	**13.74**	**13.69**	**13.61**	**13.57**	**13.52**	**13.48**	**13.46**	
4.64	4.60	4.56	4.53	4.50	4.46	4.44	4.42	4.40	4.38	4.37	4.36	5
9.77	**9.68**	**9.55**	**9.47**	**9.38**	**9.29**	**9.24**	**9.17**	**9.13**	**9.07**	**9.04**	**9.02**	
3.96	3.92	3.87	3.84	3.81	3.77	3.75	3.72	3.71	3.69	3.68	3.67	6
7.60	**7.52**	**7.39**	**7.31**	**7.23**	**7.14**	**7.09**	**7.02**	**6.99**	**6.94**	**6.90**	**6.88**	
3.52	3.49	3.44	3.41	3.38	3.34	3.32	3.29	3.28	3.25	3.24	3.23	7
6.35	**6.27**	**6.15**	**6.07**	**5.98**	**5.90**	**5.85**	**5.78**	**5.75**	**5.70**	**5.67**	**5.65**	
3.23	3.20	3.15	3.12	3.08	3.05	3.03	3.00	2.98	2.96	2.94	2.93	8
5.56	**5.48**	**5.36**	**5.28**	**5.20**	**5.11**	**5.06**	**5.00**	**4.96**	**4.91**	**4.88**	**4.86**	
3.02	2.98	2.93	2.90	2.86	2.82	2.80	2.77	2.76	2.73	2.72	2.71	9
5.00	**4.92**	**4.80**	**4.73**	**4.64**	**4.56**	**4.51**	**4.45**	**4.41**	**4.36**	**4.33**	**4.31**	
2.86	2.82	2.77	2.74	2.70	2.67	2.64	2.61	2.59	2.56	2.55	2.54	10
4.60	**4.52**	**4.41**	**4.33**	**4.25**	**4.17**	**4.12**	**4.05**	**4.01**	**3.96**	**3.93**	**3.91**	
2.74	2.70	2.65	2.61	2.57	2.53	2.50	2.47	2.45	2.42	2.41	2.40	11
4.29	**4.21**	**4.10**	**4.02**	**3.94**	**3.86**	**3.80**	**3.74**	**3.70**	**3.66**	**3.62**	**3.60**	
2.64	2.60	2.54	2.50	2.46	2.42	2.40	2.36	2.35	2.32	2.31	2.30	12
4.05	**3.98**	**3.86**	**3.78**	**3.70**	**3.61**	**3.56**	**3.49**	**3.46**	**3.41**	**3.38**	**3.36**	
2.55	2.51	2.46	2.42	2.38	2.34	2.32	2.28	2.26	2.24	2.22	2.21	13
3.85	**3.78**	**3.67**	**3.59**	**3.51**	**3.42**	**3.37**	**3.30**	**3.27**	**3.21**	**3.18**	**3.16**	
2.48	2.44	2.39	2.35	2.31	2.27	2.24	2.21	2.19	2.16	2.14	2.13	14
3.70	**3.62**	**3.51**	**3.43**	**3.34**	**3.26**	**3.21**	**3.14**	**3.11**	**3.06**	**3.02**	**3.00**	
2.43	2.39	2.33	2.29	2.25	2.21	2.18	2.15	2.12	2.10	2.08	2.07	15
3.56	**3.48**	**3.36**	**3.29**	**3.20**	**3.12**	**3.07**	**3.00**	**2.97**	**2.92**	**2.89**	**2.87**	
2.37	2.33	2.28	2.24	2.20	2.16	2.13	2.09	2.07	2.04	2.02	2.01	16
3.45	**3.37**	**3.25**	**3.18**	**3.10**	**3.01**	**2.96**	**2.89**	**2.86**	**2.80**	**2.77**	**2.75**	
2.33	2.29	2.23	2.19	2.15	2.11	2.08	2.04	2.02	1.99	1.97	1.96	17
3.35	**3.27**	**3.16**	**3.08**	**3.00**	**2.92**	**2.86**	**2.79**	**2.76**	**2.70**	**2.67**	**2.65**	
2.29	2.25	2.19	2.15	2.11	2.07	2.04	2.00	1.98	1.95	1.93	1.92	18
3.27	**3.19**	**3.07**	**3.00**	**2.91**	**2.83**	**2.78**	**2.71**	**2.68**	**2.62**	**2.59**	**2.57**	
2.26	2.21	2.15	2.11	2.07	2.02	2.00	1.96	1.94	1.91	1.90	1.88	19
3.19	**3.12**	**3.00**	**2.92**	**2.84**	**2.76**	**2.70**	**2.63**	**2.60**	**2.54**	**2.51**	**2.49**	
2.23	2.18	2.12	2.08	2.04	1.99	1.96	1.92	1.90	1.87	1.85	1.84	20
3.13	**3.05**	**2.94**	**2.86**	**2.77**	**2.69**	**2.63**	**2.56**	**2.53**	**2.47**	**2.44**	**2.42**	
2.20	2.15	2.09	2.05	2.00	1.96	1.93	1.89	1.87	1.84	1.82	1.81	21
3.07	**2.99**	**2.88**	**2.80**	**2.72**	**2.63**	**2.58**	**2.51**	**2.47**	**2.42**	**2.38**	**2.36**	
2.18	2.13	2.07	2.03	1.98	1.93	1.91	1.87	1.84	1.81	1.80	1.78	22
3.02	**2.94**	**2.83**	**2.75**	**2.67**	**2.58**	**2.53**	**2.46**	**2.42**	**2.37**	**2.33**	**2.31**	
2.14	2.10	2.04	2.00	1.96	1.91	1.88	1.84	1.82	1.79	1.77	1.76	23
2.97	**2.89**	**2.78**	**2.70**	**2.62**	**2.53**	**2.48**	**2.41**	**2.37**	**2.32**	**2.28**	**2.26**	
2.13	2.09	2.02	1.98	1.94	1.89	1.86	1.82	1.80	1.76	1.74	1.73	24
2.93	**2.85**	**2.74**	**2.66**	**2.58**	**2.49**	**2.44**	**2.36**	**2.33**	**2.27**	**2.23**	**2.21**	
2.11	2.06	2.00	1.96	1.92	1.87	1.84	1.80	1.77	1.74	1.72	1.71	25
2.89	**2.81**	**2.70**	**2.62**	**2.54**	**2.45**	**2.40**	**2.32**	**2.29**	**2.23**	**2.19**	**2.17**	
2.10	2.05	1.99	1.95	1.90	1.85	1.82	1.78	1.76	1.72	1.70	1.69	26
2.86	**2.77**	**2.66**	**2.58**	**2.50**	**2.41**	**2.36**	**2.28**	**2.25**	**2.19**	**2.15**	**2.13**	

ν_2 = degrees of freedom for denominator

Table 5   99th and 95 Percentile Values of the *F* Distribution (Continued)

95th Percentile in Lightface Type; 99th Percentile in Boldface Type;
ν_1 = Degrees of Freedom for Numerator

ν_2 = degrees of freedom for denominator

ν_2	1	2	3	4	5	6	7	8	9	10	11	12
27	4.21	3.35	2.96	2.73	2.57	2.46	2.37	2.30	2.25	2.20	2.16	2.13
	7.68	**5.49**	**4.60**	**4.11**	**3.79**	**3.56**	**3.39**	**3.26**	**3.14**	**3.06**	**2.98**	**2.93**
28	4.20	3.34	2.95	2.71	2.56	2.44	2.36	2.29	2.24	2.19	2.15	2.12
	7.64	**5.45**	**4.57**	**4.07**	**3.76**	**3.53**	**3.36**	**3.23**	**3.11**	**3.03**	**2.95**	**2.90**
29	4.18	3.33	2.93	2.70	2.54	2.43	2.35	2.28	2.22	2.18	2.14	2.10
	7.60	**5.42**	**4.54**	**4.04**	**3.73**	**3.50**	**3.33**	**3.20**	**3.08**	**3.00**	**2.92**	**2.87**
30	4.17	3.32	2.92	2.69	2.53	2.42	2.34	2.27	2.21	2.16	2.12	2.09
	7.56	**5.39**	**4.51**	**4.02**	**3.70**	**3.47**	**3.30**	**3.17**	**3.06**	**2.98**	**2.90**	**2.84**
32	4.15	3.30	2.90	2.67	2.51	2.40	2.32	2.25	2.19	2.14	2.10	2.07
	7.50	**5.34**	**4.46**	**3.97**	**3.66**	**3.42**	**3.25**	**3.12**	**3.01**	**2.94**	**2.86**	**2.80**
34	4.13	3.28	2.88	2.65	2.49	2.38	2.30	2.23	2.17	2.12	2.08	2.05
	7.44	**5.29**	**4.42**	**3.93**	**3.61**	**3.38**	**3.21**	**3.08**	**2.97**	**2.89**	**2.82**	**2.76**
36	4.11	3.26	2.86	2.63	2.48	2.36	2.28	2.21	2.15	2.10	2.06	2.03
	7.39	**5.25**	**4.38**	**3.89**	**3.58**	**3.35**	**3.18**	**3.04**	**2.94**	**2.86**	**2.78**	**2.72**
38	4.10	3.25	2.85	2.62	2.46	2.35	2.26	2.19	2.14	2.09	2.05	2.02
	7.35	**5.21**	**4.34**	**3.86**	**3.54**	**3.32**	**3.15**	**3.02**	**2.91**	**2.82**	**2.75**	**2.69**
40	4.08	3.23	2.84	2.61	2.45	2.34	2.25	2.18	2.12	2.07	2.04	2.00
	7.31	**5.18**	**4.31**	**3.83**	**3.51**	**3.29**	**3.12**	**2.99**	**2.88**	**2.80**	**2.73**	**2.66**
42	4.07	3.22	2.83	2.59	2.44	2.32	2.24	2.17	2.11	2.06	2.02	1.99
	7.27	**5.15**	**4.29**	**3.80**	**3.49**	**3.26**	**3.10**	**2.96**	**2.86**	**2.77**	**2.70**	**2.64**
44	4.06	3.21	2.82	2.58	2.43	2.31	2.23	2.16	2.10	2.05	2.01	1.98
	7.24	**5.12**	**4.26**	**3.78**	**3.46**	**3.24**	**3.07**	**2.94**	**2.84**	**2.75**	**2.68**	**2.62**
46	4.05	3.20	2.81	2.57	2.42	2.30	2.22	2.14	2.09	2.04	2.00	1.97
	7.21	**5.10**	**4.24**	**3.76**	**3.44**	**3.22**	**3.05**	**2.92**	**2.82**	**2.73**	**2.66**	2.60
48	4.04	3.19	2.80	2.56	2.41	2.30	2.21	2.14	2.08	2.03	1.99	1.96
	7.19	**5.08**	**4.22**	**3.74**	**3.42**	**3.20**	**3.04**	**2.90**	**2.80**	**2.71**	**2.64**	**2.58**
50	4.03	3.18	2.79	2.56	2.40	2.29	2.20	2.13	2.07	2.02	1.98	1.95
	7.17	**5.06**	**4.20**	**3.72**	**3.41**	**3.18**	**3.02**	**2.88**	**2.78**	**2.70**	**2.62**	**2.56**
55	4.02	3.17	2.78	2.54	2.38	2.27	2.18	2.11	2.05	2.00	1.97	1.93
	7.12	**5.01**	**4.16**	**3.68**	**3.37**	**3.15**	**2.98**	**2.85**	**2.75**	**2.66**	**2.59**	**2.53**
60	4.00	3.15	2.76	2.52	2.37	2.25	2.17	2.10	2.04	1.99	1.95	1.92
	7.08	**4.98**	**4.13**	**3.65**	**3.34**	**3.12**	**2.95**	**2.82**	**2.72**	**2.63**	**2.56**	**2.50**
65	3.99	3.14	2.75	2.51	2.36	2.24	2.15	2.08	2.02	1.98	1.94	1.90
	7.04	**4.95**	**4.10**	**3.62**	**3.31**	**3.09**	**2.93**	**2.79**	**2.70**	**2.61**	**2.54**	**2.47**
70	3.98	3.13	2.74	2.50	2.35	2.23	2.14	2.07	2.01	1.97	1.93	1.89
	7.01	**4.92**	**4.08**	**3.60**	**3.29**	**3.07**	**2.91**	**2.77**	**2.67**	**2.59**	**2.51**	**2.45**
80	3.96	3.11	2.72	2.48	2.33	2.21	2.12	2.05	1.99	1.95	1.91	1.88
	6.96	**4.88**	**4.04**	**3.56**	**3.25**	**3.04**	**2.87**	**2.74**	**2.64**	**2.55**	**2.48**	**2.41**
100	3.94	3.09	2.70	2.46	2.30	2.19	2.10	2.03	1.97	1.92	1.88	1.85
	6.90	**4.82**	**3.98**	**3.51**	**3.20**	**2.99**	**2.82**	**2.69**	**2.59**	**2.51**	**2.43**	**2.36**
125	3.92	3.07	2.68	2.44	2.29	2.17	2.08	2.01	1.95	1.90	1.86	1.83
	6.84	**4.78**	**3.94**	**3.47**	**3.17**	**2.95**	**2.79**	**2.65**	**2.56**	**2.47**	**2.40**	**2.33**
150	3.91	3.06	2.67	2.43	2.27	2.16	2.07	2.00	1.94	1.89	1.85	1.82
	6.81	**4.75**	**3.91**	**3.44**	**3.14**	**2.92**	**2.76**	**2.62**	**2.53**	**2.44**	**2.37**	**2.30**
200	3.89	3.04	2.65	2.41	2.26	2.14	2.05	1.98	1.92	1.87	1.83	1.80
	6.76	**4.71**	**3.88**	**3.41**	**3.11**	**2.90**	**2.73**	**2.60**	**2.50**	**2.41**	**2.34**	**2.28**
400	3.86	3.02	2.62	2.39	2.23	2.12	2.03	1.96	1.90	1.85	1.81	1.78
	6.70	**4.66**	**3.83**	**3.36**	**3.06**	**2.85**	**2.69**	**2.55**	**2.46**	**2.37**	**2.29**	**2.23**
1,000	3.85	3.00	2.61	2.38	2.22	2.10	2.02	1.95	1.89	1.84	1.80	1.76
	6.66	**4.62**	**3.80**	**3.34**	**3.04**	**2.82**	**2.66**	**2.53**	**2.43**	**2.34**	**2.26**	**2.20**
∞	3.84	2.99	2.60	2.37	2.21	2.09	2.01	1.94	1.88	1.83	1.79	1.75
	6.64	**4.60**	**3.78**	**3.32**	**3.02**	**2.80**	**2.64**	**2.51**	**2.41**	**2.32**	**2.24**	**21.8**

Continued

Table 5   99th and 95 Percentile Values of the *F* Distribution (Continued)

95th Percentile in Lightface Type; 99th Percentile in Boldface Type;
ν_1 = Degrees of Freedom for Numerator

14	16	20	24	30	40	50	75	100	200	500	∞	ν_2
2.08	2.03	1.97	1.93	1.88	1.84	1.80	1.76	1.74	1.71	1.68	1.67	27
2.83	**2.74**	**2.63**	**2.55**	**2.47**	**2.38**	**2.33**	**2.25**	**2.21**	**2.16**	**2.12**	**2.10**	
2.06	2.02	1.96	1.91	1.87	1.81	1.78	1.75	1.72	1.69	1.67	1.65	28
2.80	**2.71**	**2.60**	**2.52**	**2.44**	**2.35**	**2.30**	**2.22**	**2.18**	**2.13**	**2.09**	**2.06**	
2.05	2.00	1.94	1.90	1.85	1.80	1.77	1.73	1.71	1.68	1.65	1.64	29
2.77	**2.68**	**2.57**	**2.49**	**2.41**	**2.32**	**2.27**	**2.19**	**2.15**	**2.10**	**2.06**	**2.03**	
2.04	1.99	1.93	1.89	1.84	1.79	1.76	1.72	1.69	1.66	1.64	1.62	30
2.74	**2.66**	**2.55**	**2.47**	**2.38**	**2.29**	**2.24**	**2.16**	**2.13**	**2.07**	**2.03**	**2.01**	
2.02	1.97	1.91	1.86	1.82	1.76	1.74	1.69	1.67	1.64	1.61	1.59	32
2.70	**2.62**	**2.51**	**2.42**	**2.34**	**2.25**	**2.20**	**2.12**	**2.08**	**2.02**	**1.98**	**1.96**	
2.00	1.95	1.89	1.84	1.80	1.74	1.71	1.67	1.64	1.61	1.59	1.57	34
2.66	**2.58**	**2.47**	**2.38**	**2.30**	**2.21**	**2.15**	**2.08**	**2.04**	**1.98**	**1.94**	**1.91**	
1.98	1.93	1.87	1.82	1.78	1.72	1.69	1.65	1.62	1.59	1.56	1.55	36
2.62	**2.54**	**2.43**	**2.35**	**2.26**	**2.17**	**2.12**	**2.04**	**2.00**	**1.94**	**1.90**	**1.87**	
1.96	1.92	1.85	1.80	1.76	1.71	1.67	1.63	1.60	1.57	1.54	1.53	38
2.59	**2.51**	**2.40**	**2.32**	**2.22**	**2.14**	**2.08**	**2.00**	**1.97**	**1.90**	**1.86**	**1.84**	
1.95	1.90	1.84	1.79	1.74	1.69	1.66	1.61	1.59	1.55	1.53	1.51	40
2.56	**2.49**	**2.37**	**2.29**	**2.20**	**2.11**	**2.05**	**1.97**	**1.94**	**1.88**	**1.84**	**1.81**	
1.94	1.89	1.82	1.78	1.73	1.68	1.64	1.60	1.57	1.54	1.51	1.49	42
2.54	**2.46**	**2.35**	**2.26**	**2.17**	**2.08**	**2.02**	**1.94**	**1.91**	**1.85**	**1.80**	**1.78**	
1.92	1.88	1.81	1.76	1.72	1.66	1.63	1.58	1.56	1.52	1.50	1.48	44
2.52	**2.44**	**2.32**	**2.24**	**2.15**	**2.06**	**2.00**	**1.92**	**1.88**	**1.82**	**1.78**	**1.75**	
1.91	1.87	1.80	1.75	1.71	1.65	1.62	1.57	1.54	1.51	1.48	1.46	46
2.50	**2.42**	**2.30**	**2.22**	**2.13**	**2.04**	**1.98**	**1.90**	**1.86**	**1.80**	**1.76**	**1.72**	
1.90	1.86	1.79	1.74	1.70	1.64	1.61	1.56	1.53	1.50	1.47	1.45	48
2.48	**2.40**	**2.28**	**2.20**	**2.11**	**2.02**	**1.96**	**1.88**	**1.84**	**1.78**	**1.73**	**1.70**	
1.90	1.85	1.78	1.74	1.69	1.63	1.60	1.55	1.52	1.48	1.46	1.44	50
2.46	**2.39**	**2.26**	**2.18**	**2.10**	**2.00**	**1.94**	**1.86**	**1.82**	**1.76**	**1.71**	**1.68**	
1.88	1.83	1.76	1.72	1.67	1.61	1.58	1.52	1.50	1.46	1.43	1.41	55
2.43	**2.35**	**2.23**	**2.15**	**2.06**	**1.96**	**1.90**	**1.82**	**1.78**	**1.71**	**1.66**	**1.64**	
1.86	1.81	1.75	1.70	1.65	1.59	1.56	1.50	1.48	1.44	1.41	1.39	60
2.40	**2.32**	**2.20**	**2.12**	**2.03**	**1.93**	**1.87**	**1.79**	**1.74**	**1.68**	**1.63**	**1.60**	
1.85	1.80	1.73	1.68	1.63	1.57	1.54	1.49	1.46	1.42	1.39	1.37	65
2.37	**2.30**	**2.18**	**2.09**	**2.00**	**1.90**	**1.84**	**1.76**	**1.71**	**1.64**	**1.60**	**1.56**	
1.84	1.79	1.72	1.67	1.62	1.56	1.53	1.47	1.45	1.40	1.37	1.35	70
2.35	**2.28**	**2.15**	**2.07**	**1.98**	**1.88**	**1.82**	**1.74**	**1.69**	**1.62**	**1.56**	**1.53**	
1.82	1.77	1.70	1.65	1.60	1.54	1.51	1.45	1.42	1.38	1.35	1.32	80
2.32	**2.24**	**2.11**	**2.03**	**1.94**	**1.84**	**1.78**	**1.70**	**1.65**	**1.57**	**1.52**	**1.49**	
1.79	1.75	1.68	1.63	1.57	1.51	1.48	1.42	1.39	1.34	1.30	1.28	100
2.26	**2.19**	**2.06**	**1.98**	**1.89**	**1.79**	**1.73**	**1.64**	**1.59**	**1.51**	**1.46**	**1.43**	
1.77	1.72	1.65	1.60	1.55	1.49	1.45	1.39	1.36	1.31	1.27	1.25	125
2.23	**2.15**	**2.03**	**1.94**	**1.85**	**1.75**	**1.68**	**1.59**	**1.54**	**1.46**	**1.40**	**1.37**	
1.76	1.71	1.64	1.59	1.54	1.47	1.44	1.37	1.34	1.29	1.25	1.22	150
2.20	**2.12**	**2.00**	**1.91**	**1.83**	**1.72**	**1.66**	**1.56**	**1.51**	**1.43**	**1.37**	**1.33**	
1.74	1.69	1.62	1.57	1.52	1.45	1.42	1.35	1.32	1.26	1.22	1.19	200
2.17	**2.09**	**1.97**	**1.88**	**1.79**	**1.69**	**1.62**	**1.53**	**1.48**	**1.39**	**1.33**	**1.28**	
1.72	1.67	1.60	1.54	1.49	1.42	1.38	1.32	1.28	1.22	1.16	1.13	400
2.12	**2.04**	**1.92**	**1.84**	**1.74**	**1.64**	**1.57**	**1.47**	**1.42**	**1.32**	**1.24**	**1.19**	
1.70	1.65	1.58	1.53	1.47	1.41	1.36	1.30	1.26	1.19	1.13	1.08	1,000
2.09	**2.01**	**1.89**	**1.81**	**1.71**	**1.61**	**1.54**	**1.44**	**1.38**	**1.28**	**1.19**	**1.11**	
1.69	1.64	1.57	1.52	1.46	1.40	1.35	1.28	1.24	1.17	1.11	1.00	∞
2.07	**1.99**	**1.87**	**1.79**	**1.69**	**1.59**	**1.52**	**1.41**	**1.36**	**1.25**	**1.15**	**1.00**	

ν_2 = degrees of freedom for denominator

Table 6 Values of Z for Given Values of r

r	.000	.001	.002	.003	.004	.005	.006	.007	.008	.009
.000	.0000	.0010	.0020	.0030	.0040	.0050	.0060	.0070	.0080	.0090
.010	.0100	.0110	.0120	.0130	.0140	.0150	.0160	.0170	.0180	.0190
.020	.0200	.0210	.0220	.0230	.0240	.0250	.0260	.0270	.0280	.0290
.030	.0300	.0310	.0320	.0330	.0340	.0350	.0360	.0370	.0380	.0390
.040	.0400	.0410	.0420	.0430	.0440	.0450	.0460	.0470	.0480	.0490
.050	.0501	.0511	.0521	.0531	.0541	.0551	.0561	.0571	.0581	.0591
.060	.0601	.0611	.0621	.0631	.0641	.0651	.0661	.0671	.0681	.0691
.070	.0701	.0711	.0721	.0731	.0741	.0751	.0761	.0771	.0782	.0792
.080	.0802	.0812	.0822	.0832	.0842	.0852	.0862	.0872	.0882	.0892
.090	.0902	.0912	.0922	.0933	.0943	.0953	.0963	.0973	.0983	.0993
.100	.1003	.1013	.1024	.1034	.1044	.1054	.1064	.1074	.1084	.1094
.110	.1105	.1115	.1125	.1135	.1145	.1155	.1165	.1175	.1185	.1195
.120	.1206	.1216	.1226	.1236	.1246	.1257	.1267	.1277	.1287	.1297
.130	.1308	.1318	.1328	.1338	.1348	.1358	.1368	.1379	.1389	.1399
.140	.1409	.1419	.1430	.1440	.1450	.1460	.1470	.1481	.1491	.1501
.150	.1511	.1522	.1532	.1542	.1552	.1563	.1573	.1583	.1593	.1604
.160	.1614	.1624	.1634	.1644	.1655	.1665	.1676	.1686	.1696	.1706
.170	.1717	.1727	.1737	.1748	.1758	.1768	.1779	.1789	.1799	.1810
.180	.1820	.1830	.1841	.1851	.1861	.1872	.1882	.1892	.1903	.1913
.190	.1923	.1934	.1944	.1954	.1965	.1975	.1986	.1996	.2007	.2017
.200	.2027	.2038	.2048	.2059	.2069	.2079	.2090	.2100	.2111	.2121
.210	.2132	.2142	.2153	.2163	.2174	.2184	.2194	.2205	.2215	.2226
.220	.2237	.2247	.2258	.2268	.2279	.2289	.2300	.2310	.2321	.2331
.230	.2342	.2353	.2363	.2374	.2384	.2395	.2405	.2416	.2427	.2437
.240	.2448	.2458	.2469	.2480	.2490	.2501	.2511	.2522	.2533	.2543
.250	.2554	.2565	.2575	.2586	.2597	.2608	.2618	.2629	.2640	.2650
.260	.2661	.2672	.2682	.2693	.2704	.2715	.2726	.2736	.2747	.2758
.370	.2769	.2779	.2790	.2801	.2812	.2823	.2833	.2844	.2855	.2866
.280	.2877	.2888	.2898	.2909	.2920	.2931	.2942	.2953	.2964	.2975
.290	.2986	.2997	.3008	.3019	.3029	.3040	.3051	.3062	.3073	.3084
.300	.3095	.3106	.3117	.3128	.3139	.3150	.3161	.3172	.3183	.3195
.310	.3206	.3217	.3228	.3239	.3250	.3261	.3272	.3283	.3294	.3305
.320	.3317	.3328	.3339	.3350	.3361	.3372	.3384	.3395	.3406	.3417
.330	.3428	.3439	.3451	.3462	.3473	.3484	.3496	.3507	.3518	.3530
.340	.3541	.3552	.3564	.3575	.3586	.3597	.3609	.3620	.3632	.3643
.350	.3654	.3666	.3677	.3689	.3700	.3712	.3723	.3734	.3746	.3757
.360	.3769	.3780	.3792	.3803	.3815	.3826	.3838	.3850	.3861	.3873
.370	.3884	.3896	.3907	.3919	.3931	.3942	.3954	.3966	.3977	.3989
.380	.4001	.4012	.4024	.4036	.4047	.4059	.4071	.4083	.4094	.4106
.390	.4118	.4130	.4142	.4153	.4165	.4177	.4189	.4201	.4213	.4225
.400	.4236	.4248	.4260	.4272	.4284	.4296	.4308	.4320	.4332	.4344
.410	.4356	.4368	.4380	.4392	.4404	.4416	.4429	.4441	.4453	.4465
.420	.4477	.4489	.4501	.4513	.4526	.4538	.4550	.4562	.4574	.4587
.430	.4599	.4611	.4623	.4636	.4648	.4660	.4673	.4685	.4697	.4710
.440	.4722	.4735	.4747	.4760	.4772	.4784	.4797	.4809	.4822	.4835
.450	.4847	.4860	.4872	.4885	.4897	.4910	.4923	.4935	.4948	.4961
.460	.4973	.4986	.4999	.5011	.5024	.5037	.5049	.5062	.5075	.5088
.470	.5101	.5114	.5126	.5139	.5152	.5165	.5178	.5191	.5204	.5217
.480	.5230	.5243	.5256	.5279	.5282	.5295	.5308	.5321	.5334	.5347
.490	.5361	.5374	.5387	.5400	.5413	.5427	.5440	.5453	.5466	.5480

Continued

Source: Albert E. Waugh, *Statistical Tables and Problems,* McGraw-Hill Book Company, Inc., New York, 1952, table A11, pp. 40–41, by permission of the publisher.

Table 6   Values of Z for Given Values of r (Continued)

r	.000	.001	.002	.003	.004	.005	.006	.007	.008	.009
.500	.5493	.5506	.5520	.5533	.5547	.5560	.5573	.5587	.5600	.5614
.510	.5627	.5641	.5654	.5668	.5681	.5695	.5709	.5722	.5736	.5750
.520	.5763	.5777	.5791	.5805	.5818	.5832	.5846	.5860	.5874	.5888
.530	.5901	.5915	.5929	.5943	.5957	.5971	.5985	.5999	.6013	.6027
.540	.6042	.6056	.6070	.6084	.6098	.6112	.6127	.6141	.6155	.6170
.550	.6184	.6198	.6213	.6227	.6241	.6256	.6270	.6285	.6299	.6314
.560	.6328	.6343	.6358	.6372	.6387	.6401	.6416	.6431	.6446	.6460
.570	.6475	.6490	.6505	.6520	.6535	.6550	.6565	.6579	.6594	.6610
.580	.6625	.6640	.6655	.6670	.6685	.6700	.6715	.6731	.6746	.6761
.590	.6777	.6792	.6807	.6823	.6838	.6854	.6869	.6885	.6900	.6916
.600	.6931	.6947	.6963	.6978	.6994	.7010	.7026	.7042	.7057	.7073
.610	.7089	.7105	.7121	.7137	.7153	.7169	.7185	.7201	.7218	.7234
.620	.7250	.7266	.7283	.7299	.7315	.7332	.7348	.7364	.7381	.7398
.630	.7414	.7431	.7447	.7464	.7481	.7497	.7514	.7531	.7548	.7565
.640	.7582	.7599	.7616	.7633	.7650	.7667	.7684	.7701	.7718	.7736
.650	.7753	.7770	.7788	.7805	.7823	.7840	.7858	.7875	.7893	.7910
.660	.7928	.7946	.7964	.7981	.7999	.8017	.8035	.8053	.8071	.8089
.670	.8107	.8126	.8144	.8162	.8180	.8199	.8217	.8236	.8254	.8273
.680	.8291	.8310	.8328	.8347	.8366	.8385	.8404	.8423	.8442	.8461
.690	.8480	.8499	.8518	.8537	.8556	.8576	.8595	.8614	.8634	.8653
.700	.8673	.8693	.8712	.8732	.8752	.8772	.8792	.8812	.8832	.8852
.710	.8872	.8892	.8912	.8933	.8953	.8973	.8994	.9014	.9035	.9056
.720	.9076	.9097	.9118	.9139	.9160	.9181	.9202	.9223	.9245	.9266
.730	.9287	.9309	.9330	.9352	.9373	.9395	.9417	.9439	.9461	.9483
.740	.9505	.9527	.9549	.9571	.9594	.9616	.9639	.9661	.9684	.9707
.750	.9730	.9752	.9775	.9799	.9822	.9845	.9868	.9892	.9915	.9939
.760	.9962	.9986	1.0010	1.0034	1.0058	1.0082	1.0106	1.0130	1.0154	1.0179
.770	1.0203	1.0228	1.0253	1.0277	1.0302	1.0327	1.0352	1.0378	1.0403	1.0428
.780	1.0454	1.0479	1.0505	1.0531	1.0557	1.0583	1.0609	1.0635	1.0661	1.0688
.790	1.0714	1.0741	1.0768	1.0795	1.0822	1.0849	1.0876	1.0903	1.0931	1.0958
.800	1.0986	1.1014	1.1041	1.1070	1.1098	1.1127	1.1155	1.1184	1.1212	1.1241
.810	1.1270	1.1299	1.1329	1.1358	1.1388	1.1417	1.1447	1.1477	1.1507	1.1538
.820	1.1568	1.1599	1.1630	1.1660	1.1692	1.1723	1.1754	1.1786	1.1817	1.1849
.830	1.1870	1.1913	1.1946	1.1979	1.2011	1.2044	1.2077	1.2111	1.2144	1.2178
.840	1.2212	1.2246	1.2280	1.2315	1.2349	1.2384	1.2419	1.2454	1.2490	1.2526
.850	1.2561	1.2598	1.2634	1.2670	1.2708	1.2744	1.2782	1.2819	1.2857	1.2895
.860	1.2934	1.2972	1.3011	1.3050	1.3089	1.3129	1.3168	1.3209	1.3249	1.3290
.870	1.3331	1.3372	1.3414	1.3456	1.3498	1.3540	1.3583	1.3626	1.3670	1.3714
.880	1.3758	1.3802	1.3847	1.3892	1.3938	1.3984	1.4030	1.4077	1.4124	1.4171
.890	1.4219	1.4268	1.4316	1.4366	1.4415	1.4465	1.4516	1.4566	1.4618	1.4670
.900	1.4722	1.4775	1.4828	1.4883	1.4937	1.4992	1.5047	1.5103	1.5160	1.5217
.910	1.5275	1.5334	1.5393	1.5453	1.5513	1.5574	1.5636	1.5698	1.5762	1.5825
.920	1.5890	1.5956	1.6022	1.6089	1.6157	1.6226	1.6296	1.6366	1.6438	1.6510
.930	1.6584	1.6659	1.6734	1.6811	1.6888	1.6967	1.7047	1.7129	1.7211	1.7295
.940	1.7380	1.7467	1.7555	1.7645	1.7736	1.7828	1.7923	1.8019	1.8117	1.8216
.950	1.8318	1.8421	1.8527	1.8635	1.8745	1.8857	1.8972	1.9090	1.9210	1.9333
.960	1.9459	1.9588	1.9721	1.9857	1.9996	2.0140	2.0287	2.0439	2.0595	2.0756
.970	2.0923	2.1095	2.1273	2.1457	2.1649	2.1847	2.2054	2.2269	2.2494	2.2729
.980	2.2976	2.3223	2.3507	2.3796	2.4101	2.4426	2.4774	2.5147	2.5550	2.5988
.990	2.6467	2.6996	2.7587	2.8257	2.9031	2.9945	3.1063	3.2504	3.4534	3.8002

r	z
.9999	4.95172
.99999	6.10303

Table 7 Percentile Values of r for ν Degrees of Freedom When ρ = 0*

ν	$r_{.95}$	$r_{.975}$	$r_{.99}$	$r_{.995}$	$r_{.9995}$	ν	$r_{.95}$	$r_{.975}$	$r_{.99}$	$r_{.995}$	$r_{.9995}$
1	.988	.997	.9995	.9999	1.000	30	.296	.349	.409	.449	.554
2	.900	.950	.980	.990	.999	35	.275	.325	.381	.418	.519
3	.805	.878	.934	.959	.991	40	.257	.304	.358	.393	.490
4	.729	.811	.882	.917	.974	45	.243	.288	.338	.372	.465
5	.669	.754	.833	.874	.951	50	.231	.273	.322	.354	.443
6	.622	.707	.789	.834	.925	55	.220	.261	.307	.338	.424
7	.582	.666	.750	.798	.898	60	.211	.250	.295	.325	.408
8	.550	.632	.716	.765	.872	65	.203	.240	.284	.312	.393
9	.521	.602	.685	.735	.847	70	.195	.232	.274	.302	.380
10	.497	.576	.658	.708	.823	75	.189	.224	.264	.292	.368
11	.476	.553	.634	.684	.801	80	.183	.217	.256	.283	.357
12	.458	.532	.612	.661	.780	85	.178	.211	.249	.275	.347
13	.441	.514	.592	.641	.760	90	.173	.205	.242	.267	.338
14	.426	.497	.574	.623	.742	95	.168	.200	.236	.260	.329
15	.412	.482	.558	.606	.725	100	.164	.195	.230	.254	.321
16	.400	.468	.542	.590	.708	125	.147	.174	.206	.228	.288
17	.389	.456	.528	.575	.693	150	.134	.159	.189	.208	.264
18	.378	.444	.516	.561	.679	175	.124	.148	.174	.194	.248
19	.369	.433	.503	.549	.665	200	.116	.138	.164	.181	.235
20	.360	.423	.492	.537	.652	300	.095	.113	.134	.148	.188
22	.344	.404	.472	.515	.629	500	.074	.088	.104	.115	.148
24	.330	.388	.453	.496	.607	1000	.052	.062	.073	.081	.104
25	.323	.381	.445	.487	.597	2000	.037	.044	.051	.058	.074
	$-r_{.05}$	$-r_{.025}$	$-r_{.01}$	$-r_{.005}$	$-r_{.0005}$		$-r_{.05}$	$-r_{.025}$	$-r_{.01}$	$-r_{.005}$	$-r_{.0005}$

Source: Reprinted abridged from R. A. Fisher and F. Yates, *Statistical Tables for Biological, Agricultural, and Medical Research,* published by Oliver & Boyd Ltd., Edinburgh, 1963, by permission of the publishers.

Table 8 Sample Sizes Required for Selected Confidence Levels and Sample Limits Error

A. Parameter in Population Assumed to Be 50 Percent and for 95 Percent Confidence Level*

Size of Population	Sample Size for Reliability of				
	±1%	±2%	±3%	±4%	±5%
1,000	**	**	**	375	278
2,000	**	**	696	462	322
3,000	**	1334	787	500	341
4,000	**	1500	842	522	350
5,000	**	1622	879	536	357
10,000	4899	1936	964	566	370
20,000	6489	2144	1013	583	377
50,000	8057	2291	1045	593	381
100,000	8763	2345	1056	597	383
500,000 to ∞	9423	2390	1065	600	384

B. Parameter in Population Assumed to Be 50 Percent and for 99 Percent Confidence Level

Size of Population	Sample Size for Reliability of				
	±1%	±2%	±3%	±4%	±5%
1,000	**	**	**	**	400
2,000	**	**	959	683	498
3,000	**	**	1142	771	544
4,000	**	**	1262	824	569
5,000	**	2267	1347	859	586
10,000	**	2932	1556	939	622
20,000	9068	3435	1688	986	642
50,000	12456	3830	1778	1016	655
100,000	14229	3982	1810	1026	659
500,000 to ∞	16056	4113	1836	1035	663

* This section of this table should be used only when the sampler is unable or unwilling to estimate a maximum (or minimum) occurrence rate to be expected. The use of this section of the table, while conservative, will result in a much larger sample size than found in other sections of the table where such an estimate is used.

** In these cases more than 50% of the population is required in the sample. Since the normal approximation of the hypergeometric distribution is a poor approximation in such instances, no sample value is given.

Source: Adapted from and extended from tables in H. P. Hill, J. L. Roth, and H. Arkin, *Sampling in Auditing* (New York: The Ronald Press, 1962) by permission of the publisher.

Table 8   Continued

C. Parameter in Population Assumed to Be over 70 Percent or under 30 Percent and for 95 Percent Confidence Level

Size of Population	Sample Size for Reliabilities of			
	±1%	±2%	±3%	±5%
1,000	*	*	473	244
2,000	*	*	619	278
3,000	*	1206	690	291
4,000	*	1341	732	299
5,000	*	1437	760	303
10,000	4465	1678	823	313
20,000	5749	1832	858	318
50,000	6946	1939	881	321
100,000	7465	1977	888	321
500,000 to ∞	7939	2009	895	322

D. Parameter in Population Assumed to Be over 70 Percent or under 30 Percent and for 99 Percent Confidence Level

Size of Population	Sample Size for Reliabilities of			
	±1%	±2%	±3%	±5%
1,000	*	*	*	360
2,000	*	*	873	436
3,000	*	*	1021	470
4,000	*	1862	1116	489
5,000	*	2053	1182	502
10,000	*	2584	1341	527
20,000	8213	2967	1437	542
50,000	10898	3257	1502	551
100,000	12231	3367	1525	554
500,000 to ∞	13557	3460	1544	557

* In these cases more than 50% of the population is required in the sample. Since the normal approximation of the hypergeometric distribution is a poor approximation in such instances, no sample value is given.

Table 8   Continued

E. Parameter in Population Assumed to Be over 85 Percent or
under 15 Percent and for 95 Percent Confidence Level

Size of Population	Sample Size for Reliabilities of			
	±1%	±2%	±3%	±4%
1,000	*	*	353	235
2,000	*	760	428	266
3,000	*	870	461	278
4,000	*	938	479	284
5,000	2474	984	491	289
10,000	3288	1091	516	297
20,000	3935	1154	530	302
50,000	4461	1195	538	304
100,000	4669	1210	541	305
500,000 to ∞	4850	1222	544	306

F. Parameter in Population Assumed to Be over 85 Percent or
under 15 Percent and for 99 Percent Confidence Level

Size of Population	Sample Size for Reliabilities of			
	±1%	±2%	±3%	±4%
1,000	*	*	485	346
2,000	*	*	640	418
3,000	*	1241	716	450
4,000	*	1384	761	467
5,000	*	1487	791	478
10,000	4583	1746	859	502
20,000	5946	1913	898	515
50,000	7237	2029	923	523
100,000	7801	2071	931	526
500,000 to ∞	8320	2106	938	528

* In these cases more than 50% of the population is required in the sample. Since the normal approximation of the hypergeometric distribution is a poor approximation in such instances, no sample value is given.

Index

Index